Operations Research
Techniques for
Management

Herbert Moskowitz and Gordon P. Wright

Krannert Graduate School of Management
and School of Management
Purdue University
West Lafayette, Indiana

PRENTICE-HALL, INC. ENGLEWOOD CLIFFS, N.J. 07632

Operations Research Techniques for Management

Library of Congress Cataloging in Publication Data

Moskowitz, Herbert.
  Operations research techniques for management

  Includes bibliographies and index.
  1. Decision-making—Mathematical models.
2. Operations research. 3. Statistical decision.
I. Wright, Gordon P., joint author. II. Title.
HD30.23.M68   658.4′034   79-1007
ISBN 0-13-637389-5

Operations Research Techniques for Management

by Herbert Moskowitz and Gordon P. Wright

COVER DESIGN BY KONODA ASSOCIATES

Printed in the United States of America

10 9 8 7 6 5 4 3 2

Prentice-Hall International, Inc., *London*
Prentice-Hall of Australia Pty. Limited, *Sydney*
Prentice-Hall of Canada, Ltd., *Toronto*
Prentice-Hall of India Private Limited, *New Delhi*
Prentice-Hall of Japan, Inc., *Tokyo*
Prentice-Hall of Southeast Asia Pte. Ltd., *Singapore*
Whitehall Books Limited, *Wellington, New Zealand*

Acknowledgments

During the six years that we spent developing this text, we received many helpful suggestions from undergraduate and graduate students at Purdue University. We have also benefited from the counsel of two outstanding teachers at Purdue University, Dennis J. Weidenaar and Emanuel T. Weiler. The constructive reviews of Dr. Grover Rodich of Portland State University, Dr. John Bernardo of the University of Kentucky, Professor Eleanor M. Birch of the University of Iowa, Professor Irwin Kruger of the University of Miami, and Professor Jay Strum of New York University have been most helpful.

The secretarial skills of Judy Kocher at Purdue University and Judy Orasky at Dartmouth College have been invaluable. Also, the consistently pleasant disposition and encouraging support of Ellen Wiggins at Purdue University was wonderful, considering the never-ending strain of the redrafts to be typed and the deadlines to be met.

We wish to acknowledge the significant long-term support received from the Krannert School of Management, John S. Day, Dean of the Krannert School, and Wilbur G. Lewellen, Professor of Management of the Krannert School.

—Herbert Moskowitz and Gordon P. Wright

To Heather and Judy

Contents

x

APPENDICES

Preface

Our goal, as both teachers and authors, is to provide our readers with a good understanding of basic operations research methodology. We have written this book for the reader who has only an algebra background.

We have used three basic strategies to achieve our goal. First, to motivate the reader, we have tried as much as possible to make the material relevant to business problems; almost every chapter begins by citing activities or examples that relate to situations that ar encountered by people in business. Then, as the chapter proceeds, numerous illustrations are included to maintain this relationship.

Our strategy has been to organize the book and individual chapters according to a simple instructional model. This model has the following components:

1. Specify what you want the student to understand.
2. Design instructional strategies to meet these goals.
3. Evaluate the degree of success achieved in meeting the objectives.

At the beginning of each chapter we have specified objectives to be attained by the readers. We believe that if the readers are successful in achieving these goals, they will obtain an important and adequate understanding of the material in a chapter. This is our third strategy.

To help the reader meet the goals that we have established, we have supplemented the text of each chapter with review questions and sometimes with review problems (most of which are analytical), with exercises, and with mini-cases. Each

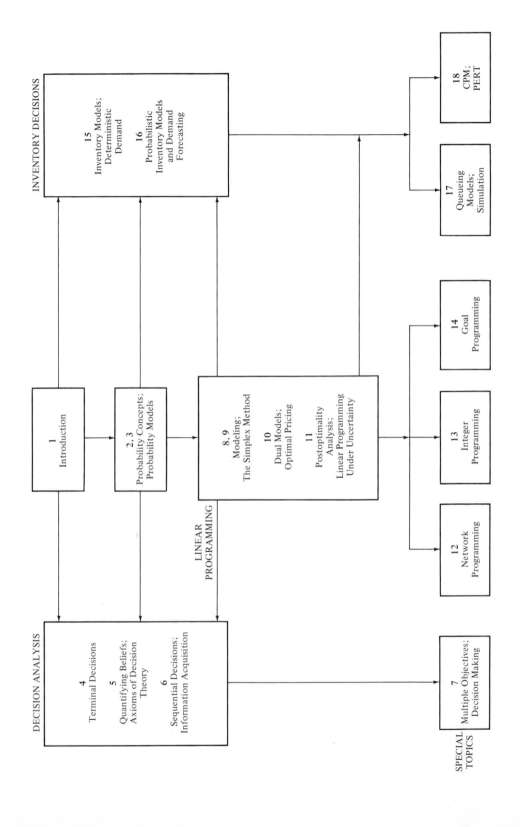

INVENTORY DECISIONS

15 Inventory Models; Deterministic Demand

16 Probabilistic Inventory Models and Demand Forecasting

18 CPM; PERT

17 Queueing Models; Simulation

1 Introduction

2, 3 Probability Concepts; Probability Models

8, 9 Modeling; The Simplex Method

10 Dual Models; Optimal Pricing

11 Postoptimality Analysis; Linear Programming Under Uncertainty

LINEAR PROGRAMMING

14 Goal Programming

13 Integer Programming

12 Network Programming

DECISION ANALYSIS

4 Terminal Decisions

5 Quantifying Beliefs; Axioms of Decision Theory

6 Sequential Decisions; Information Acquisition

7 Multiple Objectives; Decision Making

SPECIAL TOPICS

section of review questions and review problems is followed by an answer section that allows our readers to check their work and get immediate feedback. The mini-cases will offer our readers various perspectives and will provide them with an opportunity for analysis and criticism.

The overall design of the book is modular as shown in the figure on page xiv. This allows for maximum flexibility in adapting the book to the objectives of a particular course in operations research. For example, Chapters 2 and 3 may be bypassed by readers who have had previous experience in statistics. Also, Chapters 2 and 3 may be omitted in a course that, for the most part, teaches the deterministic models of operations research.—*Herbert Moskowitz and Gordon P. Wright*

*Operations Research
Techniques for
Management*

PART I   Probability and Decision Making

CHAPTER 1
Introduction to Operations Research

OBJECTIVES. Upon completion of this chapter, you should be able to:

1. Have a perspective of what operations research is about and how it can improve managerial decision making.
2. Understand the concept of modeling, the different types of models that can be constructed, and the nature and development of a mathematical model.
3. Understand the five major steps in operations research: (a) problem definition, (b) model construction, (c) model solution, (d) model validation, and (e) implementation.
4. See how a linear programming and decision analysis model are constructed in two managerial applications.

1.1. MANAGERIAL DECISION MAKING AND THE NEED FOR OPERATIONS RESEARCH

This is a book about managerial decision making and how to make better managerial decisions. The decisions we are concerned with are complex, important decisions: those that require careful thought and deliberation in exercising the management function and those that would benefit from the use of mathematical models to aid the decision-making process.

We consider managerial decision making to be a process whereby a manager when confronted with a problem chooses a specific alternative course of action from a set of possible available courses of action. In most cases there is some uncertainty about the future, so that we cannot be sure of the ultimate consequences of the decision that is chosen. How do such (or any) decision situations arise? Decision making is a response to a decision problem, which generally arises as a result of a discrepancy between existing conditions and the manager's (and hopefully the organization's) goals or objectives.

3

1.1.1. Types of Decisions and Their Constituent Elements

Figure 1.1 illustrates several general types of decision situations that a manager might encounter. These situations include:

1. Decisions under *certainty* (where all the facts are known for sure) versus *uncertainty* [where the event that will occur (state of nature) is not known for sure but a probability or odds can be assigned to its possible occurrence].
2. *Static* decisions (decisions made once and only once) versus *dynamic* decisions (where a sequence of interrelated decisions are made either simultaneously or over several time periods).
3. Decisions where the opponent is *nature* (e.g., the weather, state of the economy) or a *thinking (rational)* opponent (developing a national energy policy where we have to consider the actions of OPEC).

Considering all possible combinations of these factors, there are eight general types of decision situations that a manager might face. For example, point 7 in Figure 1.1 represents a dynamic decision situation where there exists uncertainty, and nature is the opponent. Scheduling production and employment levels each month in the face of uncertain future sales is an illustration of such a decision situation.

The elements of any decision consist of:

1. A decision-making unit (individual, group, organization, or society).
2. A set of possible actions that may be taken to solve the decision problem.
3. A set of possible states that may occur.
4. A set of consequences associated with each possible action and state that may occur.
5. The relationship between the consequences and values of the decision-making unit.

Of course, in a real decision-making situation, definition and generation of the alternatives, states, and consequences are perhaps the most difficult, but nevertheless crucial, aspects of the decision problem.

1.1.2. What Makes Decision Making Complex?

Why do complex decision-making situations arise in the first place? One reason is that in our contemporary society, economic, political, technological, environmental, and competitive factors interact in a highly complicated fashion. For example, the selection of a site for a new plant must be based on the availability of the labor force, access to raw materials and markets, the attitude of the community, environmental and ecological considerations, the possibility of wage increases by indigenous companies in the area to avoid drainage of their work force, and so forth.

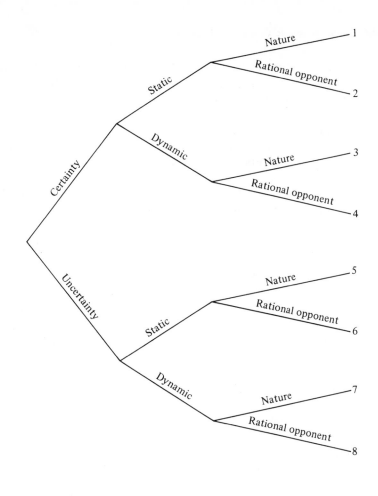

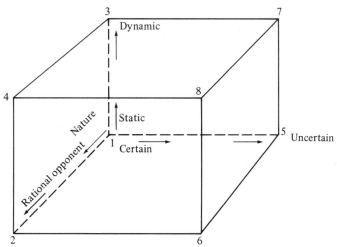

Figure 1.1. Taxonomy of decision situations.

Other factors that may complicate decision-making are that the organization (perhaps unknowingly) may be pursuing incompatible goals, the responsibility and authority for decision making may be greatly diffused within the organization, and the environment within which the organization operates may be dynamic and uncertain.

In more fundamental terms, we can say that, in general, the difficulties or complexities of making decisions (even relatively simple ones) are due to:

1. The decision makers or decision-making units—their values, goals (which may be inconsistent with the organization's), risk attitudes, and their beliefs or knowledge of the situation.
2. The limited resources and capabilities of the organization and its people.
3. The complexity of the decision situation:
   (a) The multiple nature of the goals and objectives attempting to be achieved.
   (b) The number of feasible alternatives to choose from.
   (c) The multiple possible events or states that can occur.
   (d) The multiple possible consequences that can result when an action is taken and a set of events occur.
4. The different preference structures among individuals in the organization.
5. The interaction of the decisions made by different decision makers.

The complexity of even a rather simple decision problem can be mind boggling. The basic premise of operations research is that it is easier to resolve complex decision problems if the factors that influence the decisions are made *visible* and *quantifiable*. It is also easier to examine and analyze a complex problem if the concepts, tools, and techniques of operations research are used to decompose the problem into simpler elements. Once this is done, the elements can be aggregated or synthesized. This will give insight into the overall problem and will provide direction on its resolution. Intrinsic in an operations research approach is the construction of a model that synthesizes the segments of an organization that are affected by the decision.

1.1.3. Benefits and Limitations of a Scientific Approach to Decision Making

Obviously, managers must and do make decisions constantly. For a given situation a formal process of decision making may result in an identical solution arrived at by intuitive means. Moreover, the fact that a decision is made within an orderly and mathematically precise framework does not mean that it will necessarily be judged, in retrospect, to have been a good decision. Uncertainty about the future consequences plays a key role here, and thus an unsatisfactory outcome can result even for the best decision that could have been made. A good poker player (i.e., a good decision maker) may lose to a poor one because of how the cards happened to fall in a particular hand. Over the long run, however, we would expect the good player to win.

Similarly, over the long run, application of a formal rational approach to decision making should also enhance the managerial decision-making process. This assertion is amply borne out by the substantial use of operations research models and techniques in both the private and public sectors of our society (business, industry, military, civil government and agencies, hospitals, etc.) and its establishment in the basic curricula of practically every business and engineering school.

How is a formal approach to decision making beneficial?

1. It provides decision makers with a set of concepts and tools that will enable them to make decisions in a logically consistent fashion, and with as much precision as possible. Stated simply, a formal approach results in better decisions.
2. It gives decision makers an improved insight into how they make their decisions, so that they can improve their own intuitive decision-making processes.
3. Formalization and quantification of the problem facilitates communication and coordination. In this way, divergent preferences and information among individuals can be reconciled and decisions coordinated.
4. Formalization of routine or repetitive decision problems (i.e., handling the daily operating activities and their monitoring for dangerous trends) frees managers to concentrate on more pressing matters, except when unusual circumstances arise, requiring review of the course of everyday action. In this way managers achieve better control of their operations and can allocate their time more efficiently.
5. Formalization facilitates the development of better organizational planning, operating, and control systems. An operations research study initiated to analyze a particular decision problem may ultimately become an integral part of the organization decision system to be employed repetitively. Thus, the cost of undertaking the first application may produce longer-run benefits and spin-off benefits not originally envisioned.
6. It serves as a matter of record, that is, of historical and current informational value. Thus, managers can trace the development of a system, new managers can quickly become familiar with the existing system, problems can be more easily traced and isolated, and revisions to the system are more easily made and made known to those involved.

There are, of course, limitations to using a formal approach to decision making. No matter how sophisticated the design of the system, a formal approach rarely ever provides all the information for action. A formal approach involves a model, and a model is not reality but an abstraction of it. Moreover, the very process of constructing a formal decision system involves subjectivity in addition to the logical manipulation of symbols and data. Therefore, managers must guard against thinking of the model as being reality, and hence accompanying solutions as being sacrosanct. In short, an operations research approach is never sufficient per se but must be tempered by the judgment supplied by knowledgeable managers.

Furthermore, a truly successful implementation of an operations research approach must apply behavioral as well as mathematical science, because the resultant system must interact with human beings. Hence, it must take into account people's capabilities and their willingness to use the system developed.

1.2. HISTORICAL PERSPECTIVE: ORIGINS AND DEVELOPMENT OF OPERATIONS RESEARCH

The manager who can make rational decisions in the face of uncertainty and unclear personal judgments is a person to be envied. Until recently, decisions were always made by the syllogistic process of deductive reasoning that we call *intuition*. However, reliance on intuition started to wane during World War II, when formal approaches to decision making (under the name of *operations research*) were extensively used. These were the origins of operations research as it exists today. To maximize the war effort, it was necessary to allocate scarce resources—in an effective manner—to the various military operations and to the activities within each operation. First the British and then the American military management commissioned large numbers of scientists to apply a scientific approach to the many strategic and tactical problems. These teams of scientists included physicists, biologists, statisticians, mathematicians, and psychologists. They were the first operations research teams. It is reported that their efforts were instrumental in winning such military encounters as the Air Battle of Britain, the Battle of the North Atlantic, and the Island Campaign in the Pacific.

Some of the investigations carried out by the British in the early days of World War II were the determination of the optimum convoy size to minimize losses from submarine attacks, the determination of the correct color of aircraft to minimize detection by submarines (or maximize the number of submarines sunk), the determination of the correct depth-charge setting, and the determination of the best way to deploy radar units to maximize potential coverage against possible enemy attacks. Some studies carried out by the Americans included the resolution of logistical problems, the invention of new flight patterns, the planning of sea mining, and the effective utilization of electronic equipment. The essence of much of these initial studies lay in simple statistical investigations.

After the war, the apparent success of the military teams attracted the attention of industry, which was seeking solutions to problems caused by the increasing complexity and specialization in organizations. This created possible goal incompatibilities and interaction effects among areas of specialization and functionalization. The result was complex decision problems. This prompted business organizations to use the formal tools of operations research.

It is possible to identify at least two other factors that contributed greatly to the rapid growth of operations research during this period. One was the substantial progress that was made in developing and improving techniques available to operations research. One example is the simplex method for solving linear programming problems, which was developed in 1947 by the American mathematician George Dantzig. Many of the standard tools of operations research, such as linear programming, dynamic programming, inventory theory, and queuing theory were relatively well developed before the end of the 1950s.

The second factor in the impressive progress of operations research was the parallel development of the digital computer. This provided the decision maker with tremendous capabilities in computational speed and information storage and retrieval. Were it not for the digital computer, operations research, with its large-scale computational problems, would not have grown to its present status.

Up until 1960, most of the formal approaches to decision making in industry were typically applied to special types of rather clearcut, repetitive, operating problems, such as those of production control and resource allocation. Since the 1960s, however, formal approaches have been applied increasingly to the less-well-structured planning problems as well. Partly as a result of this, a more general technology has emerged for imposing logical structure on the reasoning that underlies *any* specific decision. This technology, based on the concepts of decision theory, has been called *decision analysis*. While decision theory appears to have originated with Bernoulli, its application to decision problems was developed much later. The key factors were the axiomatization by von Neumann and Morgenstern (1947), and the fusing of the concepts of utility and subjective probability into an axiomatized theory of decision making under uncertainty by Savage (1954).

Thus, the term "operations research" as we use it, encompasses all managerial problems that are amenable to both the standard concepts and techniques of operations research as well as decision analysis.

1.3. THE NATURE OF OPERATIONS RESEARCH

As the discipline of operations research developed, many names were designed to capture the subtle nuances of each particular domain of activity in the field. Labels that are frequently used are "operations research," "operations analysis," "systems analysis," "decision analysis," "cost–benefit analysis," "management science," "decision science," and others. There is no point in listing further designations or attempting to explain the differences among the various labels, as these would only create more heat than light.

For convenience, and with reasonable accuracy, we can simply define operations research as the scientific method applied to problem solving and decision making for management, which embodies all of these labels. An operations research approach involves:

1. Constructing a symbolic (usually mathematical) model that extracts the essential elements of a real-life decision problem which is inherently complex and

uncertain, so that a solution relevant to the decision maker's objectives can be optimized.
2. Examining and analyzing the relationships that determine the consequences of the decisions made and comparing the relative merit of alternative actions against the decision maker's objectives.
3. Developing a solution technique, including the mathematical theory, if necessary, that yields an optimal value based on the decision maker's objective.

Operations Research applies to both the tactical (problems that are repetitive in nature and do not require subjective inputs) and strategic problems of the organization. Tactical problems are concerned with the daily or ongoing activities of the organization. Examples of this sort include production scheduling and inventory control, balancing assembly-line facilities, facility maintenance and repair, inspection plans for quality control and auditing, and number of counters to serve a queue. Strategic problems have a planning and more global orientation, thus bearing on the daily operations of an organization only indirectly. Illustrations of such problems include developing a long-term program for plant expansion, selecting plant sites, determination of our strategic posture for deterrance, allocation of resources for space exploration, development of programs to aid the needy, increasing the education of disadvantaged minorities, and promoting urban development.

1.3.1. Characteristics of Operations Research

Perhaps the best way of grasping the unique nature of operations research is to examine its outstanding characteristics and qualities.

FOCUS. The primary focus of an operations research study is on decision making. That is, the main results of the analysis must directly and unambiguously have implications for managerial action.

AREAS OF APPLICATION. Operations research is applied to problems that are concerned with conducting and coordinating the operations or activities within an organization. The nature of the organization is irrelevant. In fact, operations research has been applied extensively in a variety of areas—such as business, industry, hospitals, and government.

METHODOLOGICAL APPROACH. Operations research utilizes the scientific method. Specifically, the process begins with the careful observation and formulation of the problem. The next step is to construct a scientific (typically mathematical or simulation) model that attempts to abstract the essence of the real problem. From this model, conclusions or solutions are obtained which are also valid for the real problem. In an iterative fashion, the model is then verified through appropriate experimentation.

OBJECTIVE. Operations research attempts to find the best or optimal solution to the problem under consideration. To do this, it is necessary to define a measure of effectiveness that takes into account the goals of the organization. This measure is then used to compare alternative actions.

INTERDISCIPLINARY TEAM APPROACH. No single individual can have a thorough knowledge of all the myriad aspects of operations research or the problems being addressed. This would require a group of individuals having diverse backgrounds and skills, indicating the need for a team approach. The team should be interdisciplinary, including individuals with skills in mathematics, statistics, economics, management, computer science, engineering, and psychology.

DIGITAL COMPUTER. Most operations research studies require the use of a computer. This may be due to the complexity of the mathematical model, the volume of data to be manipulated, or the computations needing to be performed. Many if not most of the techniques you will study in this text are available as "canned" programs, thus eliminating the need of solving many problems by hand.

1.4. MODEL BUILDING: A SYSTEMS APPROACH

1.4.1. Models and Modeling

As you study this text, keep in mind that the most important skills that you can learn are the formulating, manipulating, and analyzing of models from a management point of view. Proficiency in these areas is more important than the mastering of specific quantitative techniques. By means of an experiential approach, using small projects and cases of some real-world management problems, we focus on modeling and analysis and let the computer do the routine computations.

Modeling is the essence of an operations research approach. Building a model helps you put the complexities and uncertainties of a decision-making problem into a logical structure that is amenable to formal analysis. Such a model specifies the decision alternatives and their anticipated consequences for all possible events that may occur, indicates the relevant data for analyzing the alternatives, and leads to meaningful and informative managerial conclusions. In short, a model is a vehicle for arriving at a well-structured view of reality.

What is a model? A model is an abstraction or an idealized representation of a real-life system. The objective of the model is to provide a means for analyzing the behavior of the system for the purpose of improving its performance. Or, if the system is not as yet in existence, to define the ideal structure of this future system indicating the functional relationships among its elements. The reliability of the solution obtained from the model depends on the validity of this model in representing the *real* system. The greater the discrepancy between the output of the model and the real world, the less accurate is the model in describing the behavior of the original system. A major advantage of modeling is that it permits one to examine the behavior of a system without interfering with ongoing operations.

In order of increasing abstraction, models may be classified generally as (1) iconic, (2) analog, or (3) symbolic. *Iconic models* are physical representations of the real system, scaled up or down. For example, a toy ship is an iconic model of a real one. *Analog models* essentially require the substitution of one property for another for the purpose of expediency in manipulating the model. After the problem is solved, the solution is reinterpreted in terms of the original system. For example, an electrical network model may be used as an analog model to study flows in a transportation system.

Finally, and most relevant for operations research, *symbolic or mathematical models* employ a set of mathematical symbols and functions to represent the decision variables and their relationships to describe the behavior of the system. The solution of the problem is then obtained by applying known mathematical techniques (such as linear programming) to the model. In operations research, a model is almost always a mathematical, and hence approximate, representation of reality. The use of mathematics as a language for model representation has the advantage of being very compact and permits us to take advantage both of high-speed computers and advanced mathematical solution techniques.

The development of the computer has led to the use of two other types of modeling in operations research: (1) simulation models and (2) heuristic models. *Simulation models* are generally computer programs that replicate the behavior of a system using the computer. The statistics describing the different measures of performance of the system are accumulated as the simulator advances on the computer. Simulation modeling is more flexible than mathematical modeling, and hence may be used to represent complex systems that could otherwise not be formulated mathematically. However, simulation does not yield general solutions such as those obtained from mathematical models. Moreover, simulation results are inferential in nature, and therefore imprecise, and the development and use of a simulation model may be quite expensive.

Heuristic models are essentially models that employ some intuitive rules or guidelines in the hope of generating new strategies which will yield improved solutions. This is in contrast to mathematical and simulation models, where the strategies are generally well defined. Heuristic models do not claim to find the optimum solution to the problem. An example of a heuristic might be: "service all customers in the line on a first-come first-served basis."

The result of a successful model-building exercise, then, is a model that will help the decision maker make the choice that is most commensurable with his goals, indicate those variables of greatest importance to the decision, and reflect the simplifying assumptions that can be introduced without distorting the basic nature of the original problem.

Always attempt to build as simple a model as possible. The advantages of a simple model are: (1) it is economical in terms of time, costs, and thinking; (2) it can be more readily understood by the decision maker; and (3) if necessary, the model can be altered readily and effectively.

1.4.2. The Nature and Structure of Mathematical Models

A mathematical model includes principally three basic sets of elements. These are (1) decision variables and parameters, (2) constraints, and (3) objective functions.

1. *Decision variables and parameters.* The decision variables are the unknowns (or decisions) which are to be determined by solving the model. The parameters are the known values that relate the decision variables to the constraints and objective function. The parameters of the model may either be deterministic or probabilistic (stochastic).
2. *Constraints.* To account for the technological, economic, and other limitations of the system, the model must include constraints (implicit or explicit) that restrict the decision variables to a range of feasible values.
3. *Objective function.* The objective function defines the measure of effectiveness of the system as a mathematical function of the decision variables. An *optimal* solution to the model is obtained when the values of the decision variables yield a best value of the objective function, subject to the constraints. A poor or inappropriate formulation of the objective function can only lead to a poor solution to the problem. A common example of this occurs when some aspects of the system are neglected. For example, in determining the optimal production level of a certain product, the objective function may reflect only the goals of the production department while neglecting the goals of marketing and finance. In such cases, the model yields a *suboptimal* solution, which may not serve the best interest of the entire organization.

We shall now consider two highly simplified problems to illustrate some of the elements and principles involved in model building and in the application of quantitative techniques to the solution of managerial problems. We have made no attempt to be realistic in these examples. However, you will find more practical and realistic examples in the chapters to follow and be given an opportunity to work on such problems in the illustrative minicases at the end of each chapter. The first problem is one that can be modeled and solved as a mathematical programming problem. The second problem employs the concepts and techniques of decision analysis to solve the decision problem.

1.4.3. Example—A Production Problem

The XYZ company produces two toy products, Bobby and Teddy bears. Each of these products must be processed through two different machines. One machine has 12 hours and the second machine has 8 hours of available capacity. Each Bobby produced requires 2 hours of time on both machines. Each Teddy produced requires 3 hours of time on the first machine and 1 hour on the second machine. The incremental profit is $6 per Bobby and $7 per Teddy sold, and the firm can sell as many units of each product as it can manufacture. The problem is to determine how many units of Bobbies and Teddies should be produced.

Suppose that you were an operations researcher and your task was to assist the XYZ Company. You would first translate XYZ Company's problem from the verbal problem description into mathematical terms, and then by utilizing the mathematical tools at your disposal, solve the newly defined mathematical problem.

Let us denote x_1 as the number of units of Bobbies to be produced and x_2 as the number of units of Teddies to be produced. Also, let P represent the total incremental profit to the company. The variables x_1 and x_2 are the decision variables of the problem. These are the variables over which the company exercises control and whose levels it seeks to establish (to maximize its profit). Since the company can make a profit of $6 and $7 on each Bobby and Teddy sold, respectively (parameters), the company's total profit is given by

$$P = 6x_1 + 7x_2.$$

This states that the firm's total profit is made up of the profit from Bobbies ($6 times the number sold) plus the profit from Teddies ($7 time the number sold). Hence, if 50 Bobbies and 100 Teddies are sold, the company's profit is 6(50) + 7(100) = $1000. The equation above is the company's (and the problem's) objective function, which it wishes to maximize. It is a linear function of the decision variables (x_1, x_2) and the parameters ($6, $7). The company wishes to select values for x_1 and x_2 that will maximize this function.

The company would like to produce as much of x_1 and x_2 as possible, since profits would go up accordingly. However, it cannot because of the constraints under which it is forced to operate. There are two: the capacity constraints on the two machines used to produce both products.

The first machine constraint, transformed into mathematical terms, is expressed as follows:

$$2x_1 + 3x_2 \leqslant 12.$$

That is, each Bobby uses 2 hours of this machine, and each Teddy uses 3 hours (these are parameters associated with the technological constraints of the problem). Hence, the total hours used in producing Bobbies and Teddies is expressed by the left-hand side of this equation. This must be equal to or less than the total hours available on this machine (= 12). If, for example, only Bobbies are produced, a maximum of 6 can be made. If only Teddies are produced, at most 4 can be made. If the company decides to produce both Bobbies and Teddies, it can produce 3 and 2 of these products respectively, 4 and 1 of them respectively, and so forth.

For the second machine, a similar constraint is

$$2x_1 + 1x_2 \leqslant 8.$$

In addition, we must impose the constraint that restrict x_1 and x_2 nonnegative. In terms of the problem, this means that the firm cannot produce negative amounts of products.

The company's problem might thus be symbolically summarized as follows:

$$\text{maximize } P = 6x_1 + 7x_2$$

$$\text{subject to} \quad 2x_1 + 3x_2 \leqslant 12$$

$$2x_1 + \ x_2 \leqslant 8$$

$$x_1, \quad x_2 \geqslant 0.$$

The preceding problem is actually a *linear programming* problem. It is a programming problem because it asks us to program or establish the levels of the decision variables to maximize (sometimes to minimize) an objective function. It is a *linear* programming problem because we are asked to maximize a linear objective function subject to linear constraints, including the nonnegativity conditions imposed on the variables. The *parameters* of the problem, that is, the coefficients of the variables in the objective function and in the constraints, as well as the constants (12 and 8 on the right-hand side of the constraints), are assumed to be deterministic (i.e., known with certainty). More particularly, however, it is not possible to produce a fraction of a bear; thus, we need another constraint on the decision variables to ensure both nonnegativity and integer conditions. That is, the nonnegativity constraint should be altered to read

$$x_1, x_2 = 0, 1, 2, 3, \ldots, \quad \text{integer.}$$

In this form, with the three dots meaning "and so forth," we are demanding that the solution be an integer solution. We now have an *integer programming* problem, that is, a problem in which a linear objective function is maximized or minimized subject to a set of linear constraints, where the decision variables can take on only integer values.

While we shall learn about techniques for solving both linear and integer programming problems, this example is simple enough to be solved intuitively. It should be evident, however, that a programmed mathematical procedure will ordinarily be preferable, if not mandatory, for problems of only slightly greater complexity than the present one.

It is clear that given a level of x_1, in order to maximize P, we want x_2 to be as large as is feasible. Further, x_1 can take on only the values 0, 1, 2, 3, and 4. The best feasible values that x_2 can take on for each value of x_1 are as follows (the larger x_2 given a fixed level of x_1, the larger the profit):

Solution Number	x_1 Level	x_2 Level	P
1	0	4	$28
2	1	3	27
3	2	2	26
4	3	2	32
5	4	0	24

Therefore, $x_1 = 3$ and $x_2 = 2$ is the optimal solution to this problem, yielding the highest profit, $32.

This example illustrates several of the ingredients of operations research. To solve the problem, it was first necessary to determine the organization's goals. We then developed functional relationships describing in mathematical terms the interactions of the relevant variables and the constraints within which a solution must lie. That is, a mathematical model was specified that restated the verbal description of the problem in symbolic terms. The parameters of the model were probably based on both objective facts and subjective assessments regarding unit profits and technological constraints. The problem could have been solved by linear programming or by integer programming methods. Instead, it was simplified and solved through a little intelligence and logic. The latter should never be overlooked in any decision problem being addressed.

1.4.4. Example—A Plant Expansion Problem

Consider a firm that is faced with a decision as to whether to remain with its present manufacturing plant, to build a small extension, or to build a large extension. Its decision is influenced by the possible future markets for its product. Let us, for simplicity, assume that the future market will be either low, medium, or high. Let us further assume that the firm is able to calculate the net profits that each of its options would bring under each possible future market condition and that the firm's goal is to obtain the highest expected profit possible. Suppose that the probabilities of a low, medium, and high market have been assessed by the firm to be $\frac{1}{4}$, $\frac{1}{4}$, and $\frac{1}{2}$, respectively. What should the firm do?

We can structure or model this discrete decision-making problem under uncertainty in terms of a set of alternative actions, a set of possible events, a consequence or value associated with each possible event and action, and probabilities (or beliefs) about the chance of each of the possible events occurring. This problem can be expressed in either a matrix or tree form, as shown in Figure 1.2.

Thus, instead of decision variables, we have a set of alternative decisions or actions from which we must choose. The constraints in this problem are implicit, and are manifested in terms of the number of alternatives the firm wishes to or can

Matrix

| Manager's Actions | FUTURE MARKET STATES (EVENTS) AND THEIR PROBABILITY OF OCCURRENCE | | | Expected Profits |
	$\frac{1}{4}$ Low	$\frac{1}{4}$ Medium	$\frac{1}{2}$ High	
Stay with present plant	$ 0	0	0	0
Build small extension	50	300	200	187.5
Build large extension	−500	100	600	200

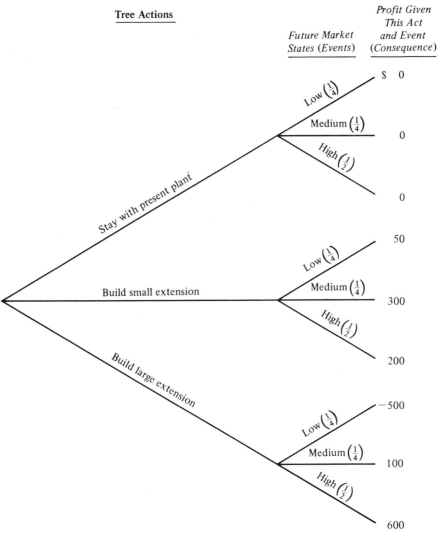

Figure 1.2. Plant expansion problem.

consider in selecting a course of action. The parameters of the problem are the event probabilities and profits associated with each action–event pair. If the state of the market was known, the firm could easily choose a preferred course of action, based on its objective of maximizing profit. For example, if the future state of the market were low, the firm would prefer to build a small extension. However, since the future state of the market is uncertain and can only be assessed in probabilistic terms, the criterion of choice (objective) is to maximize expected value. The expected value appropriate to each option is shown in Figure 1.2, calculated from the payoffs for each of the options and the probabilities of the future states of the market. For example, for the action build a large extension,

$$\text{expected profit} = (-500)\left(\tfrac{1}{4}\right) + (100)\left(\tfrac{1}{4}\right) + 600\left(\tfrac{1}{2}\right) = \$200.$$

The optimal action would be to build the large extension.

1.4.5. Commentary

Real-world problems are not as simple as the ones given in the examples. Frequently, the organization's objectives cannot be stated as precisely and compactly as we have done. Frequently, historical data are not available or sufficiently complete to permit anything more than rough estimates of the relevant parameters. Frequently, the problem is so complex that the construction and solution of an appropriate mathematical model become an onerous if not impossible task, and alternative procedures must be relied upon. Frequently, the mathematical techniques required for the solution of the model are relatively obscure or as yet undiscovered. Frequently, analysts arrive at conclusions that disagree with their employers' intuition, and getting their suggestions implemented becomes an interesting problem in human relations.

1.5. THE PROCESS OF OPERATIONS RESEARCH

The process of operations research involves the following five major steps:

1. Formulation and definition of the problem.
2. Construction of the model.
3. Solution of the model.
4. Validation of the model.
5. Implementation of the results.

1.5.1. Formulation and Definition of the Problem

This phase of the process requires (1) a precise description of the goals or objectives of the study, (2) identification of the controllable or decision variables and uncontrollable variables of the decision system, and (3) recognition of the restrictions or constraints on the variables and system. Establishing the bounds of the system and the options open is a matter of judgment. One must be careful to define the system in such a way so as not to suboptimize: for example, to define a goal which can represent only a portion of the system and which may actually prove harmful for the entire organization; or fail to account for all possible decision alternatives and constraints resulting in an inadequate solution.

1.5.2. Construction of the Model

This is the detail phase of the process. First, the operations researcher must decide on the most suitable model for representing the system. Such a model should specify quantitative relationships for the objective and constraints of the problem in terms of its decision variables. It should provide parameter estimates, either obtained from historical or subjective data, or formally estimated by some statistical mechanism. A time horizon must be chosen. So must a determination be made as to whether to treat the system as deterministic or probabilistic. The model can be a mathematical, simulation, or heuristic model, depending upon the complexity and solvability of the mathematical relationships.

1.5.3. Solution of the Model

Given the model, along with its parameters as specified by historical, technological, and judgmental data, the operations researcher then calculates or derives a mathematical solution. If the model fits into one of the well-known mathematical models such as linear programming, an optimal solution may be obtained by using these techniques. The various mathematical techniques for arriving at such solutions comprise much of the contents of this text. On the other hand, if the mathematical relationships of the model are too complex to permit analytic solutions, then a simulation approach may be more appropriate. If simulation or heuristic models are used, the search for optimality must be replaced by the search for "good" solutions.

In addition to the solution of the model, one must also perform *sensitivity analysis*, that is, determine the behavior of the system to changes in the system's parameters and specifications. This is done because the input data (parameters) may not be accurate or stable, and the structural assumptions of the model may not be valid. Sensitivity analysis is an essential part of this phase of the process and must not be overlooked.

1.5.4. Validation of the Model

Validating a model requires determining if the model can reliably predict the actual system's performance. It also involves testing the structural assumptions of the model (i.e., the variables, functional relationships, etc.) to ascertain their validity. A common approach for testing the validity of a model is to compare its performance with past data available for the actual system. The model will be valid if, under similar input conditions, it can reasonably reproduce the past performance of the system. Of course, there is no assurance that the future performance of the system will continue to duplicate its past history. Thus, one must always be on guard for possible changes in the system over time and adjust the model accordingly.

1.5.5. Implementation

Implementation should really begin at the initiation of the operations research study. We cannot overemphasize the importance of having those managers who will act on the results of the study *on the team* that analyzes the problem. Otherwise, the project is likely to be judged only as an interesting, but academic or inconclusive exercise.

If the model is used more than once in analyzing decision problems, each time the model must be revised to account for the specifics of the problem and current data. Because the model may be used repeatedly, documentation of the model and plans for its updating are not only desirable but necessary.

1.6. CONTEMPORARY OPERATIONS RESEARCH APPLICATIONS

Operations research has had an increasing impact on organizational management and decision making in recent years, both in the public and private sectors of our society. Both the number and the variety of its applications continue to grow rapidly, and much of this growth has paralleled the growth of the computer. Operations research is being used widely in the military, government, and business and industry. Many industries, including aircraft and aerospace, automobile, computer, communication, electronics, electric power, mining, paper, petroleum, transportation, and so on, have made widespread use of operations research.

More specifically, consider some of the problems that have been solved by particular techniques of operations research. Mathematical programming has been used successfully in the modeling and solution of problems concerned with the assignment of personnel, assignment of jobs to machines, blending of materials, feed and product mix problems, diet problems, distribution and transportation, energy, ecology (pollution), and investment portfolios, to mention just a few.

Dynamic programming has been successfully applied to such problems as planning and advertising expenditures, distributing sales effort, and production scheduling.

Decision analysis has been applied to problems in controlling hurricanes, water pollution, medicine, law, nuclear safety, space exploration, new product decisions, advertising expenditures, research and development, and so forth. Queuing theory has had application in solving problems concerned with traffic congestion, servicing machines subject to breakdown, determining the level of a service force, air traffic scheduling, design of dams, job shop scheduling, and hospital operations. Other concepts and techniques, such as inventory theory, simulation, and PERT, also have been successfully applied in a multitude of problem contexts.

1.7. OPERATIONS RESEARCH CONCEPTS AND TECHNIQUES COVERED

This section will briefly introduce each of the operations research methods that will be covered in this text. The purpose of the section is to show you the types of analyses that are available and some of the problems to which these analyses can be applied. This section like the text is divided into three parts: (1) Probability and Decision Making, (2) Mathematical Programming and Optimization, and (3) Operations Research Applications. The first two parts deal essentially with concepts and solution techniques that can be generally applied to models representing systems from different operational environments. The third part, as its title implies, deals with applications that are characterized generally by special model formulations.

1.7.1. Probability and Decision Making

PROBABILITY CONCEPTS, MODELS, AND TECHNIQUES. These are useful when coping with decision making in an uncertain environment. The concepts of probability are discussed and methods are indicated for using and computing probabilities. Bayes' theorem for probability revision (revising beliefs in light of new information) is presented and applied. Applications of probability to decision making are included.

DECISION ANALYSIS. Bayesian decision theory or decision analysis presents a powerful method for making decisions, especially when only limited information is available. We first discuss such concepts as decision matrices, decision trees, decision criteria, expected monetary value, expected utility, and value of information. We also distinguish between individual and group decisions and suggest how differences among individual members of a group might be reconciled.

We then proceed to discuss how beliefs and tastes can be quantified via subjective probability distributions and utility functions. The notion of risk is discussed as well as the method for computing expected utilities and choosing on the basis of the criterion of expected utility maximization.

Decision-tree diagramming and analysis are presented using the extensive and normal forms of analysis, and the backward induction process to choose the optimal strategy is developed. Typologies of managerial behavior in information processing, information acquisition, and strategy selection are discussed based on experimental and realistic observations. Cases and problems discussed in this area include new product development, company acquisition alternatives, equipment selection, quality control, production management, oil exploration, and auditing.

MULTIPLE OBJECTIVES. Organizational objectives are multifaceted. We discuss some techniques for measuring the multiple objectives of an organization and how to choose among alternatives having multiple objectives. Applications of these techniques are included.

1.7.2. Mathematical Programming and Optimization

LINEAR PROGRAMMING. This is perhaps the best-known and applied operations research technique. Linear programming is a mathematical technique for determination of the optimal allocation of scarce resources when the objective function and constraint sets are linear. It is an efficient way of solving such problems when a choice must be made from alternatives too numerous to evaluate intuitively or by other conventional methods.

The nature and limitations of linear programming, modeling applications, graphical solutions, and possible solution outcomes (such as conditions under which a unique solution, infinite solution, degenerate solution, or no solution occurs) as viewed geometrically are first discussed.

The simplex method and simplex tableau are then presented using the Gauss–Jordan method for solving systems of linear equations as the underlying basis for the simplex computational procedure. In this way, the simplex method is easily grasped and remembered rather than becoming a mechanical routine which is quickly forgotten once the course examination is over with. Complications and their resolution and artificial variables are also discussed using the simplex tableau. Applications include production forecasting, financial planning, and media-selection.

Additional topics covered in linear programming are duality and its economic interpretation, sensitivity (or postoptimality) analysis, and special types of linear programming algorithms, such as transportation models. Applications of linear programming include production planning, requirements planning, and production–inventory–purchasing.

INTEGER PROGRAMMING. Integer programming applies when the values of the decision variables are restricted to integers. The nature of integer programming problems, model-building applications, formulations, "modeling tricks," and solution procedures and sensitivity analysis are presented. One popular solution procedure discussed is branch and bound (more formally called "implicit enumeration"). Applications include financial management and plant location.

GOAL PROGRAMMING. Goal programming deals with problems having multiple objectives. It is a technique quite similar to linear programming, which has become very popular in the last several years. The history, concepts, application areas, and limitations of goal programming are discussed. Also discussed are the methods and processes of goal programming. Here we compare goal programming to linear programming, demonstrate model formulations through case applications, and use the graphical and simplex method as a solution routine. Applications include production scheduling, transportation problems, portfolio analysis, constrained regression, and crop selection in agriculture.

1.7.3. Operations Research Applications

INVENTORY THEORY AND MODELS. These aid in the control of inventory costs by minimizing the total cost of purchasing, carrying, and being short of inventory. Inventory control models for deterministic and probabilistic demand are discussed. Models useful in dealing with quantity discounts, multiple products, and stochastic models are discussed at some length, along with applications. Forecasting methods, such as the moving average and exponential smoothing, are also presented and applied.

WAITING-LINE (QUEUING) MODELS AND SIMULATION MODELS. Queuing theory studies random arrivals at a servicing or processing facility of limited capacity. Such models have been applied to study job shop flows, banking operations, air traffic scheduling and control, and so on. Such models allow management to predict lengths of future waiting lines, average time spent in the line or system by an individual awaiting service, and needed facility additions. Analytic techniques of queuing theory can be used to solve waiting-line problems, but simulation is virtually always used, owing to the complexity of a real system.

The nature and techniques of simulation are also presented and applied to problems in inventory control, decision theory, and to oil transport operation.

CPM AND PERT: NETWORKING. Networking models enable managers to cope with the complexities and interdependencies involved in large projects. Much of this application has been in the construction and aerospace and defense industries. Techniques covered include CPM and PERT. Linear programming is also applied to solve such problems.

REFERENCES   BROWN, R. V. "Do Managers Find Decision Theory Useful?" *Harvard Business Review*, May–June 1970, 78–89.

MJOSUND, A. "The Synergy of Operations Research and Computers." *Operations Research*, **20** (5), 1975, 1057–1064.

RAIFFA, H. *Decision Analysis*. Reading, Mass.: Addison-Wesley Publishing Co., Inc., 1968.

SAVAGE, L. J. *The Foundations of Statistics*. New York: John Wiley & Sons, Inc., 1954.

SCHLAIFER, R. *Analysis of Decisions Under Uncertainty*. New York: McGraw-Hill Book Company, 1969.

VON NEUMANN, J., and O. MORGENSTERN. *Theory of Games and Economic Behavior*. Princeton, N.J.: Princeton University Press, 1947.

WAGNER, H. M. *Principles of Operations Research*. Englewood Cliffs, N.J.: Prentice-Hall, Inc., 1969.

WAGNER, H. M. "The ABC's of OR." *Operations Research*, **19**, 1971, 1259–1281.

KEY CONCEPTS

Operations research
Decisions
   certainty/uncertainty
   static/dynamic
   nature/rational opponent
Elements of a decision
   decision making unit
   actions
   states
   objective consequences
   subjective consequences
Models
   iconic
   analog
   symbolic
   simulation
   heuristic

Structure of mathematical models
   decision variables
   parameters
   constraints
   objective function
Process of operations research
   definition of problem
   model construction
   model solution
   model validation
   model implementation

REVIEW QUESTIONS

1.1. Herbert Simon has said that management is synonymous with decision making. Do you agree or disagree? State your reasons.

1.2. Eight general types of decision situations have been identified. Give an example of each of these decision situations and show that your example fits.

1.3. Select a decision-making situation and relate it in terms of the elements of a decision. Do you agree that all or most decision processes can be thought of in terms of the explicit elements that have been stated in the text?

1.4. Give an example of an organizational problem where there may be incompatible or conflicting goals among organizational members or departments. How can the tendency for the objectives of an organization and those of its members to diverge be corrected?

1.5. What is a good decision? Cite a good decision that turned out badly. Give examples of good and bad business or public decisions, such as by presidents of educational or other institutions.

1.6. Using an example decision situation, discuss the benefits and limitations of using a formal approach to decision making.

1.7. The objective of any private business organization is to maximize profit. Comment.

1.8. What are the most important qualities distinguishing successful from unsuccessful managers? Where do decision-making skills fall on your list? Which of these qualities can be enhanced by formal education, for example, at a school of business or management. Which do you think you have to be born with? Which can only be learned on the job?

1.9. What post-World War II factors played a key role in the development of operations research?

1.10. How do you view the role of science in management and decision making in terms of concept, approach, and application?

1.11. What is the function of models in decision making? Name the types of models. What are the advantages of models? What are the pitfalls of models?

1.12. Give examples of iconic, analog, symbolic, simulation, and heuristic models.

1.13. A good deal has been written and said about the use of "operations research techniques" in managerial decision making. Discuss their value, limitations, and future. Be as specific as possible by discussing specific applications.

1.14. Using the steps in the process of conducting an operations research study, explain how you would apply such an approach to (a) developing a new product for consumer use; (b) allocating the national budget.

ANSWERS TO REVIEW QUESTIONS

1.1. *Agree.* Decision making is the core of management. *All* activities require managerial decisions, even the implementation of decisions already made.

1.2. *Type 1—Static, certainty, nature.* Example: Deciding whether or not to insulate your home, knowing what the weather will be like in the future.

Type 2—Static, certainty, rational opponent. Examples: Deciding at what price to sell your product, knowing that your chief competitor has set his price at a certain level, *or* deciding which television program to put in a certain time slot, knowing what the rival networks have slotted for the same time.

Type 3—Dynamic decision, certainty, nature. Example: Selecting manpower needs for the next 12 months, knowing what sales will be in each month.

Type 4—Dynamic, certainty, rational opponent. Example: Setting production levels for the next 12 months, knowing the quantities your chief competitor will produce.

Type 5—Static, uncertainty, nature. Example: Deciding whether or not to buy flood (or any other type) insurance for the next year.

Type 6—Static, uncertainty, rational opponent. Example: Deciding on an energy policy, not knowing what OPEC will do regarding the price of crude petroleum.

Type 7—Dynamic, uncertainty, nature. Example: Setting production levels for the next 12 months, not knowing what future sales will be.

Type 8—Dynamic, uncertainty, rational opponent. Example: Deciding how much money to allocate (budget) for pollution control over the next 10 years, not knowing what the Environmental Protection Agency (EPA) will do.

1.3. Consider a simple decision situation where someone is trying to decide whether or not to carry an umbrella to work on a certain day.

In this case, the *decision making unit* is an individual. The *set of possible actions* consists of (1) carrying an umbrella and (2) not carrying an umbrella.

The *set of possible states* which may occur are (1) rain and (2) no rain.

The *consequences* associated with each possible action–state pair are:

1. Carry umbrella—rain → stay dry
2. Carry umbrella—no rain → stay dry, have inconvenience
                             of carrying umbrella
3. Do not carry umbrella—rain → get wet
4. Do not carry umbrella—no rain → stay dry

The relationship between consequences and the values of an individual is the relative worth to the individual of the four consequences enumerated above.

It would seem that most decision processes can be thought of in these terms, even those which have only one possible state of nature (decisions under certainty). In this case, each action will have only one consequence.

1.4. An example might be a business organization which has the goal of *maximizing* profits. Employed by the firm are salesmen who are paid on a commission basis. These salesmen, in order to *maximize* their compensation, will tend to sell those items with the largest selling price, not (necessarily) those with the highest profit margin.

In this case and in general, the solution would be to design a different system for compensation and/or evaluation such that the individual who attempts to *maximize* his own goals will also be working toward furthering the goals of the organization as a whole.

1.5. A good decision is one in which the elements of the decision problem are considered and incorporated in a rational, logical manner. Operation research provides a formal way to decompose a problem into its simpler elements to facilitate analysis.

An example of a hypothetical "good" decision that turned out badly would be an even money bet on a football game between the Superbowl champions and a winless expansion team. Most would agree that there is a much greater probability than .50 that the championship team would win. But if the expansion team happened to win in this particular case, the outcome would be "bad." Yet, over the long view we would expect that a person taking such a bet would generally come out ahead.

1.6. Advantages of the formal approach include:

1. The formal approach provides decision makers with a set of concepts and tools that will enable them to make decisions in a logically consistent fashion, and with as much precision as possible.
2. The formal approach gives decision makers an improved insight into how they make their decisions.
3. Formalization and quantification of the problem facilitate communication.
4. Formalization of routine or repetitive decision problems frees the manager to concentrate on more pressing matters.
5. Formalization facilitates the development of better organizational planning, operating, and control systems.
6. It serves as a matter of record—that is, of historical and current informational value.

Limitations of the formal approach include:

1. Managers might have a tendency to regard the model as reality and place too much faith in the results.
2. The model may not be able to incorporate important nuances of the real system, making it dysfunctional.
3. The formal approach does not take into account decision implementation, which is a behavioral and psychological problem.

1.7. *False.* Many other objectives are possible such as maximization of stock price, certain social and humanitarian goals, enhancement of public image or prestige, and so on.

1.8. Important qualities of successful managers would include ability to make rational decisions and motivate people to implement decisions. Decision-making skills are very important and include quantitative and mathematical (logical) skills. While decision making as well as motivational skills can, by and large, be learned through formal education, practical on-the-job experience is also necessary.

1.9. The following factors contributed to the postwar development of operations research.

1. Increasing complexity and specialization in organizations.
2. Progress made in developing and improving techniques available to operations research.
3. Development of the digital computer.

1.10. Operations research is the scientific method applied to problem solving for management. The approach involves:

1. Constructing a model which abstracts the elements of a real life decision problem.
2. Examining and analyzing the relationships that determine the consequences of decisions.

3. Developing a solution technique that yields an optimal value based on the decision maker's objective.

Operations research can be applied to both repetitive problems (production scheduling, inventory control, and so on) and strategic problems (selecting plant sites, deciding on R and D projects, and so on).

1.11. Models are an attempt to put the complexities and uncertainties of a decision-making problem into a logical structure amenable to formal analysis. The function of a model is to serve as a tool for analyzing the behavior of a system for the purpose of providing insights into its operation and improving its performance. Models may be iconic, analog, or symbolic.

Advantages of models include (1) allowing one to analyze a system without interfering with its ongoing operations and (2) allowing one to make this analysis much quicker and with much less expense than if the analysis were made while working with the real system.

The major disadvantage of models, especially of complex systems, is that the model may not capture the reality of the situation, especially if there are constraints (budgeting or time) on formulation and/or data collection.

1.12. Examples of "iconic," "analog," "symbolic," "simulation," and "heuristic" are:

Iconic: Toy ship, link trainer for airplane pilots.
Analog: Electrical network representing a transportation system.
Symbolic: Modeling the arrival of customers at a bank by using symbols and equations to relate interarrival time, maximum queue size, time spent in queue, etc.
Simulation: Modeling an inventory system and finding out such things as average stock level, number of stockouts, etc., by simulating the operation several thousand times.
Heuristic: Servicing customers in a line on a first come, first serve basis.

1.13. The benefits and limitations of operations research techniques were discussed in (1.6). The future will see more classes of problems being attacked by operations research techniques as these techniques grow in sophistication and become better known and understood.

1.14. For each case, one would need to construct a model, analyze the consequences of any and all possible actions, and choose that action which promises to optimize the objective.

EXERCISES   **1.1.** Ace manufacturing has the option of producing two products during periods of slack activity. For the next week, production has been scheduled so that the milling machine is free 20 hours and skilled labor will have 16 hours of available time. Product 1 requires 8 hours of machine time and 4 hours of skilled labor input. Product 2 requires 4 hours of machine time and 4 hours of skilled labor input. Product 1 contributes $7 per unit to profit, and product 2 contributes $5 per unit to profit (not including skilled labor or machine time cost). Formulate a mathematical model of this problem in terms of (1) decision variables and parameters, (2) constraints, and (3) objective function. (*Hint:* It is a linear programming problem.) What is the optimal decision?

1.2. A farm manager has to choose between purchasing 500, 600, or 800 store cattle for paddock fattening. The profit from fattening will depend on whether the grazing season is good, fair, or poor. The manager's personal beliefs about the season are that there is a 0.4, 0.2, and 0.4 chance of a good, fair, and poor season, respectively. If the manager buys 500 cattle, his profits will be $10,000, $5000, and $3000 if the season is good, fair, and poor, respectively. If he purchases 600 cattle, profits will be $12,500, $6000, and $0 for a good, fair, and poor season, respectively. And if he buys 800 cattle, they will be $17,000, $8000, and −$5500 for a good, fair, and poor season, respectively. Formulate this decision problem under uncertainty in terms of alternatives, events (and event probabilities), and consequences. Draw a decision matrix and decision tree of the problem. Using the criterion of expected profit, select a best course of action. Comment on your choice.

CHAPTER 2
Probability Concepts and Techniques

OBJECTIVES. Upon successful completion of this chapter, you should be able to:

1. Cite examples of business situations that can be better understood and predicted through the use of probabilities.
2. Use Venn diagrams to describe and interpret business situations.
3. Determine and correctly manipulate probability assignments of uncertain business events.
4. Revise probability predictions of uncertain business events by the use of subjective information and empirical data.

2.1. INTRODUCTION

A manager, management scientist, operations researcher, financial analyst, marketing analyst, accountant, production planner, auditor, personnel specialist, labor negotiator, and so forth, who has never been asked to make a decision in the face of *uncertainty*, is almost certainly from an environment radically different from anything imaginable. For example, if he is a stock broker, then he is able to *predict with certainty* the rate of return of any portfolio. If he is a new product manager, then he is able to *predict with certainty* future sales and profits of a new product just entering the market. If he is a distribution manager, then he is able to *predict with certainty* the distribution schedule of a product so that a shipment arrives on time to satisfy sales at each demand center. If his responsibility in a personnel department is personnel placement, then he is able to *predict with certainty* how well a candidate for employment will perform a particular assignment.

The obvious conclusions to be drawn from the preceding remarks is that, in the world of business, decisions are being made daily in the face of uncertainty. In fact, you, your classmates, and others already recognize the problem of making a decision under uncertainty. Consider some comments that you or the others have probably made. "It is a high-risk decision." "It will never happen." "It is a low-risk stock with expected increasing returns." "We must enter the market to stay competitive and hope for the best." "It is highly likely that future demand will exceed present production capacity."

Do you as a student of management science and future business decision maker require a book containing probability concepts to help you understand uncertainty? Do you need to understand decision analysis techniques based on probability concepts in order to make good decisions? The answers to these two questions depend upon the seriousness and complexity of the decision problems you will be faced with. Some sensible decisions obviously can be made on a largely intuitive basis.

However, other problems you may regard as more serious, and for these you will find your intuition less reliable. For example, do you recommend that the firm open a new factory and, if so, in what location and why in this location? Which of the new products should we begin manufacturing? How many accounts should I audit to maximize the likelihood of detecting fraud? Which alterations should you, as Treasurer, make in next year's proposed budget?

While you may feel adequately equipped for the "smaller" decisions and for some "complex" or "high-risk" decisions, you probably have and will in the future admit to being perplexed by the more complicated decisions. Our goal in this chapter and in the succeeding chapters on probability models and decision analysis is threefold:

1. To make clear the precise nature of the difficulties that can arise in understanding decision making under uncertainty.
2. To investigate what assumptions and further knowledge are required to overcome these difficulties.
3. To follow through to the point of making decisions under uncertainty.

We have emphasized that we do not regard probability models and decision analysis as necessary tools for the solving of trivial problems. We also do not make the claim that all complex decision problems can be solved by studying the concepts and techniques in this book. But there are many situations in industry, government, technology, and education where a careful analysis of the uncertainty present is undoubtedly beneficial. An understanding of some of the basic concepts of probability (Chapter 2) and an understanding of some standard probability models (Chapter 3) not only can be of aid in pinpointing which problems are immediately amenable to solution but also highlight those aspects of other decision problems which require further investigation before a truly satisfactory solution can emerge. A number of interesting and challenging problems and projects will be used to illustrate the concepts and principles of probability models, and then we will go on to a study of the practice of decision making under uncertainty. We begin our study with the presentation of some basic concepts of probability models.

2.2. RANDOM EXPERIMENTS, SAMPLE SPACE, AND UNCERTAINTY

The basic concept in probability models is that of a *random experiment*: an experiment whose outcome cannot be determined in advance.

2.2.1. Example—The Cola and Orange Soda Experiment

To describe this experiment, assume that *two* individuals are given a choice between a bottle of cola (C) and a bottle of orange soda (O). Arbitrarily designate the first coordinate a of a pair (a, b) to denote the choice of the first individual, $a = C$ or $a = O$, and the coordinate b for the choice of the second individual, $b = C$ or $b = O$. A suitable choice of the four possible *outcomes* of this *random experiment* or *random observation* is now afforded by the pairs

$$(C, C), \quad (C, O), \quad (O, C), \quad (O, O),$$

where (C, C) denotes the outcome that both individuals choose colas, (C, O) denotes the outcome that the first individual chooses a cola and the second the orange soda, and so forth.

The set of all possible *outcomes* of a *random experiment* is called the *sample space* of that experiment.

2.2.2. Example—Sample Space of Example 2.2.1

In the cola and orange soda experiment, the sample space is the set

$$S = \{(C, C), (C, O), (O, C), (O, O)\}.$$

Note that S contains four outcomes. We use the notation $N(A)$ to denote the number of outcomes in the set A. Thus, $N(S) = 4$ in Example 2.2.2.

2.2.3. Example—The Ice Cream Purchasing Experiment

To describe this experiment, suppose the Sealcrest Dairy Inc. (SDI) produces three brands of vanilla ice cream for their commercial customers, denoted by a, b, and c. SDI's management is interested in the brand purchased by a particular customer over time on a weekly basis. Each week that the customer purchases ice cream from SDI is considered a *trial* or *observation* of this experiment, and the sample space for one trial is $\{a, b, c\}$. We let $S_1 = \{a, b, c\}$ denote the sample space for one trial (or one purchase) of this experiment.

Next consider three successive trials (or three successive purchases) of this experiment for the customer. The sample space for the second trial is $S_2 = \{a, b, c\}$ and the sample space for the third trial is $S_3 = \{a, b, c\}$. Note, in this case, that $S_1 = S_2 = S_3$. The sample space for all three trials (purchases) is the set

$$S = \begin{bmatrix} (a, a, a), & (a, a, b), & (a, a, c) \\ (a, b, a), & (a, b, b), & (a, b, c) \\ (a, c, a), & (a, c, b), & (a, c, c) \\ (b, a, a), & (b, a, b), & (b, a, c) \\ (b, b, a), & (b, b, b), & (b, b, c) \\ (b, c, a), & (b, c, b), & (b, c, c) \\ (c, a, a), & (c, a, b), & (c, a, c) \\ (c, b, a), & (c, b, b), & (c, b, c) \\ (c, c, a), & (c, c, b), & (c, c, c) \end{bmatrix}.$$

Note that $N(S_1) = N(S_2) = N(S_3) = 3$ and $N(S) = 27$.

A sample space containing a small number of outcomes may be conveniently presented graphically by a rectangular coordinate system or a tree diagram. In general, tree diagrams are more tractable than coordinate systems, especially when outcomes are triples or of higher dimension. For example, the cola and orange soda experiment can be conveniently represented by the use of two-dimensional coordinates (Figure 2.1). The sample space for the ice cream purchasing experiment is represented by a tree diagram (Figure 2.2). Clearly, the ice cream purchasing experiment would be quite difficult to depict by three-dimensional coordinates. Note that tree diagrams provide an organized way of listing all the possible outcomes in a sample space.

It is important to note that no matter how a sample space S is constructed, written, or diagrammed, the outcomes in S must not contain any duplicates; that is

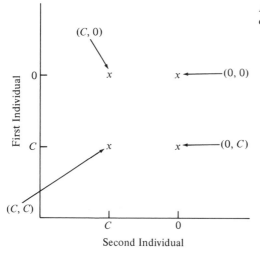

Figure 2.1. Sample space for the cola and orange soda experiment of Example 2.2.1.

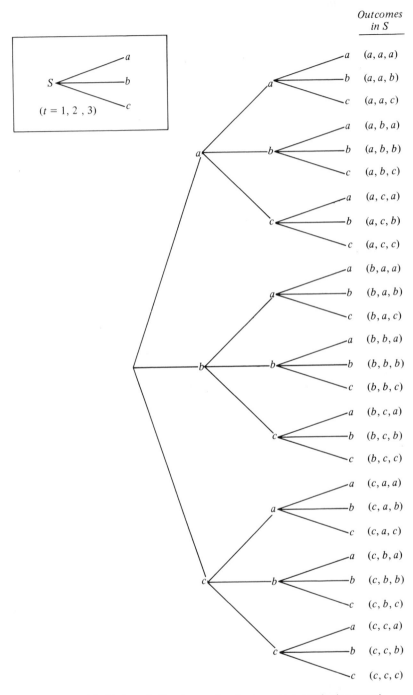

Figure 2.2. Listing of all outcomes for the ice cream purchasing experiment of Example 2.2.3.

35 *S* must be *mutually exclusive. S* must contain all possible outcomes of the random experiment; that is, *S* must be *collectively exhaustive.*

2.2.4. Example—Traffic Counting Experiment

Consider the random experiment of counting the number of cars crossing an intersection during a specified time interval. The sample is

$$S = \{0, 1, 2, \ldots \}.$$

Note that $N(S) =$ infinity $= \infty$.

2.3. EVENTS

An *event* is a subset of a sample space. If a sample space S contains n outcomes, $N(S) = n$, then there are a total of 2^n *events* in S.

2.3.1. Example—Price-Change Forecasting

Tomorrow's closing price for wheat on the Chicago Board of Trade is to be classified as

$$lower = L$$
$$same = S$$
$$higher = H$$

when compared to its opening price. What will occur tomorrow, the comparison of the opening and closing price of wheat, is obviously a *random experiment.*

QUESTION. How would you describe the following events, one or more of which will occur tomorrow on the Chicago Board of Trade?

1. Sample space.
2. The event "closing price of wheat is the same or lower than its opening price."
3. The event "closing price of wheat is the same or higher than its opening price."

Is your sample space S given in (1):

4. Mutually exclusive?
5. Mutually exhaustive?

Answers

1. S = {lower, same, higher}
   = {L, S, H}.
2. "Same or lower" = {same, lower}
   = {S, L}.
3. "Same or higher" = {same, higher}
   = {S, H}.
4. S is *mutually exclusive* since it contains no duplicate outcomes.
5. S is *mutually exhaustive* since it contains *all* possible outcomes of the random experiment.

2.3.2. Example—Events in the Cola and Orange Soda Experiment

Consider Example 2.2.2. $N(S) = 4$, so there are $2^4 = 16$ events in S. Using the capital letters $E_1, E_2, \ldots, E_{16}$ to denote the 16 events in S we have

$$E_1 = \{(C, C)\}, \quad E_2 = \{(C, O)\}, \quad E_3 = \{(O, C)\}, \quad E_4 = \{(O, O)\},$$

$$E_5 = \{(C, O), (C, C)\}, \quad E_6 = \{(C, C), (O, C)\}, \quad E_7 = \{(C, C), (O, O)\},$$

$$E_8 = \{(C, O), (O, C)\}, \quad E_9 = \{(C, O), (O, O)\}, \quad E_{10} = \{(O, C), (O, O)\},$$

$$E_{11} = \{(C, C), (C, O), (O, C)\}, \quad E_{12} = \{(C, C), (C, O), (O, O)\},$$

$$E_{13} = \{(C, O), (O, C), (O, O)\}, \quad E_{14} = \{(C, C), (O, C), (O, O)\},$$

$$E_{15} = \{(C, C), (C, O), (O, C), (O, O)\} = S, \quad E_{16} = \varnothing.$$

Note that one of the 16 events in S is E_{15}, which is S, the sample space. Also note that the "empty event," denoted by $\varnothing$, the event containing no outcomes, is also assumed to be an event in S.

We most often use the notation $E_1, E_2, \ldots$ to denote events, as in Example 2.3.2, or capital letters, such as $A, B, C, \ldots$.

A set of events defined over some sample space is said to be *mutually exclusive*, or *disjoint*, if no outcome is contained in more than one of these events. That is, a collection of events $\{E_1, E_2, \ldots, E_m\}$ is *mutually exclusive*, or *disjoint*, if no two events have any sample outcomes in common. This can be stated precisely by use of the symbol "$\cap$," which stands for intersection of two events. If events E_i and E_j contain no common outcomes, that is, if $E_i \cap E_j = \varnothing$ for all i and j ($i \neq j$, $i = 1, \ldots, m$ and $j = i, \ldots, m$), then the E_i's are said to be *mutually exclusive*.

QUESTION. Which events in Example 2.3.1 are mutually exclusive?

Answer. None of the events are mutually exclusive, since for

(1) and (2):   {lower, same, higher} ∩ {same, lower} = {same, lower}
                        S ∩ $\{S, L\}$ = $\{S, L\}$
(1) and (3):   {lower, same, higher} ∩ {same, higher} = {same, higher}
                        S ∩ $\{S, H\}$ = $\{S\}$
(2) and (3):   {same, lower}   ∩ {same, higher} =   {same}
                     $\{S, L\}$ ∩ $\{S, H\}$ = $\{S\}$.

Note that every pair of events contains at least one common outcome.

2.3.4. Examples—Mutually Exclusive Events

From Examples 2.2.2 and 2.3.2:

1. $E_1 \cap E_2 = \varnothing$, $E_1 \cap E_3 = \varnothing$, $E_1 \cap E_4 = \varnothing$, $E_2 \cap E_3 = \varnothing$, $E_2 \cap E_4 = \varnothing$, $E_3 \cap E_4 = \varnothing$. Thus, the collection of events $\{E_1, E_2, E_3, E_4\}$ is mutually exclusive.
2. $E_1 \cap E_5 = \{(C, C)\}$, $E_1 \cap E_6 = \{(C, C)\}$, $E_1 \cap E_7 = \{(C, C)\}$, $E_1 \cap E_8 = \varnothing$, $E_1 \cap E_9 = \varnothing$, $E_1 \cap E_{10} = \varnothing$, so the collection of events $\{E_1, E_5, E_6, E_7\}$ is *not* mutually exclusive, since there are at least two events in the collection which have a common outcome.
3. Note that $E_8 \cap E_{11} = \{(C, O), (O, C)\}$ and $E_8 \cap E_{13} = \{(C, O), (O, C)\}$. Thus, the collection $\{E_8, E_{11}, E_{13}\}$ is not mutually exclusive. Also, we note that every outcome in E_8 is also in E_{11}, and every outcome in E_8 is in E_{13}. Hence, we say that E_8 is a subevent of E_{11} (E_8 is a subset of E_{11}) and E_8 is a subevent of E_{13}, denoted by use of the symbol "$\subset$" (inclusion). Thus,

$$E_8 \subset E_{11} \quad \text{and} \quad E_8 \subset E_{13}.$$

By this time you have noted that E_{11} contains two outcomes which are in E_8, (C, O) and (O, C). However, (C, C) is in E_{11} and is not in E_8. Hence, E_{11} is not a subset of E_8. We have $E_8 \subset E_{11}$ and $E_{11} \not\subset E_8$. Similarly, $E_8 \subset E_{13}$ but $E_{13} \not\subset E_8$, since (O, O) is in E_{13} but not in E_8. You are now aware of the fact that another way to say that two events are equal, "$A = B$," is that A must be a subevent in B and B must be a subevent in A. That is,

$$A \subset B \quad \text{and} \quad B \subset A.$$

A collection of events defined over the same sample space are said to be *collectively exhaustive* if their *union* is equal to the sample space. The *union* of a collection of events is defined to be the event consisting of all outcomes from the events in the collection. We use the symbol "$\cup$" to denote union of two events. In Example 2.3.2 we note, for example, that

$$E_1 \cup E_2 = \{(C, C), (C, O)\}$$
$$E_2 \cup E_5 = \{(C, O), (C, C)\}$$

and
$$E_1 \cup E_2 \cup E_5 = \{(C, O), (C, C)\}.$$

A collection of m events are said to form a partition of S if the m events are mutually exclusive and collectively exhaustive.

2.3.5. Example—Venn Diagrams for Disjoint or Mutually Exclusive Events

See Figure 2.3.

The following equations refer to the middle diagram in Figure 2.3.

$$E_1 \cap E_2 = \varnothing, \quad E_1 \cap E_3 = \varnothing, \quad E_1 \cap E_4 = \varnothing,$$
$$E_2 \cap E_3 = \varnothing, \quad E_2 \cap E_4 = \varnothing, \quad E_3 \cap E_4 = \varnothing.$$

Note in the right-hand diagram of Figure 2.3 that the events A and B partition S. That is,

$$A \text{ intersect } B = A \cap B = \text{empty set} = \varnothing$$

and
$$A \text{ union } B = A \cup B = \text{sample space} = S.$$

Figure 2.3

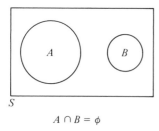

$A \cap B = \phi$

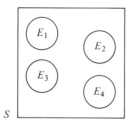

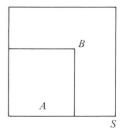

$A \cap B = \phi$ and
$A \cup B = S$

2.3.6. Example—Venn Diagram of a Partitioned Sample Space

See Figure 2.4.

Referring to Figure 2.4,

$$A_i \cap A_j = \emptyset \qquad (\text{for } i \neq j, i = 1, \ldots, 8, j = 1, \ldots, 8)$$
$$S = A_1 \cup A_2 \cup A_3 \cup A_4 \cup A_5 \cup A_6 \cup A_7 \cup A_8.$$

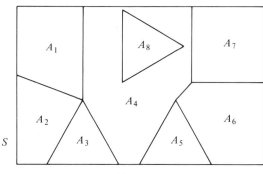

Figure 2.4

2.3.7. Example—Composite Events

For the ice cream purchasing experiment, Example 2.2.3, consider the two events

$$E_1 = \{\text{customer never switches brands}\}$$
$$= \{(a, a, a), (b, b, b), (c, c, c)\}$$

and
$$E_2 = \{\text{customer switches brands exactly once}\}$$

$$= \left\{ \begin{array}{llll} (a, a, b), & (a, a, c), & (a, b, b), & (a, c, c) \\ (b, a, a), & (b, b, a), & (b, b, c), & (b, c, c) \\ (c, a, a), & (c, b, b), & (c, c, a), & (c, c, b) \end{array} \right\}.$$

and the event

$$E_3 = \{\text{customer switches at most once}\}$$
$$= \{\text{customer never switches brands}\} \cup \{\text{customer switches exactly once}\}$$
$$= E_1 \cup E_2 \qquad (\text{note that } E_1 \text{ and } E_2 \text{ are disjoint}).$$

The events E_1, E_2, and E_3 are called *composite events*, since they contain more than one outcome.

2.4. UNCERTAINTY

Uncertainty refers to the outcome of an experiment. If the number of possible outcomes of an experiment is at least two, that is, $N(S) \geqslant 2$, where S is the sample space, and each outcome may occur, then the outcomes are said to be *uncertain*. Such an experiment is often called a *random experiment* or a *stochastic experiment*.

The purchasing sequence of the customer in Example 2.2.3 is *uncertain*. Will the customer in Example 2.2.3 choose ice cream brand a on three adjacent purchase occasions? That is, will outcome (a, a, a) occur? Or, will his purchase sequence be brand a, brand b, and brand a? That is, will outcome (a, b, a) occur? The number of cars that cross an intersection during a specified time interval is *uncertain* (Example 2.2.4).

As we mentioned previously, we will be concerned with decision problems where there is "uncertainty." How does one quantify—measure—predict uncertainty? The answer is by use of the theory of probability. We would agree that in all the random experiments considered so far *the outcomes are uncertain*. However, while many experiments have uncertain outcomes, some may be less uncertain or more uncertain than others. For example, the experienced manager of an automobile dealership may believe that, for next week's sales, it is *nearly certain* that he will sell 21 or less new automobiles, *somewhat uncertain* that he will sell 14 or less automobiles, and he is *very uncertain* as to whether he will sell 8, 9, or 10 automobiles.

What do such terms as *nearly certain*, *somewhat uncertain*, and *very uncertain* mean, and how does one compare such statements? All these questions are answered by the use of *probabilities*.

> Probability is a number between zero and 1 that is used to measure uncertainty.

The more *certain* an event, the closer the probability is to 1. The more *unlikely* an event, the closer the probability is to zero. For *very uncertain events*, the probability of assignment can be difficult.

2.5. PROBABILITY ASSIGNMENTS—THE NATURE OF PROBABILITY

We consider three different types of probability assignments of events over a sample space.

2.5.1. Subjective Probability Assignments

The first type of assessment is what we call subjective. It may differ from individual to individual, or from week to week for the same individual.

Frequently in a business decision there are no historical data (empirical evidence) available for estimating the likelihood of various outcomes.

For example, consider a retailer facing the problem of whether or not to order 100 Martian toy dolls for the Christmas selling season. Let us assume that the retailer knows that the space-exploration syndrome has peaked, but nevertheless, there is and will continue to be considerable interest in science fiction-type TV shows, which have a large children's audience. He believes it is very likely, say with odds of 9 : 1, that he will have enough dolls on hand to meet demand. That is, his *subjective estimate* is 0.9 that he will have enough dolls on hand to meet demand.

Other examples of subjective probability assignments are provided by those who trade on the stock market. An "active" stock trader who believes (he assigns a high likelihood of occurrence) that a stock will have a considerable increase in price tomorrow will buy the stock today. If he owns stock that he believes (he assigns a high likelihood of occurrence) will have a considerable decrease in price tomorrow, he will sell his stock today.

Your decision to play black jack and my decision not to play black jack in Las Vegas are an indication of different probability assessments about winning. It is important to note in a subjective assignment of probabilities that personal experience often becomes the basis of the probability assignment because historical information (data) may not be available.

Consider the situation where an executive of a large U.S. oil firm must decide whether to build a new refinery or continue with the existing facilities. Now the *success* of his decision (and possibly his job) depends for the most part on whether or not there is an Arab oil embargo in the next two years. A probability assigned to the occurrence of the event "an Arab oil embargo occurs in the next two years" would be a subjective estimate. A *long* history of oil embargos which can be projected into the future with confidence is not directly available. It may be useful and probably necessary for the executive to gather evidence from other executives as well as from the appropriate personnel in the U.S. State Department. Then using this additional information plus his judgment he assigns a probability to the event "an Arab oil embargo occurs in the next two years." However, there could be considerable disagreement from one executive to another about the accuracy of such probability assessments.

2.5.2. *Logical Probability*

The second type of probability assignment is what one might call logical. A logical probability assignment is usually based on considering the "obvious" and the symmetry of an experiment. One of the classic and standard examples is the experiment of tossing a six-sided die. Assuming that the die is well balanced, you would assign equal probabilities of $\frac{1}{6}$ to each possible outcome (1 or 2 or 3 or 4 or 5 or 6) in a toss of the die. Other examples abound in games of chance. For example, the different draws from a well-shuffled deck of cards all have well-defined (and sometimes difficult to compute) probabilities.

2.5.3. The Relative-Frequency or
Experimental Interpretation of Probability

You now know that a probability is a measure of the likelihood of the occurrence of an event of interest. However, there still may be some confusion as to the interpretation of a probability. For example, what does it mean to say that the probability is $\frac{2}{11}$ that you will receive an A in this course? What does it mean to say that the probability is $\frac{4}{10}$ that your stock in XYZ Company will show a price increase tomorrow? What does it mean that the probability is 0.33 (or 33%) that a typical Thursday night TV viewer will see a particular soap commercial? What does it mean that the probability is $\frac{4}{13}$ that John Doe will default on his automobile loan? These questions lead to a third interpretation of probability, called the *frequency* interpretation.

If we are interested in determining (or estimating) the probability of some event, and we can perform (or observe) a large number of trials of an experiment (event) and then count the number of times the event occurs, we are able to compute what is called an *experimental probability*.

Let E be the event of interest. Then the relative-frequency approach to probability assignment is given by the formula

$$\text{probability of event } E \text{ occurring} = \frac{\text{number of trials (times) } E \text{ occurred}}{\text{total number of trials}}$$

$$(2.5.1)$$

The following shorthand notation is commonly used for denoting the probability of an event occurring. If A is an event, the $P(A)$ stands for the probability of A occurring. Thus, in formula (2.5.1) we have

$$P(E) = \frac{N(E)}{\text{total number of trials}} \qquad (2.5.2)$$

where, as you recall, $N(E)$ is the total number of outcomes in E.

2.5.4. Example—The Tucker and Edsel Experiment

Suppose that over a period of 12 months, the pricing policy of two supposedly competitive automobile dealerships have been observed—the Tucker Agency and the Edsel Agency. Their prices have been observed to increase, remain unchanged, and decline, as shown in Tables 2.1 and 2.2.

Table 2.1. The Tucker Agency
(selling price in thousands of dollars,
January–December)

Aug.	Sept.	Oct.	Nov.	Dec.	Jan.	Feb.	Mar.	Apr.	May	June	July
3.0	3.1	2.9	2.8	3.1	3.2	3.2	3.1	3.2	3.3	3.0	3.0

Table 2.2. The Edsel Agency
(selling price in thousands of dollars,
January–December)

Aug.	Sept.	Oct.	Nov.	Dec.	Jan.	Feb.	Mar.	Apr.	May	June	July
2.9	3.0	2.8	2.7	2.8	3.0	3.2	3.2	3.1	3.0	3.1	3.2

From Tables 2.1 and 2.2 we are able to construct Tables 2.3 and 2.4. Table 2.3 shows that for the past 12 months (or 12 observations) there were 5 months (or 5 observations) during which the price of a Tucker increased, 2 months (or 2 observations) during which the price remained unchanged, and 4 months (or 4 observations) during which the price declined. Since in 4 out of 11 observations Tucker prices decreased, the *probability, empirically estimated or relative-frequency-determined*, of Tucker's price declining, during *any* arbitrarily chosen (randomly chosen) month is $\frac{4}{11} = 0.364$. By dividing all entries in Tables 2.3 and 2.4 by 11, the number of observations, we can obtain *empirical* probabilities of price changes for both automobiles as shown in Tables 2.5 and 2.6.

Table 2.3. The Tucker Agency

Selling Price	Number of Times (months)
Increases	5
Unchanged	2
Declines	4
	11

Table 2.4. The Edsel Agency

Selling Price	Number of Times (months)
Increases	6
Unchanged	1
Declines	4
	11

Table 2.5. The Tucker Agency
(data obtained from Table 2.3)

Event Future Selling Price (compared to this month's price)	Event Symbol	Number of Months	Probability of Occurrence, $P(E_i)$
Increases	E_1	5	$\frac{5}{11} = 0.454$
Unchanged	E_2	2	$\frac{2}{11} = 0.182$
Decreases	E_3	4	$\frac{4}{11} = 0.364$
		11	1.000

Table 2.6. The Edsel Agency
(data obtained from Table 2.4)

Event Future Selling Price (compared to this month's price)	Event Symbol	Number of Months	Probability of Occurrence, $P(E_i)$
Increases	E_4	6	$\frac{6}{11} = 0.545$
Unchanged	E_5	1	$\frac{1}{11} = 0.091$
Decreases	E_6	4	$\frac{4}{11} = 0.364$
		11	1.000

From Table 2.5, we have the following empirically estimated probabilities for any arbitrarily chosen future month:

$$P(\text{Tucker prices increase}) = P(E_1)$$
$$= 0.454$$
$$P(\text{Tucker prices are unchanged}) = P(E_2)$$
$$= 0.182$$
$$P(\text{Tucker prices decrease}) = P(E_3)$$
$$= 0.364.$$

Similarly, from Table 2.6,

$$P(\text{Edsel's price increase}) = P(E_4)$$
$$= 0.545$$
$$P(\text{Edsel's price is unchanged}) = P(E_5)$$
$$= 0.091$$
$$P(\text{Edsel's price decreases}) = P(E_6)$$
$$= 0.364.$$

2.6. RULES OF PROBABILITY (POSTULATES OF PROBABILITY)

One basic postulate is that a probability must be a number between 0 to 1, inclusive. That is, if E is an event, then $0 \leqslant P(E) \leqslant 1$. In particular, if $E = S =$ sample space ("the sure event"), then $P(S) = 1$. If $E = \varnothing =$ the null event, then $P(\varnothing) = 0$.

2.6.1. Example—Auditing an Accounts Receivable File

During *last month's audit* 2500 accounts in an accounts receivable file were audited and subsequently classified into one of three categories: error-free, minor (contains minor errors), and major (contains major errors). The frequency of occurrence of each classification is given in Table 2.7. During a *future audit*, an

Table 2.7. Audit Results—Accounts Receivable File

Account Categories	Event	Number of Accounts	Probability of Occurrence
Error-free	A	2000	$P(A) = 0.80$
Minor	B	400	$P(B) = 0.16$
Major	C	100	$P(C) = 0.04$
		2500	1.00

arbitrarily selected account will either be an *A* or *B* or *C*, where *A* denotes error-free, *B* denotes minor errors, and *C* denotes major errors. We let $P(A)$, $P(B)$, and $P(C)$ given in Table 2.7 be the probabilities of *A* or *B* or *C* occurring, respectively, for an arbitrarily selected account in a *future* audit.

2.6.2. Rules of Addition

We know that the events *A*, *B*, and *C* in Example 2.6.1 are mutually exclusive and exhaustive. Thus, the sum of the probabilities of a randomly chosen account being error-free (event *A*), minor (event *B*), or major (event *C*) must be equal to 1.00. This statement is often called the *special rule of addition*. That is, if events *A*, *B*, and *C* are mutually exclusive and exhaustive, then

$$P(A) + P(B) + P(C) = 1$$
$$0.80 + 0.16 + 0.04 = 1.$$

It is usually written

$$P(A \text{ or } B \text{ or } C) = P(A) + P(B) + P(C).$$

The statement "*A* or *B* or *C*" is frequently written $A \cup B \cup C$, where the symbol $\cup$ is read "union." The Venn diagram in Figure 2.5 illustrates the data given in Table 2.7. Note that the events *A*, *B*, and *C* in Figure 2.5 are mutually exclusive. That is,

$$A \cap B = \varnothing, \quad A \cap C = \varnothing, \quad \text{and} \quad B \cap C = \varnothing.$$

Also note that the events *A*, *B*, and *C* partition *S*, since $A \cup B \cup C = S$.

In Example 2.6.1 we note that the probability that an account selected at random is error-free (event *A* occurs), $P(A)$, plus the probability that it contains at least one error (the "complement" of *A* occurs, written as event A^c occurs), $P(A^c)$, must logically equal 1. This is expressed by saying

$$P(A) + P(A^c) = 1. \tag{2.6.1}$$

Equation (2.6.1) can also be stated as

$$P(A) = 1 - P(A^c) \tag{2.6.2}$$

or
$$P(A^c) = 1 - P(A), \tag{2.6.3}$$

Figure 2.5

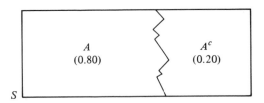

S *Figure 2.6*

where, again, A^c denotes the *complement* of event A. Equation (2.6.2) is called the *complement rule* of probability. Figure 2.6 illustrates the complement rule of probability.

The special rule of addition also applies when it is desired to find the probability that a randomly chosen account is either error-free or a major account, either A or C, written as $A \cup C$. From Table 2.7 we have the following probabilities:

Account Categories	Event	Probability
Error-free	A	$P(A) = 0.80$
Major	C	$P(C) = \underline{0.04}$
		0.84

Thus,
$$P(A \text{ or } C) = P(A \cup C) = P(A) + P(C)$$
$$= 0.80 + 0.04$$
$$= 0.84.$$

The Venn diagram in Figure 2.7 illustrates these events and their associated probabilities. Note that in this figure

$$(A \cup C)^c = B \text{ and } P((A \cup C)^c) = 1 - P(A \cup C)$$
$$= 1 - 0.84 = 0.16.$$

Events in many applications may not be mutually exclusive. To illustrate this, consider the data given in Table 2.8. Suppose that 60% of the accounts in the accounts receivable file have balances of $10,000 or more and 40% of the accounts have balances of less than $10,000. Let D be the event that an account selected at

Figure 2.7

Error free A (0.80)	Not error free and not major $(A \cup C)^c$ (0.16)	Major C (0.04)

Table 2.8. Audit Results—Accounts Receivable File

Accounts	Event	Probabilities
Error-free with a balance less than $10,000	$A \cap D$	0.50
Error-free with a balance equal to or greater than $10,000	$A \cap D^c$	0.30
Error-free	A	0.80
Contains more than one error	A^c	0.20
Balance of more than $10,000	D	0.60
Balance of less than $10,000	D^c	0.40

random has a balance of more than $10,000. Then

$$P(D) = 0.60 \quad (\text{or } 60\%)$$

and

P(account selected at random has a balance equal to or less than $10,000)

$$= P(D^c)$$
$$= 1 - P(D) = 0.40 \quad (\text{or } 40\%).$$

What is the probability that an account selected at random from the file will either have a balance of more than $10,000 *or* be error-free? That is, $P(A \cup D) = ?$ There is some chance that the account selected will be both error-free *and* have a balance of more than $10,000. Hence, there is an overlapping of outcomes resulting in A (error-free) and D (a balance of more than $10,000) that can occur at the same time. The probability that this can happen is called the *joint probability* of A and D. It is usually written $P(A \cap D)$, where the symbol "$\cap$" is read intersection. To compute $P(A \cup D)$, we apply the general rule of addition.

The *general rule of addition* is

$$P(A \text{ or } D) = P(A \cup D)$$
$$= P(A) + P(D) - P(\text{both } A \text{ and } D) \quad (2.6.4)$$
$$= P(A) + P(D) - P(A \cap D).$$

Solving for $P(A \text{ or } D)$ by use of the probabilities given in Table 2.8 gives

$$P(A \text{ or } D) = P(A \cup D)$$
$$= P(A) + P(D) - P(A \cap D)$$
$$= 0.80 + 0.60 - 0.50$$
$$= 1.40 - 0.50$$
$$= 0.90.$$

It seems logical that the joint probability of an error-free account and a balance of more than $10,000 should be subtracted once or it will be included twice in finding the probability that an account chosen at random will either be error-free or will have a balance of more than $10,000.

Before proceeding to the rules for multiplying probabilities, let us first review the rules discussed so far for manipulating probabilities.

Definition   *Let S be a sample and P(E) a function that associates a number with each event E in S. Then P(E) is called a probability function provided that the following rules hold:*

Rule 1   For any event A in S, $0 \leqslant P(A) \leqslant 1$.

Rule 2 $P(S) = 1$.

Rule 3   For any sequence $E_1, E_2, \ldots$ of disjoint events,

$$P(E_1 \cup E_2 \cup \cdots) = P(E_1) + P(E_2) + \cdots .$$

Some other properties of probabilities that follow from the preceding three rules are:

Property 1 $P(\varnothing) = 0$, where $\varnothing$ is the event containing no outcomes.

Property 2   For any two events A and B of S, $P(A \cup B) = P(A) + P(B) - P(A \cap B)$, where $P(A \cap B)$ is the probability of the *joint occurrence* of events A and B.

Property 3   If A and B are events of S and $A \subset B$, then $P(A) \leqslant P(B)$.

Property 4   If A is any event in S and A^c its complement ($A \cap A^c = \varnothing$ and $A \cup A^c = S$), then

$$P(A^c) = 1 - P(A)$$

or

$$P(A) = 1 - P(A^c).$$

2.7. CONDITIONAL PROBABILITIES

A *conditional probability is the probability that an event will happen given that another event happens.*

2.7.1. Example—R & G Soap Company Examination

During the past several years (starting in 1960) the R & G Soap Company administered a written test to each prospective management trainee during the campus interview. A review of the 10-year-period statistics (1960–1969) of those hired and their success with R & G is summarized in Table 2.9. An explanation of the statistics in Table 2.9 is as follows. R & G hired 300 trainees during 1960–1969, of which 200 scored 70 or higher on the test and 100 scored less

Table 2.9. 1960–1969 R & G Soap Company Examination—First Interview Testing

Interview Test Score (*out of* 100 possible points)	PRESENT STATUS			Total
	Senior Management Position (S)	Junior Management Position (J)	Dismissed (D)	
70 or higher (H)	20	120	60	200
Less than 70 (L)	10	50	40	100
	30	170	100	300

than 70 on the first test. Of the 200 trainees who scored 70 or higher on the test, 140 (= 20 + 120) were successful with R & G and 60 of the 200 were dismissed. Twenty of the 140 advanced to senior management positions and 120 advanced to junior management positions. Of those 100 trainees who were hired and who scored less than 70, 60 (= 10 + 50) are considered a success at R & G, and 40 of the 100 who scored less than 70 were dismissed by R & G. Ten of the 60 have advanced to senior management positions and 50 of the 60 advanced to junior management positions.

Can we use these data to estimate the likelihood or probability that a newly hired trainee will advance to senior management *given* that he scores 70 or higher on the test. That is,

$$P(\text{a newly hired trainee advances to senior management} \mid \text{a score of 70 or higher on the interview test}) = ? \tag{2.7.1}$$

The vertical bar "|" is read as "given that." Before the bar, the event S is given whose probability we are interested in; after the bar we are given the event H that has occurred or will certainly occur. Using capital letters to denote events, we can express the probability statement in (2.7.1) as

$$P(S|H) = ?$$

From Table 2.9 we note that 200 trainees (200 observations) scored 70 or higher. That is, $N(H) = 200$. Also, from Table 2.9, 20 of those who scored 70 or higher advanced to a senior position. That is, $N(H \cap S) = 20$; so it is reasonable that

$$P(S|H) = P\left(\overset{(S)}{\text{advances to a senior position}} \mid \overset{(H)}{\text{scores 70 or more}} \right)$$

$$= \frac{N(H \cap S)}{N(H)} = \frac{20}{200} = 0.10.$$

Note that in computing $P(S|H)$ we only considered those 200 trainees who score 70 or higher—we did not consider all 300 trainees. That is, our sample space is those trainees who score 70 or more, "excluding" trainees who score less than 70.

QUESTION. What is the probability that a newly hired trainee will advance to senior management *given* that he scores low on the interview test?

Answer $P(S|L) = P\left(\overset{(S)}{\text{advances to a senior position}} \Big| \overset{(\text{given})}{\text{scores less than 70}}\right)$

$$= \frac{N(S \cap L)}{N(L)} = \frac{10}{100} = 0.10.$$

QUESTION. What are the probabilities that a newly hired trainee will advance to junior management *given* how he scores on the interview test?

Answer. The trainee either will score low (H) or (L). Thus,

$$P(J|H) = \frac{N(J \cap H)}{N(H)} = \frac{120}{200} = 0.60$$

and

$$P(J|L) = \frac{N(J \cap L)}{N(L)} = \frac{50}{100} = 0.50.$$

QUESTION. What is the probability that a new trainee who scores low on the test will eventually be dismissed by R & G?

Answer

P(trainee is dismissed given that he scores low on the test)

$$= P(D|L) = \frac{N(D \cap L)}{N(L)} = \frac{40}{100} = 0.40.$$

QUESTION. What is the probability that a trainee who scores high on the test will eventually be dismissed by R & G?

Answer

P(trainee is dismissed given that he scored high on the test)

$$= P(D|H) = \frac{N(D \cap H)}{N(H)} = \frac{60}{200} = 0.30.$$

Table 2.10 summarizes all the preceding computations of conditional probabilities.

Table 2.10. 1960–1969 R & G Soap Company Examination

Given Interview Test Score	CONDITIONAL PREDICTIONS			
	Senior Management Position (S)	Junior Management Position (J)	Dismissed (D)	Total
High (H)	0.10	0.60	0.30	1.00
Low (L)	0.10	0.50	0.40	1.00

51

Note in Table 2.10 that $P(S|H) = P(S|L) = 0.10$. That is, there is a 10% chance that a trainee will advance to a senior management position regardless of whether he scores high or low on the campus interview test. Also note in Table 2.10 that it is more likely that a trainee who scores low on the test will be dismissed than a trainee who scores high. That is,

$$P(D|L) = 0.40 > 0.30 = P(D|H).$$

Suppose that instead of Table 2.9 you were given *fewer data* (less information) about the 300 trainees hired during 1960–1969. Specifically, assume that all the data available to you are those given in Table 2.11.

Table 2.11. 1960–1969 R & G Soap Company

SUCCESSES		Dismissed (D)	Total
Senior Management Position (S)	Junior Management Position (J)		
30	170	100	300

What are *missing* from Table 2.11 are the test score data. All you know is the number who are successful, 30 and 70, and the number 100, the number of those dismissed out of 300 trainees. Using Table 2.11, we have the following estimates:

$$P(\text{trainee becomes a senior manager}) = P(S) = \frac{30}{300} = \frac{1}{10} = 0.100$$

$$P(\text{trainee becomes a junior manager}) = P(J) = \frac{170}{300} = \frac{17}{30} = 0.567$$

$$P(\text{trainee is dismissed}) = P(D) = \frac{100}{300} = \frac{1}{3} = \frac{0.333}{1.000},$$

which is also listed in Table 2.12. Note that $P(S) + P(J) + P(D) = 1.0$. That is, either a newly hired trainee becomes a success, an S or J, with R & G or is dismissed, D.

Now from Table 2.10 we have $P(S|H) = 0.10$, which is equal to $P(S)$ given in Table 2.12. That is,

$$P(S|H) = 0.10 = P(S).$$
$$\uparrow \qquad\qquad \uparrow$$
from Table 2.10   from Table 2.12

Table 2.12. 1960–1969 R & G Soap Company[a]

SUCCESSES		Dismissed (D)	Total
Senior Management Position (S)	Junior Management Position (J)		
0.100	0.567	0.333	1.000

[a]Probabilities computed from Table 2.11.

That is, the prediction of success to the senior management level for a trainee who scores high (70 or more) on the test is the same as the prediction when you do not know the trainee's test score, $P(S|H) = P(S)$.

Note also that

$$P(J|H) = 0.600 \neq P(J) = 0.567.$$

from Table 2.10   from Table 2.12

That is, you will underpredict success at the junior level $P(J) = 0.567$ if you are *not aware* that he scores H (70 or more). We have

$$P(J|H) = 0.600$$

and
$$P(J) = 0.567$$

giving an underprediction of 0.033. Similarly, $P(D|H) \neq P(D)$. Thus, in some cases a conditional probability is equal to the unconditional probability, and in some cases it is not.

This leads us to the definition of *independent events*.

Definition   *We say that two events A and B are independent if the probability of A occurring given that B occurs, P(A|B), is equal to the probability of A occurring, P(A).*

That is, if $P(A|B) = P(A)$, then A and B are said to be *independent events*. If $P(A|B) \neq P(A)$, then A and B are said to be *dependent events*.

From Tables 2.10 and 2.12 we see that events H and J are dependent, since

$$P(J|H) = 0.60 \neq P(J) = 0.567.$$

Events H and D are dependent, since

$$P(D|H) = 0.30 \neq P(D) = 0.333.$$

Events L and J are dependent, since

$$P(J|L) = 0.50 \neq P(J) = 0.567.$$

Events L and D are dependent, since

$$P(D|L) = 0.40 \neq P(D) = 0.333.$$

Events L and S are independent, since

$$P(S|L) = 0.10 = P(S) = 0.10.$$

Events S and H are independent, since

$$P(S|H) = 0.10 = P(S) = 0.10.$$

An intuitive explanation of independence of two events is as follows.

> **Definition** *Two events are independent if knowledge about one does not help at all in assessing probabilities concerning the other.*

For example, suppose you are asked to assess the probability that a newly hired trainee at R & G will be dismissed. Assume that you do not know his interview test score. So from Tables 2.11 or 2.12 your estimate is $\frac{100}{300} = 0.333$. That is,

$$P(D) = 0.333.$$

Suppose at a later time you are told that he scored low (less than 70) on his test. You now have the *additional information* given in Tables 2.9 and 2.10. Your estimate of dismissal is now $\frac{40}{100} = 0.40$. That is,

$$P(D|L) = 0.40.$$

Since $P(D|L) = 0.40 \neq P(D) = 0.333$, the events D and L are not independent. That is, D and L are dependent events and your estimate of the likelihood of dismissal will *depend* upon whether or not you know his test score.

Consider Table 2.9 again. The entries in Table 2.9 tell us that out of 300 trainees 20 scored high and advanced to a senior position, $N(H \cap S) = 20$, 120 scored high and advanced to a junior management position, $N(H \cap J) = 120$, and 60 scored high and were dismissed, $N(H \cap D) = 60$. So if we divide the end numbers in the first row of Table 2.9 by 300, we obtain the joint probabilities $P(H \cap S)$, $P(H \cap J)$, and $P(H \cap D)$, and the marginal probability $P(H)$. For example,

$$P(H \cap S) = \frac{N(H \cap S)}{N(S)} = \frac{20}{300} = 0.067,$$

which is the joint probability that a trainee scores high and is advanced to a senior position.

Dividing all the numbers in Table 2.9 by 300, we obtain the probabilities given in Table 2.13.

The entries in Table 2.13 are *joint probabilities*. For example, P(trainee scores 70 or higher *and* is dismissed) $= P(H \cap D) = 0.200$, or 20 percent, and P(trainee scores less than 70 and becomes a senior manager) $= P(L \cap S) = 0.033$, or 3.3%.

The probabilities in the right column and bottom row in Table 2.13 (both labeled "total") are called *marginal probabilities*. For example,

$$P(\text{trainee scores 70 or higher}) = P(H) = 0.667$$
$$P(\text{trainee is dismissed}) = P(D) = 0.333.$$

Table 2.13. 1960–1969 R & G Soap Company
(obtained by dividing every entry in Table 2.10 by 300)

| Interview Test Score | JOINT PROBABILITIES | | | Total |
	Senior Management (S)	Junior Management (J)	Dismissed (D)	
70 or higher (H)	0.067	0.400	0.200	0.667
Less than 70 (L)	0.033	0.167	0.133	0.333
Total	0.100	0.567	0.333	1.000

Marginal probabilities give predictions concerning only one event. For example, in Table 2.13 we have

$$P(S) = 0.100 \qquad P(H) = 0.667$$
$$P(J) = 0.567 \qquad P(L) = 0.333$$
$$P(D) = 0.333 \qquad \overline{1.000}$$
$$\overline{1.000}$$

Note that the sum of the marginal probabilities given in the bottom row or the right-hand column sum to 1. They should sum to 1 since S, J, and D are mutually exclusive and exhaustive events and H and L are mutually exclusive and exhaustive events.

2.8. REVISING PROBABILITIES—BAYES' FORMULA

The conditional probability that event A will occur given that event B occurred is *not* always the same as the conditional probability that event B will occur given that event A occurred. That is, $P(A|B)$ is not always equal to $P(B|A)$. Now we know that

$$P(A|B) = \frac{P(A \cap B)}{P(B)} \qquad (2.8.1)$$

and

$$P(B|A) = \frac{P(A \cap B)}{P(A)}. \qquad (2.8.2)$$

Note that the denominators are different when comparing (2.8.1) and (2.8.2). Multiplying (2.8.1) on both sides by $P(B)$ yields

$$P(A \cap B) = P(B)P(A|B). \qquad (2.8.3)$$

Multiplying (2.8.2) on both sides by $P(A)$ yields

$$P(A \cap B) = P(A)P(B|A). \qquad (2.8.4)$$

Equations (2.8.3) and (2.8.4) are called the *multiplication rule* for computing the joint probability of A and B regardless of whether or not A and B are independent events. Recall that two events A and B are independent if $P(A \cap B) = P(A)P(B)$ or, equivalently, $P(A|B) = P(A)$ or, equivalently, $P(B|A) = P(B)$.

We can describe formula (2.8.3) as follows. For events A and B to *simultaneously occur*, event B must occur, but if B occurred, event A should also occur. A similar interpretation of (2.8.4) follows immediately.

2.8.1. Example—Multiplication Rule for Computing a Joint Probability

Let A be the event that the price of gasoline increases next month and let B be the event that gasoline increases in the succeeding month. The following probability assessments are available.

$$P(A) = 0.2, \quad P(B) = 0.4, \quad \text{and} \quad P(A|B) = 0.15.$$

QUESTION. What is the probability that the price of gasoline will increase in each of the next 2 months?

Answer

P(price increase next month *and* the month after)

$$= P(A \cap B) = P(B)P(A|B) \quad [\text{applying formula (2.8.3)}]$$
$$= (0.4)(0.15)$$
$$= 0.06.$$

QUESTION. What is the probability that the price of gasoline increases next month *or* increases the month after?

Answer

P(price increases next month *or* the month after)

$$= P(A \cup B) = P(A) + P(B) - P(A \cap B) \quad [\text{applying formula (2.6.4)}]$$
$$= 0.2 + 0.4 - 0.06$$
$$= 0.54.$$

QUESTION. Are price changes during the next 2 months independent?

Answer. Price changes during the next 2 months are independent if

$$P(A|B) = P(A). \tag{2.8.5}$$

However, $P(A|B) = 0.15$ and $P(A) = 0.2$. Thus, the price changes are dependent.

2.8.2. Example—Auditing and the Probability-Tree Diagram

A convenient method to use in applying the multiplication rules (2.8.3) and (2.8.4) is the probability-tree diagram. Suppose, for example, that an accounts receivable file containing 50 accounts is to undergo a *partial* audit. It is believed that 10% contain major errors. That is, it is believed that 5 of the 50 accounts contain major errors. Now the auditor is to select three accounts randomly. Figure 2.8 gives the probability-tree diagram for this audit where M_1, M_2 and M_3 denote

Figure 2.8. Probability tree diagram for auditing three accounts from a file of size 50.

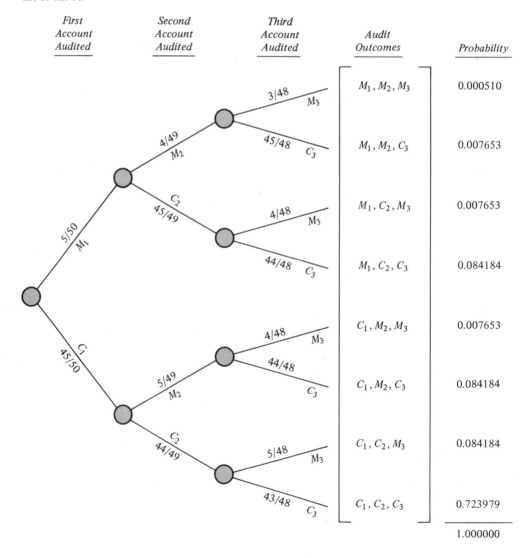

that the first, second, and third contain major errors, respectively, and C_1, C_2, and C_3 denote that the first, second, and third accounts audited are correct.

Each audit outcome is represented by a branch in the diagram in Figure 2.8. The probability of each outcome is indicated alongside its branch. Note in Figure 2.8 that there are two branches for each account audited—one for major errors and one for no errors. Finally, note in Figure 2.8 that each path (a path equals three branches) defines an outcome of the entire audit.

The outcomes of each account audited are not independent, since after one account is audited it is not considered (not replaced in the file) again for auditing. For example, if the first account audited contains major errors (M_1 occurs), there are only 4 accounts left in the file, of a total of 49, containing major errors. Thus, if M_1 occurs, the likelihood of M_2 occurring is $\frac{4}{49}$, which is a conditional probability. Technically we are saying the following:

$$P(M_1) = P(\text{first account contains major errors}) = \tfrac{5}{50}$$

$$P(M_2|M_1) = P(\text{second account contains major errors} \mid$$

$$\text{first account contains major errors})$$

$$= \tfrac{4}{49}.$$

QUESTION. What is the probability that the first *and* the second account contain major errors: that is, that $P(M_1 \cap M_2) = ?$

Answer. Applying the multiplication rule (2.8.4) with $A = M_1$ and $B = M_2$ gives

$$P(M_1 \cap M_2) = P(M_1)P(M_2|M_1)$$

$$= \left(\tfrac{5}{50}\right)\left(\tfrac{4}{49}\right)$$

$$= 0.008163 \quad \text{(slightly less than 1\%).}$$

QUESTION. What is the probability that the first account audited contains major errors *and* the second account audited is correct: that is, that $P(M_1 \cap C_2) = ?$

Answer $\qquad\qquad P(M_1) = \tfrac{5}{50} \quad \text{and} \quad P(C_2|M_1) = \tfrac{45}{49}.$

Applying (2.8.4) with $A = M_1$ and $B = C_2$ gives

$$P(M_1 \cap C_2) = \left(\tfrac{5}{50}\right)\left(\tfrac{45}{49}\right)$$

$$= 0.091837.$$

Note that the $P(C_2|M_1) = \tfrac{45}{49}$ since after M_1 occurs, we are left with 49 accounts in the file, 45 of which are correct.

QUESTION. What is the probability that the third account audited contains major errors *given* that the first *and* second accounts contained major errors|: that is, that $P(M_3|M_1 \cap M_2) = ?$

Answer
$$P(M_3|M_1 \cap M_2) = \tfrac{3}{48},$$

since *after* the first two accounts are audited we are left with 3 of 48 which contain major errors.

QUESTION. What is the probability that all three accounts audited contain major errors: that is, that $P(M_1 \cap M_2 \cap M_3) = ?$

Answer
$$P(M_1 \cap M_2 \cap M_3) = P(M_3|M_1 \cap M_2)P(M_1 \cap M_2), \qquad (2.8.6)$$

by letting $A = M_1 \cap M_2$ and $B = M_3$ in the multiplication rule (2.8.4). Thus,

$$P(M_1 \cap M_2 \cap M_3) = P(M_3|M_1 \cap M_2)P(M_1 \cap M_2)$$
$$= \left(\tfrac{3}{48}\right)(0.008163)$$
$$= 0.000510.$$

QUESTION. What is the probability that all three accounts audited are correct: that is, that $P(C_1 \cap C_2 \cap C_3) = ?$

Answer. Applying rule (2.8.4) gives

$$P(C_1 \cap C_2 \cap C_3) = P(C_3|C_1 \cap C_2)P(C_1 \cap C_2).$$

To determine $P(C_1 \cap C_2)$, we use (2.8.4):

$$P(C_1 \cap C_2) = P(C_2|C_1)P(C_1) = \left(\tfrac{44}{49}\right)\left(\tfrac{45}{50}\right).$$

Thus,

$$P(C_1 \cap C_2 \cap C_3) = P(C_3|C_1 \cap C_2)P(C_2|C_1)P(C_1)$$
$$= \left(\tfrac{43}{48}\right)\left(\tfrac{44}{49}\right)\left(\tfrac{45}{50}\right)$$
$$= 0.723979.$$

Figure 2.8 gives the *joint* probabilities for all the possible audit outcomes in the right-hand column.

2.8.3. Bayes' Formula

Let us begin by reviewing the definition of conditional probability and the multiplication rule of probability. We have

$$P(A|B) = \frac{P(A \cap B)}{P(B)} \left.\begin{array}{c} \\ \\ \end{array}\right\} \quad \begin{array}{l} \text{definition of} \\ \text{conditional} \end{array} \qquad (2.8.7)$$

and
$$P(B|A) = \frac{P(A \cap B)}{P(A)} \qquad \text{probability} \qquad (2.8.8)$$

$$P(A \cap B) = P(B)P(A|B). \qquad \text{(multiplication rule)} \qquad (2.8.9)$$

By substituting the expression for the joint probability $P(A \cap B)$ in (2.8.9) into (2.8.8), we obtain

$$P(B|A) = \frac{P(A|B)P(B)}{P(A)},$$
(2.8.10)

which is Bayes' formula. Note in (2.8.10) that $P(B|A) = P(A|B)$ if $P(A) = P(B)$.

Of what use is Bayes' formula, given in (2.8.10)? Bayes' formula is a powerful method of *evaluating new information* in order to revise *prior estimates* of the probability of events of interest. When correctly used it can be of tremendous aid in making decisions based upon probabilities. We shall illustrate the usefulness of Bayes' formula given in (2.8.10), by the use of several examples.

2.8.4. Example—Applying Bayes' Formula

Consider a firm that has two assembly lines, 1 and 2, both producing electronic calculators. Assume that you have purchased a calculator and it turns out to be *defective*.

QUESTION 1. What is the probability that your calculator was produced on line 1?

QUESTION 2. What is the probability that your calculator was produced on line 2?

To answer both these questions we need to have information about both assembly lines. First, let:

L_1 = event that the calculator is produced on line 1

L_2 = event that the calculator is produced on line 2

A = event that a calculator is defective.

Now it is known that line 1 produces 60% of all calculators produced. Thus, we have

$$P(L_1) = 0.60 \ (60\%) \quad \text{and} \quad P(L_2) = 0.40 \ (40\%).$$

We are now in a position to answer both questions.

Answer to Question 1

$P($your calculator was produced on line 1$) = P(L_1) = 0.60 \ (60\%)$.

Answer to Question 2

$P($your calculator was produced on line 2$) = P(L_2) = 0.40 \ (40\%)$.

The answers above seem reasonable if one *assumes* that the rate of producing defective calculators *is the same* for both assembly lines. We call

$$P(L_1) = 0.60 \quad \text{and} \quad P(L_2) = 0.40$$

prior estimates of which line produced the defective calculator.
    Suppose that you are given the following *additional information*:

10% of the calculators produced on line 1 are defective
20% of the calculators produced on line 2 are defective.

That is, let D denote the event that a defective calculator is produced. Then the additional information can be expressed as

$$P(D|L_1) = 0.10 \quad (10\%)$$
and
$$P(D|L_2) = 0.20 \quad (20\%).$$

QUESTION. How can this additional information be used to revise your prior estimates?

Answer. By using Bayes' formula (2.8.10), we have

$$P(L_1|D) = \frac{P(D|L_1)P(L_1)}{P(D)}$$

$$= \frac{(0.10)(0.60)}{0.14}$$

$$= 0.429,$$

where

$$P(D) = P(D|L_1)P(L_1) + P(D|L_2)P(L_2)$$
$$= (0.10)(0.60) \quad + (0.20)(0.40) \qquad \text{(applying the multiplication rule)}$$
$$= 0.06 \qquad\qquad +0.08$$
$$= 0.14.$$

Also,
$$P(L_2|D) = \frac{P(D|L_2)P(L_2)}{P(D)}$$

$$= \frac{(0.20)(0.40)}{0.14}$$

$$= 0.571.$$

$P(L_1|D) = 0.429$ and $P(L_2|D) = 0.571$ are called the *posterior estimates*. Note that your prior (original) estimates are

$$P(L_1) = 0.60 \quad \text{and} \quad P(L_2) = 0.40,$$

and using the additional information concerning the rate of defectives produced by each line and Bayes' formula gives the posterior estimates:

$$P(L_1|D) = 0.429 \quad \text{and} \quad P(L_2|D) = 0.571.$$

Table 2.14 summarizes the preceding calculations.

Table 2.14. Applying Bayes' Formula

Event	Prior Estimates, $P(L_i)$	Likelihood, $P(D|L_i)$	Joint Probabilities, $P(L_i \cap D)$	Posterior Estimates, $P(L_i|D)$
Line 1 (L_1)	0.6	0.1	0.06	0.06/0.14 = 0.429
Line 2 (L_2)	0.4	0.2	0.08	0.08/0.14 = 0.571
	1.00		$P(D) = 0.14$	1.000

2.8.5. Example—Determining Posterior Probabilities Using Probability-Tree Diagrams

Probability-tree diagrams are often useful in determining posterior probabilities. To show this, we consider the following problem.

Banks Security Incorporated has 10 clerks, one of whom is an embezzler. You, as head of security, select one clerk at random and require that he submit to a polygraph test. Suppose that the chosen clerk passes the test. What is the probability that the chosen clerk is the embezzler?

First define the following relative events:

S = polygraph test is passed
E = chosen clerk is the embezzler
E^c = chosen clerk is not the embezzler.

Prior to the polygraph test, it seems reasonable to use the estimates

$$P(E) = 0.10 \quad \text{and} \quad P(E^c) = 0.90,$$

since only one of the 10 clerks is embezzling. These are your *prior probabilities*. They are the best estimates of E and E^c before obtaining additional empirical evidence, such as the results of the polygraph test. The prior probabilities are shown along with the indicated events in Figure 2.9.

The initial two branches in Figure 2.9 indicate that the selected clerk may be either embezzling (E) or not embezzling (E^c), with the probabilities given on the corresponding branches.

The reliability of polygraph tests varies from individual to individual. Based on past experiences, it is estimated that 5% of those lying will pass the test and 1% of those who are honest will fail the test. Thus, we have the following likelihoods or

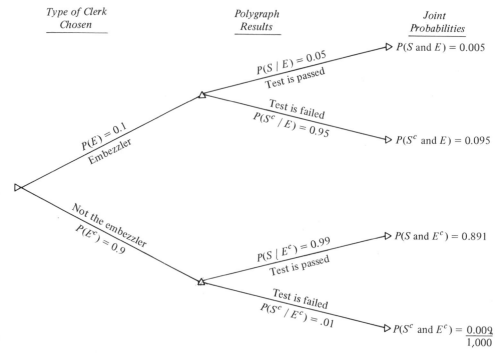

Figure 2.9. Sequence of events in chronological order.

conditional probabilities:

$$P(S|E) = 0.05 \quad \text{and} \quad P(S^c|E) = 1 - P(S|E) = 0.95$$
$$P(S^c|E^c) = 0.01 \quad \text{and} \quad P(S|E^c) = 1 - P(S^c|E^c) = 0.99.$$

The second set of four branches indicates the outcomes of the polygraph test, pass (S) or fail (S^c). The probabilities for each of these events depend upon the type of clerk chosen, embezzler or not the embezzler, so they are treated as conditional probabilities.

Figure 2.10 is the probability tree for the denoting the information received from the polygraph test (the experiment). The initial events in Figure 2.10 are the polygraph test results—the first set of information received. Note that the sequence of information received in Figure 2.10 is the reverse of Figure 2.9.

To obtain the joint probabilities to be placed at the end of the last branches in Figure 2.9, we apply the multiplication law of probabilities. For example,

$$P(S \text{ and } E) = P(S \cap E) = P(E)P(S|E)$$
$$= (0.1)(0.05) = 0.005.$$
$$P(S \text{ and } E^c) = P(S \cap E^c) = P(E^c)P(S|E^c)$$
$$= (0.9)(0.99) = 0.891.$$

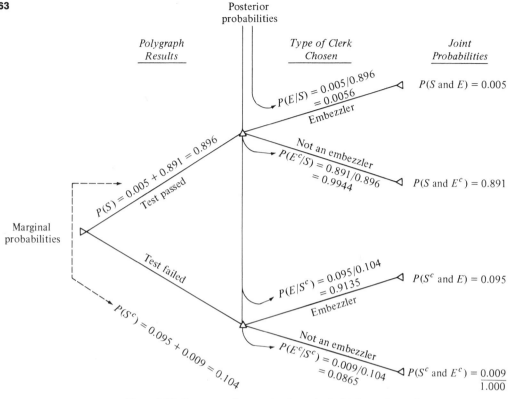

Figure 2.10. Sequence of events in chronological information order.

All four of these marginal probabilities are not put at the end of branches in Figure 2.9. Next the marginal probabilities for each branch in the first set of branches of Figure 2.10 are determined using the addition law. That is,

$$P(S) = P(S \text{ and } E) + P(S \text{ and } E^c)$$
$$= 0.005 + 0.891$$
$$= 0.896$$
$$P(S^c) = P(S^c \text{ and } E) + P(S^c \text{ and } E^c)$$
$$= 0.095 + 0.009$$
$$= 0.104.$$

Finally, the conditional probabilities in the second set of branches in Figure 2.10 are determined. Each of these conditional probabilities is determined by dividing the end-point joint probability by the respective initial point marginal probability. For example,

$$P(E|S) = \frac{P(S \cap E)}{P(S)} = \frac{0.005}{0.896}$$
$$= 0.0056$$

and
$$P(E^c|S^c) = \frac{P(S^c \cap E^c)}{P(S^c)} = \frac{0.009}{0.104}$$
$$= 0.0865.$$

Note that our original probability assessments are $P(E) = 0.10$ and $P(E^c) = 0.90$ and our posterior assessments are $P(E|S) = 0.0056$ and $P(E^c|S) = 0.9946$. Thus, the likelihood that the chosen clerk is the embezzler decreased from 10% to 0.56% as a result of the result of the polygraph test (he "passed").

REFERENCES   Freund, J. E. *Modern Elementary Statistics*. Englewood Cliffs, N.J.: Prentice-Hall, Inc., 1967.

Freund, J. E. *Mathematical Statistics*, 2nd ed. Englewood Cliffs, N.J.: Prentice-Hall, Inc., 1971.

Goldberg, S. *Probability, an Introduction*. Englewood Cliffs, N.J.: Prentice-Hall, Inc., 1960.

Hamburg, M. *Statistical Analysis for Decision Making*. New York: Harcourt Brace Jovanovich, Inc., 1970.

KEY CONCEPTS

Random experiment
Sample space; outcomes
Trial or observation
Mutually exclusive or disjoint
Collectively exhaustive
Events
  empty or null event
  mutually exclusive or disjoint
    events
  collectively exhaustive events
  partition
  composite events
Venn diagrams
Uncertain outcomes
Probability assignments
  subjective probabilities
  logical probabilities
  relative frequencies

Rules of probability
  special rule of addition
  complement rule
  general rule of addition
Conditional probabilities
Independent events
Joint probabilities
Marginal probabilities
Revising probabilities
  Bayes' formula
  prior probabilities
  posterior probabilities

REVIEW PROBLEMS

2.1. The possible demand for the ensuing year at Generous Electric Company is any *integer* number between 2 and 10, inclusive, in billion kilowatt-hours. Construct the event set for each of the following events.
(a) Demand is not less than 6 nor more than 9.
(b) Demand is less than or equal to 5.
(c) Demand is greater than 8.
(d) Demand is at most 3.

2.2. For the following quality control situation, indicate whether the events are mutually exclusive and, if not, state why.

Electronic calculators are inspected and rejected if any one of the following events occurs:

$$A = \text{addition key fails} \qquad B = \text{all keys fail.}$$

2.3. Executive Search Inc. specializes in placing marketing managers. It classifies clients in terms of skills and years of experience. The skills are technical and administrative. No one candidate possesses both skills. Experience categories are 1 year or less, between 1 and 5 years, and 5 years or more. At present there are 100 executives on file with skills and experience summarized in the following table:

Experience	SKILL		Total
	Technical	Administrative	
1 Year or less	30	5	35
Between 1 and 5 years	15	15	30
5 Years or more	5	30	35
Total	50	50	100

Suppose that you select at random one executive's file. Determine the following probabilities:
(a) P(technical)
(b) P(administrative)
(c) P(technical and 5 years or more experience)
(d) P(5 years or more experience technical) given a technical executive is selected.

2.4. A manufacturing company is considering the introduction of a new product. Based on past experiences with similar products, management has made the following probability assignments concerning the expected sales volume for the new product.

Prior Probabilities

Expected Sales Volume	Probability
High (H)	0.7
Low (L)	0.3
	1.0

Management has available for use a consumer test panel that can evaluate the new product as well as forecast expected sales. The table on page 66 gives the panel's "track record" in new product evaluations.

That is,

$$P(PH|H) = 0.6 \qquad P(PL|H) = 0.4$$
$$P(PH|L) = 0.3 \qquad P(PL|L) = 0.7.$$

Panel's Prediction (*Given*)	*ACTUAL SALES VOLUME*	
	High (H)	*Low (L)*
High (*PH*)	0.6	0.3
Low (*PL*)	0.4	0.7
	1.0	1.0

Suppose the test panel concludes (predicts) that the product will have low expected sales. That is, they conclude that the new product will be a "*PL*."

Using Bayes' rule, revise the original prior probability assignments of the new product being an *H* and an *L*.

ANSWERS TO REVIEW PROBLEMS

2.1. The sample space for this experiment is

$$S = \{2, 3, 4, 5, 6, 7, 8, 9, 10\}.$$

(a) The event that demand is not less than 6 nor more than 9 is the set {6, 7, 8, 9}.
(b) {2, 3, 4, 5}
(c) {9, 10}
(d) {2, 3}

2.2. *A* and *B* are not mutually exclusive, since if *B* occurs (all keys fail), then *A* must occur (addition key fails). In fact, $A \subset B$.

2.3. (a) P(technical) = (number with technical skills)/
(total number of executives) $= \frac{50}{100} = 0.5$.
(b) P(administrative) = (number with administrative skills)/
(total number of executives) $= \frac{50}{100} = 0.5$.
(c) P(technical *and* 5 years or more experience)
= (number with technical skills who have 5 years
or more experience)/(total number of executives)
$= \frac{5}{100} = 0.05$.
(d) P(5 years or more experience|technical)

$$= \frac{P(5 \text{ years or more experience and technical})}{P(\text{technical})}$$

$$= \frac{0.05}{0.5} = 0.1 \quad \text{or} \quad 10\%.$$

2.4. Using the multiplication, we have

$$P(PL) = P(PL|H)P(H) + P(PL|L)P(L)$$
$$= (0.4)(0.7) + (0.7)(0.3)$$
$$= 0.49.$$

Now
$$P(H|PL) = \frac{P(PL|H)P(H)}{P(PL)}$$
$$= \frac{(0.4)(0.7)}{0.49}$$
$$= 0.571.$$

Similarly,
$$P(L|PL) = \frac{P(PL|L)P(L)}{P(PL)}$$
$$= \frac{(0.7)(0.3)}{0.49}$$
$$= 0.429.$$

EXERCISES **2.1.** Monthly sales of color TV sets at Wilson Electronics totals between 1 and 20 sets, inclusive.
(a) What is the sample space for each month's sales?
(b) What sales would be included in the event "10 or more"?
(c) What sales (outcomes) would be included in the event "12 or less"?
(d) What sales (outcomes) would be included in the event "6 or more"?
(e) What sales (outcomes) would be included in the event "15 or less"?

2.2. A quality control specialist road tests four automobiles daily. Each of the four automobiles tested are selected randomly from the assembly line, road-tested, and then classified as a winner (W) or a lemon (L). Each outcome of his daily tests (random experiment) must describe the condition of the four automobiles. Describe, using a tree diagram, the sample space for this random experiment.

2.3. From a Venn diagram show that the event A^c (not A) $\cap$ B^c (not B) and $A \cup B$ (A or B) are mutually exclusive and collectively exhaustive. Also show that $P(A \cup B) + P(A^c \cap B^c) = 1$.

2.4. Let A be the event that next year's sales exceed \$2 million. Let B be the event that next year's sales are less than \$3 million.
(a) Is the joint probability that both events A and B occur, $P(A \text{ and } B \text{ occur}) = P(A \cap B)$, less than, equal to, or greater than 1? State why.
(b) Is $P(A) + P(B)$ less than, equal to, or greater than 1? State why.
(c) Is $P(A \text{ or } B \text{ occur}) = P(A \cup B)$ less than, equal to, or greater than 1? State why.

2.5. Consider the following table of conditional probabilities estimated using personnel data on 1000 management trainees.

Management Trainees (conditional probabilities)

Psychological Test Prediction (Given)[a]	STATUS OF THE 1000 TRAINEES		Total
	Success (S)	Dismissed (D)	
Success (PS)	0.80	0.20	1.00
Failure (PF)	0.60	0.40	1.00

[a]$P(PS) = 0.50$ and $P(PF) = 0.50$.

(a) How many of the original 1000 trainees are still with the firm? That is, $1000P(S) = ?$

(b) How many of the original 1000 trainees were dismissed by the firm? That is, $1000P(D) = ?$

(c) Determine the joint probabilities needed to complete the following table.

Management Trainees (joint probabilities)

Psychological Test Prediction	STATUS OF THE 1000 TRAINEES		Total
	Success (S)	Dismissed (D)	
Success (PS)	?	?	?
Failure (PF)	?	?	?
Total	?	?	?

2.6. Assume that it is true that events A and B are independent. That is, assume it is true that

$$P(A|B) = P(A) \quad \text{and} \quad P(B|A) = P(A).$$

You are given the probability assessments that $P(A) = 0.45$ and $P(B) = 0.80$.

(a) What is $P(A \text{ and } B) = P(A \cap B) = ?$

(b) What is $P(A \text{ or } B) = P(A \cup B) = ?$

2.7. Consider the following table of joint probabilities.

Change in Sales	Increase Advertising (IA)	Do Not Increase Advertising (NIA)	Total
Sales increase (SI)	0.20	0.40	0.60
Sales remain constant or decrease (NSI)	0.20	0.20	0.40
Total	0.40	0.60	1.00

(a) Determine the probability that sales will increase if advertising is increased.

(b) What is the probability advertising was increased if sales increased?

(c) $P(\text{SI}|\text{IA}) + P(\text{NSI}|\text{IA}) = ?$
$P(\text{SI}|\text{NIA}) + P(\text{NSI}|\text{NIA}) = ?$

(d) $P(\text{IA}|\text{SI}) + P(\text{NIA}|\text{SI}) = ?$
$P(\text{IA}|\text{NSI}) + P(\text{NIA}|\text{NSI}) = ?$

(e) Describe in words the conditional probability obtained from the table that has the value $0.40/0.60 = \frac{2}{3}$.

2.8. Super Star Vitamins Inc. conducted a controlled experiment last year on 350 typical American housewives. Of the 350 housewives, 200 took Super Star's Brand X vitamins and the remaining 150 took another leading vitamin. At the end of the study, the husbands of each of the housewives were asked to answer the question: "Do you love your wife more (M), about the same (S), or less (*L*) than you did one year ago?" The results of the study are given in the following table.

| Husband's Attitude | VITAMIN TAKEN | | Total |
	Brand X	Another Leading Vitamin	
More (*M*)	110	50	160
Same (*S*)	50	50	100
Less (*L*)	40	50	90
Total	200	150	350

(a) Using the data above, what can you conclude about the ability of Brand X to affect the attitude of husbands toward their wives? That is, is "husband's attitude" independent or dependent on the use of Brand X?

(b) Perform a similar analysis for the other leading vitamin.

2.9. Jack Foster is Marcey Department store's best salesman. Sixty-five percent of the customers he waits on make a purchase (it is assumed that the purchasing behavior of any two customers is independent). Two customers, *A* and *B*, enter Marcey's and both are waited on by Foster. What is your estimate of the probability that Foster will make a sale to *A* or *B*? That is, *P*(*A* or *B* or both make a purchase from Foster) = ? What is the probability that both will make a purchase: that is, that $P(A \cap B) = ?$

2.10. WV Automobiles are produced in four plants in Western Europe, which we shall label *A*, *B*, *C*, and *D*. Plant *A* produces 25%, plant *B* produces 25%, plant *C* produces 40%, and plant *D* produces 10% of WV's total annual output. The manager of customer relations for WV believes (his subjective estimate) that 2%, 4%, 6%, and 1% of the automobiles produced in *A*, *B*, *C*, and *D*, respectively, are junk. If you were to purchase a WV automobile and it turned out to be a piece of junk, what would be the likelihood that it was produced at plant *A*? Plant *D*?

CASE 2.1 Illustrative Case Study
Involving Computation of Probabilities

INTERNATIONAL CONSTRUCTION CO. (SELECTING CONSTRUCTION PROJECTS IN THE MIDEAST) Assume that you are the chief executive of International Construction Incorporated. Your firm has been asked to bid on two major construction projects in the Middle East: Syria and Saudi Arabia. The Syrian project involves the construction of a new petrochemical plant in the city of Aleppo and the Saudi Arabian project involves the construction of a dam on the Oman River.

Both projects require different engineering skills and equipment. The construction firm that can present the best combination of skills and equipment will have an important advantage in contract negotiations with both governments.

Upon inquiry with the U.S. State Department, you have concluded that the most critical aspect of the chemical project in Aleppo is whether or not Syria becomes a decidedly socialist regime. If Syria goes socialistic, then most U.S. State Department experts believe that there is a probability of 0.2 (20%)

that the chemical plant will *not* be built by a Western company. If Syria does not go socialistic, this probability is reduced to 0.1 (10%). Your estimate is that the probability is 0.3 (30%) for Syria to become a socialist regime.

You also have from the State Department subjective estimates of the dam project on the Oman River. To your surprise, you find that the Saudi Arabian government is disturbed by the news stories regarding the nuclear power plant the United States plans to build in Egypt. Should the nuclear plant be built, it is estimated there is only 1 chance in 10 that Saudi Arabia will let a contract to a Western company for the dam construction. The odds are changed to 50–50 if the power plant is not constructed. State Department experts believe there is a 40% chance that the United States will build a nuclear plant in Egypt.

Question. International Construction Company can only bid on one of the projects. If you accept the subjective probability assessments of the State Department and the other information, which contract would you advise International to bid on so as to maximize their probability of success?

CHAPTER 3
Probability Models for Decision Making

OBJECTIVES: Upon successful completion of this chapter, you should be able to:

1. Explain and illustrate the concept of a random variable.
2. Explain and illustrate the concept of a probability distribution.
3. Define, illustrate, and use the mean, variance, and standard deviation statistics.
4. Explain the basic assumptions of several important probability distributions.
5. Apply probability distributions to a variety of business problems.

3.1. INTRODUCTION

We are now ready to study some additional tools that are useful in analyzing business situations involving uncertainty. In Chapter 2 we studied several important concepts of probability. In particular we reviewed several different business problems that involved random outcomes and random events with associated probabilities. Often such outcomes and events may be expressed as *variables*. Because the value of the variable is uncertain we refer to it as a *random variable*. Probabilities assigned to each possible *value* for this variable constitutes a probability distribution.

The three basic concepts to be illustrated are:

Random Variable. Any rule that associates with each outcome of an experiment a corresponding number is called a random variable.

Value. The number that a random variable associates with a particular outcome is called the value of the variable for that outcome.

Distribution. A list containing both the values of the random variable and its corresponding probabilities is called the distribution of the random variable.

3.1.1. Example—Employee Selection

Two employees are selected at random (with replacement) from a list of which 70% of the employees are male. The number X of males in the sample is a random variable. The outcomes of the experiment are (m, m), (m, f), (f, m), and (f, f), where (m, m) denotes the outcome that two men are selected, (m, f) denotes a male selected first and a female selected second, (f, m) denotes a female selected first and a male second, and (f, f) denotes the outcome that two females are chosen.

A random variable X is assigned values according to the following rule:

$X = 2$ if outcome (m, m) occurs
$X = 1$ if either outcome (m, f) or (f, m) occurs
$X = 0$ if outcome (f, f) occurs.

From the tree diagram in Figure 3.1, we can obtain the distribution of X shown in Table 3.1:

$$P(X = 2) = P((m, m) \text{ selected}) \qquad\qquad = 0.49$$
$$P(X = 1) = P((m, f) \quad or \quad (f, m) \text{ selected}) = 0.21 + 0.21 = 0.42$$
$$P(X = 0) = P((f, f) \text{ selected}) \qquad\qquad = 0.09.$$

The distribution of a variable can be represented by a graph called a *histogram*. Figure 3.2 shows the histogram for the distribution of X. The histogram consists of nonoverlapping rectangles with equal bases, one centered at each value of the variable, with height proportional to the probability that the variable has that probability. Thus, the heights of the rectangles in Figure 3.2 are proportional to 9, 42, and 49.

Figure 3.1. Tree diagram: employee selection.

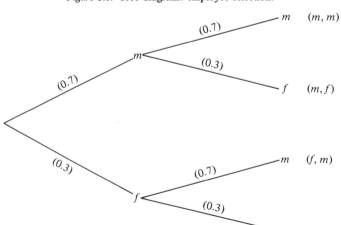

Table 3.1. Distribution of X: Employee Selection

Sample Outcome	Value of X (how many males chosen)	Probability Distribution of X
(m, m)	2	$(0.7)(0.7) = 0.49$
(m, f)	1	$(0.7)(0.3) = 0.21$
(f, m)	1	$(0.3)(0.7) = 0.21$
(f, f)	0	$(0.3)(0.3) = \underline{0.09}$
		1.00

Figure 3.2. Histogram: employee selection.

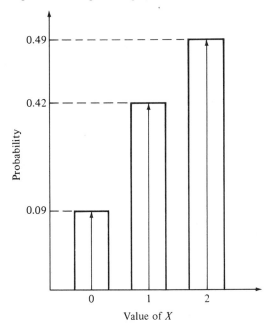

Value of X	Probability Distribution of X
0	0.09
1	0.42
2	0.49
	$\overline{1.00}$

3.1.2. Example—Finding the Distribution of the Number of Errors

The experiment is to audit three accounts in an accounts receivable file. Let E_i denote the outcome that the ith account audited is in error and O_i denote the outcome that there is no error, $i = 1, 2,$ and 3.

Let X be a random variable ("a counting variable") which gives the number of accounts in error found in the audit. Since there are three accounts *to be audited*,

$$X = 0, 1, 2, \text{ or } 3.$$

What is the probability distribution of X?

Assume from prior information that 10% of the accounts in the file contain errors. That is, we know that

$$P(E_i) = 0.10 \quad \text{(for } i = 1, 2, 3)$$

and

$$P(O_i) = 0.90 \quad \text{(for } i = 1, 2, 3).$$

How the probability distribution of X is determined is evident from columns 1 and 2, Table 3.2. The two columns on the left give the outcomes of the experiment and their probability assignments. For example, the outcome that the first two accounts contain no errors and the third does, that is, (O_1, O_2, E_3), has the following probability assignment:

$$P(O_1, O_2, \text{ and } E_3 \text{ occurs}) = P(O_1)P(O_2)P(E_3) = (0.9)(0.9)(0.1) = 0.081.$$

The two columns on the right in Table 3.2 give the probability distribution of X. Note that the arrows in the table illustrate a mapping from *one or more* of the original sample points onto each value of X: 0, 1, or 2. Also note that

$$P(X = 0) + P(X = 1) + P(X = 2) + P(X = 3) = 1$$
$$0.001 \quad + \quad 0.027 \quad + \quad 0.243 \quad + \quad 0.729 \quad = 1,$$

as expected, since either zero ($X = 0$), or one ($X = 1$), or two ($X = 2$), or three ($X = 3$) accounts will be found in error when auditing the three accounts. The histogram representation of the distribution of X is shown in Figure 3.3.

In Examples 3.1.1 and 3.1.2 we note that the value of a random variable is uncertain, depending on the occurrence of some event. Next consider the sales prediction problem of California Ketchup Inc. (CKI).

Table 3.2. Constructing the Probability Distribution of X: Audit Errors

(1) Probability Assignment, $P(s)$	(2) Sample Outcomes, s	(3) Values of $X : x$	(4) $P(X = x)$
$(0.1)(0.1)(0.1) = 0.001$	$(E_1, E_2, E_3) \longrightarrow$	3	0.001
$(0.1)(0.1)(0.9) = 0.009$	(E_1, E_2, O_3)		
$(0.1)(0.9)(0.1) = 0.009$	$(E_1, O_2, E_3) \Longrightarrow$	2	0.027
$(0.9)(0.1)(0.1) = 0.009$	(O_1, E_2, E_3)		
$(0.1)(0.9)(0.9) = 0.081$	(E_1, O_2, O_3)		
$(0.9)(0.1)(0.9) = 0.081$	$(O_1, E_2, O_3) \longrightarrow$	1	0.243
$(0.9)(0.9)(0.1) = 0.081$	(O_1, O_2, E_3)		
$(0.9)(0.9)(0.9) = 0.729$	$(O_1, O_2, O_3) \longrightarrow$	0	0.729
$\overline{1.000}$			$\overline{1.000}$

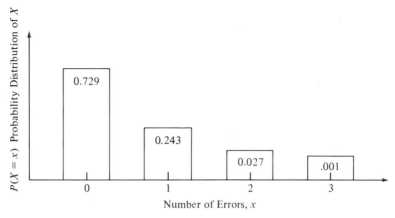

Figure 3.3. Histogram: audit errors.

Table 3.3. CKI Ketchup Sales During Last 100 Weeks (number of cases)

Quantity Sold S	Number of Weeks	Distribution of S
100	2	$\frac{2}{100} = 0.02$
101	3	$\frac{3}{100} = 0.03$
102	7	$\frac{7}{100} = 0.07$
103	4	$\frac{4}{100} = 0.04$
104	13	$\frac{13}{100} = 0.13$
105	9	$\frac{9}{100} = 0.09$
106	9	$\frac{9}{100} = 0.09$
107	10	$\frac{10}{100} = 0.10$
108	10	$\frac{10}{100} = 0.10$
109	15	$\frac{15}{100} = 0.15$
110	18	$\frac{18}{100} = 0.18$
$\overline{1155}$	$\overline{100}$	$\overline{1.00}$

3.1.3. Example—Sales Prediction

Let S be next week's sales of California Ketchup. Obviously, S is a random variable. Assume that the sales department of CKI has kept a record of the number of cases sold during the past 100 weeks, as shown in the first two columns of Table 3.3. The third column of Table 3.3 gives an estimate of the probability distribution of S *using past sales history*.

For example, we predict that there is a 10% chance that next week's sales will be 107 cases: $P(S = 107) = \frac{10}{100} = 0.10$.

QUESTION. What is the probability that next week's sales S will be *at most* 102 cases?

Answer

P(next week's sales will be at most 102 cases)

$$= P(S = 100 \text{ or } 101 \text{ or } 102)$$
$$= P(S = 100) + P(S = 101) + P(S = 102)$$
$$= 0.02 \qquad + 0.03 \qquad + 0.07$$
$$= 0.12 \quad \text{or} \quad 12\%.$$

QUESTION. What is the probability that next week's sales will be *less than* 100?

Answer. $P(S < 100) = 0$, since weekly sales are always at least 100 or more cases.

QUESTION. What is the probability that next week's sales will be equal to or greater than 100?

Answer. $P(S \geqslant 100) = 1.0$ or 100%, since weekly sales are always equal to or greater than 100 cases.

QUESTION. What is the probability that next week's sales will be equal to or less than 110 cases?

Answer. $P(S \leqslant 110) = 1.0$ or 100%, since weekly sales are always equal to or less than 110 cases.

QUESTION. What is the probability that next week's sales will be between 106 cases and 110 cases?

Answer. $P(106 < S < 110) = P(S = 107) + P(S = 108) + P(S = 109)$
$$= 0.10 \qquad + 0.10 \qquad + 0.15$$
$$= 0.35 \quad \text{or} \quad 35\%.$$

3.2. DISCRETE PROBABILITY DISTRIBUTIONS

Usually, the distribution function of a random variable is characterized by two derived numbers: its *mean* and its *variance*. Such a description of a distribution function is valuable in many business applications.

Let X be a random variable. Let x_i ($i = 1, \ldots, n$) be the possible values that X can assume, and let $P(x_i) = P(X = x_i)$ be the probability that X assumes the value x_i. If we denote the *mean* by $\bar{X}$ and the variance by var(X), we have

$$\bar{X} = \sum_{i=1}^{n} x_i P(x_i) \tag{3.2.1}$$

$$\text{var}(X) = \sum_{i=1}^{n} \left(x_i - \bar{X}\right)^2 P(x_i). \tag{3.2.2}$$

Formula (3.2.2) can be simplified for *computational* purposes as

$$\text{var}(X) = \sum_{i=1}^{n} x_i^2 P(x_i) - (\bar{X})^2. \tag{3.2.3}$$

The *mean*, often called the *expected value* of X, is an estimate of the value of X *to be expected* from an experiment. The variance of X, var(X), is a measure of the *expected scatter* or *expected dispersion* of achieved values of X about its expected value, $\bar{X}$.

3.2.1. Example—Estimating Expected Rate of Return

The following table gives the probability distribution of R, the rate of return or investment to be achieved in purchasing a new machine.

Possible Rate of Return, R	Probability Distribution of R, $P(r_i)$
$r_1 = 10\%$	0.25
$r_2 = 12\%$	0.50
$r_3 = 14\%$	0.25
	$\overline{1.00}$

QUESTION. What is the expected or mean rate of return?

Answer. Using formula (3.2.1), we have

$$\bar{R} = (10\%)P(R = 10\%) + (12\%)P(R = 12\%) + (14\%)P(R = 14\%)$$
$$= (10\%)(0.25) + (12\%)(0.50) + (14\%)(0.25)$$
$$= 12\%.$$

QUESTION. What is the variance or expected dispersion of rate of return R about its mean $\bar{R}$?

Answer. To use formula (3.2.3) we first perform the calculations shown in the following table.

Variance Calculation for Rate of Return

Values of R	(Values of R)² = r²	Probability, P(r_i)	r_i²P(r_i)
$r_1 = 10\%$	100	0.25	25
$r_2 = 12\%$	144	0.50	72
$r_3 = 14\%$	196	0.25	49
			$\overline{146}$

Using formula (3.2.3), we have

$$\text{var}(R) = \sum_{i=1}^{3} r_i^2 P(R = r_i) - (\overline{R})^2$$

$$= 146 - (12)^2$$

$$= 2.$$

3.2.2. Example—Measuring Expected Sales

In the data of Table 3.3 we can determine an *expected* volume for next week's sales by multiplying the values of the random variable S by the individual probabilities, as shown in the last column of Table 3.4. Thus, expected sales $\overline{S}$ is equal to 106.45 cases. That is,

$$\overline{S} = \sum_{i=1}^{10} s_i P(s_i) = 106.45 \text{ cases.}$$

$\overline{S}$ is also often called a *weighted average*.
   The *arithmetic average* is

$$\frac{100 + 101 + \cdots + 110}{11} = \frac{1155 \text{ cases}}{11} = 105 \text{ cases.}$$

The computation of the expected variability of next week's sales about an expected sales of $\overline{S} = 106.45$ cases is obtainable from the computations given in Table 3.5. Thus, variation of sales, S, about expected sales, $\overline{S}$, is, using formula (3.2.3),

$$\text{var}(S) = \sum_{i=1}^{11} s_i^2 P(s_i) - (\overline{S})^2$$

$$= 11,339.69 - (106.45)^2$$

$$= 11,339.69 - 11,331.60$$

$$= 8.09 (\text{cases})^2.$$

Table 3.4. Determining Expected Sales[a]

(1) *Values of the Random Variable S, s_i*	(2) *Probability Distribution of S, $P(s_i)$*	(3) = (1) × (2) *Expected Value Computations*
$s_1 = 100$	$P(s_1) = 0.02$	2.00
$s_2 = 101$	$P(s_2) = 0.03$	3.03
$s_3 = 102$	$P(s_3) = 0.07$	7.14
$s_4 = 103$	$P(s_4) = 0.04$	4.12
$s_5 = 104$	$P(s_5) = 0.13$	13.52
$s_6 = 105$	$P(s_6) = 0.09$	9.45
$s_7 = 106$	$P(s_7) = 0.09$	9.54
$s_8 = 107$	$P(s_8) = 0.10$	10.70
$s_9 = 108$	$P(s_9) = 0.10$	10.80
$s_{10} = 109$	$P(s_{10}) = 0.15$	16.35
$s_{11} = 110$	$P(s_{11}) = 0.18$	19.80
	$\overline{1.00}$	$\overline{S} = \overline{106.45}$ cases

[a]From Table 3.3.

Table 3.5. Measuring the Variation of Sales About Expected Sales

Values of S, s_i	s_i^2	$P(s_i)$	$s_i^2 P(s_i)$
100	10,000	0.02	200.00
101	10,201	0.03	306.03
102	10,404	0.07	728.28
103	10,609	0.04	424.36
104	10,816	0.13	1,406.08
105	11,025	0.09	992.25
106	11,236	0.09	1,011.24
107	11,449	0.10	1,144.90
108	11,664	0.10	1,166.40
109	11,881	0.15	1,782.15
110	12,100	0.18	2,178.00
		$\overline{1.00}$	$\overline{11,339.69}$

Another statistic commonly used is the *standard deviation* of a random variable defined by $SD(X) = \sqrt{\text{var}(X)}$. Thus, in Example 3.2.1 we have that the standard deviation of rate of return = $SD(R) = \sqrt{\text{var}(R)} = \sqrt{2} = 1.41\%$. In Example 3.2.2 we have $SD(S) = \sqrt{\text{var}(S)} = \sqrt{8.09} = 2.84$ cases.

3.3. SOME SPECIAL DISCRETE DISTRIBUTIONS

There are several important discrete probability distributions which recur often in business applications, such as the *binomial distribution*, *Poisson distribution*, *hypergeometric distribution*, and the *multinomial distribution*.

3.3.1. Binomial Distribution

$$\text{values of } X: \quad 0, 1, 2, \ldots, n$$

$$\text{distribution of } X: \quad f(x) = P(X = x) = \binom{n}{x}\theta^x(1 - \theta)^{n-x} \qquad (3.3.1)$$

$$\text{mean of } X: \quad \overline{X} = n\theta \qquad (3.3.2)$$

$$\text{variance of } X: \quad \text{var}(X) = n\theta(1 - \theta). \qquad (3.3.3)$$

A binomial distribution most often can be thought of as a model of a sequence of trials (or experiments), where each trial has two possible outcomes. For example:

success or failure   correct or incorrect

reject or accept   purchase or nonpurchase

pass or fail   member or nonmember.

Technically, a binomial variable must satisfy the following three properties:

Property 1 There must be a fixed number of repeated trials (observations) that are statistically independent (n = number of trials).

Property 2 Each trial must be a Bernoulli variable; that is, each trial must result in a *success* or a *failure*.

Property 3 All trials must have identical probabilities of success, θ, so that the probability of failure, $1 - \theta$, is also a constant for each trial.

3.3.2. Example—Binomial Distribution and Telephone Polling

Assume that the TV viewing audience of the Bowling for Peanuts show constitutes 30% of the total TV viewing audience. That is, the program has a market share of 30%.

QUESTION. What is the probability that exactly one viewer in a random sample (random telephone poll) of five viewers will be watching Bowling for Peanuts?

Answer. Using the binomial formula (3.3.1), with

$$n = 5 \qquad \text{(sample size)}$$
$$\theta = 0.30 \qquad \text{(market share)}$$
$$x = 1 \qquad \text{(exactly one viewer)}$$

yields
$$f(x = 1) = \binom{5}{1}(0.3)^1(1-.3)^{5-1}$$
$$= 5(0.3)^1(0.7)^4$$
$$= 5(0.3)(0.2401)$$
$$= 0.3602 \quad \text{or} \quad \text{approximately 36\%.}$$

QUESTION. What is the probability that more than half of those viewers called will be watching Bowling for Peanuts?

Answer. Using the binomial formula (3.3.1), with

$$n = 5$$
$$\theta = 0.30,$$

we need to compute

$$P(\text{more than half}) = P(X > 3)$$
$$= P(X = 3 \text{ or } 4 \text{ or } 5 \text{ "successes"})$$
$$= P(X = 3) + P(X = 4) + P(X = 5)$$
$$= \binom{5}{3}(0.3)^3(0.7)^2 + \binom{5}{4}(0.3)^4(0.7)^1 + \binom{5}{5}(0.3)^5(0.7)^0$$
$$= (0.1323) + (0.0284) + (0.0024)$$
$$= 0.1631 \quad \text{or} \quad \text{approximately 16\%.}$$

Also note in Example 3.3.2 that the expected number of viewers (prior to sampling) is

$$\bar{X} = n\theta = 5(0.3) = 1.5 \text{ viewers} \qquad [\text{using formula (3.3.2)}]$$

with an expected dispersion of

$$\text{var}(X) = n\theta(1 - \theta) = 5(0.3)(0.7) = 1.05 (\text{viewers})^2 \qquad [\text{using formula (3.3.3)}]$$

Table I in Appendix A gives

$$P(X = x) = f(x) = \binom{n}{x}\theta^x(1 - \theta)^{n-x}$$

for several values of n and θ.

3.3.3. Example—Binomial Distribution and Quality Control

From past data it has been estimated that a production line produces defective items at a rate of 10%. Each day five items are randomly selected from the line and inspected.

QUESTION. What is the probability that 60% or less of the sample [(0.60)(5) = 3 items] will be defective?

Answer. In this problem we have $n = 5$ (sample size) and $\theta = 0.10$ (or 10% defective items). Thus,

$$
\begin{aligned}
P(X < 3) &= P(X = 0) + P(X = 1) + P(X = 2) + P(X = 3) \\
&= 0.5905 + 0.3280 + 0.0729 + 0.0081 \\
&= 0.9995.
\end{aligned}
$$

The probability $(0.5905) = P(X = 0)$ was obtained from Table I using $n = 5$, $x = 0$, and $\theta = 0.10$, the probability $(0.3280) = P(X = 1)$ was obtained from Table I using $n = 5$, $x = 1$, and $\theta = 0.10$; and so forth.

QUESTION. What is the expected weekly number of defective items?

Answer $\overline{X} = n\theta = 5(0.10) = 0.5$ defective item.

QUESTION. What is the expected variation of sample defectives about the expected number of defectives?

Answer

$$
\begin{aligned}
\text{var}(X) &= n\theta(1 - \theta) \\
&= 5(0.10)(0.90) \\
&= 0.45(\text{item})^2.
\end{aligned}
$$

QUESTION. What is the standard deviation of sample defectives?

Answer

$$
\begin{aligned}
\text{SD}(X) &= \sqrt{\text{var}(X)} \\
&= \sqrt{0.45(\text{item})^2} \\
&= 0.67 \text{ item.}
\end{aligned}
$$

3.3.4. *Example—Binomial Distribution and Mail-Order-House Advertising*

A mail-order house expects a 20% rate of response from circulars mailed to households. What types of response is expected from a test mailing to 20 randomly selected households. That is, answer the following questions.

QUESTION. How many responses are expected from the test mailing?

Answer. Using $n = 20$ and $\theta = 0.20$ in the binomial formula (3.3.1), we have $\overline{X} = n\theta = 20 (0.20) = 4$. Thus, we expect four responses for every 20 mailings.

QUESTION. What is the probability of receiving at least one response from the 20 mailings?

Answer

$$P(X \geqslant 1) = 1 - P(X = 0)$$

$$= 1 - \binom{20}{0}(0.20)^0(0.80)^{20}$$

$$= 1 - 0.0115$$

$$= 0.9885 \quad \text{or} \quad 98.85\%.$$

$\theta = \text{probability of success}$

3.3.5. Geometric Distribution

$$\text{values of } X: \quad 1, 2, 3, \ldots \qquad (n = \infty)$$

$$\text{distribution of } X: \quad f(x) = P(X = x) = \theta(1 - \theta)^{x-1} \qquad (3.3.4)$$

$$\text{mean of } X: \quad \overline{X} = \frac{1}{\theta} \qquad (3.3.5)$$

$$\text{variance of } X: \quad \text{var}(X) = \frac{1 - \theta}{\theta^2}. \qquad (3.3.6)$$

A geometric variable represents "the number of trials" ($X = 1$ or 2 or 3 or ...) until the "first success." Recall that a binomial variable represents the "number of successes" in n trials.

3.3.6. Example—Geometric Distribution and Quality Control

Review Example 3.3.3

Suppose that a production line is to be sampled until a defective item is found. Using an error rate of $\theta = 0.20$ (or 20%), consider the following questions.

QUESTION. How many items would you expect to be tested until one is found to be defective?

Answer

$$\overline{X} = \frac{1}{0.20} = 5 \text{ items.}$$

QUESTION. What is the probability that the first item found to be defective is the fourth item tested?

Answer

$$P(X = 4) = \theta(1 - \theta)^3$$

$$= (0.20)(0.80)^3$$

$$= 0.1024.$$

QUESTION. What is the probability that the first item found to be defective is the sixth item tested?

Answer
$$P(X = 6) = (0.20)(0.80)^5$$
$$= 0.0655.$$

QUESTION. What is the probability that the first defective item found is *not* the first item tested?

Answer

P(first defective is not the first item tested) $= P(X \neq 1)$
$$= P(X = 2 \text{ or } 3 \text{ or } 4 \text{ or } \dots)$$
$$= 1 - P(X = 1) = 1 - 0.20 = 0.80.$$

3.3.7. *Negative Binomial Distribution*

values of X: $x = k, k + 1, k + 2, \dots$

distribution of X: $f(x) = P(X = x) = \binom{x-1}{k-1}\theta^k(1 - \theta)^{x-k}$ (3.3.7)

mean of X: $\bar{X} = \dfrac{k}{\theta}$ (3.3.8)

variance of X: $\text{var}(X) = \dfrac{k}{\theta}\left(\dfrac{1}{\theta} - 1\right).$ (3.3.9)

A negative binomial variable represents the "number of the trial in which the kth success occurs." So if $k = 1$, we have the geometric distribution being a special case of the negative binomial distribution. That is, letting $k = 1$ in (3.3.7) yields

$$f(x) = \binom{x-1}{1-1}\theta^1(1 - \theta)^{x-1}$$
$$= \binom{x-1}{0}\theta^1(1 - \theta)^{x-1}$$
$$= \theta(1 - \theta)^{x-1},$$

which is indeed the distribution of a geometric variable.

3.3.8. *Example—Negative Binomial Distribution and TV Telephone Polling*

Review Example 3.3.2

How many phone calls would you expect to have to make until you have contacted 12 viewers of the program?

Using the negative binomial formula (3.7) with $k = 12$ and $\theta = 0.3$ yields

$$\bar{X} = \frac{k}{\theta} = \frac{12}{0.3} = 40 \text{ telephone calls.}$$

Also, note that

$$\text{var}(X) = \frac{k}{\theta}\left(\frac{1}{\theta} - 1\right) = \left(\frac{12}{0.3}\right)\left(\frac{1}{0.3} - 1\right) = 93.33(\text{viewer})^2$$

What is the probability that the sixth person contacted will be the fourth viewer who is watching the program? Let $x = 6$, $k = 4$, and $\theta = 0.30$ in (3.3.7). Then

$P(\text{4th success occurs on call number 6}) = P(X = 6)$

$$= f(6) = \binom{6-1}{4-1}(0.3)^4(1 - 0.3)^{6-4}$$

$$= \binom{5}{3}(0.3)^4(0.7)^2$$

$$= \left(\frac{5 \cdot 4}{2 \cdot 1}\right)(0.0081)(0.49) = 0.04 \quad (4\%).$$

3.3.9. Example—Negative Binomial Distribution and Quality Control

Review Example 3.3.3

QUESTION. On the average, how many items need to be tested until 5 defective items are found?

Answer $\qquad X = \frac{k}{\theta} = \frac{5}{0.10} = 50$ items.

QUESTION. What percentage of the time (performing daily tests) would you find that the fifth defective item is the tenth item tested?

Answer. Let $\theta = 0.10$ and $k = 5$ in (3.7). Then

$$P(X = 10) = \binom{9}{4}(0.10)^5(0.90)^5$$

$$= 0.0007 \quad \text{or} \quad \text{less than 1\% of the time.}$$

3.3.10. Hypergeometric Distribution

Assume that a sample space or a population S can be partitioned into two subsets A and B ($A \cap B = \varnothing$, $A \cup B = S$) such that

$$N(A) = a \qquad N(B) = b.$$

Thus, $N(S) = N(A) + N(B) = a + b$.

Assume that the a's and b's represent two dissimilar attributes of the population. Examples are:

a = success   and b = failure
a = pass   and b = fail
a = correct   and b = incorrect
a = prefers brand X and b = prefers brand Y   etc.

Then $P(\text{a sample of } n \text{ from } S \text{ will contain exactly } x \text{ } a\text{'s}) = \dfrac{\binom{a}{x}\binom{b}{n-x}}{\binom{a+b}{n}},$

which is the distribution of a hypergeometric random variable.

values of X: $0, 1, \ldots, \min(a, n)$

distribution of X: $P(X = x | n \text{ observations}) = \binom{a}{x}\binom{b}{n-x} \Big/ \binom{a+b}{n}$ (3.3.10)

mean of X: $\bar{X} = \dfrac{na}{a+b}$ (3.3.11)

variance of X: $\text{var}(X) = \dfrac{nab(a+b-n)}{(a+b)^2(a+b-1)}$ (3.3.12)

3.3.11. Example—The Hypergeometric Distribution and Quality Control

Suppose it is "known" that 4 out of every sequence of 20 automobiles off the assembly line at MG Motors require extensive reworking. Suppose that 2 automobiles are selected from a sequence of 20. What is the likelihood that exactly *one* automobile will require extensive reworking? Let $a = 4$, $b = 16$, and $n = 2$ in the hypergeometric distribution. Then,

$$P(X = 1 | \text{sample of } n = 2) = \binom{4}{1}\binom{16}{1} \Big/ \binom{20}{2}$$

$$= \frac{(4)(16)}{(10)(19)} = \frac{64}{190} = 0.34.$$

In a sample of size $n = 10$, from a sequence of 20 automobiles, how many automobiles do you *expect* to require extensive reworking?

$$\bar{X} = \frac{na}{a+b} = \frac{(10)(4)}{20} = 2.0.$$

3.3.12. Example—The Hypergeometric Distribution and Personnel Selection

Suppose that a manager randomly selects $n = 4$ names from a file containing $a + b = 15$ job applicants, $a = 10$ of whom have previous managerial experience. Consider the following questions.

QUESTION. What is the probability that none of the selected applicants has previous managerial experience?

Answer. Let $n = 4$, $a = 10$, and $b = 5$ in (3.10). Then

$$P(X = 0|4 \text{ observations}) = \binom{10}{0}\binom{5}{4} \bigg/ \binom{15}{4}$$

$$= \frac{5}{1365} = 0.0037 \quad \text{or} \quad \text{less than 1\%.}$$

QUESTION. What is the probability that exactly one applicant has previous experience?

Answer $P(X = 1|4 \text{ observations}) = \binom{10}{1}\binom{5}{3} \bigg/ 1365$

$$= 0.7326 \quad \text{or} \quad \text{slightly greater than 70\%.}$$

3.3.13. Multinomial Distribution

The binomial distribution deals with independent trials (observations) with two outcomes and is a special case of the *multinomial distribution*. The multinomial distribution is concerned with independent trials in which there can be *more than two outcomes*.

Suppose that we have an experiment (observation) which can have k possible mutually exclusive outcomes $E_1, E_2, \ldots, E_k$ with respective probabilities $\theta_1, \theta_2, \ldots, \theta_k$ which add up to 1: $\theta_1 + \theta_2 + \cdots + \theta_k = 1$. For example, consider the problem of observing a randomly selected customer's brand choice, where

E_1: customer purchases Jamaican sugar
E_2: customer purchases Hawaiian sugar
E_3: customer purchases Taiwan sugar,

with $\theta_1 = 0.35 = P(E_1)$, $\theta_2 = 0.40 = P(E_2)$, and $\theta_3 = 0.25 = P(E_3)$. Note that

$$\theta_1 + \theta_2 + \theta_3 = 1$$
$$0.35 + 0.40 + 0.25 = 1.$$

If we repeat this experiment n times and the θ_i's remain constant, what is the probability of exactly x_1 occurrences of outcome E_1; x_2 occurrences of outcome

$E_2, \ldots$, and x_k occurrences of outcome E_k? For example, in the brand-purchasing problem, suppose that we plan to observe $n = 10$ customers' brand choices (sample size of $n = 10$). Then we can ask, for example, what is the probability of $x_1 = 3$ purchases of Jamaican sugar, $x_2 = 4$ purchases of Hawaiian sugar, and $x_3 = 3$ purchases of Taiwan sugar? Note that

$$x_1 + x_2 + x_3 = n$$
$$3 + 4 + 3 = 10.$$

To answer the preceding questions, we note that the n observations are independent. Thus, the probability of any sequence of outcomes is equal to the product of their separate probabilities; that is,

$$\theta_1^{x_1} \theta_2^{x_2} \cdots \theta_k^{x_k}.$$

Furthermore, the number of distinct sequences yielding the stated number of results of each possible such sequence

$$\binom{n}{x_1, x_2, \ldots, x_k} = \frac{n!}{x_1! x_2! \cdots x_k!},$$

which is the number of ways to permute n things taken all at a time when x_1 are alike, x_2 are alike, $\ldots$, and x_k are alike. Since all these outcomes are mutually exclusive and have the same probability of occurrence, the total probability of x_1 occurrences of E_1, x_2 occurrences of $E_2, \ldots$, and x_k occurrences of E_k is

$$\binom{n}{x_1, x_2, \ldots, x_k} \theta_1^{x_1} \theta_2^{x_2} \cdots \theta_k^{x_k} = \frac{n!}{x_1! x_2! \cdots x_k!} \theta_1^{x_1} \theta_2^{x_2} \cdots \theta_k^{x_k}. \quad (3.3.13)$$

In the brand-purchasing problem, we have

$$\binom{10}{3, 4, 3}(0.35)^3(0.40)^4(0.25)^3 = \frac{10!}{3!4!3!}(0.35)^3(0.40)^4(0.25)^3$$
$$= (4200)(0.043)(0.026)(0.016)$$
$$= 0.0751 \quad \text{or} \quad \text{about 7.5\%.}$$

3.3.14. Example—Production Line Sampling

Assume that a production line produces a product that is either E_1, E_2, or E_3.

E_1: acceptable
E_2: is reworkable into an acceptable product
E_3: is defective and must be destroyed.

Assume (from past experience) that 90% of all the units produced are acceptable, 7% must be reworked, and 3% must be destroyed. Thus, $\theta_1 = 0.90$, $\theta_2 = 0.07$, and $\theta_3 = 0.03$. Suppose that quality control tests 10 units each day, where each unit is tested for being an E_1, an E_2, or an E_3. What is the probability that tomorrow's sample will contain 8 E_1's and 2 E_2's? We have

$$\binom{10}{8,\,2,\,0}(0.90)^8(0.07)^2(0.03)^0 = \frac{10!}{8!2!0!}(0.90)^8(0.07)^2$$
$$= (45)(0.430)(0.005)$$
$$= 0.097 \quad \text{or} \quad \text{approximately } 10\%.$$

3.3.15. Poisson Distribution

Consider the problem of determining the probability distribution, as well as the mean and variance, of the *number of arrivals* at a complaint department in a large department store during a specified time interval of length t.
Let

$$X_t = \text{number of arrivals (or complaints) during the interval } [0, t].$$

If the following properties hold, then X_t is said to have the *Poisson distribution*.

Property 1 The number of arrivals appear to come in *independently*. That is, the occurrence of a number of arrivals in a given time interval has no effect on the number of arrivals during any other time interval.

Property 2 The likelihood of two or more arrivals during a "small" time interval is very small compared to the likelihood of one arrival during the same time interval.

Property 3 The probability distribution of the number of arrivals during any given time interval depends only on the length of the time interval. Specifically, the longer the time interval, the more arrivals tend to come in.

Thus, if a variable X_t satisfies all three properties, we say that X_t has the *Poisson distribution*.

$$\text{values of } X_t: \quad 0, 1, 2, \ldots$$

$$\text{distribution of } X_t: \quad f(n) = P(X_t = n) = \frac{e^{-\lambda t}(\lambda t)^n}{n!} \tag{3.3.14}$$

$$\text{mean of } X_t: \quad \overline{X}_t = \lambda t \tag{3.3.15}$$

$$\text{variance of } X_t: \quad \text{var}(X_t) = \lambda t. \tag{3.3.16}$$

The parameter λ is called the *rate of arrivals*.
Suppose that the arrival rate at the complaint department is 7 per hour. Then

$\lambda = 7$ and

$$P(8 \text{ arrivals during any one hour}) = P(X_1 = 8)$$

$$= \frac{e^{-7(1)}[7(1)]^8}{8!}$$

$$= \frac{(0.000912)(5,764,801)}{40,320} = 0.1304.$$

$$P(4 \text{ arrivals between } 10:00 \text{ A.M. and } 10:30 \text{ A.M.}) = P(X_{1/2} = 4)$$

$$= \frac{e^{-7(1/2)}\left[7\left(\frac{1}{2}\right)\right]^4}{4!}$$

$$= \frac{e^{-7/2}\left(\frac{7}{2}\right)^4}{4!}$$

$$= \frac{(0.030)(150.06)}{24} = 0.188.$$

Also, $E(X_t) = 7t$ and $\text{var}(X_t) = 7t$.

Table II in Appendix A gives

$$P(X_t = n) = \frac{e^{-\lambda t}(\lambda t)^n}{n!}$$

for several values of λt.

3.3.16. Example—Predicting Power Failure

Suppose that the number of yearly breakdowns, "blackouts," of electricity generation in Tucson Arizona, follows a Poisson distribution with $\lambda = 1$. Thus,

$$P(X_t = n) = \frac{e^{-1t}(1 \cdot t)^n}{n!} \qquad (n = 0, 1, 2, \dots).$$

The expected number of breakdowns in 2 years is

$$\bar{X} = E(X_2) = \lambda t = (1)(2) = 2.$$

$$P(\text{no breakdown occurs}$$

$$\text{over the next 12 months}) = P(X_1 = 0)$$

($t = 1$ year)

$$= \frac{e^{-1(1)}(1(1))^0}{0!}$$

$$= e^{-1} = 0.3679.$$

$$P(\text{no breakdown occurs in 2 years}) = P(X_2 = 0)$$

$(t = 2 \text{ years})$
$$= \frac{e^{-1(2)}[1(2)]^0}{0!} = 0.1353.$$

$$\begin{array}{c} P(\text{no breakdown occurs} \\ \text{in the next 6 months}) = P(X_{1/2} = 0) \end{array}$$

$\left(t = \tfrac{1}{2} \text{ year}\right)$
$$= \frac{e^{-1(1/2)}\left[1\left(\tfrac{1}{2}\right)\right]^0}{0!} = 0.6065.$$

$$\begin{aligned} P(\text{two or more breakdowns next year}) = 1 - \big[& P(\text{zero breakdowns occur next year}) \\ & + P(\text{one breakdown occurs next year}) \big] \end{aligned}$$

$(t = 1 \text{ year})$
$$= 1 - \big[P(X_1 = 0) + P(X_1 = 1) \big]$$
$$= 1 - (0.3679 + 0.3679)$$
$$= 0.2642.$$

These probabilities can be obtained directly from Table II in Appendix A.

3.3.17. Example—Predicting Pipeline Explosions

Suppose that State-Wide National Gas Company has found that the average number of pipeline explosions in a metropolitan area occur at the rate of 0.5 per week. Also, it is known that the number of explosions over time has the Poisson distribution. Thus, $\lambda = 0.5$ and

$$P(X_t = n) = \frac{e^{-0.5t}(0.5t)^n}{n!} \qquad n = 0, 1, \ldots .$$

For example,

$$P(0 \text{ explosions in 2 weeks}) = P(X_2 = 0) = \frac{e^{-0.5(2)}[0.5(2)]^0}{0!} = 0.3679$$

and the expected number of explosions during next year $= E(X_{52}) = (0.5)(52) = 26.$

3.4. CONTINUOUS DISTRIBUTIONS AND PROBABILITY DENSITIES

In the preceding section several random variables were discussed whose possible values were "separated" or "discrete," such as the number of accounts containing errors in a (binomial) sample of size n, the number of arrivals at a bank in a specified time interval (Poisson distribution), the number of service completions in a specified time interval (Poisson distribution), and so on. We now turn to random variables which are, more properly and conveniently, regarded as ranging over a *continuum* of values. Examples are the *weight* of a carload of grain, the *time* between arrivals of customers at a service center, and so forth.

3.4.1. The Exponential Distribution

Recall that the distribution of a Poisson variable X_t is given by

$$P(X_t = n) = \frac{e^{-\lambda t}(\lambda t)^n}{n!},$$

where X_t = number of arrivals during a time interval of length t

$$E(X_t) = \lambda t$$

$$\text{var}(X_t) = \lambda t.$$

Let T be the *elapsed time* until the first customer arrival in a Poisson stream of arrivals. Note that T is a continuous valued random variable with $0 \leqslant T < \infty$. Consider the event

the first arrival occurs after time $t = T > t$.

Now

$$(T > t) = \text{the first arrival occurs after time } t$$

"occurs" if (the number of arrivals during the interval of length t is zero) = (X_t = 0). The "converse" of the statement above also holds. That is, the ("number" of arrivals during the interval of length t is zero) = (X_t = 0) *occurs* if ($T > t$). In summary,

$$(T > t) = (X_t = 0).$$

That is, the two events are equal, and

$$P(T > t) = P(X_t = 0) = \frac{e^{-\lambda t}(\lambda t)^0}{0!} = e^{-\lambda t}.$$

Since $P(T \leqslant t) + P(T > t) = 1$, we have

$$P(T \leqslant t) = 1 - P(T > t)$$
$$= 1 - e^{-\lambda t}.$$

In summary, the *distribution of an exponential distributed random variable* is given by

$$F(t) = P(T \leqslant t) = 1 - e^{-\lambda t} \qquad (t \geqslant 0) \qquad (3.4.1)$$

with

$$E(T) = \bar{T} = \frac{1}{\lambda} \tag{3.4.2}$$

and

$$\text{var}(T) = \frac{1}{\lambda^2}. \tag{3.4.3}$$

For example, assume that arrivals occur at a Poisson rate of $\lambda = 1.2$ per week. Then T denotes the *time between arrivals* with expectation $\bar{T} = 1/1.2 = 0.83$ week and variance $\text{var}(T) = 1/(1.2)^2 = 0.69(\text{week})^2$.

3.4.2. Example—Computation of Idle Times

Suppose that delivery trucks arrive "randomly" (Poisson arrivals) at a loading dock of a department store at the rate of 4 per hour. That is,

$$P(n \text{ trucks arrive in } t \text{ hours}) = P(X_t = n) = \frac{e^{-4t}(4t)^n}{n!} \qquad (n = 0, 1, \dots)$$

with an expectation of $\bar{X}_t = 4t$ trucks every t hours.

Since 4 trucks arrive per hour, we have $\lambda = \frac{4}{60} = \frac{1}{15}$ arrival per minute. Thus, using (4.1), we have

$$P(\text{time between arrivals} \leqslant t \text{ minutes}) = 1 - e^{-\lambda t}$$
$$= 1 - e^{-(1/15)t} \qquad (t \geqslant 0)$$

with $\bar{T} = 1/\lambda = 1/\frac{1}{15} = 15$ minutes (= expected time between any two arrivals) and $\text{var}(T) = 1/(\frac{1}{15})^2 = 225$. Also,

$$P\left(\begin{array}{l}\text{dock crew will have to wait less than} \\ 15 \text{ minutes before a truck arrives}\end{array}\right) = P(T < 15)$$
$$= 1 - e^{-15/15}$$
$$= 1 - e^{-1}$$
$$= 1 - 0.368$$
$$= 0.632,$$

where e^{-1} is found in Table III in Appendix A.

$$P\left(\begin{array}{l}\text{dock crew will have to wait at least} \\ 15 \text{ minutes before a truck arrives}\end{array}\right) = P(T > 15)$$
$$= 1 - P(T \leqslant 15)$$
$$= 1 - 0.632$$
$$= 0.368.$$

3.4.3. Example—The Exponential Distribution and Reliability Predictions

An important application of the exponential distribution is in establishing requirements for the reliability of equipment which is expected to fail at some future time period. The operating requirements are often given in terms of mean time between failure, which for the exponential distribution is given in (3.4.2) as

$$\overline{T} = \frac{1}{\lambda} \quad (= \text{mean time between failures}),$$

where λ is the *rate* of failures. Recall that the mean time between failure is the inverse of the rate of failure.

Consider WV TV sets which must be designed so that 60% of them last more than 100 hours.

QUESTION. What should the expected time between failures be in order to achieve desired percent probability that failure occurs after 100 hours of operation?

Answer
$$0.60 = P(T > 100) = 1 - P(T \leqslant 100)$$
$$= 1 - (1 - e^{-\lambda 100})$$
$$= e^{-\lambda 100}.$$

Thus, we need a λ such that $e^{-\lambda(100)} = 0.60$. From Table III we see that $e^{-x} = e^{-0.5} = 0.606$, which is close to 0.60. Thus, if we let $\lambda(100) = 0.5$ or $\lambda = 0.5/100 = 0.005$, we can achieve the desired reliability of 60%. Thus, the desired mean time between failures is $1/\lambda = 1/0.005 = 200$ hours.

QUESTION. For $1/\lambda = 200$ hours, what percentage of WV TV sets will fail after 100 and before 300 hours of operation?

Answer
$$P(100 < T < 300) = P(T < 300) - P(T < 100)$$
$$= 1 - e^{-(0.005)(300)} - \left[1 - e^{-(0.005)(100)} \right]$$
$$= e^{-0.5} - e^{-1.5}$$
$$= 0.607 - 0.223$$
$$= 0.384 \quad \text{or} \quad 38.4\% \text{ will fail.}$$

3.4.4. The Normal Probability Distribution

The normal distribution is very important in business applications. In many instances the normal distribution is a reasonable approximation for a prior probability distribution for business decisions. The normal probability function is a

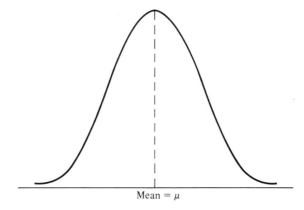

Mean = μ

Figure 3.4. Normal probability distribution.

smooth, symmetric, continuous, bell-shaped curve, as shown in Figure 3.4. We have

$$
\begin{aligned}
\text{values of } X: \quad &\text{between } -\infty \text{ and } \infty \\
\text{mean of:} \quad &\overline{X} = \mu \\
\text{variance of } X: \quad &\text{var}(X) = \sigma^2 \\
\text{distribution:} \quad &P(X \leqslant x) = N\!\left(\frac{x - \mu}{\sigma}\right),
\end{aligned}
$$

where $N[(x - \mu)/\sigma]$ is the shaded total area under the normal curve as shown in Figure 3.5.

Before discussing the computation of normal probabilities $P(X \leqslant x) = N[(x - \mu)/\sigma]$, we will give and discuss some important properties of normal distributed random variables.

Figure 3.5. Standard normal function.

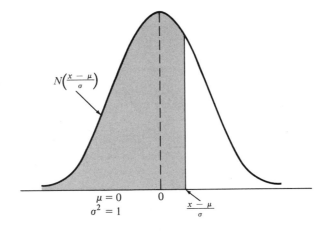

$N\!\left(\frac{x - \mu}{\sigma}\right)$

$\mu = 0$
$\sigma^2 = 1$

0

$\frac{x - \mu}{\sigma}$

First recall that the square root of the variance of any random variable X, $\sqrt{\operatorname{var}(X)} = \sqrt{\sigma^2} = \sigma$ is called the *standard deviation* of X. Then a normal variable X with mean μ and standard deviation σ has the following properties (Figure 3.6):

1. Approximately 0.50 (50%) of the area under the normal curve lies within ± 0.67 standard deviation from the mean μ. That is,

$$P\big[\,\mu - (0.67)\sigma \leqslant X \leqslant \mu + (0.67)\sigma\,\big] = 0.50.$$

2. Approximately 0.68 (68%) of the area under the normal curve lies within ± 1 standard deviation from the mean μ. That is,

$$P(\mu - \sigma \leqslant X \leqslant \mu + \sigma) = 0.68.$$

3. Approximately 0.95 (95%) of the area under the normal curve lies within ± 1.96 standard deviations from the mean μ:

$$P(\mu - 1.96\sigma \leqslant X \leqslant \mu + 1.96\sigma) = 0.95.$$

A normal distribution with $\mu = 0$ (mean of zero) and $\sigma = 1$ (standard deviation of 1) is said to be a *standard normal distribution*. If a normal variable has a mean other than zero and a standard deviation other than 1, we may "standardize" the distribution. The ability to standardize normal variables is one of its useful properties and allows us to use tables to determine normal probabilities.

Let X be a normal variable with $E(X) = \mu$ and var $= \sigma^2$. To standardize X, we define a standardized normal variable Z as follows:

$$Z = \frac{X - \bar{X}}{\operatorname{SD}(X)} = \frac{X - \mu}{\sigma}.$$

It can be shown that $E(Z) = 0$ and $\operatorname{var}(Z) = 1$.

Figure 3.6. Areas under the normal curve corresponding to $k\sigma$ values.

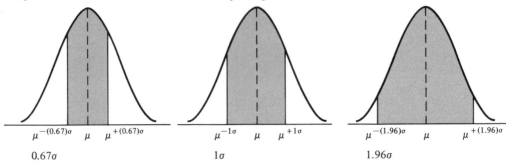

Thus, any general normal distribution with given mean μ and given standard deviation σ can be converted into the standard normal distribution with mean 0 and standard deviation of 1 by use of the Z transformation.

That is, let X be a normal random variable with mean μ and standard deviation σ. Then

$$
\begin{aligned}
P(X \leqslant x) &= P(\mu + \sigma Z \leqslant x) \\
&= P\left(Z \leqslant \frac{x - \mu}{\sigma}\right) \\
&= N\left(\frac{x - \mu}{\sigma}\right),
\end{aligned}
\tag{3.4.4}
$$

where values of $N(\ )$ are given in Table IV in Appendix A.

Also, for a normal random variable X with mean μ and standard deviation σ and for any two numbers a and b, with $a < b$, we have

$$
P(a \leqslant X \leqslant b) = N\left(\frac{b - \mu}{\sigma}\right) - N\left(\frac{a - \mu}{\sigma}\right).
\tag{3.4.5}
$$

As a result of (3.4.4) and (3.4.5), we can determine normal probabilities using the table of values for $N(Z)$ given in Table IV in Appendix A.

3.4.5. Example—Normal Probabilities: Standard Normal Probability Table

Let X be a normal random variable with mean $\mu = 16$ and standard deviation $\sigma = 5$. Determine the following probabilities.

1. $P(11 \leqslant X \leqslant 21)$
2. $P(X > 26)$
3. $P(X < 12)$
4. $P(X \leqslant 21)$

Solutions

1. Using formula (3.4.5), we have

$$
\begin{aligned}
P(11 \leqslant X \leqslant 21) &= N\left(\frac{21 - 16}{5}\right) - N\left(\frac{11 - 16}{5}\right) \\
&= N(1) - N(-1) \\
&= 0.8413 - 0.1587 \\
&= 0.6826.
\end{aligned}
$$

This probability is illustrated in Figure 3.7.

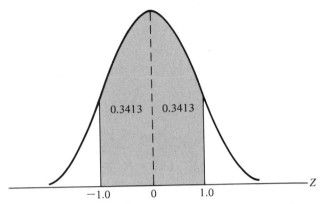

Figure 3.7. Areas under standard normal curve for $\sigma = \pm 1$.

2. $P(X > 26) = 1 - P(X \leqslant 26)$. Using formula (3.4.5), we have

$$P(X > 26) = 1 - P(X \leqslant 26)$$
$$= 1 - N\left(\frac{26 - 16}{5}\right)$$
$$= 1 - N(2)$$
$$= 1 - 0.9772$$
$$= 0.0228.$$

3.
$$P(X < 6) = N\left(\frac{12 - 16}{2}\right)$$
$$= N(-2)$$
$$= 0.0228.$$

4.
$$P(X \leqslant 21) = N\left(\frac{21 - 16}{5}\right)$$
$$= N(1)$$
$$= 0.8413.$$

3.4.6. Example—Sales Prediction Model

Sales of winter coats are known to have a normal distribution with mean sales of 36 per day and a standard deviation of 9 per day. From the previous formulas we know the following.

1. There is a 50% chance that daily sales X will be between approximately 30 and 42 coats, since $\mu - (0.67)\sigma = 30$ and $\mu + (0.67)\sigma = 42$.
2. There is a 68% chance that daily sales X will be between 27 and 45 coats inclusive since $\mu - (1)\sigma = 27$ and $\mu + (1)\sigma = 45$.

3. There is at least a 95% chance that daily sales X will be between 19 and 54 coats, since $\mu - (1.96)\sigma = 18.36$ and $\mu + (1.96)\sigma = 53.64$.

Consider the following questions.

QUESTION. What is the probability that sales will be less than 12 coats on any given day?

Answer
$$P(X < 12) = N\left(\frac{12 - 36}{9}\right)$$
$$= N(-2.67)$$
$$= 0.0038 \quad \text{(less than 1\% chance)}.$$

QUESTION. How many coats should the store carry in order to have at most a 10% chance of being understocked?

Answer. Let n be the number of coats to have on hand. Then we want to determine n such that $P(\text{sales exceed } n) = P(X > n) \leqslant 0.10$. Now

$$P(X > n) = 1 - P(X \leqslant n)$$
$$= 1 - N\left(\frac{n - 36}{9}\right).$$

Thus, what value of n satisfies the equation

$$1 - N\left(\frac{n - 36}{9}\right) \leqslant 0.10$$

or
$$N\left(\frac{n - 36}{9}\right) \geqslant 0.90?$$

Now in Table IV in Appendix A we see that a value of $Z = 1.29$ yields $N(1.29) = 0.9015$. Thus, if we let $Z = 1.29 = (n - 36)/9$ or $n = 48$, we have

$$N\left(\frac{48 - 36}{9}\right) \geqslant 0.90$$

as shown in Figure 3.8.

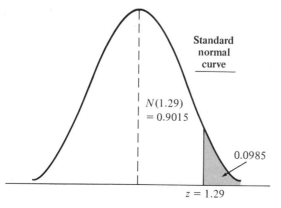

Figure 3.8. Sales prediction solution.

Standard normal curve

$N(1.29) = 0.9015$

0.0985

$z = 1.29$

3.4.7. Example—Weight Prediction

The Maui Nut Company packages mixed nuts in 1-pound amounts. The packaging equipment usually packages normally distributed weights with mean of $\mu = 1.05$ pounds with a standard deviation of $\sigma = 0.05$ pound.

Now

$$P\left(\begin{array}{l}\text{a randomly selected package will contain}\\\text{less than 1 pound}\end{array}\right) = P(X < 1)$$

$$= N\left(\frac{1 - \mu}{\sigma}\right) = N\left(\frac{1 - 1.05}{0.05}\right)$$

$$= N(-1)$$

$$= 0.1587,$$

as illustrated in Figure 3.9.

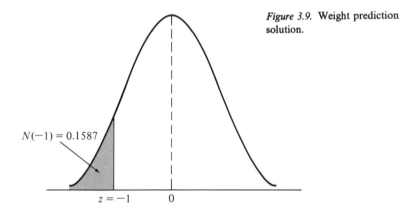

$N(-1) = 0.1587$

$z = -1$ 0

Figure 3.9. Weight prediction solution.

REFERENCES   ANDERSON, T. W., and S. L. SCLOVE. *Introductory Statistical Analysis*. Boston: Houghton Mifflin Company, 174.

CLELLAND, R. C., J. S. DE CANI, and F. E. BROWN. *Basic Statistics with Business Applications*, 2nd ed. New York: John Wiley & Sons, Inc., 1973.

DIXON, W., and F. MASSEY, JR. *Introduction to Statistical Analysis*, 3rd ed. New York: McGraw-Hill Book Company, 1969.

EHRENFIELD, S., and S. LITTAUER. *Introduction to Statistical Method*. New York: McGraw-Hill Book Company, 1964.

EZEKIEL, M., and K. FOX. *Methods of Correlation and Regression Analysis*, 3rd ed. New York: John Wiley & Sons, Inc., 1959.

FRUEND, J., and F. WILLIAMS. *Modern Business Statistics*, 2nd ed. Englewood Cliffs, N.J: Prentice-Hall, Inc., 1969.

HUFF, D. *How To Lie with Statistics*. New York: W. W. Norton & Co., Inc., 1954.

LAPIN, L. L. *Statistics for Modern Business Decisions*. New York: Harcourt Brace Jovanovich, Inc., 1973.

MOOD, A. M., F. A. GRAYBILL, and D. C. BOES. *Introduction to the Theory of Statistics*, 3rd ed. New York: McGraw-Hill Book Company, 1974.

NETER, J., W. WASSERMAN, and G. WHITMORE. *Fundamental Statistics for Business and Economics*, 4th ed. Boston: Allyn and Bacon, Inc., 1973.

PETERS, W. S. *Readings in Applied Statistics*. Englewood Cliffs, N.J: Prentice-Hall, Inc., 1969.

ROBBINS, H., and J. V. RYZIN. *Introduction to Statistics*. Chicago: Science Research Associates, Inc., 1975.

SUMMERS, G., and W. PETERS. *Statistical Analysis for Decision Making*. Englewood Cliffs, N.J: Prentice-Hall, Inc., 1968.

TANUR, J. M., ET AL. (EDS.). *Statistics: A Guide to the Unknown*. San Francisco: Holden-Day, Inc., 1972.

KEY CONCEPTS

Random variable	Negative binomial distribution
value	Hypergeometric distribution
distribution	Multinomial distribution
histogram	Poisson distribution
Expected value; mean	Exponential distribution
Variance; standard deviation	Normal distribution
Binomial distribution	Standard normal distribution
Geometric distribution	Standard normal table

REVIEW PROBLEMS

3.1. A random X has the following probability distribution:

Values of X, x	Probability Distribution of X, $P(X = x)$
$1	$\frac{1}{3} = P(X = 1)$
2	$\frac{1}{3} = P(X = 2)$
3	$\frac{1}{3} = P(X = 3)$
	1.0

(a) Determine the cumulative distribution of X.
(b) Determine the expected value or mean value of X.
(c) Determine the variance of X.
(d) Determine the standard deviation of X.

3.2 A random sample of 5 weeks using 1978 sales data yielded the following data.

Observation	Sales (000s)
1	$500
2	200
3	300
4	400
5	500
	1900

Estimate the average 1978 weekly sales using the data above.

3.3. The distribution of price changes X (increase = success, no increase = failure) during n consecutive weeks is given by the following model:

$$P(x \text{ increases in price}) = P(X = x)$$
$$= \binom{n}{x}\theta^x(1 - \theta)^{n-x} \quad \text{(binomial distribution)}$$

where $\theta = 0.5$.
(a) For any randomly chosen week, what is the probability that the price will increase?
(b) What is the expected number of price increases during the next 52 weeks?
(c) What is the expected variation of price increases about the expected number of price increases during the next 52 weeks?
(d) What is the probability that two or less price increases occur during the next 4 weeks?
(e) What is the probability that more than two price increases occur during the next 4 weeks?

3.4. Telephone inquiries occur randomly at the Master Bank Credit Office at an expected rate of 300 per hour. Determine the probability that:
(a) One inquiry occurs during a given 1-minute period.
(b) At least two inquiries occur during a given 1-minute period.
(c) The time between the first and the second inquiry is at most 4 minutes.
(d) The time between any two consecutive inquiries is at most 4 minutes.
(e) The time between any two consecutive inquiries is at least 4 minutes.

3.5. Oil in the Alcan pipeline is moved by means of a large network of pump stations. The time until failure (or breakdown) of the network is normally distributed with $\mu = 12$ months and $\sigma = 1$ month.
(a) What is the probability that the pipeline will operate more than 10 months without a breakdown?
(b) What is the probability that the pipeline will operate between 10 and 14 months without a breakdown?

3.1. (a) Let $F(x) = P(X \leqslant x)$ denote the cumulative distribution of X. Then

$$F(1) = P(X \leqslant 1) = P(X = 1) = \tfrac{1}{3}$$
$$F(2) = P(X \leqslant 2) = P(X = 1) + P(X = 2)$$
$$= \tfrac{1}{3} + \tfrac{1}{3} = \tfrac{2}{3}$$
$$F(3) = P(X \leqslant 3) = P(X = 1) + P(X = 2) + P(X = 3)$$
$$= \tfrac{1}{3} + \tfrac{1}{3} + \tfrac{1}{3} = 1.$$

We can list the *cumulative* distribution of X in a table as follows:

Values of X, x	Cumulative Distribution of X, $P(X \leqslant x)$
1	$\tfrac{1}{3} = P(X \leqslant 1)$
2	$\tfrac{2}{3} = P(X \leqslant 2)$
3	$1 = P(X \leqslant 3)$

(b)
$$\overline{X} = \text{mean or expected value of } X$$
$$= \sum_x xP(X = x)$$
$$= (1)\left(\tfrac{1}{3}\right) + (2)\left(\tfrac{1}{3}\right) + 3\left(\tfrac{1}{3}\right)$$
$$= 2.$$

(c)
$$\text{var}(X) = \text{variance of } X$$
$$= \sum_x x^2 P(X = x) - (\overline{X})^2$$
$$= (1)\left(\tfrac{1}{3}\right) + (2)^2\left(\tfrac{1}{3}\right) + (3)^2\left(\tfrac{1}{3}\right) - (2)^2$$
$$= \tfrac{2}{3}.$$

(d)
$$\text{SD}(X) = \text{standard deviation of } X$$
$$= \sqrt{\text{var}(X)}$$
$$= \sqrt{\tfrac{2}{3}}$$
$$= 0.8165.$$

3.2 $\overline{X} = \frac{\$1900}{5} = \$380.$

3.3. (a) $\theta = 0.5$ or there is a 50% chance on any randomly chosen week that the price will increase.

(b) $\overline{X} = n\theta$
$$= 52(0.5)$$
$$= 26, \text{ or one can expect 26 price increases during the next 52 weeks.}$$

(c)
$$\text{var}(X) = n\theta(1 - \theta)$$
$$= 52(0.5)(0.5)$$
$$= 13.$$

(d) P(number of price increases is equal to or less than 2)

$$= P(X \leqslant 2) = P(X = 0) + P(X = 1) + P(X = 2)$$

$$= \binom{4}{0}(0.5)^0(0.5)^4 + \binom{4}{1}(0.5)^1(0.5)^3 + \binom{4}{2}(0.5)^2(0.5)^2$$

$$= 0.0625 + 0.2500 + 0.3750 \qquad \text{(using Table I)}$$

$$= 0.6875.$$

(e) P(number of price increases is greater than 2)

$$= P(X > 2) = 1 - P(X \leqslant 2)$$

$$= 1 - 0.6875 \qquad \text{given in part (d)}$$

$$= 0.3125.$$

3.4 Let X_t be the number of inquiries during time period t (in minutes). Since the expected arrival rate is 300 per hour, we have an expected arrival rate of $300/60 = 5$ per minute. Thus, $E(X_t) = 5t$ (t in minutes) and

$$P(X_t = n) = \frac{e^{-5t}(5t)^n}{n!}.$$

(a) Here $t = 1$ minute and $n = 1$.

$$P(X_1 = 1) = \frac{e^{-5}(5)^1}{1!}$$

$$= 0.0337.$$

(b)
$$P(X_1 \geqslant 2) = 1 - [P(X_1 = 1) + P(X_1 = 0)]$$

$$= 1 - \left[\frac{e^{-5}(5)^1}{1} + \frac{e^{-5}(5)^0}{0!} \right]$$

$$= 1 - (0.0337 + 0.0067)$$

$$= 0.9596.$$

Let T be the time between any two consecutive inquiries. Then, since inquiries occur in a Poisson fashion, we have

$$P(T \leqslant t \text{ minutes}) = 1 - e^{-5t} \qquad (t \geqslant 0),$$

which is the exponential distribution with *mean* time between arrivals

$$= E(T) = \tfrac{1}{5} = 0.20 \text{ minute.}$$

(c)
$$P(T \leqslant 4) = 1 - e^{-20}$$

$$= 1.000 \qquad \text{(approximately 1)}$$

(d) Same as in part (c).

(e)
$$P(T > 4) = 1 - P(T \leqslant 4)$$
$$= 1 - (1 - e^{-20})$$
$$= e^{-20}$$
$$= 0.000 \quad (\text{approximately } 0).$$

3.5. Let X be the time failure occurs. Then,

$$P(X \leqslant x \text{ months}) = N\left(\frac{x - 12}{1}\right).$$

(a)
$$P(X > 10 \text{ months}) = 1 - P(X \leqslant 10)$$
$$= 1 - N\left(\frac{10 - 12}{1}\right)$$
$$= 1 - N(-2)$$
$$= 1 - 0.0228$$
$$= 0.9772.$$

(b)
$$P(10 < X < 14) = P(X < 14) - P(X \leqslant 10)$$
$$= N\left(\frac{14 - 12}{1}\right) - N\left(\frac{10 - 12}{1}\right)$$
$$= N(2) - N(-2)$$
$$= 0.9772 - 0.0228$$
$$= 0.9544.$$

EXERCISES

EXPECTED
VALUE
AND VARIANCE

3.1. The following table gives the probability distribution of a random variable X.

	x	$P(X = x)$
	0	0.1
	1	0.2
values of $X \rightarrow$	2	0.3
	3	0.4
		1.0

(a) What is the mean value of X?
(b) What is the variance of X?
(c) What is the standard deviation of X?

EXPECTED
VALUE
AND VARIANCE

3.2. The purchasing agent for XYZ Department Stores purchases two makes of color TV sets, brand A and brand B. The following data were obtained from past sales observations of 60 units each of set A and B.
(a) Which set requires more expected service calls?
(b) Which set has the lowest dispersion about its average number of service calls?

| Number of | SAMPLES FROM | |
Service Calls	Set A	Set B
0	10	4
1	20	20
2	20	10
3	10	26
	60	60

BINOMIAL DISTRIBUTION

3.3. An automobile loan may either be repaid to the finance company or not repaid. The finance company considers repayment a "success." Assume that 90% of all automobile loans are repaid. What is the probability that 10 out of every 15 loans will be repaid?

GEOMETRIC DISTRIBUTION

3.4. McGee Consultants Inc. bid on a large number of government contract proposals. The probability distribution of the number of bids made until a success is given by the following model:

$$P(\text{success occurs on bid number } x) = \theta(1 - \theta)^{x-1}$$

where $x = 1, 2, \ldots$ and $\theta = 0.05$.

(a) What is the probability that the first success occurs after the second bid?
(b) What is the probability that the first success occurs between bids 2 and 6?

BINOMIAL DISTRIBUTION

3.5. An auditor for MTA Inc. must use a fixed policy in the evaluation of the accounts receivable file at ZYX Manufacturing. ZYX has 5000 such accounts. The auditor considers the accounts receivable file to be "acceptable" if 2% or less of the accounts contain errors. However, if 6% or more are in error, then MTA's policy is to conduct a complete audit of all 5000 accounts.

Since this is a large number of accounts, 5000, the auditor plans to audit a random sample of 20 accounts. His decision will be: certify the accounts receivable file if at most 0, 1, or 2 accounts of the 20 investigated are found in error; otherwise, if 3 or more of the accounts contain errors, conduct a complete audit of all 5000 accounts.

(a) If it is *true* that 2% or 100 accounts are in error, what is the probability that the auditor will certify the accounts receivable file? What is the probability that he will decide to conduct a complete audit?
(b) If it is *true* that 6% or 300 accounts contain mistakes, what is the probability that the auditor will conduct a complete audit? What is the probability that he will certify the accounts receivable file?

NEGATIVE BINOMIAL DISTRIBUTION

3.6. Titanic Corporation will have its kth president in year X where X has the following distribution:

$$P(X = x \text{ years}) = \binom{x-1}{k-1}\theta^k(1 - \theta)^{x-k},$$

where $x = k, k + 1, \ldots,$ and $\theta = 0.5$.

107

Assume that you are now the second president of Titantic,
(a) What is the probabilty that you will survive for 4 years? What is the probability that your successor will take office in 4 years?
(b) What is the probability that the fifth president of Titantic will take office exactly 7 years from now?

NEGATIVE BINOMIAL DISTRIBUTION **3.7.** McGee Consultants Inc. bid on a large number of government contract proposals. The probability distribution that the kth success (or the kth bid won by McGee) occurs on bid number x is given by

$$P(X = x) = \binom{x-1}{k-1}\theta^k(1-\theta)^{x-k},$$

where $x = k, k+1, \ldots,$ and $\theta = 0.05$.
(a) How many bids can McGee expect to make until he receives 10 contracts?
(b) What is the probability that McGee will receive his fourth contract on bid number 6?

MULTINOMIAL DISTRIBUTION **3.8.** Kentucky Fast Foods buys a truckload of fryers from three suppliers at the following rates:

Supplier	Rate
I	$\theta_1 = 0.20$ (or 20% of the time)
II	$\theta_2 = 0.30$ (or 30% of the time)
III	$\theta_3 = 0.50$ (or 50% of the time)

For Kentucky's next 10 purchases, determine the following:
(a) Probability that I sells 3, II sells 4, and III sells 3 truckloads to Kentucky Fast Foods.
(b) Probability that I sells 6 and III sells 4.
(c) Probability that III sells 10.

MULTINOMIAL DISTRIBUTION **3.9.** A set of n accounts randomly selected from a file is to be audited. The status of the file is considered acceptable if the following occurs:

$\theta_1 = $ at most 0.01 or 1% of the sample contain major errors,

$\theta_2 = $ at most 0.09 or 9% or less contain minor errors

and $\theta_3 = $ at least 0.90 or 90% contain no errors.

Assume that a random sample of $n = 100$ accounts is taken. Assume that the accounts in the file are such that *exactly* 1% contain major errors, 9% contain minor errors, and 90% contain no errors. What is the probability that your sample upon completion of the audit will show 1% major errors, 9% minor errors, and 90% no errors?

HYPERGEOMETRIC DISTRIBUTION **3.10.** In a test market population consisting of 10 males who tried Manno Shaving Lotion, 6 are impressed and believe it is an improvement over their currently used lotion, but 4 do not think so. What is the probability that a random sample of size 5 taken from the test market population (drawn without replacement) includes exactly 3 impressed customers?

HYPERGEOMETRIC DISTRIBUTION **3.11.** Sixty percent of all mechanics employed by WV dealers in the United States are considered incompetent. The WV dealer in Indianapolis presently employs 15 mechanics. Three mechanics are selected randomly, without replacement, at the Indianapolis dealership and given a battery of examinations to determine their mechanical ability. What is the probability that all three will be judged incompetent?

POISSON DISTRIBUTION **3.12.** Determine using Table II, the following Poisson probabilities.
(a) $P(X = 3)$ with $\lambda t = 2$.
(b) $P(X = 3)$ with $\lambda t = 0.9$.
(c) $P(X \leqslant 4)$ with $\lambda t = 5$.
(d) $P(X < 6)$ with $\lambda t = 5$.

POISSON DISTRIBUTION **3.13.** Records are kept on the number of hourly paid workers who arrive late for work each day at the XYZ assembly plant. In a period of 200 days, 400 instances of late arrival were recorded on the time clocks. Assume that the number of late arrivals per day has the Poisson distribution.
(a) What is the expected number of late arrivals per day?
(b) What is the expected number of late arrivals per 20 days?
(c) What is the variance of the number of late arrivals per day?
(d) What is the variance of the number of late arrivals per 20 days?
(e) What is the probability of exactly 2 late arrivals on any given day?
(f) What is the probability of exactly 10 late arrivals in 5 days?

POISSON DISTRIBUTION **3.14.** The Good Ride Taxi Company in Altoona has 100 cabs in its fleet. Each cab has, on the average, 2 flat tires per hour. Flat tires are known to occur randomly for each cab.

Good Ride estimates that each hour one of their cabs is "down" due to a flat costs the firm $5 in lost revenue. What is Good Ride's expected lost revenue for each cab per 24-hour day due to flat tires? What is Good Ride's expected lost revenue per 7-day week due to flat tires? What is Good Ride's expected lost revenue per year ($= 365$ days $= 365 \times 24 = 8760$ hours)?

EXPONENTIAL DISTRIBUTION **3.15.** At an XYZ discount store, the number of customers arriving per hour has Poisson distribution with mean arrival rate of $\lambda = 60$ per hour. Assume that XYZ is open 10 hours per day. In an hour, say between 9:00 A.M. and 10:00 A.M., 50 customers entered the store. What is the probability that in the next 10 minutes, 10:00 A.M. to 10:10 A.M., at least one customer will enter the store?

EXPONENTIAL DISTRIBUTION **3.16.** Suppose that the *time* needed for a computer terminal to service a typical customer has an exponential distribution with a mean service time of 30 seconds.
(a) What is the probability that the service time needed for any randomly chosen customer will exceed 4 minutes?

(b) What percentage of the terminal customers will require service times between 1 and 2 minutes?

EXPONENTIAL DISTRIBUTION **3.17.** Compute the following exponential probabilities using Table III in Appendix A.
(a) $P(X_1 > 4)$ with $\lambda t = 0.5$.
(b) $P(X_1 < 2)$ with $\lambda t = 0.4$.
(c) $P(10 < X_1 < 30)$ with $\lambda t = 0.1$.
(d) $P(X_1 > 2)$ with $\lambda t = 0.4$.

STANDARD NORMAL DISTRIBUTION (TABLE IV) **3.18.** The random variable X is normally distributed with mean $\mu = 16$ and standard deviation $\sigma = 9$. Determine, using Table IV, the following probabilities:
(a) $P(X \geqslant 25)$.
(b) $P(X \leqslant 16)$.
(c) $P(12 \leqslant X \leqslant 16)$.
(d) $P(11 \leqslant X \leqslant 19)$.

NORMAL DISTRIBUTION **3.19.** A wood-cutting machine is designed to cut logs at a length of 10.50 inches. In fact, the lengths cut are normally distributed with a mean of $\mu = 10.50$ inches and a standard deviation of $\sigma = 0.20$ inch. An acceptable tolerance of 0.30 inch is allowed. What percentage of the cut logs are within tolerance? That is, what percentage of the cut logs has length between 10.20 inches and 10.80 inches?

NORMAL DISTRIBUTION **3.20.** It has been estimated that the weekly gasoline requirement at XYZ Trucking Inc. is approximately normally distributed with an average of $\mu = 10,000$ gallons with a standard deviation of $\sigma = 500$ gallons. XYZ is supplied weekly with gasoline. What must XYZ's gasoline storage capacity be in order that the probability that its supply will be exhausted does not exceed 0.05 (or 5%)?

NORMAL PROBABILITIES **3.21.** The charge accounts at ZYX department store have an average balance of $\mu = \$100$ with a standard deviation of $\sigma = \$50$. Assume that the accounts receivable balances are normally distributed. Determine:
(a) The percentage of accounts with balances exceeding $120.
(b) The percentage of accounts with balances between $90 and $110.
(c) The percentage of accounts with balances less than $90.

CASE 3.1 Illustrated Case Study

PREDICTING GROUP (COMMITTEE) DECISIONS The object of this case is to show how probability models can be used to *predict* committee decisions. The problem you are asked to consider involves choosing among gambles (decisions in real life are often gambles because the outcomes may be uncertain). Upon completion of this case you will have used a model for *predicting the decision* of a committee based on your knowledge of the preferences and choices of its individual members, the committee structure, and how they vote. Such knowledge is important for understanding how committees formally and informally function.

Assume that you are asked to study a committee composed of *n* members, each of whom have individual preferences for either one or the other of two possible courses of action, say a risky versus a conservative action, and who must make a decision as a group, choosing one of the two courses of action that are diagrammed in Figure 3.10.

Your goal is to predict the choice of the committee and to answer the following questions:

1. What are the effects of the following *voting rules* on the final choice:
   (a) Dictatorial (D)
   (b) Unanimity (U)
   (c) Simple majority rule (MR)?
2. What is the effect of *committee size* on its choice?

Figure 3.10

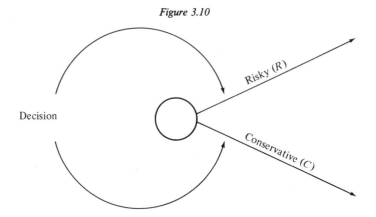

PART A. ASSUMPTIONS. Assume that (1) the probability of selecting action *R* or *C* is identical for all individual members; (2) for the dictatorial voting rule (*D*), any individual in a given group is equally likely to be the dictator; and (3) all individuals *must* choose either one of the two actions *R* or *C*. [An individual cannot choose not to choose (il faut parier!); the committee can, however.]

Question 1. Compute the probability that the group will either choose the risky action, conservative action, or not be able to make a choice as a function of the group size for each voting rule. [*Hint:* Use tables of the binomial distribution.) Your prediction model is

$$P_C(R) = b(x; n, \theta) = \binom{n}{x}\theta^x(1 - \theta)^{n-x},$$

where $P_C(R)$ = probability that the committee chooses the risky action

x = number of individuals choosing the risky action *R*

n = committee size

θ = probability of each individual choosing the risky action.

Do the preceding analysis for $\theta = 0.5$ and $\theta = 0.2$. What conclusion, if any, can you make from your analysis?

Question 2. If there were more than two (say three) alternative courses of action, how would you perform the computations? That is, what probability model (e.g., multinomial, hypergeometric, etc.) is the most appropriate? Propose a probability model and discuss how you would use it in studying a committee's voting behavior.

PART B. ASSUMPTIONS. Assume that (a) only assumptions (2) and (3) of Part A hold, (b) the preferences of each individual on the committee are known, and (c) the committee is of size $n = 3$.

Question 3. List all the possible individual preference patterns. What is the probability of the committee choosing the risky (R) or conservative (C) action, or making no choice (NC) at all, for the various voting rules?

CHAPTER 4
Decision Theory and Decision Analysis: Terminal Decisions

OBJECTIVES. Upon successful completion of this chapter, you should be able to:

1. Structure a terminal decision problem in the form of a decision or payoff matrix and a decision tree.
2. Specify and apply the alternative non-probabilistic and probabilistic choice criteria that can be used in making a decision.
3. Calculate the expected value of perfect information (EVPI).
4. Perform sensitivity analysis on how the probability assignments affect the decision.
5. Represent actions by a probability distribution of its possible outcomes.

4.1. INTRODUCTION

Chapters 4 through 6 deal with the problem of making decisions under conditions of uncertainty. Much of life, of course, involves the making of choices under uncertainty, that is, choosing from some set of alternative courses of action in situations where one is uncertain about the actual consequences of each course of action. Often, however, we must make a choice and are frequently concerned that it is a best or optimal choice.

In today's fast-moving technology the need for sound, rational decision making by business, industry, and government is vividly and sometimes (perhaps all too often) disquietingly apparent. Consider, for example, the area of design and development of new and improved products and equipment. Typically, development from invention to commercialization is expensive and fraught with *uncertainty* regarding both technical and marketing success. Product development problems related to research and development (R&D), production, finance, and marketing activities, both of a tactical and strategic nature abound. In R&D, for example, decision makers might be faced with the problem of choosing whether to pursue a parallel versus sequential strategy (i.e., pursuing two or more designs simultaneously versus developing the most promising design, and if it fails, going to the next most promising design, and so on). In production, they may have to decide on a production method or process for manufacture; also whether to lease, subcontract, or manufacture, or select a quality control plan. In finance, they may have to decide whether to invest in a new plant, equipment, research programs, marketing facilities, even risky orders. In marketing, they may have to determine the pricing scheme, whether to do market research and what type and amount of it, the type of advertising campaign, and so on.

Each of these decision problems are characteristically complex. It is almost impossible for any decision maker to intuitively take full account of all the factors impinging on the decision simultaneously. It thus would be useful to find some way of decomposing such decision problems that will allow a decision maker to think through the implications of one set of factors at a time in a rational (consistent) manner.

Decision analysis provides a rich set of concepts and techniques to aid the decision maker in dealing with complex decision problems under uncertainty. The decision analysis formulation considers explicitly both the preference structure of the individual decision maker and the uncertainties that characterize the situation. An exposure to the concepts of decision analysis rapidly makes one aware of the common shortcomings in several more informal approaches (such as intuition) to such decision problems. A particular benefit of this approach is its facility for communication and analysis among individuals involved and affected by the decision problem.

Decision analysis is concerned with the making of rational (consistent) decisions, notably under conditions of uncertainty. That is, it helps the decision maker answer the question, "What is the best alternative I can select in light of the information I now have?" (which normally is incomplete and uncertain). Decision analysis enables the decision maker to analyze a complex situation with many different alternatives, states, and consequences. The major objective is to choose a course of action that is consistent with the basic values (tastes) and knowledge (beliefs) of the decision maker. It is a prescriptive rather than descriptive approach. That is, it presents the concepts and methods for how one should choose, but it does not purport to describe how people really make decisions.

In this and the next two chapters we shall introduce some of the concepts of decision analysis, and show, in a practical way, how to apply these principles and techniques to resolve decision problems under uncertainty. To illustrate the value of this approach you will have the opportunity (through minicases at the end of the chapters) to compare and discuss your own decision-making behavior on several problems involving decisions in R&D, production, marketing, and so on, with that obtained from a formal decision analysis. In presenting the concepts, emphasis will be placed on generating an intuitive, managerially oriented interpretive view of the fundamental ideas and procedures, as well as their application in a variety of actual decision contexts. Decision trees, measuring and revising beliefs based on new information, risk preference, value of information, and sensitivity analysis are several of the key concepts to be discussed. These chapters should provide you with new tools for formulating, analyzing, and making effective decisions under uncertainty. It should also serve to sharpen your ability to be an aware, critical, and appropriately cynical consumer of such formal analysis.

In this chapter we shall discuss the concepts and techniques of decision analysis when a single terminal decision must be made on the basis of the decision maker's current information state; that is, sequential decisions and opportunities to acquire further information before deciding are not considered. Such a decision is called a *terminal decision*. The discussion in this chapter will raise issues which require that we step back and deal with certain fundamental questions that form the underlying basis of decision analysis. Thus, in Chapter 5 we discuss the fundamental axioms of decision theory (rules of logical decision making) and the questions of how to measure subjective probabilities (beliefs) and utilities (tastes). These, of course, are critical inputs (parameters) to any decision model. In Chapter 6 we discuss the concepts and techniques of decision analysis when sequential decisions are made and/or there is opportunity to acquire additional information before deciding.

To facilitate our exposition, we will adopt three primary policies: (1) to avoid the use of mathematics when there is no real need for it, (2) to restrict the discussion principally to discrete problems, and (3) to explain the various methods of decision analysis through a simple concrete example. We shall now begin with an example, which we shall carry throughout the chapter to illustrate the concepts, structure, and techniques of formally making terminal decisions under uncertainty.

4.1.1. An Example—Stocking Tennis Shorts

You are the owner of a tennis shop and must decide how many men's tennis shorts to order for the summer season. For a particular type of short, you must order in batches of 100. If you order 100 shorts, your cost is $10 per short; if you order 200, your cost is $9 per short; and if you order 300 or more shorts, your cost is $8.50 per short. Your selling price is $12, but if any are left unsold at the end of the summer, you will sell them for half-price. For the sake of simplicity, you believe that demand for this short will be either 100, 150, or 200. Of course, you cannot sell more shorts than you stock. If, however, you understock, there is a goodwill loss equivalent to $0.50 for each short a person wants to buy but cannot because it is out of stock. Furthermore, you must place the order now for the forthcoming summer season; you cannot wait to see how the demand is running for this short before you order, or place several orders.

4.2. CHARACTERISTICS OF A DECISION PROBLEM

The problem described above, in fact any decision problem, has certain common characteristics. These characteristics constitute the formal description of the problem and provide the structure for a solution. The decision problem under study may be represented by a model in terms of the following elements:

1. *The decision maker.* He is responsible for making the decision. He is viewed as an entity, and may be a single individual, committee, company, nation, and so forth. In the example above, he is the tennis shop owner.
2. *Alternative courses of action.* An important part of the decision maker's task is to specify and describe his alternatives. Given that the alternatives are speci-

fied, the decision involves a choice among the alternative courses of action. When the opportunity to acquire information is available, the decision maker's problem is to choose the best information source or sources and a best overall strategy. A strategy is a decision rule indicating which action should be taken contingent upon a specific observation received from the chosen information source. In the problem above, three alternative courses of action are open: (a_1) order 100, (a_2) order 200, and (a_3) order 300.

3. *Events.* These are the situations or states of the environment, not under the control of the decision maker, which may occur. Under conditions of uncertainty, the decision maker does not know for certain which event will occur when he decides. It is worth pointing out that the true event may be a matter of fact, unknown to the decision maker (For example, is Italy longer than California? This is a fact, which may not be known to you.), or, it may be a future event (For example, the outcome of a horserace is unknown until a bet is made and the race is run.).

The events are defined to be mutually exclusive and collectively exhaustive. This means that one and only one of all possible events specified will occur. Events are synonymously called "states," "states of nature," "states of the world," or "payoff relevant events."

Uncertainty is measured in terms of probabilities assigned to the events. One of the distinguishing characteristics of decision analysis is that these probabilities can be subjective (reflecting the decision maker's state of knowledge or beliefs), or objective (i.e., theoretically or empirically determined).

The decision maker must identify and specify the events as well as assess their probabilities of occurrence. In the example above, the events are (θ_1) demand is 100, (θ_2) demand is 150, and (θ_3) demand is 200.

4. *Consequences.* The consequences, which must be assessed by the decision maker, are a measure of the net benefit or payoff received by him. The consequence that results from a decision depends not only on the decision but also on the event that occurs. Thus, there is a consequence associated with each action–event pair. Consequences are synonymously called "payoffs," "outcomes," "benefits," or "losses." They are conveniently summarized in a "payoff matrix" or "decision matrix," which displays the consequences of all action–event combinations. For example, in the tennis shop owner's decision problem, if he orders 100 shorts and demand turns out to be 100, the consequence is that the owner will make a profit of $100.

It should be pointed out that the consequences should reflect the subjective values of the decision maker. That is, they should represent the decision maker's preferences or values for the corresponding objective consequences. In other words, the objective consequences will necessarily have to be transformed into "utilities" which reflect the subjective value of the consequences to the decision maker. Hence, the decision maker's utility function will need to be assessed. To simplify the discussion, we shall assume, unless otherwise stated, that the consequence values given have been already transformed into utilities. This issue will, however, be taken up in Chapter 5 when discussing the question of measuring a decision maker's utility function and extracting his risk preference from it.

The elements of a terminal decision problem, when there is no opportunity to acquire information, are depicted in Figure 4.1 (the dashed area containing the inquiry function and data are excluded). There exists a set of events θ with probabilities of occurrence $p(\theta)$ and a set of actions A. Associated with each action and event is an *objective* consequence made up of benefits b and costs c, which is determined through an objective consequence function composed of benefit and cost functions β and γ. An objective consequence (b,c) is transformed into a *subjective* consequence or utility through the decision maker's utility function ν. Given these elements and structure of a decision problem, the fundamental notion of decision analysis, which is derived from certain axioms of rational behavior, states that the decision maker should:

1. Assign personal probabilities to the events and utilities to the consequences associated with each action–event pair.
2. Compute an *expected* utility for each action.
3. Choose the action that *maximizes* expected utility.

Figure 4.1. Flow diagram of the decision theoretic process.

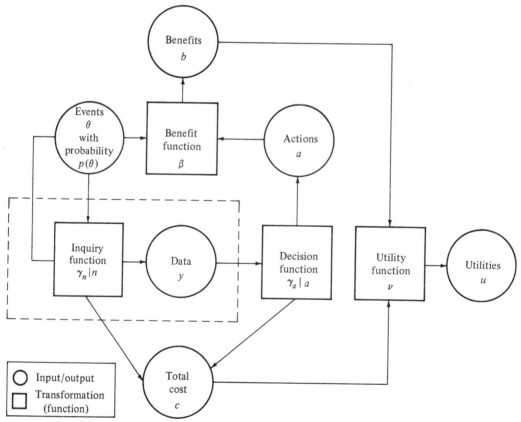

The decision maker may also have the option of acquiring more information about the consequence associated with the courses of action under evaluation through an inquiry function (information source) which relates the events to messages (Figure 4.1). Under this situation the decision maker acts on the basis of the message or datum y received by means of a decision function or strategy. This information is generally cost incurring in itself, will delay the decision, and will be usually less than perfectly reliable or informative. Bayes' theorem is used to revise one's probabilities or beliefs based on the new information. Decision analysis provides a basic conceptual model for determining what information should be acquired when, and what choice to make after its receipt. This will be covered in Chapter 6.

4.2.1. The Payoff (Decision) Matrix

The decision matrix for our tennis shop owner's problem is depicted in Table 4.1. In the payoff matrix the actions are listed on the left along the rows, the states are listed at the top of the matrix along the columns, and the possible consequences are listed in the matrix cells, one consequence associated with each action–event pair. The consequences are determined from the following consequence function: If supply is greater than demand (i.e., if $S > D$), then profit is equal to $D(R - C) - (C - 6)(S - D)$. If demand is greater than supply (i.e., if $D > S$), then profit is equal to $S(R - C) - 0.50(D - S)$. R is the per unit revenue (selling price), C is the relevant unit cost. The parameter \$6 is the half-price end of summer selling price for unsold goods and \$0.50 is the goodwill loss per short.

If the event that will occur were known with certainty beforehand by the decision maker, for example θ_2 (demand will be 150), then the owner would merely have to look down column θ_2 in the payoff matrix and choose the action that yields the highest payoff [i.e., max(175, 300, 150) = 300], which indicates that he should order 200 shorts. However, in the real world, the context of decision problems is such that since the states of nature lie beyond the control of the decision maker, he does not know with certainty which specific event will occur (or is true). The choice of the optimal course of action in the face of uncertainty is the crux of the decision maker's problem.

Although the term "uncertainty" refers to the decision maker's ignorance about which event will occur (or which event is the "true" event), he may also feel

Table 4.1. Payoff (Decision) Matrix for Tennis Shop Owner's Problem

Action \ Event	DEMAND θ_1: 100	θ_2: 150	θ_3: 200
a_1: order 100	200	175	150
a_2: order 200	0	300	600
a_3: order 300	−150	150	450

uncertain about various aspects of the "consequences." For instance, if the tennis shop owner was not sure of his goodwill loss, then some of the profits in the decision matrix would be uncertain. Such thoughts may lead one to expand the formulation of the problem to include greater detail and scope. Whether to do so or otherwise depends on how complex (and how realistic) you want the model to be. See, for example, Raiffa (1968) for a further discussion on this.

It should be noted that some authors differentiate between what they call "decision making under risk" (decision making when the state of the world is not known but probabilities for the various possible states are known) and "decision making under uncertainty" (decision making when the state of the world is not known and probabilities for the various possible states are not known). Under the subjective interpretation of probability, as discussed in Chapter 2, it is always possible to assess probabilities for the possible events, or states of the world. Hence, the "risk versus uncertainty" dichotomy is extremely artificial (in fact, it is nonexistent according to the subjective interpretation of probability), and in this book any decision-making problem in which the state of the world is not known for certain is called decision making under uncertainty. The term "risk" is reserved for discussions relating to utility, which is covered in Chapter 5.

4.3. CHOICE CRITERIA

Having examined the fundamental elements and structure of decision problems under uncertainty, we now look at various criteria that may be used in selecting a course of action. We first investigate decision-making criteria that have been developed which are based solely on the payoff matrix. These criteria have been developed, at least in part, to avoid the assessment of probabilities. Such criteria ignore the probabilistic nature of decision making under uncertainty. Here we shall explore the following choice criteria: (1) dominance (inadmissibility), (2) maximin, (3) maximax, (4) Hurwicz α, and (5) minimax regret or opportunity loss. We shall then explore criteria when the decision maker is willing to assign a probability distribution to the events. The criteria discussed here are (1) Laplace and (2) maximizing expected value (MEV).

4.3.1. Nonprobabilistic Choice Criteria

This type of decision-making situation has no prior probability distribution; that is, it is characterized by complete ignorance of any probability distribution on the states of nature. While one might argue that this situation is somewhat rare in a real situation, various scholars of decision making under uncertainty have proposed various decision criteria to solve such problems.

DOMINANCE. The dominance principle is not so much a way of selecting an action or strategy as it is a way of deciding what actions or strategies to eliminate from consideration. Dominance states that, if for each event the consequence of action a_1 is at least as desirable as the consequence of another action a_2, and is more desirable for at least one event, then action a_2 is dominated or inadmissible and therefore should not be chosen. Use of this widely accepted principle would result in the elimination of the tennis owner's action to order 300 shorts (a_3), since no matter what demand occurs, this action will always result in less profit than would result if he chose to order 200. Action a_3 is therefore dominated by action a_2, leaving the owner to decide between a_1 and a_2.

MAXIMIN: WALD. The maximin criterion (or criterion of pessimism) was suggested by Abraham Wald. Under this principle, the decision maker assumes that once he has chosen a course of action, nature would be malevolent (with an implicit probability of 1) and hence would select the event that minimizes the decision maker's payoff. Wald suggested that the decision maker should choose a course of action so that he would receive as large a payoff as possible under such circumstances. In other words, "pick the best of the worst" or "maximize the minimum." Stated another way, choose an action whose worst consequence is as good as the worst consequence of every other action.

The results of applying this criterion to the tennis shop owner's problem is shown below (action a_3: order 300 is dominated; therefore, it is no longer considered as a viable action):

Action	Minimum Payoff
→ a_1: order 100	150
a_2: order 200	0

Therefore, the best action, assuming that nature will always be malevolent, is to choose a_1: order 100, since this action has the maximum minimum payoff. Obviously, maximin is an ultraconservative criterion, since it hedges against the worst thing that can happen. A businessman following maximin would probably cease to be in business, since most everything he does might lose money, whereas if he does nothing he incurs no monetary losses (and makes no profit!). It seems most reasonable to argue that a decision maker should take into account the probabilities of occurrence of the different possible events. As an extreme example, if the event that results in the minimum payoff for a given act is rare (say, 1 chance in 1 million of occurring), it would generally not seem to make sense to concentrate on this possible occurrence. Despite these negative remarks about maximin there are situations, for example, in game theory, where it appears to be a good method for selecting a strategy.

MAXIMAX. Where maximin is overly pessimistic, maximax is superoptimistic. This criterion would only appeal to a highly venturesome person. Maximax chooses the act that is the "best of the best." This is tantamount to choosing an action whose best consequence is as good as the best consequence of each other action. In the tennis example problem, maximax would choose a_2: order 200.

Action	Maximum Payoff
a_1: order 100	200
$\rightarrow a_2$: order 200	600

The criticisms of this criterion are similar to those of maximin. Nobody seriously recommends maximax as a good choice criterion, as it ignores losses and does not consider the chances of occurrence of the different possible events. The remaining choice criteria require fuller use of the consequence and corresponding value matrix.

HURWICZ–α INDEX. Leonid Hurwicz, a contemporary econometrician asked: "Why should we always assume that nature will be malevolent?" Suppose that the decision maker was an optimist and felt confident about his chances of getting a good event. If he were a complete optimist, he would always assume that nature will kindly select the event that will yield him the highest possible payoff for the action or strategy he selected.

Therefore, the best strategy, assuming that nature is kind, is a_2: order 200 (maximax). However, Hurwicz did not envision that a rational decision maker should be completely optimistic. But he did suggest that if a decision maker did feel optimistic, he should be able to state his degree of optimism. Thus, the notion of the coefficient of optimism was introduced. The coefficient of optimism is a means by which the decision maker considers both the largest and smallest payoffs, and weights them in accordance with his own feeling of optimism and pessimism. For example, suppose that the decision maker had a coefficient of optimism of $\frac{1}{3}$. This means that, in effect, the decision maker has implicitly assigned a probability of occurrence of 1/3 to his maximum payoff and 2/3 to his minimum payoff. By Hurwicz's criterion we would determine the expected value of each action, assuming that either the maximum or the minimum will occur with the probabilities above; that is,

$$H_i = \alpha C_{\max} + (1 - \alpha) C_{\min} \tag{4.3.1}$$

and select the largest H_i value. A value of α near 1 reflects an optimistic decision maker, since, when $\alpha = 1$, Hurwicz α is the same as maximax. A value of α near zero reflects a pessimistic decision maker since, when $\alpha = 0$, Hurwicz α is the same as maximin. A value of α near $\frac{1}{2}$ would reflect a neutral attitude toward the fates. The results of applying the Hurwicz criterion ($\alpha = \frac{1}{3}$) to the example problem are as follows:

Action	C_{max}: Maximum Payoff	C_{min}: Minimum Payoff	Expected Payoff
a_1: order 100	200	150	167
$\rightarrow a_2$: order 200	600	0	200

Thus, a_2: order 200 would be chosen. The obvious shortcomings of this criterion include (1) the difficulty of assigning α a specific value, (2) the ignoring of all intermediate consequence values for each action when more than two events exist, and (3) the inability to choose a particular action when all actions have the same best and worst consequences.

MINIMAX REGRET: SAVAGE. Savage, the noted statistician, pointed out that after a decision has been made and the event has occurred, the decision maker may experience regret because he now knows what event has occurred and wishes perhaps that he had selected a different action. Savage proposed that the decision maker should attempt to minimize his maximum regret. Savage's criterion requires the development of a regret or opportunity loss matrix, and use of minimax to select an action. Regret is defined as the difference between the actual payoff and the payoff one could have received if one knew which event was going to occur.

To use the minimax regret criterion, first convert the payoff matrix into a corresponding regret matrix. This is done by subtracting each entry in the payoff matrix from the *largest* entry in its column. The largest entry in a column will have zero regret. The resulting matrix is called a *regret matrix* or an *opportunity loss matrix*.

Table 4.2 depicts the regret matrix for our example problem. A regret, computed as described above, represents the *difference* in value between what one obtains for a given action and a given event and what one could obtain if he knew beforehand that the given event was, in fact, the true event. In the example, if you order 100 units (a_1) and demand is 150 units (θ_2), then your regret is $125 since you could have gotten $125 more by ordering 200 units had you known beforehand that demand would actually be for 150 units. If, however, you had ordered 200 units (a_2) and demand is 150 units, your regret is zero, since you could not have chosen a better action if you had known in advance that demand would be 150 units. The

Table 4.2. Value and Regret (Opportunity Loss) Matrix for Tennis Shop Owner's Problem

PAYOFF MATRIX

Action \ Event	DEMAND θ_1: 100	θ_2: 150	θ_3: 200
a_1: order 100	$200	175	150
a_2: order 200	0	300	600

REGRET MATRIX

Action \ Event	DEMAND θ_1	θ_2	θ_3
a_1: order 100	0	125	450
a_2: order 200	200	0	0

optimum action under this criterion is a_2, and is determined as follows:

Action	Maximum Regret (Opportunity Loss)
a_1	450
$\rightarrow a_2$	200

In the event that the original table was in terms of losses (costs), one picks out the smallest loss for each event and subtracts it from each row entry. Each entry in the regret table is now the opportunity loss associated with an act–event combination. The cells where the smallest loss appeared before, now show zeros. Here, the minimax criterion is applied as before.

The objections raised against the maximin and maximax criteria also apply to minimax regret. But there are also other objections that can be raised against it. One objection arises when the payoffs (gains or losses) are stated in terms of utility. The utility functions we shall discuss in Chapter 5 do not allow one to subtract utility numbers and conclude something about the differences. In other words, it is generally not possible to say that the regret of going from a utility of 20 utils to a utility of 10 utils is half as dissatisfying as going from a utility of 100 utils to 80 utils. This is also true of temperature measurement, that is, we have no basis for saying that an increase in temperature from 70°F to 80°F is half as uncomfortable as going from 80°F to 100°F. Thus, it is doubtful that differences in utility as we have defined it reflect regrets in the same sense as differences in, for example, monetary gains.

Another criticism lies in its sensitivity to alternatives not selected by it. We could, for example, add or subtract an alternative to our decision problem such that it would change our choice from a_2 to a_1. Thus, while the new alternative is not chosen by minimax regret, its mere presence could change our choice from a_2 to a_1.

4.3.2. Probabilistic Choice Criteria

The remaining two choice criteria to be discussed have a probability distribution associated with the events. Both of these criteria use expected value; that is, where each action or strategy is assigned an expected value computed from its consequences or payoffs along with the probabilities assigned to the events. Each expected value method says to select an action whose expected value is at least as large (small, if working with losses) as the expected value of every other action.

LAPLACE: PRINCIPLE OF INSUFFICIENT REASON. If we are completely ignorant of which event might occur, we could behave as though the states were equally likely, that is, assign each event the same probability, calculate the expected payoff (loss) for each act, and choose the act with the largest (smallest) expected payoff (loss). Thus, we would treat the problem as though we had a uniform probability distribution over the events and, if the payoffs were stated in terms of utility, we would solve the problem by finding that action which maximized the expected utility.

The name of this method comes from Pierre-Simon, Marquis de Laplace, a mathematician of the early nineteenth century who espoused the view that when one is faced with a set of events and has insufficient reason to suppose one will occur rather than another, the events ought to be considered equally likely.

For our example problem the probability assigned to each event would thus be $\frac{1}{3}$. The expected value for each action is then

$$EV(a_1) = \tfrac{1}{3}(200) + \tfrac{1}{3}(175) + \tfrac{1}{3}(150) = \$175$$

$$EV(a_2) = \tfrac{1}{3}(0) + \tfrac{1}{3}(300) + \tfrac{1}{3}(600) = \$300.$$

Therefore, the Laplace criterion would choose a_2, since its expected value is higher.

When we think of assigning probabilities to the events, it is generally rare that we will be completely ignorant of the situation; hence, we would not give each event the same probability of occurring. In such situations the Laplace criterion would be inappropriate and one is naturally led into using the more general expected value method.

MAXIMIZING EXPECTED VALUE (MEV). As previously indicated, a maximum expected value criterion says the following: (1) assign a probability to each event with the probabilities summing to 1; (2) compute the expected value of each action by multiplying each value by its corresponding probability and summing these products; (3) choose an action whose expected value is largest. In other words, the "expected value of an act" is the weighted average of the payoffs under that act, where the weights are the probabilities of the various mutually exclusive events that can occur.

In a realistic decision problem it would be reasonable to suppose that a decision maker would have some idea of the likelihood of occurrence of the various events and that this knowledge would help him choose a course of action. For example, in our illustrative problem, if the tennis shop owner felt very confident that sales (demand) would be 200 units, this would tend to move him toward ordering 200 tennis shorts (a_2). By the same reasoning, if he was highly confident that sales (demand) would be 100 units, he would only order 100 shorts. If there are many possible events and many possible courses of action, the problem becomes complex, and the decision maker clearly needs some orderly method of processing all the relevant information. Such a systematic procedure is provided by the computation of the expected value of each course of action, and the selection of that act which yields the highest of these expected values. We shall also see how this method can be adjusted for the computation of expected utilities rather than expected payoffs in cases where the maximization of expected payoffs is not an appropriate criterion of choice.

To illustrate the calculations using the MEV criterion, suppose that the tennis shop owner (on the basis of past data, experience, and instinct) assigns the following subjective probability distribution to the events:

Event	Probability, $p(\theta)$
θ_1: demand is 100	0.5
θ_2: demand is 200	0.3
θ_3: demand is 300	0.2
	$\overline{1.0}$

Note that if demand is 100, it cannot be 200 (i.e., events are mutually exclusive), and the probabilities sum to 1, as they should (i.e., events are collectively exhaustive). The owner's expected value for each act is shown in Table 4.3. Using the MEV criterion, the tennis shop owner should choose a_2: order 200 shorts, with an expected value of $210.

Table 4.3. Tennis Shop Owner's Expected Profits

	ACT a_1:	*ORDER 100 UNITS*	
Event	Probability	Profit	Weighted Profit
θ_1: demand is 100	0.5	$200	$100.0
θ_2: demand is 200	0.3	175	52.5
θ_3: demand is 300	0.2	150	30.0
	$\overline{1.0}$		$\overline{\$182.5}$

Expected profit = $182.5.

	ACT a_2:	*ORDER 200 UNITS*	
Event	Probability	Profit	Weighted Profit
θ_1: demand is 100	0.5	$ 0	$ 0.0
θ_2: demand is 200	0.3	300	90.0
θ_3: demand is 300	0.2	600	120.0
			$\overline{\$210.0}$

Expected profit = $210.0.

It should be reemphasized that the consequences and event probabilities can be interpreted as objective or subjective. Objective consequences (values) represent "physical" quantities such as dollars, units of time, and so forth. Subjective consequences (values) represent the decision maker's relative preferences or values for the corresponding consequences. It is called "subjective" since its entries are directly related to the decision maker's preferences in the particular problem situation.

MINIMIZING EXPECTED OPPORTUNITY LOSS (EOL). A useful concept in the analysis of decisions under uncertainty is that of "opportunity loss," which has previously been described when discussing Savage's minimax regret criterion. The calculation of expected opportunity loss proceeds in a completely analogous manner to the calculation of expected value. That is, we use the probabilities of events as weights and determine the weighted average opportunity loss for each act. The objective is to select the act having the *minimum* EOL. The calculation of the EOLs for the two actions in the tennis shop owner's problem is given in Table 4.4 (refer to the lower part of Table 4.2 for the opportunity losses). If he selects the act which minimizes EOL, he will choose a_2: order 200 units. Note that this is the same act that he selected under the criterion of MEV. It can be proved that the best action according to the criterion of MEV is also best using minimization of EOL. It also should be noted that opportunity losses are not accounting losses, but represent foregone opportunities.

Table 4.4. Expected Opportunity Losses (EOLs) in the Tennis Owner's Problem

ACT a_1:   ORDER 100 UNITS

Event	Probability	Opportunity Loss	Weighted Opportunity Loss
θ_1: demand is 100 units	0.5	$ 0	$ 0.0
θ_2: demand is 150 units	0.3	125	37.5
θ_3: demand is 200 units	0.2	450	90.0
	1.0		$127.5

EOL(a_1) = $127.5.

ACT a_2:   ORDER 200 UNITS

Event	Probability	Loss	Weighted Opportunity Loss
θ_1: demand is 100 units	0.5	$200	$100.0
θ_2: demand is 150 units	0.3	0	0.0
θ_3: demand is 200 units	0.2	0	0.0
	1.0		$100.0

EOL(a_2) = $100.0.

4.3.3. Summary

The results of employing the seven criteria to our decision-making problem under uncertainty are summarized as follows:

Criterion	Optimal (Best) Act
Dominance	Did not select best act (eliminated a_3)
Maximin (Wald)	a_1.
Maximax	a_2
Hurwicz α	a_2
Laplace	a_2
MEV (min. EOL)	a_2

Five out of the six criteria (not counting dominance) chose a_2. Only Wald's criterion chose a_1 (the least risky or most conservative action). However, this may not be the usual situation. In other examples, each of the criteria might select a different action. Therefore, in general, under conditions of uncertainty, the selection of the decision criterion can be of crucial importance. The choice of criterion or criteria must be left to the decision maker and is dictated by his own attitude and company policy. Some of the shortcomings and invalidities of the various criteria have already been indicated. Wald's criterion will, in many cases result in a firm doing nothing or doing no new business. Hurwicz's criterion does not consider all the payoffs, only the maximum and minimum. Savage's criterion is pessimistic and evaluates the strategies in terms of opportunity loss. Opportunity loss becomes generally invalid when using the subjective preferences (utilities) of the decision maker. Laplace's criterion seems invalid since there usually is sufficient reason to believe that a decision maker is not completely ignorant of a situation, and thus the assignment of equally likely probabilities is unreasonable.

Throughout the remainder of this text, for decision-making problems under uncertainty, we will use the choice criterion of MEV, minimize EOL, or maximize expected utility, unless otherwise indicated.

4.4. EXPECTED VALUE OF
PERFECT INFORMATION (EVPI)

Up to this point, we have considered situations in which the decision maker chooses among alternative courses of action on the basis of the information he has (i.e., his *prior information*) without attempting to acquire further information before he makes his decision. The probabilities used in computing the expected value of an action, as shown in Table 4.3 for example, are termed prior probabilities to indicate that they represent probabilities established prior to obtaining additional information through testing, experimentation, or sampling. Choosing an optimal act based on MEV is often referred to as *prior analysis*.

In Chapter 6 we consider the question of deciding whether or not it is worth gathering additional information (which is rarely if ever perfectly reliable) and if so, what information to gather and what actions to take based on the information received. Before asking this question, it is first desirable to ask, "What is perfect information worth?" Suppose that in our tennis shop owner's problem, perfect information about the demand for the particular tennis short in question is worth $100 and the survey under consideration to find out what demand will be costs $200. In this case we would not have the survey conducted, since it would be irrational to pay $200 for information worth $100. To make such judgments we need to determine the expected value of perfect information (EVPI). There are three ways EVPI can be calculated.

We first calculate the *expected value under certainty* (i.e., having perfect information) and subtract this from the *expected value under uncertainty* (the best action chosen using MEV). First, we have said that under uncertainty we would take action a_2 in our tennis example and get an MEV of $(0.5)(0) + (0.3)(300) + (0.2)(600) = \$210$ (Table 4.3). This is the expected value under uncertainty. To obtain the expected value under certainty, we now ask: "What is your expected value if you can choose your action *after* learning the true event (demand), that is, after obtaining perfect information?" Clearly, the availability of perfect information allows you to obtain a profit of $200 if θ_1 obtains, since you would choose action a_1 over a_2 in this situation. If θ_2 obtains you would realize a profit of $300, since action a_2 would be preferred to a_1. And, similarly, if you knew that θ_3 would occur, you would earn a profit of $600 since you would also choose a_2 over a_1. To understand and compute the expected value under certainty, it is necessary to adopt a long-run relative frequency point of view. That is, we must weight each of these profits by the prior probabilities of each of these events occurring. In other words, from a relative frequency viewpoint, these probabilities are now interpreted as the proportion of times a perfect predictor would forecast that each of the given events would occur if the current situation were faced repeatedly. Each time the predictor makes a forecast the decision maker chooses the optimal payoff action. The calculation of the expected profit with perfect information is shown in Table 4.5 and is equal to $310. The EVPI is thus $\$310 - \$210 = \$100$. This is the *expected* (average) profit that could be gained if the tennis shop owner had perfect information about future demand.

Table 4.5. Calculation of Expected Profit Under Certainty

Event \ Action	DEMAND $P(\theta_1) = 0.5$ θ_1: 100	$P(\theta_2) = 0.3$ θ_2: 150	$P(\theta_3) = 0.2$ θ_3: 200
a_1: order 100	200^a	175	150
a_2: order 200	0	300^a	600^a

Expected profit under certainty = $200(0.5) + 300(0.3) + 600(0.2) = \$310$.

^{a}Optimal consequences (and actions) for a given event.

4.4.2. Method 2

Another way of performing this computation is as follows. The tennis shop owner's best act *under uncertainty* is to choose a_2. Suppose that he knew θ_1 would occur. Then he would wish to choose a_1 over a_2, his choice under uncertainty. The gain in profit between choosing a_2 over a_1 when θ_1 occurs is $200, but θ_1 would occur only 50% of the time. Hence, on the average, he would gain $100 if he chose a_2 over a_1 when θ_1 was known to occur. However, if θ_2 or θ_3 occurred, the tennis shop owner would still be content with a_2, the decision he made under uncertainty. Hence, only his action would change if θ_1 were known to occur. His overall expected gain, then, under perfect information is $100, which is the EVPI.

4.4.3. Method 3

The expected opportunity loss (EOL) of choosing the optimal act under conditions of uncertainty in the tennis shop owner's problem was also shown earlier to be equal to $100. That is this amount represented the minimum value among the expected opportunity losses associated with each action. This value is equal to the EVPI. To intuitively see why this is so, consider what the EOL would be under perfect information; it would be equal to zero. That is, there would be no opportunity losses if the decision maker knew which event would occur and behaved rationally. Thus, under uncertainty, he would do the best he could, that is, minimize his EOL. It can be mathematically proved that EVPI = EOL of the optimal act under uncertainty. Another term used for the EOL of the optimal act under uncertainty is the *cost of uncertainty*. This term stresses the cost of making the best decision under uncertainty, which would be eliminated if perfect information were known. Hence, the cost of uncertainty is also equal to the EVPI. In short, *EVPI, EOL of the optimal action under uncertainty, and the cost of uncertainty are equivalent.*

It is interesting to note that the EV (expected value) plus the EOL is constant for all acts, and their sum, which is $310 in our example, is the EV under certainty. Observe from Table 4.6 that action a_2 has a maximum EV and a minimum EOL.

By similar reasoning we can define what we mean by the more general term "value of information." Specifically, this is the expected value of the optimal action under a better information state (i.e., after additional information is received) minus the expected value of the optimal action given the present (prior) information state. It is a measure of the improvement of the decision as a result of new information. We will say more about this in Chapter 6 when we deal with the

Table 4.6. Relationship Among EV, EOL, and Expected Value Under Certainty

	ACT	
	a_1	a_2
EV	182.5	210
EOL	127.5	100[a]
	310.0[b]	310[b]

[a]Minimum EOL, which is equal to the EVPI.
[b]Expected value under certainty.

question of whether or not to buy more information. In sum, the EVPI serves as a gross measure for determining whether it is worthwhile or not to purchase information or analyze whether it is worthwhile to do so.

4.5. SENSITIVITY ANALYSIS

Placing probabilities on events is a difficult task which many managers may be reticent to do, at least to any degree of precision. In some cases they may prefer to say: "I think the probability of this event happening is between 0.5 and 0.7." Under these circumstances, as in any managerial decision setting, it is useful to perform sensitivity analysis to determine how the probability assessments affect the decisions. Analogous situations occur when more than one individual has assessed a probability distribution on the events, such as in a group decision-making situation, or when the manager and an expert consultant make probability assessments, which turn out to be different.

Sensitivity analysis can be performed as follows. Find the sets of probability distributions where a given action is always preferred to the other actions, that is, whose expected value is highest. This can be done simply by equating the expected value of a given act to all the other acts and solving for the bounding probabilities. To show this, reconsider the tennis shop owner's problem. The expected value of acts a_1 and a_2 stated in terms of the event probabilities are

$$\text{EV}(a_1) = 200p(\theta_1) + 175p(\theta_2) + 150[1 - p(\theta_1) - p(\theta_2)]$$
$$\text{EV}(a_2) = 0p(\theta_1) + 300p(\theta_2) + 600[1 - p(\theta_1) - p(\theta_2)],$$

where $p(\theta_3) = 1 - p(\theta_1) - p(\theta_2)$, since the events are mutually exclusive and collectively exhaustive, and thus must sum to 1. The conditions under which a_1 is as preferred or more preferred to a_2 is when $\text{EV}(a_1)$ is equal to or greater than ($\geqslant$) $\text{EV}(a_2)$. Using the right-hand sides of these expected values, we get

$$200p(\theta_1) + 175p(\theta_2) + 150[1 - p(\theta_1) - p(\theta_2)]$$
$$\geqslant 0p(\theta_1) + 300p(\theta_2) + 600[1 - p(\theta_1) - p(\theta_2)].$$

Solving this inequality, we obtain the expression

$$2p(\theta_1) + p(\theta_2) \geqslant \tfrac{18}{13}.$$

This gives us the expression for determining all possible probability values for $p(\theta_1)$ and $p(\theta_2)$ [$p(\theta_3)$ would be determined implicitly], for which a_1 would be preferred to a_2. Of course, the basic probability axioms must not be violated; that is, all probabilities must be equal to or greater than 0 but equal to or less than 1. Also, the sum of the probabilities for events 1, 2, and 3 must sum to 1.

An easier way to visualize the conditions under which a given action is better than another is to graph the resulting inequality. This is shown in Figure 4.2. Note that graphing can only be done when the number of events is at most equal to four.

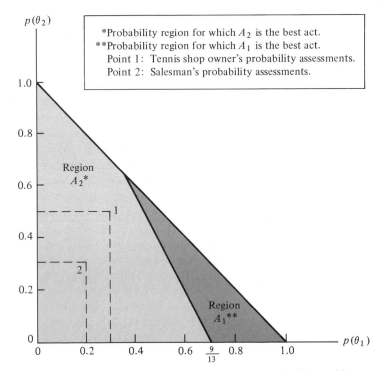

Figure 4.2. Sensitivity analysis of tennis shop owner's decision problem.

Suppose that in addition to the tennis owner's probability assessment, the tennis short salesman (a good friend of his) gives the following honest assessment of the demand: $p(\theta_1) = 0.2$, $p(\theta_2) = 3$, $p(\theta_3) = 5$. This, as seen from Figure 4.2 or from the EV calculations, would also result in the owner choosing a_2 (point 2 in Figure 4.2). Hence, there is no choice conflict resulting from these two different probability assessments. In fact, most of the area of the graph in Figure 4.2 contains a_2 as the preferred choice. It is only when $p(\theta_1)$ becomes relatively high that a_1 is preferred.

4.6. DECISION TREES

An alternative way to structure a decision problem pictorially is in terms of a *tree diagram* or *decision tree*. A decision tree chronologically depicts the sequence of actions and outcomes as they unfold. A decision tree is presented for the tennis shop owner's problem in Figure 4.3. The first fork (node) corresponds to the action chosen by the decision maker and the second fork corresponds to the event. The numbers at the end of these terminal branches are the corresponding payoffs (alternatively, losses could be used in place of payoffs). For example, the owner can follow either branch a_1 or branch a_2; that is, he can choose either act a_1 or a_2 (a_3 was dominated and therefore eliminated). Assuming that he follows path a_1, he comes to another juncture, which is a chance fork. Chance now determines whether the event that will occur is θ_1, θ_2, or θ_3. If chance takes him down the θ_1 path, the terminal payoff is \$200; the corresponding payoffs are indicated for the other paths. An analogous interpretation holds if he chooses to follow branch a_2. Thus the decision diagram depicts the basic structure of the decision problem in schematic form. In Figure 4.3, additional information is superimposed on the diagram to represent the analysis and solution to the problem.

The decision analysis process represented in Figure 4.3 is called *backward induction*. We imagine ourselves as located at the right-hand side of the tree diagram, where the payoffs are. Let us consider first the upper three paths denoted θ_1, θ_2, and θ_3. To the right of these symbols we enter the respective probability assignments 0.5, 0.3, and 0.2 as given in the original problem. These represent the probabilities assigned by chance of following these three paths, after the decision maker has selected act a_1. Moving back to the chance fork from which these three paths emanate, we can calculate the expected monetary value of being located at that fork. This expected monetary value is \$182.5 and is calculated in the usual way; that is,

$$\$182.5 = (0.5)(\$200) + (0.3)(\$175) + (0.2)(\$150).$$

This value is entered at the chance fork under discussion. It represents the value of standing at that fork after choosing act a_1, as chance is about to select one of the three paths. The analogous figure entered at the lower chance fork is \$210. Therefore, imagining ourselves as being transferred back to node 1, where the little square represents a fork at which the decision maker can make a choice, we have

Figure 4.3. Decision tree for tennis shop owner's problem.

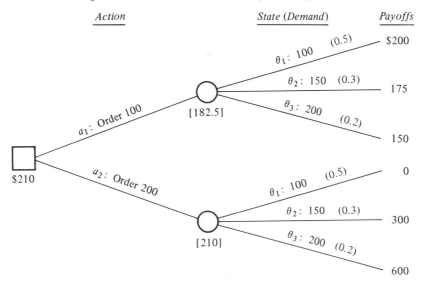

the alternatives of selecting act a_1 or act a_2. Each of these acts leads us down a path at the end of which is a risky option whose expected profit has been indicated. Since following path a_2 yields a higher expected payoff than path a_1, we block off a_1 (using a double slash) as a nonoptimal course of action. This is indicated in Figure 4.3 by the two vertical lines. Hence, a_2 is the optimal course of action, and it has the indicated expected payoff of $210.

Thus, the decision-tree diagram reproduces in compact schematic form the analysis given in Table 4.3. An analogous diagram could be constructed in terms of opportunity losses. However, it is much more customary to use tree diagrams to portray analyses in terms of payoffs rather than opportunity losses.

Tree diagrams are particularly useful in representing complex decision-making problems with sequences of actions and events over time, as you shall see in Chapter 6, for it is convenient to add more branches and forks to the diagram. Such complex problems are very difficult to represent clearly in tabular (matrix) form.

4.6.1. Actions as Outcomes of Probability Distributions

It is often useful to represent the outcomes of each action by means of a discrete probability distribution, especially when "risk" (in addition to expected value) is also considered as a basis of choice. To do this, we simply treat the possible outcomes of a given decision as values of a random variable having specified probabilities. Figure 4.4 depicts actions a_1 and a_2 as probability distributions on their respective outcomes.

Probability Distributions

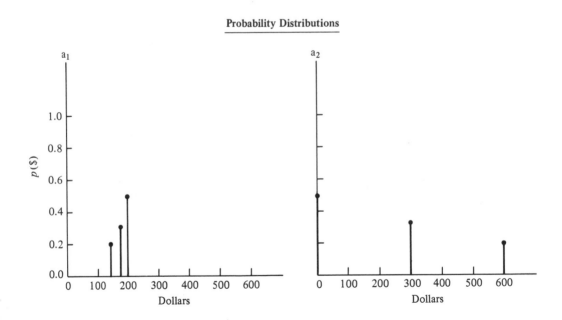

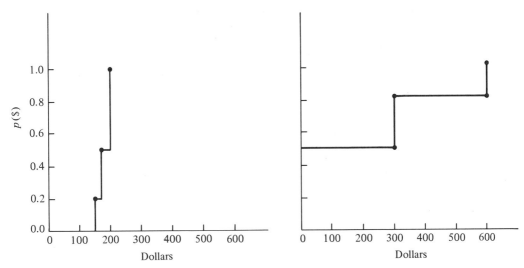

Figure 4.4. Probability distribution of outcomes for each action in tennis shop owner's problem.

4.7. SUMMARY

Decision analysis concerns itself with choosing the best act from a set of possible acts, given uncertainty as to the event which may exist. By the use of maximizing expected value, this can be accomplished in a manner that is consistent with the decision maker's beliefs and tastes (values).

A prime contribution of this procedure is that it focuses attention on all possible events and requires a calculation of the consequences of each act and each possible state of nature. Even if the analysis stopped with the structuring of the problem in the form of a decision matrix, decision tree, or set of probability distributions of outcomes for each action, this would be a contribution to the art of decision making. But by the use of the criterion of maximizing expected value, it is possible to go further. For a decision maker to stop with the use of nonprobabilistic criteria is not justified in view of the techniques that are available for incorporating uncertainty into the analysis.

The advocacy of the maximizing expected value criterion implies measurable utility relationships. While in the real business world, the input data for decisions are generally in the form of dollars, not measures of utility, it will not always be appropriate to base a decision on expected monetary value.

REFERENCES   CHERNOFF, H., and L. E. MOSES. *Elementary Decision Theory*. New York: John Wiley & Sons, Inc., 1959.

FISHBURN, P. C. "Decision Under Uncertainty: An Introductory Exposition." *Journal of Industrial Engineering*, **17**(7), 1966, 341–53.

HALTER, A. N., and G. W. DEAN, *Decisions Under Uncertainty*. Cincinnati, Ohio: South-Western Publishing Co., 1971.

LUCE, R. D., and H. RAIFFA. *Games and Decisions*. New York: John Wiley & Sons, Inc., 1957.

MILLER, D. W., and M. K. STARR. *Executive Decisions and Operations Research*. Englewood Cliffs, N.J.: Prentice-Hall, Inc., 1960.

RAIFFA, H. *Decision Analysis*. Reading, Mass.: Addison-Wesley Publishing Co., Inc., 1968.

WALD, A. INC., *Statistical Decision Functions*. New York: John Wiley & Sons, Inc., 1950.

WEISS, L. *Statistical Decision Theory*. New York: McGraw-Hill Book Company, 1961.

WINKLER, R. L. *Introduction to Bayesian Inference and Decision*. New York: Holt, Rinehart and Winston, Inc., 1972.

KEY CONCEPTS

Payoff (decision) matrix
Nonprobabilistic choice criteria
  dominance
  maximin: Wald
  maximax
  Hurwicz-index
  Minimax regret: Savage
Probabilistic choice criteria
  Laplace: principle of insufficient
    reason
  maximizing expected value
  minimizing expected opportunity
    loss

Expected value of perfect
  information (EVPI)
  cost of uncertainty
Sensitivity analysis
Value of information
Decision trees

REVIEW QUESTIONS

4.1. Do you think decisions under certainty occur very often in your day-to-day actvities or in the day-to-day work of your organization? Explain your answer and justify with examples.

4.2. Do situations arise where it is impossible to assess probabilities for uncertain events? Can you provide examples?

4.3. Is the minimization of uncertainty a real consideration in managerial decision making? What practical steps do managers take to minimize uncertainty? Do you think there is any relation between managerial success and the minimization of uncertainty?

4.4. What is a payoff matrix? What is a decision tree? Is there any benefit in representing a decision problem in either of these forms? Under what circumstances is a decision tree a better representation of the problem than a decision matrix?

4.5. Consider a decision problem under uncertainty that you are currently faced with or have been confronted with in the past. State the characteristics of any decision problem under uncertainty and specifically relate these characteristics to your particular problem. Represent the problem in both a payoff matrix and decision tree.

4.6. State the nonprobabilistic choice criteria of a decision problem under uncertainty. State the probabilistic choice criteria. Evaluate these criteria as a basis for choice.

4.7. What do we mean by expected value of perfect information (EVPI)? Make up an example and indicate how you would compute EVPI.

ANSWERS TO REVIEW QUESTIONS

4.1 Because the future is never perfectly predictable, decisions are never made under conditions of complete certainty; however, there are degrees of uncertainty.

The uncertainty may manifest itself in the payoffs involved in a set of action-state combinations, or in the states of nature themselves. For example, the decision to buy a car has uncertainty in the future price of gasoline (state of nature) and in how much one will enjoy the car after it has been bought (payoffs).

4.2. There may be examples where, because of a complete lack of information, a decision maker cannot distinguish between different states of nature. In public policy issues, such as determining the effect of a contaminant in drinking water, there may be no way of identifying the long-term hazard of such a contaminant. However, even in these cases, probabilities may still be assigned. For example, equal probabilities can be assigned to the possible outcomes envisioned. To demonstrate what this means, let us assume that we asked someone who was totally unfamiliar with the stock market whether the Dow Jones Index was above or below 900. This person could assign probabilities of 0.5 to each of the two possible events.

4.3. *Yes.* Managers may acquire information (at some cost) in order to reduce uncertainty in a decision problem. Furthermore, a manager may decide on a course of action which has a smaller expected payoff in order to reduce uncertainty and guarantee a certain minimum outcome. There certainly is a relationship between managerial success and reduction of uncertainty. Executives who are right are successful; those who are often wrong are unsuccessful.

4.4. A payoff matrix is a matrix whose entries are the outcomes (utilities) associated with each action-state of nature pair. A decision tree chronologically depicts the sequence of actions and outcomes in a decision problem. The benefit in depicting a decision problem in these forms is that one can see clearly the relationships among actions, states, and possible consequences. A decision tree is particularly useful in representing complex decision-making problems involving sequences of actions and events over time. Such complex problems are very difficult to represent clearly in tabular form.

4.5. The characteristics of a decision problem under uncertainty are:

1. The decision maker.
2. Alternative courses of action.

3. Possible events or states of nature.
4. Outcomes or consequences which occur when a particular action is taken and a particular state of nature obtains.

4.6. The nonprobabilistic choice criteria include:

1. Dominance, which is not so much a method for selecting an optimal strategy as for eliminating suboptimal ones.
2. Maximin, or maximizing the minimum payoff, is used when the decision maker is pessimistic.
3. Maximax, or maximizing the maximum payoff, is used when the decision maker is optimistic. Both maximin and maximax ignore a large portion of the information in the payoff matrix.
4. Hurwicz, which weighs the best and worst outcomes according to the degree of optimism of the decision maker. Again it utilizies only a small amount of information from the payoff matrix.
5. Minimax regret, or minimize the maximum opportunity loss of choosing the wrong action.

The probabilistic choice criteria include:

1. Laplace, where all events are assigned equal probabilities and the highest expected payoff is the basis for choosing an action.
2. MEV, or maximizing expected payoffs, with different probabilities assigned to the states of nature either subjectively or objectively.

The probabilistic criteria are generally considered to be superior to the nonprobabilistic criteria, since they utilize a greater proportion of the information in the payoff matrix.

4.7. The EVPI is the difference between the expected payoff under certainty and the expected payoff of the optimal action under the current information state. It provides a ceiling above which we would not be willing to pay any money for sample information. To illustrate, consider the following problem with the payoff matrix given below:

	θ_1	θ_2	θ_3
a_1	6	2	-3
a_2	4	4	-10
a_3	-2	2	20

$$P(\theta) = 0.8 \qquad P(\theta_2) = 0.1 \qquad P(\theta_3) = .1$$

The expected payoff of each action is given as:

$$E(a_1) = 0.8(6) + 0.1(2) + 0.1(-3) = 4.7$$
$$E(a_2) = 0.8(4) + 0.1(4) + 0.1(-10) = 2.6$$
$$E(a_3) = 0.8(-2) + 0.1(2) + 0.1(20) = 0.6$$

Therefore the optimal action is a_1. If we knew the state of nature that would occur, we would receive an expected payoff of

$$0.8(6) + 0.1(4) + 0.1(20) = 7.2$$

The EVPI is thus $(7.2 - 4.7)$ or 2.5.

EXERCISES

4.1. The possible price of General Motors common stock tomorrow will be either higher, the same, or lower. Are these events mutually exclusive? Collectively exhaustive? What is wrong with assessing the prior probabilities as 0.5, 0.4, and 0, respectively?

4.2. The owner of a tennis shop finds that in his first month of business he sold 125 wood tennis rackets, 50 aluminum rackets, and 25 steel rackets. Based solely on these data, what prior probability distribution would you formulate for the type of tennis racket sold?

4.3. Suppose that it is an overcast Sunday morning and you have 100 people coming for cocktails in the afternoon. You have a nice garden and your house is not too large; so weather permitting, you would like to set up the refreshments in the garden and have the party there. It would be pleasant, and your guests would be more comfortable. On the other hand, if you set up the party for the garden and after all the guests arrive it begins to rain, the refreshments will be ruined, your guests will get wet, and you will surely wish you had decided to have the party in the house. Define the acts, events, and consequences and represent the problem in a payoff table.

4.4. An investor has the objective of achieving the maximum possible rate of return. Assume that he has only three possible investments (his strategies): speculative stocks, high-grade stocks, or bonds. Also, assume that only three possible states of nature can occur: war, peace, depression. Ignore all nuances of capital gains, taxes, and so on, and assume that the investor has determined his rates of return (in percent) for each of the nine act–state combinations as shown in the table. What is the optimal action using the various nonprobabilistic choice criteria in this chapter?

Action \ Event	θ_1: War	θ_2: Peace	θ_3: Depression
a_1: speculative stocks	20	1	−6
a_2: high-grade bonds	9	8	0
a_3: bonds	4	4	4

4.5. You are given the following payoff matrix:

(a) Apply the following nonprobabilistic choice criteria to select an optimal action: (1) dominance, (2) maximin, (3) maximax, (4) Hurwicz ($\alpha = \frac{1}{3}$), and minimax regret.

(b) Apply the Laplace criterion to the same problem.

Event / Action	θ_1	θ_2	θ_3	θ_4	θ_5
a_1	− 100	160	40	200	0
a_2	60	80	140	40	100
a_3	20	60	− 60	20	80
a_4	− 20	− 100	− 140	− 40	400

(c) Compare your choices under these various criteria.

(d) Criticize each of these criteria.

(e) Suppose that the following prior probability distribution has been assessed:

Event	Probability
θ_1	0.08
θ_2	0.10
θ_3	0.50
θ_4	0.12
θ_5	0.20

Using the criterion of expected value, what is the optimal act?

(f) Which decision in this problem do you prefer and why?

4.6. A processor of frozen vegetables has to decide what crop to plant in a particular area. Suppose that there are only two strategies: to plant cabbage or to plant cauliflower. Suppose, further, that the states of nature can be summarized in three possibilities: perfect weather, variable weather, and bad weather. On the basis of weather records, it is determined that the probability of perfect weather is 0.25, variable weather is 0.50, and bad weather is 0.25. The dollar yields of the two crops under these different conditions are known and the utility of the company can be assumed to be measured by dollar amounts as shown in the following payoff table. What action should the decision maker select?

Events / Actions	θ_1: Perfect	θ_2: Variable	θ_3: Bad
a_1: plant cabbage	$40,000	$30,000	$20,000
a_2: plant cauliflower	70,000	20,000	0

4.7. The Mocheck Company has developed a new product which it is considering marketing. The cost of marketing is $500,000. If its product is preferred to its competitor, and if it is marketed, the company anticipates factory gross sales of $1,500,000. If it is worse than its competitor, then, if marketed, the gross sales is estimated to be $250,000. If they do not market it, they can and will sell the new product idea to their competitors for $500,000 if it is a superior product or $150,000 if it is inferior. The decision whether to market or to sell the idea must be made now, although the positive confirmation of the relative superiority or inferiority of the product will not be available until some weeks from now. Should they market the product?

4.8. The Rodney Sportswear Company has designed two new tennis short styles for next year, "Wimbledon" and "Forest Hills." The company can produce either or both or neither of the two styles. Thus, they must select one of four actions available to them: Wimbledon only, Forest Hills only, both, or neither. The cost of production, all of which must be borne in advance, if a model design is to be produced, is $50,000 for either of the models; but it is $125,000 for both together, because of the strain on capacity involved in producing two styles. The profit, including all income and costs except production cost, is $100,000 per style if the style is successful, and zero if the style is unsuccessful. What is the best course of action?

4.9. Consider the following payoff matrix:

Action \ Event	θ_1	θ_2	θ_3
a_1	$10	$6	$3
a_2	5	8	4
a_3	2	5	9

The prior probability distribution assessed by the decision maker is

Event	$P(Event)$
θ_1	$\frac{1}{4}$
θ_2	$\frac{1}{2}$
θ_3	$\frac{1}{4}$

(a) Specify the opportunity loss matrix.
(b) Compute the expected value of perfect information (EVPI) three different ways.
(c) If nearly perfect information about which event is true could be bought for $2, would you buy it?

4.10. You have the opportunity to participate in one of two business ventures. The first venture (A_1), should it be successful, would earn you a profit of $100,000; should it be a failure, you will lose $100,000. The second venture (A_2), should it turn out to be successful, would earn you $10,000; if it fails, it will cost you $10,000.

(a) Draw a decision-tree diagram of each venture.

(b) Using dollars as the random variable, represent the outcomes of each venture as a probability distribution.

(c) Which venture do you prefer and why?

(d) Looking at each probability distribution of outcomes for each venture, how would you define risk?

CASE 4.1   Illustrative Case Study
Involving a Comparison Between
Intuitive and Expected Value Analysis

THE LASER CIRCUIT   You are about to perform an exercise where you will be asked to make
(LASCI)   decisions in a product development situation which involves uncertainty and
DEVELOPMENT   rank your decisions in order of preference. Although the actual development
PROJECT   project from which the following exercise was derived was much more complex and did not have all the information so readily available as will be the
case here, we shall, to simplify matters, look only at simple cases where the
data and available courses of action will be specified explicitly. You will
choose from among the series of alternative courses of action given in each
exercise. Your choices should be based solely on the information initially given
in the scenario and on the evidence accumulated after specific actions are
taken.

In all cases you will assume that all incomes or outgoes will take place in
the very near future, or, alternatively, that these can be considered the present
worths of all future case flows that are affected by your decision. All amounts
are considered to be net after taxes.

You are asked to make these choices in your capacity as a *corporate
decision maker*, not as a private individual dealing with your own funds. Try to
give responses that represent the actual action you would take if presented
with this choice at work *today*. Top management wants to know what you
would *actually do*, not what you feel you should do or what we might expect
you to do. One further comment: It is recognized that information gained
within a task may prove to have important applications external to the project.
The potential for such learning may justify certain choices that would not be
preferred solely on the basis of their contribution to the immediate task. For
example, both people in the project and the organization conducting it may
have other concurrent responsibilities and longer-term goals. As a result, some
activities may be undertaken to generate information that is justified in part by
its contribution to other organizational activities, to the establishment of
technical capabilities which will have more distant payoffs, or to the satisfaction of personal, professional goals of the investigators. You are *not* to permit
these factors to influence your choice; that is, your decisions should be based
strictly on the immediate task.

Description of Project. Your firm has just assigned you the responsibility for
developing a new switching circuit as a modular component for a laser device.
The laser device will be designed to emit large single impulses of light energy.

The laser requires a substantial amount of energy to activate the light emitter, the ruby. Once the proper energy level is reached, the ruby will emit a strong and sudden surge of light energy through the use of mirror reflections located at both ends of the ruby. During the energy buildup period, which is of split-second duration, it is necessary to remove in some manner the reflective capacity at both ends of the ruby. A control crystal is to be inserted between one end of the ruby and the mirror. The control crystal stands in the way of the reflection until the maximum ruby energy level is reached, at which time it allows the light beam to pass through to the mirror and on to the next step in the emission of the light beam. The timing of the control crystal on opening and closing is critical in achieving the proper emission. The critical element of the device is the circuit that controls the sudden single light energy impulse. The switching circuit is to initiate and terminate a control pulse with far greater precision than any presently existing circuit.

The switching circuit must meet the following two performance specifications:

1. Fast switching action, or opening time, no greater than 10 nanoseconds.
2. The switch is to close the crystal within less than 100 nanoseconds after the peak pulse has been achieved.

These specifications are firm requirements; that is, it is not anticipated that they will be reformulated or redefined, and they must be achieved if the project is to be successful.

Task. In this section you will have *three* technical approaches available for the LASCI project. You will be asked to rank, on the response sheets provided, your relative preferences for *all* the available courses of action. Your available actions will only involve making a "critical decision"—which particular technical approach or approaches to breadboard (the term "breadboard" denotes a crudely built device used solely to demonstrate its functionability).

Project Information. You are given a budget of $400,000, and 3 months to complete the project. At the time this project was formally approved, analysis of the problem had been complete and three technical approaches had been identified, one using a circuit incorporating conventional tubes, another designed around a single newly developed tube which you called the betatron, and a third which uses a different type of circuit incorporating another newly developed tube called the thetatron. All three of these approaches are quite different in design and are independent of each other in the sense that knowledge gathered about one does not affect the outcome of the others.

All three technical approaches were conceived by three engineers working in concert. You have available one of these engineers and a technician for the LASCI Project. The technician can only be used to perform tasks commensurate with his position title, that is, to provide assistance and support to the engineer or engineers responsible for development of a given technical approach. The other two engineers are each currently working on separate projects under your cognizance. You will not allow an engineer to split his duties by working on more than one approach at a time, since experience dictates that this is highly undesirable. Because of time limitations, a sequential strategy (i.e., building one breadboard, for each approach, at a time until a successful one is found) is out of the question. However, you can pursue two or three approaches simultaneously, but this means additional development costs as well as taking one or both of the engineers responsible for conception of the technical approaches off the project or projects each is currently working on. In either case, if either engineer is removed from the project he is currently working on and placed on the LASCI Project, the chances of success of each of the other projects is reduced by 0%, which is estimated to be equivalent to $0 lost to the firm.

You estimate that a successful conventional circuit design would be worth $478,300 to the company. In comparison with the conventional approach use of the single betatron tube would offer a simpler, more reliable circuit, and one that was sufficiently easier to manufacture, to offer an additional cost saving of $150,000 and would be worth an additional $121,700 to the firm over and above any cost savings, for the quantity expected. In comparison with the conventional approach, use of the thetatron device would offer an additional cost saving of $100,000 and would be worth an additional $211,700 to the firm over and above any cost savings, for the quantity expected.

You are sure that either of the three approaches could be developed to satisfy the project's specification, given enough time and money. However, within the time and cost budget, you estimate that there was a 30% chance that the conventional circuit would not meet specifications, a 50% chance that the betatron would not meet specifications, and a 50% chance that the thetatron could not meet specifications.

The end result of the project was to be a prototype built in the manufacturing shop from the drawings released to you. In order to work out the design details of the circuit and to identify and resolve unanticipated problems in design, you planned to design and build a breadboard model of the complete circuit. This would take 3 months and cost (in labor, materials, and equipment) $60,000 for the conventional design, $100,000 for the betatron design, and $120,000 for the thetatron design. The "critical decision" you are faced with is the choice of which design to follow in construction of a breadboard model.

As indicated previously, you have the option of pursuing more than one technical approach simultaneously (since the budget constraint = $400,000). If you pursue a parallel approach you will incur the following additional costs over and above the breadboard costs:

Breadboard Parallel Approach Options	Additional Out-of-Pocket Costs
Conventional and betatron	$107,000
Conventional and thetatron	108,000
Betatron and thetatron	87,500
Conventional, betatron, and thetatron	111,000

You must now choose what you think is a best course of action for conducting this development project. Your choices must be made on the basis of the development situation presented.

1. Subjectively rank (8 is best) your relative preferences for all eight available courses of action. Specifically state your reasons for your choices (i.e., describe exactly how you went about making your choices).
2. Draw a decision matrix of the development problem and compute the expected values for each alternative. Compare these results to your subjective rankings.
3. Discuss the notion of a parallel approach. What are its advantages and disadvantages? Develop some rule of thumb for determining under what circumstances a parallel approach might be beneficial in managerial practice.

CHAPTER 5
Decision Analysis: Quantifying Beliefs and Tastes and the Axioms of Decision Theory

OBJECTIVES. Upon successful completion of this chapter, you should be able to:

1. Understand several ways in which risk might be perceived.
2. Specify alternative methods of measuring a single attribute utility function for a decision maker.
3. Specify the general characteristics of various types of utility functions in terms of risk attitude.
4. Measure subjective probabilities and subjective probability distributions.
5. State and illustrate a set of axioms of rational behavior that is fundamental to the development of decision theory.

5.1. INTRODUCTION

Decision theory is concerned with selecting an alternative from among a set of alternatives; it is an attempt to give structure and rationale to the different conditions under which decisions are made. Although there are widely diverse opinions about the application and limits of decision theory, authors generally agree on their concept of the basic decision-making situation: the decision maker must choose between multiple alternatives. These are referred to as *actions* (or *strategies*). The choice of any one action results in a payoff or outcome. If decision makers knew the payoff associated with each action, they would simply be able to choose the action that had the largest payoff. However, most decision situations are characterized by incomplete information; thus predictions are made about payoffs, which are often specified under various conditions we have called "events" or "states of nature." Decisions are said to be made under conditions of certainty and uncertainty, reflecting various degrees of information and understanding that a decision maker has about a particular situation or problem.

Decision theorists contend that in making decisions from among multiple alternatives, individuals make selections from among alternatives by assigning a preference or utility value to each alternative. Thus, the decision maker is faced with two basic problems involving judgment:

1. How to quantify (or measure) his utility for various payoffs.
2. How to quantify his judgments concerning the probability of the occurrence of each possible event.

A choice of a best or optimal action (or strategy) is determined by choosing the action having the highest expected utility. The expected utility of each action is determined by multiplying the utility of each event by its probability of occurrence and adding the products.

In this chapter we first focus on the questions of how to measure the utility of consequences and the subjective probability of events. We then briefly examine the fundamental axioms (or psychological assumptions) of decision theory, which lead us to choose an action or strategy based on the maximization of expected utility.

We shall begin with an example, which we shall carry throughout much of the chapter, to illustrate the concepts and techniques to be discussed.

5.1.1. Example—Selection of New Product Development Strategies

As project manager of a research and development department you have been assigned the responsibility for development of a new switching circuit as a modular component for a laser device. You are given a budget of $300,000 and 3 months to complete the project. Two technical approaches have been identified, one using a circuit incorporating conventional tubes, and another designed around a single newly developed tube which you called the betatron.

You estimate that a successful conventional circuit design would be worth $478,300 to the company. In comparison with the conventional approach, use of the single betatron tube would offer a simpler, more reliable circuit, and one that was sufficiently easier to manufacture, to offer an additional cost saving of $150,000 and would be worth an additional $121,700 to the firm over and above any cost savings, for the quantity expected.

You are sure that either of the two approaches could be developed to satisfy the project's specifications given enough time and money. However, within the time and cost budget, you estimate that there was a 30% chance that the conventional circuit would not meet specifications and a 50% chance that the betatron would not meet specifications.

The end result of the project was to be a prototype built in the manufacturing shop from the drawings released by you. In order to work out the design details of the circuit and to identify and resolve unanticipated problems in design, you planned to design and build a breadboard (functional) model of the complete circuit. This would take 3 months and cost (in labor, materials, and equipment) $60,000 for the conventional design and $100,000 for the betatron design. The "critical decision" you are faced with is the choice of which design to follow in construction of a breadboard model.

You have the option of pursuing more than one technical approach simultaneously (since the budget constraint is equal to $300,000). If you pursue a parallel approach you will incur the following additional costs of $107,000. What is the best course of action for conducting this development project?

5.2. EMV MAXIMIZATION AS A DECISION CRITERION

The decision tree and payoff matrix for this problem are shown in Figure 5.1. By arranged coincidence the expected monetary value (EMV) for each of the three actions—build conventional breadboard (A_2), build betatron breadboard (B_2), and build both of these breadboards simultaneously (A_2B_2)—is $275,000. Thus, based solely on an EMV maximization criterion, all three alternatives are equally good and one should be indifferent among these three alternatives.

But would you really be indifferent among these three alternative courses of action? To answer this, let us view each action as a gamble that can be represented by a discrete probability distribution of its outcomes, as shown in Figure 5.2. Note that for each action there is a "risk" of losing money, manifested by an amount lost

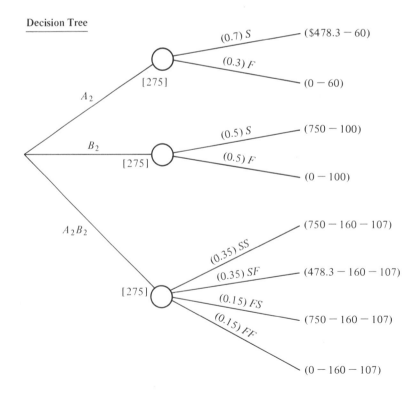

Decision Tree

$P(E)$	0.35	0.35	0.15	0.15	
E A	$A_2 : S$ $B_2 : S$	S F	F S	F F	EMV
A_2	418.3	418.3	−60.0	−60.0	275
B_2	650.0	−100.0	650.0	−100.0	275
$A_2 B_2$	483.0	211.3	483.0	−267.0	275

Figure 5.1. Decision tree (page 146) and payoff matrix of R&D example.

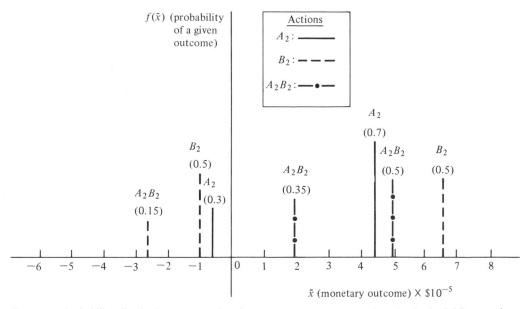

Figure 5.2. Probability distributions representing the monetary outcomes of each action in the R&D example.

and a probability of losing that amount. You, as the decision maker, might not be willing to tolerate the prospect of a loss of $100,000 or more (e.g., such a loss might cost you your job, or might force your firm into a very difficult financial position), but you might be willing and able to bear the financial strain of a $60,000 loss. Hence, you would choose A_2 over the other alternatives, since one cannot lose more than $60,000 with A_2, whereas $100,000 and $267,000 could be lost with alternatives B_2 and $A_2 B_2$, respectively.

In the above, EMV maximization could not be used as the criterion because all alternatives yielded the same EMV. But suppose that this was not the case. What might be some objections for using EMV maximization as the choice criterion? The main argument that can be advanced against EMV as a criterion of choice between available options is that it is generally appropriate only to decisions that are repeated many times. This argument is based on the fact that the outcome in a single decision is that resulting from choice of one of the options and an unknown future state of nature. It is only in many repeated decisions of the same type that the average outcome approaches the expected value. For example, in the new product example just considered, the outcome of developing the betatron is either a gain of $650,000 or a loss of $100,000. The fact that the expected value is a $275,000 gain may be very little consolation to the project manager (and perhaps the company) if the betatron turns out to be a failure. A prudent manager might not wish to risk an outcome of $-\$100,000$ that would occur with the betatron alternative if it turned out to be a failure. He might be tempted to develop the conventional circuit to avoid the 50% chance of a $100,000 loss in the single decision situation confronting him. In this way, he risks a $60,000 loss with only a 30% chance of occurring.

Thus, while expected value provides a decision maker with helpful information, it can, however, obscure the presence of an intolerably high potential loss or an exceptionally alluring potential gain. In essence, expected value is a statistic summarizing an entire distribution of outcomes. The decision maker basing his decisions solely on such a summary statistic could, then, be led to make choices that are inconsistent with his psychological preferences and attitudes toward risk.

The decision maker basing selections on the expected value criterion, over the long run, does better *on the average* than will the decision maker who relies on any other criterion—but only if the "run" is long enough and the decision maker both survives the short-term ups and downs and is a continual participant in comparable decision problems. Thus, to reduce uncertainty and moderate the potential short-term swings, the decision maker might choose the action that provides a satisfactory return subject to a tolerable *risk*.

How might *risk* be defined? Risk might be thought of in a variety of ways (actually there is no one precise definition of risk). It might be viewed as:

1. The variance (or dispersion) of the probability distribution of outcomes associated with a given action;
2. The probability of a monetary loss [i.e., $p(\tilde{x} \leq \$0)$, where x is the dollar outcome]; or
3. The probable loss (i.e., the sum of the products of the losses times their probabilities).

For example, the variance of the outcomes associated with action A_2 is

$$\text{var}(A_2) = \sum_x (x - \mu_x)^2 f(x)$$
$$= (418,300 - 275,000)^2 (0.7) + (-60,000 - 275,000)^2 (0.3)$$
$$= \$75,900.$$

The probability of a loss for A_2 is 0.3, and the 'probable loss' for A_2 is ($60,000)(0.3) = $18,000. Other rules for or definitions of risk could also be stated.

The choice preference rankings based on the risk criteria above are shown in Table 5.1. Note that B_2 is always the highest risk alternative, while A_2 and A_2B_2 are the lowest risk alternatives, depending on one's definition of risk.

Of these three risk criteria, perhaps the measure that is most commonly used is variance. One place where variance is used as the measure of risk is in portfolio analysis in finance. In making a portfolio decision, one attempts to make a trade-off between expected return on investment and variance. Variance (as well as the other risk measures) is a summary statistic of a probability distribution, as is expected value. Reliance on these statistics for decision-making purposes may not be entirely appropriate, since such measures may not capture the psychological preferences and risk attitudes of the decision maker.

In the next section we discuss the notion of utility as a decision criterion, which presents an orderly procedure for arriving at an optimal decision that is commensurate with the decision maker's psychological preferences and risk attitudes. This is done by first obtaining a decision maker's utility function and then using this utility function to calculate the expected utility (rather than EMV) of all possible actions. The optimal action is the one that maximizes expected utility. On a broader basis, such a procedure provides an analyst, attempting to advise management, with a tool for suggesting policies that are best for management in the light of management's expressed goals, values, and needs. The latter property is of considerable importance to the modern manager, who is usually overburdened with problems and who is, consequently, compelled to delegate decision-making authority to subordinates.

Table 5.1. Risk and Choice Preference Rankings
(1 is most preferred)

Action	$P(\tilde{x} < \$0)^b$	RISK CRITERIA^a Probable Loss^c	Variance
A_2	2 (0.3)	1 (−$18,000)	2 ($74,900)
B_2	3 (0.5)	3 (−$50,000)	3 ($141,000)
A_2B_2	1 (0.15)	2 (−$40,050)	1 ($67,140)

^{a}Numbers in parentheses are the actual "risk" values.

^{b}Probability of a loss.

^{c}Probable loss is defined as the sum of the products of the losses times the probability of the loss [e.g., for A_2 it is $(-\$60,000)(0.3) = -\$18,000$].

5.3. EXPECTED UTILITY MAXIMIZATION AS A DECISION CRITERION

Assume that you are given a choice in each of the following five decision situations:

Situation 1 a_1: The certainty of receiving $1

   or

   a_2: on the flip of a fair coin, $10 if it comes up heads, or − $1 if it comes up tails.

Situation 2 b_1: The certainty of receiving $100

or

b_2: on the flip of a fair coin, $1000 if it comes up heads, or − $100 if it comes up tails.

Situation 3 c_1: The certainty of receiving $1000

or

c_2: on the flip of a fair coin, $10,000 if it comes up heads, or − $1,000 if it comes up tails.

Situation 4 d_1: The certainty of receiving $10,000

or

d_2: on the flip of a fair coin $100,000 if it comes up heads, or − $10,000 if it comes up tails.

Situation 5 e_1: The certainty of receiving $10,000

or

e_2: a payment of 2^n, where n is the number of times a fair coin is flipped until heads comes up. If heads appears on the first toss, you receive $2; if the coin shows tails on the first toss and heads on the second, you receive $4; two tails in a row followed by heads yields $8; and so forth. However, you are allowed to participate only once; the sequence stops with the first showing of heads.

Most people would probably choose a_2, b_2, c_1, d_1, and e_1. The choices a_2 and b_2 would be those chosen by an EMV maximization criterion since EMV(a_1) = $4.50 is greater than the certain choice of a_2 = $1, and EMV($b_2$) = $450 is greater than $100. However, in situations 3, 4, and 5, c_1 would probably be preferred to c_2, even though EMV(c_2) = $4500 is greater than $1000, and d_1 would be preferred to d_2 even though EMV(d_2) = $45,000 is greater than $10,000. In situation 5, the EMV of e_2 is infinite; that is,

$$EMV(e_2) = \tfrac{1}{2}(\$2) + \tfrac{1}{4}(\$4) + \tfrac{1}{8}(\$8) + \cdots$$
$$= \$1 + \$1 + \$1 + \cdots$$
$$= \infty,$$

yet e_1 would be preferred to e_2 by practically all people.

In the first four decision situations, most people would tend to change their decision criterion away from maximizing EMV as soon as the thought of losing a large sum of money (say $1000) was too painful despite the pleasure to be gained from possibly obtaining a large sum (say, $10,000). At this point, the individual faced with such a choice would not be considering EMV but would be instead thinking solely of utility. In this sense, *utility* refers essentially to the pleasure (utility) or displeasure (disutility) one would derive from certain outcomes. In essence we are saying that the individual's displeasure from losing $1000 is greater than the pleasure of winning many times that amount. In situation 5, no prudent person would choose the gamble e_2 in preference to the certainty of a relatively modest amount obtained by choosing e_1. This problem, known as the famous St.

Petersburg paradox, led Daniel Bernoulli to the first investigations of utility rather than EMV as a basis of decision making.

Since most people would choose c_1, d_1, and e_1 rather than the alternatives with greater monetary expectation, it seems reasonable to conclude that people do not always make decisions according to an EMV criterion. What, then, is an alternative criterion for decision making? Von Neumann and Morgenstern (1944) constructed a framework that was consistent with choices such as c_1, d_1, and e_1. They argued that decisions were made so as to maximize expected *utility* rather than EMV. If you selected c_1 over c_2, we would conclude that alternative c_1 had more utility for you than alternative c_2. If you were indifferent between c_1 and c_2, we would conclude that each alternative had the same utility to you. Indifference would be defined as your willingness to take either result at random, or have a third party make the choice for you. It is possible to derive generalizations about a person's utility function for some attribute or commodity (usually money) that are consistent with logic and observation of repeated decisions. It thus seems plausible to presume that people make decisions so as to maximize expected utility rather than expected value. This is not a painless choice, for EMV is an unambiguous, relatively easy to calculate concept. It would be quite expedient if we were able to associate different monetary or nonmonetary outcomes with measures of the decision maker's preferences (i.e., utilities). A complex set of alternatives might thus be transformed into utility measures for purposes of decision making.

The von Neumann–Morgenstern (NM) measure of utility is a special type of cardinal measure (some would say it is a special type of ordinal measure). It measures utility in situations involving risk for the individual decision maker. The use of this utility measure allows us to predict which of several lotteries (or gambles) a person will prefer and thus enables a manager to make the decision for his employer. Sometimes the employer will make decisions inconsistent with his utility function, but this type of inconsistency can generally be rectified if the employer reflects on his decisions.

One of our purposes in this chapter is to relate money (or, more generally, any attribute) to a utility index, and to derive generalizations about this relationship in situations involving risk. Any utility function is the result of a person's attitude towards risk. There are no right or wrong answers (although inconsistencies may arise because of misunderstandings). Thus, if you are asked, "What certain amount will you accept instead of engaging in a lottery (or gamble) involving a 0.5 probability of winning $1000 or losing $500," the answer is a personal preference rather than a mathematical calculation. (If such a question is asked to 100 people, it is likely that close to 100 different answers will be obtained.)

What is the usefulness of cardinal utility theory? There are at least four possible levels of usefulness:

1. It serves as a frame of reference to aid in understanding decision-making behavior in situations involving risk and uncertainty.
2. It serves as a means of predicting decisions in uncertain situations.
3. It serves as a means of improving choice consistency in uncertain stiuations.
4. It serves as an aid toward making "better" decisions under conditions of uncertainty.

5.4. DERIVING A DECISION MAKER'S UTILITY FUNCTION

To be of use in decision making, utility values (i.e., subjective preferences) must be assigned to all possible outcomes. In many circumstances, such outcomes are nonmonetary in nature. For example, in making a decision regarding a job, one has to weigh such factors as geographical area, quality of work, advancement potential, and so on, as well as the salary. It is possible to assign utility values to such outcomes. However, in most business decision problems, a monetary consequence is of major importance. Hence, we shall illustrate how to evaluate one's utility function for money. The same procedure, however, applies to nonmonetary outcomes. However, most decisions involve multiple objectives and values. This will be discussed in Chapter 7.

In assessing utility functions, two things should be pointed out. First, since an expression of subjective feelings is involved, one may question the degree of accuracy of the utility function. However, unless the decision-making problem is highly sensitive to slight changes in the utility function (a rare situation), it should not be too difficult to derive a utility function that is a reasonable approximation of an individual's preferences.

Second, it should be noted that a person's utility function will not necessarily remain constant over time. As wealth and other factors in his life change, his values change, thereby modifying his utility function in some manner.

The assessment of a person's utility function (as is the case with the assessment of his subjective probability function) involves the pinning down in quantitative terms of subjective feelings that may not have been thought of before in a precise quantitative way. At least four approaches for doing this may be distinguished: (1) direct measurement, (2) the von Neumann–Morgenstern (NM) or standard reference contract method, (3) the modified NM method, and (4) the Ramsey method.

The direct measurement approach involves asking a series of questions of the type: "Suppose I were to give you an outright gift of $100. This $100 comes from a philanthropist whose resources are limitless. How much money would you need to make you twice as happy as the $100 would make you feel?" The answers to a sequence of such questions enable the plotting of a utility curve (or more precisely, a value curve) against whatever arbitrarily chosen utility (value) scale is desired (Figure 5.3). However, it is a very gross approach, is not concerned with uncertainty and, for many people, cannot be expected to be as precise as other methods.

The other three approaches deal with the question of risk attitude directly and ask the decision maker to compare certain gambles to sure sums of money, or gambles to gambles. For example, in the new product development problem, a question might be to have the project manager choose between receiving $200,000 for *certain* versus a *gamble* (lottery) with equal chances of winning $1,000,000 and losing $500,000. Through such questioning, one can find some riskless value that would make the project manager indifferent. This value is called the *certainty equivalent* of the gamble. Usually, for such sums of money, the certainty equivalent is less than the expected value of the gamble and we then say that the decision maker is risk-averse. The measurement procedure is continued with different

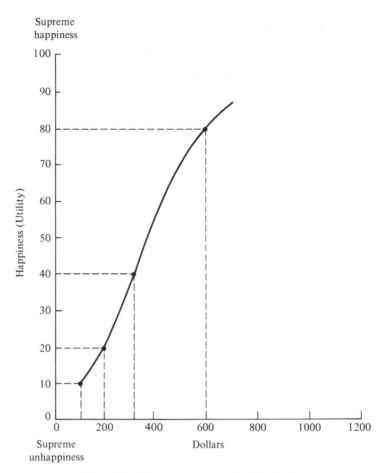

Supreme
happiness

Supreme
unhappiness

Dollars

Happiness (Utility)

Figure 5.3. Direct measurement of utility (value).

gambles until a good idea can be formed concerning the decision maker's risk attitude. The risk attitude is plotted in the form of a utility function and subsequently used to choose the best alternative based on the criterion of maximizing expected utility.

In this chapter we shall discuss the NM and modified NM methods, since these methods seem to work best in practice. For a good account of the Ramsey method, see the book by Davidson, Suppes, and Siegel (1957).

The first step in deriving a utility function by the NM methods is to determine two monetary outcome values as reference points. For convenience, we look at the most favorable and least favorable monetary outcomes and then select two values at least as favorable and at least as unfavorable as these values for our reference points. The utilities of these extreme outcomes are arbitrarily selected. For convenience, we might assign utility values of 1 and zero, respectively, to these monetary values. For example, in our new product development decision problem, the monetary outcomes ranged from −$267,000 to $750,000. For expediency, we thus might choose extreme values of $-\$500,000$ and $\$1,000,000$, assigning a zero utility to $-\$500,000$ and a utility of 1.0 to $\$1,000,000$. That is,

$$U(-\$500,000) = 0 \quad \text{and} \quad U(\$1,000,000) = 1.0.$$

The choice of the utility values of zero and 1 is arbitrary. Other values, such as -100 and $+100$, or -332 and $+400$, could have also been selected. In this sense, the utility scale is like that for temperature. Both the Fahrenheit and Celsius scales measure temperature but have different readings for the boiling point of water ($212°$ and $100°$, respectively) and for the freezing point ($32°$ and $0°$, respectively).

5.4.1. NM Method

The standard reference contract or NM method is based on the concept of certainty equivalence. If outcome x_1 is preferred to x_2, and x_2 is preferred to x_3, then (by the continuity postulate, to be discussed later) there exists a probability p such that

$$pU(x_1) + (1-p)U(x_3) = U(x_2). \tag{5.4.1}$$

For specified values of x_1, x_2, and x_3, the utility of x_2 can be determined by questioning to find the value of p at which x_2 is the *certainty equivalent* of the gamble involving x_1 and x_3 (i.e., what value of p will make you indifferent to the gamble and receiving x_2 for certain?), $U(x_1)$ and $U(x_3)$ being given values on an arbitrary scale. For example, if $U(x_1)$ is set at 1 and $U(x_3)$ at zero, then $U(x_2) = p$ [i.e., $(p)(1) + (1-p)(0) = U(x_2)$]. By finding the values of p corresponding to an array of values of x_2 between x_1 and x_3, the utility curve may be plotted for values of x from x_1 to x_3.

Let us illustrate this procedure on the new product development problem. Using the maximum and minimum values, we define a "reference contract" (alternative B) as one in which there is a probability p of winning $\$1,000,000$ and a probability $(1-p)$ of losing $\$500,000$. We define another alternative (alternative A) as receiving a given amount of money with complete certainty. The alternatives are then:

Alternative A: a given amount of money with certainty ("certain cash")

Alternative B: a reference contract with

> probability p of winning $\$1,000,000$
> probability $(1-p)$ of losing $\$500,000$.

The project manager is then asked to indicate his preference between A and B for a series of different values of p and levels of "certain cash." This process can be classified by considering Table 5.2. Alternative A (certain cash) is listed in the left-hand column. Alternative B, providing either $\$1,000,000$ with probability p or

Table 5.2. Choice Table for Finding Indifference Points for the Derivation of Utility Function [a]

Certain Dollars (A) (e.g., Cash)	Possible Company Incomes (B)	Chances Out of 10 That Development Outcome Will Be $1,000,000 or −$500,000 (Probabilities)										
	1,000,000	0	1	2	3	4	5	6	7	8	9	10
	−500,000	10	9	8	7	6	5	4	3	2	1	0
$1,110,000		A	A	A	A	A	A	A	A	A	A	A
1,000,000		A	·	·	·	·	·	·	·	·	·	I
900,000		A	·	·	·	·	·	·	·	·	·	B
800,000		A	·		·	·	·	·	·	·	·	B
700,000		A	·	·		·	·	·	·	·	·	B
600,000		A	·	·		·	·	·	·	·	·	B
500,000		A	·	·		·	·	·	·	·	A	B
400,000		A	·	·	·	·	·	·	·	·	I	B
300,000		A	·	·	·	·	·	·	·		B	B
200,000		A	·	·	·	·	·	·	A	A / I	·	B
100,000		A	·	·	·	·	·	·	A	B	·	B
0		A	·	·	·	·	A	I	·	·		B
−100,000		A	·	·	·	·	A	I	B	·	·	B
−200,000		A	·	·	·	·	A	B	·	·	·	B
−300,000		A	·	A	A	A	I	·	·	·	·	B
−400,000		A	A	A	I	I / B	B	·	·	·	·	B
−500,000		I	I / B	I / B	B	·	·	·	·	·	·	B
−600,000		B	B	B	B	B	B	B	B	B	B	B

[a] 1. You will be given a series of choices where

   A = income of $X with complete certainty

   B = income of $Y with probability p or income of $Z with probability (1 − p).

   Fill out the table with A, B, or I (indifferent). For example, to fill cell X, ask yourself: "Which do I prefer, $1,110,000 certain income (A), or an uncertain income alternative (B) consisting of $1,000,000 with probability 1 in 10 and −$500,000 with probabilities 9 in 10?"

2. Try to think of this as income possibilities for the firm from a given product development activity. Alternative A might be to sell a particular product development idea to another firm for cash—no uncertainty. Alternative B might be to develop the idea in house—considerable uncertainty. Obviously, A is preferred, so A is marked in cell X.

3. Continue this procedure until you find a point where you are "indifferent" between A and B. Make the decision, taking into account your firm's current financial position. Try to think of this as an action you would really have to take, once you make a decision. Proceed in this fashion to find indifference points in each of the columns.

4. There are no "correct" answers. Just try to respond as realistically as possible.

5. Take as long as you wish to make your decisions, and use pencil and paper if you wish.

6. Note that due to the broad dollar intervals for each row, a cell could have multiple choices if a shift in preference occurs in a given dollar interval defined by that cell.

— $500,000 with probability 1 − p, is listed across the top. The project manager is then asked to indicate for each cell in each column whether he prefers A or B or is indifferent. Taking one column at a time, the entire table is completed. For example, start from the bottom of the first column of Table 5.2. Do you, as project manager, prefer losing $600,000 certain cash (A) or a gamble (B) with probability 0.0 of winning $1,000,000 and probability 1.0 of losing $500,000? Alternative B is obviously preferred. Moving up to the next cell, ask a similar question: Do you prefer losing $500,000 certain cash (A) or a gamble (B) with probability 0.0 of winning $1,000,000 and probability 1.0 of losing $500,000? These alternatives are obviously identical and we write "indifferent." We ask a similar question as we move to the next cell and we find that A is clearly preferred. We have the same experience as we move to each remaining cell in the first column. We use this procedure to fill in the balance of the table. However, it will take considerable reflection and introspection to find the indifference cells in the other columns (try it!). Obviously, except for the first and last columns, we would expect different decision makers to select a different pattern of "indifference" points. Their selection would depend, for example, on the initial wealth position of the decision maker and on his or her general attitude toward risks. Presenting the options in this way allows the decision maker to check as he or she goes along for internal consistency. For example, if the pattern of indifference points is not monotonically increasing or is wildly erratic, this is immediately apparent to the decision maker.

Figure 5.4. Utility function obtained from Table 5.2.

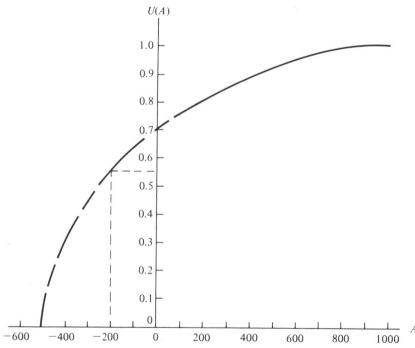

In completing Table 5.2, the project manager indicated his indifference point at $-\$250,000$ in the column where $p = 0.5$. The utility of $-\$250,000$ was derived as follows:

$$U(-\$250,000) = pU(\$1,000,000) + (1-p)U(-\$500,000)$$
$$= \tfrac{1}{2}(1) + \tfrac{1}{2}(0)$$
$$= \tfrac{1}{2}.$$

The indifference points obtained in Table 5.2 are now plotted in Figure 5.4 and a curve is fitted through the 10 points. Figure 5.4 then shows what amount of certain cash is equivalent, in the project manager's opinion, to a gamble in which there is a probability p of winning $\$1,000,000$ or a probability $(1-p)$ of losing $\$500,000$.

5.4.2. Modified NM Method

The modified NM method uses neutral probabilities of $p = 0.5 = 1 - p$ (to overcome the problem that some people have preferences for certain probabilities that would bias the results obtained from using the NM method). Questions are posed to determine the certainty equivalent x_2 for a 50–50 chance of x_1 or x_3, arbitrary utilities again being set for x_1 and x_3. Thus, we have

$$0.5U(x_1) + 0.5U(x_3) = U(x_2). \tag{5.4.2}$$

If $U(x_1)$ is arbitrarily set at 1 and $U(x_3)$ at zero, then $U(x_2) = 0.5$. In a similar fashion, the certainty equivalent may be established for the 50–50 gamble of x_1 and x_2, say x_4, which will have a utility of

$$U(x_4) = 0.5U(x_1) + 0.5U(x_2) = 0.75;$$

and for the 50–50 gamble of x_2 and x_3, say x_5, which will have a utility of

$$U(x_5) = 0.5U(x_2) + 0.5U(x_3) = 0.25.$$

By such further linked questions, additional points on the utility curve may be established. Again, suppose that we assign the following utilities to the extreme monetary values in our new product development problem,

$$U(\$1,000,000) = 1 \quad \text{and} \quad U(-\$500,000) = 0.$$

Now that we have arbitrarily defined two points on the project manager's utility function, let us next formulate the following two alternatives: (1) a gamble that offers a 50–50 chance at winning $\$1,000,000$ and losing $\$500,000$; and (2) one that offers a sure amount of money.

Suppose that you had to choose between this gamble (call this action B) and some sure amount of money (call this action A). How much would this sure amount of money be such that you would be indifferent between that sure amount of money and the gamble (i.e., such that the sure amount of money is as equally attractive as the gamble)? Suppose, you said $-\$250,000$. Since, you are indifferent to these two options, they must have the same utility, or, more properly speaking, the same expected utility. The expected utility of any set of mutually exclusive outcomes resulting from a decision is the sum of the products of the utility of each of the outcomes and its probability of occurrence. The expected utility of this alternative is the sum of the utility assignments to the possible events, weighted by the appropriate probabilities. In this case,

$$U(B) = \tfrac{1}{2}U(\$1,000,000) + \tfrac{1}{2}U(-\$500,000)$$
$$= \tfrac{1}{2}(1) + \tfrac{1}{2}(0)$$
$$= 0.5$$

since

$$U(B) = U(-\$250,000)$$
$$U(A) = U(B)$$
$$U(B) = 0.5.$$

Thus, the expected utility of the first option (B) is 0.5 utile. The utility of the sure $-\$250,000$ (A) is its utility times 1. The project manager's indifference says that, for him, these two options have the same utility. Therefore, his utility for $-\$250,000$ must, on the scale chosen, be 0.5 utile also. The concept of utility assessment by the modified NM method is depicted in Figure 5.5.

We now have three points through which the project manager's utility function passes. Additional utility evaluations may be made in a similar manner. For example, pose an alternative that offers a 50–50 chance of gaining $\$1,000,000$ and

Figure 5.5. Utility assessment (notion of risk preference and certainty equivalence).

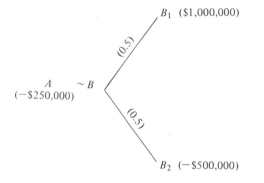

B_1 ($\$1,000,000$)

A
$(-\$250,000)$ ~ B

(0.5)

(0.5)

B_2 $(-\$500,000)$

Note:

$\$1,000,000 > $ (preferred to) $\$100,000 > -\$500,000$

$U(A_2) = 0.5U(B_1) + 0.5U(B_2)$

without loss of quality let $U(B_1) = 1, U(B_2) = 0$

Then $U(A) = 0.5\,(1) + 0.5(0)$

$U\,(-\$250,000) = 0.5$

$100,000. Find the sum that must be offered with certainty to make him or her indifferent to the 50–50 gamble. Suppose that he says $75,000. Then

$$U(\$75,000) = \tfrac{1}{2} U(\$1,000,000) + \tfrac{1}{2} U(\$100,000)$$
$$= \tfrac{1}{2}(1.0) + \tfrac{1}{2}(0.5)$$
$$= 0.75.$$

Next, pose the alternative involving a 50–50 chance of gaining $100,000 or losing $500,000. The project manager would certainly consider this gamble unfavorable, and in fact would be willing to pay some amount to be relieved of this gamble (in the same way that one buys insurance to be relieved of a risk). Suppose that he was indifferent between this gamble and paying a sure sum of $420,000. Then

$$U(-\$420,000) = \tfrac{1}{2} U(\$100,000) + \tfrac{1}{2} U(-\$500,000)$$
$$= \tfrac{1}{2}(0.5) + \tfrac{1}{2}(0)$$
$$= 0.25.$$

We now have five points of his utility function shown in Table 5.3 and Figure 5.4. These can be connected by a smooth curve to approximate the project manager's utility function over the entire range of from $-\$500,000$ to $\$1,000,000$.

Table 5.3. Assessed Utilities

Monetary Outcome, M ($)	Utility, $U(M)$
− 500,000	0.00
−420,000	0.25
−250,000	0.50
75,000	0.75
1,000,000	1.00

Note that, to be consistent, the project manager, for example, should be indifferent between a gamble (C), which offered him an equal chance of winning $1,000,000 or losing $500,000, and another gamble (D), which offered him an equal chance of winning $400,000 or losing $250,000. That is,

$$U(C) = \tfrac{1}{2} U(\$1,000,000) + \tfrac{1}{2} U(-\$500,000) = \tfrac{1}{2}(1) + \tfrac{1}{2}(0) = \tfrac{1}{2}$$
$$U(D) = \tfrac{1}{2} U(75,000) + \tfrac{1}{2} U(-420,000) = \tfrac{1}{2}(0.75) + \tfrac{1}{2}(0.25) = \tfrac{1}{2}.$$

If this is not true, his assessments are inconsistent and should be revised.

5.5. GENERAL TYPES AND CHARACTERISTICS OF UTILITY FUNCTIONS

The utility function depicted in Figure 5.4 rises consistently from the lower left to the upper right side of the figure; that is, it is monotonically increasing. In other words, the utility curve has a positive slope throughout. This is a general characteristic of utility functions. It simply implies that people ordinarily attach greater utility to a larger amount of money than to a smaller amount of money (i.e., they prefer more money to less). Economists refer to such a psychological trait as a "positive marginal utility for money."

5.5.1. General Types of Utility Functions

Three general types of utility functions can be distinguished and are depicted in Figure 5.6. (Of course, the curves discussed below are by no means the only possible forms for utility functions.) The concave-downward shape illustrates the utility curve of an individual who has a diminishing marginal utility for money, although the marginal utility is always positive (slope of curve is positive but decreasing as the dollar amount increases). This type of utility function characterizes a "risk avoider." Note that the slope of this curve decreases as the amount

Figure 5.6. Some general types of utility functions.

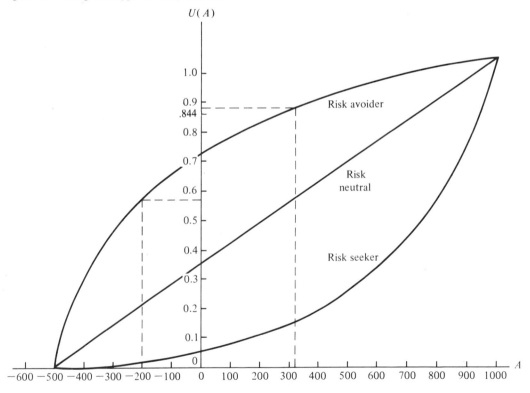

of gain increases, while the slope of this curve increases as the amount of loss increases. This implies that the utility of a given amount of gain is less than the disutility of an equal amount of loss; also, as the dollar gain increases, it becomes personally less valuable. A person characterized by such a utility function would prefer a small but certain monetary gain to a gamble whose EMV is greater but may involve a larger but unlikely gain, or a large and not unlikely loss.

The linear function in Figure 5.6 depicts the behavior of a person who is 'neutral" or "indifferent" to risk. For such a person every increment of say, $1000, has an associated constant increment of utility (slope of utility curve is positive and constant). That is, he values an additional dollar of income just as highly regardless of whether it is the first dollar of gain or the 100,000th dollar of gain. This type of individual would use the criterion of EMV in making a decision because by so doing he would also maximize expected utility.

In Figure 5.6 is also shown the utility function for a "risk preferer" or "risk seeker." Note that the slope of the utility curve increases as the dollar amount increases. This implies that the utility of a given amount of gain is greater than the disutility of a given amount of loss. This individual subjectively values each dollar of gain more highly. This type of person willingly accepts gambles that have a smaller EMV than an alternative payoff received with certainty. He will also take an "unfair" bet in the sense that he will choose an action whose EMV is negative. In the case of such an individual, the attractiveness of a possibly large payoff in the gamble tends to outweigh the fact that the probability of such a payoff may indeed be exceedingly small.

Most individuals have utility functions in which for small changes in money amounts, the slope does not change very much. Hence, over these ranges of money outcomes, the utility function may approximately be considered as linear, having a constant slope. However, in considering courses of action in which one of the consequences is very adverse or in which one of the payoffs is very favorably large, individuals can be expected to depart from the maximization of expected monetary value as a criterion to decision making. For many business decisions, where the monetary consequences may represent only a small fraction of the total assets of the business unit, the use of maximization of expected monetary payoff may constitute a reasonable approximation to the decision-making criterion of maximization of expected utility. In other words, in such cases the utility function may often be treated as approximately linear over the range of monetary payoffs considered.

Figure 5.7 shows another shape for an individual's utility function [suggested by Friedman and Savage (1948)]. It typifies some individuals, who appear to be risk takers for some decisions (such as gambling) and risk avoiders for other decisions (such as purchasing insurance). It shows, for example, why an individual might simultaneously (1) buy fire insurance to protect against a potentially large loss when the cost of the premium is greater than the expected monetary value of the loss, and (2) buy a lottery ticket that promises a potentially large gain when the cost of the ticket is greater than the expected monetary value of the lottery. In the first instance, the individual is comparing a small dollar outlay to the small probability of a very large loss; therefore, he is operating on the "conservative"

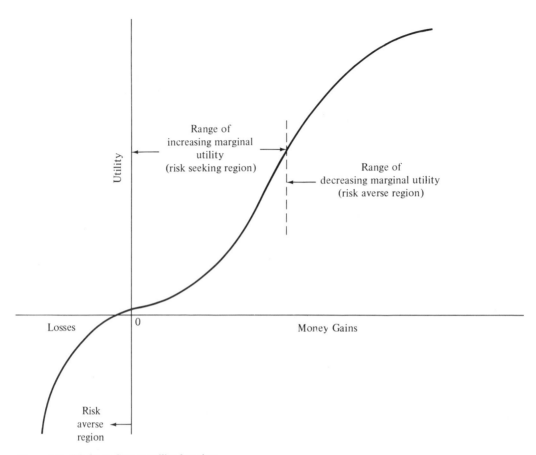

Figure 5.7. Friedman-Savage utility function.

portion of his utility curve to the left of his initial position in Figure 5.7. In the second instance, he is comparing a small dollar outlay to the small probability of a very large gain; therefore, he is operating mainly on the "gambler" portion of his utility curve to the right of his initial position.

5.5.2. Risk Premium

The risk premium is defined as the difference between the EMV and the cash or certainty equivalent of a gamble. The sign and magnitude of the risk premium reveals something about the individual's attitude toward risk. For two individuals presented with the same gamble, the one with the higher risk premium is the more risk-averse. For a given individual, the risk premium will generally not be the same at different parts of his utility function. In fact, many risk-averse utility functions have the property of decreasing risk aversion. In other words, the individual becomes less risk-averse as his money amount increases. Consider the following choices in the new product development problem:

Alternative A: Receive X for certain

Alternative B: Receive \$1,000,000 with probability $\frac{1}{2}$ and receive $-\$500,000$ with probability $\frac{1}{2}$.

Suppose the project manager says that $X = \$100,000$ makes him indifferent between the two alternatives. Then, as we have previously shown, $U(\$100,000) = 0.50$ and \$100,000 can be thought of as a "cash or certainty equivalent" for the gamble (alternative B). The risk premium would be

$$\begin{aligned}\text{risk premium} &= \text{EMV} - \text{certainty equivalent}\\ &= \$250,000 - \$100,000\\ &= \$150,000.\end{aligned}\tag{5.5.1}$$

It is the largest amount the project manager is willing to pay to avoid the risk in the gamble (B). Because of the risk in B, he is willing to pay a risk premium to avoid the gamble even though the gamble is perfectly fair in terms of money. A graphical interpretation of risk premium is shown in Figure 5.8.

The concept of a risk premium provides another way to investigate the general shape of a person's utility function. For a risk avoider, whose utility function is concave, as in Figure 5.8, the risk premium for a gamble (or for any situation in which the payoff is uncertain) is positive. For a risk taker, whose utility function is

Figure 5.8. Risk premiums for various utility functions.

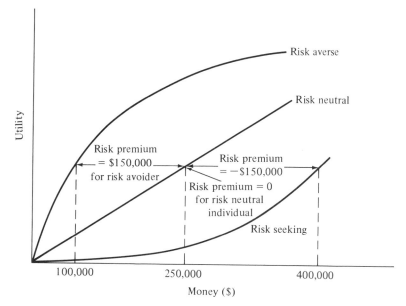

convex, as in Figure 5.6, the risk premium is negative (= $250,000 − 400,000 = − $150,000). The negative risk premium indicates that a project manager with such a utility function, instead of willing to pay a premium to avoid the risk in such a gamble, is willing to pay a premium (above and beyond the EMV) to be able to participate in the gamble. For a person whose utility function is linear, as also shown in Figure 5.6, the risk premium is always $0, since the cash equivalent of a gamble is always equal to the expected monetary payoff of the gamble. For a person with a utility function such as that in Figure 5.7, the risk premium is positive for some gambles, negative for other gambles, and zero for yet other gambles. For instance, for gambles involving large potential losses, the risk premium will generally be positive, whereas for gambles involving only small potential losses (and small or moderate potential gains), the risk premium is likely to be negative.

5.6. USING THE UTILITY FUNCTION

Since a utility function represents the subjective attitude of a decision maker to risk, his utility function should be used to make choices in decision problems under uncertainty. All one simply needs to do is to determine, for a given alternative, the utilities associated with the possible monetary outcomes, then compute an expected utility (EU), and choose the action that maximizes EU. To illustrate this application and to show the effect on the choice made of alternative shapes of utility functions, consider once again the new product development problem (Figure 5.1). The problem is set out in Table 5.4 using the three utility functions in Figure 5.6. The initial problem at the top is in terms of dollar payoffs, showing all three actions with the same EMV (i.e., $A_2 \sim B_2 \sim A_2B_2$, where "$\sim$" denotes indifference). When the same problem is solved with a linear utility function, we find the expected utility (EU) equal for all three actions. Thus, when the utility function is linear, maximizing EMV will also maximize EU. If we now solve the same problem with the risk-averse utility function, we find that A_2 provides the highest expected utility (i.e., $A_2 > A_2B_2 > B_2$, where "$>$" denotes preferred to). This is in line with our intuition: such an individual is "conservative" in the sense that in a risky situation he prefers the actions with the least risk, even though all have the same EMV (see Table 5.1). On the other hand, if we use the utility function associated with a "risk seeker" then B_2 provides the highest expected utility (i.e., $B_2 > A_2B_2 > A_2$). Such an individual is a "gambler" in the sense that he will choose the action with the greatest risk (B_2) even though all the alternatives have the same EMV. His utility function shows that he values very highly the small chance of a very large gain.

It should be stressed that there is nothing "irrational" in the behavior of either of these individuals. For example, if the "risk seeker" is offered two actions with the same two possible monetary outcomes, he will choose the action that has the

Table 5.4. Presentation of New Product Development Decision Problem with the Three Types of Utility Functions Shown in Figure 5.6

$P(\theta)$ $\quad \theta$ A	0.35 $A_2:S$ $B_2:S$	0.35 S F	0.15 F S	0.15 F F	EMV	Choice Preference
Initial Problem						
A_2	418.3	418.3	−60.0	−60.0	275	
B_2	650.0	−100.0	650.0	−100.0	275	$A_2 \sim B_2 \sim A_2B_2$
A_2B_2	483.0	211.3	483.0	−267.0	275	
					EU	
Risk Neutral						
A_2	0.60	0.60	0.30	0.30	0.51	
B_2	0.74	0.28	0.74	0.28	0.51	$A_2 \sim B_2 \sim A_2B_2$
A_2B_2	0.65	0.47	0.65	0.16	0.51	
Risk Avoider						
A_2	0.90	0.90	0.70	0.70	0.84	
B_2	0.95	0.67	0.95	0.67	0.81	$A_2 > A_2B_2 > B_2$
A_2B_2	0.92	0.83	0.92	0.49	0.82	
Risk Seeker						
A_2	0.20	0.20	0.05	0.05	0.155	
B_2	0.35	0.04	0.35	0.04	0.195	$B_2 > A_2B_2 > A_2$
A_2B_2	0.23	0.11	0.23	0.02	0.1565	

higher probability of the more favorable outcome. Hence, even a risk seeker prefers less risk to more risk given the same monetary outcomes.

Once we have obtained the utility function for a decision maker and also obtained the probabilities in a given decision situation, a certainty equivalent of a given action can be obtained directly from the utility function. In our new product development example, the expected utility of action A_2 for the risk-averse utility function was 0.844. Reading from the risk-averse utility function in Figure 5.6 we see that a utility of 0.844 corresponds to a monetary outcome of about $310,000. Hence, we say that the amount $310,000 is the certainty equivalent associated with taking action A_2. One could also ask the decision maker directly for a certainty equivalent of a given action and avoid all the manipulation we have done in this chapter. However, it is highly likely that a decision maker would have considerable difficulty in coming up with such a certainty equivalent, especially in complex decision problems; and would probably respond inconsistently over repeated trials.

The certainty equivalent can also be used in another way. Our procedure so far has called for obtaining probabilities of various events and a utility function as inputs to the decision-making process. We could forego this and come up with certainty equivalents directly. However, the real value of the approach used in this chapter is that once having obtained a utility function, we can apply our procedure to many different decision problems. Hence, in addition to fostering consistency through structure, the utility approach facilitates expediency and efficiency.

5.7. SUBJECTIVE PROBABILITY

Probability is the language of communication about uncertainty. One view of probability, which is fundamental to the decision analysis philosophy, is to view it as a degree of belief (or knowledge) about an event, and thus it is intimately tied to the person making the probability assignment. This interpretation of probability is the subjective interpretation as discussed in Chapter 2. Probability represents a state of information, and it is only natural that two persons can make different probability assignments to the same event, since they are likely to have different experiences and beliefs (everyone is entitled to his own opinion).

5.7.1. The Concept of Subjective Probability

Probability can be viewed as a number on a scale, or a yardstick, used to measure uncertainty. Consider the two events in the new product development problem: success of the betatron design, or its complement failure. If you were certain that the betatron design would be successful, you would assign a probability of 1 to this event [and a probability of zero to the probability of the betatron design failing; i.e., $p(B_2) = 1$ and $\underline{p(\bar{B}_2^c)} = 0$]. If you were sure the betatron design would fail, then $p(B_2) = 0$ and $p(\bar{B}_2^c) = 1$. If however, you were completely uncertain (i.e., totally ignorant) about the chances of the betatron design succeeding, then $p(B_2) = 0.5$ and $p(\bar{B}_2) = 0.5$. Thus, for the two events, the degree of uncertainty or knowledge about a given event ranges from 0.5 (completely uncertain) to 1.0 (completely certain). For three events the degree of uncertainty would range from $\frac{1}{3}$ (each of the three events is equally likely) to 1, and so forth. The concept of subjective probability is especially useful when assessing the likelihood of one-time events, such as a forthcoming presidential election or a sporting event. It not only applies to predicting future events, but also to assessing one's knowledge regarding historical or existing facts; for example, the likelihood of Italy being longer than California, the probability of the gross national product being greater than $500 billion in 1962, and so forth.

Two features of personal or subjective probability are (1) that it imposes the difficult responsibility to be honest with oneself, and (2) that it requires a coherent person to formulate opinions. It is extremely difficult to be honest with one's self. Scoring rules (reward functions) and other procedures, however, have been developed to motivate people to give honest probability assessments (Winkler, 1967b).

A coherent person is one who does not allow "book" to be made against him. He cannot be put into a position in which he is always paying no matter what happens; that is, if a person is offered a sequence of bets, he will not accept all of them, which would leave him with a negative net. Of course, people make mistakes; but if a mistake is pointed out to a coherent person, he will correct it. Savage has shown that if a person is coherent (consistent), his probability function will obey the fundamental postulates of probability (Chapter 2); that is, the probability that he associates with each event is zero or positive, the probability of the entire sample space is equal to 1 (i.e., the probability of all mutually exclusive and collectively exhaustive events sum to 1), and that if two events are disjoint (i.e., mutually exclusive), the probability of either of the events occurring is equal to the sum of their probabilities.

5.7.2. Measuring Subjective Probabilities

How can subjective probabilities be measured? There are many ways in which this can be done. The reader is referred to Winkler (1967a) and Huber (1974) and the references cited therein for the many ways in which subjective probabilities can be measured.

Broadly speaking, there are two basic ways in which subjective probabilities can be measured. One way is by direct questioning; that is, ask the decision maker for a probability associated with the event in question. The second way is indirect and determined from the preferred choices revealed by the decision maker when confronted with two bets. One bet is based on a reference process such as a probability wheel. This is a disk with two sectors, one shaded and the other unshaded. A pointer is spun in the center of the disk and finally lands in either the shaded or unshaded sector (see Figure 5.9). A simple twist changes the relative

Figure 5.9. A probability (Borel) wheel.

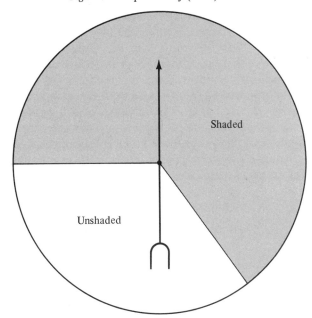

areas of the two sectors and thereby also the probabilities for the pointer landing in the two sectors.

The probability wheel can be used in two ways. The decision maker can be asked to bet on either of two comparable bets: (1) a fixed event (e.g., in the new product development problem a bet that "the conventional design will be successful"), or (2) landing in the shaded sector. The proportion of the shaded area to the total area in the wheel is then varied until the decision maker becomes indifferent between betting on the event in question (conventional design successful) or on the pointer falling in the shaded area. When indifference has been obtained, the proportion of the shaded area to the total area in the wheel is assigned as the probability of the event.

As an example, consider the question of assigning a probability to the event that the conventional design in the new product development problem will be successful. We first consider the following two comparable bets: [*Note:* The value of the bets in terms of winning or losing is immaterial as long as they are meaningful and as long as they are comparable (the same) for bets 1 and 2]:

Bet 1 If the conventional design is successful you personally win, say, $1000; otherwise, you lose, say, $1000.

Bet 2 If I spin the pointer on the probability wheel and it falls in the shaded region specified you win $1000; otherwise, you lose $1000.

QUESTION. Which bet do you choose; bet 1 or bet 2? If the decision maker prefers bet 2, he is implying that the probability of falling in the shaded region is greater than the probability of the conventional design being successful since the two bets have identical payoffs (i.e., the bets are comparable). We thus reduce the shaded region of the wheel and ask the same question. If, now, bet 1 is preferred to bet 2, that shows that the probability of the conventional design being successful is greater than the probability of the pointer falling in the shaded region. We then increase the proportion of the wheel's shaded region and ask the decision maker to choose between bets 1 and 2. Eventually, he will be indifferent between the two bets, which implies that the probability of the pointer falling in the shaded region of the wheel (i.e., the proportion of the total area that is shaded) is equal to the decision maker's subjective probability of a successful conventional design occurring. Mathematically, we have the following:

Bet 1: $p(A_2) \cdot (\$1000) + [1 - p(A)](-\$1000)$

Bet 2: $p(S) \cdot (\$1000) + [1 - p(S)](-\$1000),$

where

$$p(A_2) = \text{probability of the conventional design being successful}$$
$$p(S) = \text{probability of the pointer falling in the shaded region.}$$

Setting the two functions equal to each other, we get

$$p(A_2)(1000) + [1 - p(A_2)](-1000) \gtreqless p(S)(1000) + [1 - p(S)](-1000)$$
$$(1000)[p(A_2) - p(S)] \gtreqless (-1000)[(1 - p(S)) - (1 - p(A_2))]$$
$$(1000)[(A_2) - p(S)] \gtreqless (-1000)[p(A_2) - p(S)]$$
$$p(A_2) - p(S) \gtreqless p(S) - p(A_2)$$
$$p(A_2) \gtreqless p(S)$$

Thus,

    if $p(A_2) > p(S)$,   bet on the conventional design (bet 1)

    if $p(A_2) < p(S)$,   bet on the wheel (bet 2)

    if $p(A_2) = p(S)$,   indifferent.

If the decision maker is assessing the probability distribution of a random variable rather than two events (such as success/failure of the conventional design), then the method of successive subdivisions can be used on the probability wheel as follows. An interval is split into two (or more) parts and the decision maker is asked to choose a part to bet on. The dividing point(s) is (are) changed until indifference is reached, and the subintervals are then assigned equal probabilities. Starting from an interval covering all possible outcomes, splitting into two parts will first give the median, then the quartiles, and so on. The most common procedure for obtaining a subjective probability distribution of an uncertain quantity is by direct assessment. There are many such direct assessment procedures (Huber, 1975; Winkler, 1967a). One such method is the fractile method for assessing a cumulative distribution function. This is discussed and applied in case 5.2. Estimates made as in PERT (Chapter 18) can also be used to assess probability distributions.

Another procedure for finding subjective probabilities is to ask the decision maker how much he would pay to have a prize of value V if the state of nature θ_1 would occur. For example, in the new product development problem the decision maker could be asked how much he would pay for a chance at $1000 if θ_1 would occur, that is, if the conventional design was successful. Various prices that the decision maker could pay are shown in Table 5.5, along with the odds that are implied by the prices and the implied subjective probabilities of the event. Thus, if a decision maker says he would pay $500 for a $1000 return should θ_1 occur, he is telling us that the odds for θ_1 occurring is $1:1$. The other odds and probabilities of Table 5.5 are associated with the prices in a similar fashion.

Given the probability of an event $p(\theta)$, we can say that the odds for θ are a to b if and only if

$$p(\theta) = \frac{a}{a + b}. \tag{5.7.1}$$

If the odds for θ are a to b, then the odds against θ are b to a. For example, if the

Table 5.5. Relationship Among Prices, Odds, and Subjective Probabilities

Price for $1000 Return If θ_1 Occurs	Subjective Probability	Odds for Event
0.500	$\frac{1}{2}$	1:1
0.667	$\frac{2}{3}$	2:1
0.750	$\frac{3}{4}$	3:1
0.375	$\frac{3}{8}$	3:5
0.330	$\frac{1}{3}$	1:2
0.706	$\frac{12}{17}$	12:5

probability of θ is 0.7, then

$$p(\theta) = \frac{7}{10} = \frac{7}{7+3}$$

and the odds for θ are 7 to 3, and against θ are 3 to 7.

Our discussion of odds and their relationship to subjective probability would apply equally as well to empirical or to logical probabilities; that is, the same interpretation in terms of odds can be given to any type of probability. In fact, one could go one step further and say that if the probability of event θ_1 is $p(\theta_1)$, one should pay no more than $p(\theta_1) \times 1000$ dollars for a chance at a $1000 return in the event that θ_1 occurs. If you agree with the last statement, we see no reason why you should not agree when the statement is turned around to read. "The probability of an event θ_1 is the price you would be willing to pay for a $1000 return to you in the event that θ_1 occurs." The difference among empirical, logical, and subjective probabilities comes down to a mere difference of interpretation as to the source of the probability statement. This distinction is an important philosophical point; but when it comes to solving decision makers' problems, the recognition of the use of the probability calculus is more important than the origin of the probability statement. The origin of the probability is unimportant because any prior probability of an event can be revised in the face of new evidence and experience via Bayes' Theorem as shown in Chapter 2.

5.8. AXIOMS OF RATIONAL DECISION MAKING

The expected utility norm prescribes how people should choose among alternative courses of action. It is based on fundamental principles or axioms that reasonable people want to obey. These axioms, which empirical studies show people do obey or want to obey, establish the existence of a "subjective probability" distribution on the events and a "utility function" on the consequences with the following property: "an action is preferred to another action if and only if (*iff*) it has a higher expected utility." There are several axiomatic systems of expected utility theory. The one we shall specify essentially follows that of Marschak (1968). The axioms are stated as follows: (1) complete ordering and transitivity, (2) admissibility, (3) irrelevance of identical outcomes, (4) independence of beliefs and tastes, (5) continuity, and (6) substitution. Let us consider each in turn.

5.8.1. Complete Ordering and Transitivity

This first axiom is composed of two parts, *comparability* and *transitivity*. This axiom states that individuals can order their preferences and this ordering is transitive. Given two alternatives, say *a* and *b*, a reasonable man can decide whether he prefers *a* to *b* or *b* to *a* or is indifferent. That is, he can *compare* alternatives and thus choose among them. He cannot, for example, refuse to compare a Shakespearean piece of literature with a Mozart composition. Alternatives should also be *transitive*. If *a* is preferred to *b* and *b* is preferred to *c*, then *a* is preferred to *c*. Also, if *a* is indifferent to *b* and *b* is indifferent to *c*, then *a* is indifferent to *c*, and so forth. In other words, circular (intransitive) judgments should not be made. For example, if a person dining out says he prefers fish to steak, and steak to chicken, he should prefer fish to chicken. It is possible, where the degree of preference is small and there are many alternatives, for a person to give preferences of pairs that are intransitive. This means that on close decisions an individual may be inconsistent. He should, however, be able to eliminate his intransitivities when reflecting upon his decisions.

5.8.2. Admissibility

This axiom eliminates from consideration those actions which are dominated. An action's result (outcome) depends, in general, not only on the action but also on the event that occurs, which is not under the decision maker's control. Action *a* is said to dominate action *b* (i.e., *b* is inadmissible) if the outcomes of *a* are sometimes (i.e., when some events take place) better than the results of *b* and are never worse. Consider for example, the following actions:

Action \ Event	θ_1	θ_2
a	$600	$1000
b	590	1000

The admissibility postulate would say that *a* is preferred to *b*. Action *b* is inadmissible or dominated by *a*, since the outcomes of taking action *a* for any event that may occur is at least as good as they are for *b*.

5.8.3. *Irrevelance of Identical Outcomes*

This axiom asserts that only outcomes that help to distinguish among alternatives should be considered when making a choice. For example, consider the matrix of outcomes measured in percent of return on a firm's investment:

Action \ Event	θ_1	θ_2	θ_3
a	20	-300	200
b	20	10	10
c	-300	-300	200
d	-300	10	10

Interpret a and b as the firm's investing in the development of alternative products. The outcomes of these actions, of course, depend on the mutually exclusive events (say, business conditions) θ_1, θ_2, and θ_3. Suppose that the firm prefers a to b. This preference cannot be due to any difference in the outcomes if the event θ_1 happens, for these outcomes are identically 20. Therefore, the firm's preference of a to b must be due to its preferring the gamble "-300 if θ_2, 200 if θ_3" to the return of 10 with certainty. But then the firm should also prefer c to d, for again, if θ_1 happens, the outcome (-300) is not affected by the firm's choice. Its preference as between c and d must depend on its preference as between the gamble "-300 if θ_2, 200, if θ_3" and the certainty of 10, just as in the previous case. By the same reasoning, if the firm is indifferent between a and b, it should be indifferent between c and d.

5.8.4. *Independence of Beliefs and Tastes*

If a decision maker's choice among actions reveals that, in his present information state, he feels that one event is more probable than another, then his subsequent choice of actions must be consistent with this view, regardless of the values placed on the outcomes. That is, his beliefs (subjective probabilities) should be independent of (i.e., not interact with) his tastes (values, utilities). He should be subject to neither wishful thinking nor to persecution mania. To illustrate this postulate, consider the following example.

Action \ Event	Fair Coin Falls Heads Up	Fair Coin Falls Tails Up
a	$1000	-500

Event Action	Inflation Rate This Year < 10%	Inflation Rate This Year > 10%
b	$1000	−$500

Suppose that when asked to choose between *a* and *b*, you choose *b*. This postulate then asserts that you should choose, for example, *d* over *c*, where actions *c* and *d* are given by

Event Action	Fair Coin Falls Heads Up	Fair Coin Falls Tails Up
c	$100	−$1000

Event Action	Inflation Rate This Year < 10%	Inflation Rate This Year > 10%
d	$100	−$1000

This relationship will hold for all other pairs of actions having a similar form. We then say that you at least prefer to bet that inflation will be ≤ 10% is more probable than a fair coin falling heads up. This is how probability is defined here. It is implicit in a choice among actions. Since the particular payoffs do not matter, we say that probabilities are independent of payoffs or, alternatively, that beliefs are independent of tastes. Without the postulate, it would be impossible to compare probabilities of events without reference to rewards. We thus postulate that whether the associated consequences are favorable or unfavorable, or have a large or small monetary value (if any), the decision maker's subjective ranking of "probabilities" of the events themselves should remain constant. The justification for this is that our true beliefs concerning some event should depend only on the event involved.

We commonly characterize individuals who do exhibit dependence between beliefs and tastes as being subject to either "wishful thinking" or to a "persecution complex." Those who evaluate an event as more likely when they get a higher-valued associated consequence in case the event happened are called "wishful thinkers." Those who behave in an opposite manner, that is, think an event is more likely if it yields a lower-valued consequence are said to suffer from a "persecution complex." A wishful thinker would believe that a plane is less likely to crash if he is a passenger in it, whereas a person with a persecution complex would believe that it would be more likely to crash if he was in it. [Note that "optimist" and pessimist" are not used here. These terms shall refer to bias in the estimation of the probabilities without necessarily a dependence on the consequences involved.] Note that this postulate, by asserting the independence of beliefs and tastes, has implicitly established the existence of beliefs defined in a particular way; that is, by a choice among actions. With the postulate adjoined to those already defined, we can construct a subjective (ordinal) probability measure.

5.8.5. Continuity

Consider three prizes, *a*, *b*, and *c*, where *a* is preferred to *b* and *b* is preferred to *c*. The continuity axiom asserts that there must exist a probability *p* such that you are indifferent to receiving prize *c* for certain or a lottery where there is a *p* chance of winning *a* and a $(1 - p)$ chance of winning *c*. For example, let $a = \$1000$, $b = \$300$, and $c = \$0$. We first make up a gamble involving *a* with probability *p* and *c* with probability $(1 - p)$. We then ask, what is the value of *p* that will make you indifferent to the lottery and *b* for certain

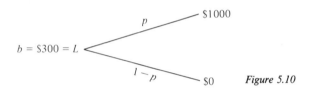

Figure 5.10

If you are willing and able to state some value of *p* (say, 0.4), then the continuity assumption is satisfied; *b* would, of course, be the *certainty equivalent* of the lottery (as we have previously discussed).

This axiom thus asserts that there is some probability of winning at which you will be indifferent between (1) gambling for a more preferable item with some risk of getting a less desired item, and (2) simply keeping what you have. This axiom was the basis for the NM approach involving a most preferred ($1000 gain) and a least preferred ($0 gain) payoff, whereby a cash equivalent function was determined.

5.8.6. Substitution

This axiom states that if you are truly indifferent between a particular gamble and a sure prize (or between two gambles), you should be willing to accept the substitution of one for the other as a payoff. For example, suppose that you were indifferent between a 50–50 chance of winning $1000 and zero dollars, and $300 for certain. Then, by the substitution axiom, we can replace the gamble with $300, since the utilities of the lottery and the sure $300 are equal. This axiom was the basis for the substitution of the various standard gambles for the certain payoffs in the payoff table.

Conformance to these six axioms implies the following less obvious rule: "The consistent man behaves as if he (1) assigns personal probabilities to events, (2) assigns numerical (cardinal) utilities to the results or outcomes of his actions, and (3) chooses the action with the highest expected utility." Thus, these six behavioral axioms provide the cornerstone of decision theory. Most of us find them quite palatable and easy to accept as principles by which reasonable people should abide. Most of us also recognize, however, that we frequently fail to abide by these principles, just as we fail to employ the decision-making procedure they imply in resolving our own problems of choice—because, perhaps, we are not quite as reasonable as we like to think we are.

5.9. SUMMARY

Decision theory deals with the science of decision making. Such a theory must consider the beliefs and tastes of the individual decision maker as inputs into the decision-making process. This provides a basis for showing why two reasonable people, when confronted with the same decision situation, will frequently make different decisions. Although we may not approve of the choice another person makes, his choice may be just as optimal as ours. For his choices, too, are governed by subjective factors, which probably are not the same as ours.

In this chapter we have developed techniques for measuring a person's tastes or values by means of a utility function. This also provided a measure of an individual's risk attitude. We also showed how a person's beliefs, in terms of subjective probabilities, can be measured implicitly from his choice among comparable bets. The existence of utilities and subjective probabilities derive from some fundamental behavioral assumptions or axioms that reasonable people want to obey. If these axioms are followed, then and only then should a decision maker choose his optimal action based on maximization of expected utility (and not necessarily EMV).

REFERENCES   DAVIDSON, D., P. SUPPES, and S. SIEGEL. *Decision Making: An Experimental Approach*. Stanford, Calif.: Stanford University Press, 1957.

FRIEDMAN, M., and L. J. SAVAGE. "The Utility Analysis of Choices Involving Risk." *Journal of Political Economy*, August 1948.

HALTER, A. N. and G. W. DEAN. *Decisions Under Uncertainty*. Cincinnati, Ohio: South-Western Publishing Co., 1971.

HUBER, G. P. "Methods for Quantifying Subjective Probabilities and Multi-Attribute Utilities." *Decision Sciences*, 5(3), 1974, 430–458.

MARSCHAK, J. "Decision Making: Economic Aspects." *International Encyclopedia of the Social Sciences*, **4**, 1968, 42–55.

RAIFFA, H. *Decision Analysis*. Reading, Mass.: Addison-Wesley Publishing Co., Inc., 1968.

SAVAGE, L. J. *The Foundations of Statistics*. New York: John Wiley & Sons, Inc., 1954.

SWALM, R. O. "Utility Theory—Insights into Risk Taking." *Harvard Business Review*, November–December 1966.

VON NEUMANN, J., and O. MORGENSTERN. *Theory of Games and Economic Behavior*. Princeton, N.J.: Princeton University Press, 1944.

WINKLER, R. L. "The Assessment of Prior Distributions in Bayesian Analysis." *Journal of the American Statistical Association*, **62**, 1967, 776–800. (a)

WINKLER, R. L. "The Quantification of Judgment: Some Methodological Suggestions." *Journal of the American Statistical Association*, **62**, 1967, 1105–1120. (b)

KEY CONCEPTS

Risk
Utility
Measuring utility functions
  direct measurement
  von Neumann-Morgenstern (NM)
  method
  modified NM method
Characteristics of utility
  functions
  risk avoider
  risk neutral
  risk seeker
Friedman-Savage utility
  function
Risk premium

Subjective probability and
  subjective probability
  distribution
  direct measurement
  indirect measurement
  fractile assessments
Axioms of decision theory
  complete ordering and
  transitivity
  admissibility
  irrelevance of identical
  outcomes
  independence of beliefs and tastes
  continuity
  substitution

REVIEW QUESTIONS

5.1. State and discuss the arguments for and against the use of maximizing expected monetary value as a choice criterion.

5.2. Define risk in your own terms. How does it relate to the concepts of risk discussed in this chapter?

5.3. Comment on the following statement: "The minimization of uncertainty is of primary consideration in managerial decision making. Hence, there is a relationship between managerial success and the successful minimization of uncertainty." What practical steps do managers take to minimize uncertainty?

5.4. What is the value of deriving a decision maker's utility function? How can his utility function be advantageously used?

5.5. Describe the various ways discussed in this chapter in which an individual's utility function can be derived. Which method do you prefer and why?

5.6. Define and illustrate the following two notions: (1) certainty equivalent and (2) risk premium.

5.7. Sketch utility functions for a person who is risk-averse, risk-seeking, risk-neutral, and a person who simultaneously buys insurance while engaging in the Irish sweepstakes.

5.8. State and illustrate the axioms of decision theory. Do you think people obey or want to obey these axioms when making decisions?

ANSWERS TO REVIEW QUESTIONS **5.1.** The primary argument against maximizing EMV as a choice criterion is that EMV is a summary statistic used to describe a distribution of possible outcomes. As such, it obscures and conceals the individual outcomes that may occur. One cannot know the maximum loss that one might suffer, the maximum gain that might be obtained, or their respective probabilities. In cases where there is the possibility of an intolerably adverse loss, this could be disastrous. Conversion of outcomes into a utility function and expected utility maximization criterion overcomes this objection by incorporating the decision maker's values and risk attitude, which is neglected with EMV maximization.

The major argument advanced in favor of maximizing EMV is that in the long run, payoffs to persons using this criterion will be higher than those to persons using any other criterion. However, this assumes that there will be a long run (repeated choice situations) and that the person will survive the short run ups and downs.

5.2. Risk should probably consist of two components:

1. The probability that something unfavorable will occur.
2. The seriousness of the unfavorable occurrence.

The above definition seems to be most closely related to definition (3) in the text, that is, risk is the probable loss. However, the probable loss is a summary statistic for part of a distribution, and it might be better to view the distribution itself in order to make a subjective determination of risk. No really clearcut definition of risk seems to exist.

5.3. Minimization of uncertainty, in and of itself, would seem to be a primary goal of management, as long as the alternative situation is tolerable to the manager. For example, consider a division manager who knows that he will be fired if his division does not show a profit. The only way he sees to achieve a profit is to gamble on the sale of a new item which, if it succeeds, will produce a profit but if it fails, will reduce profits even more. Because the alternative to increased uncertainty is intolerable, the manager decides to gamble.

Usually, however, the manager will act to reduce uncertainty whenever he can. This will probably be done by accepting a smaller sure payoff rather than by gambling on the prospect of a very large payoff with also a chance of a large loss. This implies that a decision maker's utility function is risk-averse.

5.4. The value of deriving a decision maker's utility function is that:

1. It serves as a means of predicting decisions under uncertainty.
2. It serves as a means of improving choice consistency in uncertain situations.
3. It serves as an aid toward making "better" decisions under conditions of uncertainty
4. It helps in understanding decision-making behavior in situations involving risk and uncertainty—e.g., the decision maker's attitude to risk.

To use a utility function, determine, for a given alternative, the utilities associated with the possible monetary outcomes, compute the expected utility, and choose the action which maximizes expected utility.

5.5. The four described approaches for measuring utility are:

1. *Direct measurement.* The decision maker is simply asked how much of something would be required to give him twice as much satisfaction or happiness as some reference amount. Further questions for half as much, three times as much, and so on, enable the plotting of a utility or, more realistically, a value scale.
2. *von Neumann–Morgenstern method.* The first step is to determine two monetary outcomes as reference points and assign arbitrary utilities to them. The decision makers are then offered a series of lotteries in which they are asked what probability would make them indifferent to the lottery and a cash equivalent amount. If the two values involved in the lottery have known utilities (our reference points), the utility of the cash equivalent can easily be calculated.
3. *Modified von Neumann–Morgenstern method.* Similar to (2), except that instead of asking for probabilities which would make lotteries and sure amounts of cash equivalent, the decision maker is presented with a lottery with a 0.5 chance of winning some amount and a 0.5 chance of losing some amount. The person is then asked for an amount which would make him or her indifferent to taking the lottery or taking the sure cash amount. Again, if the utilities of the lottery amounts are known (reference points), the utility of the cash equivalent can be easily calculated.
4. *Ramsey method.*

5.6. A certainty equivalent for a lottery is an amount of money (or any other commodity or service) which would make a decision maker indifferent to accepting the gamble implied by the lottery to the amount of money, commodity, or service. The risk premium of a lottery is the difference between the expected monetary value of the lottery and the certainty equivalent.

5.7. The utility functions are:

Risk-averse: concave utility function
Risk-seeking: convex utility function
Risk-neutral: linear utility function
Insurance and Irish sweepstakes buyer: Friedman-Savage utility-function; concave and convex in various regions.

5.8. Axioms of decision theory:

1. *Comparability and transitivity.* States that people can compare alternatives and order them transitively. For example if a group of people prefer baseball to football, and also football to hockey, they should also prefer baseball to hockey.
2. *Admissibility.* If, for every state of nature that could occur action a results in at least as high a payoff as action b, then action a should be preferred. For example:

		STATE OF NATURE OR EVENT		
		θ_1	θ_2	θ_3
Action	a	6	14	10
	b	2	14	9

In the table above, action a should be preferred.

3. *Irrelevance of identical outcomes.* Only outcomes which distinguish between alternatives should be considered when making a choice. To illustrate, consider the following table

			EVENT		
		θ_1	θ_2	θ_3	θ_4
Action	a	− 100	50	30	120
	b	− 100	25	40	120

Here, only θ_2 and θ_3 should be considered in deciding between actions a and b.

4. *Independence of beliefs and tastes.* This states that a person's like or dislike of a particular outcome should not influence his estimate of the probability of that event occurring, and vice versa.
5. *Continuity.* If a is preferred to b and b is preferred to c, then there exists some probability p such that a person is indifferent to receiving b for certain or a lottery where there is a p chance of winning a and a $(1 - p)$ chance of winning c.
6. *Substitution.* If one is truly indifferent between a particular gamble and a sure prize (or between 2 gambles), one should be willing to accept the substitution of one for the other as payoff.

EXERCISES **5.1.** Mr. Berry has a utility index of 0.5 for a loss of $1000, and 1.0 for a profit of $3000. He claims that he is indifferent between $300 and a 0.5 chance of a $1000 loss and a 0.4 chance of $3000 profit. What is his certainty equivalent? What is his utility for $300? Calculate Mr. Berry's EMV. Is Mr. Berry risk-prone, risk-neutral, or risk-averse?

5.2. Mr. Comiskey has a utility value for $-\$100$ of 0.5. His utility value for $200 is 0.7. He claims that he is indifferent between $200 for certain and a 50–50 gamble at winning $2000 or losing $100, respectively. What is his utility for $2000?

5.3. Mr. King has the following utilities (U) for various sums of money (M):

M	U
$1000	10
$500	4
$0	1

What probabilites should be assigned to $1000 and $0 that would make him indifferent between a gamble involving these outcomes and $500 for certain?

5.4. Consider three farm managers who have to choose between purchasing 500, 600, or 800 store cattle for paddock fattening. The profit from fattening will depend on whether the grazing season is good, fair, or poor. The managers' personal strengths of conviction about these events are that here is a 0.4 chance of a good season, a 0.2 chance of a fair season, and a 0.4 chance of a poor season. The total net profits on the deal in thousands of dollars are shown in the payoff table:

Action	Event	PROBABILITIES, $P(\theta)$		
		0.4: Good	0.2: Fair	0.4: Poor
A_1: buy 500		20	10	6
A_2: buy 600		25	12	0
A_3: buy 800		34	16	−11

Assume that the farm managers' utilities (U) for the consequences are:

$	U_1	U_2	U_3
34,000	58.14	26.86	69
25,000	45.00	17.50	51
20,000	37.00	13.00	41
16,000	30.24	9.76	33
12,000	23.16	6.84	25
10,000	19.50	5.50	21
6,000	11.94	3.06	13
0	0	0.40	0
−11,000	−30.58	−11.36	−21

(a) For each manager, compute the expected utility for each action and choose the optimal action. Is the managers' utility function risk-averse, risk-neutral, or risk-prone?

(b) Compute the EMV of each action and choose the optimal action based on this criterion.

(c) Compare the optimal choices using the various criteria in parts (a) and (b) and discuss the results.

5.5. A. Whinston has the following utility function for money:

U ($)	$
− 800	− 10,000
−2	− 200
−1	− 100
0	0
250	10,000

He is currently faced with the following two decision problems: (1) Should he pay a $100 premium to insure against a potential $10,000 fire loss when he knows that the insurance company has calculated the chance of fire on his type of property to be 1 in 200? (2) Should he invest $100 in an oil-drilling venture where the geologist has said that there is only 1 chance in 200 of striking oil with the expectation of a $10,000 profit and a 199-out-of-200 chance of losing the $100 investment? Comment on the decisions made in relation to those that would have been made if Mr. Whinston used the criterion of maximizing EMV. What type of utility function does Whinston have?

5.6. The following matrix gives the payoffs resulting from your accepting six bets $(b_1, \ldots, b_6)$. The events H and T are, respectively: "A tossed fair coin will fall *heads* up" and " . . . *tails* up."

	H	T	Rank	Cash Equivalents
b_1	$1500	$ − 500	_____	_____
b_2	500	500	_____	_____
b_3	0	1000	_____	_____
b_4	500	0	_____	_____
b_5	6000	− 5000	_____	_____
b_6	510	490	_____	_____

(a) Rank each of the six bets in order of preference.

(b) Assign cash equivalents to each bet.

(c) Compute the mean and variance of each bet.

(d) Plot your rankings of each bet as a function of its variance on a graph.

(e) Derive your utility function based on your cash equivalents for the six bets and plot your utility function.

(f) Discuss the results.

5.7. W. Lewellen, a married man with three children, has a steady job that pays him about $15,000 per year. He can easily afford the necessities of life, but few of the luxuries. Mr. W's father, who died recently, carried a $6000 life insurance policy. Mr. W. would like to invest this money in stocks. He is well aware of the secure "blue-chip" stocks and bonds that would pay approximately 6% on his investment. On the other hand, Mr. W has heard that the stocks of a relatively unknown Company X might double their present value if a new product currently in production is favorably received by the buying public. However, if the product is unfavorably received, the stocks would decline in value.

Imagine that you are advising Mr. Lewellen. Listed below are several probabilities or odds that Company X stocks will double their value.

(a) Please check the lowest probability that you would consider acceptable for Mr. W to invest in Company X stocks.

_____ Place a check here if you think Mr. Lewellen should not invest in Company X stocks no matter what the probabilities.

_____ The chances are 9 in 10 that the stocks will double their value.

_____ The chances are 7 in 10 that the stocks will double their value.

_____ The chances are 3 in 10 that the stocks will double their value.

_____ The chances are 1 in 10 that the stocks will double their value.

(b) Discuss this decision problem in terms of utilities. Show that the higher the probability marked, the more risk-averse the decision.†

5.8. In this chapter, we have presented two methods (NM and Modified NM) for assessing a single attribute utility function under uncertainty, based on the *continuity postulate*—i.e.,

$$U(x_2) = pU(x_1) + (1 - p)U(x_3).$$

Using the continuity postulate, suggest alternate procedures for determining an individual's utility function. How cognitively meaningful are these alternative procedures relative to the NM and Modified NM methods?

5.9. Using one of the standard reference devices mentioned in the chapter (e.g., Borel Wheel, spinner) assess your uncertainty about the following events:
(a) A woman will become President of the United States by the year 1992.
(b) Life will be discovered somewhere in space other than earth by the year 2000.
(c) A major world wide depression will occur within the next 10 years.

5.10. You have been asked to forecast sales for next year on one of your company's new products. Your best prediction of sales is 10,000 units. The marketing manager asks what you can say about the degree of uncertainty in your forecast. To answer this, you examine your past forecasting performance

---

†This is one of 12 questions taken from N. Kogan and M. A. Wallach, *Risk Taking: A Study in Cognition and Personality* (New York: Holt, Rinehart and Winston, Inc., 1964).

and believe that:

(a) Sales will turn out to be greater than your forecast about as often as it would turn out to be less.

(b) About half the time, sales would be expected to be between 30% below and 20% above your forecast. When sales fall outside this range, they are equally likely to fall above it as below it.

(c) Only about once in 100 times would sales be expected to be less than half your forecast, and on only about once in 100 times would sales be expected to be more than three times your forecast.

Construct a cumulative distribution function (CDF) representing your degree of uncertainty in your forecast. How accurate would you say your forecast is?

CASE 5.1   Illustrative Case Study
Involving Utility Assessment

GRADES IN   Using the NM method, derive your utility function for grades by answering
MANAGEMENT   the following set of questions. Suppose that you had the following choice to
SCIENCE   make in determining your grade for a course in management science. You can
take a C for certain or pick your grade from a bowl that contains 20 D's and
20 B's. Would you take the C for certain or pick from the bowl?

Assignment. In each of the following situations, indicate your choice (check the alternative you prefer):

Take C for certain	Pick from a bowl of
_____	___ 36 D's and 4 B's
_____	___ 32 D's and 8 B's
_____	___ 28 D's and 12 B's
_____	___ 24 D's and 16 B's
_____	___ 20 D's and 20 B's
_____	___ 16 D's and 24 B's
_____	___ 12 D's and 28 B's
_____	___ 8 D's and 32 B's
_____	___ 4 D's and 36 B's

Take B for Certain	Pick from a bowl of
_____	___ 36 C's and 4 A's
_____	___ 32 C's and 8 A's
_____	___ 28 C's and 12 A's
_____	___ 24 C's and 16 A's
_____	___ 20 C's and 20 A's
_____	___ 16 C's and 24 A's
_____	___ 12 C's and 28 A's
_____	___ 8 C's and 32 A's
_____	___ 4 C's and 36 A's

Take C for certain	Pick from a bowl of
_____	___ 36 D's and 4 A's
_____	___ 32 D's and 8 A's
_____	___ 28 D's and 12 A's
_____	___ 24 D's and 16 A's
_____	___ 20 D's and 20 A's
_____	___ 16 D's and 24 A's
_____	___ 12 D's and 28 A's
_____	___ 8 D's and 32 A's
_____	___ 4 D's and 36 A's

CASE 5.2   Illustrative Case Study Involving the Assessment
of Probability Distributions of Uncertain Quantities

EXERCISE IN
SUBJECTIVE
FORECASTING

Introduction to Fractiles. Many of our activities as executive decision makers and in our personal lives require that we deal with uncertainty, with unknown or uncertain things. We estimate about next year's sales level when making advertising commitments or ordering raw materials, we guess about the weather when planning a weekend or vacation trip, and so on. And we often find ourselves expressing our uncertainty by phrases such as "probable," "possible, but unlikely," and "almost certain." The problem with expressions of that sort is that they lack precision—they mean different things to different people or to the same person in different circumstances. One way to get around this ambiguity is to assign *numbers* to correspond to your feelings of uncertainty. A familiar device is the use of betting odds to describe your degree of conviction about the occurrence of a particular outcome. Such betting odds can be expressed as, or easily converted to, the standard mathematical probabilities used by statisticians and others in the formal analysis of problems involving uncertainty.

In thinking about the uncertain quantities (u.q.'s) in this assessment exercise, you will be given a probability and asked to decide what is the corresponding value of the u.q., rather than the more common method of starting with a value of the u.q. and estimating its probability. For example, the first u.q. is, "number of your classmates who prefer wine to beer." *Rather than* being asked a question like

1. What are the chances (or "what is the probability . . . ") that the number preferring wine is 9 or less?
   Ans.: Probability is _____ .

You will be given a probability, say 0.25 (which is the same as 25%, or 1 chance in 4), and asked to fill in the blank in this statement:

2. I think there is a 0.25 probability that _____ or fewer of my classmates prefer wine.

This is the number of classmates preferring wine that, according to your estimate, corresponds to a probability of 0.25. The number you fill in the blank is called your "0.25 fractile" for this u.q.

Another assessment to make will be:

3. I think there is a 0.50 probability that _____ or fewer of my classmates prefer wine.

(The 0.50 probability is the same as the "50–50" or "even" betting odds, or 1 chance out of 2.) Your answer here is your "0.50 fractile."

Suppose, when you selected a number to be the 0.25 fractile, you wrote "19" in the blank in statement 2. The *actual* number preferring wine if we take a poll will be either (a) less than or equal to your choice, or (b) larger than your choice. You have said that the probability it is "less than or equal to 19" was 0.25. The total probability of the two outcomes must equal 1.00. Therefore, if the "less than or equal to" probability is 0.25, the "larger than" probability must be 0.75 (i.e., 1.00 − 0.25). When you select a number, say 28, to be the 0.50 fractile in statement 3, you are saying that you think there is a 0.50 probability that the number of classmates preferring wine will be less than or equal to this value, "28." And that implies (by the "total = 1.00" rule) that the probability the actual number turns out to be larger than the 0.50 fractile is also 0.50. Consequently, in your opinion, it is just as likely for the actual value to be larger than the 0.50 fractile as it is to be less than or equal to this number. Check this conclusion—if the number you filled in statement 3 is "28," then you should feel that it is just as likely that the number of classmates preferring wine is less than or equal to 28 as it is that this number will turn out to be greater than 28. If you do not feel this way for 28, change this number until you find the value for which it is a true description of your feelings.

The 0.01 fractile is the number such that you feel there is only 1 chance in 100 (a 0.01 probability) that the actual number of classmates preferring wine will turn out to be as few or fewer than this fractile. Similarly, the 0.99 fractile is the number of classmates such that the odds are 99 to 1 that the actual number preferring wine will be less than or equal to this fractile.

Illustration of the Probability Assessment Procedure. Suppose that you were asked to assess the position of the Dow Jones Index (DJI) on January 1, 1979. Consider the following assessments:

Fractile	0.01	0.25	0.50	0.75	0.99
DJI	750	800	900	1020	1170

The writer of this assessment is saying that he thinks there is an even chance (50–50) that on January 1 the DJI will be 900 or below. He feels that there is a 0.25 chance (1 in 4) that the DJI will be equal to or less than 800, and he feels that there is a 0.75 chance (3 in 4) that it will be equal to or below 1020. He feels also that there is a 0.5 chance that the DJI will be between 800 and 1020. He feels that there is only 1 chance in 100 that the DJI will be equal to or less than 750, and he feels that there is 1 chance in 100 that the DJI will be greater than 1170. His median value of the DJI is 900.

The Exercise. The purpose of this exercise is to see how well you can subjectively forecast by assessing cumulative probability distributions for uncertain quantities (u.q.'s) or events. The uncertain quantities under consideration have to do with the behavior and opinions of this class on three questions. These questions are given below. You are asked to estimate, in the form of a cumulative probability distribution, the way you think the class as a whole will be divided up in its answers to these questions.

Taking the first question as an example, the uncertain quantity is how many in this class would accept a 50–50 gamble on a business venture where your firm could lose $500,000 if the venture fails, or gain $1,500,000 if the venture succeeds. The uncertain quantity should be interpreted to be *how many in the class accept the gamble.*

In class we shall discuss how the class members split in answering each question and how well the assessed distributions describe your uncertainty surrounding these values. The interest and value of the class discussion, in part, will come from the revelation of whether you and others in the class tend to be too tight in your assessments, or too loose, or generally biased in an upward or downward direction.

Using the assessment procedure discussed, evaluate the fractiles requested for the three u.q.'s of this exercise and enter your answers in the space provided on the answer sheet.

Questions

1. Would you accept a 50–50 gamble on a venture where your firm could lose $500,000 if the venture is a failure, or gain $1,500,000 if the venture is successful?

       Accept _____   Reject _____

2. Do you think that the Dow Jones Industrial Index (DJI) on January 1, 1980, will be above 1100?

       Yes _____   No _____

3. Do you think that the use of nuclear power for meeting our national energy needs should be stopped?

       Yes _____   No _____

LIST OF UNCERTAIN QUANTITIES

1. The number in the class who would *accept* the gamble described in Question 1.
2. The number in the class who believe that the DJI on January 1, 1980, will be above 1100.
3. The number in the class who are against the use of nuclear power to meet our national energy needs.

Answer Sheet for the Assessment of Fractiles. For each of the following uncertain quantities, please assess the 0.50 fractile first, then the 0.25 and the 0.75 fractiles, and last the 0.01 and 0.99 fractiles.

Uncertain Quantities	FRACTILES				
	0.01	0.25	0.50	0.75	0.99
			Median		
1. Number of class members accepting venture	——	——	——	——	——
2. Number of class members who believe DJI will be above 1100 on Jan. 1, 1980	——	——	——	——	——
3. Number of class members against the use of nuclear power for meeting our national energy needs	——	——	——	——	——

CHAPTER 6

Decision Analysis:
Sequential and
Information
Acquisition
Decisions

OBJECTIVES. To be able to:

1. Perform decision-tree analysis on sequential decision problems by the process of backward induction.
2. Perform *prior, posterior,* and *preposterior* decision-tree analysis on information acquisition decision problems by the process of backward induction.
3. Determine the value of acquiring further information.
4. Perform decision-tree analysis using both extensive and normal forms of analysis.
5. Specify some typologies of actual managerial behavior in information acquisition decision problems under uncertainty.

6.1. INTRODUCTION

In Chapter 4 we were concerned with what are called *single-stage* or *static decision* problems, where the decision maker selects one action at a single point in time. Often, however, decision problems involve making a sequence of decisions before a problem is resolved—that is, there are occasions where the entire set of decisions at different points in time should be evaluated at the same time that the initial decision is made. Moreover, in real-world decision problems, it is often possible to acquire more information on which to base a decision through, for example, analysis, laboratory experimentation, field testing, sampling inspection, market research, industrial espionage, and so forth, before a terminal decision is made. In this chapter we shall consider such decision problems and show how they can be structured and analyzed by use of decision-tree analysis. As we have indicated at the end of Chapter 4, we shall make use of the decision tree as an efficient and instructive method for structuring and evaluating these more complex decision problems. In doing so, notationally, we shall again use *squares* to refer to *decision forks* (nodes) and *circles* to represent *chance forks* (nodes). At a decision fork, the decision maker is in control and decides which action to take. At a chance fork, the decision maker is no longer in control and the outcome (or choice) is left to chance. Creation of a decision-tree diagram requires, simply, that the act forks and event forks representing the acts and events relevant to a particular decision problem be arranged in sequence, with the base of the tree representing the time nearest the present and the tips of the rightmost branches representing the most distant future being considered. Usually the fork at the base of the decision tree is an act fork, representing the immediate decision with which the analysis is most concerned.

6.2. SEQUENTIAL DECISIONS

Let us use an example to show how we may analyze sequential decision problems by a decision-tree analysis.

6.2.1. Example—Company Acquisition Alternatives: The Case of Hi Voltage Transformer

The President of Solar Phasic Industries, J. P. Cash, is interested in buying the Hi Voltage Transformer Company. He sees the possibility of large profits occurring to Hi Voltage if business is good. By purchasing it now, large returns can be made in 2 years, when it would be sold.

Hi Voltage's stock is currently held by two families, the Edisons and the Franklins. They have agreed to sell all their stock now for $1 million, or half now for $600,000 and the rest in 1 year based upon the profit picture at that time.

Cash sees the following alternatives available to him. One is to buy all the stock now and sell at the end of 2 years. On the other hand, if he buys only half, he can purchase the rest in 1 year and sell all at the end of the second year. Or he could hold his initial purchase and not buy the second half, then sell it at the end of the second year. A third alternative is not to purchase any stock but instead to purchase 2-year Treasury bills.

His returns are influenced by the business conditions. If business is good the first year, the price of the second 50% of stock will sell at $800,000. If it is bad, it will sell for $300,000. However, if business is good the first year, it may be bad during the second, and vice versa. All these events influence what the payoffs could be when J. P. plans to sell his shares of Hi Voltage.

To resolve the chances of these states of nature facing Cash, G. N. Potash, Solar's chief economist, was called in to develop estimates of future events. He gathered data and projected future events. Potash said that in the first year, there is a 60% chance of good business and 40% of bad. In the second year, if business is good in the first, there is a 70% chance it will be good in the second and 30% chance of bad. If the first year is bad, there is a 40% chance of good times and 60% of bad in the second year.

C. T. Smart, Solar's chief systems analyst, was also called upon to help. He computed the net present value of all possible alternatives available, based upon the expected payoffs for each possible outcome. They are presented in Table 6.1. Cash can reap up to $800,000 or lose $700,000, depending upon what decision he makes and the events that occur in future.

J. P. sat at his desk reviewing the information from Potash and Smart. He has to make a decision in the next few days or lose the opportunity to buy into the

Table 6.1 Possible Payoffs

Alternative	BUSINESS CONDITIONS Year 1	BUSINESS CONDITIONS Year 2	Net Present Value (NPV) Payoffs (000s)
Buy 100%	Good	Good	$ 800
(single purchase)	Good	Bad	− 500
	Bad	Good	600
	Bad	Bad	− 700
Buy 50%	Good	Good	300
	Good	Bad	0
	Bad	Good	100
	Bad	Bad	− 100
Buy 100%	Good	Good	600
(double purchase)	Good	Bad	− 600
	Bad	Good	500
	Bad	Bad	− 400
Buy Treasury bills			50

company. The Edison and Franklin families have received other inquiries about selling.

6.2.2. Decision-Tree Analysis

A decision-tree diagram of this problem is shown in Figure 6.1. Starting from the first decision fork at the extreme left of Figure 6.1, Cash is initially confronted with three alternative courses of action: (1) to purchase 100% of Hi Voltage's stock now (a_1); (2) to purchase 50% of their stock now (a_2); or (3) not to purchase any Hi Voltage stock but instead to buy Treasury bills (a_3). Action a_1 is a one-time (terminal) decision. If Cash chooses a_1, he has no further recourse. The payoff resulting from this decision is out of his hands, for it depends on economic conditions in the first and second years, of which there are four mutually exclusive possibilities.

If Cash decides to purchase only 50% of Hi Voltage's stock now (a_2), depending upon next year's business conditions, he can then decide (next year) whether or not to purchase the remaining 50% of the stock. He has four possible strategies here: (1) he can purchase the remaining stock regardless of business conditions in the first year; (2) he can purchase the remaining stock only if business conditions are good in the first year; (3) he can purchase the stock only if business conditions are bad in the first year; and (4) he does not purchase the remaining stock regardless of business conditions in the first year.

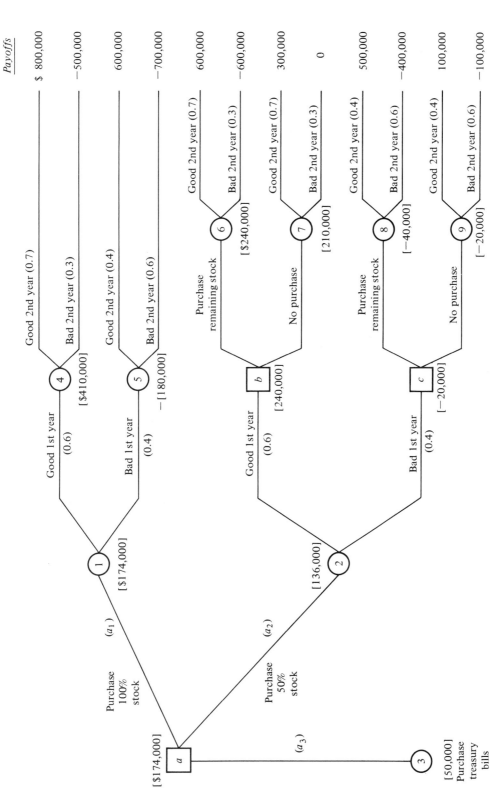

Figure 6.1. Discrete decision tree of Cash's problem.

Table 6.2 Expected Payoffs:
      Initially Purchase All Hi Voltage Stock

(1) Year 1	(2) Year 2	(3) = (1 × 2) Joint Probability	(4) Payoff (000s)	(5) = (3 × 4) Expected NPV (000s)
0.6	0.7	0.42	$800	$336
0.6	0.3	0.18	− 500	− 90
0.4	0.4	0.16	600	96
0.4	0.6	0.24	− 700	− 168
		1.00		174

Table 6.3. Expected Payoffs:
      Initially Purchase 50% of stock

(1) Year 1	(2) Year 2	(3) = (1) × (2) Joint Probability	(4) Payoff (000s)	(5) = (3) × (4) Expected NPV (000s)

Strategy 1: If good or bad first year, purchase remaining stock.

0.6	0.7	0.42	$600	$252
0.6	0.3	0.18	− 600	− 108
0.4	0.4	0.16	500	80
0.4	0.6	0.24	− 400	− 96
				128

Strategy 2: If good first year, purchase remaining stock; if bad first year, no purchase.

0.6	0.7	0.42	600	252
0.6	0.3	0.18	− 600	− 108
0.4	0.4	0.16	100	16
0.4	0.6	0.24	− 100	− 24
				136

Strategy 3: If good first year, no purchase; if bad first year, purchase remaining stock.

0.6	0.7	0.42	300	126
0.6	0.3	0.8	0	0
0.4	0.4	0.16	500	80
0.4	0.6	0.64	− 400	− 96
				110

Strategy 4: If good or bad first year, no purchase second year.

0.6	0.7	0.42	300	126
0.6	0.3	0.18	0	0
0.4	0.4	0.16	100	16
0.4	0.6	0.64	− 100	− 24
				118

We could argue intuitively that strategy (2) is better than the three other strategies, simply because strategies (1) and (4) make no use of the information gained in the first year, while strategy (3) misuses the information, that is, takes actions that are not consistent with the information. (We shall verify this in our formal analysis.) With the information presented in the decision tree, we can proceed to find the best decision or sequence of decisions for Cash's decision problem. We shall assume that Cash's objective is to maximize EMV.

For the terminal action of purchasing 100% of Hi Voltage's stock immediately (a_1), the expected value is equal to $174,000, as shown in Table 6.2. The expected values of the four feasible strategies associated with the initial action of purchasing 50% of Hi Voltage's stock now (a_2) are also calculated and are shown in Table 6.3. The optimal strategy if Cash purchased 50% of the stock initially would be to purchase the remaining stock if business were good the first year, and not to purchase any more stock if business were bad the first year $(= \$136,000)$. Thus, of the six available sequences of actions, the optimal one is to simply purchase 100% of the stock now (a_1), since it has the highest EMV.

6.2.3. The Process of Backward Induction

We can perform the decision-tree analysis in a more efficient way, by working backward from the end branches of the tree diagram to the first decision fork, optimizing as we go along (i.e., carrying forward only the best action, while eliminating all inferior ones). This is known as the process of *backward induction*, where we work from right to left, each event fork being replaced by its certainty equivalent [i.e., by the sure sum (in this case EMV) which the decision maker assesses as equivalent to the risky prospect represented by the event fork]. For example, from Figure 6.1, we can compute the EMV of purchasing 100% stock immediately as follows:

1. Compute the expected value (certainty equivalent) at chance nodes 4 and 5:

$$\text{node 4:} \quad 800,000(0.7) + (-500,000)(0.3) = \$410,000$$
$$\text{node 5:} \quad 600,000(0.4) + (-700,000)(0.6) = -\$180,000.$$

2. Compute the expected value at chance node 1 using the expected values calculated at chance nodes 4 and 5:

$$\text{node 1:} \quad 410,000(0.6) + (-180,000)(0.4) = \$174,000.$$

Thus, the expected value of purchasing 100% stock immediately is $174,000. Using this backward induction, certainty equivalent approach we have reduced the decision tree associated with action a_1 to its ultimate reduced form (Figure 6.2).

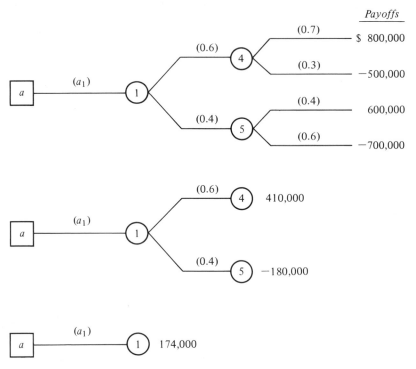

Figure 6.2. Certainty equivalent of initially purchasing 100% stock.

Let us now proceed to compute the optimal strategy for purchasing 50% stock immediately (a_2):

1. Compute the EMV's at chance nodes 6 and 7; also for chance nodes 8 and 9;

   node 6: $600{,}000(0.7) + (-600{,}000)(0.3) = \$240{,}000$

   node 7: $300{,}000(0.7) + (0)(0.3) = \$210{,}000$

   node 8: $(500{,}000)(0.4) + (-400{,}000)(0.6) = -\$40{,}000$

   node 9: $(100{,}000)(0.4) + (-100{,}000)(0.6) = -\$20{,}000.$

2. To determine the optimal action to take at decision node *b*, compare the EMV's associated with nodes 6 and 7 and choose the action whose node has the highest EMV [i.e., choose to purchase the remaining stock (node 6) and discard the action associated with node 7]. A double slash is used to indicate that the no purchase action should be discarded at decision node *b*. Thus, *if business conditions are good the first year*, the best action to take is to purchase the remaining stock in the second year.

3. Similarly, to determine the optimal action at decision node c, compare the EMV's at nodes 8 and 9 and choose the action whose node has the highest EMV (i.e., choose the no purchase action and discard the action of purchasing the remaining stock). Thus, if business conditions are bad the first year, the best action to take is not to purchase any more stock in the second year.

4. Next, compute the EMV at chance node 2:

$$\text{node 2:} \quad 240{,}000(0.6) + (-20{,}000)(0.4) = \$136{,}000.$$

This says if 50% of the stock is initially purchased, the best strategy is to purchase the remaining stock if first-year business conditions are good; and if first-year conditions are bad, not to make any further stock purchase. The expected value of this strategy is $136,000. Note again that by using this backward-induction certainty equivalent approach, we have reduced the initial action a_2 to its ultimate reduced form, as shown in Figure 6.3.

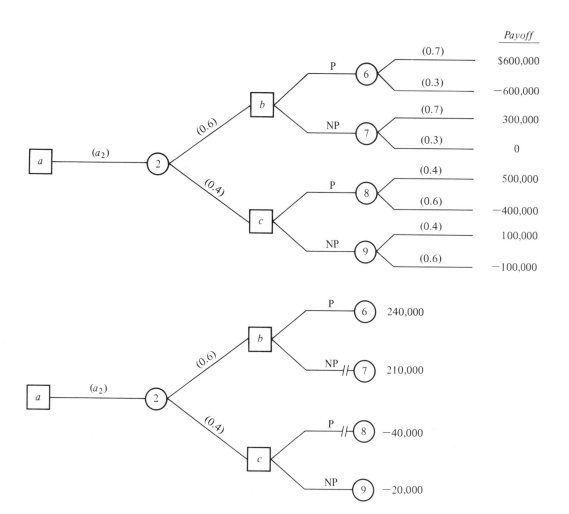

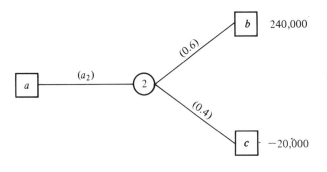

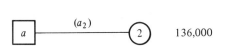

P–Purchase remaining stock
NP–Don't purchase remaining stock

Figure 6.3. Optimal certainty equivalent of initially purchasing 50% stock (continued from page 195).

Figure 6.4. Discrete payoff distributions (see section 6.2.4).

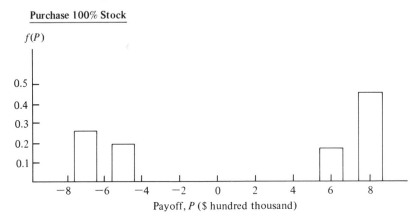

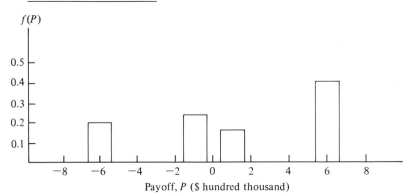

To make the optimal decision at decision node a, note the expected values (certainty equivalents) of our three initial choices: purchase 100% of stock (node 1 = \$174,000), purchase 50% stock (node 2 = \$136,000), and purchase Treasury bills (node 3 = \$50,000). The optimal decision at decision node a is to purchase 100% of stock, since it has the highest EMV.

6.2.4. Representing Strategies as Outcomes of Discrete Probability Distributions

It is often useful to represent the outcomes of each action or strategy (Tables 6.2 and 6.3) in terms of a discrete probability distribution, as shown for several of Hi Voltage Transformer's possible actions and sequences of actions in Figure 6.4. Such a representation illuminates the potential shortcomings of an EMV maximization criterion by portraying the "risks" (potential losses) involved in taking a given action or strategy (the cumulative probability distribution is perhaps an even more informative representation). When the decision maker's utility function is unobtainable, such a representation provides a surrogate approach to expected utility maximization as a basis of choice.

6.3. INFORMATION ACQUISITION

Often in real decision problems, it is possible to gain more information on which to base a decision through analysis, experimentation, testing, sampling, and so forth. In such situations two basic choices must be made: (1) choice of inquiry or information sources (including the null case, not to acquire any information); that is, what information to acquire and when, and (2) choice of a strategy or decision rule in response to the messages, data, observations, or outcomes received from a chosen information source. Again, by strategy we mean a precise set of instructions explaining what action is to be taken under every possible message or outcome received from a given information source. In essence, a strategy is a contingency plan for responding to all possible messages received from an information source.

To illustrate the development of the decision-tree analysis in such decision situations, let us consider the following simplified case situation.

6.3.1. Example—Cactus Petroleum: Analyzing Oil Exploration Strategies

An oil wildcatter for Cactus Petroleum must decide whether to drill (act a_1) or not drill (act a_2) a well on a particular piece of the company's property in northern Oklahoma. He is uncertain whether the hole is dry (state θ_1), wet (state θ_2), or soaking (state θ_3), but he believes the probabilities for these states to be:

$$P(\text{dry}) = 0.5 \qquad P(\text{wet}) = 0.3 \qquad P(\text{soaking}) = 0.2.$$

The cost of drilling is $70,000. If the well is judged to be soaking, the revenue would be $270,000. But if the well is wet, the revenue would be $120,000.

At a cost of $10,000, the wildcatter could take seismic soundings that will help determine the underlying geological structure at the site. The soundings will disclose whether the terrain below has (a) no structure (outcome NS)—that's bad, or (b) open structure (outcome OS)—that's so-so, or (c) closed structure (outcome CS)—that's really hopeful. In the past, oil wells that have been dry, wet, or soaking have had the following distributions of seismic test outcomes:

Seismic Test Outcome: $P(O|\theta)$

Well Type	O_1 (NS)	O_2 (OS)	O_3 (CS)	
θ_1: dry	0.6	0.3	0.1	1.0
θ_2: wet	0.3	0.4	0.3	1.0
θ_3: soaking	0.1	0.4	0.5	1.0

The oil wildcatter must decide what to do: should he drill or not drill immediately, or should he take seismic soundings, and if so, what actions should he take for each seismic test outcome. You are called in as a decision analyst to help him with his problem. What would you recommend based on the criterion of EMV maximization?

6.3.2. Analysis—Optimal Action
Without Experimentation and EVPI

As noted in Table 6.4, the determination of EMV for this simple two-act, two-state case merely involves calculations of a weighted payoff for each act:

$$E(a_1) = -70,000(0.5) + 50,000(0.3) + 200,000(0.2)$$
$$= \$20,000$$
$$E(a_2) = \$0.$$

In the absence of any further information, the decision maker who wished to maximize EMV would choose to drill (a_1).

More realistically, the decision maker may elect to delay his terminal decision by conducting seismic soundings in order to gather more information regarding the probabilities attached to alternative states that affect the consequences of each course of action.

As developed in Chapter 4, the concept of EVPI provides useful information regarding how much the decision would be improved if such a test were perfectly

Table 6.4. Decision Matrix: Oil Wildcatter Problem

Act \ Event	$P(\theta_1) = 0.5$ θ_1: dry	$P(\theta_2) = 0.3$ θ_2: wet	$P(\theta_3) = 0.2$ θ_3: soaking
a_1: drill	$\$ - 70{,}000$	$50{,}000^a$	$200{,}000^a$
a_2: don't drill	0^a	0	0

^{a}Optimal act for a given event.

reliable. Thus, it provides a rough measure as to whether it is worthwhile gathering more information. One method of computing EVPI, discussed in Chapter 4, is to first determine the value of the decision made under perfect information and then subtract this value from the best decision that can be made given the current information state. That is, if we had perfect information regarding which state would obtain, we would behave as follows: if θ_1 obtains, we would *not drill* since the payoff is higher for a_2; if θ_2 or θ_3 obtains, we would *drill* since the return is higher for act a_1. Therefore, the EVPI, which is the difference between the optimal EMV under perfect information and the optimal EMV under the current uncertainty (i.e., before testing), is

$$\text{EVPI} = \sum_{i=1}^{3} p(\theta_j)\max_i \left[c(\theta_j, a_i) \right] - \max_i E(a_i)$$
$$= \left[0(0.5) + 50{,}000(0.3) + 200{,}000(0.2) \right] - 20$$
$$= \$35{,}000,$$

where $c(a_i, \theta_j)$ is the consequence or payoff associated with a given action and state of nature. Therefore, we should be willing to pay up to \$35,000 for sample information, but no more. Of course, sample information is generally *not* perfect, so the amount we should expect to pay should be less than \$35,000. Since the cost of the seismic test is \$10,000, we should examine its potential value to our decision process. That is, it may be worthwhile to perform the seismic test.

6.3.3. Decision-Tree Diagramming and Analysis: Extensive Form

Figure 6.5 represents a decision tree of this problem which summarizes the pertinent payoffs and probabilities associated with the null test and seismic test. By following the path e_0 (no test) of Figure 6.5, we note the same data which are shown in Table 6.4. As before, we designate the *decision* forks (or nodes) with a box, while the chance forks (nodes) are designated by a circle. It is clear that in the absence of experimentation, the decision maker would select a_1 (drill), leading to an EMV of \$20,000. We, as before, use a double slash to eliminate the nonoptimal actions; hence, the path labeled a_2 is blocked off by a double slash. This part of the analysis is known as *prior analysis*. It refers to the manner in which a terminal act is

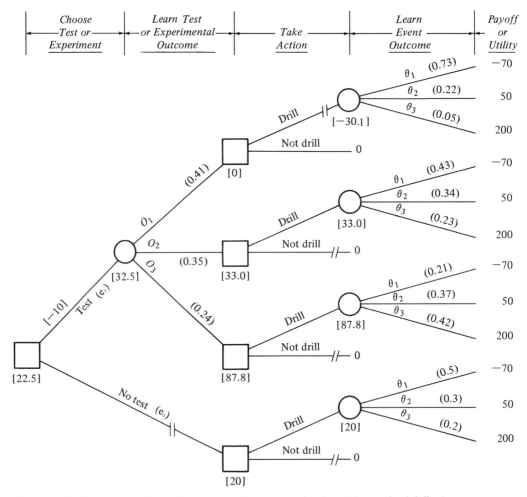

Figure 6.5. Decision tree analysis of cactus petroleum: extensive form (thousands of dollars).

chosen on the basis of prior probabilities alone (our current information state or beliefs).

The path labeled e_1 traces out the strategies associated with the opportunity to conduct a seismic test at the cost of $10,000. Note how the tree in Figure 6.5 traces out the chronology of choices and events, as they would occur over time. That is, we first perform the seismic test. Three possible test outcomes can occur—NS(O_1), OS(O_2), and CS(O_3). Whichever of these test outcomes occur, we will then have to decide whether or not to drill. After taking our action, we then learn which state is true (θ_1, θ_2, or θ_3); this results in a certain payoff to us. Note that there are a total of eight strategies associated with seismic testing. Can you define them?

The seismic test is not completely reliable, as indicated by the conditional probabilities stated in the problem. That is, the test outcome would not disclose without some error which event θ_1, θ_2, or θ_3 is true. [If the test was perfectly reliable, then $P(O_1|\theta_1)$, $P(O_2|\theta_2)$, and $P(O_3|\theta_3)$, where O_k and θ_j denote the test outcome and state of nature, respectively, would all be equal to 1, and all the other conditional probabilities would be equal to zero.]

To evaluate the e_1 path, we first need to determine the values of the following probabilities: (1) $p(O_k)$, the probabilities of the three possible test outcomes, and (2) $p(\theta_j|O_k)$, the posterior probabilities of the states of nature given the test outcomes. We can do this using Bayes' theorem:

$$p(\theta_j|O_k) = \frac{p(\theta_j \cap O_k)}{p(O_k)}$$

$$= \frac{p(\theta_j) \cdot p(O_k|\theta_j)}{\sum_{j=1}^{3} p(\theta_j \cap O_k)}.$$

The results of these computations are shown in Table 6.5.

Table 6.5. Obtaining the Probabilities in Cactus Petroleum: Bayes' Theorem

$P(O_k|\theta_j)$			
θ_j \ O_k	O_1	O_2	O_3
θ_1	0.6	0.3	0.1
θ_2	0.3	0.4	0.3
θ_3	0.1	0.4	0.5

$P(\theta_j)$	
θ_j	$P(\theta_j)$
θ_1	0.5
θ_2	0.3
θ_3	0.2

$P(O_k)$	
O_k	$P(O_k)$
O_1	0.41
O_2	0.35
O_3	0.24

$P(O_k \cap \theta_j)$				
θ_j \ O_k	O_1	O_2	O_3	
θ_1	0.30	0.15	0.05	0.5
θ_2	0.09	0.12	0.09	0.3
θ_3	0.02	0.08	0.10	0.2
	0.41	0.35	0.24	

$P(\theta_j|O_k)$			
θ_j \ O_k	O_1	O_2	O_3
θ_1	0.73	0.43	0.21
θ_2	0.22	0.34	0.37
θ_3	0.05	0.23	0.42

Now we can place the probabilities at the appropriate points on the decision tree of Figure 6.5. Given that we decide to test, one of three test outcomes will occur with probabilities $p(O_1) = 0.41$, $p(O_2) = 0.35$, and $p(O_3) = 0.24$. For each of these possible test outcomes we must choose either one of two actions—to drill or not drill. Given a test outcome and a specific course of action, one of three states will occur with probabilities $p(\theta_1|O_k)$, $p(\theta_2|O_k)$, and $p(\theta_3|O_k)$. For example, if the test outcome is O_1(NS), then $p(\theta_1|O_1) = 0.73$, $p(\theta_2|O_1) = 0.22$, and $p(\theta_3|O_1) = 0.05$. Observe and compare the values of the posterior probabilities [e.g., $p(\theta_1|O_1)$, $p(\theta_2|O_1)$, $p(\theta_3|O_1)$] to the prior probabilities [$p(\theta_1) = 0.5$, $p(\theta_2) = 0.3$, $p(\theta_3) = 0.2$]. Note that, if the test outcome is O_1, we would expect $p(\theta_1|O_1)$ to be greater than $p(\theta_1)$, since a no-structure-test indication would increase our confidence or belief that the well is really dry, as Bayes' theorem indicates.

We are now ready to choose our best strategy for experimentation and action. First, we compute the optimal strategy associated with performing a seismic test, using the process of backward induction. That is, we start from the tips of the tree and work backwards, always choosing the path with the highest certainty equivalent (EMV). The expected values of the optimal action associated with each test outcome is computed in Table 6.6 and shown in Figure 6.5. Thus, the optimal

Table 6.6. Posterior and Preposterior Analysis of Seismic Test

Test Outcome (O_k)	State (θ_j)	ACT		$P(\theta_j|O_k)$
		Drill	Don't Drill	
No structure	Dry	−70,000	0	0.73
	Wet	50,000	0	0.22
	Soaking	200,000	0	0.05
	EMV	−30,100	0	
Open	Dry	−70,000	0	0.43
structure	Wet	50,000	0	0.34
	Soaking	200,000	0	0.23
	EMV	33,000	0	
Closed	Dry	−70,000	0	0.21
structure	Wet	50,000	0	0.37
	Soaking	200,000	0	0.42
	EMV	87,800	0	
		$P(O_k)$	EMV	
No structure		0.41	0	0
Open structure		0.35	33,000	11,500
Closed structure		0.24	87,800	21,000

Prior expectation of
EMV posterior to
seismic tests: $32,500 - 10,000 = \$22,500.$

$$EVSI = EMV_{test} - EMV_{no\ test}$$
$$= 32,500 - 20,000 = \$12,500.$$

strategy for seismic testing is: if O_1 (NS) occurs, we should not drill; if O_2 (OS) or O_3 (CS) occurs, we should drill. We refer to this part of the analysis, which deals with the optimal choice and evaluation of an action subsequent to all experimentation or testing (i.e., after learning the test outcome) as *posterior analysis*.

The decision maker's immediate problem, however, is to decide whether or not to perform a seismic test. To analyze this aspect of the problem, we must continue with the backward-induction process. That is, to find the expected value of the optimal test strategy (before performing the test), we must next multiply the probability of the test outcomes times the expected value of each respective optimal posterior act:

$$\text{Value of optimal strategy for seismic test} = (0.41)(0) + (0.35)(33,000)$$
$$+ (0.24)(87,800)$$
$$= \$32,500$$

After subtracting the cost of the seismic test, the net expected return is $22,500. This part of the analysis is known as *preposterior analysis*, since we evaluate the value of performing the test using, of course, the optimal strategy *before* we have learned the particular results of the test.

Since the value of performing the test ($= \$22,500$) is $2500 greater than the optimal no test alternative ($= \$20,000$), the seismic test should be performed, and if the test outcome is O_1 (NS), do not drill; if the test outcome is either O_2 (OS) or O_3 (CS), drill.

We can also represent each phase of our analysis in terms of the consequences of the various actions or strategies to be taken in terms of discrete probability distributions. For example, Figure 6.6 represents the optimal no test alternative, the optimal posterior actions, and optimal posterior strategy in the form of discrete probability distributions on the consequences.

6.3.4. Decision-Tree Diagramming and Analysis: Normal Form

The decision problem, of the type we have just analyzed, can be analyzed in two basic ways. The first way we have just considered consists of four principal steps: (1) structure the decision tree in extensive form (chronologically), (2) assign payoffs or utilities at the tips of the branches, (3) assign probabilities at all chance forks or nodes, and (4) compute expected values using the process of backward induction. This four-step procedure has been called the *extensive form of analysis*. In this form, the decision maker can be viewed as a participant in a *game against chance (or nature)* in which he makes his choice, sits back and waits for his opponent (chance) to make its move, and then makes his next choice in light of chance's countermove.

There is a second mode of analysis, called the *normal form of analysis*, which gives an equivalent solution to the extensive form of analysis. The normal form of analysis does not require the assessment of prior probabilities at the outset, but brings these judgmental probabilities into the analysis, at the very last step.

In the normal form of analysis, we start by considering *all feasible strategies* for experimentation and action. For each such strategy we shall ask: What is the expected value of this strategy if θ_1 happens to be true; if θ_2 happens to be true; and if θ_3 happens to be true? If we observe that strategy A is better (i.e., has a higher expected value) than strategy B when θ_1, θ_2, and θ_3 are true, then we shall simply say that A dominates B; that is, A is preferred to B. If, however, A is sometimes better than B and sometimes worse than B when θ_1, θ_2, or θ_3 is true, then we shall have to compute the unconditional expected value of a given strategy

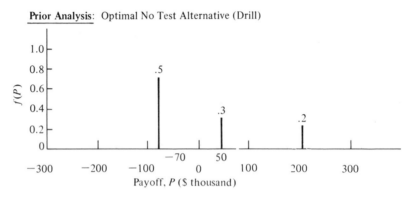

Prior Analysis: Optimal No Test Alternative (Drill)

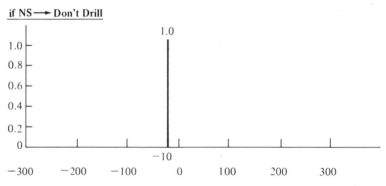

Posterior Analysis: Optimal Strategy (if NS, don't drill; if OS or CS, drill)

if NS → Don't Drill

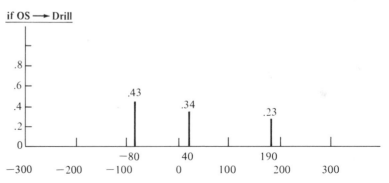

if OS → Drill

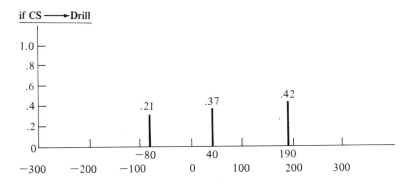

if CS ──▶ Drill

Preposterior Analysis: Optimal Strategy (if NS, don't drill; if OS or CS, drill)

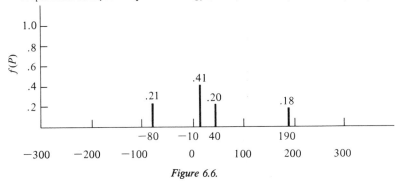

Figure 6.6.

by weighting its expected values associated with each state of nature (θ) by the prior probabilities of their occurrence.

To illustrate the procedure, consider once again Cactus Petroleum's problem. In the normal form of analysis, we start out by listing all feasible pure strategies for experimentation and action. In this problem there are 10 such pure strategies, labeled $S_1, S_2, \ldots, S_{10}$, as shown in Table 6.7. Each of these strategies gives a complete description of precisely what the decision maker will do in each and every contingency that may arise. In brief, there are two strategies for e_0 (no test) and eight strategies for e_1 (seismic test). For example, S_4 (for the seismic test) is defined as follows: if the test outcome is NS, don't drill (DD); and if the test outcome is either OS or CS, drill (D). The problem, in normal form, can be conveniently depicted in the form of a tree diagram as shown in Figure 6.7. Going from left to

Table 6.7. Listing of Strategies in Cactus Petroleum

Strategy / Outcome	S_1	S_2	S_3	S_4	S_5	S_6	S_7	S_8	S_9	S_{10}
				e_1					e_0	
NS	DD	DD	DD	DD	D	D	D	D	D	DD
OS	DD	DD	D	D	DD	DD	D	D	D	DD
CS	DD	D	DD	D	DD	D	DD	D	D	DD

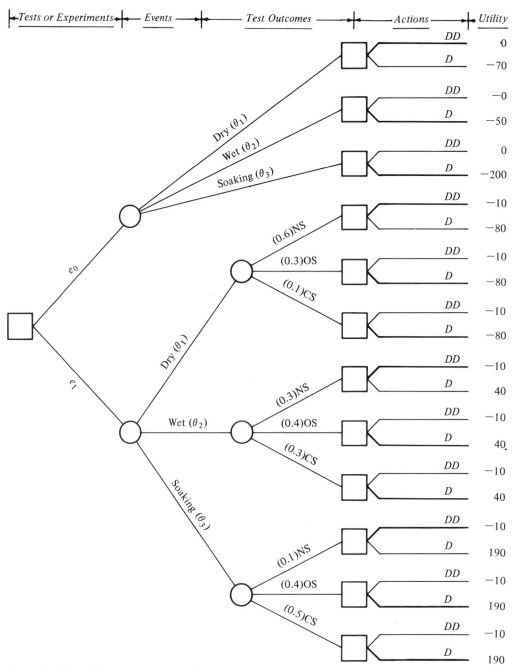

Figure 6.7. Normal form tree: cactus petroleum.

right, the tree is drawn in the following sequence: (1) experiments or tests considered, (2) states of nature, (3) test outcomes, (4) actions, and (5) payoffs or utilities. The probabilities shown (in parentheses) are the $P(O_k|\theta_j)$'s.

The next step is to evaluate each strategy *conditional on θ_1 being true, θ_2 being true, and θ_3 being true.* To make the discussion concrete, let us conditionally evaluate strategy S_4 (darkened lines in Figure 6.7). Strategy S_4, given θ_1, θ_2, and θ_3, leads to the following respective conditional EMVs (in thousands of dollars):

$$\text{EMV}(S_4|\theta_1) = (0.6)(-10) + (0.3)(-80) + (0.1)(-80)$$
$$= -\$38$$
$$\text{EMV}(S_4|\theta_2) = (0.3)(-10) + (0.4)(40) + (0.3)(40)$$
$$= \$25$$
$$\text{EMV}(S_4|\theta_3) = (0.1)(-10) + (0.4)(190) + (0.5)(190)$$
$$= \$170.$$

Thus, the *joint conditional evaluation* of strategy S_4 is represented by the vector $(-38, 25, 170)$. Table 6.8 represents the joint conditional evaluations of all our 10 strategies for e_0 and e_1.

Our next step is to determine the set of admissible (nondominated) strategies. As previously indicated, strategy A dominates strategy B when it is as good as or better than strategy B for all states of nature (θ). Thus, $S_{10}(0, 0, 0)$ dominates $S_1(-10, -10, -10)$; $S_4(-38, 25, 170)$ dominates $S_5(-52, 5, 15)$; and so forth. Considering the different strategies, we find that the set of admissible pure strategies is $\{S_2, S_3, S_4, S_9, S_{10}\}$. The unconditional expected value of each admissible strategy is then determined by multiplying each conditional evaluation (given θ) by its prior probability, $p(\theta)$. For example, for S_4,

$$\text{EMV}(S_4) = (0.5)(-38) + (0.3)(25) + (0.2)(170)$$
$$= \$22.5.$$

The EMVs for each admissible strategy are given in Table 6.8. Note that the optimal strategy for experimentation and action is identical to that obtained with the extensive form of analysis.

Table 6.8 Joint (Vector of) Conditional Evaluations of All Strategies

Strategy State of Nature	S_1	$S_2{}^a$	$S_3{}^a$	$S_4{}^{a,\,b}$	S_5	S_6	S_7	S_8	$S_9{}^a$	$S_{10}{}^a$
D: θ_1 (0.5)	-10	-17	-31	-38	-52	-59	-73	-80	-70	0
W: θ_2 (0.3)	-10	5	10	25	5	20	25	40	50	0
S: θ_3 (0.2)	-10	90	70	170	15	110	90	190	200	0
EMV		11	2.5	22.5					20	0

[a]Admissible strategies.
[b]Optimal strategy.

To summarize, let us briefly contrast the extensive and normal forms of analysis. First, while the two approaches differ in the way the decision maker analyzes the problem, both modes of analysis lead to identical solutions. The extensive-form decision tree is a chronological tree which is simpler to envision conceptually than the normal-form tree. The extensive form of analysis preassigns prior probabilities to the states of nature and through the process of backward induction optimizes on a best strategy. The normal form of analysis first finds the set of admissible strategies by enumerating and evaluating all feasible strategies, then assigns prior probabilities to the states of nature and finds an optimal strategy. The extensive form is thus simpler both computationally and conceptually. In fact, for even relatively small problems, a normal form of analysis may not be feasible, owing to the large number of feasible strategies that would have to be evaluated. Thus, most decision-tree analysis is done in extensive form.

6.4. TYPOLOGIES OF MANAGERIAL BEHAVIOR

The process of performing a formal decision analysis is intended to assist the decision maker in making decisions under conditions of uncertainty. Without the use of such a formal tool of analysis, especially in complex decision situations, decisions left solely to the intuition of the decision maker often turn out to be inferior. Many studies performed by psychologists and management scientists have demonstrated the value of decision analysis by pointing out human deficiencies in processing information and deciding. Some general typologies of suboptimal behavior (with respect to the Bayesian decision theoretic norm) observed in both experimental and realistic situations are indicated below for the prototypical type of managerial decision situation discussed in section 6.3. That is, an action or choice must be made under uncertainty, but there exists the chance of buying information to reduce the uncertainty. Thus, the decision maker makes a choice on whether or not to gather additional information and, if so, how and how much. After learning the informational results (if any), he makes a choice conditioned on these results. In making choices on such a decision problem, three cognitive functions (or tasks) are involved: (1) information processing, (2) information acquisition (e.g., choice of experimentation including the "null" case of foregoing experimentation), and (3) strategy selection (choice of actions in response to experimental outcomes). A flow diagram of these three constituent mental functions is shown in Figure 6.8.

1. *Information processing behavior.* Five typologies of behavior have been typically observed in human information processing.
   (a) *Bayesians or near-Bayesians.* Those whose posterior beliefs based on new information correspond to that obtained using Bayes' theorem.
   (b) *Prior information disregarders.* Those who revise their beliefs solely on the basis of the new information received from an inquiry source (experiment, test, etc.) that is, irrespective of their prior beliefs, hence give no weight to prior information.

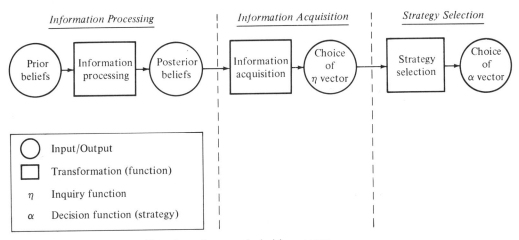

○	Input/Output
□	Transformation (function)
η	Inquiry function
α	Decision function (strategy)

Figure 6.8. Constituent mental functions of manager's decision process.

    (c) *Inquiry source disregarders.* Those who apparently treat a given informative, inquiry source as if it were informationless, that is, those who cling to their prior beliefs irrespective of the informational value of the new information.

    (d) *Subjective or intuitive processors.* Those who simply respond in a suboptimal, but coherent manner (i.e., obey the probability axioms) but whose responses cannot be replicated using simple rules.

    (e) *Aberrants (incoherents).* Those whose responses explicitly or implicitly violate the probability axioms.

By and large, most decision makers are not type (a). Moreover, humans typically tend to process information conservatively. That is, upon receipt of new information, individuals tend to revise their posterior probability assessments in the same direction as Bayes' theorem would indicate, but the revision is typically too small. Thus, people behave as if the data are less informative than they truly are.

    2. *Information acquisition behavior.* Three general typologies of behavior have been observed in acquiring information:

    (a) *Optimal (Bayesian) purchasers.* Those who purchase information identically to that suggested by a formal decision analysis.

    (b) *Underpurchasers.* Those who purchase too little information relative to the Bayesian decision theoretic norm.

    (c) *Overpurchasers.* Those who purchase more than the amount suggested by the Bayesian decision theoretic norm.

Typically, most managers (and people in general) tend to overpurchase information. Moreover, human beings seem to prefer to acquire information in parallel (i.e., seek data simultaneously from different sources) rather than in a sequential fashion, even when sequential information acquisition is the preferred procedure from a Bayesian viewpoint.

3. *Strategy selection behavior*. Five basic typologies of behavior have been observed when managers select strategies based on experimental outcomes.

   (a) *Observation–action matcher (OAM)*. Those who at least the majority of the time match terminal actions with observations. (For example, assume in the new product development problem in Chapter 5 that a decision maker initially chooses to experiment on two circuit designs simultaneously—say, a conventional and a betatron circuit; if both experimental outcomes are successful, he would build both breadboards; if the conventional or betatron experiment were successful only, he would only build that respective breadboard; if both experiments failed, he would drop the project.)

   (b) *Information waster (IW)*. Those who purchase information but disregard it in their decisions—a form of illogical or aberrant behavior. (For example, assuming again that the new product manager initially chooses to experiment on the conventional circuit, he would still choose to build the conventional breadboard regardless of the conventional circuit experimental outcome.)

   (c) *Information misuser (IM)*. Those who purchase information and act in antithesis to at least one of the observations—a form of illogical or aberrant behavior. (For example, assuming that the manager initially chooses to experiment on the conventional circuit, if the outcome were successful, he would then choose the betatron breadboard design; otherwise, he would select the conventional breadboard.)

   (d) *Bayesians (B)*. Those whose strategies would correspond to the decision theoretic norm.

   (e) *Other (O)*. The remainder.

Most managers seem to fit in categories (a) and (b); very few seem to fit in category (c).

6.5. SUMMARY

In this chapter we have developed methods for performing a decision-tree analysis of sequential decision problems and decision problems, where there is an opportunity to acquire information prior to making a terminal decision. The real managerial value of a decision-tree analysis is obtained when it is applied to such complex decision problems—where there exist many alternative actions, information sources, states of nature, future decision periods, and so on. In brief, a decision-tree analysis aids and improves the decision process in at least the following ways:

1. It *structures the decision process* into constituent parts, forcing the manager to analyze his decision problem in an orderly, rational manner.

2. It helps the manager to *enumerate all feasible alternatives and outcomes* (some initially not considered, and others not worth considering) into a workable set.

3. It *communicates the decision-making process* to organizational members, quantifying each subjective belief, subjective preference, and each assumption in a concise manner. If a group decision is involved, this facilitites the reconciliation of differences.

4. It *documents* the decision process for historical purposes.

5. It serves as a *management-by-exception* device, to isolate subjective inputs which the decisions are sensitive to, and therefore need to be assessed more accurately.

6. *It is often used with a computer*, thus permitting detailed sensitivity analysis of the various subjective inputs, assumptions, and so on, on the choices made.

REFERENCES CHERNOFF, H., and L. E. MOSES. *Elementary Decision Theory*. New York: John Wiley & Sons, Inc., 1959.

HALTER, A. N., and G. W. DEAN. *Decisions Under Uncertainty*. Cincinnati, Ohio: South-western Publishing Co., 1971.

RAIFFA, H. *Decision Analysis*. Reading, Mass: Addison-Wesley Publishing Co., Inc., 1968.

WINKLER, R. L. *Introduction to Bayesian Inference and Decision*. New York: Holt, Rinehart and Winston, Inc., 1972.

KEY CONCEPTS Sequential decisions
Information acquisition decisions
Decision-tree analysis: extensive
   form
   decision-tree diagram
   backward induction
   prior, posterior, and preposterior
    analysis

Decision-tree analysis: normal form
   decision-tree diagram
   computational procedure
Typologies of managerial behavior
   information processing
   information acquisition
   strategy selection

REVIEW QUESTIONS

6.1. What are the two basic choices that constitute the essence of decision theory? Illustrate these choices using an example.

6.2. Define and illustrate the concept of a strategy in decision-making problems under uncertainty.

6.3. In performing a decision-tree analysis in extensive form, one performs prior, posterior, and preposterior analysis. Define and illustrate these three forms of analysis. What are the differences among these forms of analysis?

6.4. A decision tree in extensive form traces out the chronology of actions and events as they would unfold in a decision problem. Enumerate the prototypical types of action and event nodes that form the basic structure of a decision problem and the basic structure of a decision tree in extensive form. Using a problem of your own choosing, sketch a decision tree of the problem in extensive form.

6.5. State and illustrate the procedure for performing a decision-tree analysis in extensive form of a decision problem, where there exists an opportunity to acquire information. State and illustrate the procedures for performing a normal form of analysis. Contrast the two modes of analysis from a theoretical and practical point of view.

6.6. Define and illustrate the notion of admissibility.

6.7. What are certainty equivalents and how can they help simplify problems of decision making under uncertainty?

6.8. Explain the process of backward induction for solving decision trees.

6.9. Of what importance is sensitivity analysis in analyzing decision-making problems under uncertainty? Illustrate how sensitivity analysis might be performed on the types of problems discussed in this chapter.

6.10. Of what value is it to represent actions or strategies in the form of probability distributions or cumulative probability distributions on the consequences (random variables)?

ANSWERS TO REVIEW QUESTIONS

6.1. The two basic choices are:

1. Choice of inquiry or information sources—i.e., what information to acquire and when.
2. Choice of a strategy or decision rule in response to the messages received from the information source.

To illustrate, a politician may be in a position where he is undecided on whether to vote for a bill because he does not know how his constituents will view his action. To make this decision, he can choose from several possible information sources—i.e., from a public opinion poll, from letters from voters, or from the advice of colleagues. He must decide which, if any, of these sources of information to use. He further must decide, in the case where an information source is chosen, what his action will be in response to messages from the selected source. For example, he may choose a simple strategy that if more than 50% of the people polled are against the bill, he will not support it.

6.2. A strategy is a decision rule which specifies a particular action in response to each chance fork of a decision tree.

To illustrate, consider a woman who is trying to decide whether or not to take an umbrella with her on a cloudy day, and who has the option of reading a weather forecast. The woman has several strategies open to her (four in all). For example, she may simply decide to carry an umbrella and not read the forecast at all. *Or*, she may decide to read the forecast, and if rain is predicted carry an umbrella, and if no rain is predicted, she will not carry an umbrella. The crucial aspect of a strategy is that it specifies in advance an action in response to all possible situations that could occur.

6.3. If a decision maker chooses a terminal act on the basis of prior probabilities alone (no information acquisition), he is using *prior* analysis. If a decision maker decides to acquire information, or at least wishes to evaluate whether or not he should acquire information, he would use *preposterior* analysis. To do this he would need to choose the optimal strategy given each possible message from the set as well as the probability of each message given his prior beliefs and the characteristics of the information system. He can then evaluate the expected value of acquiring information and decide if it is worthwhile. The process of calculating an optimal action given a particular test outcome has occurred is called *posterior* analysis.

6.4. The two types of action nodes are (1) which, if any, information source to use and (2) what decision rule or strategy to use in response to messages from the information source chosen.

The two types of event nodes are (1) messages from the information source and (2) terminal ultimate events which determine the ultimate payoffs.

The procedure for performing a decision-tree analysis in extensive form includes:

1. Calculation of probabilities associated with all chance forks. These calculations will utilize prior probabilities in Bayes' theorem along with conditional probabilities describing the reliability of the information source.
2. The calculation of a certainty equivalent which replaces the "lottery" implied at a chance fork.
3. The elimination of actions which result in a lower expected utility or certainty equivalent.

The normal form of analysis does not use prior probabilities until the final step. In order to perform this type of analysis, one must first enumerate all possible strategies. Then, using the conditional probabilities describing the reliability of the information system, one calculates the expected value of each strategy conditional on each state of nature occurring. This leads to a j-vector of conditional consequences for each strategy—assuming j possible states of nature. The final step is to use prior probabilities to calculate an unconditional expected utility for each strategy and choose the strategy having the highest expected utility.

The normal form, in contrast to the extensive form of analysis, introduces prior subjective probabilities at the final step rather than at the first. The extensive form is easier to use in practice, especially when there are a large number of strategies to consider.

6.6. An admissible strategy is one that is nondominated—i.e., there exists no strategy which has as good or better a payoff for every possible state of nature. To illustrate, suppose we have the following matrix indicating payoffs of four strategies conditional on three states of nature:

	θ_1	θ_2	θ_3
S_1	2	3	-1
S_2	6	7	8
S_3	-2	-2	5
S_4	4	10	12

Here strategies 1 and 3 are inadmissible–no matter what state of nature occurs, strategies 2 and 4 are better and therefore are admissible.

6.7. Certainty equivalents are the sure amounts of a commodity or service a decision maker feels is equivalent to a lottery involving the same object. In other words, the decision maker would be indifferent to accepting the certainty equivalent or the lottery. Certainty equivalents are useful for working through a decision tree, since they enable one to replace a chance fork with an equivalent sure amount, thus simplifying the tree by removing branches.

6.8. Once the decision tree has been filled in with the probabilities at all chance forks using prior probabilities and conditional probabilities describing the information system as inputs into Bayes' theorem, we are ready to use backward induction. Starting at the tips of the tree and working backwards, we sequentially replace all chance forks with certainty equivalents, and block off all action forks which have lower certainty equivalents. This leads to an optimal strategy and a calculation of an expected payoff.

6.9. Sensitivity analysis enables one to predict how the solution to a problem changes as the inputs change. For example, in a decision problem, we may wish to determine how small changes or errors in prior probabilities affect our choice of an optimal strategy. If we find that small changes affect strategies drastically, we may decide to gather more information in an effort to assess probabilities more precisely. If we find that the optimal decision is not very sensitive to changes in probabilities, we may be confident that we have selected an optimal strategy, without having to do any further analysis.

6.10. Probability distributions, as opposed to expected values, depict all possible outcomes and portray the risks or potential losses involved in taking a given action or strategy. The expected value, being a summary statistic, does not enable one to get any idea of the maximum potential loss or gain as do probability distributions or cumulative probability distributions.

EXERCISES **6.1.** A plant manager has the option of having a process in his plant set up by the process operator or by a setup man. If the process operator performs his own setup, the fraction of the items produced which are defective will be 0.10, 0.20, or 0.40. If the process is set up by a setup man, however, the plant manager can be certain that the process will produce items with a fraction defective of 0.10. It costs an additional $12.00 to have the setup man do the setting up. The item is produced in lots of 100 (total of good and bad items). Each defective item is repaired by hand at a cost of $1 per item.

(a) Select and state two principles of choice which are appropriate for solving the plant manager's problem as one of uncertainty (i.e., complete ignorance beyond the information given above). For each principle of choice, recommend whether the process should be set by the process operator or by the setup man.

(b) Suppose that on the basis of his records of past performance, the plant manager finds that setups by the process operator have led to the various fraction defectives with the following relative frequencies:

Fraction Defective of Items Produced	Relative Frequency of Fraction Defective
0.10	0.40
0.20	0.50
0.40	0.10

Using minimum expected cost as the choice criterion, recommend whether the process should be set up by the process operator or by the setup man.

(c) Assume that the process has been set up by the process operator. Two items have been produced and inspected. If one of the two items is defective, should the plant manager have the operator complete the rest of the lot or should he have the process reset up by the setup man?

6.2. The Mocheck Manufacturing Company has developed a new product which it is considering marketing. The cost of marketing is $1,000,000. There are only two possible states of nature. Either it is preferred to its competitor or it is not: if it is preferred, and if it is marketed, the company will enjoy factory gross sales of $3,000,000. If it is worse than its competitor, then, if marketed, the gross sales will be $500,000. The cost of production is zero. If they do not market it, they can and will sell the new product idea to their competitors for $1,000,000 if it is a superior product, or $300,000 if it is inferior. Assume that, for these amounts, the utility of money is linear. The decision whether to market or sell the idea must be made now, although the positive confirmation of the relative superiority or inferiority of the product will not be available until some weeks from now.

(a) Should they market the product if the probability of the new product's superiority is 0.8? Which course of action should be taken and what is the expected return?

(b) In addition, a market test yields results (i.e., a particular test outcome) which indicate that it is a superior product. The test result, X_1, is such that, if it really is a superior product, this outcome has a probability of occurrence of 0.9. If the product is inferior, the probability of this test outcome is 0.3. With this new evidence, which course of action should be taken and what is the expected return?

(c) Assume an environment of complete certainty about the probabilities of possible outcomes. What is the expected return under perfect information?

6.3. Professor Cooper, head of graduate admissions at a large university, has long watched the performance of his six committee members, professors 1, 2, 3, 4, 5, and 6, who provided judgments of the kind: "This student would (would not) successfully finish the program if admitted to graduate school." Here is what Professor Cooper thinks of them: Professor 1 is always right. Professor 2 is wrong half of the time. Professor 3 is wrong in one out of six cases. When the student successfully finishes the program, Professor 4 is always correct in saying so; but he is wrong half the time when the student does, in fact, not finish the program. Professor 5's optimism goes further: he always says the student will complete the program. Finally, Professor 6 is known to be always wrong.

For what follows you will completely trust Professor Cooper's judgment. Describe each of the six committee member's judgmental reliability by a 2×2 "likelihood matrix," whose elements are the conditional probabilities of the two possible judgments ("would complete program, would not complete program"), given the student's true state.

6.4. Suppose that a coin is either two-headed or that it is a balanced coin with heads on one side and tails on the other. We cannot inspect the coin, but at a cost of 5 cents we can flip it once, observe whether it comes up heads or tails, and then we must decide whether it is two-headed or not. Furthermore, there is a penalty of $2 if our decision is wrong, and no penalty (or rewards) if our decision is right.
(a) Determine the optimal strategy for experimentation and action using the extensive form of analysis.
(b) Determine the optimal strategy for experimentation and action using the normal form of analysis.

6.5. The product manager for a large firm is faced with choosing between two advertising campaigns for his product. The monetary return from sales generated by each of two campaigns (called a_1 and a_2, respectively), will depend upon the prevailing market conditions, which can be either good (θ_1) or bad (θ_2). The manager believes that a 50–50 chance exists for the occurrence of θ_1 versus θ_2. The monetary returns for each action–state combination are summarized below:

Advertising Campaign Problem

Act \ State	θ_1	θ_2
a_1	800	-500
a_2	0	0

The manager may elect to delay his terminal decision in order to gather information regarding which state is more likely to occur. Suppose that he has the following data-gathering options prior to making a terminal choice:
(a) e_0—do not experiment, but make a terminal choice now.
(b) e_1—purchase a perfect survey service; the cost of this survey is $250,000.
(c) e_2—purchase a survey that is 75% reliable; the cost of this survey is $75,000.
Using whatever analysis is at your disposal, determine what the marketing manager should do.

6.6. A decision is to be made as to whether or not to perform a *complete audit* of an accounts receivable file. Substantial errors in the file can result in a loss of revenue to the company. However, conducting a *complete audit* is expensive.

It has been estimated that the average cost of auditing one account is $6. However, if a *completed audit* is conducted, resulting in the true but *unknown* proportion p of the accounts in error being reduced, then the loss of revenue may be significantly reduced.

The audit manager has the option of first conducting a *partial audit* prior to his decision on the *complete audit*. Using the *prior* probability distribution and *payoffs* given in the table below, develop a single auditing plan based on a *partial audit* of three accounts. (*Note:* Work with opportunity losses.)

Prior Distribution: Payoff Table

		CONDITIONAL COST	
Proportion of Accounts in Error, p	Prior Probability of p, $P(p)$	Do Not Audit (NCA)	Complete Audit (CA)
0.05	0.2	$1,000	$10,000
0.50	0.7	10,000	10,000
0.95	0.1	29,000	10,000

(a) Develop the opportunity loss matrix.
(b) Structure the problem in the form of a decision tree. Specify all actions, sample outcomes, and events. Indicate opportunity losses and probabilities at all points on the tree. Show all calculations.
(c) Develop the conditional probability matrix.
(d) Develop the joint probability matrix.
(e) Is this plan better than not conducting a partial audit?
   (1) What is the expected opportunity loss (EOL) with no partial auditing?
   (2) What is the expected value of perfect information (EVPI)?
   (3) EOL (sampling, $n = 3$, $c = $?). (*Note:* c is the acceptance number.)
   (4) What is the expected value of sample information (EVSI)?
   (5) Which of the preceding sampling plans is better?
   (6) State how you would calculate the optimal sample plan.

CASE 6.1 Illustrative Case Study
Involving Sequential Decision Making

GOVERNMENT PROCUREMENT OF MAINTENANCE EQUIPMENT James Dean is a government project manager responsible for urgently acquiring three pieces of aircraft maintenance equipment. All three pieces, a specially designed and configured systems analyzer, maintenance stand, and hydraulic lift are needed to meet new Air Force maintenance requirements for certain aircraft.

Dean sees two options for obtaining the equipment: (1) to order from a contractor (A) who is under heavy schedule pressure to meet certain commercial airline orders but who can give competitive prices because of his proposed use of new technology to reduce costs; and (2) to order from his usual producer (B), who has the equipment in stock but at a significantly higher cost. The costs indicated to Dean by the two contractors are as follows:

	CORPORATION A (cost + fixed-fee contract)	CORPORATION B (fixed-price contract)
Systems analyzer, S	$100K (S)	$200K (S')
Maintenance stand, M	200K (M)	500K (M')
Hydraulic lift, H	400K (H)	700K (H')
	$700K	$1400K

Having obtained these costs, Dean wants to analyze his various options to determine which strategy might be best for the government. He assesses the chances of Corporation A delivering the various equipment as:

	ASSESSMENT OF PROBABILITY OF DELIVERY	
	On Time	Too Late
Systems analyzer, S	0.8	0.2
Maintenance stand, M	0.7	0.3
Hydraulic lift, H	0.5	0.5

He thinks that the probabilities assessed are independent; that is, a piece of equipment delivered on time does not change the likelihood that a subsequent delivery will be on time.

Dean's contracting officer lays down the following constraints on the procurement flexibility: "Dean, you have two options—buy all three from B, because we have an obvious sole-source justification, or all three from Corporation A. That is, once you start your procurement, you must buy all three pieces of equipment from the same company, unless at any time Corporation A cannot deliver; in that case, you, of course, will pay Corporation A for that piece of equipment under your cost-plus contract and then purchase that piece of equipment and the remaining piece of equipment from Corporation B under a fixed-price contract. Since the systems analyzer has the first pressing deadline, you must buy it first, then either the maintenance stand or the hydraulic lift. Also, Corporation A has enough capacity to work on only one machine at a time."

Dean knows that he must prepare an analysis to support his decision for acquiring the equipment. Obviously, the best he can do costwise is with Corporation A, buying all three pieces of equipment for $700K; the worst is with Corporation B at $1400K. It all seems straightforward; nevertheless, while preparing his decision briefing, nagging doubts arise in his mind. If he goes with Corporation A, with Corporation B in a fall-back position, he realizes he might be required to pay more than twice Corporation A's price for the whole process. It might then be irrational to go with Corporation A, and he starts vacillating in his choice between the two.

1. As Dean, indicate, without doing any explicit analysis, which strategy you would recommend. Then indicate what further analyses you would want to perform and what information these analyses could reveal for decision making.
2. Diagram the decision problem with a decision tree.
3. Using the backward-induction process, determine the best strategy.
4. If you were Dean, would you adopt the best strategy? Why?

CASE 6.2   Illustrative Case Study
Involving Information Acquisition Decisions

CITY PLANNING   The small town of Mesquite must decide whether or not to develop a new
STRATEGIES FOR   ground-water supply. If they choose to develop it, the quantity of water will be
WATER RESOURCES   either "high" or "low." The objective of the town is to minimize costs of
DEVELOPMENT   development. The town may make a geological survey costing $5000 to measure the quantity of water in the aquifer. Results of such a survey will be categorized as "great," "good," or "poor." If the quantity is "high," the benefit, not including geological survey costs, is $50,000. If the quantity is "low," there will be a cost of $100,000 excluding geological survey costs. Note that the sale of surplus water may offset the cost if the quantity is "high." A cost of $60,000 will be incurred if the alternative to ground-water development is chosen.

The local water planners feel that the a priori probability of a "high" quantity of water in a nearby aquifer is 0.4. Given they knew that a "high" quantity would result, the planners would assign a probability of 0.6 to the likelihood that the geological survey was "great," 0.3 to the likelihood it is "good," and 0.1 to the likelihood it is "poor." The corresponding probabilities, given that the quantity would be "low," are 0.1 "great," 0.3 "good," and 0.6 "poor."

Question. What is the best strategy to follow in this problem? That is, should a geologic survey be conducted and should the town develop the ground water?

CHAPTER 7
Multiple Objectives and Decision Making

OBJECTIVES. To be able to:

1. Understand some of the different types of multiattribute utility models that can be applied to decision problems having multiple conflicting objectives under conditions of certainty and uncertainty.
2. Distinguish between noncompensatory and compensatory multiattribute utility models in terms of their assumptions, applicability, and differences in the results obtained in various decision situations.
3. Understand the relationship between various multiattribute utility models and mathematical programming models.

7.1. INTRODUCTION

Up to this point, the concepts and models we have developed have been applicable to decision problems where there existed a single objective or criterion, say, for example, profit or cost. The actions could be evaluated based on this criterion or its utility transform, and an optimal action could be chosen.

In most real decision situations, the choice of the best action must be based on multiple aspects or criteria. That is, each action has associated with it a set or vector of various consequences. For example:

In *personal life*, the *job* we choose may depend on its prestige, location, salary, advancement opportunities, working conditions, and so forth. The *car* we buy may be characterized in terms of price, horsepower, and riding comfort. The *vacation* site we choose may be described by such attributes or dimensions as climate, social opportunities, sports activities, and so on.

In *business*, the manager's or business executive's choice of *corporate strategy* would depend on the company's profits over time, its stock price, share of market, goodwill, labor relations, corporate image, societal obligations, and so forth. The manager's choice of a *secretary* may depend on her typing and shorthand skills, attractiveness, and cooperativeness. His or her choice of a *pricing policy* for a new product would depend on profitability, market share, prevention of competitive entry, and so on. The company's choice of a computer would depend on such factors as speed, memory capacity, input–output capability, maintainability, service and support from the manufacturer, and so on.

In *government*, the choice of a weapons system for the military may be selected on the basis of vulnerability, reliability, cost, yield, and so on. The choice of a national energy policy would have to consider such factors as costs, ecology, international politics, social problems, health problems, and so on.

In *medicine*, the choice of treatment may depend on cost, probability of side effects, probability of cure, probability of complications, probability of relapse, days in bed with various levels of discomfort, and so on.

This chapter is concerned with precisely these sorts of problems, that is, choosing an alternative course of action when there are multiple conflicting objectives (we say alternatives are multiattributed; that is, they have multiple consequences). Considering the pervasiveness of this type of problem, it is perhaps surprising that only recently has serious attention been given by scientists to the development of various models and techniques for dealing with multiple objective (multiattribute) decision making. Managerial interest in the multiattribute decision problem has increased considerably, reflecting the fact that managers themselves have become cognizant of the complexity of alternatives, even in the "profit-conscious" private sector of our society. Thus, developments in both technique and substantive interest have prompted application of formal analytical approaches to this class of problems.

In this chapter we shall consider various techniques and models for dealing with multiattribute decision problems. In rather gross terms, the problem is: "How can a decision maker choose the best of several alternative actions when each action will result in a set or vector of outcomes and where each outcome can at best be described only in terms of its performance characteristics on many diverse dimensions or attributes?"

The general problem is first described in terms of an illustrated case example. We then introduce various kinds of multiattribute choice models for dealing with decision problems under certainty and provide a classification scheme for these models. The models are then illustrated numerically in terms of our case example and points of similarity and difference are discussed. We then deal with the more complex multiattribute problem under uncertainty (of which certainty is a special case).

7.2. EXAMPLE—WEAPONS SYSTEM SELECTION PROBLEM

Suppose, for a particular anticipated military requirement, that within the general U.S. military mission a choice must be made among designs for a future aircraft weapon system. Assume that a multiple-incentive contract has been awarded to a particular contractor. Three feasible types of system designs are being considered by the government contractor—call them a_1, a_2, and a_3. To simplify matters, no parallel design efforts are feasible; that is, the contractor cannot consider simultaneous development of more than one design alternative, nor sequential development of a second or third design alternative if the first fails to achieve expectations.

7.2.1. Defining Goals, Attributes, and Criteria

The relevant attributes in this decision problem would be generated by careful political–military consideration of the particular requirement within the overall mission (the "supergoal" or "meta-goal") and also future uses of the proposed system. Let us assume that the following three subgoals have been identified: (1) performance effectiveness, (2) scheduled development completion, and (3) system development cost. Performance, reflected in terms of expected target destruction, may be further decomposed into its subgoals of probability of reaching target, expected destruction if target is reached and future usage possibilities. These attributes, in turn, could be decomposed still further to yield such meaningfully measurable specifications as speed, distance, delivery (reaction) time, vulnerability, accuracy, reliability, and so on. The decomposition process could, of course, continue further.

The decision maker would initially generate a reasonably exhaustive menu of relevant attributes at each level. The extent of the partitioning of attributes would depend on the levels necessary to capture the essence of the problem and to obtain some rational prospect of measurability. This last statement is a really substantive issue of major importance, that is: "Are the attributes defined a sufficiently rich and meaningful set of descriptors to capture the essence of the problem area?" This issue will be circumvented by assuming that this is, in fact, so in our example problem. Not all the attributes generated, however, need to be used, since some may be redundant while others may not serve to discriminate among alternatives. An example of the first case would be the redundancy contained in the attributes of speed, distance, and delivery time; an example of the second case would be if the same yield applied to all systems. Figure 7.1 exhibits the hierarchy of attributes associated with the example problem.

Suppose such a logical analysis has occurred and the attributes remaining are delivery (reaction) time, range, schedule, cost, and vulnerability (the numbered attributes in Figure 7.1). The characterization of each system in terms of these attributes is given in Table 7.1. We shall assume that the attribute values are known uniquely for each event (or are expected values), although in many decision situations (especially in research and development) this information would be uncertain. The extra complication of uncertainty about attribute values is later considered briefly.

An alternative design is thus defined in terms of a vector or set of consequences, one consequence associated with each relevant attribute. For example, alternative design a_1 is characterized by a delivery time of 5 hours, a range of 6000 nautical miles, a completion time of within 3 years, a cost of $14 million per system, and an average vulnerability.

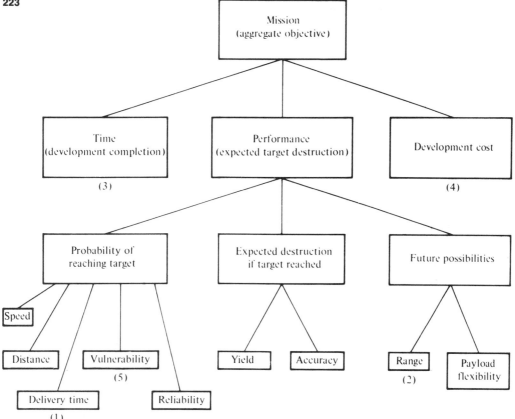

Figure 7.1. Hierarchy of objectives, subgoals, and specifications.

Table 7.1. Systems Development Decision Problem

	ALTERNATIVE DESIGN		
Attribute	a_1	a_2	a_3
(1) Delivery time (hours)	5	3	2
(2) Range (nautical miles)	6000	4000	5000
(3) Schedule (years)	3	2	4
(4) Cost ($\$ \times 10^6$)	14	16	12
(5) Vulnerability (high–low)	Average	High	Low

The value of the first four attributes in Table 7.1 is expressed quantitatively. The fifth attribute, vulnerability, is expressed qualitatively as high, average, or low. The quantitative attributes possess a more or less natural measure or metric. Qualitative attributes, while also expressible in terms of numerical ratings, require some type of judgmental or subjective metric to be imposed.

7.3. SOME CONSIDERATIONS INVOLVING MULTIATTRIBUTE DECISIONS

Assuming that we are restricted to the information given in Table 7.1, which alternative design should we choose? The choice, of course, will depend on the nature of the mission. If the decision maker wants the system with the greatest range, he would choose a_1. For the system with the lowest vulnerability, he would choose a_3. If, however, he wanted the system with the fastest delivery time, he would also choose a_3. By thus focusing on a single attribute only, he could justify the choice of any one system. But since all five attributes affect mission effectiveness, the decision maker must decide considering all five attributes.

Decision theory and decision analysis apply strongly to this goal-oriented systems decision situation. The decision maker undertakes the systems effort to achieve known goals and objectives. He considers only those alternatives and criteria which, to the best of his knowledge, significantly influence the success of the effort. He can, therefore, compare outcomes. Moreover, the decision maker can choose in accordance with the criterion of utility maximization (i.e., assign utilities to the multiattribute consequences of each action) or, in the case of uncertainty, expected utility maximization (i.e., assign probabilities to events and utilities to the multiattribute consequences, compute expected utilities, and choose the alternative with the highest expected utility). The utility or expected utility concept is theoretically sound, and the mathematical details are not involved. Unfortunately, however, there are currently many difficulties which limit the applicability of decision theory for the analysis of real-world problems. One key limitation is the difficulty of assessing utility functions. For decisions where consequences are adequately described by a single variable, existing utility assessment methods are adequate. However, when many variables are required to describe the consequences being considered, then utility assessment becomes more difficult. It is perhaps unrealistic to expect a decision maker to come up with a utility value without providing him with some means of sorting out the attribute information for each alternative.

Let us now consider some of the methods available to a decision maker for dealing with a multiattribute decision problem.

7.3.1. Processing of Attribute Information

If we examine the three alternative designs in Table 7.1, we note that decision makers would probably process the attribute information in two basic ways:

1. They could try to collapse each candidate design into a single utility number that represents the design's overall value or worth.
2. They could try to arrive at a decision by procedures that retain the individuality of the various attributes in the information processing steps; that is, use procedures that do not require interattribute comparisons.

An example of the first procedure would be to assign "importance weights" (i.e., scaling factors) to each of the attributes after, say, assigning a utility to each attribute value.[†] The weights, w_j, could then be used to arrive at an aggregated utility $U(a_i)$ for each alternative by taking a weighted linear combination of the attribute values associated with each alternative:

$$U(a_i) = \sum_{j=1}^{m} w_j u(a_{ij}) \quad (\text{for} \quad i = 1, \ldots, n; j = 1, \ldots, m),$$

where $m = 5$ and $n = 3$ in our case example. Note that this approach has effectively transformed or mapped each multiattribute design configuration into a single overall or aggregated utility.

An example of the second method of processing attribute information would be to assign satisfactory–unsatisfactory levels for each attribute separately and then to find that design, if any exists, that meets all satisfactory (acceptable) criterion levels. For example, we could define minimum acceptable design standards on delivery of 3 hours, range of 5000 miles, schedule of 2 years, cost of $12 million per system, and not worse-than-average vulnerability. If no design meets all these specifications, one or more of the acceptable levels could be relaxed until at least one design is acceptable. If two or more designs are acceptable, then some other procedure, including the possibility of specification tightening (i.e., changing the satisfactory–unsatisfactory levels), could be used. Note, however, that this second procedure retains the individuality of the attributes; that is, a low delivery time cannot compensate for or offset a short range. In short, tradeoffs are not permissible in this case.

7.3.2. Nature of Decision Maker's Task

The decision maker's evaluative task may take different forms, ranging from making a numerical assignment of overall utility (mission effectiveness in our example) to each design to merely dividing the designs into acceptable versus unacceptable subsets. Again, the choice of response measures reflects the purposes of the investigation. If only a single design is to be selected (the more likely situation in our example), one may wish to find only the maximal element of the set and hence not be concerned with a complete ranking among the remaining $n-1$ designs. If a winner and runner-up are to be selected, these designs must be strictly ranked within this subset. Also, in terms of overall evaluation, each design

[†]As will be described later, the w_j may be elicited directly from the decision maker (e.g., via gambles in risky situations) or may be derived from a statistical procedure, such as multiple regression analysis, that considers the decision maker's overall evaluative responses to varied combinations of the attribute levels. This weight is *not*, in general, a measure of the "relative importance" of each attribute, but reflects the relative importance of each attribute going from its *worst* to its *best* value, where "worst" and "best" values are those used in determining the individual unidimensional utility functions on each attribute. Alternately stated, w_j is a measure of the relative importance of these *changes* in the attribute values, not of the attributes themselves.

must be strictly better than the remaining designs with no ordering required within the remaining designs.

If only a subset of designs is to be picked for subsequent evaluation, we need only establish that all designs of the preferred subset exceed, in overall utility, all designs of the unpreferred subset. No ranking of designs within each subset is required.

7.4. MULTIATTRIBUTE MODELS AND TECHNIQUES

For the purposes of formalism, let us first introduce some notation. Let a set of alternatives $\{a\}$ be given, each alternative a_i being characterized by a set or vector $a_i = (a_{ij}, \ldots, a_{im})$, where a_{ij} is the value (not necessarily numerical) of the jth attribute for alternative a_i. It is assumed that a preference ordering (not necessarily monotonic) is defined on each attribute. That is, we can indicate our preferences for different values of a given attribute. For example, we prefer more range to less range, a shorter delivery time to a longer delivery time, and so forth. We thus write

$$a_{1j} \geqslant a_{2j}$$

and
$$a_{1j} > a_{2j} \qquad (7.4.1)$$

to indicate that the value of the jth attribute of alternative 1 (a_{1j}) is not worse or, rather, is better than the value of the jth attribute of alternative 2. For example, for the second attribute, range ($j = 2$), $a_{12} > a_{22}$, since $a_{12} = 6000$ and $a_{22} = 4000$.

Having established this notation, we next consider the principal ways in which attribute information of the type illustrated in Table 7.1 can be processed in order to arrive at a choice. Two basic approaches discussed earlier can be utilized and are classified as compensatory and noncompensatory models:

1. *Noncompensatory models* do not permit tradeoffs between or among attributes. Comparisons are made on an attribute-by-attribute basis, and in general the multidimensional characterizations are not amalgable into a single utility number. In other words, the full dimensionality of the attribute space is generally retained (although there are exceptions).
2. *Compensatory models* permit tradeoffs between attributes. That is, in these models, changes (perhaps small changes only) in one attribute can be offset by opposing changes in any other attribute. With compensatory models a single utility is assigned to each multidimensional characterization representing an alternative. Tradeoffs between attributes are generated by different characterizations that have equal utilities. Thus, the full dimensionality of the attribute space is reduced to a single overall dimension of utility.

Figure 7.2 categorizes and depicts the models and techniques to be examined in

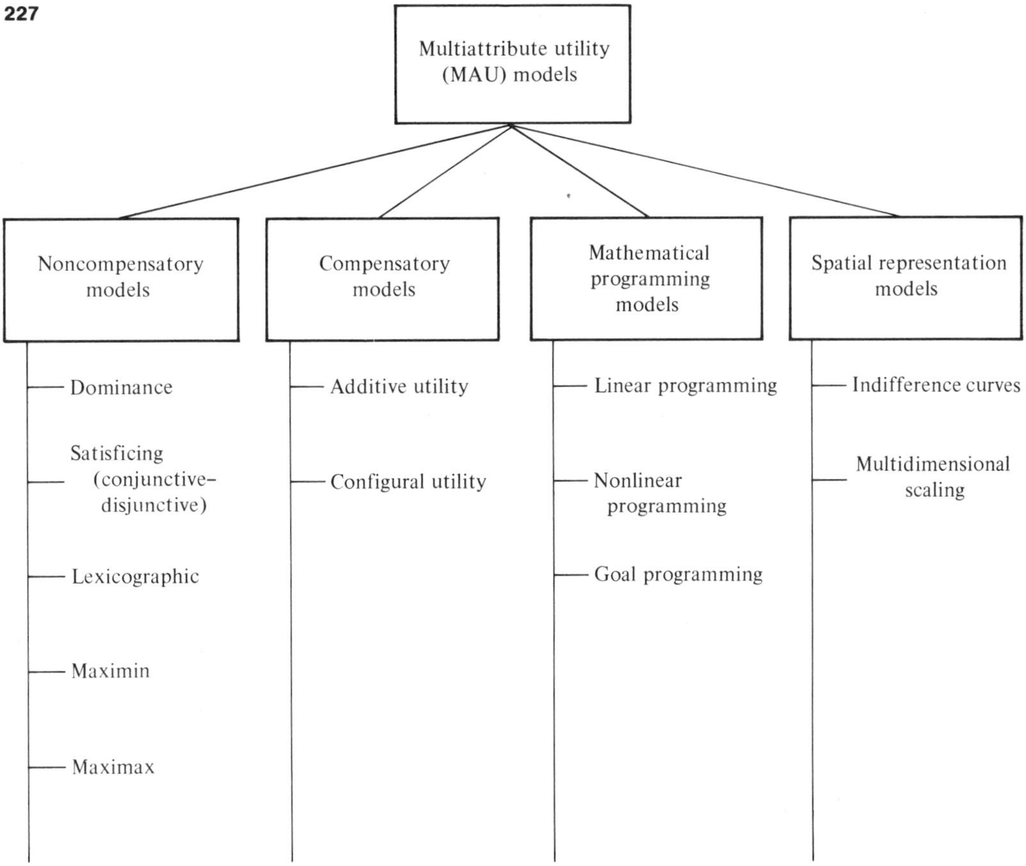

Figure 7.2. Multiattribute utility models and techniques.

this chapter. Note in Figure 7.2 that mathematical programming and spatial representation models are treated as special categories of MAU models. These classes of models have been listed separately because (1) their scope warrants their separate treatment, and (2) they do not purely fit into compensatory or noncompensatory classifications. For example, linear programming can be viewed as a compensatory model, goal programming as a noncompensatory model. A more extensive discussion of multiattribute models and techniques can be found in (Keeney and Raiffa, 1973; MacCrimmon, 1973).

7.4.1. Noncompensatory Models

The following models are *noncompensatory* multiattribute utility models: (1) dominance models, (2) satisficing models (conjunctive and disjunctive), (3) lexicographic models, (4) maximin (or minimax) models, and (5) maximax models. Let us consider each in turn.

DOMINANCE MODELS. We can reduce the number of alternatives that need to be examined by eliminating those that are "dominated"; alternative a_1 is said to dominate alternative a_2 if

$$a_{1j} \geqslant a_{2j} \qquad \text{(for all } j \text{ attributes)}$$

and, further, $\qquad a_{1j} > a_{2j} \qquad \text{(for at least one of the } j \text{ attributes).} \qquad (7.4.2)$

That is, when comparing all alternatives, if one alternative has at least as good or higher attribute values for all attributes, we say that this alternative *dominates* the others. In other words, the utility of a_1 is greater than the utility of a_2 ($U(a_1) > U(a_2)$), and thus a_1 is preferred to a_2 ($a_1 > a_2$). The elimination leaves us with undominated (also called *admissible*, *Pareto-optimal*) alternatives only.

In Table 7.1 none of the three alternatives is dominated (i.e., each of them is admissible). For example, in comparing design a_1 to design a_2, delivery time is worse for a_1 (5 versus 3 hours), range is better (6000 versus 4000 nautical miles), schedule is worse (3 versus 2 years), cost is better ($14 versus $16 million), and vulnerability is better (average versus high). If, however, alternatives a_1 and a_2 had the same delivery time and scheduled completion date, a_1 would dominate a_2, since a_1's range, cost, and vulnerability are better than a_2's (6000 versus 4000 nautical miles, $14 versus $16 million, and average versus high, respectively). In this manner, dominance can be a useful method for simplifying a decision problem by reducing the size of the problem. Dominance is not a very powerful method for making a final decision, however, because there are usually a large number of alternatives remaining after the method is applied (especially when a large number of attributes are involved). When employing the dominance criterion: (1) numerical information about attribute values is unnecessary, (2) no assumption concerning the decision maker's degree of preference for particular attribute values is implied, and (3) nor does dominance require the decision maker to assess the relative importance of each of the attributes.

SATISFICING MODELS. There are two types of satisficing models we shall consider: conjunctive and disjunctive. Both conjunctive and disjunctive models are not usually employed to order alternatives but rather to dichotomize them into *acceptable–unacceptable* categories.

With *conjunctive* models we specify a minimal value g_j (*aspiration level, cutoff value, threshold value, goal level*) for each attribute, and we say that alternative a_i is "acceptable" if it dominates (or is not worse than) $g_1, \ldots, g_m$. In other words, all the standards or goals must be achieved or surpassed in order for the alternative to be acceptable.

In our weapons systems development example, suppose that the decision maker specified the following minimal requirements: delivery time, not greater than 3 hours; range, not less than 4000 miles; scheduled completion date, within 4 years or less; cost, not greater than $14 million; and vulnerability, not worse than average. Given these minimal acceptable values, only a_3 satisfies all these requirements and therefore is the only acceptable alternative.

With *disjunctive* models we specify a maximum value h_j for each *critical* attribute m, and we say that alternative a_i is "acceptable" if it surpasses that maximum value on each critical attribute. In the disjunctive form, only one or more standards must be exceeded for an alternative to be acceptable. Disjunctive models thus evaluate alternatives on the basis of their maximum rather than their minimum level. For purposes of illustration, suppose that a delivery time equal to or less than 2 hours or low vulnerability were essential for partitioning the set of alternatives into acceptable versus unacceptable designs. If so, each design would be compared on the basis of this attribute level only and all designs that met or surpassed the criteria levels of a delivery time of 2 hours and low vulnerability would be accepted. Only alternative a_3 would thus be acceptable.

As with the dominance model, after applying a satisficing model, we are often still left with a number of feasible alternatives. Satisficing is, however, a more powerful technique than dominance because it can be used interactively by successively raising (or lowering) the aspiration levels. Its drawbacks are that it requires knowledge of the aspiration levels and that alternatives do not get credited (penalized) for especially good (bad) attribute values. The satisficing models, similar to dominance models, do not require interattribute comparisons nor that the attribute information be in numerical form. We need only know which value is preferred, other things being equal. Further, with satisficing (as with dominance) we do not need information on the relative importance of the attributes. In a sense, though, the information requirements for satisficing are greater than those for dominance because we need to have information on the minimal (or maximal) acceptable attribute values. It should be noted again that if we simply use minimum (or maximum) cutoff values for each of the attributes, none of the alternatives receives credit (penalties) for especially good (bad) attribute values.

Dominance and satisficing are two noncompensatory procedures that treat multiattribute decision problems in their full dimensionality. While both of these methods are effective in reducing the set of alternatives to be evaluated in a final choice, they are relatively weak in making the final choice, although satisficing procedures may be strengthened by applying them iteratively. Dominance uses an alternative by alternative comparison, where every alternative is compared to each other. Satisficing, however, involves an alternative to standard (goal) comparison, where each alternative is compared with a minimal or maximal goal vector.

In the remaining noncompensatory procedures, the m attributes characterizing an alternative are reduced to a single dimension.

LEXICOGRAPHY. Lexicographic models are distinguished from the preceding models in that the processing of attribute data proceeds sequentially. Alternatives are first ranked in accordance with the most important attribute (goal). If all alternatives can be ordered with respect to the most important attribute, the remaining attributes are not considered. However, if some alternatives are tied on the most important attribute, the decision maker proceeds to the next most important attribute for resolving the subset of tied alternatives. The process continues sequentially until all alternatives are ranked or until all m attributes have been considered.

Thus, we can define a lexicographic model as follows. Suppose that we have m attributes and these attributes are ranked such that attribute 1 is more important than attribute 2, attribute 2 is more important than attribute 3, and so forth. Consider two alternative actions a_1 and a_2 having the following attribute levels:

$$a_1 = (a_{11}, a_{12}, \ldots, a_{1m})$$
$$a_2 = (a_{21}, a_{22}, \ldots, a_{2m}).$$

Then, by lexicographic ordering, a_1 is preferred to a_2 ($a_1 > a_2$) if $a_{11} > a_{21}$, irrespective of the relationship between a_{1j} and a_{2j} for $j > 1$. If $a_{11} = a_{21}$, then the choice between a_1 and a_2 is based on the relative values of the second attributes a_{12} versus a_{22}. If $a_{12} = a_{22}$, the choice is made by reference to the third attribute (i.e., a_{13} versus a_{23}), and so on.[†]

Generally speaking, lexicographic models assume separate and independent utility functions for each attribute and a preference ordering for attributes. Hence, the lexicographic model is noncompensatory and cannot be represented by a single or overall utility. No consideration is given to attribute k if it is possible to rank all alternatives with regard to attribute j, the most important attribute.

In the weapons system development example, suppose that delivery time is the most important attribute. Since a_3 has the fastest delivery time, it is the preferred alternative. If, say, a_2 and a_3 had the same delivery time and this was less than a_1, then a_1 is eliminated from consideration and a_2 and a_3 are compared on the next most important dimension (e.g., range). Action a_3 would then be chosen since its range is greater than a_2.

In making a choice, a combination of the three preceding methods is suggested as being both very reasonable and computationally simple. That is, we might use a satisficing model first, then dominance, and finally lexicography.

The dominance, satisficing, and lexicographic models are noncompensatory in the sense that alternatives can be evaluated on an attribute-by-attribute basis across all attributes. That is, no interattribute comparisons have been made; hence, in using these models, the scale of one attribute does not need to be commensurable (or comparable) with the scales of other attributes. For example, one attribute could be expressed in terms of hours and another in terms of nautical miles, as is the case in our systems development example. Moreover, attribute values have not been required to be numerical.

We shall now review two noncompensatory models—maximin and maximax—which characterize each alternative by a single overall utility and require attribute values to be numerical and commensurable to allow interattribute com-

---

[†]A procedure very similar to lexicography is the elimination by aspects approach discussed by Tversky (1972), and a similar approach put in a mathematical programming framework by Halter and Dean (1971). Like lexicography, it examines one attribute at a time, making comparisons among alternatives. However, these procedures differ slightly in that they eliminate alternatives which do not satisfy some standard. Moreover, Tversky's approach does not order attributes in terms of importance, but rather, in terms of their likely ability to discriminate among alternatives.

parability. This requires us to place all attribute-value information on a comparable numerical scale.

Let us first examine the question of quantifying the nonnumerical values associated with the qualitative attribute of vulnerability, shown in Table 7.1. One common quantification procedure is to construct a scale associating the qualitative terms with numbers on the scale. For example, we might choose a 100-point scale and calibrate it in one of several ways. We could start with the end points, giving 100 points to the maximum attribute value that is practically or physically realizable and 0 points to the minimum attribute value that is practically or physically realizable. The midpoint would also be a basis for calibration, since it would be the breakpoint between values that are favorable (e.g., better than average) and values that are unfavorable (e.g., worse than average). The type of scaling used could be of major importance in the final choice made, but since our principal interest is not in scaling but rather in the models (that either require or do not require scaling), we shall assume that one scaling procedure is selected and is used consistently.[†] Thus, we can proceed by assigning attribute values more favorable than "average," a score of more than 50 points, while values less favorable would be assigned less than 50 points.

Taking our only qualitative attribute of vulnerability, assume that the decision maker assigns a value of 30 to high vulnerability, 50 to average vulnerability, and 90 to low vulnerability. The scale values for vulnerability are diagrammed in Figure 7.3. When the numerical values on the scale in Figure 7.3 are substituted for the corresponding qualitative vulnerability values in Table 7.1, we obtain Table 7.2.

Table 7.2. Assigning Quantitative Values to Qualitative Attributes

Attribute	ALTERNATIVE DESIGN		
	a_1	a_2	a_3
(1) Delivery time (hours)	5	3	2
(2) Range (nautical miles)	6000	4000	5000
(3) Schedule (years)	3	2	4
(4) Cost ($ $\times$ 10^6)	14	16	12
(5) Vulnerability (100, high; 0, low)	50	30	90

It should be obvious that numerical assignments such as those given above are highly arbitrary. Many other scales are possible. This type of scaling assumes that a scale value of 90 is three times as favorable as a scale value of 30. For example, for vulnerability an attribute value of "low" is three times as favorable as one of "high." Furthermore, it assumes that the difference between "low" and "high" vulnerability is the same as the difference between "very low" and "average"

[†]For the case of certainty, such scaling is often called a *value function*; for the case of uncertainty it is called a *utility function*. For a discussion of scaling, see Green and Wind (1973) and Torgenson (1958).

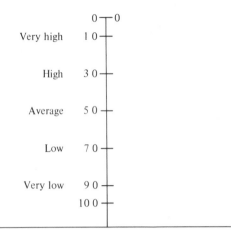

Figure 7.3. Assignment of values on a numerical scale, for vulnerability.

vulnerability (40 scale points). Further, the combination of values across attributes implies that the difference between any two specific values (say, "high" and "low") is the same for each attribute; that is, that the difference between "low" and "high" vulnerability is the same as the difference between "low" and "high" systems cost (assuming that we put cost values on a comparable scale).

Even after the qualitative attribute values have been quantified, we must still make all the numerical values comparable. Using the scaling procedure described above, let us assume that the decision maker has derived comparable numerical values for the effectiveness of each alternative in achieving each criterion (attribute) on the same 0 to 100 scale, as shown in Table 7.3. We are now in a position to review the two noncompensatory procedures of maximin and maximax.

Table 7.3. Comparable Numerical Values to System Attributes

Normalized Importance Weights	Attribute	ALTERNATIVE DESIGN		
		a_1	a_2	a_3
0.55	Delivery time	30	50	75
0.25	Range	60	40	50
0.10	Schedule	52	80	40
0.05	Cost	68	60	80
0.05	Vulnerability	50	30	90

MAXIMIN. The maximin procedure selects the alternative with the largest minimum value of any attribute. In symbols,

$$\max\{a_i\} \min_j a_{ij} \qquad (7.4.3)$$

The maximin method can be used only when interattribute values are comparable. The method uses what could be called a specialized degenerate weighting, since the weighting, which may be different for each alternative, assigns a weight of "1" to the worst attribute value and a weight of "0" to all others. The method requires that, for each alternative, the decision maker compare all attribute values in order to identify the poorest value. This poorest attribute value is then used to represent the alternative. The rule for the decision maker, then, is to select that alternative with the maximum of these minimum values.

The only time maximin is applicable is when the overall performance of the alternative is determined by the weakest attribute (e.g., the weakest link in a chain). In our weapon systems development problem, for example, the decision maker would decide on an aircraft design by determining the worst characteristic of each design having the least worst characteristic.

In applying the maximin procedure to our example, we note in Table 7.3 that the lowest attribute value for a_1 is 30 (for delivery time); the lowest attribute value for a_2 is 30 (for vulnerability); the lowest attribute value for a_3 is 40 (for schedule). Since the largest of these three minimum values is 40, a_3 would be selected because it has the *maximum–minimum* value (in the event of ties other criteria would have to be used to make the final selection). It should be evident that this method utilizes only a small part of the available information in making a final choice— only one attribute per alternative. Thus, even if an alternative is clearly superior in all but one attribute, another alternative that is only average on all attributes would be chosen over it. The maximin procedure, then, can have obvious shortcomings in decision situations.

MAXIMAX. The maximax procedure selects the alternative with the largest highest value of any attribute. In symbols,

$$\max\{a_i\} \max_{j} a_{ij}. \tag{7.4.4}$$

In contrast to the maximin method, the maximax method represents an alternative by its best attribute value. It, too, requires a high degree of comparability and utilizes a specialized, degenerate weighting (with a weight of "1" assigned to the best attribute and "0" to all others). In both maximax and minimax cases the final choice is made by considering only one attribute per alternative, which is generally undesirable. Both methods assume all attributes to be interchangeable in the sense that it does not matter which one we maximize.

This method is applicable when the alternatives, which are described by multiattributes, can be specialized in use to one attribute and the decision maker has no a priori requirement as to which attribute this is. For example, the decision maker in our weapons systems development problem might wish to choose a weapons system based on each design's outstanding characteristic, choosing the design having the most highly developed single capability. Although this procedure might seem useful in a single instance, it is clearly inadequate when considering the whole multiattribute problem.

In Table 7.3, under the maximax procedure, the highest attribute value for a_1 is 68 (for cost), the highest value for a_2 is 80 (for scheduled completion date), and the highest value for a_3 is 90 (for vulnerability). Maximizing these maximum values would then lead to a choice of a_3.

7.4.2. Compensatory Models

Compensatory models, like maximin and maximax, are used to ultimately describe all alternatives in terms of single overall utility numbers. These models, like maximin and maximax, require that attribute-value information be placed on a comparable numerical scale. Moreover, we must consider the relative importance of each attribute. The basic steps in the procedure are: (1) to quantify all attribute values on a comparable numerical scale for all alternatives (as was done in Table 7.3); (2) to assign relative "importance weights" (the weights have been normalized to sum to 1; this reflects the relative importance of each attribute as a percentage of the total) to the attribute values, reflecting their influence on the overall utility; and (3) for each alternative, use addition and/or multiplication operations across attributes to derive an overall utility measure.

The term "compensatory" is used in the sense that a low value on some attribute can be compensated (or "traded off") for by a high value on some other attribute. The various ways in which attribute values compensate for one another serve, in part, to distinguish the models. The models described in the section are:

1. The *additive utility model*.
2. *Configural utility models* (i.e., quasi-additive, multiplicative), including compensatory approximations of the conjunctive–disjunctive models.
3. *Spatial representation models*, in which the dimensional arguments constitute a space of more limited dimensionality than the original attribute space. Within this reduced space, however, the utility model is assumed to be compensatory.
4. *Mathematical programming models*.

Before considering each type of model in turn, we shall first discuss the concept of making tradeoffs.

MAKING TRADEOFFS. A principal function of a manager is to make tradeoffs among multiple attributes in a decision problem. For example, the manager may trade off risk for profit in choosing a new product or venture, reliability for cost in selecting a weapons system, long-term health hazards resulting from side effects for a short-term cure of an ailment in deciding on whether to introduce a new drug, etc. A tradeoff is simply a statement of how much of one attribute a person would be willing to give up in order to obtain a specified gain in some other attribute, and vice versa.

One approach for making tradeoffs and using this as a basis for evaluating alternatives in a decision problem would be to ask a decision maker to make tradeoffs until this person is indifferent between the outcomes describing a given actual alternative (O_1) and a prescribed (reference) set of outcomes (O_1^1)—i.e., $O_1 \sim O_1^1$. The decision maker could do the same for each actual alternative being considered—e.g., if there were two alternatives, the decision maker would also make tradeoffs such that $O_2 \sim O_2^1$. This tradeoff process would be structured such that the reference outcomes O_1^1 and O_2^1 would have the same value for all attributes except one. Since the outcome vectors O_1^1 and O_2^1 would be equal for all attributes but one, it would be easy to select one of them. If O_1^1 were preferred to O_2^1 this would imply that alternative a_1 would be preferred to a_2, since $O_1 \sim O_1^1 > O_2 \sim O_2^1$.

Let us illustrate the use of making tradeoffs on the weapons system development problem depicted in Figure 7.1, considering only alternatives a_1 and a_2. We will use the following respective reference attribute values for delivery time, range, schedule, and vulnerability: (3, 4000, 3, 13, average). That is, for each alternative, tradeoffs will be made on cost to achieve these same values on these attributes; in the end, only the value for the cost attribute will generally be different among the alternatives.

To demonstrate the process on alternative a_1 suppose we ask the decision maker, how much of an increase in cost he would be willing to tolerate before he would be indifferent between a_1 [represented by (5, 6000, 3, 14, average)] and another alternative represented by the outcomes (3, 6000, 3, ?, average). That is, if delivery time is reduced from 5 to 3 hours, how much of an increase in cost is he willing to trade off for this reduction in delivery time such that he would be indifferent between a_1 and the partially described alternative (3, 6000, 3, ?, average)? Suppose he says one million dollars. Then (5, 6000, 3, 14, average) $\sim$ (3, 6000, 3, 15, average). To continue, next we say, let us take the alternative we have just identified (3, 6000, 3, 15, average), and let us reduce range to 4000 miles. How much does the cost have to be reduced to make the decision maker indifferent? Suppose he says two million dollars. Then (3, 6000, 3, 15, average) $\sim$ (3, 4000, 3, 13, average). The tradeoffs made by the decision maker for alternative a_1 are summarized in the table (we assume that expressions of indifference are transitive):

Decision Maker's Indifference	Tradeoff
(5, 6000, 3, 14, average) $\sim$ (3, 6000, 3, 15, average)	Reduce delivery time by 2 hours for a cost increase of $1 million
(3, 6000, 3, 15, average) $\sim$ (3, 4000, 3, 13, average)	Reduce cost by $2 million for a 2000 mile reduction in range

Let us repeat this process with the decision maker for alternative a_2. There is no need to make tradeoffs with respect to delivery time or range since these values for

a_2 correspond to the reference values. However, we need to make tradeoffs on schedule and vulnerability. We therefore ask, if we increase schedule completion from 2 to 3 years how much of a reduction in cost will he tolerate such that he would be indifferent between a_2 (3, 4000, 2, 16, high) and the partially described alternative (3, 4000, 3, ?, high). Suppose the decision maker says $1.5 million. Then (3, 4000, 2, 16, high) $\sim$ (3, 4000, 3, 14.5, high). We then say, let us take the alternative we have just identified (3, 4000, 3, 14.5, high), and let us reduce vulnerability to average. How much does the cost have to be increased to make him indifferent? Suppose the decision maker says 1.75 million dollars. Then (3, 4000, 3, 14.5, high) $\sim$ (3, 4000, 3, 16.25, average). The tradeoffs made by the decision maker for alternative a_2 are summarized in the table.

Decision Maker's Indifference	*Tradeoff*
(3, 4000, 2, 16, high) $\sim$ (3, 4000, 3, 14.5, high)	Increased schedule completion by 1 year for a cost reduction of $1.5 million
(3, 4000, 3, 14.5, high) $\sim$ (3, 4000, 3, 16.25, average)	Reduce vulnerability to average for a cost increase of $1.75 million

Finally, we see that a_1 and a_2 are represented by identical outcomes except for cost—i.e., $a_1 = $ (3, 4000, 3, *13*, average) and $a_2 = $ (3, 4000, 3, *16.25*, average). Obviously, since a_1 is cheaper than a_2, *ceteris paribus*, a_1 is preferred to a_2.

This process of making tradeoffs is straightforward, conceptually simple, and applies to the case of uncertainty as well as certainty. It provides a useful means of evaluating several distinct alternatives that have multiple attributes. It does not require any particular assumptions about the preferences of the decision maker. All that is required is that at least one attribute be measurable on a continuous scale—e.g., dollars. Unfortunately this process can be tedious and time consuming, particularly if there are many attributes and alternatives. Other more formal approaches and models may be preferable in these cases.

ADDITIVE MODEL. This model has received the most attention and has been the most widely applied of all MAU models. The basic form of this model, as previously stated, is

$$U(a_i) = \sum_{j=1}^{m} w_j u(a_{ij}) \qquad (\text{for } i = 1, 2, \ldots, n; j = 1, 2, \ldots, m). \quad (7.4.5)$$

The w_j denote relative importances assigned to each of the attributes, reflecting their contribution to the overall utility. In essence each $w_j u(a_{ij})$ reflects the component utility of the value of the jth attribute associated with the ith alternative, that is, can be written as

$$U(a_i) = \sum_{j=1}^{m} u_{ij}, \qquad (7.4.6)$$

where $u_{ij} = w_j(u)a_{ij}$. Thus, in this model the utility of an alternative is equal to the sum of the utilities of its parts.

To illustrate the use of the model, let us again consider the weapons system development problem and assume a linear additive utility model applies. Suppose also that the importance weights reflecting the decision maker's tastes have also been determined for each of the attributes and have been normalized as shown in Table 7.3. Using equation (7.4.5), that is, multiplying these weights by the corresponding attribute values for each alternative and summing across alternatives, yields the following weighted averages (overall utilities):

$$U(a_1) = 42.60 \qquad U(a_2) = 53.00 \qquad U(a_3) = 63.25.$$

For example, $U(a_1)$ is determined as follows:

$$U(a_1) = 0.55(30) + 0.25(60) + 0.10(52) + 0.05(68) + 0.05(50) = 42.60.$$

The optimal action is a_3, since its utility is highest.

CONFIGURAL (NONLINEAR) UTILITY MODELS. Configural MAU models allow for more complex functions than the simple linear additive model of equation (7.4.5) or (7.4.6). For example, if we assume just two attributes and the attribute values interact, we would have the following configural model:

$$U(a_i) = w_1 u(a_{i1}) + w_2 u(a_{i2}) + w_3 u(a_{i1}, a_{i2}) \qquad (7.4.7)$$

where a_{i1} and a_{i2} are the values of the first and second attributes of the ith alternative, respectively:

$$U(a_i) = u_{i1} + u_{i2} + u_{i1, i2}, \qquad (7.4.8)$$

where u_{i1} and u_{i2} are the component utilities of the first and second attribute values and $u_{i1, i2}$ is the component utility contributed by the interaction effect. The interaction effect simply implies that each attribute is not valued unto itself, that is, cannot be separated into utilities for each individual attribute. In our weapons system problem, for example, a fast delivery time might not be valued independently of range, vulnerability, or any other attribute. A linear additive model could thus be unrealistic and lead to misleading conclusions if, for example, a fast delivery time is of little value unless the range is long and vulnerability is average or better. In sum, attributes cannot often be considered separately and added together as in equation (7.4.5).

Two other types of configural models that can be thought of as compensatory approximations to the conjunctive and disjunctive satisficing models described earlier are briefly mentioned. For the conjunctive model, approximation

$$U(a_i) = \prod_{j=1}^{m} u(a_{ij})^{w_j}, \qquad (7.4.9)$$

where the w_j are constants to be derived. The formulation above can be expressed in logarithmic form as

$$\log U(a_i) = \sum_{j=1}^{m} w_j \log u(a_{ij}). \qquad (7.4.10)$$

Equation (7.4.10) has the familiar linear additive form of equation (7.4.5) and thus can be solved in that fashion.

The disjunctive model approximation requires the selection of a set of maximal values h_j for all j attributes. These values are set arbitrarily above the highest values attainable for each alternative on a given attribute. The model is written as

$$U(a_i) = \prod_{j=1}^{m} \left(1/h_j - u(a_{ij})\right)^{w_j} \qquad (7.4.11)$$

or, in logarithmic form, as

$$\log U(a_i) = \sum_{j=1}^{m} \left[-w_j \log \left(h_j - u(a_{ij}) \right) \right], \qquad (7.4.12)$$

where the model represented by equation (7.4.8) is in the linear additive form of equation (7.4.5).

Other types of configural (nonlinear) models could be postulated. Suffice it to say that by suitable transformations it is often possible to represent these models in a linear additive form that is amenable to such procedures as regression analysis.

Let us conclude this section by saying that there are two basic methods for estimating the parameter values of compensatory MAU models: (1) *inference* from past choice data using a statistical model such as regression analysis, and (2) *direct query*. A good and readable account of these procedures is given and illustrated in Huber (1974).

SPATIAL REPRESENTATION MODELS. There are two types of these models. Both types will now be briefly considered.

INDIFFERENCE CURVES: Indifference curves, long used in economics, show the combinations of attribute values that are equally preferred. The alternatives to be evaluated are points on these indifference curves, and by identifying the indifference curve on which they lie, a complete ordering among the alternatives can be generated. In essence, this procedure is simply a graphical form for making tradeoffs. A feasible procedure for obtaining indifference curves is given by MacCrimmon and Toda (1969), and further discussion of indifference-curve representations is covered in Easton (1973).

To illustrate their use, suppose that in our weapons system development problem, the choice among alternatives a_1, a_2, and a_3 boiled down to the attribute values associated with delivery time and cost. Assume that indifference curves representing the decision maker's preferences have been developed as shown in Figure 7.4. Note that the closer the indifference curve is to the origin, the more it is preferred, since for a given delivery time, the indifference curve closer to the origin

Figure 7.4. Indifference curves for weapons system development problem.

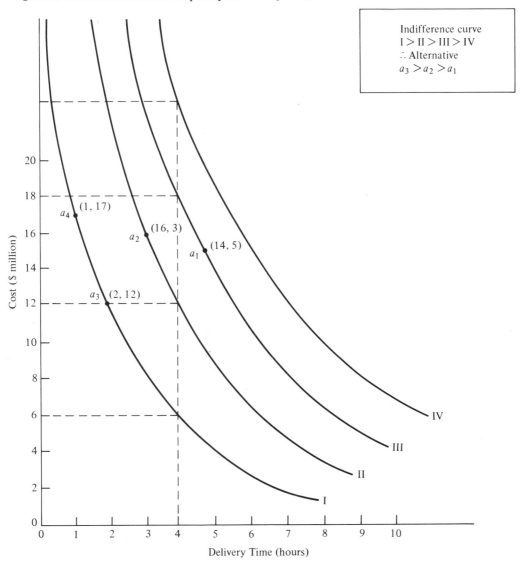

has a lower cost. Hence, indifference curve I > II > III > IV (where " > " means "preferred to"). Thus, in our weapons system problem, $a_3 > a_2 > a_1$ (" > " means "preferred to"), since I > II > III. Suppose there exists a fourth alternative a_4, which also falls on indifference curve I. Its delivery time and cost are 1 hour and \$17 million, respectively. Then we are indifferent between a_3 and a_4 because they both lie on the same indifference curve. In essence we are saying that the decision maker is willing to trade off a \$5 million increase in cost per system for a 1-hour reduction in delivery time.

MULTIDIMENSIONAL SCALING: These models are characterized by four attributes. These are:

1. A set of specified alternatives, in some cases with vague or unknown attribute values.
2. A procedure for obtaining intra- and interattribute judgments, or an aggregated judgment.
3. The construction of a spatial representation.
4. The identification of ideal configurations and the choice rule based on the proximity of alternatives to these ideal configurations.

The techniques of multidimensional scaling comprise a large body of literature too numerous to be covered in this text. The interested reader is referred to Green and Wind (1973) and references cited therein.

In multidimensional scaling the decision maker's orderings of the proximities of pairs of alternatives can be used to construct a multidimensional spatial representation. Alternatives are represented by points in this space. The points that are close together are assumed to be close together in terms of preference. The decision maker is asked to locate his ideal alternative in this space and then the distance from the ideal point is measured (using a Euclidean or other measure) in order to rank the alternatives in terms of preference.

MATHEMATICAL PROGRAMMING MODELS. This general class of models has the following set of common characteristics:

1. A *large* or *infinite* set of *alternatives*.
2. A set of technological, economic, or preference *constraints*.
3. An *objective function* that is compensatory.
4. An *algorithm* (e.g., the simplex method of linear programming) which converges toward an optimum solution.

The three basic types of mathematical programming models, covered in later chapters of this text are: (1) linear (noninteger or integer) programming, (2) nonlinear programming, and (3) goal programming. A fourth and recent model might be classified as multicriterion or interactive multicriterion programming. For a brief description of this method, the interested reader is referred to MacCrimmon (1973) and references cited therein.

LINEAR AND NONLINEAR PROGRAMMING: A regular linear (nonlinear) programming model may be viewed as a multiple attribute decision model in the following sense. The variables are the attributes, the linear (nonlinear) constraints are conjunctive constraints on combinations of attributes, and there is a linear (nonlinear), compensatory objective (utility) function. The object is to maximize or minimize the objective function subject to the constraints.

In contrast to the usual MAU models, there is not a small explicit list of alternatives from which to choose but rather a large or infinite set of feasible alternatives implicitly defined by the set of constraints. Efficient solution algorithms such as the simplex method of linear programming are used to find the optimal alternative by putting together the best combination or set of feasible attribute (variable) values. Typical types of MAU functions solvable by various mathematical programming algorithms are given in Table 7.4.

GOAL PROGRAMMING: In a goal programming formulation, the decision maker specifies acceptable or desired levels on single attribute values (i.e., one-variable constraints) or on combinations of attributes (i.e., multivariable constraints), and these serve as the primary goals. Instead of trying to maximize or minimize the objective function directly, as in linear (nonlinear) programming, the deviations among goals and what can be achieved within the given set of constraints are to be minimized. This is done with standard mathematical programming algorithms. In the simplex algorithm of linear programming, such deviations are called "slack" or "surplus" variables. These deviational variables take on a new significance in goal programming. The deviational variable is represented in two dimensions--positive and negative deviations from each subgoal or goal. Then the objective function becomes the minimization of these deviations, based on the relative importance or priority assigned to them.

The distinguishing characteristic of goal programming is that goals are satisfied in an ordinal sequence; that is, goals which are ranked in order of priority (importance) by the decision maker are satisfied sequentially by the solution algorithm. Obviously, it is not always possible to achieve every goal to the extent desired by management. In this sense goal programming may be viewed as a *lexicographic* procedure. In the sense that the decision maker attempts to achieve a "satisfactory" level of multiple objectives rather than the best possible outcome for a single objective (as with linear programming), goal programming is a *satisficing* procedure.

7.5. SUMMARY

In this chapter we have discussed four major classes of MAU models: (1) noncompensatory, (2) compensatory, (3) spatial representation, and (4) mathematical programming. It should be clear at this point that we could also take an eclectic approach by using a combination of these models. For example, in the weapons

Table 7.4. MAU Functions Solvable by Mathematical Programming Algorithms (parameters estimated by multiple regression)

MAU Model	Functional Form	Conditions	Algorithm
Linear additive	$U = \sum_{i=1}^{n} b_i x_i$, where x_i = fixed utility of the ith attribute, b_i = importance weight of the ith attribute	Linear constraints	Linear programming
Quasi additive (configural)	$U = \sum_{i=1}^{n} b_i x_i + \sum\sum_{i<j} b_{ij} x_i x_j$	Linear constraints	Quadratic programming
	$U = \sum_{i=1}^{n} b_i x_i + \sum\sum_{i<j} b_{ij} x_i x_j + \cdots + \sum\sum \cdots \sum_{i<j\cdots<n} x_i x_j \cdots x_n$	All b_i and b_{ij}'s are nonnegative (nonpositive) in the context of minimization (maximization)	Geometric programming
Multiplicative (configural)	$U = \prod_{i=1}^{n} x_i^{b}$ (parameters estimated using the log transformed model: $\log U = \sum_{i=1}^{n} b_i \log x_i$)		Geometric programming
General polynomial[a] (configural)	$U = \sum_{j=1}^{m} c_j \prod_{i=1}^{n} x_i^{b_{ij}}$, where $\prod_{i=1}^{n} x_i^{b_{ij}}$ = fixed utility of the jth term, c_j = importance weight of the jth term	All c_j's are nonnegative (nonpositive) in the context of minimization (maximization)	Geometric programming
Linear additive with risk[b]	$U = \sum_{i=1}^{n} b_i x_i - \sum_{\substack{i=1 \\ i=j}}^{n} \sum_{j=1}^{n} x_i x_j \sigma_{ij}$, where σ_{ij} is an $n \times n$ covariance matrix and $\sigma_{ij} = 0$ for $i \neq j$	Linear constraints	Stochastic quadratic programming

[a] See Balachandran and Gensch (1974) for procedures for estimating the parameters of this function by regression.

[b] Parameters estimated using random coefficients regression models (RCRMs); see Hildreth and Houck (1968), Hsiao (1973), and Swamy (1970).

system development problem we could have easily used satisficing, dominance, and lexicography in choosing a design configuration. The types of combinations selected will generally depend on the nature and complexity of the multiple-objective decision problem, the type of response that is requested, and so forth.

In this chapter we have so far focused on riskless-choice models that involve multiattribute alternatives. We have avoided the added complexity of uncertainty. This can be manifested in two ways: (1) there can be uncertainty about the events, and (2) there can be uncertainty about the attribute values.

Suppose, in our weapons system development problem, that the attribute values for each alternative are contingent upon whether a certain technological breakthrough occurs. We would then have two possible events that could occur. Different attribute values (as shown in Table 7.5) would be associated with each. Assuming that a compensatory MAU model is applicable (e.g., the linear additive model), we can reduce Table 7.5 into the three-action/two-event decision matrix shown in Table 7.6, where the cell values $U(a_i, \theta_j)$ are now aggregated utilities obtained by applying the compensatory model to each alternative for each event. We may then apply the expected utility norm (i.e., maximize expected utility) in choosing the best alternative.

If the attribute values are uncertain, we could do one of several things. First, and simplest, is to use *expected* values for each attribute value and then treat the problem as one of riskless choice. A second and more computationally demanding procedure is to use an interval or range of values rather than a point estimate of attribute values. A third and the most complex way to account for attribute value uncertainty is by introducing probability distributions. Procedures for using the

Table 7.5. Development Decision Problem

Attribute	EXISTING TECHNOLOGY, θ_1 ALTERNATIVE DESIGNS			TECHNOLOGICAL BREAKTHROUGH, θ_2 ALTERNATIVE DESIGNS		
	a_1	a_2	a_3	a_1	a_2	a_3
Delivery time (hours)	5	3	2	0.5	2	2
Range (nautical miles)	6000	4000	5000	10,000	8000	8000
Schedule (years)	3	2	4	2	2	2
Cost ($\$ \times 10^6$)	14	16	12	9	10	10
Vulnerability (high–low)	Average	High	Low	Low	Average	Low

Table 7.6. Amalgamated Decision Matrix of Table 7.5

State / Alternative	θ_1	θ_2
a_1	$U(a_1, \theta_1)$	$U(a_1, \theta_2)$
a_2	$U(a_2, \theta_1)$	$U(a_2, \theta_2)$
a_3	$U(a_3, \theta_1)$	$U(a_3, \theta_2)$

noncompensatory and compensatory models we have discussed when a range or probability distributions of values are given are discussed by MacCrimmon (1968). For configural and stochastic MAU models fitting a mathematical programming formulation, quadratic programming and stochastic programming models and solution algorithms are available.

More recent advances in multiattribute utility measurement under uncertainty have been developed principally by Keeney (1972). An excellent description of how to use Keeney's concepts to perform a decision analysis can be found in Keeney (1973) and Keeney and Raiffa (1976). A discussion of Keeney's method follows in the Appendix to this chapter.

REFERENCES   BALACHANDRAN, V., and D. H. GENSCH. "Solving the 'Marketing Mix' Problem Using Geometric Programming." *Management Science*, **21**(2), 1974, 160–171.

CHURCHMAN, C. W., A. L. ACKOFF, and E. L. ARNOFF, *Introduction to Operations Research*. New York: John Wiley & Sons, Inc., 1957, Chap. 6.

EASTON, A. *Complex Managerial Decisions Involving Multiple Objectives*. New York: John Wiley & Sons, Inc., 1973.

ECKENRODE, R. T. "Weighting Multiple Criteria." *Management Science*, **12**(3), 1965.

GREEN, P. E., and W. WIND. *Multiattribute Decisions in Marketing: A Measurement Approach*. Hinsdale, Ill.: Dryden Press, 1973.

GUSTAFSON, D. H., G. K. PAI, and G. C. KRAMMER. "A 'Weighted Aggregate' Approach to R&D Project Selection." *AIIE Transactions*, **3**(1), 1971, 22–31.

HALTER, A. N., and G. W. DEAN. *Decisions Under Uncertainty*. Cincinnati, Ohio: South-Western Publishing Co., 1971, Chap. III.

HILDRETH, C., and J. P. HOUCK. "Some Estimators for a Linear Model with Random Coefficients." *Journal of the American Statistical Association*, **63**, June 1968, 584–595.

HSIAO, C. "Statistical Inferences for a Model with Both Random Cross-Sectional and Time Effects," Technical Report No. 83. Institute for Mathematical Studies in the Social Sciences, Stanford University, January 1973.

HUBER, G. P. "Methods for Quantifying Subjective Probabilities and Multiattribute Utilities." *Decision Sciences*, **5**(3), 1974, 430–458.

KEENEY, R. L. "Multiplicative Utility Functions," Technical Report No. 70. Operations Research Center, MIT, Mar. 1972.

KEENEY, R. L. "A Decision Analysis with Multiple Objectives: The Mexico City Airport." *Bell Journal of Economics and Management Science*, 1973, 101–117.

KEENEY, R. L., AND RAIFFA, H., *Decisions With Multiple Objectives: Preferences and Value Tradeoffs*, New York: John Wiley & Sons, Inc., 1976.

MacCrimmon, K. R. "An Overview of Multiple Objective Decision Making," in J. L. Cochrane and M. Zeleny (eds.), *Multiple Criteria Decision Making*. University of South Carolina Press, Columbia, S.C., 1973.

MacCrimmon, K. R. "Decision Making Among Multiple-Attribute Alternatives: A Survey and Consolidated Approach," Memorandum RM-4823-ARPA. Rand Corporation, Santa Monica, Calif., December, 1968.

MacCrimmon, K. R. and M. Toda. "The Experimental Determination of Indifference Curves." *The Review of Economic Studies*, **36**(4), 1969, 433–450.

Moskowitz, H. "Robustness of Linear Models for Decision Making—Some Comments." *OMEGA*, 1977.

Raiffa, H. "Preferences for Multi-attributed Alternatives," RM-5868-DOT/RC. The Rand Corporation, Santa Monica, Calif., April 1969.

Swamy, P. A. V. B. "Efficient Inference in a Random Coefficient Regression Model." *Econometrica*, **38**, March 1970, 311–323.

Torgenson, W. S. *Theory and Methods of Scaling*. New York: John Wiley & Sons, Inc., 1958.

Tversky, A. "Choice by Elimination." *Journal of Mathematical Psychology*, **9**, 1972, 341–367.

KEY CONCEPTS

Goals, attributes, criteria
Noncompensatory models
  dominance
  satisficing: conjunctive,
    disjunctive
  lexicographic
  maximin
  maximax

Compensatory models
  additive
  configural
  spatial representation
  mathematical programming
Tradeoffs
Preferential independence
Utility independence

REVIEW QUESTIONS

7.1. Consider some personal or professional decisions you might have to make. For each decision, state the multiattributed consequences involved.

7.2. What are the two ways in which multiattributed information can be processed? Using a decision problem, illustrate these two ways.

7.3. What is a noncompensatory MAU model? Compensatory model?

7.4. State, describe, and illustrate the noncompensatory MAU models.

7.5. State, describe, and illustrate the compensatory MAU models.

7.6. What is the difference between a disjunctive and conjunctive satisficing MAU model? Illustrate using an example.

7.7. What is the difference between an additive model and a configural MAU model? Illustrate using an example.

7.8. Two spatial representation models are indifference curves and multidimensional scaling. Describe these models in general.

7.9. Generally describe the techniques of linear programming and goal programming, highlighting their differences.

7.10. Do you agree with the statement, "MAU models really only apply to problems in the public sector, since in the private sector there is only one goal: to make a profit." Defend your answer.

ANSWERS TO
REVIEW
QUESTIONS

7.1. Examples of decisions and their multiattributed consequences are as follows:

Selecting a job: Salary, location, prestige, opportunity for advancement, fringe benefits.

Buying a home: distance from a school, distance from work, cost, type of neighborhood, age of home.

7.2. The two ways that multiattributed information can be processed are:

1. Find a value which represents the overall utility of an alternative.
2. Retain the information on each attribute level and utility and use procedures which do not require interattribute comparisons.

To illustrate the two approaches, consider a decision to choose the best stereo system from a group of five. The decision maker has on hand ratings of reliability, sound quality, and styling from a leading consumer magazine (0 to 10 scale). The first approach might be implemented by adding all three scale values and choosing the highest total. The second approach would be illustrated with a decision rule that looked at only the most important attribute and chose the system with the highest level of that attribute.

7.3. A noncompensatory model is one that does not permit tradeoffs between or among attributes. A compensatory model is one that does allow tradeoffs—i.e., changes in the level of one attribute may be compensated for by opposing changes in one or more of the other attributes.

7.4. Noncompensatory models include:

1. Dominance models which allow the decision maker to eliminate alternatives that are no better than some other alternative for *every* attribute. This means that, in comparing alternatives, if one alternative has at least as good as or higher attribute values for all attributes, this alternative dominates the others.
2. Satisficing models:
   (a) These include conjunctive models which classify an alternative as acceptable if it meets specified minimal values for each attribute.
   (b) Satisficing models also include disjunctive models which classify an alternative as acceptable if it surpasses a specified maximum value on one or more *critical* attributes.

3. Lexicographic models require that attributes be ranked in order of importance. If all alternatives can be ordered with respect to the most important attribute, the remaining attributes are not considered. However, if some alternatives are tied on the most important attribute, the decision maker proceeds to the next most important attribute for resolving the subset of tied alternatives. This continues until all alternatives are ranked or until all attributes are considered.
4. Maximin models choose the alternative with the largest minimum value of any alternatives. These models require comparison of attribute values in order to identify the poorest value.
5. Maximax models choose the alternative with the largest highest value of any alternative. These models also require comparability of attributes.

7.5. Compensatory models include:

1. The additive utility model which specifies that the utility of an alternative is equal to the sum of the utilities of its parts (the various attribute levels).
2. Configural utility models which specify that the utility of an alternative is some nonlinear combination of the utilities of its parts.
3. Spatial representation models in which the dimensional arguments constitute a space of more limited dimensionality than the original attribute space. Two types are indifference curves and multidimensional scaling models.
4. Mathematical Programming models which include (a) linear and nonlinear programming models in which the variables are attribute levels and the objective function is the utility function and (b) goal programming models.

7.6. To illustrate disjunctive and conjunctive models, consider the following three alternatives and their attribute levels for 4 attributes

		Attribute Value			
		1	2	3	4
	1	7	4	1	5
Alternative	2	6	6	4	2
	3	1	4	4	2

A conjunctive model specifies minimum values for each alternative which must be met or exceeded in order for an alternative to be "acceptable." Suppose that we require the four attributes each to be at least at a level of 2 in order to be acceptable. Under this criterion, only alternative 2 would be accepted.

A disjunctive model specifies a maximum value for each of several *critical* attributes, and states that an alternative is "acceptable" if it surpasses that maximum value for each critical attribute. To illustrate, suppose that attribute 2 having a level greater than or equal to 4 and attribute 4 having a level equal to or less than 2 were essential for partitioning the three alternatives into acceptable and unacceptable regions. Then both alternatives 2 and 3 would be accepted.

7.7. To illustrate the difference between an additive and a configural utility model, consider again the three alternatives considered in 7.6.

An additive model assumes that the decision maker can assign weights which denote the "relative importance" of each of the four attributes. The utility of an alternative is then found by summing up the products of the weights and attribute levels for all alternatives. For example, suppose the "importance weights" are 0.5, 0.2, 0.1, and 0.2. Then the utility of alternative 1 would be

$$U(\text{alt. 1}) = 0.5(7) + 0.2(4) + 0.1(1) + 0.2(5)$$
$$= 3.5 + 0.8 + 0.1 + 1.0 = 5.4$$

Likewise, alternatives 2 and 3 would have utilities of 5.0 and 2.1 and alternative 1 would be chosen.

A configural model uses some other function to relate overall utility to attribute levels. One example might be a model where overall utility is determined by the product of all attribute levels. Using this model, alternative 1 would have a utility of 140 ($7 \times 4 \times 1 \times 5$), and alternatives 2 and 3 would have utilities of 288 and 32, respectively. Thus alternative 2 should be chosen as having the highest utility.

7.8. Indifference curves show combinations of attribute values that are equally preferred. The alternatives to be evaluated are points on these indifference curves, and by identifying the indifference curve on which they lie, it is possible to generate a complete ordering among the alternatives. In essence, this procedure is simply a graphic form for making tradeoffs. In theory, if there are n attributes, indifference hyperplanes of dimension $(n - 1)$ can be used to represent preferences. In practice, usually two attributes are as many as a decision maker can handle. Here the indifference region is defined with a line.

Multidimensional scaling models are characterized by:

1. A set of specified alternatives.
2. A procedure for obtaining intra- and interattribute judgments, or an aggregated judgment.
3. The construction of a spatial representation.
4. The identification of ideal configurations and the choice rule based on the proximity of alternatives to these ideal configurations.

7.9. A linear or nonlinear programming model may be viewed as a multiple attribute decision model in the following sense: the variables are attributes (which usually may take on an infinite number of values), the constraints are conjunctive constraints on combinations of attributes, and there is a linear or nonlinear compensatory objective (utility) function.

In goal programming models, the decision maker specifies desired levels of combinations of attributes and these serve as the primary goals. The objective of goal programming is to minimize deviations from the desired levels of variable combinations. This minimization is performed based on the relative importance or priority assigned to the goals.

The features that distinguish goal programming from linear or nonlinear programming models are (1) the former allows for more than one goal to be considered at a time and (2) goal programming considers goals separately and in order of their importance.

7.10. False. Although making a profit is *usually* (but not always) the primary goal, there may be and usually are other goals—e.g., enhancement of public image, minimizing damage to environment, maximization of stock price, establishment of stable dividend policy, market share, etc.

EXERCISES **7.1.** Assume that you are evaluating 10 craftsmen at your shop in order to select the best person to create a special, important project. All of the craftsmen are given the same amount of material to work with and then asked to create to meet certain size and configuration dimensions. These specifications are not easy to meet because of the material being used and the need to create something novel. All 10 craftsmen have been evaluated based on the attributes shown in the following table.

	(1)	(2)	(3)	(4)	(5)	(6)	(7)
	PHYSICAL MEASUREMENTS				ATTRIBUTES		
	Base length	Width	Depth	Length			
Craftsman	(inches)	(inches)	(inches)	(feet–inches)	Smoothness[a]	Lustre[a]	Creativity[a]
1	34	24	35	5–3	9	7	8
2	34	26	36	5–4	7	4	10
3	36	24	37	5–7	8	10	2
3	35	24	35	5–4	6	6	4
5	39	25	37	5–6	3	5	3
6	34	23	34	5–5	8	4	2
7	36	24	40	5–6	1	7	7
8	34	25	33	5–2	10	4	8
9	35	24	36	5–6	4	2	9
10	37	26	38	5–8	7	10	7

[a]A score of 10 represents highest rating.

Assume that the "ideal" art form would be 5 feet 8 inches in length with base length, width, and depth measurements of 37 inches, 26 inches, and 37 inches, respectively, and smoothness, lustre, and creativity rating scores of 10 points each (the maximum possible). Moreover, assume that for any of the seven attributes (criteria), component utility declines monotonically and symmetrically as the attribute values and physical measurements depart from the ideal profile.

(a) Use the dominance model to eliminate craftsmen. Show which craftsmen are eliminated.

(b) Is the dominance model a compensatory or noncompensatory model?

(c) Does the dominance model require intraattribute and interattribute comparisons?

(d) What are some of the major shortcomings of the dominance model?

(e) Under what circumstances or in what way is the dominance model best used?

(f) As the number of attributes or criteria increases, does the dominance model become more functional or more dysfunctional? Why?

7.2. Suppose that you are interested in partitioning the group of 10 craftsmen into acceptable and unacceptable groupings prior to final evaluation. To qualify for acceptance a craftsman's work must have satisfied the following attribute values: (1) base length $\geqslant$ 36 inches; (2) width $\geqslant$ 24 inches; (3) depth $\geqslant$ 36 inches; (4) length $\geqslant$ 5 feet 6 inches; (5) smoothness, lustre, and creativity, each greater than or equal to 3.

(a) Is this a compensatory or a noncompensatory model? Is this a conjunctive or disjunctive model? Why?

(b) Which craftsmen are acceptable; unacceptable?

7.3. Suppose you thought that either a large base length ($\geqslant$ 37 inches) or extremely high creativity (a rating of 10) was essential for partitioning the set into acceptable versus unacceptable craftsmen (i.e., assume that craftsmen profiles are now represented by only the above two attributes).

(a) Which craftsmen are acceptable; unacceptable? Why?

(b) What type of MAU model is being used—compensatory or noncompensatory?

7.4. The following shows the ranking of attributes in the craftsmen evaluation in terms of importance, with 1 being the most important and 7 the least important.

Attribute	Ranking (*preference ordering of attributes*)
Creativity	1
Lustre	2
Smoothness	3
Base length	4
Width	5
Depth	6
Length	7

Using a lexicographic MAU model, select the best craftsmen.

7.5. Suppose, for the data in Exercise 7.1, that we consider a MAU model in which utility increases monotonically with increases in smoothness, creativity, and lustre rating scores, but not so in terms of increases in base length, width, depth, and length. For the latter four factors, utility is assumed to decline symmetrically as the craftsman's work departs on either side from the ideal values stated in Exercise 7.1. We thus can state the following linear additive MAU model:

$$U(a_i) = \sum_{j=1}^{7} U(a_{ij}) \qquad (i = 1, \ldots, 10)$$

or $$U(a_i) = \sum_{j=5}^{7} w_j a_{ij} - \sum_{j=1}^{4} w_j |a_{ij} - z_j| \qquad (i = 1, \ldots, 10),$$

where w_j = importance weight attached to the jth attribute

a_{ij} = *actual* rating or measurement associated with the ith craftsman on the jth attribute

z_j = prespecified ideal level on the jth attribute (given in Exercise 7.1)

Note that for attributes 1 through 4, as the absolute difference between the attribute level and ideal level decreases, utility should increase.

(a) Using the data in the table of Exercise 7.1, develop a new table which places all attribute values on a comparable numerical, 0 to 10, scale. To do this apply the formula $|a_{ij} - z_j|$ to obtain rating scores for each alternative on the four physical dimensions of base length, width, depth, and length. The rating scores on smoothness, lustre, and creativity remain the same.

(b) After placing all values on a comparable numerical scale, you assign the following importance weights to each of the attributes (based on a 0 to 1 scale with weights adding up to 1):

Attribute	Importance
Base length	0.10
Width	0.10
Depth	0.05
Length	0.05
Smoothness	0.15
Lustre	0.20
Creativity	0.35
	1.00

Using the linear additive model above and "importance weights," determine the best craftsman.

(c) Comment on the appropriateness of the linear additive MAU model for choosing the best craftsman.

7.6. Assume that you are responsible for certain capital budgeting expenditure decisions in your company. You have nine projects before you and must choose the best from among the set of these nine available projects. The criteria used in evaluating each project are: (a) discounted cash flow rate of return (DCF rate), (b) payback period, (c) net present value, and (d) stability of annual earnings. The nine projects and their expected performance with respect to the four criteria are shown in the table on page 252.

A project is considered "unacceptable" if either its DCF rate is less than 10%, payback period is greater than 5 years, its present value is negative, or its stability of annual earnings is rated less than 5 on a scale from 1 to 10. Moreover, the DCF rate is deemed more important than the payback period, which is considered more important than net present value. Stability of annual earnings is considered to be least important.

Project	DCF Rate (%)	Payback Period (years)	Net Present Value (100,000)	Rating of Stability of Annual Earnings (10 highest)
A	16	6	1	7
B	13	5	4	5
C	10	3	5	9
D	14	4	−2	6
E	16	4	3	6
F	10	4	3	8
G	11	2	3	10
H	12	4	4	7
I	16	5	2	5

(a) Using a satisficing (conjunctive) model, then dominance, and finally lexicography in that order, choose the best project or projects.
(b) Criticize the use of these models in this problem.

7.7. Suppose you were offered two jobs having the characteristics shown in the table.

Characteristics	Job A	Job B
Starting salary ($)	$20,000	14,000
Commuting travel time (minutes)	40	15
Population of city (millions)	2	0.2
Advancement opportunity	Average	High

(a) Using the tradeoff approach, find the starting salary that would make you indifferent between Job A and another job alternative with a 15-minute commuting time, a city population of one million, and an average advancement opportunity. Do the same for Job B. Which job would you prefer?
(b) Look at the original descriptions for Jobs A and B. Indicate which job you prefer based on these original descriptions. Does your preference in part (b) agree with your preference in part (a)?

7.8. Let us consider the problem of you selecting a job and, for purposes of simplicity, let us assume that there are just three attributes you would be considering about each job: (1) starting salary, (2) commuting time, and (3) size of the city. Assume also that for the set of alternatives considered you have determined the best and worst values for each attribute to be as follows:

Attributes	RANGE	
	Best	Worst
Starting salary ($)	$20,000	$10,000
Commuting time (minutes)	15	75
Size of city (millions)	5	0.5

(a) Using your own preferences, test for preferential independence (PI) and utility independence (UI) of these attributes.

(b) Assuming that the attributes are both preferentially and utility independent, illustrate specifically how you would assess the utility functions for each of the attributes.

(c) Again, assuming that the independence assumptions are satisfied, illustrate precisely how you would obtain the scaling factors $k_i(i = 1, \ldots, 3)$ and K.

7.9. Consider the problem of a decision maker who must decide between two possible locations for a new plant which his company is planning to build. To determine the "best" location, he lists six criteria that must be considered. He then ranks these outcomes in terms of his considered judgment of their relative importance (best, worst). The criteria and their importance are listed in the following table.

Criterion	Dimension	Importance Rank
1. Cost of land and building plant	Dollars invested	3
2. Site desirability	Preference rating (10 best–1 poorest)	1
3. Cost of labor	Dollar expense	5
4. Community relations	Cooperation rating (10 best–1 poorest)	2
5. Raw material supply	Quality and cost (10 best–1 poorest)	4
6. Transportation facilities	Convenience and cost (10 best–1 poorest)	5

Three locations are being considered. The outcome values in terms of each criterion for each of the locations considered are as follows:

Location	Criterion 1	2	3	4	5	6
A	$2,000,000	5	5	8	7	2
B	1,500,000	7	9	7	10	4
C	1,000,000	3	6	4	7	9

Using a lexicographic model, choose the best plant location.

CASE 7.1 Illustrative Case Study
Involving Linear Additive MAU Models Developed by Regression

MODELING
ADMISSIONS
COMMITTEE
DECISIONS

You have been asked to develop a model that represents admissions committee decisions on students applying to the graduate business school of a large prominent university. This model is intended to describe the admissions committee's decision-making process and assist in making admission decisions. The school requires all applicants to take the Graduate Records Exam (GRE), to provide a grade transcript of past work, and to obtain letters of recommendation from three professors or work supervisors. Once this information is supplied to the admissions committee, each of the five members separately rates the applicants on a rating scale. The scale has the following verbal labels attached to each point: (1) reject now, (2) defer rejection but looks weak, (3) defer, (4) defer acceptance but looks strong, (5) accept now, and (6) accept now and offer financial support. The numerical values of this scale are then averaged over the committee members to obtain an overall rating of the applicant by the committee. This rating is a judgment or prediction of how well the applicant will do in graduate school.

In making admissions choices, the committee members agree that the four most important factors considered are: (1) overall undergraduate grade-point average, out of 6 (GPA); (2) the quality of the undergraduate institution (QI); (3) the total raw score GRE (i.e., the sum of the raw scores on the verbal part and quantitative part); and (4) the recommendations (R), where 5 is the highest and 1 is the lowest.[†] These are the attributes or criteria, that is, the independent variables in this multiattribute utility (MAU) model. The average rating (AR) made by the admissions committee at the time a student's application was processed is the overall utility, or dependent variable.

The table at the foot of the page lists admissions data and committee ratings taken from a sample of 15 students. The members of the committee arrive at an overall rating for these students by taking some linear combination of the criteria (i.e, a linear additive utility model is appropriate).

Student	AR	GRE	GPA	QI	R
1	4	550	4.7	3	4
2	3	497	4.8	3	4
3	6	710	5.8	6	5
4	5	620	5.5	5	5
5	1	350	4.5	2	4
6	2	490	4.4	3	4
7	3	512	4.6	4	4
8	3	507	5.2	2	5
9	5	650	4.9	6	4
10	4	500	5.3	4	5
11	3	490	4.8	5	5
12	5	550	5.4	4	4
13	4	580	5.1	5	2
14	4	460	5.3	5	5
15	2	480	4.7	3	3

[†]The index for rating the quality of the institution is based on Cass and Birnbaum's (1968) rating of selectivity given at the end of their book, *Comparison Guide to American Colleges*. The verbal categories of selectivity are given numerical values according to the following rule: most selective, 6; highly selective, 5; very selective (+), 4; very selective, 3; selective, 2; not mentioned, 1.

(a) Assuming a linear additive utility model, use regression analysis to model the admissions committee's ratings (AR).

(b) Do the factor weights derived agree with your feelings regarding how much importance or weight should be attached to each of the criteria used in making admissions decisions?

(c) What other factors do you think the admissions committee should consider? How might these factors or criteria be built into the model?

(d) How good or accurate is this model for predicting admissions decisions? What regression and correlation statistics can we use in measuring the goodness of fit?

(e) Discuss the benefits and drawbacks of using this MAU model (or any MAU model) as a basis for making admission decisions.

References for Case 7.1

CASS, J., and M. BIRNBAUM. *Comparative Guide to American Colleges.* New York: Harper & Row, Publishers, 1968.

DAWES, R. M. "A Case Study of Graduate Admissions: Application of Three Principles of Human Decision Making." *American Psychologist*, **26**(2), 1971, 180–188.

CHAPTER 7 APPENDIX

MAU Assessment Under Uncertainty

Recently, Keeney (1972) has developed a method for assessing MAU functions for the case when the multiple outcomes or consequences of a decision situation are uncertain. In principle, we could handle such a decision situation with the tools of utility assessment already developed in Chapter 5 for a single attribute. That is, we would generate a utility assessment in the form of a multivariate expression based on the decision maker's stated preferences over lotteries or gambles in which the outcomes were simply described in multidimensional terms. To illustrate, consider a decision maker who characterizes a house in terms of cost and location. He considers $65,000 to be the highest amount he would pay and $45,000 the smallest amount that provides him with the quality house he would need. He regards the worst possible alternative as a house at $65,000 in neighborhood A (a lower-middle-class neighborhood in a poor school district), and conventionally we would assign such a house a utility of 0. The best possible alternative would be a house at $45,000 in neighborhood B (an upper-middle-class neighborhood in an excellent school district). We would assign this house a utility of 1. We could then map his utility function by asking him to specify a value of p for which he would be indifferent between

L_1:   a house of x dollars in neighborhood C

and L_2:   \$45,000 in neighborhood B with probability p or
\$65,000 in neighborhood A with probability $1 - p$.

This is diagrammed in Figure 7A.1.

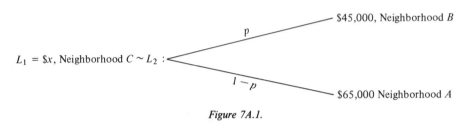

Figure 7A.1.

The expressed value of p would be the utility assessment for a house costing \$$x$ in neighborhood C (see NM method in Chapter 5). This perfectly rational multidimensional extension of the methods in Chapter 5 fails in application simply because such assessments (especially when we go beyond two dimensions) are virtually impossible for most human beings to make meaningfully. Thus, such an assessment process is impractical and unacceptable to most decision makers.

7A.1. KEENEY'S METHOD

Keeney proposed a method that gives conditions under which we may circumvent the practical difficulty of obtaining certainty equivalents for multidimensional outcomes. His basic approach is to assess utility functions for each attribute, one at a time using any of the methods in Chapter 5. Keeney shows how these single attribute utility functions can then be combined, either *additively* or *multiplicatively*, to produce the MAU function. The decision maker is thus faced with the considerably simpler task of considering his preferences for only one attribute at a time, holding all the other attribute consequences constant for assessment purposes. This method has been used quite extensively in such real applications as selecting alternative airport locations for the Mexico City Airport (Keeney, 1973), water resources planning and management, nuclear power plant location, and energy-generation planning, to mention a few. Keeney's method is now illustrated using a simplified airport site selection decision. For a more formal development of the method, the reader is referred to Keeney (1972, 1973) and Keeney and Raiffa (1976).

Suppose that in choosing among alternative nuclear power locations a decision maker (such as a public utility, an interest group, or a constituency) considers three attributes to be of concern: (1) cost (x_1), safety (x_2), and reliability (x_3). There may, of course, be measurement difficulties in specifying, for example, a variable that measures the safety of a location. This might be either scaled subjectively or be more objectively defined in terms of the number of people dying and injured per 10 years from a nuclear power plant failure.

Employing the NM technique discussed in Chapter 5, the decision maker is asked to respond to questions about preferences with respect to lotteries on gambles involving costs (x_1), assuming that safety (x_2) and reliability (x_3) are held constant at satisfactory levels. In this way, the decision maker has assessed a *conditional* utility function $u_1(x_1)$. Similarly, *conditional* utility functions for safety $u_2(x_2)$ and reliability $u_3(x_3)$ are also obtained.

We now need to combine these conditional utility functions into an overall or aggregate MAU function for nuclear power plant locations, $U(x_1, x_2, x_3)$. Keeney has shown that if the decision maker's preferences exhibit the properties of *preferential independence* (PI) and *utility independence* (UI), this amalgamation process is either *additive* or *multiplicative* and can be rather easily performed.[†] The concepts of preferential independence and utility independence are first illustrated and then the process of combining the conditional utility functions into an overall MAU function is indicated.

7A.1.1. Preferential Independence (PI)

Assume that the decision maker restricts the attribute values to the following ranges:

> cost: $200–750 million
> safety: 1–500 people killed and injured per 10 years
> reliability: 0.60–0.98.

Preferential independence simply denotes that the decision maker's willingness to trade off cost for safety is independent of the level of system reliability. Similarly, preferential independence means that his willingness to trade off cost for reliability is independent of the level of safety, and so on. Preferential independence may be tested using questions of the following type. Suppose that we fix reliability at 0.90 and consider two sites; one with a cost of $300 million and a safety level of 200 persons injured or killed in 10 years, and the second with a cost of $500 million and a safety level of x_2 persons injured or killed per 10-year period. For what value of x_2 would these sites be indifferent to the decision maker?

Suppose that the decision maker answers $x_2 = 100$ persons per 10-year period. We then change the level of reliability to say 0.70 and repeat the question, and

---

[†]Preferential independence concerns only ordinal preferences and no probabilistic elements are involved. It involves the ranking of *consequences*. Utility independence, on the other hand, concerns the cardinal preferences of the decision maker and involves the ranking of *lotteries* (hence, probabilistic elements are involved). For the riskless case, verification of preferential independence implies an additive multiattribute *value* function (utility independence is not applicable as no probabilistic elements are involved). For the risky case, both preferential independence and utility independence need to be verified to assure the existence of either an additive or a multiplicative multiattribute *utility* function (Keeney and Raiffa, 1976).

suppose that the answer is still 100. We then repeat the question for various levels of reliability over its full range. If the answer is always $x_2 = 100$, we then know that cost and safety are preferentially independent (x_1 PI x_2). Analogous questioning would be used to determine if x_1 PI x_3 and x_2 PI x_3.

7A.1.2. Utility Independence (UI)

Utility independence is similar in concept and approach. The fundamental issue is whether the utility function for cost $u_1(x_1)$ is independent of the levels of safety and reliability. This can be tested by assessing several utilities for cost at various levels of safety and reliability. If the conditional utilities obtained are independent of the other attribute levels [i.e., $u_1(x_1)$ remains constant over different safety and reliability levels], then utility independence holds.

7A.1.3. Determining the MAU Function

Given the PI and UI conditions are satisfied among the attributes, it can be shown that the MAU function for the nuclear power plant siting decision will be either one of two forms. The *additive* form is

$$U(x_1, x_2, x_3) = k_1 u_1(x_1) + k_2 u_2(x_2) + k_3 u_3(x_3) \tag{7A.1}$$

and the *multiplicative* form is

$$\begin{aligned}
U(x_1, x_2, x_3) = {}& k_1 u_1(x_1) + k_2 u_2(x_2) + k_3 u_3(x_3) \\
& + K k_1 k_2 u_1(x_1) u_2(x_2) + K k_1 k_3 u_1(x_1) u_2(x_2) \\
& + K k_2 k_3 u_2(x_2) u_3(x_3) + K^2 k_1 k_2 k_3 u_1(x_1) u_2(x_2) u_3(x_3).
\end{aligned} \tag{7A.2}$$

The k_i and K are scaling constants that must be determined to obtain $U(x_1, x_2, x_3)$. Note that if $K = 0$ in (7A.2), the multiplicative form reduces to the additive form of (7A.1). The additive form is thus a special case of the multiplicative MAU model. It turns out that if the k_i sum to 1, the appropriate model is the additive model (since K is 0 under this condition). If the k_i do not sum to 1, the multiplicative model is appropriate.

The remaining question is how to assess the k_i scaling factors. Let us illustrate this by assessing the scaling factor for cost, k_1. The decision maker is asked to consider the alternative a_1 whose outcomes have *cost at its most preferred level* and the *other two attributes at their least preferred level* [i.e., $a_1 = (200, 500, 0.60)$ corresponding to (x_1^*, x_{2*}, x_{3*}), respectively, where the superscript asterisk represents the most preferred level of a given attribute and the subscript asterisk the least preferred level]. He is then asked to choose between a_1 and a gamble, a_4, involving all attributes at their most preferred levels (200, 1, 0.98) with probability

P, and the least preferred attribute levels (750, 500, 0.60) with probability $1 - P$. As before, the decision maker is asked to state the value of P for which he would be indifferent between a_1 and a_2. This is diagrammed in Figure 7A.2.

$$a_1: (x_1^*, x_{2*}, x_{3*}) = (200, 500, 0.60) \sim a_2 = \begin{cases} P & (x_1^*, x_2^*, x_3^*) = (200, 1, 0.98) \\ 1-P & (x_{1*}, x_{2*}, x_{3*}) = (750, 500, 0.60) \end{cases}$$

Figure 7A.2.

For a_1, our scaling convention fixes $u_1(200) = 1$, $u_2(500) = 0$, $u_3(0.60) = 0$. Substituting these values into (7A.2) yields $u(a_1) = k_1$. For the gamble a_2, $u(200, 1, 0.98) = 1$ and $u(750, 500, 0.60) = 0$. Equating the utilities for a_1 and a_4 results in $k_1 = P$. Thus, the decision maker's stated value for P is k_1. Similarly, k_2 and k_3 are obtained. If $k_1 + k_2 + k_3 = 1$, the additive model should be used since K will be equal to zero. If not, we set all the attributes at their most preferred levels, making their utilities equal to 1, substitute these utilities along with the known values of k_i into the multiplicative model of (7A.2), and solve for the unknown K. K will turn out to have a value between -1 and 0. To illustrate, suppose that $k_1 = 0.2$, $k_2 = 0.4$, and $k_3 = 0.1$. Since $\Sigma k_i = 0.7$, the multiplicative model is appropriate. We substitute into (7A.2),

$$\begin{aligned} 1 = & \ 0.2(1) + 0.4(1) + 0.1(1) \\ & + K(0.2)(0.4)(1)(1) + K(0.2)(0.1)(1)(1) \\ & + K(0.4)(0.1)(1)(1) + K^2(0.2)(0.4)(0.1)(1)(1)(1) \end{aligned}$$

and solve for K.

By employing the Keeney procedure, we would obtain our overall MAU function with considerably less cognitive strain on the decision maker than employing gambles with multidimensional outcomes as was done at the beginning of this section. It should, however, be stressed that under uncertainty the Keeney procedure is valid only if preferential independence and utility independence hold among the attributes.

PART II   *Mathematical Programming and Optimization*

CHAPTER 8
Linear Programming: Modeling and Geometric Interpretation

OBJECTIVES: Upon successful completion of this chapter, you should be able to:

1. Give several examples of linear programming models of business problems.
2. List and explain the assumptions of a linear programming model.
3. Construct linear programming models of business problems.
4. Be able to discuss the properties of optimal solutions to linear programming models.

Mathematical programming is perhaps the most developed area of operations research. It covers such topics as:

Linear Programming   Chapters 8, 9, 10, and 11
Network Programming   Chapter 12
Integer Programming   Chapter 13

and several other variants of programming methods, such as

Goal Programming   Chapter 14

In this chapter and the following three chapters we concentrate on linear programming decision models and their solution techniques.

8.1. EXAMPLES OF MANAGEMENT DECISION PROBLEMS SOLVABLE BY LINEAR PROGRAMMING METHODS

A linear programming model provides an efficient method for determining an optimal decision (or an optimal strategy or an optimal plan) chosen from a large number of possible decisions. The optimal decision is the one that meets a specified objective of management, subject to various restrictions and constraints. For example, an *optimal decision* could be a decision that yields the highest or maximum profit or the lowest or minimum cost.

The *characteristics* of business problems amenable to solution using linear programming is well defined. However, the number, diversity, and dimensions of such problems falling within the linear programming framework is extremely impressive.

8.1.1. Example—Profit-Maximization Problem: Product Mix Decisions

Tennessee Furniture Inc. (TFI) specializes in the production of two types of Early American dining tables. Each table requires a different amount of construction time and painting time. TFI would like to determine the number of units of each type of table to produce daily which will yield the maximum profit.

8.2. CONSTRUCTING LINEAR PROGRAMMING MODELS

We now list what is required in order to construct a linear programming model.

Requirement 1. Objective Function. There must be an *objective* (or goal or target) the firm wants to achieve. For example, maximize dollar profits, minimize dollar cost, maximize total expected potential customers, minimize total time, and so forth.

Requirement 2. Restrictions and Decisions. There must be *alternative courses of action* or *decisions*, one of which will achieve the objective.

Requirement 3. Linear Objective Function and Linear Constraints. We must be able to express the decision problem incorporating the objective and restrictions on the decisions using only *linear equations* and *linear inequalities*. That is, we must be able to state the problem as a linear programming model.

8.2.1. Example—TFI Funiture Incorporated (Continued)

Let us consider TFI's problem in Example 8.1.1 of determining how many units of each table to make and sell. TFI produces Virginia (V)- and Massachusetts (M)-type Early American tables. TFI realizes a profit (= net selling price minus variable manufacturing cost) of $200 and $240 from selling a Virginia table and Massachusetts table, respectively. TFI is experiencing a high demand for both tables. Consequently, management believes that it can sell all the tables it can produce. Now both tables require processing time in the construction room (C) and the painting room (P). The production requirements and daily capacities are summarized in Table 8.1.

Table 8.1. TFI Production Table

Resources Required to produce 1 unit	PRODUCT		Resources Available (Capacity)
	Virginia, V	Masschusetts, M	
Construction time, C (hours)	6	12	120
Painting time, P(hours)	8	4	64
Unit profit	$200	$240	

Note that TFI has limited production capacity. That is, tables V and M share two production facilities, construction (C) and painting (P), both of which have limited daily capacities that must be considered *scarce resources*.

Each table must be processed in both the construction (C) and the painting department (P). To produce 1 table V requires 6 hours of time of C and 8 hours of P. To produce 1 table M requires 12 hours of C and 4 hours of P. We also note that TFI has a daily capacity of 120 hours of C and 64 hours of P. Thus, to determine the best or optimal mix of tables V and M to produce daily, TFI must allocate its limited capacity (scarce resources) of departments C and P in a manner that will best achieve its objective.

CONSTRUCTION OF THE LINEAR PROGRAMMING MODEL FOR TFI

Step 1. To construct the decision model, we first must define TFI's *decision variables*. They are:

$$x_V = \text{number of Virginia tables to produce daily}$$

$$x_M = \text{number of Massachusetts tables to produce daily.}$$

Step 2. Next we must define the objective or goal of TFI in terms of its decision variables. To do this, we introduce what is called the *objective function*. This function shows the relationship between output, x_V and x_M, and profit. Let $Z = $ profit. Then

$$\$200x_V = \text{total profit from sale of type } V \text{ tables}$$

$$\$240x_M = \text{total profit from sale of type } M \text{ tables.}$$

Thus,

$$\text{profit} = Z = \$200x_V + \$240x_M \qquad \text{(TFI's objective function)}$$

TFI's objective is to choose an x_V and an x_M that

$$\text{maximizes profit} = \text{maximize } Z = \$200x_V + \$240x_M.$$

Step 3. Define the *capacity restrictions* using x_V and x_M. The time used per day in making the two products must not exceed the total time available in the processing departments C and P. Using Table 8.1 we note that the hours required to make 1 V table times the number of V tables produced, x_V, plus the hours required to make 1 M table times the number of M tables produced, x_M, must be *equal to or less than* the time available in each processing department. We have

	(6 hours for 1 V)	$\times$	(number of V's produced)
	6	$\times$	x_V
plus	(12 hours for 1 M)	$\times$	(number of M's produced)
+	12	$\times$	x_M
(must be equal to or less than)		the	(capacity of department C)
$\leqslant$			120

That is,

$$6x_V + 12x_M \leqslant 120.$$

Similarly, for department P,

$$8x_V + 4x_M \leqslant 64.$$

Step 4. Restrict all decision variables to be *nonnegative*. For TFI this means

$$x_V \geqslant 0 \quad \text{and} \quad x_M \geqslant 0.$$

The linear programming model for TFI can be summarized as follows:

SUMMARY OF THE LINEAR PROGRAMMING MODEL FOR TFI

Choose production levels x_V and x_M which

maximize $Z = 200x_V + 240x_M$ (objective function)

and satisfy

$$6x_V + 12x_M \leqslant 120 \quad (C \text{ time})$$
$$8x_V + 4x_M \leqslant 64 \quad (P \text{ time})$$
(restrictions)

$$x_V \geqslant 0$$
$$x_M \geqslant 0.$$

QUESTIONS. What is TFI's expected daily profit if they produce $x_V = 5$ Virginia tables and $x_M = 5$ Massachusetts tables? How much construction time per day is used by this plan? How much painting time per day is used by this plan?

Answers

$$\text{daily profit} = Z = 200x_V + 240x_M$$
$$= 200(5) + 240(5)$$
$$= \$2200.$$
$$\text{construction capacity used} = 6x_V + 12x_M$$
$$= 6(5) + 12(5)$$
$$= 90 \text{ hours.}$$

This production plan leaves TFI with an *excess* of $120 - 90 = 30$ hours per day of construction capacity.

$$\text{painting capacity used} = 8x_V + 4x_M$$
$$= 8(5) + 4(5)$$
$$= 60 \text{ hours.}$$

The plan leaves an *excess* of $64 - 60 = 4$ hours per day of painting time.

QUESTION. Suppose that TFI was restricted to only producing Virginia tables. What is the maximum number of Virginia tables they can produce under this restriction? What will this yield in profit?

Answer. Consider the construction-time restriction with $x_M = 0$. We have

$$6x_V + 12x_M \leqslant 120$$
$$6x_V + 12(0) \leqslant 120$$

or

$$6x_V \leqslant 120.$$

Thus, the largest value we can assign to x_V is $\frac{120}{6} = 20$ tables. Note that $6(20) = 120$ hours. For example, if we let $x_V = 21$, then $6(21) = 126$ *exceeds* daily available construction time by $126 - 120 = 6$ hours.

Next, consider the painting-time restriction with $x_M = 0$. We have

$$8x_V + 4x_M \leqslant 64$$

or

$$8x_V + 4(0) \leqslant 64$$

or

$$8x_V \leqslant 64.$$

Thus, the largest we can assign to x_V is $\frac{64}{8} = 8$ tables without exceeding the available daily painting time of 64 hours.

Each capacity restriction must not be violated. Thus, the largest value of x_V is 8 tables, yielding a profit of

$$Z = 200x_V + 240x_M$$
$$= 200(8) + 240(0)$$
$$= \$1600.$$

QUESTION. Suppose that TFI was restricted to producing only Massachusetts tables. What is the maximum number of Massachusetts tables they can produce under this restriction? What will this yield in profit?

Answer. Let $x_V = 0$ in both capacity restrictions. Then we have $12x_M \leqslant 120$ or $x_M \leqslant \frac{120}{12} = 10$ in the construction capacity restriction and we have $4x_M \leqslant 64$ or $x_M \leqslant \frac{64}{4} = 16$ in the painting-time restriction. Thus, the largest value we can assign to x_M is the minimum of 10 and 16, which is 10 tables, without violating either restriction. This solution yields a daily profit of

$$Z = 200x_V + 240x_M$$
$$= 200(0) + 240(10)$$
$$= \$2400.$$

Note that if TFI is restricted to producing only one product, then it is optimal (yields the highest profit) to produce Massachusetts tables, yielding a profit of \$2400, which is \$800 more than only producing Virginia tables.

8.2.2. Example—Hawaii Stores Inc.

The advertising department of Hawaii Stores Inc. (HSI) must plan next month's advertising strategy for a new line of color TV sets. HSI's goal is to reach *at least* 36% of high-income households and 60% of middle-income households. Two different media are under consideration:

HDAL TV—Honolulu
The Honolulu Times.

Marketing studies have shown that

1. TV advertising reaches 2% of high-income households and 3% of middle-income households per commercial in Hawaii.
2. Newspaper advertising reaches 3% of high-income households and 6% of middle-income households per ad in Hawaii.

Newspaper advertising costs \$500 per ad and TV advertising costs \$2000 per commercial. HSI's goal is to obtain at least a minimal exposure of 36% of high-income households and 60% of middle-income households at minimum advertising costs.

PROBLEM. Assuming that a person viewing both the ad and the commercial will count as a double exposure (exposure greater than 100% is possible), construct a linear programming model for HSI.

Step 1—HSI's Decision Variables. Let

$$x_N = \text{number of newspaper ads}$$

and $\qquad\qquad\quad x_T = \text{number of TV commercials.}$

Step 2—HSI's Objective Function. Choose x_N and x_T to

minimize total advertising costs = minimize $Z = \$500x_N + \$2000x_T.$

Step 3—HSI's Constraints or Goals

$$(3\%)x_N + (2\%)x_T \geqslant 36\% \qquad \text{(high-income households)}$$
$$(6\%)x_N + (3\%)x_T \geqslant 60\%. \qquad \text{(middle-income households)}$$

Step 4. $x_N \geqslant 0$ and $x_T \geqslant 0.$

THE HSI MODEL

Choose x_N and x_T to minimize $Z = 500x_N + 2000x_T$ subject to the constraints on x_N and x_T that

$$3x_N + 2x_T \geqslant 36$$
$$6x_N + 3x_T \geqslant 60$$

$$x_N \geqslant 0$$
$$x_T \geqslant 0.$$

QUESTION. Will an advertising plan of $x_N = 6$ ads and $x_T = 6$ ads meet both of HSI's exposure goals?

Answer. No. For high-income households, we have

$$3x_N + 2x_T = 3(6) + 2(6)$$
$$= 30\%,$$

which is $(36 - 30 =)$ 6% below the goal of 36%. For middle-income households, we have

$$6x_N + 3x_T = 6(6) + 3(6)$$
$$= 54\%,$$

which is 6% below the goal of 60% for middle-income households.

QUESTION. Will an advertising plan of $x_N = 8$ ads and $x_T = 6$ ads meet both of HSI's exposure goals?

Answer. Yes. For high-income households, we have

$$3x_N + 2x_T = 3(8) + 2(6)$$
$$= 36\%,$$

which meets exactly the goal of 36%. For middle-income households, we have

$$6x_N + 3x_T = 6(8) + 3(6)$$
$$= 66\%,$$

which is 6% above the goal of 60%.

8.3. SOLUTIONS TO LINEAR PROGRAMMING MODELS

Graphs are usually not the best method for solving real-world linear programming problems since we can draw in at most three dimensions. However, a graphical solution of a three (or less)-dimensional problem is effective in understanding the structure of linear programming models. Graphs are also of tremendous aid in understanding the characteristics of optimal solutions to linear programming models.

8.3.1. Graphical Procedure—Maximization

Step 1. Plot the constraints of the linear programming problem on a graph.

Step 2. Locate all the corner points of the graph.

Step 3. Test all the corner points to see which yields the maximum profit.

8.3.2. Example—TFI's Product Mix Problem

Consider the linear programming model given in Example 8.2.1:

maximize $Z = 200x_V + 240x_M$

subject to

$$6x_V + 12x_M \leqslant 120 \quad \text{(construction capacity)}$$
$$8x_V + 4x_M \leqslant 64 \quad \text{(painting capacity)}$$

$$x_V \geqslant 0, \quad x_M \geqslant 0.$$

Step 1—Plotting the Constraints. Plot the constraints of the model with product x_V shown on the horizontal axis and x_M on the vertical axis. Figure 8.1 shows the x_V and x_M axis.

The inequality (or inequation)

$$6x_V + 12x_M \leqslant 120$$

can be plotted on the graph by first plotting the boundary of the constraint.

The boundary of

$$6x_V + 12x_M \leqslant 120$$

is defined by the line

$$6x_V + 12x_M = 120.$$

Straight lines are easily plotted by finding the two end points where the line intersects the x_V and x_M axis and then joining the two points by a straight line. The two end points can be found by setting one variable equal to zero in the equation and solving for the other variable and doing this for both variables.

Figure 8.1

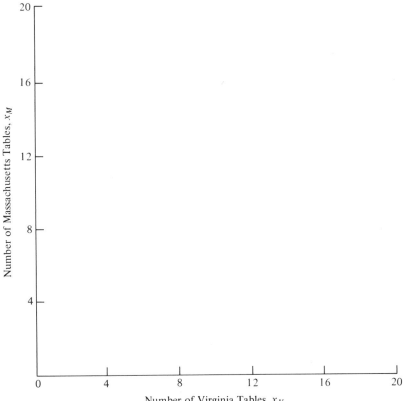

Let $x_V = 0$. Then $6(0) + 12x_M = 120$. Or, dividing both sides by 12 we obtain $x_M = \frac{120}{12} = 10$. Thus, our first point P_1 is $(0, 10)$. See Figure 8.2.

Next, let $x_M = 0$ in $6x_V + 12x_M = 120$. Then $6x_V = 120$ or $x_V = \frac{120}{6} = 20$. Thus, our second point P_2 is $(20, 0)$. Locating these two points $P_1 = (0, 10)$ and $P_2 = (20, 0)$ and joining them gives the straight line P_1-P_2 shown in Figure 8.2.

At point $P_1 = (0, 10)$ we are producing $x_V = 0$ of type V tables and $x_M = 10$ of type M tables. We are at what is called a *boundary point* of the inequality $6x_V + 12x_M \leqslant 120$ since $6(0) + 12(10) = 120$. At point P_1 we are using all of the 120 hours of processing time in department C for producing type M tables.

Similarly, at point $P_2 = (20, 0)$ we are producing $x_V = 20$ of type V tables and $x_M = 0$ of type M tables. As with point P_1, point P_2 is also a boundary point of the inequality

$$6x_V + 12x_M \leqslant 120$$

since

$$6(20) + 12(0) = 120.$$

At P_2 we are using all the 120 hours of processing time available in department C to produce only type V tables.

Figure 8.2. Graph of the equation $6x_V + 12x_M = 120$.

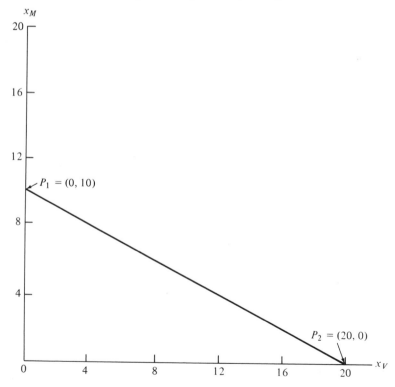

Now any combination of type V and M tables on the line P_1 and P_2 will also use up all 120 hours of department C's capacity. For example, for points on line P_1–P_2 (see Figures 8.2 and Figure 8.3), we have:

V Tables	M Tables	$6x_V + 12x_M$ = Number of Units of Department C's Capacity Used
$x_V = 4$	$x_M = 8$	$6(4) + 12(8) = 120$ hours
$x_V = 8$	$x_M = 6$	$6(8) + 12(6) = 120$ hours
$x_V = 12$	$x_M = 4$	$6(12) + 12(4) = 120$ hours
$x_V = 16$	$x_M = 2$	$6(16) + 12(2) = 120$ hours

Now suppose that TFI can only sell 4 of type V and 4 of type M. This point is shown in the shaded area of Figure 8.3. We have

$$6(4) + 12(4) = 72 \text{ hours}$$

of C used. Thus, we have a *slack* of $120 - 72 = 48$ hours of C. Hence, the shaded area in Figure 8.3, including the boundary, is the graphic representation of the

Figure 8.3. Graph of the inequality $6x_V + 12x_M \leqslant 120$.

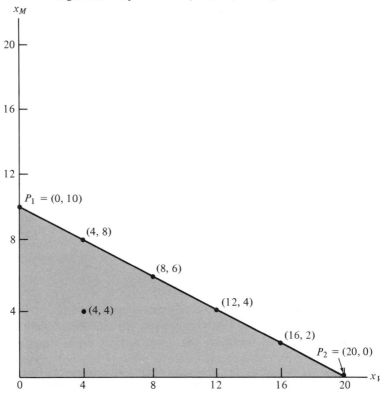

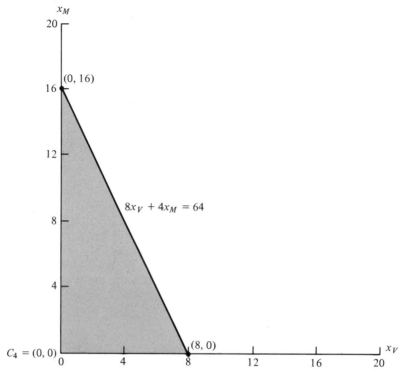

Figure 8.4. Graph of the capacity constraint $8x_V + 4x_M \leqslant 64$.

inequality

$$6x_V + 12x_M \leqslant 120.$$

We can similarly graph the second inequality:

$$8x_V + 4x_M \leqslant 64. \qquad \text{(painting capacity)}$$

The two boundary points are found by letting $x_M = 0$ and solving:

$$8x_V + 4(0) = 64,$$

yielding $x_V = \frac{64}{8} = 8$.

Similarly, with $x_V = 0$,

$$8(0) + 4x_M = 64,$$

or $x_M = \frac{64}{4} = 16$. Thus, the two boundary points are $x_M = 0$, $x_V = 8$ and $x_V = 0$ and $x_M = 16$. These two boundary points are shown in Figure 8.4. The shaded area in Figure 8.4 are values of x_M and x_V that satisfy the inequality $8x_V + 4x_M \leqslant 64$.[†]

[†]Any combination of type V and type M tables falling within and on the boundary of the shaded area in Figure 8.4 will satisfy the capacity restriction in the painting department.

In order to build a complete V or M table, both production centers must be used. This means that the best or optimal combination of tables must fall within the shaded area *common to both* Figures 8.3 and 8.4. That is, we first need to graph the two original inequalities, $6x_V + 12x_M \leqslant 120$ and $8x_V + 4x_M \leqslant 64$, on the same x_V and x_M axis. Next, in this graph determine values for x_V and x_M which are satisfying both simultaneously. The result of this graphing is shown in Figure 8.5.

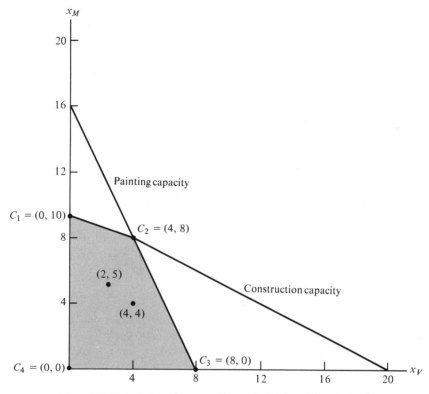

Figure 8.5. Plot of TFI's two capacity constraints [feasible solutions].

Any point (x_V, x_M) in the shaded area, or on the boundary of the shaded area, does not exceed either of the capacities of the two production centers. That is, the shaded area, including its boundary, contains all possible production levels x_V and x_M for tables V and M that satisfy both of the following two inequalities:

$$6x_V + 12x_M \leqslant 120 \text{ hours} \qquad \text{(construction capacity)}$$
$$8x_V + 4x_M \leqslant 64 \text{ hours.} \qquad \text{(painting capacity)}$$

For example, if $x_V = 4$ and $x_M = 4$, then

$$6(4) + 12(4) = 72 \text{ hours} < 120 \text{ hours}$$

and

$$8(4) + 4(4) = 48 \text{ hours} < 64 \text{ hours.}$$

See Figure 8.5. Also, for

$$x_V = 2 \quad \text{and} \quad x_M = 5,$$

$$6(2) + 12(5) = 72 \text{ hours} < 120 \text{ hours}$$

and $\qquad\qquad 8(2) + 4(5) = 36 \text{ hours} < 64 \text{ hours}.$

Thus, as illustrated in Figure 8.5, every solution (x_V, x_M) that lies within the shaded area and on the boundary of the shaded area is called a *feasible solution*. That is, a feasible solution (or a feasible production plan) is a solution that *simultaneously satisfies all the constraints* of the linear programming model.

TFI could produce that number of each table corresponding to any point in the set of feasible solutions; all of them are feasible. However, the goal of TFI is to maximize total profit, where profit is expressed by the equation

$$Z = 200x_V + 240x_M.$$

To complete the graphical procedure we need to incorporate profit $Z = 200x_V + 240x_M$ in the graph. To do this, we use the following property of every linear programming model in *step 3* of the graphical procedure:

A maximum profit occurs at a corner point of the set of feasible solutions.

Step 2—Locating the Corner Points. Locate all the corner points of the set of feasible solutions. In Figure 8.6, there are four corner points to the set of feasible production plans (the shaded area, including the boundary of Figure 8.6). They are:

$$C_1 = (0, 10), \quad C_2 = (4, 8), \quad C_3 = (8, 0), \quad \text{and} \quad C_4 = (0, 0).$$

How was point $C_2 = (4, 8)$ determined? $C_2 = (4, 8)$ can be located by constructing an accurate graph. Another method is to find the *simultaneous solution* to the two equations

$$6x_V + 12x_M = 120$$
$$8x_V + 4x_M = 64$$

since the point $C_2 = (4, 8)$ is at the intersection of these two lines.

To solve for the x_V and x_M which satisfies both equations, we divide the first equation by the number 3:

$$\frac{6x_V + 12x_M}{3} = \frac{120}{3}$$
$$2x_V + 4x_M = 40$$

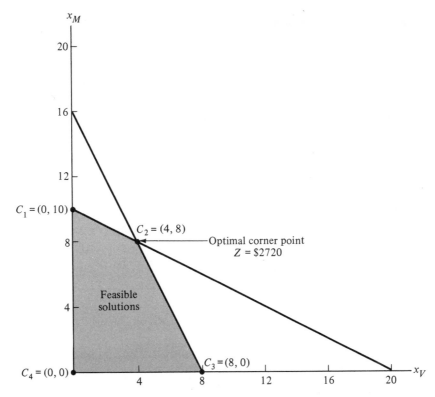

Figure 8.6. Feasible production plans for TFI; corner points are C_1, C_2, C_3, C_4.

and subtract from it the second equation. This yields

$$2x_V + 4x_M = 40$$
$$-8x_V - 4x_M = -64$$
$$\overline{-6x_V = -24.}$$

Then dividing both sides by -6 yields

$$x_V = -\frac{-24}{6} = 4.$$

To solve for x_M we substitute $x_V = 4$ into either equation, say the first equation, yielding

$$6(4) + 12x_M = 120$$

or $$24 + 12x_M = 120$$

or $$12x_M = 120 - 24$$

or $$12x_M = 96$$

or $$x_M = \frac{96}{12} = 8.$$

Thus, we have $x_V = 4$ and $x_M = 8$. That is,

$$C_2 = (4, 8).$$

Step 3—Testing the Corner Points. Test all the corner points to see which yields the maximum profit.

Corner Points	Profit = Z = $200x_V + 240x_M$
$(x_V, x_M) = (0, 0)$	$Z = 200(0) + 240(0) = \$0$
$(x_V, x_M) = (0, 10)$	$Z = 200(0) + 240(10) = \$2400$
$(x_V, x_M) = (4, 8)$	$\boxed{Z = 200(4) + 240(8) = \$2720}$
$(x_V, x_M) = (8, 0)$	$Z = 200(8) + 240(0) = \$1600$

The corner point having the greatest profit ($2720) is $C_2 = (4, 8)$, as shown in Figure 8.6.

The property of a linear programming model that maximum profit occurs at a corner point of the set of feasible solutions may be illustrated graphically. Consider again the profit function given by the equation

$$Z = 200x_V + 240x_M.$$

Since Z is unknown, we first let profit Z equal some dollar amount we know can occur for feasible values of x_V and x_M, say $Z = \$960$. Then we plot $Z = \$960 = 200x_V + 240x_M$ on the graph containing the set of feasible solutions as shown in Figure 8.7. The profit line $\$960 = 200x_V + 240x_M$ has been plotted as a dashed line in Figure 8.7, with end points determined as follows.

First, let $x_M = 0$ in $960 = 200x_V + 240x_M$. Then

$$200x_V = 960 \quad \text{or} \quad x_V = 4.8.$$

Next, let $x_V = 0$ in $960 = 200x_V + 240x_M$. Then

$$240x_M = 960 \quad \text{or} \quad x_M = \tfrac{960}{240} = 4.$$

The two end points $(x_V, x_M) = (4.8, 0)$ and $(x_V, x_M) = (0, 4)$ of the profit line $\$960 = 200x_V + 240x_M$ are illustrated in Figure 8.7.

We can plot other profit lines for values of Z other than $960, say $1200, $1600, $2720, and so forth. Since TFI's goal is to maximize total profit, we increase profit Z say $960 to $1200 and plot the profit line:

$$Z = \$1200 = 200x_V + 240x_M.$$

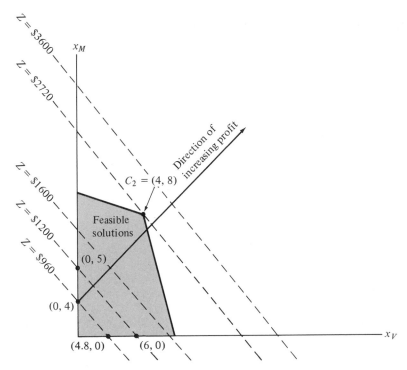

Figure 8.7. Plotting the profit function $Z = 240x_V + 240x_M$.

The end points of the profit line $\$1200 = 200x_V + 240x_M$ are

$$x_V = 0, \qquad x_M = \tfrac{1200}{240} = 5$$

and
$$x_V = \tfrac{1200}{200} = 6, \qquad x_M = 0$$

as shown in Figure 8.7.

Notice in Figure 8.7 that the two profit lines $\$1200 = 200x_V + 240x_M$ and $\$960 = 200x_V + 240x_M$ are *parallel*. These two profit lines differ by $\$1200 - \$960 = \$240$ contribution to total profit. Together, they indicate the *direction of increasing profit*, as shown by the large arrow in Figure 8.7. Thus, by increasing Z we obtain profit lines increasing in the direction of increasing profit, as illustrated in Figure 8.7. Note there is a limit as to how large a profit we can achieve by use of a feasible production plan. Thus, we see in Figure 8.7 that the highest allowable profit line Z occurs at the corner point $C_2 = (4, 8)$ of the set of feasible solutions. At $C_2 = (4, 8)$ we have

$$Z = 200x_V + 240x_M$$
$$= 200(4) + 240(8)$$
$$= \$2720.$$

A value of Z greater than \$2720 can only be achieved by an infeasible production plan. For example, let $Z = \$3600$. The profit line is

$$\$3600 = 200x_V + 240x_M,$$

which, as shown in Figure 8.7, lies completely outside the set of feasible production plans.

In summary, we increase Z as shown in Figure 8.7, so that the profit lines move parallel to each other until they intersect the set of feasible production levels at the point $C_2 = (4, 8)$, which yields a maximum profit of

$$Z = 200(4) + 240(8) = \$2720.$$

8.3.3. *Graphical Procedure—Minimization*

Many business problems require the *minimization* of some objective function instead of maximization. The graphical procedure for minimization is the same as that for maximization with a slight modification in step 3. Step 3 for minimization should read: *Test* all corner points to see which yields the *minimum* total cost.

8.3.4. *Example—Hawaii Stores Inc.*

Consider the linear programming model given in Example 8.2.2:

minimize $Z = 500x_N + 2000x_T$

subject to	$3x_N +$	$2x_T \geqslant 36$	(high-income households)
	$6x_N +$	$3x_T \geqslant 60$	(middle-income households)
	$x_N \geqslant 0,$	$x_T \geqslant 0.$	

Step 1—Plotting the Constraints. We first plot the constraint

$$3x_N + 2x_T \geqslant 36$$

by first plotting the end points of the line

$$3x_N + 2x_T = 36.$$

If $x_T = 0$, then

$$3x_N = 36 \quad \text{or} \quad x_N = \tfrac{36}{3} = 12.$$

So one end point is $x_N = 12$ and $x_T = 0$, which is denoted by $P_1 = (12, 0)$ in Figure 8.8. Next, if $x_N = 0$, then

$$2x_T = 36 \quad \text{or} \quad x_T = \tfrac{36}{2} = 18.$$

Thus, the other end point of the line $2x_N + 2x_T = 36$ is $x_N = 0$ and $x_T = 18$, which is denoted by P_2 in Figure 8.8.

We see in Figure 8.8 that every point within the shaded area and every point on the boundary of the shaded area satisfies the inequality $3x_N + 2x_T \geqslant 36$. For example, $(x_N, x_T) = (16, 20)$ lies within the shaded area of Figure 8.8, since

$$3x_N + 2x_T = 3(16) + 2(20)$$
$$= 88 > 36.$$

Next we graph the line

$$6x_N + 3x_T = 60.$$

The end points are P_3 with $x_N = 10$, $x_T = 0$ and P_4 with $x_N = 0$ and $x_T = 20$, as shown in Figure 8.9.

Figure 8.8. Graph of the inequality $3x_N + 2x_T \geqslant 36$, with $x_N \geqslant 0$, $x_T \geqslant 0$.

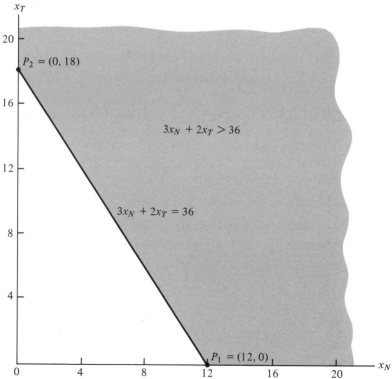

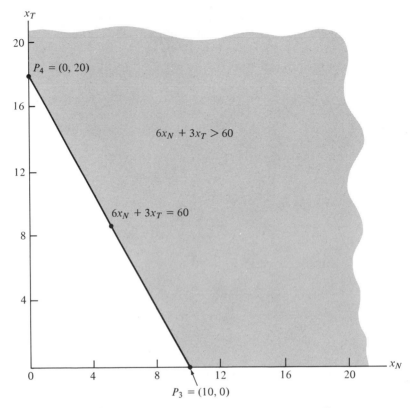

Figure 8.9. Graph of the inequality $6x_N + 3x_T \geqslant 60$.

The set of values for x_N and x_T that satisfies both of the constraints

$$3x_N + 2x_T \geqslant 36$$
$$6x_N + 3x_T \geqslant 60$$

is the shaded area common to both Figures 8.8 and 8.9, as shown in Figure 8.10.

Step 2—Locating the Corner Points. From Figure 8.10 we note that there are three corner points, C_1, C_2, and C_3, in the set of feasible solutions. By inspection of Figure 8.10 it is easily seen that

$$C_1 = (0, 20)$$

and
$$C_3 = (12, 0).$$

C_2 is obtained by finding the simultaneous solution to the two equations

$$3x_N + 2x_T = 36$$
$$6x_N + 3x_T = 60.$$

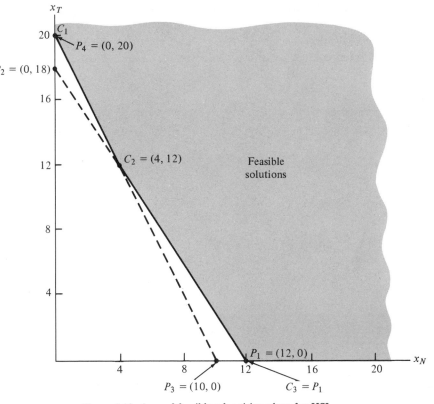

Figure 8.10. Area of feasible advertising plans for HSI.

To solve for C_2 we multiply the first equation by 3 and subtract from it the second equation multiplied by 2:

$$3(3x_N + 2x_T) = 3(36)$$
$$- 2(6x_N + 3x_T) = -2(60)$$

This yields

$$9x_N + 6x_T = 108$$
$$\underline{-12x_N - 6x_T = -120}$$
$$-3x_N = -12$$

or
$$x_N = \frac{-12}{-3} = 4.$$

Substituting $x_N = 4$ into $3x_N + 2x_T = 36$ yields

$$3(4) + 2x_T = 36$$

or
$$2x_T = 36 - 3(4) = 24$$

or
$$x_T = \tfrac{24}{2} = 12.$$

Thus, $C_2 = (4, 12)$, as shown in Figure 8.10.

Step 3—Testing the Corner Points. Test all the corner points to see which yields the minimum cost.

Corner Point	Advertising Cost $= Z = 500x_N + 2000x_T$
$C_1 = (x_N, x_T) = (0, 20)$	$Z = 500(0) + 2000(20) = \$40,000$
$C_2 = (x_N, x_T) = (4, 12)$	$Z = 500(4) + 2000(12) = \$26,000$
$C_3 = (x_N, x_T) = (12, 0)$	$Z = 500(12) + 2000(0) = \$6,000$

Thus, the optimal advertising plan is

$$x_N = 12, \qquad x_T = 0, \quad \text{and} \quad \text{total cost } Z = \$6000.$$

Figure 8.11. Plotting the cost function $Z = 500x_N + 2000x_T$.

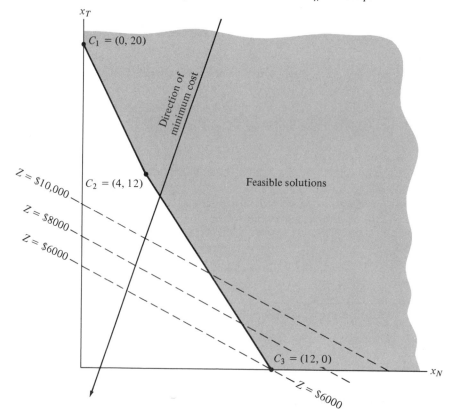

Note that instead of profit lines we have cost lines in this problem. That is, the objective function is

$$Z = 500x_N + 2000x_T$$

and HSI's goal is to choose feasible values for x_N and x_T which minimize Z. Consider a cost of $10,000. That is, let $Z = \$10,000$ and consider the cost line

$$10,000 = 500x_N + 2000x_T,$$

as shown in Figure 8.11. The parallel cost line $\$8000 = 500x_N + 2000x_T$ is also shown in Figure 8.11. Thus, we can immediately determine the direction of minimum cost as shown by the arrow in Figure 8.11. We also see that the lowest value of Z for a feasible advertising plan occurs at the corner point C_3, with $x_N = 12$, $x_T = 0$ and $Z = \$6000$.

8.4. CHARACTERISTICS OF LINEAR PROGRAMMING PROBLEMS

In this section, we will review some of the basic properties of a linear programming problem—specifically, we will discuss proportionality, additivity, divisibility, and optimality.

8.4.1. Proportionality

The objective function and every restriction on the decision variables must be linear in a linear programming model. That is, the measure of effectiveness (profit or cost) in the objective function and the amount of each resource used must be proportional to the value of each decision variable considered individually.

8.4.2. Additivity

In a linear programming model it is necessary that each variable be "additive" with respect to profit (or cost) and the amount of resources used.

For example, suppose that a company is considering the production of two types of tables. Suppose that the profit would be $\$100x_1$ if x_1 units of the first table are sold and the second table is not produced at all. Suppose that $\$120x_2$ would be the profit from selling the second table in the amount of x_2 units if $x_1 = 0$. The two products are additive with respect to profit only if the total profit would be $\$100x_1 + \$120x_2$ when both $x_1 > 0$ and $x_2 > 0$. However, for example, if $x_1 > 0$ and $x_2 > 0$ units are sold, and total profit $= \$100x_1 + \$120x_2 - \$2x_1x_2$, then profit is not additive.

8.4.3. Divisibility

In many business problems it is frequently the case that the decision variables would have physical significance only if they have integer values. Thus, another limitation of linear programming in obtaining an optimal solution is that fractional levels of the decision variables must be allowed.

8.4.4. Optimality

In a linear programming problem a maximum profit solution or a minimum cost solution always occurs at a corner point of the set of feasible solutions.

REFERENCES BIERMAN, H., C. P. BONINI, and W. H. HAUSMAN. *Quantitative Analysis for Business Decisions*, 4th ed. Homewood, Ill.: Richard D. Irwin, Inc., 1973.

DAELLENBACH, H. G., and E. J. BELL. *User's Guide to Linear Programming*. Englewood Cliffs, N.J.: Prentice-Hall, Inc., 1970.

DANTZIG, G. B. *Linear Programming and Extensions*. Princeton, N.J.: Princeton University Press, 1963.

DRIEBEEK, N. J. *Applied Linear Programming*. Reading, Mass.: Addison-Wesley Publishing Co., Inc., 1969.

HILLIER, F. S., and G. J. LIEBERMAN. *Introduction to Operations Research*, 2nd ed. San Francisco: Holden-Day, Inc., 1974.

HOROWITZ, I. *An Introduction to Quantitative Business Analysis*, 2nd ed. New York: McGraw-Hill Book Company, 1972.

KIM, C. *Introduction to Linear Programming*. New York: Holt, Rinehart and Winston, Inc., 1972.

KWAK, N. K. *Mathematical Programming with Business Applications*. New York: McGraw-Hill Book Company, 1973.

LAPIN, L. *Quantitative Methods for Business Decisions*. New York: Harcourt Brace Jovanovich, Inc., 1976.

LEVIN, R., and C. KIRKPATRICK. *Quantitative Approaches to Management*, 3rd ed. New York: McGraw-Hill Book Company, 1975.

SHAMBLIN, J. E., and G. T. STEVENS, JR. *Operations Research—A Fundamental Approach*. New York: McGraw-Hill Book Company, 1974.

SIMMONS, D. M. *Linear Programming for Operations Research*. San Francisco: Holden-Day, Inc., 1972.

287

STRUM, J. E. *Introduction to Linear Programming*. San Francisco: Holden-Day, Inc., 1972.

TAHA, H. A. *Operations Research: An Introduction*. New York: Macmillan Publishing Co., Inc., 1971.

WAGNER, H. M. *Principles of Operations Research with Applications to Managerial Decisions*. Englewood Cliffs, N.J.: Prentice-Hall, Inc., 1975.

KEY CONCEPTS

Maximize profit	Feasible solutions
Minimize cost	Infeasible solutions
Objective function	Corner point solutions
Interrelated decisions; variables	Optimal solutions
Restrictions	
inequations	
equations	

REVIEW PROBLEMS

8.1. Consider the following linear programming model. Choose x_1 and x_2 to

$$\text{minimize } Z = 25x_1 + 30x_2$$

$$\text{subject to} \quad x_1 + 2x_2 \leqslant 4$$

$$x_1 + \quad x_2 \geqslant 1$$

$$x_1 \geqslant 0, \quad x_2 \geqslant 0.$$

(a) Which symbols represent the decision variables?
(b) Which expression represents the objective function?
(c) Is $x_1 = 1$ and $x_2 = 2$ a feasible solution?
(d) Is $x_1 = 2$ and $x_2 = 1$ a feasible solution?
(e) Is the feasible solution $x_1 = 3$ and $x_2 = \frac{1}{2}$ a "better solution" than the feasible solution $x_1 = 1$ and $x_2 = 1$?

8.2. Plot each of the following constraints. Indicate which side of the constraint represents *nonnegative* feasible solutions.
(a) $x_1 + 2x_2 \geqslant 4$
(b) $x_1 + 2x_2 = 4$
(c) $x_1 + 2x_2 \leqslant 4$

8.3. Plot the cost function $Z = x_1 + x_2$ for costs of $Z = \$10$ and $\$20$. Denote on the graph the direction of decreasing costs. Also, denote on the graph the direction of increasing costs.

8.4. Plot the profit function $Z = 2x_1 + 4x_2$ for profits of $Z = \$16$ and $Z = \$20$. Denote on the graph the direction of increasing profit. Also, denote on the graph the direction of decreasing profit.

8.5. Consider the following linear programming problem:

$$\text{maximize } Z = 2x_1 + 3x_2$$

$$\text{subject to} \quad x_1 \qquad \leqslant 5$$

$$x_2 \leqslant 5$$

$$x_1 + x_2 \leqslant 8$$

$$x_1 \geqslant 0, \quad x_2 \geqslant 0.$$

Find an optimal (profit-maximizing) solution to this problem.

ANSWERS TO
REVIEW
PROBLEMS

8.1. (a) x_1 and x_2 denote the decision variables.

(b) The cost function $Z = 25x_1 + 30x_2$ represents the objective function.

(c) $x_1 = 1$ and $x_2 = 2$ is an unfeasible solution since it violates the first constraint $x_1 + 2x_2 \leqslant 4$. That is, $1 + 2(2) = 5 > 4$.

(d) $x_1 = 2$ and $x_2 = 1$ is a feasible solution since it satisfies both constraints and the nonnegativity restrictions. Check:

$$\text{constraint 1:} \quad x_1 + 2x_2 \leqslant 4$$

$$(2) + 2(1) = 4$$

$$\text{constraint 2:} \quad x_1 + x_2 \geqslant 1$$

$$(2) + (1) = 3 > 1$$

$$\text{nonnegativity:} \quad x_1 \geqslant 0, \quad x_2 \geqslant 0$$

$$2 > 0, \quad 1 > 0.$$

(e) The feasible solution $x_1 = 3$ and $x_2 = \frac{1}{2}$ yields a cost $Z = 25(3) + 30(\frac{1}{2}) = \$90$. The feasible solution $x_1 = 1$ and $x_2 = 1$ yields a cost $Z = 25(1) + 30(1) = \$55$. Hence, the solution $x_1 = 1$ and $x_2 = 1$ is better than the solution $x_1 = 3$ and $x_2 = \frac{1}{2}$.

8.2. (a) The end points of $x_1 + 2x_2 = 4$ may be determined as follows. Let $x_1 = 0$ in the equation $x_1 + 2x_2 = 4$. Then $2x_2 = 4$ or $x_2 = 4/2 = 2$. Thus, one end point is $x_1 = 0$ and $x_2 = 2$. Similarly, let $x_2 = 0$ in the equation $x_1 + 2x_2 = 4$. Then $x_1 = 4$ and the other end point is $x_1 = 4$ and $x_2 = 0$. Both end points are plotted in Figure 8.12. The set of feasible solutions to $x_1 + 2x_2 \geqslant 4$ are those points on the line and in the shaded area. For example, testing (4, 4) for feasibility, we have $4 + 2(4) = 12 > 4$. The point (0, 0) is infeasible since $0 + 2(0) < 4$.

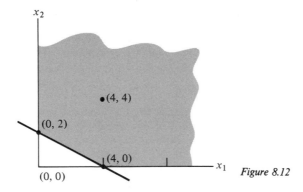

Figure 8.12

(b) The nonnegative feasible solutions to $x_1 + 2x_2 = 4$ are only those points on the line $x_1 + 2x_2 = 4$, as shown in Figure 8.13. For example, $(1, 1)$ is infeasible since $(1) + 2(1) = 3 < 4$. The point $(4, 4)$ is also infeasible since $4 + 2(4) = 12 > 4$. However, $x_1 = 3$, $x_2 = \frac{1}{2}$ is feasible since $3 + 2(\frac{1}{2}) = 4$.

(c) The set of nonnegative feasible solutions to the inequality $x_1 + 2x_2 \leqslant 4$ is on the boundary and within the shaded area of Figure 8.14. For example, $(1, 1)$ is feasible since $1 + 2(1) = 3 < 4$ but $(3, 3)$ is infeasible since $3 + 2(3) = 9 > 4$.

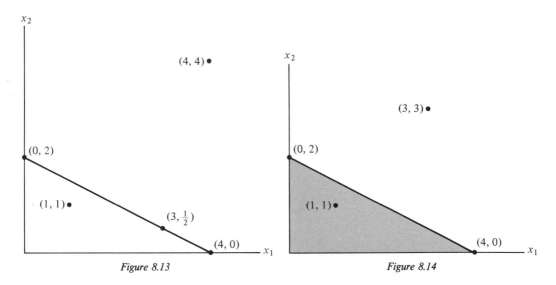

Figure 8.13   Figure 8.14

8.3. Let $Z = \$10$ in the cost function $Z = x_1 + x_2$. Then we have $10 = x_1 + x_2$ with end points $x_1 = 0$, $x_2 = 10$ and $x_1 = 10$, $x_2 = 0$. Similarly, letting $Z = \$20$ in the cost function yields $20 = x_1 + x_2$ with end points $x_1 = 0$, $x_2 = 20$ and $x_1 = 20$, $x_2 = 0$. The two resulting parallel lines are shown in Figure 8.15 along with the directions of increasing and decreasing total cost.

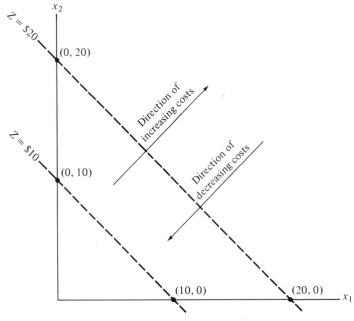

Figure 8.15

8.4. Let $Z = \$16$ in the profit function $Z = 2x_1 + 4x_2$. Then we have $\$16 = 2x_1 + 4x_2$ with end points $x_1 = 0$, $x_2 = \frac{16}{4} = 4$ and $x_1 = \frac{16}{2} = 8$, $x_2 = 0$. Next, let $Z = \$20$ in the profit function $Z = 2x_1 + 4x_2$. Then we have $20 = 2x_1 + 4x_2$ with end points $x_1 = 0$, $x_2 = \frac{20}{4} = 5$ and $x_1 = \frac{20}{2} = 10$, $x_2 = 0$. Both parallel profit functions are illustrated in Figure 8.16 along with the directions of increasing and decreasing total profit.

Figure 8.16

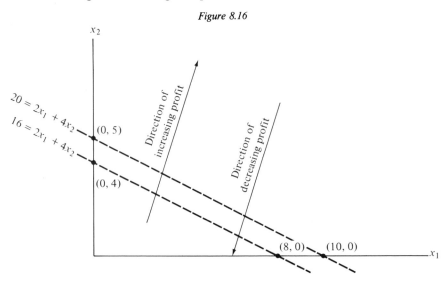

8.5. To solve this problem, we use the graphical procedure.

Step 1—Plot the Constraints. There are three constraints to be plotted. The corresponding equations and their end points are as follows:

Constraint	End Points
$x_1 \leqslant 5$	$x_1 = 5, x_2 = 0$
$x_2 \leqslant 5$	$x_1 = 0, x_2 = 5$
$x_1 + x_2 \leqslant 8$	$x_1 = 0, x_2 = 8 \quad \text{and} \quad x_1 = 8, x_2 = 0$

Using the end points given in the table, we next plot the set of feasible solutions as shown in Figure 8.17. The set of feasible solutions is denoted by the shaded area, including its boundary. Note that there are five corner points.

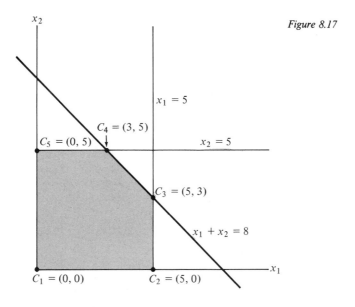

Figure 8.17

Step 2—Determine the Corner-Point Solutions. We see from the figure above that there are five corner-point solutions.

$$C_1 = (0,0), \quad C_2 = (5,0), \quad C_3 = (5,3), \quad C_4 = (3,5), \quad \text{and} \quad C_5 = (0,5).$$

C_3 and C_4 are determined by determining the points of intersection of the constraint equations. C_3 occurs at the intersection of $x_1 = 5$ and $x_1 + x_2 = 8$. Thus, substituting $x_1 = 5$ into $x_1 + x_2 = 8$ yields $x_2 = 3$ and we have $C_3 = (5, 3)$. C_4 occurs at the intersection of $x_2 = 5$ and $x_1 + x_2 = 8$. Substituting $x_2 = 5$ into $x_1 + x_2 = 8$ yields $x_1 = 3$. Thus, $C_4 = (3, 5)$.

Step 3—Determine the Profit-Maximizing Corner-Point Solution. The five corner points and their associated profits are as follows:

CORNER POINT			Profit
	x_1	x_2	$= Z = 2x_1 + 3x_2$
C_1	0	0	$\$0 = 2(0) + 3(0)$
C_2	5	0	$10 = 2(5) + 3(0)$
C_3	5	3	$19 = 2(5) + 3(3)$
C_4	3	5	$21 = 2(3) + 3(5)$
C_5	0	5	$15 = 2(0) + 3(5)$

Thus, the optimal solution occurs at C_4 with $x_1 = 3$, $x_2 = 5$, yielding a profit of $21.

EXERCISES

PRODUCTION PROBLEM **8.1.** The Maine Snowmobile Company manufactures two kinds of machines, each requiring a different manufacturing technique. The Deluxe machine requires 18 hours of labor, 9 hours of testing, and yields a profit of $400. The Standard machine requires 3 hours of labor, 4 hours of testing, and yields a profit of $200. There are 800 hours of labor and 600 hours of testing available each month.

A marketing forecast has shown that the monthly demand for the Deluxe model to be no more than 80, and monthly demand for the Standard machine to be no more than 150. Management wants to know the number of each model to produce monthly that will maximize total profit. Formulate this as a linear programming problem.

PRODUCTION PROBLEM **8.2.** Texas Electronics Incorporated (TEI) is considering adding new minicomputers to its product line in order to increase profit. Three new computers have been designed and evaluated. Each will require a $300,000 investment. Computer 1 has an expected sales of 50,000 units per year with a profit contribution of $20 per unit. Computers 2 and 3 have an expected annual sales of 300,000 units and 100,000 units, respectively, with profit contributions of $5 and $10. TEI has allocated 800 hours of technician time to be available each month for the new products. Computers 1, 2, and 3 require 1.00, 0.20, and 0.50 technician-hour per unit, respectively. The automated packing and shipping system presently used in the plant will also have to be used for the new computers. This system can pack and ship at most 25,000 boxes of minicomputers. Computer 1 is packed 1 unit to a box. Computers 2 and 3 are each packed 4 units to a box. Construct a linear programming model to determine the most profitable new production decisions for TEI.

TRANSPORTATION PROBLEM **8.3.** The Fargo Water Co. has three reservoirs with estimated daily inflows of 15, 20, and 25 million liters of fresh water, respectively. On each day they must supply four areas, A, B, C, and D, whose expected demands are 8, 10, 12, and

15 million liters, respectively. The cost of pumping per million liters is as follows:

Reservoirs	*A*	*B*	*C*	*D*
		AREA		
1	2	3	4	5
2	3	2	5	2
3	4	1	2	3

Formulate the Fargo Water Co. problem as a linear programming model. Assume that excess water can be disposed of at no cost to the company.

COMMODITY TRADING PROBLEM

8.4. The Kansas Company is in the commodity trading business. It buys and sells corn for cash. It owns a warehouse with a capacity of 50,000 bushels. On January 1, they expect to have an initial stock of 10,000 bushels of corn and a cash balance of 200,000. The estimated corn prices per bushel for the following quarter are as follows:

Month	Buying Price	Selling Price
January	$2.85	$3.10
February	3.05	3.25
March	2.90	2.95

The corn is delivered in the month in which it is bought and cannot be sold until the next month. Both buying and selling corn are done strictly on a "cash on delivery" basis. The company would like to have a final inventory of 20,000 bushels of corn at the end of the quarter. Management would like to set a buying and selling policy that maximizes the total net return for the 3-month period. Formulate this as a linear programming problem.

PERSONNEL PLANNING PROBLEM

8.5. The Atlanta Tollway Authority has the following minimal daily requirements for toll keepers:

Period	Clock Time (24-Hour Day)	Minimal Number of Tollkeepers Required
1	6 A.M.–10 A.M.	8
2	10 A.M.–2 P.M.	6
3	2 P.M.–6 P.M.	8
4	6 P.M.–10 P.M.	7
5	10 P.M.–2 A.M.	5
6	2 A.M.–6 A.M.	3

Tollkeepers report to the toll booths at the beginning of each period and work for 8 consecutive hours. The Authority wants to determine the minimal number of tollkeepers to employ so that there will be sufficient number of personnel available for each period. Formulate this as a linear programming problem.

PRODUCTION SMOOTHING PROBLEM

8.6. Consider the problem of scheduling the production of a product for each of the next 4 weeks. The production cost of the item is $100 for the first 2 weeks and $150 for the last 2 weeks. The weekly demands are 7, 8, 9, and 10 units. Demand each week must be satisfied. The plant can produce a maximum of 9 units each week. In addition, the company can employ overtime during the third and fourth weeks. This increases the weekly production by an additional 2 units, but the cost of production increases $58 per item. Excess production can be stored at a cost of $3 an item. How should the production be scheduled so as to minimize the total costs? Formulate this as a linear programming problem.

PRODUCT MIX PROBLEM

8.7. A company manufactures three products, labeled A, B, and C. Each unit of product A requires 1 hour of engineering service, 8 hours of direct labor, and 4 pounds of material. To produce 1 unit of product B, it required 3 hours of engineering, 3 hours of direct labor, and 3 pounds of material. Each unit of product C requires 2 hours of engineering, 4 hours of direct labor, and 2 pounds of material. There are 80 hours of engineering, 800 hours of labor, and 300 pounds of material available each month. The profit data are as follows:

	PRODUCT A		PRODUCT B		PRODUCT C	
Sales (units)	Unit Profit ($)		Sales (units)	Unit Profit ($)	Sales (units)	Unit Profit ($)
0–40	10		0–50	6	0–100	5
40–100	9		50–100	4	Over 100	4
100–150	8		Over 100	3		
Over 150	6					

Formulate a linear programming model to determine the most profitable product mix.

PRODUCTION PLANNING MODEL

8.8. In the Chemical Division of the MS Corporation two products (A and B) are made; the same two operations are required in the manufacture of each. The production of B also results in a by-product, C; some of this by-product can be sold at a profit, but beyond a certain quantity (12 units) it must be destroyed because of lack of demand. The unit profits on products A and B, respectively, are $4 and $9. The by-product C, sells at a price to yield a $2 unit profit. If C cannot be sold, the unit cost of destruction is $1. The process yields 3.1 units of C for each unit of B produced. Forecasts indicate that the demand for A and B is limited. Unit processing times: A, 2.6 hours on operation 1 and 3.3 hours on operations 2; B, 4.7 hours on operation 1 and 4.6 hours on operation 2. Available times: 60 hours of operation 1 and 65 hours of operation 2. Assume that the products are divisible, so that fractional units are acceptable. This formulation will solve the problem:

$$\text{maximize } Z = 4x_1 + 9x_2 + 2x_3 - 1x_4$$

$$\text{subject to} \quad 2.6x_1 + 4.7x_2 \quad\quad \leqslant 60 \tag{1}$$

$$3.3x_1 + 4.6x_2 \quad\quad \leqslant 65 \tag{2}$$

$$x_3 \leqslant 12 \tag{3}$$

$$3.1x_2 = x_3 + x_4 \tag{4}$$

$$x_1, x_2, x_3, x_4 \geqslant 0. \tag{5}$$

(a) Explain the meaning of each variable and each constraint in the model above.

(b) In the formulation of this problem, what will prevent the value of x_4 from becoming positive whenever x_3 is less than 12?

8.9. Consider the following linear programming model:

$$\text{minimize } Z = x_1 - 3x_2 + 4x_3$$

$$\text{subject to} \quad x_1 + x_2 + x_3 \geqslant 10$$

$$x_1 + 2x_2 \quad\quad \leqslant 7$$

$$x_1 \geqslant 0, \quad x_2 \geqslant 0, \quad x_3 \geqslant 0.$$

(a) What expression represents total cost?

(b) Which symbols represent the decision variables?

(c) Do the following values of the decision variables constitute a feasible solution?

$$x_1 = 3, \quad x_2 = 2, \quad x_3 = 2.$$

(d) Do the following values of the decision variables constitute a feasible solution?

$$x_1 = 2, \quad x_2 = 2, \quad x_3 = 6.$$

(e) Do the following values of the variables constitute a feasible solution?

$$x_1 = 2, \quad x_2 = -2, \quad x_3 = 6.$$

(f) Which of the following feasible solutions is best relative to total cost Z?

feasible solution 1: $x_1 = 1,$ $\quad x_2 = 3,$ $\quad x_3 = 6$
feasible solution 2: $x_1 = 4,$ $\quad x_2 = 0,$ $\quad x_3 = 6$
feasible solution 3: $x_1 = 1,$ $\quad x_2 = 2,$ $\quad x_3 = 8.$

8.10. Explain why an optimal solution to a linear programming model must be a feasible solution, but not every feasible solution must be an optimal solution.

8.11. Plot each of the following restrictions. Show which side of the restriction represents the infeasible solutions.

$$\text{(1)} \quad x_1 + 2x_2 \geqslant 4$$
$$\text{(2)} \quad x_1 + 2x_2 \leqslant 4$$
$$\text{(3)} \quad x_1 \qquad \geqslant 4$$
$$\text{(4)} \quad x_1 \qquad \leqslant 4$$
$$\text{(5)} \quad x_1 - 2x_2 \geqslant 4.$$

Assume in each case that $x_1 \geqslant 0$ and $x_2 \geqslant 0$.

8.12. Plot the objective function

$$z = 2x_1 + 3x_2$$

for values of

$$z = 6 \quad \text{and} \quad z = 18.$$

In what direction should you shift this objective function on a graph if you want to minimize the value of z?

8.13. Plot the objective function

$$z = 3x_1 + 2x_2$$

for values of

$$z = 6 \quad \text{and} \quad z = 18.$$

In what direction should you shift this objective function on a graph if you want to maximize the value of z?

8.14. Consider the following linear programming model:

$$\text{maximize } Z = 3x_1 + 2x_2$$

$$\text{subject to} \qquad x_1 \qquad \leqslant 6$$
$$x_2 \leqslant 6$$
$$x_1 + x_2 \leqslant 9$$

$$x_1 \geqslant 0, \qquad x_2 \geqslant 0$$

(a) Give an example of an *infeasible solution* to this linear programming problem.
(b) Give an example of a *feasible solution* to this linear programming problem.
(c) Find, by use of the graphical procedure, an optimal solution to this linear programming problem.

8.15. Consider the following linear programming model:

$$\text{minimize } Z = 3x_1 + 2x_2$$

$$\text{subject to} \quad x_1 \geqslant 9$$

$$x_1 + x_2 \geqslant 12$$

$$x_1 \geqslant 0, \quad x_2 \geqslant 0.$$

(a) Give an example of an *infeasible solution* to this linear programming problem.
(b) Give an example of a *feasible solution* to this linear programming problem.
(c) Find, by use of the graphical procedure, an optimal solution to this linear programming problem.

8.16. Consider the following linear programming model:

$$\text{maximize } Z = 3x_1 + 2x_2$$

$$\text{subject to} \quad x_1 \geqslant 9$$

$$x_1 + x_2 = 12$$

$$x_1 \geqslant 0, \quad x_2 \geqslant 0.$$

(a) Give an example of an *infeasible solution* to this linear programming problem.
(b) Give an example of a *feasible solution* to this linear programming problem.
(c) Find, by use of the graphical procedure, an optimal solution to this linear programming problem.

8.17. Using the graphical procedure, find the value of x_1 and x_2 that will

$$\text{maximize } Z = 9x_1 + 5x_2$$

$$\text{subject to} \quad 2x_1 + 2x_2 \leqslant 12$$

$$x_1 + 2x_2 \leqslant 8$$

$$x_1 - 4x_2 \geqslant 4$$

$$x_1 \geqslant 0, \quad x_2 \geqslant 0.$$

AUDIT PLANNING PROBLEM **8.18.** New York Auditing Inc. (NYAI) is a public accounting firm that specializes in preparing tax returns as well as auditing small firms in the metropolitan area. NYAI is concerned over how many tax returns and audits should be carried out each month to achieve maximum revenue. There are 800 staff-time hours and 160 review-time hours available. An average audit requires 40 hours of staff time, 10 hours of review time, and yields a gross profit of $300. An average tax return requires 8 hours of staff time, 2 hours of review time, and yields a gross profit of $100.

(a) What are NYAI's decision variables? Develop the constraints and the objective function for the linear programming model. Plot the constraints and identify the area of feasible solutions.

(b) Beginning at the policy "do nothing," move on the boundary of the set of feasible solutions, explaining the rationale of each move, until the optimal decision is found. What is the value of the objective function at this decision?

PRODUCTION PLANNING PROBLEM **8.19.** North Carolina Weaving Industries (NCWI) has a synthetic fiber manufacturing plant in Raleigh which processes two different fibers, designated F_1 and F_2, on the same production line. Production is limited in the spinning department by a requirement for 20 hours per thousand pounds for fiber F_1 and 40 hours per thousand pounds for fiber F_2, with a maximum available spinning time of 2000 hours per month. In the drawing department, the requirements are 60 hours per thousand pounds for fiber F_1 and 80 hours for fiber F_2, with a maximum available machine time of 4800 hours per month. For the cutting department, the requirements are 100 hours per thousand pounds for F_1 and 60 hours per thousand pounds for F_2, with a maximum time of 6000 hours per month. Sales constraints limit production of fiber F_1 to a maximum of 25,000 pounds per month.

How much of each fiber should be produced in order to maximize profits if the profit contribution for fiber F_1 is \$100 per thousand pounds and for fiber F_2 is \$150 per thousand pounds?

Construct a linear programming model for NCWI. Graph the constraints, identify the set of feasible solutions, and determine the optimal decision by computing the value of the objective function at each of the corner points of the set of feasible solutions. Also determine, through the use of different parallel profit lines, the optimal decision for NCWI.

PRODUCT MIX PROBLEM **8.20.** Florida Oranges Inc. (FOI) must determine the optimal number of box cars for its "super" and "average" oranges to pick, pack, and ship each week. Available labor includes 4000 hours of picking and packing time. Thirty hours of labor is required to pick and pack a car load of super oranges and 15 hours are required for the average oranges. FOI has a maximum amount of cash on hand each week of \$60,000. Two hundred dollars in cash outflows is required for each boxcar of average oranges produced and \$300 for each boxcar of super oranges. The profit contribution per box car is \$2000 for the average and \$2500 for the super. FOI wishes to determine the optimal mix of box cars by type of oranges that will maximize profit each week. Construct a linear programming model for FOI's problem. Determine the best decision for FOI by plotting the constraints of your model, identify the area of feasible solutions, and determining corner points.

PRODUCT MIX PROBLEM **8.21.** Colorado Beef Inc. (CBI) processes two grades of beef, each of which requires different production and preparation techniques. CBI is questioning its present production policy. Because the beef market is a seller's market, CBI can sell all the beef it can process at the price of \$180 per ton for grade A and \$150 per ton for grade B. This is the price payable to CBI, f.o.b. at the Denver plant. Cost accounting has estimated that direct labor costs will be 40% of the price CBI receives per ton for either grade of beef. Processing costs other than labor and exclusive of slaughtering and packing costs are $25 per ton for each grade. Slaughtering and packing costs for grade A beef are $30 per ton and for grade B beef are $50 per ton.

The capacity of the slaughtering and packing plant is limited to 2000 man-hours per day. Each ton of grade A requires 1.5 hours of processing and each ton of grade B requires 1.0 hour of processing in the slaughtering and packing plant. Labor is available in an almost unlimited supply.

Construct a profit-maximizing linear programming model for CBI. Determine the best product mix by plotting the constraints of your model, identify the area of feasible solutions, and its corner points.

PRODUCTION PLANNING MODEL

8.22. Arizona Air Conditioning Inc. (AAI) wishes to begin production of two new air conditioners by using excess time available on three production lines. These lines perform successive steps in the production process. Each of the two new air conditioners must pass through all three lines before the manufacturing process is complete. The first conditioner requires 4 hours of processing on line 1, 8 hours on line 2, and 6 hours on line 3. The second conditioner requires 4, 10, and 12 hours respectively, on the three lines. There is a limited amount of time available on each of the three lines each month, since they are already in use in producing other air conditioners. The excess time available each month is 120 hours on line 1, 240 hours on line 2, and 360 hours on line 3. The expected profit contribution for the first air conditioner is $100 and for the second air conditioner it is $150 per unit.

The objective of AAI is to maximize profit. Formulate a linear programming model for AAI. Plot the constraints of your model, identify the area of feasible solutions, and determine all the corner points. What is the maximum number of air conditioners of the first type that could be made? What is the maximum number of air conditioners of the second type that could be made? What is an optimal production plan for AAI?

CHAPTER 9
Linear Programming:
The Simplex Method

OBJECTIVES. Upon successful completion of this chapter, you should be able to:

1. Solve a linear programming problem using the simplex method.
2. Explain in detail why the simplex method finds optimal solutions to linear programming problems.
3. Determine when a linear programming problem has multiple optimal solutions.
4. Determine when a linear programming problem has no solution.

9.1. INTRODUCTION

Several business problems were formulated as linear programming problems in Chapter 8. However, we were only able to solve for an optimal solution if the problems had two or less decision variables. The *simplex method*, with the aid of the computer, can solve linear programming problems with several thousand variables and several thousand constraints.

As with the graphical procedure, the *simplex method* finds the optimal (least cost or maximum profit) corner-point solution of the set of feasible solutions. That is, regardless of the number of decision variables and regardless of the number of constraints, the simplex method uses the key property of a linear programming problem, which is:

> A linear programming problem always has an optimal solution occurring at a corner-point solution.

The simplex method is a systematic and efficient procedure for finding corner-point solutions and testing corner-point solutions for optimality. The simplex method stops (or terminates) once an optimal solution is found.

The approach we shall use in presenting the simplex method is to apply it to a problem we have already solved by the graphical procedure. The problem we shall use is TFI's product mix problem (Example 8.3.1 in Chapter 8), which is

9.1.1. Example

The set of feasible solutions to the programming problem below is illustrated in Figure 9.1.

maximize $Z = 200x_V + 240x_M$ (objective function)   (O)

subject to $6x_V + 12x_M \leqslant 120$ (construction-time restriction)   (a)

$8x_V + 4x_M \leqslant 64$ (painting-time restriction)   (b)

$x_V \geqslant 0, \quad x_M \geqslant 0.$ (nonnegativity restriction)

We already know that a profit-maximizing solution occurs at a corner-point solution. That is, we only need to test the corner points to determine the optimal or profit-maximizing solution. Consider the following corner-point evaluations for the

Figure 9.1. Feasible solutions.

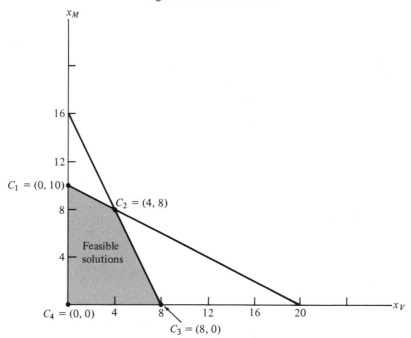

feasible solutions given in Figure 9.1.

$$\text{for } C_1 = (0, 10): \quad Z = 200(0) + 240(10) = \$2400$$
$$\text{for } C_2 = (4, 8): \quad Z = 200(4) + 240(8) = \$2720$$
$$\text{for } C_3 = (8, 0): \quad Z = 200(8) + 240(0) = \$1600$$
$$\text{for } C_4 = (0, 0): \quad Z = 200(0) + 240(0) = \$0.$$

Thus, the profit-maximizing solution is $C_2 = (4, 8)$ yielding a profit of \$2720.

9.2. BASIC CONCEPTS IN THE SIMPLEX METHOD

9.2.1. Slack Variables

The simplex method requires that the constraints be equations (or equality constraints) rather than inequations (or inequality constraints). Now any inequation can be converted to an equation by adding a nonnegative quantity to the "smaller side of the inequation."

Consider the construction capacity constraint given in (a). Adding a nonnegative variable s_1, called a *slack variable*, we have

$$6x_V + 12x_M + s_1 = 120. \tag{a'}$$

In (a') s_1 is the number of construction hours that $(6x_V + 12x_M)$ falls short of the 120 available hours. For example, if we produce $x_V = 4$ and $x_M = 3$ tables of type V and M, respectively, then we use $6(4) + 12(3) = 60$ hours of construction time, which leaves an excess of $s_1 = 120 - 60 = 60$ hours of "slack" construction time. That is, let

$$s_1 = \text{amount of unused construction time.}$$

Then

$$\text{(construction time used)} + \text{(unused construction time)} = 120$$

or $\qquad\qquad 6x_V + 12x_M \qquad + \qquad\qquad s_1 \qquad\qquad = 120.$

Similarly, we let s_2 be the slack variable denoting the number of unused painting hours in the painting capacity constraint given in (b). We have

$$8x_V + 4x_M + s_2 = 64. \tag{b'}$$

It is important to note that slack variables can never be negative. For example,

$$x_V = 9, \qquad x_M = 0, \qquad s_2 = -8$$

303 satisfies (b'):

$$8x_V + 4x_M + s_2 = 64$$
$$8(9) + 4(0) + (-8) = 64.$$

However, $x_V = 9$ and $x_M = 0$ does not satisfy the original constraint (b):

$$8x_V + 4x_M \leqslant 64 \tag{b}$$

since

$$8(9) + 4(0) = 72 > 64.$$

Thus far we have shown how slack variables may be used to convert inequations to equations.

SUMMARY

ORIGINAL LINEAR PROGRAMMING PROBLEM

maximize $Z = 200x_V + 240x_M$ $\hspace{2cm}$ (O)

subject to $\hspace{1cm}$ $6x_V + 12x_M \leqslant 120$ $\hspace{0.5cm}$ (construction) $\hspace{1cm}$ (a)

$\hspace{3.3cm}$ $8x_V + 4x_M \leqslant 64$ $\hspace{0.7cm}$ (painting) $\hspace{1.2cm}$ (b)

$\hspace{2.5cm}$ $x_V \geqslant 0, \hspace{0.5cm} x_M \geqslant 0.$

Let

$\hspace{1cm}$ s_1 = number of hours of unused construction time

$\hspace{1cm}$ s_2 = number of hours of unused painting time.

$\hspace{3cm}$ s_1 and s_2 are slack variables.

LINEAR PROGRAMMING PROBLEM INCORPORATING SLACK VARIABLES

maximize $Z = 200x_V + 240x_M + 0s_1 + 0s_2$ $\hspace{2cm}$ (O')

subject to $\hspace{1cm}$ $6x_V + 12x_M + 1s_1 + 0s_2 = 120$ $\hspace{1.5cm}$ (a')

$\hspace{3.3cm}$ $8x_V + 4x_M + 0s_1 + 1s_2 = 64$ $\hspace{1.5cm}$ (b')

$\hspace{2.5cm}$ $x_V \geqslant 0, \hspace{0.5cm} x_M \geqslant 0, \hspace{0.5cm} s_1 \geqslant 0, \hspace{0.5cm} s_2 \geqslant 0.$

Note that the unit profits associated with the two slack variables are both $0. This reflects the fact that the *unused* construction time and the *unused* painting time in the amounts s_1 and s_2, respectively, contribute nothing to profit.

9.2.2. Basic Variables and Basic Feasible Solutions

The set of feasible solutions to the new problem given in (a′) and (b′) cannot be graphed since we now have four variables. Thus, we need to use an alternative procedure to find feasible solutions. A solution to equations (a′) and (b′) is any set of four numbers, one for each variable, which satisfies (a′) and (b′) simultaneously.

Following are five examples of solutions to (a′) and (b′):

solution (1): $x_V = 0,$ $x_M = 0,$ $s_1 = 120,$ $s_2 = 64.$

solution (2): $x_V = 8,$ $x_M = 0,$ $s_1 = 72,$ $s_2 = 0.$

solution (3): $x_V = 0,$ $x_M = 1,$ $s_1 = 108,$ $s_2 = 60.$

solution (4): $x_V = 1,$ $x_M = 10,$ $s_1 = -6,$ $s_2 = 16.$

solution (5): $x_V = 20,$ $x_M = 0,$ $s_1 = 0,$ $s_2 = -96.$

Note that solutions (1), (2), and (3) also satisfy the nonnegativity restrictions. Thus, they are *feasible* solutions. Note in solution (4) that the slack variable s_1 is negative, $s_1 = -6 < 0$. This violates the nonnegativity restriction. Thus, solution (4) is an *infeasible* solution. Similarly, s_2 is negative in solution (5). Thus, solution (5) is also an infeasible solution.

How do we find feasible solutions to (a′) and (b′)? We know how to solve *two* equations for *two* variables. This we did several times in Chapter 8. But, (a′) and (b′) have *two* equations and *four* variables.

If we have *more* variables than equations, we can set the extra variables equal to zero, obtaining a system having an equal number of variables and constraints. Such a solution is called a *basic solution* and, of course, we are interested in finding basic solutions for which the variables all have nonnegative values.

A *basic feasible solution* to equations (a′) and (b′) is a solution with *at most two* (= number of equations) variables having positive values and the remaining variables having the value zero.

Solutions (1) and (2) comprise a basic feasible solution to (a′) and (b′). That is,

solution (1): $x_V = 0,$ $x_M = 0,$ $s_1 = 120,$ $s_2 = 64$
                  nonbasic variables   basic variables

solution (2): $x_M = 0,$ $s_2 = 0,$ $x_V = 8,$ $s_1 = 72$
                  nonbasic variables   basic variables

are both basic feasible solutions.

The variables that have positive values in a basic feasible solution are called *basic variables*, while those remaining variables having the value of zero are called *nonbasic variables*. Thus, in the basic feasible solution (1),

s_1 and s_2 are the basic variables
x_V and x_M are the nonbasic variables.

In solution (2),

x_V and s_1 are the basic variables
x_M and s_2 are the nonbasic variables.

Note that in solution (3):

$$x_V = 0, \qquad x_M = 1, \qquad s_1 = 108, \qquad s_2 = 60$$

has three variables which are positive. Thus, solution (3) is a feasible solution but *not a basic feasible solution*.

9.2.3. Basic Feasible Solutions and Corner-Point Solutions

Using Figure 9.1 we see that every corner point in the set of feasible solutions *corresponds to* a basic feasible solution of equations (a') and (b').

The first two columns of Table 9.1 list the four corner points of the set of feasible solutions. The values of s_1 and s_2 are obtained by substituting the corresponding values of x_V and x_M into equations (a') and (b').

Table 9.1. Basic Feasible Solutions

	x_V (from Figure 9.1)	x_M	s_1 [From (a') and (b')]	s_2 [From (a') and (b')]
C_1:	0	10	0	24
C_2:	4	8	0	0
C_3:	8	0	72	0
C_4:	0	0	120	64

QUESTION. Consider equations (a') and (b').

$$6x_V + 12x_M + 1s_1 + 0s_2 = 120 \qquad \text{(a')}$$

$$8x_V + 4x_M + 0s_1 + 1s_2 = 64. \qquad \text{(b')}$$

How was the basic feasible solution given in the third line of Table 9.1 determined?

Answer. We have two equations and four variables. Setting $x_M = 0$, $s_2 = 0$ in (a')
and (b'), we have

$$6x_V + 1s_1 = 120$$
$$8x_V \quad\quad = 64,$$

yielding $x_V = 8$ and $s_1 = 72$.

QUESTION. How was the basic feasible solution given in line 2 of Table 9.1
determined?

Answer. Setting $s_1 = 0$ and $s_2 = 0$ in (a') and (b'), we have

$$6x_V + 12x_M = 120$$
$$8x_V + 4x_M = 64,$$

yielding $x_V = 4$ and $x_M = 8$.
A summary of the important facts presented so far is as follows:

1. There is a corner point of the set of feasible solutions which yields the
   maximum profit.
2. Each corner point of the set of feasible solutions corresponds to a basic
   feasible solution of the constraint *equations* (obtained by adding slack variables to the inequations).
3. Every basic feasible solution corresponds to a corner-point solution of the set
   of feasible solutions.

Thus, from (1), (2), and (3) we now know that in order to find a profit-maximizing solution to a linear programming problem we need to find that basic
feasible solution that yields the highest profit.

9.2.4. The Simplex Method

The steps of simplex for solving a linear program problem is illustrated
in Figure 9.2. We now illustrate in detail each step of the simplex method using the
LP model given in Example 8.3.1.

$$\text{maximize } Z = 200x_V + 240x_M \quad\quad (O)$$

$$\text{subject to} \quad 6x_V + 12x_M \leqslant 120 \quad\quad (a)$$

$$8x_V + 4x_M \leqslant 64 \quad\quad (b)$$

$$x_V \geqslant 0, \quad x_M \geqslant 0.$$

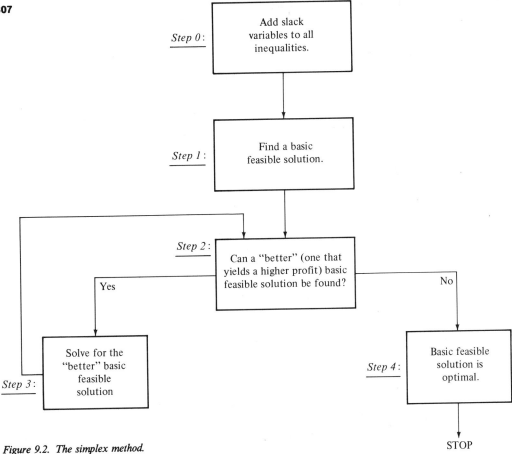

Figure 9.2. The simplex method.

Step 0—Add Slack Variables to All Inequations. Also, add the same slack variables to the objective function, each with a unit profit of $0. Let

$$s_1 \text{ be the slack variable for (a)}$$

and $\qquad s_2 \text{ be the slack variable for (b).}$

Then we have

LP MODEL

maximize $Z = 200x_V + 240x_M + 0s_1 + 0s_2$ $\qquad\qquad (O')$

subject to $\qquad 6x_V + 12x_M + 1s_1 + 0s_2 = 120$ $\qquad\qquad (a')$

$\qquad\qquad\qquad 8x_V + 4x_M + 0s_1 + 1s_2 = 64$ $\qquad\qquad (b')$

$$x_V \geqslant 0, \qquad x_M \geqslant 0, \qquad s_1 \geqslant 0, \qquad s_2 \geqslant 0.$$

Step 1—Find an Initial Basic Feasible Solution to the System of Equations (a') and (b'). This can be done in the *LP model* by inspection. Let

$$\left\{ \begin{array}{l} s_1 = 120 \\ s_2 = 64 \end{array} \right\} \quad \text{and} \quad \left\{ \begin{array}{l} x_V = 0 \\ x_M = 0 \end{array} \right\}.$$

basic
variables   nonbasic
variables

This solution yields a profit of

$$Z = 200x_V + 240x_M + 0s_1 + 0s_2$$
$$= 200(0) + 240(0) + 0(120) + 0(64)$$
$$= \$0.$$

Note in Figure 9.1 that this initial basic feasible solution corresponds to the corner point C_4 with $x_V = 0$ and $x_M = 0$.

Also, note that we have 2 equations and 4 variables in (a') and (b'). Thus, in performing Step 1 we set $4 - 2 = 2$ variables equal to 0, $x_V = 0$ and $x_M = 0$, in order to obtain an initial basic feasible solution.

Step 2—Find a Better Basic Feasible Solution. We are now in the *iterative* phase of the method. That is, note in Figure 9.2 that we go to step 3 and back to step 2 and keep repeating these two steps until we have an optimal basic feasible solution terminating at step 4.

At each iteration the simplex method moves from the current basic feasible solution to an *adjacent* basic feasible solution. This iteration, steps 2 and 3, requires that one nonbasic variable, called the *entering basic variable*, replace a basic variable, called the *leaving basic variable*, in the current solution. Which variable should enter the basis?

Consider again the *LP model*:

$$\text{maximize } Z = 200x_V + 240x_M + 0s_1 + 0s_2 \qquad (O')$$

$$\text{subject to} \qquad 6x_V + 12x_M + 1s_1 + 0s_2 = 120 \qquad (a')$$

$$8x_V + 4x_M + 0s_1 + 1s_2 = 64 \qquad (b')$$

$$x_V \geqslant 0, \qquad x_M \geqslant 0, \qquad s_1 \geqslant 0, \qquad s_2 \geqslant 0.$$

The current basic variables are s_1 and s_2 with values 120 and 64, respectively. The current nonbasic variables are x_V and x_M, both with zero values.

The only candidates to become the *entering basic variable* are the two nonbasic variables x_V and x_M. Which one do we choose? The new basic variable must yield an improvement (yield a higher profit) over the current basic feasible solution. Therefore, we choose that nonbasic variable which will increase profit Z by the *greatest rate*.

Consider the original objective function (O'):

$$Z = 200x_V + 240x_M + 0s_1 + 0s_2 \qquad (O')$$

It is obvious that profit Z will be increased at the *greatest rate* if x_M has a value greater than zero. That is, in *step O* we determined an initial basic feasible solution with $x_V = 0$, $x_M = 0$, $s_1 = 120$, and $s_2 = 64$, yielding a profit of $Z = \$0$. Now both x_V and x_M have positive unit profit coefficients, \$200 and \$240, respectively. Since both coefficients are positive and \$240 > \$200, we can increase Z from \$0 to a positive dollar value if x_M has a value greater than 0.

QUESTION. What is the increase in profit Z per unit increase in x_V?

Answer. The coefficient of x_V in Z is $+\$200$. Thus, the increase in Z is \$200 per unit increase in x_V.

QUESTION. What is the increase in profit Z per unit increase in x_M?

Answer. The coefficient of x_M in Z is $+\$240$. Hence, Z increases \$240 per unit increase in x_M.

Step 3—Solve for the New or "Better" Basic Feasible Solution. Step 3 has two parts: determining the variable to leave the basis *and* solving for the new values of the basic variables.

The *leaving basic variable* is not a matter of free choice. First, recall that the current basic variables are s_1 and s_2. Also, recall that we chose x_M to be the entering basic variable.

Our goal is to choose a basic variable for removal, either s_1 or s_2, so that the entering variable x_M can have as large a value as possible without violating any of the constraints in the model. The determination of the leaving variable caused by the entering variable x_M is shown in Table 9.2.

In row 1 of Table 9.2 we show constraint (a') of the LP model. In row 2 of Table 9.2 we show constraint (b') of the LP model. Note in row 1 that the

Table 9.2 Determining the Leaving Basic Variable

Current Basic Variables	Constraints	Upper Bounds for x_M
Row 1: s_1 (a')	$6x_V + 12x_M + 1s_1 + 0s_2 = 120$ or $s_1 = 120 - 6x_V - 12x_M - 0s_2$	$\frac{120}{12} = 10$ ←
Row 2: s_2 (b')	$8x_V + 4x_M - 0s_1 + s_2 = 64$ or $s_2 = 64 - 8x_V - 4x_M - 0s_1$	$\frac{64}{4} = 16$ ←

minimum $= 10$

constraint (a′) is written twice as:

$$6x_V + 12x_M + 1s_1 + 0s_2 = 120$$

and

$$s_1 = 120 - 6x_V - 12x_M - 0s_2.$$

We use the second equivalent form of (a′), with the current basic variable s_1 appearing by itself on the left-hand side, to facilitate determining the largest feasible value of x_M. Recall that *only* x_M is to become positive, and x_V is to *remain* equal to zero, $x_V = 0$. Thus, we see in row 1, with x_V fixed at zero, that the largest feasible value for x_M is 10. If we let x_M have a value greater than 10, then s_1 must become negative. But this violates the restriction that all variables, including slack variables, must be nonnegative.

Similarly, we see in row 2, with the current basic variable s_2 on the left-hand side, that the largest feasible value for x_M is 16.

x_M has to satisfy both constraints (a′) and (b′). Hence, x_M must equal the minimum of 10 and 16, which is 10. That is, we let $x_M = 10$ in (a′), and as shown in row 1 in Table 9.2, s_1 becomes the *leaving basic variable*.

QUESTION. Why do we obtain an infeasible solution by letting x_M be greater than 10, say $x_M = 16$?

Answer. If we let $x_M = 16$, then for constraint (a′) to hold (see row 1 in Table 9.2),

$$\begin{aligned}
s_1 &= 120 - 6x_V - 12x_M - 0s_2 \\
&= 120 - 6(0) - 12(16) - 0s_2 \\
&= 120 - 192 \\
&= -72.
\end{aligned}$$

But $s_1 = -72$ violates the restriction that all variables must be positive or zero.

QUESTION. Why does s_1 become the leaving basic variable when we let $x_M = 10$?

Answer. s_1 becomes the leaving basic variable because the minimum ratio $120/12 = 10 = x_M$ occurs in constraint (a′) (see row 1 in Table 9.2). That is, our initial basic feasible solution is $x_V = 0$, $x_M = 0$, $s_1 = 120$, and $s_2 = 64$. Now constraint (a′) says that

$$s_1 = 120 - 6x_V - 12x_M - 0s_2.$$

So if we keep $x_V = 0$ and let x_M become positive, we have

$$\begin{aligned}
s_1 &= 120 - 6x_V - 12x_M - 0s_2 \\
&= 120 - 6(0) - 12x_M - 0s_2 \\
&= 120 - 12x_M.
\end{aligned}$$

Now

$$s_1 = 120 - 12x_M \geqslant 0$$

if

$$120 \geqslant 12x_M$$

or

$$\frac{120}{12} \geqslant x_M$$

or

$$10 \geqslant x_M.$$

We now have determined that the leaving basic variable is to be s_1. Thus,

$$s_1 = 0 \quad \text{and} \quad x_M = 10$$

is the new value of x_M.

Step 3 (cont.)—Find the Values of the Remaining Basic Variables. We now have identified both the entering and leaving basic variable. Next we must determine the new values of the remaining basic variables. To accomplish this step we need to convert the original system of equations—(O'), (a'), and (b')—into a new equivalent system of equations such that each equation *contains one and only one basic variable with a coefficient of + 1.* This can be accomplished by use of the following two operations:

O_1: multiplying an equation (on both sides) by a nonzero constant

O_2: adding a multiple of one equation to another equation.

Consider again the objective function and the original set of constraint equations:

$$\text{objective function:} \quad Z - 200x_V - 240x_M - 0s_1 - 0s_2 = \quad 0 \qquad (O')$$

$$\text{row 1:} \qquad\qquad 6x_V + \quad 12x_M + \quad s_1 + 0s_2 = 120 \qquad (a')$$

$$\text{row 2:} \qquad\qquad 8x_V + \quad 4x_M + 0s_1 + 1s_2 = \quad 64. \qquad (b')$$

Recall that x_M is to replace s_1 as the basic variable in (a').

Note that we have written the objective function above as:

new version of
the objective function:

$$Z - 200x_V - 240x_M - 0s_1 - 0s_2 = 0. \qquad (O')$$

Both the original version and the new version are *equivalent.* All we have done in constructing the new from the original is move each term involving a variable on the right-hand side of the original to the left-hand side, yielding the new version of the objective function.

Note that x_M has a coefficient of $+12$ in (a'). Using operation 1, O_1, we first multiply both sides of (a') by $\frac{1}{12}$:

$$(\tfrac{1}{12})(6x_V + 12x_M + 1s_1 + 0s_2) = (\tfrac{1}{12})(120) \qquad\qquad [(\tfrac{1}{12})(a')]$$

$$\tfrac{1}{2}x_V + 1x_M + \tfrac{1}{12}s_1 + 0s_2 = 10. \qquad\qquad [(a'') = (\tfrac{1}{12})(a')]$$

We now have

$$Z - 200x_V - 240x_M - 0s_1 - 0s_2 = 0 \qquad\qquad (O')$$

$$\tfrac{1}{2}x_V + 1x_M + \tfrac{1}{12}s_1 + 0s_2 = 10 \qquad\qquad (a'')$$

$$8x_V + 4x_M + 0s_1 + 1s_2 = 64. \qquad\qquad (b')$$

Recall that our goal is to have one and only one basic variable in each equation. Since x_M is to be in (a''), we must eliminate it from (O') and (b'). This we accomplish by use of operation 2, O_2. We replace (O') by (O'') and replace (b') by (b''), where

$$(O'') = (O') + (240)(a'')$$

and

$$(b'') = (b') + (-4)(a'').$$

This yields

$$Z - 80x_V + 0x_M + 20s_1 - 0s_2 = 2400 \qquad\qquad (O'')$$

$$\tfrac{1}{2}x_V + 1x_M + \tfrac{1}{12}s_1 + 0s_2 = 10 \qquad\qquad (a'')$$

$$6x_V + 0x_M - \tfrac{1}{3}s_1 + 1s_2 = 24. \qquad\qquad (b'')$$

Note the following in (O''), (a''), and (b''):

1. Z appears only in (O''), the new basic variable x_M appears only in (a''), and the remaining basic variable s_2 appears only in (b'').
2. Since the nonbasic variables (variables with zero values) are x_V and s_1, we see in (O'') that

$$\text{profit} = Z = \$2400.$$

3. Since $x_V = 0$ and $s_1 = 0$, we see in (a'') that

$$x_M = 10.$$

4. Since $x_V = 0$ and $s_1 = 0$, we see in (b'') that

$$s_2 = 24.$$

Referring to Figure 9.1 we see that we have moved from

corner-point solution $C_4 = (0, 0)$: $x_V = 0$ and $x_M = 0$

to   corner-point solution $C_1 = (0, 10)$: $x_V = 0$ and $x_M = 10$

and profit has increased from $0 to $2400.

QUESTION. To determine the new basic feasible solution given in (O''), (a''), and (b'') we performed operations O_1 and O_2 on the original equations (O'), (a'), and (b'). The statement was made that "performing operations O_1 and O_2 leads to an equivalent system." What is meant by the phrase "equivalent system?"

Answer. Two systems of equations are called equivalent if a solution of one system is also a solution of the other system, and vice versa.
     Recall that we moved from an

$$\begin{matrix} \text{initial} \\ \text{basic} \\ \text{solution} \end{matrix} \left\{ \begin{aligned} x_V &= 0 \\ x_M &= 0 \\ s_1 &= 120 \\ s_2 &= 64 \\ \text{profit } Z &= \$0 \end{aligned} \right\} \begin{matrix} \text{to a} \\ \text{new} \\ \text{basic} \\ \text{solution} \end{matrix} \left\{ \begin{aligned} x_V &= 0 \\ x_M &= 10 \\ s_1 &= 0 \\ s_2 &= 24 \\ \text{profit } Z &= \$2400 \end{aligned} \right\}.$$

We now return to step 2.

Step 2. Can a "better" basic feasible solution be found? That is, is the current basic solution given above optimal? To answer this question, we look at the profit equation (O''):

form (1): $Z - 80x_V + 0x_M + 20s_1 - 0s_2 = 2400$ (O'')
       (profit)

or

form (2): $Z = 2400 + 80x_V - 0x_M - 20s_1 + 0s_2.$ (O'')
       (profit)

Recall that for the current basic solution

$$x_V = 0 \quad \text{and} \quad s_1 = 0.$$

Looking at (O'') it is obvious that the value of $Z = $ profit will be increased if x_V has a value greater than zero. Note that x_V has a coefficient of -80 in form 1 and a coefficient of $+80$ in form 2. Thus, the increase in $Z = $ profit will be $80 per unit increase in x_V.

QUESTION. For the current basic solution we have $s_1 = 0$. What is the increase in Z = profit per unit increase in s_1?

Answer. Since s_1 has a coefficient of $+20$ in form (1) or equivalently a coefficient of -20 in form (2), Z = profit will increase \$ -20 per unit increase in s_1. That is, profit = Z will *decrease* \$20 per unit increase in s_1. Thus, we can find a better (or greater profit) solution only if x_V has a positive value. Thus, x_V becomes the *entering basic variable*.

Step 3—Solve for the New Basic Feasible Solution. The determination of which variable, x_M or s_2 should leave the basic given that x_V is the entering basic variable is shown in Table 9.3.

   Equations (O''), (a''), and (b'') are given in rows 0, 1, and 2, respectively. Note that the minimum of ∞, 20, and 4 occurs in row 2. Thus, s_2 becomes the leaving variable and x_V will have a value of 4 in the new solution.

Table 9.3

Current Basic Variables	Equations (keep $s_1 = 0$)	Upper Bound for x_V
Z	(O''): $Z - 80x_V + 0x_M + 20s_1 - 0s_2 = 2400$ or $Z = 2400 + 80x_V - 0x_M - 20s_1 + 0s_2$	Infinity = ∞
x_M	(a''): $\frac{1}{2}x_V + 1x_M + \frac{1}{12}s_1 + 0s_2 = 10$ or $x_M = 10 - \frac{1}{2}x_V - \frac{1}{12}s_1 - 0s_2$	$10/\frac{1}{2} = 20$
s_2	(b''): $6x_V + 0x_M - \frac{1}{3}s_1 + 1s_2 = 24$ or $s_2 = 24 - 6x_V - 0x_M + \frac{1}{3}s_1$	$\frac{24}{6} = 4$

minimum = 4

QUESTION. Why not let x_V have a value of 20?

Answer. If $x_V = 20$, then in constraint (b''),

$$s_2 = 24 - 6x_V - 0x_M + \frac{1}{3}s_1$$
$$= 24 - 6(20) - 0x_M + \frac{1}{3}(0)$$
$$= 24 - 120$$
$$= -96.$$

But all variables, including slack variables, must be nonnegative.
   If x_V replaces s_2 in equation (b''), then we need to eliminate x_V from (O'') and (a'') using the row operations O_1 and O_2.

Our present system is

$$Z - 80x_V + 0x_M + 20s_1 - 0s_2 = 2400 \qquad (O'')$$

$$\tfrac{1}{2}x_V + 1x_M + \tfrac{1}{12}s_1 + 0s_2 = 10 \qquad (a'')$$

$$6x_V + 0x_M - \tfrac{1}{3}s_1 + 1s_2 = 24. \qquad (b'')$$

To replace s_2 by x_V in (b'') we multiply both sides of (b'') by $\tfrac{1}{6}$:

$$(\tfrac{1}{6})(6x_V + 0x_M - \tfrac{1}{3}s_1 + 1s_2) = (\tfrac{1}{6})(24)$$

or
$$1x_V + 0x_M - \tfrac{1}{18}s_1 + \tfrac{1}{6}s_2 = 4. \qquad (b''')$$

Replacing (b'') by $(\tfrac{1}{6})$(b''), we have

$$Z - 80x_V + 0x_M + 20s_1 - 0s_2 = 2400 \qquad (O'')$$

$$\tfrac{1}{2}x_V + 1x_M + \tfrac{1}{12}s_1 + 0s_2 = 10 \qquad (a'')$$

$$1x_V + 0x_M - \tfrac{1}{18}s_1 + \tfrac{1}{6}s_2 = 4. \qquad (b''')$$

Now it remains to eliminate x_V from (a'') and (O'') using operation O_2. To accomplish this, we replace (a'') by (a'') + $(-\tfrac{1}{2})$(b''') and replace (O'') by (O'') + (80)(b''').

Performing both of these replacement operations yields:

$$Z + 0x_V + 0x_M + \tfrac{140}{9}s_1 + \tfrac{40}{3}s_2 = 2720 \qquad (O''')$$

$$0x_V + 1x_M + \tfrac{1}{9}s_1 + -\tfrac{1}{12}s_2 = 8 \qquad (a''')$$

$$1x_V + 0x_M + -\tfrac{1}{18}s_1 + \tfrac{1}{6}s_2 = 4. \qquad (b''')$$

From (O'''), (a'''), and (b'''), we see that our new basic feasible solution is

$$\text{profit} = Z = \$2720$$

$$\text{basic variables} \begin{Bmatrix} x_V = 4 \\ x_M = 8 \end{Bmatrix} \quad \text{with nonbasic variables} \begin{Bmatrix} s_1 = 0 \\ s_2 = 0 \end{Bmatrix}.$$

Referring to Figure 9.1 we see that we have moved from

$$\text{corner-point solution } C_1 \begin{Bmatrix} x_V = 0 \\ x_M = 10 \\ Z = \$2400 \end{Bmatrix} \quad \text{to} \quad \text{corner-point solution } C_2 \begin{Bmatrix} x_V = 4 \\ x_M = 8 \\ Z = \$2720 \end{Bmatrix}.$$

Note that the new basic feasible solution yielded a net increase in profit of $\$2720 - \$2400 = \$320$ over the previous basic feasible solution. We now return to step 2 to find a better solution.

Step 2. Is the current basic feasible solution optimal? To answer this question we look at the profit equation (O'''):

$$\text{form (1):} \quad Z + 0x_V + 0x_M + \tfrac{140}{9}s_1 + \tfrac{40}{3}s_2 = 2720 \qquad (O''')$$

or

$$\text{form (2):} \quad Z = 2720 - 0x_V - 0x_M - \tfrac{140}{9}s_1 - \tfrac{40}{3}s_2. \qquad (O''')$$

It is clear from (O''') that profit Z will *decrease* if either s_1 or s_2 has a value that is greater than zero. Hence, the new basic feasible solution is optimal and we go to step 4.

Step 4—Optimal Solution

$$\begin{cases} x_V = 4 \\ x_M = 8 \\ Z = \$2720 \end{cases} \quad \text{and} \quad \begin{cases} s_1 = 0 \\ s_2 = 0 \end{cases}.$$

QUESTION. What is the decrease in the value of Z per unit increase in s_1?

Answer. Since s_1 has a coefficient of $+\tfrac{140}{9}$ in form (1) of (O'''), Z will *decrease* $\$\tfrac{140}{9}$ per unit increase in s_1.

QUESTION. What is the decrease in the value of Z per unit increase in s_2?

Answer. Since s_2 has a coefficient of $+\tfrac{40}{3}$ in form (1) of (O'''), Z will decrease $\$\tfrac{40}{3}$ per unit increase in s_2.

**SUMMARY OF THE FACTS LEARNED THUS FAR
ABOUT THE SIMPLEX METHOD**

1. The simplex method finds an optimal corner-point solution (or an optimal basic feasible solution).
2. The simplex method is a *change-of-basis* method. *One* variable enters the basis, the *entering basic variable*, and *one* variable leaves the basis, the *leaving basic variable*. That is, the simplex method is a "one-variable-at-a-time" procedure.
3. A change-of-basis method involves the replacing of a system of constraint equations by an *equivalent* system of constraint equations.
4. In a system of constraint equations, *one equation* can be replaced by *an equivalent equation* by application of either or both of the following operations.

O_1: replace an equation by itself times a nonzero constant.

O_2: replace an equation by itself *added to* a constant times another constraint equation.

5. The simplex method requires that the objective function be expressed in the form where every basic variable has a coefficient of 0.

6. The simplex method requires that each basic variable appear in one and only one constraint equation.

9.2.5. The Simplex Method in Detached Coefficient Form

The *detached coefficient form* of a linear programming problem, commonly called the *simplex tableau*, is an important device to use with the simplex method.

To illustrate its use we again consider the TFI problem given in Example 9.1.1. The two constraint equations and the profit function,

$$\text{equation 1:} \qquad 6x_V + 12x_M + 1s_1 + 0s_2 = 120$$

$$\text{equation 2:} \qquad 8x_V + 4x_M + 0s_1 + 1s_2 = 64$$

$$\text{profit:} \qquad Z - 200x_V - 240x_M - 0s_1 - 0s_2 = 0,$$

can be represented in detached-coefficient form as shown in Tableau 9.2.1. The tableau completely defines the constraints and the objective function of TFI's problem. The first column identifies the basic variables for the first basic feasible solution. The last column gives the value of each of the basic variables. Thus, from Tableau 9.2.1, $s_1 = 120$, $s_2 = 64$, and $Z = \$0$.

Tableau 9.2.1

	Basic Variable	Z	x_V	x_M	s_1	s_2		Value
(a′)	s_1	0	6	12	1	0	=	120
(b′)	s_2	0	8	4	0	1	=	64
(O′)	Z	1	−200	−240	0	0	=	0

We first need to understand certain key terms before applying steps 2 and 3 of the simplex method to a problem given in detached coefficient form. They are:

Pivot column

Pivot row

Pivot number.

The *pivot column* is the column of coefficients that is associated with the nonbasic variable that has been chosen to become the entering basic variable.

The *pivot row* is the row of coefficients containing the current basic variable, which has a coefficient of $+1$, that is chosen to be the leaving basic variable.

The *pivot number* is the coefficient at the intersection of the pivot column and pivot row.

To illustrate these three terms and the use of the simplex tableau, we now apply the simplex method to Tableau 9.2.1. Steps 0 and 1 have already been performed and the initial basic feasible solution is given in Tableau 9.2.1.

Step 2—Find a Better Basic Feasible Solution. The basic feasible solution in Tableau 9.2.1 is not optimal since the coefficients of x_V and x_M in the profit function in row (O') are negative, -240 and -200, respectively.

That is, profit Z will increase if x_V or x_M has a value greater than 0. Thus, by inspecting Tableau 9.2.1, we know that:

Each variable coefficient in row (O') indicates how much profit Z will decrease per unit increase in that variable.

To find a better solution:

We choose that variable to become the entering basic variable which has the *most negative* coefficient in the objective function row (O') of the simplex tableau.

Here we choose x_M to be the entering basic variable. Thus, the x_M column becomes the pivot column, as shown in a second version of Tableau 9.2.1.

Tableau 9.2.1

	Basic Variable	Z	x_V	x_M	s_1	s_2		Value
(a')	s_1	0	6	12	1	0	=	120
(b')	s_2	0	8	4	0	1	=	64
(O')	Z	1	-200	-240	0	0	=	0

pivot column

Step 3—Determine the Variable to Leave the Basis. We now must determine which of the current basic variables, s_1 or s_2, is to become the leaving basic variable.

Recall that:

> The variable chosen to be the leaving basic variable is the current basic variable that allows the entering basic variable x_M to have the largest value possible without violating any of the constraints of the model.

To decide which variable leaves we use the basic variable column, the pivot column, and the value column of Tableau 9.2.1 and compute value-coefficient ratios as shown below.

	Basic Variable	x_M	Value	Value/Coefficient Ratio	
Row (a')	s_1	12	120	$\frac{120}{12} = 10$	minimum ratio
Row (b')	s_2	4	64	$\frac{64}{4} = 16$	= 10
	Z	−240	0		

The minimum of 10 and 16 is 10 which occurs in row (a'), where s_1 is the current basic variable. Thus, row (a') of Tableau 9.2.1 becomes the *pivot row* and s_1 becomes the *leaving basic variable*. Thus, x_M replaces s_1 in the basis.

In summary:

> The pivot row, and hence the leaving basic variable, is the row that has the smallest value/coefficient ratio where we ignore ratios (and hence rows) and where the denominator is 0 or negative.

Both the pivot column (the entering basic variable) and the pivot row (the leaving basic variable) are blocked out below in our next version of Tableau 9.2.1. The number at the intersection of the pivot column and the pivot row is $+12$. Thus, $+12$ is the *pivot number*.

Tableau 9.2.1

	Basic Variable	Z	x_V	x_M (pivot number)	s_1	s_2		Value
(a')	s_1	0	6	12	1	0	=	120
(b')	s_2	0	8	4	0	1	=	64
(O')	Z	1	−200	−240	0	0	=	0

pivot column   pivot row

Step 3 (cont.)—Find the New Basic Feasible Solution. To make a change of basis using the simplex tableau, we require the following:

1. The pivot number be converted to a $+1$ and the entering basic variable replace the leaving basic variable in the basic variable column.
2. Each of the remaining coefficients in the pivot column be converted to 0.

To accomplish (1) we divide each coefficient in the pivot row by the pivot number. That is, we replace row (a′) by row (a″), where $(a'') = (\frac{1}{12})(a')$ (Note that we are applying operation O_1.) This leads to the new tableau, 9.2.1′.

Tableau 9.2.1′

	Basic Variable	Z	x_V	x_M	s_1	s_2		Value
(a″)	x_M	0	$\frac{1}{2}$	1	$\frac{1}{12}$	0	$=$	10
(b′)	s_2	0	8	4	0	1	$=$	64
(O′)	Z	1	-200	-240	0	0	$=$	0

To accomplish (2) we replace (b′) by $(b'') = (b') - 4(a'')$ and replace (O') by $(O'') = (O') + 240(a'')$. [Note that we are applying operation O_2.] Performing the above row multiplications and additions in Tableau 9.2.1′ yields the new simplex tableau, 9.2.2.

Tableau 9.2.2

	Basic Variable	Z	x_V	x_M	s_1	s_2		Value
(a″)	x_M	0	$\frac{1}{2}$	1	$\frac{1}{12}$	0	$=$	10
(b″)	s_2	0	6	0	$-\frac{1}{3}$	1	$=$	24
(O″)	Z	1	-80	0	20	0	$=$	2400

In Tableau 9.2.2 we now have

$$\begin{Bmatrix} x_M = & 10 \\ s_2 = & 24 \\ Z = \$2400 \end{Bmatrix} \text{ and } \begin{Bmatrix} s_1 = 0 \\ x_V = 0 \end{Bmatrix}.$$

This completes step 3 of the simplex method.

You can substitute the preceding values for the four variables into the original model in nondetached coefficient form to verify they constitute a feasible solution and yield a profit $Z = \$2400$.

Is the basic solution in Tableau 9.2.2 optimal? To answer this question we return to step 2 of the simplex method.

Step 2—Find a Better Basic Feasible Solution. We note in row (O'') of Tableau 9.2.2 that the nonbasic variable x_V has a coefficient of -80. Hence, profit Z will increase above $\$2400$ if x_V has a positive value. Thus, x_V becomes the pivot column (or x_V becomes the entering basic variable).

Step 3—Solve for the Better Basic Feasible Solution. By determining the minimum-value coefficient ratio, row (b'') becomes the pivot row (or s_2 becomes the leaving basic variable) and $+6$ is the pivot number. This is shown below for Tableau 9.2.2.

Tableau 9.2.2

Basic Variable	Z	x_V	x_M	s_1	s_2		Value
(a″) x_M	0	$\frac{1}{2}$	1	$\frac{1}{12}$	0	=	10
(b″) s_2	0	6	0	$-\frac{1}{3}$	1	=	24
(O″) Z	1	-80	0	20	0	=	2400

pivot number   pivot column   pivot row

Using the pivot column, the x_V column, and the value column of Tableau 9.2.2 we obtain:

Basic Variable	x_V	Value	Value / Coefficient
(a″) x_M	$\frac{1}{2}$	10	$10/\frac{1}{2} = 20$
(b″) s_2	6	24	$\frac{24}{6} = 4$
(O″) Z	-80	2400	minimum = 4

Since the minimum of 20 and 4 occurs in row (b''), s_2 becomes the leaving basic variable, to be replaced by x_V, and (b'') becomes the pivot row.

Step 3 (cont)—Find the Values of the Remaining Basic Variables. In step 3 we need to:

1. Convert the pivot number in the pivot column to a $+1$ and replace the leaving basic variable by the entering basic variable in the pivot column.
2. Convert the remaining coefficients in the pivot column to 0.

To accomplish part 1, we replace row (b″) in Tableau 9.2.2 by (b‴), where (b‴) = $(\frac{1}{6})$(b″). The new row (b‴) is shown below in Tableau 9.2.2′.

Tableau 9.2.2′

Basic Variable		Z	x_V	x_M	s_1	s_2		Value
(a″)	x_M	0	$\frac{1}{2}$	1	$\frac{1}{12}$	0	=	10
(b‴)	x_V	0	1	0	$-\frac{1}{18}$	$\frac{1}{6}$	=	4
(O″)	Z	1	−80	0	20	0	=	2400

pivot column   pivot row

To accomplish part 2, we replace row (a″) by row (a‴), where (a‴) = (a″) + $(-\frac{1}{2})$(b‴); and replace row (O″) by row (O‴), where (O‴) = (O″) + (80)(b‴). The result of performing these row multiplications and row additions in Tableau 9.2.2′ is shown in Tableau 9.2.3.

Tableau 9.2.3

Basic Variable		Z	x_V	x_M	s_1	s_2		Value
(a‴)	x_M	0	0	1	$\frac{1}{9}$	$-\frac{1}{12}$	=	8
(b‴)	x_V	0	1	0	$-\frac{1}{18}$	$\frac{1}{6}$	=	4
(O‴)	Z	1	0	0	$\frac{140}{9}$	$\frac{40}{3}$	=	2720

The new basic feasible solution is

$$\text{basic variables} \begin{Bmatrix} x_M = 8 \\ x_V = 4 \end{Bmatrix} \quad \text{and} \quad \text{nonbasic variables} \begin{Bmatrix} s_1 = 0 \\ s_2 = 0 \end{Bmatrix}$$

and the profit Z = \$2720.

Step 2—Find a Better Basic Feasible Solution. The solution given in Tableau 9.2.3 is optimal since the coefficients of the nonbasic variables s_1 and s_2 are both positive. Thus, we terminate at step 4.

Step 4—Current Basic Feasible Solution Is Optimal.

9.3. THE SIMPLEX METHOD
AND ARTIFICIAL VARIABLES

In the preceding example we were able to let the slack variables be the initial basic variables. However, this may not be possible, as shown by the following example.

9.3.1. Example—Surplus Variables

$$\text{maximize } Z = 3x_1 - 2x_2 \qquad (O)$$

$$\text{subject to} \qquad 2x_1 + 3x_2 \leqslant 6 \qquad (a)$$

$$x_1 - x_2 \geqslant 2 \qquad (b)$$

$$x_1 \geqslant 0, \qquad x_2 \geqslant 0.$$

Inequality (a) can be replaced by equation (a′):

$$2x_1 + 3x_2 + s_1 = 6, \qquad (a')$$

where s_1 is a slack variable ($s_1 \geqslant 0$).
Next consider constraint (b):

$$x_1 - x_2 \geqslant 2.$$

In this constraint feasible values of x_1 and x_2 must be such that $x_1 - x_2$ is equal to or *greater than* 2. Thus, $x_1 = 8$ and $x_2 = 2$ is feasible since $x_1 - x_2 = 8 - 2 = 6$. Also, $x_1 = 10$ and $x_2 = 2$ is feasible since $x_1 - x_2 = 10 - 2 = 8$, which is 6 units greater than 2. Thus, to convert $x_1 - x_2 \geqslant 2$ to an *equivalent equation*, we must *subtract* a variable from its left side. That is,

$$x_1 - x_2 \geqslant 2 \qquad (b)$$

is equivalent to

$$x_1 - x_2 - s_2 = 2, \qquad (b')$$

where $s_2 \geqslant 0$.
The variable s_2 is called a *surplus variable* since it denotes the amount by which $x_1 - x_2$ *exceeds* 2. Thus, s_2 also must be equal to or greater than zero, $s_2 \geqslant 0$.

The original LP model is equivalent to

LP MODEL

maximize $Z = 3x_1 - 2x_2 + 0s_1 + 0s_2$ (O')

subject to $2x_1 + 3x_2 + s_1 \quad\quad = 6$ (a')

               $x_1 - x_2 \quad\quad - s_2 = 2$ (b')

           $x_1 \geqslant 0, \quad x_2 \geqslant 0, \quad s_1 \geqslant 0, \quad s_2 \geqslant 0.$

PROBLEM. Determine an initial basic feasible solution.

Solution. We need two basic variables since the LP model has two equations. We can let s_1 be the basic variable for (a') with a value of 6:

$$s_1 = 6 \text{ in (a')}.$$

In (b') the choice is not obvious. We cannot let s_2 be the basic variable in (b') since s_2 would have to equal -2, but $s_2 = -2$ is unfeasible. However, we may use what is called an *artificial variable*, A, in (b') as a basic variable as follows. This is accomplished by replacing

$$\text{(b'):} \quad x_1 - x_2 - s_2 = 2$$

with

$$\text{(b''):} \quad x_1 - x_2 - s_2 + A = 2, \quad \text{where } A \geqslant 0.$$

The new variable is artificial in the sense that the only value the new variable can have, in order for a feasible solution to have a physical interpretation, is zero. That is,

$$\text{(b'):} \quad x_1 - x_2 - s_2 = 2 \quad\quad \text{(original constraint)}$$

is equivalent to

$$\text{(b''):} \quad x_1 - x_2 - s_2 + A = 2 \quad \text{(artificial equivalent constraint)}$$

only if $A = 0$.

Let M be the unit profit associated with the artificial variable A. Then we have

$$\text{Maximize} \quad Z = 3x_1 - 2x_2 + 0s_1 + 0s_2 + MA \quad\quad\quad \text{(O'')}$$

$$\text{subject to} \quad 2x_1 + 3x_2 + s_1 \quad\quad\quad = 6 \quad\quad \text{(a')}$$

$$x_1 - x_2 \quad\quad - s_2 + A = 2 \quad\quad \text{(b'')}$$

$$x_1 \geqslant 0, \quad x_2 \geqslant 0, \quad s_1 \geqslant 0, \quad s_2 \geqslant 0, \quad A \geqslant 0.$$

$$\text{basic} \atop \text{variables} \left\{ {s_1 = 6 \atop A = 2} \right\} \quad \text{and} \quad {\text{nonbasic} \atop \text{variables}} \left\{ {x_1 = 0 \atop {x_2 = 0 \atop s_2 = 0}} \right\}.$$

QUESTION. How can we eliminate an artificial variable from the basis by use of the simplex method?

Answer. To eliminate an artificial variable from the basis, we make it costly to have a value greater than zero. For example, let the artificial variable in (O'') of the LP model have a unit profit

$$M = \$ - 1000.$$

Then total profit for the preceding basic solution is

$$
\begin{aligned}
Z &= 3x_1 - 2x_1 + 0s_1 + 0s_2 + MA \\
&= 3(0) - 2(0) + 0(6) + 0(0) + (-1000)(2) \\
&= \$ - 2000,
\end{aligned}
$$

which is obviously a "very low" profit. Recall that the simplex method finds a profit-maximizing solution. Thus, the simplex method should be able to find a feasible solution to the LP model with a profit greater than $\$ - 2000$ with the variable $A = 0$.

Let's apply the simplex method to the LP model with $M = \$ - 1000$. In detached-coefficient form, we have Tableau 9.3.1.

Tableau 9.3.1

	Basic Variable	Z	x_1	x_2	s_1	s_2	A		Value
(a′)	s_1	0	2	3	1	0	0	=	6
(b″)	A	0	1	−1	0	−1	1	=	2
(O'')	Z	1	−3	2	0	0	1000	=	0

Note in Tableau 9.3.1 that the artificial variable appears in the profit function given in row (O''). To eliminate A from row (O'') we perform the following row operation: replace (O'') by (O'''), where $(O''') = (O'') + (-1000)(b'')$. This yields Tableau 9.3.2.

Tableau 9.3.2

	Basic Variable	Z	x_1	x_2	s_1	s_2	A		Value
(a')	s_1	0	2	3	1	0	0	=	6
(b'')	A	0	1	−1	0	−1	1	=	2
(O''')	Z	1	−1003	1002	0	1000	0	=	−2000

Applying the simplex method to Tableau 9.3.2 leads, after two iterations, to Tableau 9.3.3.

Tableau 9.3.3

	Basic Variable	Z	x_1	x_2	s_1	s_2	A		Value
(a''')	s_2	0	0	$\frac{5}{2}$	$\frac{1}{2}$	1	−1	=	1
(b'''')	x_1	0	1	$\frac{3}{2}$	$\frac{1}{2}$	0	0	=	3
(O''''')	Z	1	0	$\frac{13}{2}$	$\frac{3}{2}$	0	1000	=	9

The basic feasible solution given in Tableau 9.3.3 is

$$\begin{matrix} basic \\ variables \end{matrix} \left\{ \begin{matrix} s_2 = 1 \\ x_1 = 3 \end{matrix} \right\} \quad \text{and} \quad \begin{matrix} nonbasic \\ variables \end{matrix} \left\{ \begin{matrix} s_1 = 0 \\ x_2 = 0 \end{matrix} \right\}$$

and the profit $Z = \$9$.

Steps 2 and 4. Since the coefficients in the profit function given in row (O''''') for the nonbasic variables are all positive, the basic feasible solution in Tableau 9.3.3 is optimal.

9.4. COMPLICATIONS IN LINEAR PROGRAMMING PROBLEMS AND THEIR RESOLUTION

≥ CONSTRAINTS. The direction of an inequality is always reversed when both sides are multiplied by −1. Therefore, if a constraint is in the wrong direction, "≥," it can be converted into an equivalent constraint in the desired direction, "≤," by changing the signs of each term on both sides. For example, $x_1 \geq -4$ is equivalent to $-x_1 \leq 4$, and $2x_1 - 2x_2 \geq 6$ is equivalent to $-2x_1 + 2x_2 \leq -6$. However, it often happens that this procedure yields a nonpositive right-hand value as in the second case: $-2x_1 + 2x_2 \leqslant -6$. To apply the simplex method to a problem with such a constraint is easily handled through the use of an artificial variable.

First let s_1 be the slack variable in $-2x_1 + 2x_2 \leqslant -6$. This yields

$$-2x_1 + 2x_2 + s_1 = -6.$$

Since this is an equation, we can multiply both sides by $a(-1)$, yielding

$$2x_1 - 2x_2 - s_1 = 6.$$

We can now think of s_1 as being a surplus variable. To specify a basic variable for this equality constraint, we can add an artificial variable A, obtaining

$$2x_1 - 2x_2 - s_1 + A = 6 \quad \text{(with } A \geqslant 0\text{)},$$

as was done in Example 9.3.1.

COST MINIMIZATION. In many business problems it is common to want to minimize instead of maximize the objective function. A minimization problem can be handled very easily by the simplex method, as illustrated by the following example.

9.4.1. Example—A Cost-Minimization Linear Programming Problem

---

LP MODEL

Choose x_1 and x_2 to

minimize $c = 1x_1 + 2x_2$ (O)

subject to $x_1 \qquad\qquad \geqslant 2$ (a)

$x_1 - x_2 \qquad \leqslant 3$ (b)

$x_1 \geqslant 0, \quad x_2 \geqslant 0.$

To convert the LP model to an equivalent maximization:

Multiply each coefficient of the decision variables in the objective function by -1.

Thus, we replace

$$\text{cost} = c = 1x_1 + 2x_2 \qquad\qquad (O)$$

by
$$\text{profit} = Z = -1x_1 - 2x_2. \qquad\qquad (O')$$

Note that cost $= c = -(1)Z = -(1)$profit.

Note in (O) and (O') that as x_1 decreases to zero, c decreases and Z increases; similarly for x_2 in (O) and (O'). Thus, the feasible optimal solution that minimizes c given in (O) also maximizes $Z(= -c)$ given in (O'). The LP model can now be stated as

---

LP MODEL

Choose $x_1 + x_2$ to

maximize $\quad Z = -1\,x_1 - 2x_2$ $\qquad\qquad\qquad (O')$

subject to $\qquad\qquad x_1 \qquad\qquad\qquad \geqslant 2 \qquad\qquad$ (a)

$\qquad\qquad\qquad\quad x_1 - x_2 \qquad\qquad \leqslant 3 \qquad\qquad$ (b)

$\qquad\qquad\qquad\quad x_1 \geqslant 0, \qquad x_2 \geqslant 0,$

---

where $Z = -\text{cost} = -c$.

Applying the simplex method to this LP problem yields Tableau 9.3.2.

	Basic Variable	Z	x_1	x_2	s_1	s_2	A		Value
(a′)	x_1	0	1	0	-1	0	1	$=$	2
(b‴)	s_2	0	0	-1	1	1	-1	$=$	1
(O'''')	Z	1	0	2	1	0	999	$=$	-2

The basic feasible solution given in Tableau 9.3.2 is

$$\text{basic variables} \begin{Bmatrix} x_1 = 2 \\ s_2 = 1 \end{Bmatrix} \quad \text{and} \quad \text{nonbasic variables} \begin{Bmatrix} x_2 = 0 \\ s_1 = 0 \end{Bmatrix}$$

and the profit $Z = -2$.

Steps 2 and 4. The solution in Tableau 9.3.2 is optimal. The maximum total profit = \$ − 2 or, in the original equivalent model, the minimum total cost $c = -(-2) = \$2$.

No Feasible Solutions. Consider the following linear programming problem.

9.4.2. Example—No Feasible Solution

Choose x_1 to

$$\text{maximize } Z = 10x_1 \tag{O}$$

$$\text{subject to} \qquad x_1 \geqslant 6 \tag{a}$$

$$x_1 \leqslant 3. \tag{b}$$

Note that (a) and (b) require that x_1 be *both* greater than or equal to 6 and equal to or less than 3, which is impossible.

That is, there is no feasible solution to this problem, and hence there can be no optimal solution to the problem.

9.4.3. Example—No Feasible Solution

$$\text{maximize } Z = 2x_1 + 3x_2 \tag{O}$$

$$\text{subject to} \qquad x_1 + x_2 \geqslant 10 \tag{a}$$

$$x_1 + x_2 \leqslant 5 \tag{b}$$

$$x_1 \geqslant 0, \qquad x_2 \geqslant 0.$$

Any values for x_1 and x_2 that satisfy (a) cannot satisfy (b), and any values for x_1 and x_2 that satisfy (b) cannot satisfy (a). That is, the sum of two numbers cannot both be equal to or greater than 10 and at the same time be equal to or less than 5.

Thus, the system of inequalities is called *inconsistent*. The graph of (a) and (b) is given in Figure 9.3.

Multiple Optimal Solutions. The simplex method stops (step 4) as soon as it finds one optimal solution. However, it is possible for a linear programming problem to have multiple optimal solutions.

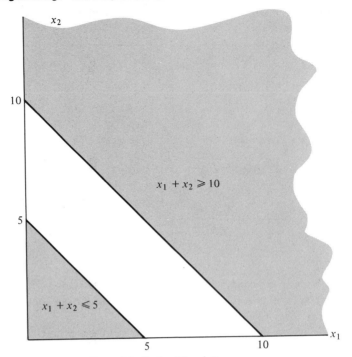

Figure 9.3. No feasible solution.

9.4.4. Example—Multiple Optimal Solutions

Consider the following linear programming problem. Choose x_1 and x_2 to

$$\text{maximize } Z = x_1 + x_2$$

$$\text{subject to} \qquad x_1 + x_2 \leqslant 10$$

$$x_1 \geqslant 0, \qquad x_2 \geqslant 0.$$

By inspection it is easily seen that

$$x_1 = 10, \qquad x_2 = 0, \quad \text{and} \quad Z = \$10$$

is an optimal solution. But so is $x_1 = 0$, $x_2 = 10$, $Z = \$10$. In fact, we can let $x_1 =$ any number between 0 and 10, say, $x_1 = n$ and let $x_2 = 10 - n$. Then $x_1 = n$, $x_2 = 10 - n$, is an optimal solution yielding a maximum profit

$$
\begin{aligned}
Z &= x_1 + x_2 \\
  &= n + (10 - n) \\
  &= \$10.
\end{aligned}
$$

Since we have an infinite number of choices for n, between 0 and 10, there is an infinite number of feasible solutions to this problem, all yielding a maximum profit of $10.

If a linear programming problem has two distinct optimal solutions, it has an infinite number of optimal solutions.

QUESTION. The simplex always finds one optimal solution. Does it also indicate the existence of other optimal solutions?

Answer. Yes.

Consider the linear programming problem given in the Tableau 9.4.1.

Tableau 9.4.1

Basic Variables	z	x_1	x_2	x_3	x_4		Value
x_1	0	1	0	3	6	=	6
x_2	0	0	1	3	2	=	9
Z	1	0	0	4	0	=	25

pivot column

pivot row

The basic feasible solution

$$\text{basic variables} \begin{cases} x_1 = 6 \\ x_2 = 9 \end{cases} \quad \text{and} \quad \text{nonbasic variables} \begin{cases} x_3 = 0 \\ x_4 = 0 \end{cases}$$

with the profit $Z = \$25$, is optimal since the coefficients of the nonbasic variables x_3 and x_4 in the profit function are $+4$ and 0, respectively. Note that if we increase x_4 and fix $x_3 = 0$, the profit Z will equal

$$Z = 25 - 4(0) - 0x_4$$
$$= 25 - 0 - 0 = 25.$$

Hence, the profit remains at $25.

Let x_4 be the entering basic variable in Tableau 9.4.1. The new basic feasible solution is given in the Tableau 9.4.2.

Tableau 9.4.2

Basic Variable	Z	x_1	x_2	x_3	x_4		Value
x_4	0	$\frac{1}{6}$	0	$\frac{1}{2}$	1	=	1
x_2	0	$-\frac{1}{3}$	1	2	0	=	7
Z	1	0	0	4	0	=	25

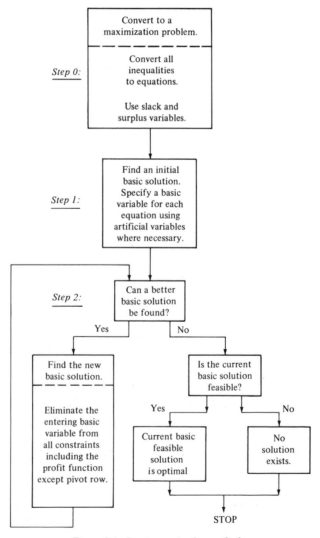

Figure 9.4. Summary: simplex method.

The basic feasible solution in Tableau 9.4.2 is also optimal with profit $= Z =$ $25.

Summary of Tableaus 9.4.1 and 9.4.2

Tableau 9.4.1	Tableau 9.4.2
$x_1 = 6$	$x_1 = 0$
$x_2 = 9$	$x_2 = 7$
$x_3 = 0$	$x_3 = 0$
$x_4 = 0$	$x_4 = 1$
$Z = \$25$	$Z = \$25$

The two solutions are distinct but both yield the same maximum profit of $Z = \$25$.

In general, we have the following rule for determining if multiple optimal solutions exist in a linear programming problem.

> If a coefficient of a nonbasic variable in the profit function is zero in an optimal simplex tableau and if that variable can have a positive value, there exist multiple optimal solutions.

Figure 9.4 provides a summary of the simplex method.

REFERENCES DAELLENBACH, H. G., and E. J. BELL. *User's Guide to Linear Programming.* Englewood Cliffs, N.J.: Prentice-Hall, Inc., 1970.

DANTZIG, G. B. *Linear Programming and Extensions.* Princeton, N.J.: Princeton University Press, 1963.

DRIEBEEK, N. J. *Applied Linear Programming.* Reading, Mass.: Addison-Wesley Publishing Co., Inc., 1969.

ECK, R. D. *Operations Research for Business.* Belmont, Calif.: Wadsworth Publishing Co., Inc., 1976.

HARTLEY, R. V. *Operations Research: A Managerial Emphasis.* Pacific Palisades, Calif.: Goodyear Publishing Co., Inc., 1976.

HILLIER, F. S., and G. J. LIEBERMAN. *Introduction to Operations Research,* 2nd ed. San Francisco: Holden-Day, Inc., 1974.

KIM, C. *Introduction to Linear Programming.* New York: Holt, Rinehart and Winston, Inc., 1972.

KWAK, N. K. *Mathematical Programming with Business Applications.* New York: McGraw-Hill Book Company, 1973.

SHAMBLIN, J. E., and G. T. STEVENS, JR. *Operations Research—A Fundamental Approach.* New York: McGraw-Hill Book Company, 1974.

SIMMONS, D. M. *Linear Programming for Operations Research.* San Francisco: Holden-Day, Inc., 1972.

STRUM, J. E. *Introduction to Linear Programming.* San Francisco: Holden-Day, Inc., 1972.

TAHA, H. A. *Operations Research: An Introduction.* New York: Macmillan Publishing Co., Inc., 1971.

WAGNER, H. M. *Principles of Operations Research with Applications to Managerial Decisions.* Prentice-Hall, Inc., Englewood Cliffs, N.J., 1975.

KEY CONCEPTS

Slack variables	Artificial variables
Basic feasible solution;	Multiple optimal solutions
corner-point solution	No feasible solution
Basic variables	Detached coefficient form of the
Nonbasic variables	simplex method
Entering basic variable	Pivot column
Leaving basic variable	Pivot row
Surplus variables	Pivot number

REVIEW PROBLEMS

9.1. Convert the following linear programming problem to an equivalent problem with all inequalities in the " $\leqslant$ " direction.

$$\text{maximize } Z = x_1 - 2x_2 \qquad (O)$$

$$\text{subject to} \quad -x_1 + x_2 \geqslant -6 \qquad (a)$$

$$x_1 \qquad \leqslant \quad 4 \qquad (b)$$

$$x_1 \geqslant 0, \qquad x_2 \geqslant 0.$$

9.2. Set up the following linear programming problem in detached-coefficient-form in a simplex tableau.

$$\text{maximize } Z = -x_1 + 2x_2 + 0s_1 + 0s_2 \qquad (O)$$

$$\text{subject to} \quad x_1 - x_2 + s_1 \qquad = 6 \qquad (a)$$

$$x_1 + \qquad s_2 = 4 \qquad (b)$$

$$x_1 \geqslant 0, \qquad x_2 \geqslant 0, \qquad s_1 \geqslant 0, \qquad s_2 \geqslant 0.$$

9.3. Consider the linear programming problem given in the following simplex tableau.

Basic Variable	Z	x_1	x_2	x_3	x_4		Value
(a) x_1	0	1	−1	0	1	=	5
(b) x_3	0	0	①	1	−2	=	10
(O) Z	1	0	−3	0	4	=	20

pivot column   pivot row

The basic feasible solution given in the tableau is not optimal, since the coefficient of x_2 in the profit function Z is -3. Why is row (b) the pivot row? That is, which variable, x_1 or x_3, is the leaving basic variable if x_2 is the entering basic variable?

9.4. The linear programming problem given in the following tableau has multiple optimal solutions. Why?

Basic Variable	Z	x_1	x_2	x_3	x_4		Value
(a) x_2	0	2	1	0	1	=	50
(b) x_3	0	1	0	1	−2	=	100
(O) Z	1	0	0	0	7	=	150

ANSWERS TO REVIEW PROBLEMS

9.1. The inequality (a): $-x_1 + x_2 \geqslant -6$ is equivalent to

$$(-1)(-x_1 + x_2) \leqslant (-1)(-6)$$

or

$$x_1 - x_2 \leqslant 6. \qquad (\text{a}')$$

Replacing (a) with (a') yields the following equivalent linear programming problem.

LP MODEL

maximize $Z = x_1 - 2x_2$ $\qquad (O)$

subject to $\quad x_1 - x_2 \qquad \leqslant 6 \quad (\text{a}')$

$\qquad\qquad\quad x_1 \qquad\qquad \leqslant 4 \quad (\text{b})$

$\qquad x_1 \geqslant 0, \qquad x_2 \geqslant 0.$

9.2. Let $s_1 = 6$ and $s_2 = 4$ be the values of the two basic variables. Note that the profit function given in (O),

$$Z = -x_1 + 2x_2 + 0s_1 + 0s_2,$$

is equivalent to

$$Z + x_1 - 2x_2 + 0s_1 + 0s_2 = 0. \qquad (O)$$

The problem in detached-coefficient form is given in the following simplex tableau.

	Basic Variable	Z	x_1	x_2	s_1	s_2		Value
(a)	s_1	0	1	-1	1	0	$=$	6
(b)	s_2	0	1	0	0	1	$=$	4
(O)	Z	1	1	-2	0	0	$=$	0

pivot column

Note that the solution given in the tableau is not optimal since if x_2 has a value greater than zero, which it can, profit $= Z$ will increase.

9.3. Row (b) is the pivot row since there is only one positive value-coefficient ratio. That is,

	Basic Variable	x_2	Value	Value-Coefficient Ratio
(a)	x_1	-1	5	∞
(b)	x_3	1	10	$\leftarrow 10 = $ minimum ratio
(O)	Z	-3	20	

pivot column

Thus, the constraint in row (b) restricts x_2 to be at most 10. Row (b) becomes the pivot row. x_3 is the leaving basic variable since it is the basic variable for the pivot row.

9.4. First, the basic feasible solution in the tableau with

$$\text{basic variables} \begin{cases} x_2 = 50 \\ x_3 = 100 \\ Z = \$150 \end{cases} \quad \text{and} \quad \text{nonbasic variables} \begin{cases} x_1 = 0 \\ x_4 = 0 \end{cases}$$

is optimal since all the coefficients in the profit function Z are zero or positive. However, note that x_1 is a nonbasic variable, $x_1 = 0$, and has a coefficient of 0 in the profit function Z. Thus, we can let x_1 be the entering basic variable and profit $= Z = \$150$ will not increase.

Letting x_1 be the entering basic variable, then x_2 becomes the leaving basic variable. The new optimal basic feasible solution is given in the following tableau.

	Basic Variable	Z	x_1	x_2	x_3	x_4		Value
(a)	x_1	0	1	$\frac{1}{2}$	0	$\frac{1}{2}$	=	25
(b')	x_3	0	0	$-\frac{1}{2}$	1	$-\frac{5}{2}$	=	75
(O)	Z	1	0	0	0	7	=	150

Thus, we have two distinct solutions, both yielding the maximum profit of $150.

EXERCISES

ADDING SLACK AND SURPLUS VARIABLES **9.1.** Convert the following system of constraints to an equivalent system of equations by using slack and surplus variables.

$$x_1 + 2x_2 \leqslant 30$$
$$2x_1 + 1x_2 \geqslant 40$$
$$3x_1 + 2x_2 = 50$$
$$x_1 \geqslant 0, \qquad x_2 \geqslant 0.$$

ADDING SLACK AND SURPLUS VARIABLES **9.2.** Convert the following systems of constraints to an equivalent system of equations.

$$x_1 + 2x_2 \leqslant 30$$
$$-2x_1 + 1x_2 \geqslant 50.$$

BASIC FEASIBLE SOLUTIONS **9.3.** Given the following system of equations,

$$2x_1 + 3x_2 + 1x_3 + 2x_5 = 40$$
$$x_1 + 2x_2 + x_4 + 2x_5 = 20$$

with $\quad x_1 \geqslant 0, \qquad x_2 \geqslant 0, \qquad x_3 \geqslant 0, \qquad x_4 \geqslant 0, \qquad x_5 \geqslant 0.$

(a) Identify an obvious basic feasible solution.
(b) Express the system in detached-coefficient form.

9.4. Consider the system

$Z = 4x_1 - 8x_2 + 0s_1 + 0s_2$

$$Z - 4x_1 - 8x_2 + 0s_1 + 0s_2 = 0$$

$$2x_1 + 2x_2 + s_1 = 10$$

$$x_1 + 2x_2 + s_2 = 20$$

with Z = profit and

$$x_1 \geqslant 0, \qquad x_2 \geqslant 0, \qquad s_1 \geqslant 0, \qquad s_2 \geqslant 0.$$

(a) Express the system in detached-coefficient form in a simplex tableau. What is an obvious basic feasible solution?

(b) Find a better (higher-profit) basic feasible solution.

CONVERTING A
LINEAR
PROGRAMMING
PROBLEM
TO STANDARD FORM
FOR SOLUTION

9.5. Convert the following linear programming problem to an equivalent problem where the objective is to maximize profit, all constraints are equations, and all decision variables are restricted to be nonnegative.

$$\text{minimize } Z = 2x_1 - 3x_2 + 4x_3$$

$$\text{subject to} \quad x_1 + 2x_2 \qquad \geqslant 6$$

$$2x_1 + \qquad x_3 \leqslant 12$$

$$x_1 \geqslant 0, \qquad x_2 \geqslant 0, \qquad x_3 \geqslant 0.$$

CONVERTING A
LINEAR
PROGRAMMING
PROBLEM
TO STANDARD FORM
FOR SOLUTION

9.6. Convert the following linear programming problem to an equivalent problem where the objective is to maximize profit, all constraints are equations, and all decision variables are restricted to be nonnegative.

$$\text{minimize } Z = x_1 - 2x_2 + 3x_3 - 4x_4$$

$$\text{subject to} \quad x_1 + x_2 \qquad \qquad \geqslant 1$$

$$x_2 + x_3 \qquad \leqslant 2$$

$$x_3 + x_4 \geqslant 3$$

$$x_1 + x_2 + x_3 + x_4 = 6$$

$$x_1 \geqslant 0, \qquad x_2 \geqslant 0, \qquad x_3 \geqslant 0, \qquad x_4 \geqslant 0.$$

9.7. Consider the linear programming problem

$$\text{maximize } Z = x_1 + 2x_2$$

$$\text{subject to} \quad x_1 + x_2 \leqslant 100$$

$$x_1 + x_2 \geqslant 50$$

$$x_1 \geqslant 0, \qquad x_2 \geqslant 0.$$

(a) Express the constraints as an equivalent system of equations.
(b) Express the equivalent system of equations and the objective function in a simplex tableau.
(c) List every basic feasible solution for the system of constraint equations.
(d) Using the objective function and the basic solutions determined in part (c), identify the optimal basic feasible solution.
(e) Confirm that your answer in part (d) is correct by solving the problem using the graphical method.

THE SIMPLEX METHOD **9.8.** Use the simplex method, find an optimal solution to the following linear programming problem.

$$\text{maximize } Z = 2x_1 + x_2$$

$$\text{subject to} \quad 2x_1 + x_2 \leqslant 10$$

$$x_2 \leqslant 5$$

$$x_1 \geqslant 0, \quad x_2 \geqslant 0.$$

THE SIMPLEX METHOD **9.9.** Using the simplex method, find an optimal solution for the following linear programming problem:

$$\text{minimize } Z = -2x_1 + x_2$$

$$\text{subject to} \quad 2x_1 + x_2 \leqslant 10$$

$$-x_2 \geqslant -5.$$

$$x_1 \geqslant 0, \quad x_2 \geqslant 0.$$

THE SIMPLEX METHOD **9.10.** Using the simplex method, find an optimal solution for the following linear programming problem.

$$\text{maximize } Z = 1x_1 + 2x_2 + 3x_3$$

$$\text{subject to} \quad x_1 + x_2 + x_3 \leqslant 30$$

$$x_1 - 2x_2 + 2x_3 \leqslant 20$$

$$x_1 \geqslant 0, \quad x_2 \geqslant 0, \quad x_3 \geqslant 0.$$

THE SIMPLEX METHOD **9.11.** Using the simplex method, find an optimal solution to the following linear programming problem.

$$\text{maximize } Z = x_1 + x_2 + 2x_3$$

$$\text{subject to} \quad x_1 + 2x_2 + x_3 = 10$$

$$x_1 - 2x_2 + x_3 \geqslant 12$$

$$x_1 \geqslant 0, \quad x_2 \geqslant 0, \quad x_3 \geqslant 0.$$

9.12. Use the simplex method to solve the following problem.

$$\text{maximize } Z = x_1 + 3x_2$$

$$\text{subject to} \quad x_1 + x_2 \geqslant 4$$

$$x_1 + 4x_2 \leqslant 12$$

$$x_2 \leqslant 6$$

$$x_1 \geqslant 0, \quad x_2 \geqslant 0.$$

Plot the set of feasible solutions using x_1 and x_2 as coordinates. Follow the steps of the simplex method graphically by interpreting the change from one basic feasible solution to the next in the set of feasible solutions.

9.13. Use the simplex method to solve the following linear programming problem.

$$\text{maximize } Z = x_1 + x_2$$

$$\text{subject to} \quad x_1 + x_2 \leqslant 20$$

$$x_1 \geqslant 0, \quad x_2 \geqslant 0.$$

Plot the set of feasible solutions using x_1 and x_2 as coordinates. Follow the steps of the simplex method by interpreting the change from one basic feasible solution to the next in the set of feasible solutions. Explain, using both the graph and the simplex tableau, why this problem has multiple optimal solutions.

9.14. Explain why the linear programming problem given in the following tableau has multiple optimal solutions. List two distinct optimal solutions.

Basic Variable	Z	x_1	x_2	x_3	x_4		Value
x_1	0	1	-1	1	0	$=$	100
x_4	0	0	1	-1	1	$=$	200
Z	1	0	5	0	0	$=$	5000

9.15. Tennessee Furniture Inc. (TFI) recently noticed that in their Nashville plant there were excess units of raw materials that could be used to produce Arkansas and Mississippi chairs. These chairs could be sold to furniture stores for $250 and $200, respectively.

The expected number of units of each raw material on hand each month and the number of units of each material required to produce a chair of each type are given in the following production table.

Each Arkansas chair requires 5 man-hours of labor and each Mississippi chair requires 4 man-hours of labor. Average labor costs at the Nashville plant

Raw Material	UNITS OF MATERIAL NEEDED TO PRODUCE A CHAIR		Units of Material on Hand (each month)
	Arkansas	Mississippi	
Wood	2	1	40
Steel bolts	5	6	30
Vinyl	3	4	20

are estimated to $5 per hour. The original unit cost of each material is given in the following cost table.

Raw Material	Unit Cost
Wood	$50
Steel bolts	2
Vinyl	25

Should TFI use the excess raw materials to produce Arkansas and Mississippi chairs? If so, how many of each? The only other alternative available to TFI is to sell for scrap the excess materials receiving 40% of their original unit cost.

MODELING AND THE SIMPLEX METHOD **9.16.** Texas Leather Inc. (TLI) receives 2000 square yards of untanned leather each month. TLI produces fancy saddles and custom seat covers. Each saddle requires 10 square yards of leather and each seat cover requires 15 square yards of leather.

Before the leather can be used for either product, it must be thoroughly tanned. The leather to be used in saddles requires 1 hour of tanning for each square yard processed; the leather to be used in seat covers requires 2 hours of tanning for each square yard processed. Two hundred hours of tanning time is available each month at TLI's plant in Houston.

The saddles sell for $1000. The seat covers sell for $275.
(a) Construct a linear programming model for TLI.
(b) Solve for the optimal mix of saddles and covers using the simplex method.

MODELING AND THE SIMPLEX METHOD **9.17.** Inhouse Electric Corporation's Dallas plant has four machines, the M1, M2, M3, and M4, which are used to build two different electronic calculators, called the Texas and the Oklahoma. The unit hourly machine requirements for each calculator are given in the following production table:

Calculator	MACHINE TIME (HOURS)			
	M1	M2	M3	M4
The Texas	0.5	0.5	1.0	1.0
The Oklahoma	1.0	0.5	1.0	1.5

The number of machine-hours available on each machine during any month at the Dallas plant is given in the following plant-capacity table:

Machine	Availability per Month (hours)
M1	150
M2	200
M3	250
M4	300

The unit contribution to profits is given in the following profitability table.

Calculator	Unit Profit
The Texas	$20
The Oklahoma	25

Determine an optimal monthly production plan for Inhouse Electric using the simplex method.

MODELING AND THE
SIMPLEX METHOD

9.18. Ed Goldman, a salesman for Tuck Tape must decide how to allocate his efforts between the different types of customers in his territory. Ed can call on either jobbers or retail outlets. A call on a jobber usually results in $20 in sales but requires on the average 2 hours of time and 10 miles of driving. A call on a retail outlet usually results in $50 in sales and requires, on the average, 3 hours of time and 20 miles of driving. Ed has a upper limit of 600 miles per week on the car. Ed also prefers not to work more than 36 hours each week.
(a) Construct a linear programming model for Ed Goldman.
(b) Solve for the optimal mix of jobbers and retail outlets using the simplex method.

MODELING AND THE
SIMPLEX METHOD

9.19. Atomic Electric (AE) manufactures two nuclear generators, the S generator (for nuclear submarines) and the P generator (for power plants). Two major manufacturing processes are used in the production of both generators. The S generator requires 500 hours of time in process A and 1000 hours of time in process B. The P generator requires 1000 hours in process A and 400 hours in process B. There are available only 6000 hours of time in process A and 4000 hours in process B each month. Profit contribution for each S generator is $500,000 and for each P generator $400,000. Atomic Electric would like to produce a combination of generators which would maximize profit per month.
(a) Prepare a linear programming model for Atomic Electric.
(b) Solve for the optimal mix of generators using the simplex method.

9.20. The Lilac Vitamin Co. plans to manufacture an inexpensive vitamin capsule using two basic ingredients, X and Y. Each unit of X contains 0.5 milligram (mg) of vitamin A, 1.0 mg of vitamin B_1, 0.2 mg of vitamin B_2 and 0.5 mg of vitamin D. Each unit of Y contains 0.5 mg of vitamin A, 0.3 mg of vitamin B_1, 0.6 mg of vitamin B_2, and 0.20 mg of vitamin D. The cost of 1 unit of X is \$0.30 and each unit of Y costs \$0.50. Each capsule must contain the minimum daily requirement of 2 mg of vitamin A, 3 mg of vitamin B_1, 1.2 mg of vitamin B_2 and 2 mg of vitamin D.

(a) Construct a linear programming model for the Lilac Vitamin Company.

(b) Solve for the minimum cost mix of X and Y using the simplex method.

CASE 9.1   Illustrative Case Study

Mr. Llewelyn is the portfolio manager of National Financial Services (NFS). NFS typically invests in large construction projects in the South Pacific. Next week Llewelyn must make a decision on three such construction projects. He has calculated the net present value, at NFS's current cost of capital, of each of the three projects as shown in the following table.

Project Name	Project Number	Net Present Value
New Zealand Lumber	1	\$120,000
Tahiti Hotels	2	\$130,000
Melbourne Meat Packing	3	\$170,000

The cash inflow and outlay of each project for the next 5 years are given in the following table.

Project Number	1	2	3	4	5[b]
1	− 10,000,000	+ 2,000,000[a]	+ 3,000,000	+ 3,000,000	+ 3,000,000
2	− 10,000,000	+ 4,000,000	+ 2,000,000	− 2,000,000	+ 2,000,000
3	0	0	− 10,000,000	+ 10,000,000	+ 10,000,000

[a]A plus sign indicates a cash inflow and a minus sign indicates a cash outflow.
[b]All cash flows are in after the fifth year of the financial planning horizon.

Llewelyn expects to have the following NFS funds to invest during the next 5 years:

Funds from Other Sources

Year	Amount of Funds
Year 1:	\$20,000,000
Year 2:	5,000,000
Year 3:	4,000,000
Year 4:	4,000,000
Year 5:	4,000,000

Assume that NFS can take any portion or all of each project. Also assume that funds not invested in the projects will be invested in the bank earning interest of 8.5%,

Problem. Using linear programming and the simplex method, determine an optimal investment plan for Llewelyn.

CASE 9.2 Illustrative Case Study

FOR COMPUTER SOLUTION

Maui Foods Inc. (MFI) is engaged in the production and exportation of potato chips. MFI is a relatively new firm and has developed a market for its products in three countries: United States, Australia, and Japan. Two grades of chips are produced called the Polynesian (highest-quality) and the Tahiti (lower-quality). Even then, only the lower-quality chips are marketable in Japan because of a licensing restriction imposed by the Japanese government. MFI exports the potato chips in case-size lots, C.I.F., from two ports: Kahalui, Hawaii (potato chips bound for Australia and Japan) and Honolulu, Hawaii (potato chips bound for the United States). MFI has available to it all the potatoes (produced in Washington) it can process into chips and sell in any given month.

MFI's production data shows that to process a case of Tahiti chips requires on the average about 15 minutes per case. Data also show that the Polynesian chips require on the average about 15 minutes per case.

MFI's labor contract calls for two 9-hour shifts (straight-time pay only) per day on a 5-day-week, 4 weeks-per-month basis. With five processing lines (cooking and packing) at the plant, this provides MFI with a total of 360 production hours per month.

A marketing research study has shown that the U.S. populace prefers the Polynesian potato chips to the Tahitian by a 2 : 1 ratio, whereas the Japanese prefer the Tahitian over the Polynesian by a 3 : 1 ratio. MFI found that total demand, in cases per month, for both chips does not exceed 4000 for the United States, 10,000 for Australia, and 3000 for Japan.

MFI is required by their bank, Honolulu National (a principal stockholder) to retain in reserve a certain percentage of the drafts loaned to the company as insurance against default by its export agent. MFI has available, or the average, $20,000 per month for this purpose. Owing to the distances and risks involved, the bank requires these reserves as a percentage of profit per case exported: United States, 10%; Japan, 20%; and Australia, 25%.

The variable production costs associated with producing a case of potato chips for export is as follows. The resources (potatoes, cooking oil, and salt) cost $4 per case. The packaging costs are about $2 a case. The processing costs (composed of labor) are on the average about $4 per hour.

The transportation costs are based on the shipping distances involved and are $5 a case for cases shipped to the United States, $6 a case to Japan, and $7 a case to Australia. Insurance costs are 5% of port cost (plant plus transportation costs).

The revenue associated with a case of each type of potato chip is as follows:

Brand	Unit Revenue per Case
U.S. Polynesian	$25
U.S. Tahiti	20
Australian Polynesian	20
Australian Tahiti	20
Japanese Polynesian	30
Japanese Tahiti	30

MFI would like to determine how many cases of each type of potato chip to produce and export to its three markets to maximize profit per month.

Assignment

1. Construct an appropriate linear programming model.
2. Solve for the optimal mix of brands using a computer program of the simplex method.

CHAPTER 10
Linear Programming: Dual Models and Optimal Pricing

OBJECTIVES: Upon successful completion of this chapter, you should be able to:

1. Formulate and interpret dual programming models.
2. Explain the importance of using dual solutions in business applications of linear programming

10.1. DUAL PROGRAMMING

We have seen how linear programming can be used to solve a wide variety of business problems involving either profit maximization or cost minimization. The decision variables in such problems were, for example, the number of tables to produce, the amount of dollars to spend on different advertising media, and so forth. In each case the optimal solution told us how company resources (e.g., raw materials, machine capacities, cash) should be allocated to reach a stated goal.

In this chapter we will see that every linear programming problem has associated with it another linear programming problem, called the *dual programming problem*. The optimal solution to the dual programming problem provides the following information with respect to the original programming problem:

> The optimal solution to the dual problem yields market prices or rents of the scarce resources allocated in the original problem.
>
> The optimal solution to the dual problem yields the optimal solution to the original problem and vice versa.

The additional information provided by an optimal solution to the dual programming problem falls under what we shall call *dual programming*.

346

Every linear programming problem has associated with it what is called a *dual programming problem*. We normally call the original linear programming problem the *primal programming problem*. To illustrate dual programming, consider the following example.

10.1.1. Example—National Business Machines

National Business Machines (NBM) produces and sells two types of typewriters: manual and electric. Each manual typewriter is sold at a profit of $40 and each electric typewriter at a profit of $60. Both typewriters must be processed (assembled and packed) through two different operations: O_1 and O_2.

NBM has the following total monthly capacities (nationwide for all plants):

$$2000 \text{ hours of } O_1$$

$$1000 \text{ hours of } O_2.$$

The number of hours of O_1 and O_2 required to produce a finished model is given in the following production table:

Operation	HOURS REQUIRED		Monthly Capacities (hours)
	Manual	Electric	
O_1	3	2	2000
O_2	1	2	1000

To produce one manual typewriter requires 3 hours of O_1 and 1 hour of O_2. To produce one electric typewriter requires 2 hours of O_1 and 2 hours of O_2. Let

x_1 = number of manual typewriters to produce each month

x_2 = number of electric typewriters to produce each month.

The following linear programming model, called the *primal problem* or *primal model*, can be used to find the optimal number of each type of typewriter to produce monthly.

PRIMAL PROBLEM

maximize $Z = 40x_1 + 60x_2$

subject to $\quad 3x_1 + 2x_2 \leqslant 2000$

$\qquad\qquad x_1 + 2x_2 \leqslant 1000$

$\quad x_1 \geqslant 0, \qquad x_2 \geqslant 0.$

If we apply the simplex method to the problem we will find that the optimal solution is to produce 500 manual typewriters per month ($x_1 = 500$) and 250 electric typewriters per month ($x_2 = 250$). The contribution to profits and overhead is $Z = \$35,000$ per month.

Given the setting of the primal problem, we now wish to focus on the dual problem, a *pricing problem*. Our goal is to determine prices at which NBM should value their resources so that they can determine the minimum total value at which they would be willing to lease or sell the resources, as appropriate. NBM would be willing to *rent* assembly and packaging capacity, hours of O_1 and O_2, on their assembly and packaging line.

Let y_1 and y_2 denote the rents per hour to be charged for O_1 and O_2, respectively. Given the availability of the resources (monthly capacities of O_1 and O_2), the total monthly rentals are

$$C = 2000y_1 + 1000y_2. \quad \text{B.E. REFT.}$$

The lowest value of this objective C is desired so that NBM may intelligently view any bids to buy or lease all the resources as a *total package*. Therefore, NBM wishes to minimize the sum of rentals.

Consider next the constraints. The prices (henceforth we shall usually use the term *prices* to include both prices and rents of resources) should all be zero or greater than zero. Obviously, no resource should have a negative price, since any resource sold (we shall use the verb *sell* to mean either sell or rent) at a negative price could more profitably be left idle. Accordingly, the following constraints must be satisfied:

$$y_1 \geqslant 0, \qquad y_2 \geqslant 0.$$

Conditions to be satisfied in the other constraints are that the prices y_1 and y_2 should be *competitive with available alternatives*. NBM has the available alternative of producing electric and manual typewriters using O_1 and O_2. For example, since 3 hours of O_1 plus 1 hour O_2 can be used to produce one manual typewriter, the value in terms of resource prices per manual typewriter is $3y_1 + 1y_2$. This price should be at least as great as what is obtained when a manual typewriter is produced—a contribution to profit of $\$40$. That is,

$$3y_1 + 1y_2 \geqslant 40.$$

Similarly, 2 hours of O_1 together with 2 hours of O_2 can be used to produce one electric typewriter and thereby generate a contribution to profits of $\$60$. Hence, the following inequality should also be satisfied:

$$2y_1 + 2y_2 \geqslant 60.$$

DUAL MODEL SUMMARY OF THE PRICING PROBLEM
(OR THE DUAL PROBLEM)

Choose prices y_1 and y_2 to

minimize $\qquad C = 2000y_1 + 1000y_2$

subject to $\qquad\qquad\qquad 3y_1 + \quad y_2 \geqslant 40$

$\qquad\qquad\qquad\qquad\qquad 2y_1 + \quad 2y_2 \geqslant 60$

$\qquad\qquad y_1 \geqslant 0, \qquad y_2 \geqslant 0.$

We now show the relationship *between the optimal solutions* of the primal model and the optimal solution of the dual model.

10.1.2. Example—Primal and Dual Optimal Solutions

Consider the primal model and the dual model of Example 10.1.1 repeated below. Also, given below are the optimal solutions to both problems.

PRIMAL MODEL

maximize $Z = 40x_1 + 60x_2$

subject to $\qquad 3x_1 + 2x_2 \leqslant 2000$

$\qquad\qquad\qquad x_1 + 2x_2 \leqslant 1000$

$\qquad\qquad x_1 \geqslant 0, \qquad x_2 \geqslant 0.$

Primal Model's Optimal Simplex Tableau

Basic Variable	Z	x_1	x_2	s_1	s_2		Value
x_1	0	1	0	$\frac{1}{2}$	$-\frac{1}{2}$	$=$	500
x_2	0	0	1	$-\frac{1}{4}$	$\frac{3}{4}$	$=$	250
Z	1	0	0	$+5$	$+25$	$=$	35,000

Optimal Solution to
_____
Primal Model: maximum profit: $Z = \$35,000$
                           basic variables: $x_1 = 500, x_2 = 250$
                           nonbasic variables: $s_1 = 0, s_2 = 0.$

Note: s_1 and s_2 are the slack variables for the primal model.

DUAL MODEL

minimize $C = 2000y_1 + 1000y_2$

subject to $\quad 3y_1 + y_2 \geqslant 40$

$\qquad\qquad\qquad 2y_1 + 2y_2 \geqslant 60$

$\qquad\qquad y_1 \geqslant 0, \qquad y_2 \geqslant 0.$

Dual Model's Optimal Simplex Tableau

Basic Variable	C	y_1	y_2	S_1	S_2	A_1	A_2		Value
y_1	0	1	0	$-\frac{1}{2}$	$\frac{1}{4}$	$\frac{1}{2}$	$-\frac{1}{4}$	$=$	5
y_2	0	0	1	$\frac{1}{2}$	$-\frac{3}{4}$	$-\frac{1}{2}$	$\frac{3}{4}$	$=$	25
C	1	0	0	$+500$	$+250$	—	—	$=$	$-35,000$

$$\underbrace{\frac{1350}{3}}\qquad \underbrace{\frac{1900}{4}}$$

Optimal Solution to
_____
Dual Model: minimum cost: $-C = \$35,000$
                         basic variables: $y_1 = 5, y_2 = 25$
                         nonbasic variables: $S_1 = 0, S_2 = 0$
                                              $A_1 = 0, A_2 = 0.$

Note: S_1 and S_2 are the surplus variables and A_1 and A_2 are the artificial variables used to determine an initial basic feasible solution to the dual model.

Several observations can be made when comparing the two optimal simplex tableaus.

Observation 1   From the dual model's optimal tableau we see that the optimal price of O_1 (packaging capacity) is $y_1 = \$5$ per hour and the optimal price of O_2 (assembly capacity) is $y_2 = \$25$ per hour. Also note that the minimum monthly value of the resources O_1 and O_2 is

$$-\max C = -(-\$35,000) = \$35,000,$$

which is exactly the same as the maximum profit attainable by producing manual and electric typewriters (the dual model was solved as an equivalent maximization problem). Why is it true that minimum cost = minimum C in the dual model equals maximum profit = maximum Z in the primal model? The answer to this question is that the relationship between the primal model and its dual model is so strong that they are in some sense two sides of the same problem. In fact, when either problem is solved by the simplex method, the solution to the other problem is obtained as a by-product. To illustrate this last statement, consider a second observation to be made when comparing the two optimal simplex tableaus.

Observation 2 Referring to the profit row in the optimal solution to the primal model note that the cost of s_1 is $5 per hour. Now, s_1 is the amount of unused O_1 and $5 per hour is the marginal value (or sometimes called shadow price) of O_1, corresponding to the dual variable y_1. Similarly, the optimal cost of s_2 is $25 per hour corresponding to the dual variable y_2. This relationship is illustrated graphically in Figure 10.1.

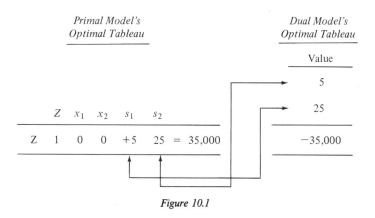

Figure 10.1

In summary, the optimal values of the dual variables, y_1 and y_2, are equal to the coefficients of the slack variables s_1 and s_2, respectively, in the profit function Z given in the primal model's optimal tableau.

In exactly the same manner, the optimal primal solution may be obtained. That is, note that the profit of S_1 in row C of the dual model is $500 per manual typewriter, which corresponds to the primal variable x_1. Similarly, the profit of S_2 in the dual model is $250 per electric typewriter which corresponds to the primal variable x_2. This relationship is shown in Figure 10.2.

In summary, the optimal values of the primal variables x_1 and x_2 are equal to the coefficients of the surplus variables S_1 and S_2, respectively, in the cost function C given in the dual model's optimal tableau.

Several other comments are appropriate concerning the optimal dual prices. First the optimal dual prices indicate whether units of resources (O_1: assembly capacity and O_2: packaging capacity) should be purchased or sold. If these *minimum prices*, $y_1 = $5 per hour of O_1 and $y_2 = $25 per hour of O_2, exist in the

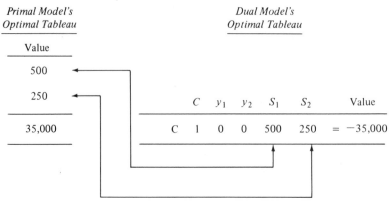

Figure 10.2

market, then NBM would be indifferent between the alternatives of producing typewriters and selling resources. If the market prices were higher than the dual minimum prices, then NBM should prefer to sell resources (or sell O_1 and O_2 time) and if the market prices were lower, then NBM should prefer to buy resources (increase capacities of O_1 and O_2). That is, the dual minimum prices give a measure for evaluating the marginal value of additional capacity of the resources. To illustrate, suppose that NBM can sell O_1 (assembly time) for $7 per hour, say to a nearby competitor, and can increase O_2 (packaging capacity) time for $20 per hour. Then NBM should be willing to sell some O_1 capacity since $2 can be earned on each hour of O_1 time sold ($7 per hour minus y_1 = $5 per hour in marginal value). Similarly, NBM should be willing to increase O_2 capacity, since $5 can be earned on each unit increase of O_2 capacity (y_2 = $25 per hour in increased profits minus $20 per hour as the cost). Of course, selling or increasing capacity will require a change in the optimal production schedule.

The minimum dual prices y_1 and y_2 are valid as given, y_1 = $5 per hour and y_2 = $25 per hour, only if the entire amounts of O_1 and O_2 are sold at these prices. If the resources (O_1 capacity and O_2 capacity) are sold piecemeal, the dual minimum prices are valid only over some range which may be small or large, depending upon the structure of the problem. Specifically, holding every other parameter in the primal model constant, *the marginal value* of a resource (such as hours of O_1 or hours of O_2), would remain constant as the availability of the resource was increased, but usually an upper limit of its range of validity will be reached and then the marginal value would drop. The reason this happens is that the availability of some other resource usually becomes limiting once enough of the first resource is made available. In a similar manner, as the availability of a resource decreases below the range of its range of validity, the marginal value of that resource increases in value. This phenomenon is what economists call "decreasing returns to scale."

The primal model is given again on the next page with its dual model.

PRIMAL MODEL

maximize $Z = 40x_1 + 60x_2$

subject to $\quad 3x_1 + 2x_2 \leqslant 2000$

$\quad\quad\quad\quad x_1 + 2x_2 \leqslant 1000$

$\quad\quad\quad\quad x_1 \geqslant 0, \quad x_2 \geqslant 0.$

DUAL MODEL

minimize $C = 2000y_1 + 100y_2$

subject to $\quad 3y_1 + \quad y_2 \geqslant 40$

$\quad\quad\quad\quad 2y_1 + \quad 2y_2 \geqslant 60$

$\quad\quad\quad\quad y_1 \geqslant 0, \quad y_2 \geqslant 0.$

Note that:

The primal model is a *maximization problem* while the dual model is a *minimization problem*. And the restrictions in the primal model are of the form less than or equal to, "$\leqslant$," while the restrictions in the dual model are of the form greater than or equal to, "$\geqslant$."

It is also obvious that there is a relationship between the coefficients and right-hand side constants between the two models. Specifically, there are three relationships. Refer to the preceding statements of the primal model and the dual model in studying these three relationships.

Relationship 1 The right-hand-side constants in the primal model are the coefficients of the variables in the objective function of the dual model (Fig. 10.3).

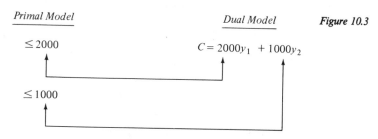

Primal Model   *Dual Model*   **Figure 10.3**

$\leqslant 2000$ $C = 2000y_1 + 1000y_2$

$\leqslant 1000$

Relationship 2   The right-hand-side constants in the dual model are the coefficients of the variables in the objective function of the primal model (Fig. 10.4).

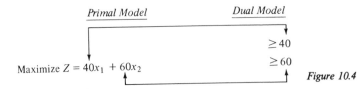

Figure 10.4

Relationship 3   Each column of constraint coefficients in the primal model becomes the coefficients in a row of the dual model (Fig. 10.5).

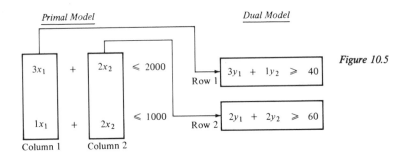

Figure 10.5

That is, coefficients in column 1 become the coefficients in row 1, and coefficients in column 2 become the coefficients in row 2.

10.2. CONSTRUCTING DUAL MODELS

In this section we give several examples of how dual models are constructed from primal models.

10.2.1. Example—Determining the Dual Model

PRIMAL MODEL

maximize $Z = 2x_1 + 3x_2 + 2x_2$

subject to $\quad x_1 + 2x_2 + 3x_3 \leqslant 4$

$\qquad\qquad 2x_1 + x_2 + x_3 \leqslant 6$

$x_1 \geqslant 0, \qquad x_2 \geqslant 0, \qquad x_3 \geqslant 0.$

Note that the primal model has three variables and two constraints.

DUAL MODEL

minimize $C = 4y_1 + 6y_2$

subject to $1y_1 + 2y_2 \geqslant 2$

$2y_1 + 1y_2 \geqslant 3$

$3y_1 + 1y_2 \geqslant 2$

$y_1 \geqslant 0, \qquad y_2 \geqslant 0.$

Note that there are three variables in the primal model and three inequalities in the dual model. Also, note that the number of constraints in the primal model equals the number of variables in the dual model. Again we see that the rows of the dual variable coefficients are the columns of primal variable coefficients. That is, in detached-coefficient form, we have

PRIMAL VARIABLE COEFFICIENTS		
x_1	x_2	x_3
1	2	3
2	1	1

DUAL VARIABLE COEFFICIENTS	
y_1	y_2
1	2
2	1
3	1

10.2.2. Example—Determining the Dual Model

PRIMAL MODEL

maximize $Z = -10x_1 + 20x_2$

subject to $x_1 + 2x_2 \leqslant 4$

$2x_1 - 3x_2 \geqslant 6$

$x_1 \geqslant 0, \qquad x_2 \geqslant 0.$

Note that the second inequality is of the form greater than or equal to. So we first convert it to an equal-to or less-than equality.

We multiply the second constraint on both sides by -1:

$$(-1)(2x_1 - 3x_2) \leqslant (-1)6$$

or

$$-2x_1 + 3x_2 \leqslant -6$$

and replace the second constraint by this equivalent constraint. This yields the following equivalent primal model.

PRIMAL MODEL

maximize $Z = -10x_1 + 20x_2$

subject to

$$x_1 + 2x_2 \leqslant 4$$
$$-2x_1 + 3x_2 \leqslant -6$$

$$x_1 \geqslant 0, \qquad x_2 \geqslant 0.$$

DUAL MODEL

minimize $C = 4y_1 - 6y_2$

subject to

$$y_1 - 2y_2 \geqslant -10$$
$$2y_1 + 3y_2 \geqslant 20$$

$$y_1 \geqslant 0, \qquad y_2 \geqslant 0.$$

10.2.3. Example—Determining the Dual Model

PRIMAL MODEL 1

maximize $Z = 10x_1 + 20x_2$

subject to

$$x_1 + 2x_2 = 4$$
$$2x_1 - 3x_2 \leqslant 7$$

$$x_1 \geqslant 0, \qquad x_2 \geqslant 0.$$

Note that the first constraint is an equation, not an inequality of the form less than or equal to. To determine the dual model, we first need to change the primal model to an equivalent model in *standard form*. By *standard form* we mean the following.

The objective is to maximize and every constraint is of the form less than or equal to, " $\leqslant$."

We note in primal model 1 that the first constraint is an equation. Thus, we replace it by the following two inequalities:

$$x_1 + 2x_2 \leqslant 4$$

and
$$x_1 + 2x_2 \geqslant 4 \quad \text{or} \quad -x_1 - 2x_2 \leqslant -4.$$

This replacement yields the following equivalent linear programming problem.

PRIMAL MODEL 2

maximize $Z = 10x_1 + 20x_2$

subject to
$$\begin{aligned}
x_1 + 2x_2 &\leqslant 4 \\
-x_1 - 2x_2 &\leqslant -4 \\
2x_1 - 3x_2 &\leqslant 7
\end{aligned}$$

$$x_1 \geqslant 0, \qquad x_2 \geqslant 0.$$

The dual of primal model 2 is given below.

DUAL MODEL

minimize $C = 4y_1 - 4y_2 + 7y_3$

subject to
$$\begin{aligned}
y_1 - y_2 + 2y_3 &\geqslant 10 \\
2y_1 - 2y_2 - 3y_3 &\geqslant 20
\end{aligned}$$

$$y_1 \geqslant 0, \qquad y_2 \geqslant 0, \qquad y_3 \geqslant 0$$

Note that the dual model above is the dual to *both* primal model 1 and primal model 2. Again, comparing the constraint coefficients of the variables in both problems:

PRIMAL VARIABLE COEFFICIENTS		DUAL VARIABLE COEFFICIENTS		
x_1	x_2	y_1	y_2	y_3
1	2	1	-1	2
-1	-2	2	-2	-3
2	-3			

shows that the column coefficients in one problem are the row coefficients in the other problem.

10.2.4. Example—Determining the Dual Model

Given the dual model of

PRIMAL MODEL 1

minimize $Z = 10x_1 - 20x_2 + 10x_3$

$$1x_1 + 1x_2 - 4x_3 \leqslant 11$$
$$2x_1 + 6x_2 + 10x_3 \leqslant 20$$

$$x_1 \geqslant 0, \quad x_2 \geqslant 0, \quad x_3 \geqslant 0.$$

Note that this is a cost-minimization problem. Thus, to determine the dual model of primal model 1, we need to first change it to an equivalent profit-maximization problem. This may be accomplished by replacing cost $= Z = 10x_1 - 20x_2 + 10x_3$ by profit $= z = -Z = -10x_1 + 20x_2 - 10x_3$. This yields the following equivalent linear programming problem.

PRIMAL MODEL 2

maximize $z = -10x_1 + 20x_2 - 10x_3$

subject to $\quad x_1 + x_2 - 4x_3 \leqslant 11$
$$2x_1 + 6x_2 + 10x_3 \leqslant 20$$

$$x_1 \geqslant 0, \quad x_2 \geqslant 0, \quad x_3 \geqslant 0.$$

---

where $-$maximum $z =$ minimum Z in primal model 1.

This leads to the following dual programming problem.

DUAL MODEL

minimize $C = 11y_1 + 20y_2$

subject to $\qquad y_1 + 2y_2 \geqslant -10$

$\qquad\qquad\qquad y_1 + 6y_2 \geqslant 20$

$\qquad\qquad -4y_1 + 10y_2 \geqslant -10$

$\qquad y_1 \geqslant 0, \qquad y_2 \geqslant 0.$

10.2.5. Example—Determining the Dual Model

PRIMAL MODEL 1

minimize $z = 10x_1 - 20x_2 + 10x_3$

subject to $\qquad x_1 + 2x_2 - 3x_3 = 6$

$\qquad\qquad 4x_1 - 11x_2 + 10x_3 \geqslant 17$

$\qquad\qquad 2x_1 + 5x_2 + 7x_3 \leqslant 9.$

To determine the correct dual model, we must first put primal model 1 in standard form. This we accomplish as follows:

1. Multiply the coefficients of the objective function by -1 to convert the minimization to a maximization.
2. Replace the first constraint by the following two equivalent constraints

$$x_1 + 2x_2 - 3x_2 \leqslant 6$$
$$-x_1 - 2x_2 + 3x_2 \leqslant -6.$$

3. Multiply the second inequality in primal model 1 by -1 on both sides so that it has the form less than or equal to.

Performing (1), (2), and (3) to primal model 1 yields the following equivalent model.

PRIMAL MODEL 2

maximize $Z = -10x_1 + 20x_2 - 10x_3$

subject to

$$x_1 + 2x_2 - 3x_3 \leqslant 6$$
$$-x_1 - 2x_2 + 3x_3 \leqslant -6$$
$$-4x_1 + 11x_2 - 10x_3 \leqslant -17$$
$$2x_1 + 5x_2 + 7x_3 \leqslant 9$$
$$x_1 \geqslant 0, \quad x_2 \geqslant 0, \quad x_3 \geqslant 0.$$

This leads to the following dual programming problem.

DUAL MODEL

minimize $C = 6y_1 - 6y_2 - 17y_3 + 9y_4$

subject to

$$y_1 - y_2 - 4y_3 + 2y_4 \geqslant -10$$
$$2y_1 - 2y_2 + 11y_3 + 5y_4 \geqslant 20$$
$$-3y_1 + 3y_2 - 10y_3 + 7y_4 \geqslant -10$$
$$y_1 \geqslant 0, \quad y_2 \geqslant 0, \quad y_3 \geqslant 0, \quad y_4 \geqslant 0.$$

Note (as a review) that the numbers on the right-hand side in one model become the coefficients of the variables in the objective function in the other model.

10.3. DETERMINING OPTIMAL SOLUTIONS FOR PRIMAL AND DUAL MODELS AND COMPLEMENTARY SLACKNESS CONDITIONS

10.3.1. Example—Primal and Dual Optimal Solutions

Consider the following profit-maximization problem.

PRIMAL MODEL

maximize $Z = 5x_1 + 70x_2$

subject to

$$3x_1 + 2x_2 \leqslant 2000$$
$$x_1 + 2x_2 \leqslant 1000$$
$$x_1 \geqslant 0, \quad x_2 \geqslant 0.$$

The optimal simplex tableau for the primal model is given below.

·Primal Model: Optimal Tableau

Basic Variable	Z	x_1	x_2	s_1	s_2		Value
s_1	0	2	0	1	-1	=	1,000
x_2	0	$\frac{1}{2}$	1	0	$\frac{1}{2}$	=	500
Z	1	30	0	0	35	=	35,000

PROBLEM. Give the dual of the primal model.

Solution

DUAL MODEL

minimize $C = 2000y_1 + 1000y_2$

subject to

$$3y_1 + 1y_2 \geqslant 5$$
$$2y_1 + 2y_2 \geqslant 70$$

$$y_1 \geqslant 0, \qquad y_2 \geqslant 0.$$

PROBLEM. Using the primal model optimal tableau, determine the optimal solution to the dual model.

Solution. The optimal values of C, y_1, and y_2 in the dual model are determined as follows:

y_1 equals the coefficient of s_1 in the profit function Z. Thus,
$y_1 = \$0$.
y_2 equals the coefficient of s_2 in the profit function Z. Thus,
$y_2 = \$35$.

$$\text{minimum cost} = C$$
$$= \text{value of } Z$$
$$= \$35,000.$$

10.3.2. Example—Primal and Dual Optimal Solutions

Consider the following profit-maximization model.

PRIMAL MODEL

maximize $Z = 60x_1 + 90x_2$

subject to $-2x_1 + 2x_2 \leqslant 3$

$-3x_1 + 6x_2 \leqslant 12$

$2x_1 + 2x_2 \leqslant 13$

$x_1 \geqslant 0, \qquad x_2 \geqslant 0.$

Adding slack variables s_1, s_2, and s_3 to the three inequality constraints yields the following equivalent linear programming problem.

PRIMAL MODEL

maximize $Z = 60x_1 + 90x_2 + 0s_1 + 0s_2 + 0s_3$

subject to $-2x_1 + 2x_2 + s_1 \qquad\qquad = 3$

$-3x_1 + 6x_2 \qquad + s_2 \qquad = 12$

$2x_1 + 2x_2 \qquad\qquad + s_3 = 13$

$x_1 \geqslant 0, \qquad x_2 \geqslant 0, \qquad s_1 \geqslant 0, \qquad s_2 \geqslant 0, \qquad s_3 \geqslant 0.$

The optimal solution to this primal model is given in the following tableau.

Primal Model Optimal Tableau

Basic Variable	x_1	x_2	s_1	s_2	s_3		Value
x_2	0	1	0	$\frac{1}{9}$	$\frac{1}{6}$	$=$	$\frac{7}{2}$
x_1	1	0	0	$-\frac{1}{9}$	$\frac{1}{3}$	$=$	3
s_1	0	0	1	$-\frac{4}{9}$	$\frac{1}{3}$	$=$	2
Z	0	0	0	$\frac{10}{3}$	$\frac{70}{2}$	$=$	495

PROBLEM 1. Give the dual model.

PROBLEM 2. List the optimal solution to the primal, including values of the slack variables, and list the optimal solution to the dual model, including values of the surplus variables.

Solution 1

DUAL MODEL

minimize $C = 3y_1 + 12y_2 + 13y_3$

subject to $\quad -2y_1 - 3y_2 + 2y_3 \geqslant 60$

$\qquad\qquad\quad 2y_1 + 6y_2 + 2y_3 \geqslant 90$

$\qquad y_1 \geqslant 0, \qquad y_2 \geqslant 0, \qquad y_3 \geqslant 0$

---

or adding surplus variables we obtain the following equivalent dual model:

EQUIVALENT DUAL MODEL

minimize $C = 3y_1 + 12y_2 + 13y_3 + 0S_1 + 0S_2$

subject to $\quad -2y_1 - 3y_2 + 2y_3 - S_1 \qquad = 60$

$\qquad\qquad\quad 2y_1 + 6y_2 + 2y_3 \qquad - S_2 = 90$

$y_1 \geqslant 0, \qquad y_2 \geqslant 0, \qquad y_3 \geqslant 0, \qquad S_1 \geqslant 0, \qquad S_2 \geqslant 0.$

Solution 2

Primal Optimal Solution	Dual Optimal Solution	Complementary Slackness
$x_1 = 3$	$S_1 = 0$	$x_1 S_1 = 0$
$x_2 = \frac{7}{2}$	$S_2 = 0$	$x_2 S_1 = 0$
$s_1 = 2$	$y_1 = 0$	$s_1 y_1 = 0$
$s_2 = 0$	$y_2 = \frac{10}{3}$	$s_2 y_2 = 0$
$s_3 = 0$	$y_3 = \frac{70}{2}$	$s_3 y_3 = 0$

Notice in the column headed "Complementary Slackness" that

$$x_1 S_1 = 0 \quad \text{and} \quad x_2 S_2 = 0$$

That is,

(value of a primal variable) × (value of the corresponding dual surplus variable) = 0

Also, notice in the column headed "Complementary Slackness" that

$$s_1 y_1 = 0, \qquad s_2 y_2 = 0, \qquad s_3 y_3 = 0.$$

That is,

(value of a primal slack variable) × (value of the corresponding dual variable) = 0.

This relationship between optimal primal and optimal dual solutions will always hold. If not, then either the primal solution or the dual solution or both are nonoptimal. This relationship between primal and dual solutions is called *complementary slackness*.

The complementary slackness conditions are conditions that a primal feasible solution and a dual feasible solution must satisfy in order for both solutions to be optimal. The conditions are given more precisely by the following four statements. First, in the dual formulation of the linear programming problem, there is a variable corresponding to every constraint of the primal and a constraint corresponding to every variable of the primal.

In Example 10.3.2 we have the following correspondences:

Dual Variable		Primal Constraint
y_1	corresponds to	$-2x_1 + 2x_2 \leqslant 3$
y_2	corresponds to	$-3x_1 + 6x_2 \leqslant 12$
y_3	corresponds to	$2x_1 + 2x_2 \leqslant 13$

Dual Constraint		Primal Variable
$-2y_1 - 3y_2 + 2y_3 \geqslant 60$	corresponds to	x_1
$2y_1 + 6y_2 + 2y_3 \geqslant 90$	corresponds to	x_2

For a primal constraint and the corresponding dual variable, the following two statements concerning an optimal solution must be true:

Statement 1   If a primal constraint is overly satisfied (i.e., the corresponding slack variable is greater than zero), then the corresponding dual variable is zero.

Note in Example 10.3.2 that only the first constraint is overly satisfied since $s_1 = 2$, $s_2 = 0$, and $s_3 = 0$. Also, note that the corresponding dual variable for the first constraint is zero, $y_1 = 0$.

Statement 2 If a dual variable is positive, the corresponding primal constraint is exactly satisfied.

Note in Example 10.3.2 that the second and third dual variables are positive, $y_2 = 10/3$ and $y_3 = 70/2$ and that the second and third constraints of the primal are exactly satisfied, $s_2 = 0$ and $s_3 = 0$.

Statements 1 and 2 may be summarized by saying that at most one term in each of the following products can be positive:

$$s_1 y_1, \quad s_2 y_2, \quad s_3 y_3.$$

That is, $s_1 y_1 = 0$, $s_2 y_2 = 0$, and $s_3 y_3 = 0$ must hold for primal and dual optimal solutions.

Next, for a dual constraint and the corresponding primal variable, the following two statements concerning an optimal solution must be true:

Statement 3 If a dual constraint is overly satisfied (i.e., the corresponding surplus variable is greater than zero), then the corresponding primal variable is zero.

Note in Example 10.3.2 that no dual constraint is overly satisfied since $S_1 = 0$ and $S_2 = 0$.

Statement 4 If a primal variable is positive, the corresponding dual constraint is exactly satisfied.

Note in Example 10.3.2 that the primal variables are positive, $x_1 = 3$ and $x_2 = 7/2$, and the corresponding dual constraints are exactly satisfied since $S_1 = 0$ and $S_2 = 0$.

Statements 3 and 4 may be summarized by saying that at most one term in each of the products $x_1 S_1$ and $x_2 S_2$ can be zero. That is, $x_1 S_1 = 0$ and $x_2 S_2 = 0$. The four complementary slackness conditions given in the preceding four statements have the following interpretations.

Statement 1 says that if a resource is not fully used in an optimal primal solution, the marginal value of that resource must be zero. That is, a company should be willing to sell units of that resource at positive prices, if possible, but unwilling to buy units of that resource.

Statement 2 says that if a company values a resource at a positive marginal price in an optimal primal solution, they should be using all of that resource in the solution.

Statement 3 says that if the minimum value of all the resources required to produce 1 unit of product *exceeds* the contribution to profits of producing 1 unit of the product, the company should produce zero units of that product.

Statement 4 says that if at an optimum solution to the primal problem the company produces some positive number of units of a product, the minimum value of the resources required to produce 1 unit of the product should exactly equal the contribution to profits earned from producing that product.

10.3.3. Example—Primal and Dual Solutions and
Complementary Slackness Conditions

PROBLEM. For the primal and dual models of Example 10.1.2 list the optimal solutions and show that the complementary slackness conditions are satisfied.

Solution

Primal Optimal Solution	Dual Optimal Solution	Complementary Slackness
$x_1 = 500$	$S_1 = 0$	$x_1 S_1 = 0$
$x_2 = 250$	$S_2 = 0$	$x_2 S_2 = 0$
$s_1 = 0$	$y_1 = 5$	$s_1 y_1 = 0$
$s_2 = 0$	$y_2 = 25$	$s_2 y_2 = 0$

QUESTION. Do the solutions for the primal and dual models of Example 10.3.1 satisfy the complementary slackness conditions?

Answer. Yes.

Primal Solution	Dual Solution	Complementary Slackness
$x_1 = 0$	$S_1 = 30$	$x_1 S_1 = 0$
$x_2 = 500$	$S_2 = 0$	$x_2 S_2 = 0$
$s_1 = 1000$	$y_1 = 0$	$s_1 y_1 = 0$
$s_2 = 0$	$y_2 = 35$	$s_2 y_2 = 0$

Since all the products in the third column are zero, the solutions in columns 1 and 2 are primal and dual optimal, respectively.

The facts learned thus far about *duality* are:

1. For any linear programming model, there exists a companion model called the dual model.
2. An optimal simplex tableau for the primal model yields the optimal solution to the dual model. Also, an optimal simplex tableau for the dual model yields the optimal solution to the primal model.
3. Feasible solutions to a primal and dual are both optimal if the complementary slackness conditions hold.

Polarex Cameras produces three models of cameras, the Broadway, Gutherie, and Hollywood. They also produce several camera accessories. Next year, based on their annual plan, they plan on selling *at least* 5000 Hollywoods, 300 Gutheries, and 240 Broadways. The excess production capacity will be used in the production of accessories, which is very profitable to Polarex.

Polarex has two plants, Albany (A) and Boston (B). Management at Polarex would like to know how many production days to allocate to each plant for the production of cameras. Cost accounting estimates that production costs per day will be $5000 at Albany and $7000 per day at Boston.

Let

$$x_1 = \text{number of camera production days at Albany}$$

$$x_2 = \text{number of camera production days at Boston.}$$

The following production table gives the maximum number of each type of camera that can be produced per day at each plant.

Daily Camera Output

Model	Albany	Boston
Hollywood	100	140
Gutheries	10	6
Broadway	4	8

That is, in one day at Albany, 100 Hollywoods, 10 Gutheries, and 4 Broadways can be produced. In one production day at the Boston plant, 140 Hollywoods, 6 Gutheries, and 8 Broadways can be produced.

Consider the following cost-minimization model:

PRIMAL MODEL

minimize $C = 5000x_1 + 7000x_2$

subject to

$$100x_1 + 140x_2 \geqslant 5000 \quad \text{(Hollywood)}$$

$$10x_1 + 6x_2 \geqslant 300 \quad \text{(Gutherie)}$$

$$4x_1 + 8x_2 \geqslant 240 \quad \text{(Broadway)}$$

$$x_1 \geqslant 0, \quad x_2 \geqslant 0.$$

QUESTION. What is the dual to the primal model above?

Answer. We first convert the primal model above to an equivalent profit-maximization model. We have

---

PRIMAL MODEL

maximize $c = -5000x_1 - 7000x_2$

subject to
$$-100x_1 - 140x_2 \leqslant -5000$$
$$-10x_1 - 6x_2 \leqslant -300$$
$$-4x_1 - 8x_2 \leqslant -240$$

$$x_1 \geqslant 0, \qquad x_2 \geqslant 0,$$

---

where $c = -C$.

Then the dual of the primal model is:

DUAL MODEL

minimize $Z = -5000y_1 - 300y_2 - 240y_3$

subject to
$$-100y_1 - 10y_2 - 4y_3 \geqslant -5000$$
$$-140y_1 - 6y_2 - 8y_3 \geqslant -7000$$
$$y_1 \geqslant 0, \qquad y_2 \geqslant 0, \qquad y_3 \geqslant 0.$$

We can convert the dual model above to the following equivalent model.

DUAL MODEL

maximize $z = 5000y_1 + 300y_2 + 240y_3$

subject to
$$100y_1 + 10y_2 + 4y_3 \leqslant 5000$$
$$140y_1 + 6y_2 + 8y_3 \leqslant 7000$$

$$y_1 \geqslant 0, \qquad y_2 \geqslant 0, \qquad y_3 \geqslant 0.$$

---

where $Z = -z$.

In summary, we have the following primal and dual models:

PRIMAL MODEL

minimize $C = 5000x_1 + 7000x_2$

subject to

$$100x_1 + 140x_2 \geqslant 5000$$
$$10x_1 + 6x_2 \geqslant 300$$
$$4x_1 + 8x_2 \geqslant 240$$

$$x_1 \geqslant 0, \quad x_2 \geqslant 0.$$

DUAL MODEL

maximize $z = 5000y_1 + 300y_2 + 240y_3$

subject to

$$100y_1 + 10y_2 + 4y_3 \leqslant 5000$$
$$140y_1 + 6y_2 + 8y_3 \leqslant 7000$$

$$y_1 \geqslant 0, \quad y_2 \geqslant 0, \quad y_3 \geqslant 0.$$

QUESTION. What is the dual of the dual model?

Answer. The primal model is the correct answer. That is, the dual of the dual programming model is the primal model.

QUESTION. The optimal solution to the primal model is given in the following tableau. What is the optimal solution to the dual model?

Primal Model—Optimal Simplex Tableau

Basic Variable	C	x_1	x_2	S_1	S_2	S_3		Value
x_1	0	1	0	$\frac{6}{800}$	$-\frac{140}{800}$	0	=	15
x_2	0	0	1	$-\frac{10}{800}$	$\frac{100}{800}$	0	=	25
S_3	0	0	0	$-\frac{56}{800}$	$\frac{240}{800}$	1	=	20
C	1	0	0	50	0	0	=	250,000

Answer. Optimal values of the dual variables are

$$y_1 = 50, \quad y_2 = 0, \quad y_3 = 0, \quad \text{and} \quad Z = 250{,}000.$$

QUESTION. What is the interpretation of Polarex's dual model?

Answer. The objective of Polarex is to minimize their total operating costs. This they can accomplish by determining the optimal number of production days at the two plants, Albany and Boston, subject to the restrictions that certain minimal amounts of each type of camera must be produced.

Let

$y_1 =$ cost Polarex would be willing to pay (say by subcontracting)
for the manufacture of *one* Hollywood camera.

Similarly, let

$y_2 =$ cost Polarex would be willing to pay
for the manufacture of *one* Gutherie camera

and $y_3 =$ cost Polarex would be willing to pay
for the manufacture of *one* Broadway camera.

Polarex requires 5000 Hollywood cameras, 300 Gutherie cameras, and 240 Broadway cameras. The total cost of meeting all their requirements is

$$Z = 5000y_1 + 300y_2 + 240y_3.$$

Polarex would like to obtain values for y_1, y_2, and y_3 which give an *upper bound* on the total cost Z which they would be willing to pay, say to a subcontractor, to meet the requirements for the three cameras subject to any other viable manufacturing alternatives. The other alternatives for Polarex are to manufacture cameras in Albany or Boston or both.

Now $100y_1 + 10y_2 + 4y_3$ is the implicit cost of operating the Albany plant for one day. Thus, Polarex must choose costs y_1, y_2, and y_3 such that

$$100y_1 + 10y_2 + 4y_3 \leqslant \$5000,$$

where \$5000 equals the daily operating cost at the Albany plant. Similarly, $140y_1 + 6y_2 + 8y_3$ is the implicit cost of operating the Boston plant for 1 day. This cost must be equal to or less than the daily operating cost of \$7000 at Boston. That is,

$$140y_1 + 6y_2 + 8y_3 \leqslant \$7000,$$

Thus, if Polarex can obtain costs of y_1, y_2, and y_3 for the manufacturing of Hollywood, Gutherie, and Broadway cameras, respectively, such that

$$140y_1 + 6y_2 + 8y_3 < \$7000,$$

then it would be economical for Polarex to not produce cameras at their Boston plant, that is $x_2 = 0$.

Note that from the optimal primal tableau that Polarex would be willing to pay \$50 ($y_1 = \$50$) to a subcontractor to manufacture one Hollywood camera. Also, note that $y_2 = \$0$ and $y_3 = \$0$ in the optimal primal tableau. Thus, Polarex would prefer to manufacture Gutherie and Broadway cameras in their Albany and Boston plants rather than subcontract their production.

10.4. COMPUTATIONAL ADVANTAGES OF DUAL PROGRAMMING

Note the following property of dual programming:

> The solution of the primal model yields the solution of the dual model, and vice versa.

This can be of considerable aid in solving linear programming problems.
Recall that:

> The number of constraints in the primal model equals the number of variables in the dual model.

Also note that:

> The number of variables in the primal problem equals the number of constraints in the dual model.

The simplex method most often finds the optimal solution in less time (less iterations) when applied to problems with fewer constraints than variables. Thus in deciding which problem to solve first, the primal or the dual model, it usually is advantageous to choose the problem with the least number of constraints. You can always obtain the solution to the other problem by reading it off the optimal simplex tableau.

REFERENCES BIERMAN, H., C. P. BONINI, and W. H. HAUSMAN. *Quantitative Analysis for Business Decisions*, 4th ed. Homewood, Ill.: Richard D. Irwin, Inc., 1973.

DAELLENBACH, H. G., and E. J. BELL. *User's Guide to Linear Programming.* Englewood Cliffs, N.J.: Prentice-Hall, Inc., 1970.

DANTZIG, G. B. *Linear Programming and Extensions*. Princeton, N.J.: Princeton University Press, 1963.

DRIEBEEK, N. J. *Applied Linear Programming*. Reading, Mass.: Addison-Wesley Publishing Co., Inc., 1969.

HILLIER, F. S., and G. J. LIEBERMAN. *Introduction to Operations Research*, 2nd ed. San Francisco: Holden-Day, Inc., 1974.

HOROWITZ, I. *An Introduction to Quantitative Business Analysis*, 2nd ed. New York: McGraw-Hill Book Company, 1972.

KIM, C. *Introduction to Linear Programming*. New York: Holt, Rinehart and Winston, Inc., 1972.

KWAK, N. K. *Mathematical Programming with Business Applications*. New York: McGraw-Hill Book Company, 1973.

LAPIN, L. *Quantitative Methods for Business Decisions*. New York: Harcourt Brace Jovanovich, Inc., 1976.

LEVIN, R., and C. KIRKPATRICK. *Quantitative Approaches to Management*, 3rd ed. New York: McGraw-Hill Book Company, 1975.

SIMMONS, D. M. *Linear Programming for Operations Research*. San Francisco: Holden-Day, Inc., 1972.

STRUM, J. E. *Introduction to Linear Programming*. San Francisco: Holden-Day, Inc., 1972.

TAHA, H. A. *Operations Research: An Introduction*. New York: Macmillan Publishing Co., Inc., 1971.

WAGNER, H. M. *Principles of Operations Research with Applications to Managerial Decisions*. Englewood Cliffs, N.J.: Prentice-Hall, Inc., 1975.

KEY CONCEPTS Dual model or dual problem
Optimal pricing
Complementary slackness conditions

10.1. Consider the following linear programming model.

PRIMAL MODEL

maximize $Z = 10x_1 + 20x_2$

subject to
$$1x_1 + 4x_2 \leqslant 8$$
$$2x_1 + 3x_2 \leqslant 6$$
$$x_1 \geqslant 0, \qquad x_2 \geqslant 0.$$

What is the dual of this primal model?

10.2. Consider the following linear programming model.

PRIMAL MODEL

minimize $C = -10x_1 - 20x_2$

subject to
$$1x_1 + 4x_2 \leqslant 8$$
$$2x_1 + 3x_2 \geqslant 6$$
$$x_1 \geqslant 0, \qquad x_2 \geqslant 0.$$

What is the dual of this primal model?

10.3. Consider the following linear programming model.

PRIMAL MODEL

maximize $Z = 2x_1 + 5x_2$

subject to
$$1x_1 + 2x_2 \leqslant 4$$
$$0x_1 + 1x_2 \leqslant 1$$
$$x_1 \geqslant 0, \qquad x_2 \geqslant 0.$$

The optimal solution to the primal model is given in the following tableau.

Optimal Tableau

Basic Variable	Z	x_1	x_2	S_1	S_2		Value
x_1	0	1	0	1	-2	$=$	2
x_2	0	0	1	0	1	$=$	1
Z	1	0	0	2	1	$=$	9

What is the dual of the primal model? Using the optimal tableau above, give the optimal solution to the dual.

10.4. Consider the following product mix problem. Let

x_1 = number of units of product 1 to produce daily.

x_2 = number of units of product 2 to produce daily.

The production of both products requires processing time in two departments, D_1 and D_2. The hourly capacities of D_1 and D_2, unit profits for products 1 and 2, and processing time requirements in D_1 and D_2 are given in the following production table.

Department	PRODUCT 1	2	Capacity (hours)
D_1	1	2	32
D_2	0	1	8
Profit	\$200	\$300	

Thus, to build 1 complete unit of product 1 requires 1 hour in D_1 and 0 hours in D_2. To build 1 complete unit of product 2 requires 2 hours in D_1 and 1 hour in D_2.

The solution to the following programming model determines the optimal product mix.

PRIMAL MODEL

maximize $Z = 200x_1 + 300x_2$

subject to

$$1x_1 + 2x_2 \leqslant 32 \quad (D_1)$$
$$0x_1 + 1x_2 \leqslant 8 \quad (D_2)$$

$$x_1 \geqslant 0, \quad x_2 \geqslant 0.$$

The optimal solution to this primal model is given in the following tableau.

Basic Variable	Z	x_1	x_2	s_1	s_2		Value
x_1	0	1	2	1	0	=	32
s_2	0	0	1	0	1	=	8
Z	1	0	100	200	0	=	6400

OPTIMAL SOLUTION

$x_1 = 32$ units $\qquad x_2 = 0$ units

$s_2 = 8$ hours $\qquad s_1 = 0$ hours

Profit $= Z = \$6400$.

Give the dual of the primal model with surplus variables included. Give the optimal solution to the dual model. Interpret the dual variables.

ANSWERS TO REVIEW PROBLEMS

10.1. Both the dual and primal models are given below.

DUAL MODEL

minimize $C = 8y_1 + 6y_2$

subject to $\qquad 1y_1 + 2y_2 \geqslant 10$

$\qquad\qquad 4y_1 + 3y_2 \geqslant 20$

$\qquad\qquad y_1 \geqslant 0, \qquad y_2 \geqslant 0.$

PRIMAL MODEL

maximize $Z = 10x_1 + 20x_2$

subject to $\qquad 1x_1 + 4x_2 \leqslant 8$

$\qquad\qquad 2x_1 + 3x_2 \leqslant 6$

$\qquad\qquad x_1 \geqslant 0, \qquad x_2 \geqslant 0.$

Note that the primal model has *two variables*, x_1 and x_2. Thus, the dual model has *two constraints*. Also, notice that the primal model has *two constraints*. Thus, the dual model has *two variables*, y_1 and y_2.

10.2. You are asked to give the dual of the following primal model.

PRIMAL MODEL

minimize $C = -10x_1 - 20x_2$ (O)

$$1x_1 + 4x_2 \leqslant 8 \quad \text{(a)}$$
$$2x_1 + 3x_2 \geqslant 6 \quad \text{(b)}$$

$$x_1 \geqslant 0, \qquad x_2 \geqslant 0.$$

To determine the dual model, we first express the primal model in standard form. By *standard form* we mean the following:

1. The goal must be to maximize the objective function.
2. All constraints must be less than or equal to, $\leqslant$, the right-hand-side values.

To accomplish (1) we replace (O) by (O'), where $(O') = (-1)(O)$. That is, (O') is constructed as follows.

$$c = -C = -(-10x_1 - 20x_2)$$
$$= \quad 10x_1 + 20x_2. \qquad (O')$$

To accomplish (2) we replace constraint (b) by (b'), where (b') = (-1)(b). That is,

$$2x_1 + 3x_2 \geqslant 6 \qquad \text{(b)}$$

is equivalent to

$$-(2x_1 + 3x_2) \leqslant -(6) \qquad \text{(b')}$$

or

$$-2x_1 - 3x_2 \leqslant -6. \qquad \text{(b')}$$

Substituting (O') for (O) and (b') for (b) yields the following equivalent primal model.

> ## PRIMAL MODEL
>
> maximize $c = 10x_1 + 20x_2$ (O')
>
> subject to $1x_1 + 4x_2 \leqslant 8$ (a)
>
> $-2x_1 - 3x_2 \leqslant -6$ (b')
>
> $x_1 \geqslant 0, \qquad x_2 \geqslant 0,$

where minimum $C = -$ maximum c.

Then the dual of the primal model is

> ## DUAL MODEL
>
> minimize $Z = 8y_1 - 6y_2$
>
> subject to $1y_1 - 2y_2 \geqslant 10$
>
> $4y_1 - 3y_2 \geqslant 20$
>
> $y_1 \geqslant 0, \qquad y_2 \geqslant 0.$

10.3. The dual of the primal model is given below.

> ## DUAL MODEL
>
> minimize $C = 4y_1 + 1y_2$
>
> subject to $1y_1 + 0y_2 \geqslant 2$
>
> $2y_1 + 1y_2 \geqslant 5$
>
> $y_1 \geqslant 0, \qquad y_2 \geqslant 0.$

The optimal solution to the dual model is as follows.

$y_1 = $ coefficient of S_1 in the profit function Z in the optimal tableau.

Thus,

$y_1 = 2$

$y_2 = $ coefficient of S_2 in the profit function Z in the optimal tableau.

Thus,

$$y_2 = 1$$
$$C = \text{maximum profit}$$
$$= \text{value of } Z \text{ in the optimal tableau.}$$

Thus, $C = \$9$.

10.4. The dual of the primal model is:

DUAL MODEL

minimize $C = 32y_1 + 8y_2 + 0S_1 + 0S_2$ (O)

subject to $1y_1 + 0y_2 - 1S_1$ $= 200$ (a)

             $2y_1 + 1y_2 -$ $S_2 = 300$ (b)

$y_1 \geqslant 0,$ $y_2 \geqslant 0,$ $S_1 \geqslant 0,$ $S_2 \geqslant 0.$

The optimal solution to the dual model is

$$
\left.\begin{aligned}
y_1 &= 200 \\
y_2 &= 0 \\
S_1 &= 0 \\
S_2 &= 100 \\
C &= \$6400
\end{aligned}\right\}
\begin{aligned}
&\text{obtained from the} \\
&\text{primal model optimal} \\
&\text{tableau}
\end{aligned}
$$

y_1 denotes the marginal increase in profit Z for an additional 1 hour of capacity in D_1. Since $y_1 = \$200$, profit Z would change from $\$6400$ to $6400 + 200 = \$6600$ with an additional hour of capacity in D_1.

y_2 denotes the increase in maximum profit given an additional hour of capacity in D_2. Since $y_2 = \$0$, an additional hour of capacity in D_2 would not change maximum profit.

Note that we have $s_2 = 8$ hours. That is, we already have an excess of 8 hours of capacity in D_2. Thus, we would expect $y_2 = 0$ or $y_2 s_2 = 0$.

Consider constraint (a) of the dual model without the surplus variable S_1. We have

$$1y_1 + 0y_2 \geqslant \$200$$

$$
\begin{bmatrix}
\textit{total value} \\
\textit{of units of } D_1 \textit{ and} \\
\textit{D}_2 \textit{ required} \\
\textit{to produce } 1 \\
\textit{unit of product } 1
\end{bmatrix}
\geqslant
\begin{bmatrix}
\textit{unit profit for} \\
\textit{product } 1
\end{bmatrix}.
$$

Thus, the inequality states that the value of the firm's D_1 and D_2 time required to produce 1 unit of product 1 has to be at least as large as the unit profit received from manufacturing and selling 1 unit of product 1.

Furthermore, if

$$1y_1 + 0y_2 > \$200$$
$$\text{value} > \text{unit profit,}$$

that is, if $S_1 > 0$, then $x_1 = 0$ (we do not produce product 1). Similarly, for constraint (b) we have

$$2y_1 + 1y_2 \geqslant \$300$$

$$\begin{bmatrix} \textit{value of the} \\ \textit{firms } D_1 \textit{ and} \\ D_2 \textit{ time re-} \\ \textit{quired to} \\ \textit{produce 1 unit} \\ \textit{of product 2} \end{bmatrix} \geqslant \begin{bmatrix} \textit{unit profit re-} \\ \textit{ceived from manu-} \\ \textit{facturing and} \\ \textit{selling 1 unit of} \\ \textit{product 2} \end{bmatrix}.$$

EXERCISES

CONSTRUCTING DUAL MODELS

10.1. Consider the following linear programming model.

> **PRIMAL MODEL**
>
> maximize $Z = 2x_1 + 3x_2$
>
> subject to $\quad 4x_1 + 5x_2 \leqslant 6$
> $\qquad\qquad 7x_1 + 8x_2 \leqslant 9$
>
> $\qquad x_1 \geqslant 0, \quad x_2 \geqslant 0.$

Give the dual of this primal model.

CONSTRUCTING DUAL MODELS

10.2. Consider the following linear programming model.

> **PRIMAL MODEL**
>
> maximize $Z = 2x_1 + 3x_2 - 4x_3$
>
> subject to $\quad 5x_1 + 6x_2 + 7x_3 \leqslant 8$
> $\qquad\qquad 8x_1 - 9x_2 + 10x_3 \leqslant 11$
>
> $\qquad x_1 \geqslant 0, \quad x_2 \geqslant 0, \quad x_3 \geqslant 0.$

Give the dual of this primal model.

10.3. Considering the following linear programming model.

> **PRIMAL MODEL**
>
> minimize $C = 2x_1 + 3x_2$
>
> subject to $\qquad 4x_1 + 5x_2 \geqslant 6$
> $\qquad\qquad\quad 7x_1 + 8x_2 \leqslant 9$
>
> $\qquad x_1 \geqslant 0, \qquad x_2 \geqslant 0.$

Give the dual of this model.

10.4. Consider the following linear programming model.

> **PRIMAL MODEL**
>
> minimize $C = 2x_1 + 3x_2 - 4x_3$
>
> subject to $\qquad 5x_1 + 6x_2 + 7x_3 \quad \leqslant \;\; 8$
> $\qquad\qquad\quad 9x_1 - 10x_2 + 11x_3 = 12$
> $\qquad\qquad\quad 13x_1 - 14x_2 + 15x_3 \geqslant 16$
>
> $\qquad x_1 \geqslant 0, x_2 \geqslant 0, x_3 \geqslant 0.$

Give the dual of this primal model.

10.5. Consider the following linear programming model.

> **PRIMAL MODEL**
>
> maximize $Z = 2x_1 + \;\; 3x_2$
>
> subject to $\qquad 1x_1 \qquad\qquad \leqslant 2$
> $\qquad\qquad\qquad\qquad 1x_2 \leqslant 2$
>
> $\qquad x_1 \geqslant 0, \qquad x_2 \geqslant 0.$

The optimal solution to the primal model is given in the following simplex tableau.

Basic Variable	Z	x_1	x_2	S_1	S_2		Value
x_1	0	1	0	1	0	=	2
x_2	0	0	1	0	1	=	2
Z	1	0	0	2	3	=	10

Give the dual of the primal model above. Using this simplex tableau, give the optimal solution to the dual model.

DUAL OPTIMAL **10.6.** The linear programming model
SOLUTION AND
COMPLEMENTARY
SLACKNESS

> **PRIMAL MODEL**
>
> maximize $Z = 2x_1 + 3x_2 - 4x_3$
>
> subject to $\quad 1x_1 + 0x_2 + \ x_3 \leqslant 4$
>
> $\qquad\qquad\quad 0x_1 + 1x_2 + 2x_3 \leqslant 6$
>
> $x_1 \geqslant 0, \qquad x_2 \geqslant 0, \qquad x_3 \geqslant 0.$

has an optimal solution given in the following tableau.

Basic Variable	Z	x_1	x_2	x_3	s_1	s_2		Value
x_1	0	1	0	1	1	0	=	4
x_2	0	0	1	2	0	1	=	6
Z	1	0	0	12	2	3	=	24

Give an optimal solution for the dual of the primal model above. Show that the optimal solution of the primal model and the optimal solution of the dual model satisfy the complementary slackness conditions.

10.7. The linear programming model

PRIMAL MODEL

minimize $C = -2x_1 - 3x_2 + 4x_3$

subject to $\quad 1x_1 + 0x_2 + 1x_3 \geqslant 4$

$\quad\quad\quad\quad 1x_1 + 1x_2 + 2x_3 \leqslant 6$

$\quad x_1 \geqslant 0, \quad x_2 \geqslant 0, \quad x_3 \geqslant 0$

has an optimal solution given in the following tableau.

Basic Variable	Z	x_1	x_2	x_3	s_1	s_2		Value
x_1	0	1	0	1	-1	0	=	4
x_2	0	0	1	1	1	1	=	2
Z	1	0	0	9	1	3	=	14

Give an optimal solution for the dual of this primal model. Show that the optimal solutions of both models satisfy the complementary slackness conditions.

10.8. The linear programming model

PRIMAL MODEL

minimize $C = -2x_1 - 3x_2 + 4x_3$

subject to $\quad 1x_1 + 0x_2 + 1x_3 \geqslant 4$

$\quad\quad\quad\quad 1x_1 + 1x_2 + 2x_3 \leqslant 6$

$\quad x_1 \geqslant 0, \quad x_2 \geqslant 0, \quad x_3 \geqslant 0.$

when solved as an equivalent profit-maximization problem has an optimal solution given in the following tableau.

Basic Variable	c	x_1	x_2	x_3	$-S_1$	S_2		Value
x_1	0	1	0	1	-1	0	=	4
x_2	0	0	1	1	1	1	=	2
c	1	0	0	9	1	3	=	14

Give an optimal solution for the dual of the primal model above. Show that the primal and dual optimal solutions satisfy the complementary slackness conditions.

INTERPRETING
DUAL OPTIMAL
SOLUTIONS

10.9. The linear programming model

PRIMAL MODEL

minimize $C = 10x_1 + 6x_2$

subject to
$$10x_1 + 5x_2 \geqslant 140 \quad (O_1)$$
$$3x_1 + 5x_2 \geqslant 105 \quad (O_2)$$
$$10x_1 + 5x_2 \geqslant 105 \quad (O_3)$$

$$x_1 \geqslant 0, \qquad x_2 \geqslant 0.$$

---

has the following interpretation:

x_1 = number of electronic engineering hours

x_2 = number of electricians hours,

where an electronic engineer costs $10 per hour and an electrician costs $6 per hour.

Both engineers and technicians can be used on a testing line where three operations are performed, O_1, O_2, and O_3. The production matrix for the department is given below.

Testing Operation	TYPE OF EMPLOYEE		Minimum Test Required per Day
	Engineer	Electrician	
O_1	10	5	$\geqslant 140$
O_2	3	5	$\geqslant 105$
O_3	10	5	$\geqslant 105$

Thus, an engineer can perform 10, 3, and 10 of tests 1, 2, and 3 per hour, respectively. An electrician can perform 5, 5, and 5 of tests 1, 2, and 3 per hour. The optimal solution to the primal model is

$$x_1 = 5 \text{ hours} \quad \text{and} \quad x_2 = 18 \text{ hours}$$

at a total cost per day of $C = \$158$. The optimal solution to the dual model is

$$y_1 = \tfrac{32}{35}, \qquad y_2 = \tfrac{2}{7}, \qquad y_3 = 0.$$

Give the dual of the primal model above. Interpret the dual model and its optimal solution.

CASE 10.1   Illustrative Case Study

HAWKS AND DOVES   The Stuffed Animal Division of Mammoth Toy Company is considering the
(AN APPLICATION   production of stuffed hawks and doves. Under present market conditions they
OF LINEAR   can sell hawks at a $10 profit and doves at a $6 profit.
PROGRAMMING)   Hawks skins are tougher and take longer to make than dove skins. The
skin machine can make 8 doves per minute, but only 4 hawks. (It can't make
both at the same time, but can easily be switched from one to the other.) The
stuffing line, on the other hand, can stuff 6 hawks per minute or it can stuff 4
doves per minute. It, too, can be changed easily from one to the other. Hawks
go through a final beak sharpening machine that has a capacity of 3.5 hawks
per minute.

Assignment

1. How many doves and hawks per 8-hour day should the division make to
maximize profits? Set up and solve as a linear programming problem.

Unless otherwise stated, the following questions are independent of each
other and are based on the original statement of the H and D problem.

2. What would you be willing to pay for additional capacity on the stuffing
line (in dollars per minute of capacity)?
3. Similarly, what would you be willing to pay for additional capacity on
the beak machine?
4. Another division wants to buy time on the skin machine. What is the
least you would sell it for (in dollars per minute of capacity)? How much
would you sell at this rate? Explain.
5. The other division wants $\frac{3}{4}$ of your skin machine capacity. How much (at
a minimum) should you charge?
6. The production manager is closely monitoring the stuffing line, which
was recently installed at large cost. To make his cost accounting records
(which are based on machine utilization) look good, he insists on a policy
of using the stuffing line to full capacity. As his assistant in charge of
scheduling what would you tell him?

7. The V.P. of production, visiting the hawks and doves line, is disturbed to observe some idle capacity on one or more of the processes. He issues an order stating that all processes are to be used to their full capacity. What would you tell him?

8. The marketing department requests that dove production be set at 3 doves per minute. What would be the cost of this policy?

9. Under the conditions of question 8, what would you be willing to pay for additional capacity on the
   (a) Skin machine?
   (b) Stuffing line?
   (c) Beak machine?
   In each case where appropriate, indicate how much extra capacity you would want at the stated rate.

10. Repeat question 9, with dove production set at 2 per minute.

Hint: Answers to some of the questions above can be facilitated by means of a graphical display of the problem.

CHAPTER 11

Linear Programming: Postoptimality Analysis and Linear Programming Under Uncertainty

OBJECTIVES. Upon successful completion of this chapter, you should be able to:

1. Perform a postoptimality analysis on profit coefficients and resources.
2. Determine optimal solutions to linear programming problems under uncertainty using the pessimistic criterion, the optimistic criterion, and the expected value criterion.

11.1. POSTOPTIMALITY ANALYSIS (SENSITIVITY ANALYSIS)

An optimal solution to a linear programming model consists of two parts: the optimal values of the decision variables and the optimal value (profit maximum or minimum cost) of the objective function.

The *parameters* in a linear programming model may be slightly or even highly inaccurate owing to the fact that they are most often based on estimates derived from data or based on "good guesses."

> Postoptimality analysis involves determining the effect on the overall optimal solution by varying the parameters.

QUESTION. What parameters in a linear programming model are usually estimates of the true but unknown parameters?

Answer. Parameters that are most often estimates of the true but unknown parameters are: coefficients (unit profits or unit costs) of the variables in the objective function, the numbers on the right-hand side of the constraints, and the coefficients of the variables in the constraints.

11.1.1. Example—National Business Machines

Consider again the National Business Machines (NBM) model given in Chapter 10. We have

$$\text{maximize } Z = 40x_1 + 60x_2$$

$$\text{subject to} \quad 3x_1 + 2x_2 \leqslant 2000$$

$$1x_1 + 2x_2 \leqslant 1000$$

$$x_1 \geqslant 0, \quad x_2 \geqslant 0.$$

Recall that the decision variables are

$$x_1 = \text{number of manual typewriters}$$
$$x_2 = \text{number of electric typewriters.}$$

The $40 and $60 in the objective function are *estimated* unit profits from selling manual and electric typewriters. The numbers 2000 and 1000 appearing on the right-hand side of the constraints represent *estimates* of the number of hours of operations O_1 and O_2 available to NBM each month. The numbers 3 and 2 in the first inequality are *estimates* of the number of hours of O_1 required to produce one manual and one electric typewriter, respectively. The numbers 1 and 2 in the second inequality are estimates of the number of hours of O_2 required to produce one manual and one electric typewriter, respectively. Thus, the NBM model has several estimated parameters.

11.1.2. Example—National Business Machines and Price Changes

For the NBM model given in Example 11.1.1, we know that maximum profit = Z = $35,000, with the optimal values for the decision variables being

$$x_1 = 500 \text{ manual typewriters}$$
$$x_2 = 250 \text{ electric typewriters.}$$

QUESTION. How much must the selling price of manual typewriters decrease ("drop") in order for NBM to only produce electric typewriters?

Answer. The unit profit of a manual typewriter is at present $40. Let D denote a decrease in its unit price. We are interested in what value or values of D will cause us to change from $x_1 = 500$ to $x_1 = 0$.

$$\text{maximize } Z = (40 - D)x_1 + 60x_2 + 0s_1 + 0s_2$$

$$\text{subject to} \quad
\begin{aligned}
3x_1 + 2x_2 + s_1 \qquad\quad &= 2000 \\
1x_1 + 2x_2 + \qquad\quad s_2 &= 1000
\end{aligned}$$

$$x_1 \geqslant 0, \qquad x_2 \geqslant 0, \qquad s_1 \geqslant 0, \qquad s_2 \geqslant 0.$$

To solve the model above (we have added slack variables s_1 and s_2), we begin with an initial simplex tableau and apply the simplex method. This yields the following two simplex tableaus.

Initial Tableau

Basic Variable	x_1	x_2	s_1	s_2		Value
s_1	3	2	1	0	=	2000
s_2	1	2	0	1	=	1000
Z	$-40 + D$	-60	0	0	=	0

Optimal Tableau
(If $-10 + D \geqslant 0$)

Basic Variable	x_1	x_2	s_1	s_2		Value
s_1	2	0	1	-1	=	1,000
x_2	$\frac{1}{2}$	1	0	$\frac{1}{2}$	=	500
Z	$-10 + D$	0	0	30	=	30,000

The basic feasible solution is:

$$\text{basic variables} \begin{cases} s_1 = 1000 \\ x_2 = 500 \text{ electric typewriters} \end{cases} \text{ and } \text{nonbasic variables} \begin{cases} s_2 = 0 \\ x_1 = 0 \text{ manual typewriters} \end{cases}$$

and profit $= Z = \$30{,}000$.

The tableau above is optimal (a profit-maximizing solution) if $-10 + D \geqslant 0$ or $D \geqslant \$10$. That is, if the decrease in price is $10 or more, $D \geqslant \$10$, the solution above is optimal with $x_1 = 0$. If the decrease in price is less than $10, $D < \$10$, then $-10 + D < 0$ and it is optimal to bring x_1 into the basis with a positive value.

For example, if:

1. Price decrease $= D = \$8$, then $-10 + 8 = -2$ and x_1 enters the basis.
2. Price decrease $= D = \$12$, then $-10 + 12 = 2$ and $x_1 = 0$.

We now consider in a more systematic way the performing of postoptimality analysis using the National Business Machines model of Example 11.1.1 to illustrate each procedure. The model, initial tableau, and final optimal tableau for the NBM model are repeated for easy reference.

NBM MODEL

maximize $Z = 40x_1 + 60x_2 + 0s_1 + 0s_2$

subject to
$$3x_1 + 2x_2 + s_1 \qquad = 2000$$
$$1x_1 + 2x_2 + \qquad s_2 = 1000$$

$$x_1 \geqslant 0, \qquad x_2 \geqslant 0, \qquad s_1 \geqslant 0, \qquad s_2 \geqslant 0.$$

Initial Tableau

Basic Variable	x_1	x_2	s_1	s_2		Value
s_1	3	2	1	0	=	2000
s_2	1	2	0	1	=	1000
Z	-40	-60	0	0	=	0

**Final Optimal Tableau
(after two iterations)**

Basic Variable	x_1	x_2	s_1	s_2		Value
x_1	1	0	$\frac{1}{2}$	$-\frac{1}{2}$	=	500
x_2	0	1	$-\frac{1}{4}$	$\frac{3}{4}$	=	250
Z	0	0	5	25	=	35,000

OPTIMAL SOLUTION

maximum profit = maximum Z = \$35,000

basic variables: $x_1 = 500$, $x_2 = 250$

nonbasic variables: $s_1 = 0$, $s_2 = 0$

(s_1 and s_2 are slack variables.)

11.1.3. Example—Right-Hand-Side Postoptimality Analysis: NBM Model and Capacity Changes

Suppose in the NBM model of Example 11.1.1 that we increase the number of hours per month of O_1 time from 2000 hours to $2000 + I_1$ hours, where I_1 denotes the actual increase in O_1 capacity.

QUESTION. For what values of I_1 do we still produce both manual and electric typewriters at a positive level? That is, for what values of I_1 do x_1 and x_2 remain basic variables?

Answer. The NBM model with I_1 added to the 2000 hours of O_1 time is:

MODIFIED NBM MODEL

maximize $Z = 40x_1 + 60x_2 + 0 \quad s_1 + 0\,s_2 \quad + 0\,s_2$ (O)

subject to $\quad 3x_1 + \quad 2x_2 + \quad s_1 \quad\quad\quad = 2000 + I_1$ (a)

$\quad\quad\quad 1x_1 + \quad 2x_2 \quad\quad\quad + s_2 = 1000$ (b)

$\quad\quad\quad x_1 \geqslant 0, \quad x_2 \geqslant 0, \quad s_1 \geqslant 0, \quad s_2 \geqslant 0.$

The results of three simplex iterations applied to the modified NBM model are given in the three following tableaus.

Tableau 11.1.1. Initial Tableau

Basic Variable	x_1	x_2	s_1	s_2		Value	
s_1	3	2	1	0	=	$2000 + I_1$	(a)
s_2	1	2	0	1	=	1000	(b)
Z	−40	−60	0	0	=	0	

Tableau 11.1.2

Basic Variable	x_1	x_2	s_1	s_2		Value	
s_1	2	0	1	-1	$=$	$1000 + I_1$	(a')
x_2	$\frac{1}{2}$	1	0	$\frac{1}{2}$	$=$	500	(b')
Z	-10	0	0	30	$=$	30,000	

Tableau 11.1.3

Basic Variable	x_1	x_2	s_1	s_2		Value	
x_1	1	0	$\frac{1}{2}$	$-\frac{1}{2}$	$=$	$500 + \frac{1}{2}I_1$	(a'')
x_2	0	1	$-\frac{1}{4}$	$\frac{3}{4}$	$=$	$250 - \frac{1}{4}I_1$	(b'')
Z	0	0	5	25	$=$	$35,000 + 5I_1$	

Notice that the only difference between the last tableau and the final optimal tableau for the unmodified NBM is the value column as shown below.

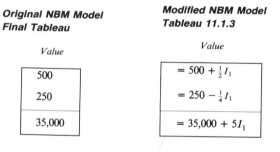

Since this is the only difference between the two tableaus, we conclude that the optimal value variables x_1 and x_2 remain in the basis with values

$$x_1 = 500 + \tfrac{1}{2}I_1$$

and

$$x_2 = 250 - \tfrac{1}{4}I_4$$

with maximum profit

$$Z = \$35,000 + 5I_1$$

provided that they remain feasible.

Note that the new value of x_1 is

$$x_1 = 500 + \tfrac{1}{2}I_1.$$

Thus, x_1 will remain feasible for positive I_1. However,

$$x_2 = 250 - \tfrac{1}{4}I_1.$$

Thus, x_2 will remain nonnegative provided that I_1 satisfies the restriction

$$250 - \tfrac{1}{4}I_1 \geqslant 0$$

or

$$(4)(250) \geqslant I_1$$

or

$$I_1 \leqslant 1000 \text{ hours.}$$

Thus, if the increase I_1 in O_1 hours available per month is less than 1000, then x_2 remains in the basis with a positive value. For example, if $I_1 = 600$ hours, then

$$x_2 = 250 - \tfrac{1}{4}(600)$$
$$= 250 - 150$$
$$= 100 \text{ electric typewriters}$$

and

$$x_1 = 500 + \tfrac{1}{2}I_1$$
$$= 500 + \tfrac{1}{2}(600)$$
$$= 800 \text{ manual typewriters.}$$

However, if $I = 1200$ hours (> 1000 hours), then

$$x_2 = 250 - \tfrac{1}{4}(1200)$$
$$= 250 - 300$$
$$= -50,$$

which is not feasible.

QUESTION. Do we need to compute all the tableaus, as done for the modified NBM problem, or can we use the original optimal NBM tableau to obtain the final modified tableau?

Answer. We can use the original optimal NBM tableau to obtain the final modified tableau.

Consider the s_1 and value columns of both tableaus:

Original Model: Final Tableau

s_1	Value
$\tfrac{1}{2}$	$= 500$
$-\tfrac{1}{4}$	$= 250$
5	35,000

Modified Model: Final Tableau

Value
$= 500 + \tfrac{1}{2}I_1$
$= 250 - \tfrac{1}{4}I_1$
$= 35,000 + 5I_1$

We see that in order to construct the value column for the modified model, we first multiply each item in the s_1 column of the original tableau by I_1. This yields

$$
\begin{array}{ccc}
s_1 & & \\
\frac{1}{2} & \times I_1 \quad = & \frac{1}{2}I_1 \\
-\frac{1}{4} & \times I_1 \quad = & -\frac{1}{4}I_1 \\
5 & \times I_1 \quad = & 5I_1 \\
\end{array}
$$

Then add the resulting column to the value column of the original tableau. This yields the modified value column shown below:

Modified Model

s_2		Value		Value
$\frac{1}{2}I_1$	+	500	=	$500 + \frac{1}{2}I_1$
$-\frac{1}{4}I_1$	+	250	=	$250 - \frac{1}{4}I_1$
$5I_1$	+	35,000	=	$35,000 + 5I_1$

QUESTION. Suppose that we increase the number of O_2 hours available each month from 1000 hours to $1000 + I_2$ hours. What is the largest value of I_2 allowed such that it is optimal for x_1 and x_2 to be positive?

Answer. Here we need the s_2 column and the value column in the final tableau of the original model. Performing a similar operation as done before for I_1 yields

Modified Model

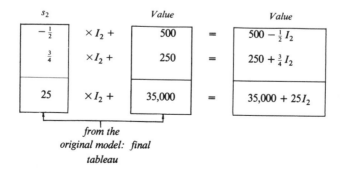

s_2		Value		Value
$-\frac{1}{2}$	$\times I_2 +$	500	=	$500 - \frac{1}{2}I_2$
$\frac{3}{4}$	$\times I_2 +$	250	=	$250 + \frac{3}{4}I_2$
25	$\times I_2 +$	35,000	=	$35,000 + 25I_2$

from the original model: final tableau

Thus, given an increase in O_2 in the amount I_2 yields

$$x_1 = 500 - \tfrac{1}{2}I_2$$

$$x_2 = 250 + \tfrac{3}{4}I_2$$

and

$$\text{profit} = Z = 35,000 + 25I_2.$$

We see that x_1 will remain nonnegative if $500 - \tfrac{1}{2}I_2 \geqslant 0$. That is, if $I_2 \leqslant (2)(500) = 1000$. x_2 will always remain positive for any positive increase I_2 since $x_2 = 250 + \tfrac{3}{4}I_2 > 0$ for $I_2 \geqslant 0$.

For example, if $I_2 = 500$ hours increase in O_2, then the optimal values of x_1 and x_2 are:

$$x_1 = 500 - \tfrac{1}{2}(500)$$

$$= 250 \text{ manual typewriters}$$

$$x_2 = 250 + \tfrac{3}{4}(500)$$

$$= 625 \text{ electric typewriters}$$

with

$$\text{profit} = Z = 35,000 + 25I_2$$

$$= 35,000 + 25(500)$$

$$= \$47,500,$$

an increase of $\$47,500 - \$35,000 = \$12,500$. If $I_2 = 1200$ hours, then

$$x_1 = 500 - \tfrac{1}{2}I_2$$

$$= -100,$$

which is not feasible.

GENERAL PROCEDURE. Let I_i be the increase in the right-hand side of the ith constraint. Then to determine the new modified value column, we perform the following operations. First, multiply each term in the s_i column of the original model's optimal tableau by I_i. Next add the resulting column to the value column of the original model's optimal tableau. This yields the following new modified value column. These operations are described below:

Modified Value		s_i		Original Value
$b_1 + a_1 I_i$	$=$	a_1	$\times I_i +$	b_1
$b_2 + a_2 I_i$	$=$	a_2	$\times I_i +$	b_2
$\vdots$	$\vdots$	$\vdots$		$\vdots$
$\vdots$	$\vdots$	$\vdots$		$\vdots$
$b_m + a_m I_i$	$=$	a_m	$\times I_i +$	b_m
$b + a I_i$		a	$\times I_i +$	b

11.1.4. Example—Right-Hand-Side
Postoptimality Analysis

Consider the following profit-maximization model.

ORIGINAL MODEL

maximize $Z = 20x_1 + 60x_2 + 0s_1 + 0s_2$

subject to
$$3x_1 + 2x_2 + s_1 \qquad = 2000 \quad \text{(hours of } O_1\text{)}$$
$$x_1 + 2x_2 + \qquad s_2 = 1000 \quad \text{(hours of } O_2\text{)}$$

$$x_1 \geqslant 0, \qquad x_2 \geqslant 0, \qquad s_1 \geqslant 0, \qquad s_2 \geqslant 0.$$

The optimal solution to the original model is given in the following final optimal simplex tableau.

Original Model: Final Tableau

Basic Variable	x_1	x_2	s_1	s_2		Value
s_1	2	0	1	-1	=	1,000
x_2	$\frac{1}{2}$	1	0	$\frac{1}{2}$	=	500
Z	10	0	0	30	=	30,000

The optimal solution is:

$$\text{maximum profit } Z = \$30,000,$$

the basic variables are s_1 and x_2 with $s_1 = 1000$ hours and $x_2 = 500$, and the nonbasic variables are x_1 and s_2 ($x_1 = 0$ and $s_2 = 0$).

QUESTION. Suppose that we increase the number of hours of O_1 by 500, $I_1 = 500$. How does the optimal solution change?

Answer. Note that we already have 1000 excess hours of O_1 in the optimal solution, $s_1 = 1000$. Thus, the optimal solution does not change. We can verify this conclusion by applying the right-hand-side postoptimality procedure with $I_1 = 1000$. We have

---

MODIFIED MODEL

maximize $Z = 20x_1 + 60x_2 + 0s_1 + 0s_2$

subject to

$$3x_1 + 2x_2 + s_1 \qquad = 3000 \quad (O_1)$$
$$x_1 + 2x_2 + s_2 \qquad = 1000 \quad (O_2)$$

$$x_1 \geqslant 0, \qquad x_2 \geqslant 0, \qquad s_1 \geqslant 0, \qquad s_2 \geqslant 0.$$

Original Model				*Modified Model*
s_1 Column		*Value Column*		*Value*
1	$\times\ 1000\ +$	1,000	$=$	2,000
0	$\times 1000\ +$	500	$=$	500
0	$\times 1000\ +$	30,000	$=$	30,000

Note that

$$s_1 = 2000 \qquad (s_1 = 1000 \text{ before})$$
$$x_1 = 500 \qquad (x_2 = 500 \text{ before})$$

The maximum profit = $30,000 (no change).

QUESTION. Suppose that we increase the number of O_2 hours available from 1000 to 2000, $I_2 = 1000$. How does this change the original optimal solution?

MODIFIED MODEL

maximize $Z = 20x_1 + 60x_2 + 0s_1 + 0s_2$

subject to

$$3x_1 + 2x_2 + s_1 \qquad = 1000 \quad (O_1)$$
$$x_1 + x_2 + \qquad s_2 = 2000 \quad (O_2)$$

$$x_1 \geqslant 0, \qquad x_2 \geqslant 0, \qquad s_1 \geqslant 0, \qquad s_2 \geqslant 0.$$

Original Model   **Modified Model**

s_2 Column		Value Column		Value
-1	$\times 1000 +$	1,000	$=$	0
$\frac{1}{2}$	$\times 1000 +$	500	$=$	1,000
30	$\times 1000 +$	30,000		60,000

Thus, for the new model we have $s_1 = 0$, $x_2 = 1000$, maximum (profit) $Z = \$60,000$, and $x_1 = 0$ and $s_2 = 0$.

11.1.5. Example—Postoptimality Analysis of the Unit Profits: NBM Price Changes

Consider the following profit-maximization model for NBM.

ORIGINAL MODEL

maximize $Z = 10x_1 + 60x_2 + 0s_1 + 0s_2$

subject to
$$3x_1 + 2x_2 + s_1 \qquad = 2000$$
$$x_1 + 2x_2 + \qquad s_2 = 1000$$

$$x_1 \geqslant 0, \quad x_2 \geqslant 0, \quad s_1 \geqslant 0, \quad s_2 \geqslant 0.$$

Note that the unit profits are \$10 and \$60 per unit for manual and electric typewriters, respectively.

The optimal simplex tableau for the original model is as follows:

Basic Variable	x_1	x_2	s_1	s_2		Value
s_1	2	0	1	-1	$=$	1,000
x_2	$\frac{1}{2}$	1	0	$\frac{1}{2}$	$=$	500
Z	20	0	0	30	$=$	30,000

The optimal solution given in the tableau above says

$$\text{produce } x_1 = 0 \text{ manual typewriters}$$
$$\text{produce } x_2 = 500 \text{ electric typewriters,}$$

which will yield a maximum of $Z = \$30,000$.

QUESTION. How much do we need to increase the unit profit of manual type-writers in order for NBM, as a profit maximizer, to start producing them at a positive level? Again, note that at a selling price of $\$10$, $x_1 = 0$. That is, x_1 is a nonbasic variable.

Answer. Let p_1 denote the increase in unit profit for a manual typewriter. This yields the following modified profit maximization model.

MODIFIED MODEL

maximize $Z = (10 + p_1)x_1 + 60x_2 + 0s_1 + 0s_2$

subject to

$$3x_1 + 2x_2 + s_1 \qquad\quad = 2000$$
$$x_1 + 2x_2 + \qquad\quad s_2 = 1000$$

$$x_1 \geqslant 0, \qquad x_2 \geqslant 0, \qquad s_1 \geqslant 0, \qquad s_2 \geqslant 0.$$

Applying the simplex method to the modified model yields the following optimal simplex tableau.

Modified Model: Optimal Tableau

Basic Variable	x_1	x_2	s_1	s_2		Value
s_1	2	0	1	-1	$=$	1,000
x_2	$\frac{1}{2}$	1	0	$\frac{1}{2}$	$=$	500
Z	$20 - p_1$	0	0	30	$=$	30,000

Note that the only difference between the original optimal tableau and the modified optimal tableau is the coefficient of x_1 in the profit function:

$$20 \text{ versus } 20 - p_1.$$

We see that if the increase in selling price p_1 is \$20 or more, then $20 - p_1 \leqslant 0$ in the modified model's optimal tableau and we can increase profit if x_1 has a positive value.

For example, if $p_1 = \$30$, then $20 - p_1 = 20 - 30 = -10$, and we can increase profit $= Z$ by letting x_1 be the entering variable. Note that this would result in s_1 becoming the leaving basic variable.

QUESTION. The unit profit of s_2, slack or excess O_2 time, in the original model is \$0. For what range of prices would it be optimal for s_2 to have a positive value?

Answer. The unit price of s_2 must increase from \$0 to \$30 or more since 30 is the coefficient of s_2 in the profit function Z in the optimal tableau. For example, if the contribution to profit of s_2 is \$40, then $\$30 - \$40 = -\$10$ would be the coefficient of s_2 in the profit function Z given in the final optimal simplex tableau. Thus, to increase profit s_2 would enter the basis at a positive value. Note that if s_2 is the entering basic variable, then x_2 becomes the leaving basic variable.

Next, consider changes (increases or decreases) in the selling prices for the basic variables in an optimal tableau. Consider again the original NBM model given below with its optimal tableau.

ORIGINAL MODEL

maximize $Z = 40x_1 + 60x_2 + 0s_1 + 0s_2$

subject to
$$3x_1 + 2x_2 + s_1 \qquad = 2000$$
$$x_1 + 2x_2 + \qquad s_2 = 1000$$

$$x_1 \geqslant 0, \quad x_2 \geqslant 0, \quad s_1 \geqslant 0, \quad s_2 \geqslant 0,$$

---

with

Original Model: Optimal Tableau

Basic Variable	x_1	x_2	s_1	s_2		Value
x_1	1	0	$\frac{1}{2}$	$-\frac{1}{2}$	=	500
x_2	0	1	$-\frac{1}{4}$	$\frac{3}{4}$	=	250
Z	0	0	5	25	=	35,000

Note that the unit contribution to profit of x_2 is \$60.

QUESTION. What is the *maximum* allowable *decrease* in x_2's unit profit such that the optimal basic solution does not change?

Answer. Let p_2 denote the amount of the decrease in the unit selling price of an electric typewriter. The modification of the original NBM model is given below.

MODIFIED MODEL

maximize $Z = 40x_1 + (60 - p_2)x_2 + 0s_1 + 0s_2$

subject to
$$3x_1 + 2x_2 + 1s_1 = 2000$$
$$x_1 + 2x_2 + 1s_2 = 1000$$

$$x_1 \geqslant 0, \quad x_2 \geqslant 0, \quad s_1 \geqslant 0, \quad s_2 \geqslant 0.$$

Tableau 11.1.1. Initial Tableau

Basic Variable	x_1	x_2	s_1	s_2		Value
s_1	3	2	1	0	=	2000
s_2	1	2	0	1	=	1000
Z	-40	$-60 + p_2$	0	0	=	0

Tableau 11.1.2

Basic Variable	x_1	x_2	s_1	s_2		Value
s_1	2	0	1	-1	=	1000
x_2	$\frac{1}{2}$	1	0	$\frac{1}{2}$	=	500
Z	$-10 - \frac{1}{2}p_2$	0	0	$30 - \frac{1}{2}p_2$	=	$30{,}000 - 500p_2$

Tableau 11.1.3. Final Optimal Tableau

Basic Variable	x_1	x_2	s_1	s_2		Value
x_1	1	0	$\frac{1}{2}$	$-\frac{1}{2}$	=	500
x_2	0	1	$-\frac{1}{4}$	$\frac{3}{4}$	=	250
Z	0	0	$5 + \frac{1}{4}p_2$	$25 - \frac{3}{4}p_2$	=	$35{,}000 - 250p_2$

Note that the solution given in Tableau 11.1.3 is optimal if the coefficients of the nonbasic variables, s_1 and s_2, in the profit function Z both have positive values. That is, the basic solution in Tableau 11.1.3 is optimal if

$$5 + \tfrac{1}{4}p_2 \geqslant 0 \qquad \text{(coefficient of } s_1)$$

$$25 - \tfrac{3}{4}p_2 \geqslant 0 \qquad \text{(coefficient of } s_2).$$

Since $p_2 \geqslant 0$, $5 + \tfrac{1}{4}p_2 > 0$ and s_1 will *never* enter the basis. But, $25 - \tfrac{3}{4}p_2$ may be negative. However, if the price decrease p_2 is at most \$100/3, then s_2 will never enter the basis with a positive value. That is, if

$$25 - \tfrac{3}{4}p_2 \geqslant 0$$

or

$$25 \geqslant \tfrac{3}{4}p_2$$

or

$$p_2 \leqslant \frac{4(25)}{3} = \frac{\$100}{3},$$

then the coefficient of s_2 in the profit function Z will be nonnegative, and therefore the basic solution in Tableau 11.1.3 will remain optimal.

11.1.6. Addition of New Products (or New Decision Variables)

NBM is considering the introduction of a third typewriter with an expected unit profit of \$45. To produce a complete new typewriter requires 2 hours of O_1 time and 3 hours of O_2. Let $x_3 =$ number of units of the new typewriter to produce monthly.

We have, in effect, $x_3 = 0$ in the previous NBM models. The new NBM model, with x_3 included in the profit function and constraints, is given below.

NEW MODEL

maximize $Z = 40x_1 + 60x_2 + 45x_3 + 0s_1 + 0s_2$

subject to
$$3x_1 + 2x_2 + 2x_3 + s_1 \qquad = 2000 \quad (O_1)$$
$$1x_1 + 2x_2 + 3x_3 + \qquad s_2 = 1000 \quad (O_2)$$

$$x_1 \geqslant 0, \quad x_2 \geqslant 0, \quad x_3 \geqslant 0, \quad s_1 \geqslant 0, \quad s_2 \geqslant 0.$$

Again, if we let $x_3 = 0$ in the new model above, then we have the original NBM model.

New Model: Initial Tableau

Basic Variable	Z	x_1	x_2	x_3	s_1	s_2		Value
s_1	0	3	2	2	1	0	=	2000
s_2	0	1	2	3	0	1	=	1000
Z	1	-40	-60	-45	0	0	=	0

New Model: Final Optimal Tableau

Basic Variable	Z	x_1	x_2	x_3	s_1	s_2		Value
x_1	0	1	0	$-\frac{1}{2}$	$\frac{1}{2}$	$-\frac{1}{2}$	=	500
x_2	0	0	1	$\frac{7}{4}$	$-\frac{1}{4}$	$\frac{3}{4}$	=	250
Z	1	0	0	40	5	25	=	35,000

Note in the final tableau that the coefficient of x_3 in the profit function Z is 40. Thus, profit $= Z$ would decrease $40 per unit increase in x_3.

Therefore, it is not desirable to enter x_3 into the basis.

11.2. LINEAR PROGRAMMING UNDER UNCERTAINTY

In linear programming models it is normal to assume that we have *perfect* knowledge about the value of all the parameters. However, as we have seen in studying postoptimality analysis, this is often not the case. Consider again the production problem of National Business Machines.

11.2.1. Example—National Business Machines

Recall that NBM produces two types of typewriters, manual and electric. NBM's monthly decisions are

x_1 = number of manual typewriters to produce monthly

x_2 = number of electric typewriters to produce monthly.

NBM's goal is profit maximization. To produce a complete typewriter requires assembling, testing, and packing time from two operations, O_1 and O_2, as given in the following production table.

NBM Production Table

Operation	HOURS REQUIRED		Hours Available Each Month
	Manual	Electric	
O_1	3	2	2000
O_2	1	2	1000

The unit profits are

$40 for a manual

and $60 for an electric typewriter.

NBM's monthly production decision problem is summarized by the following linear programming model:

NBM MODEL

maximize $Z = 40x_1 + 60x_2$

subject to $\quad 3x_1 + 2x_2 \leqslant 2000 \quad (O_1)$

$\quad\quad\quad\quad\quad x_1 + 2x_2 \leqslant 1000 \quad (O_2)$

$\quad\quad\quad\quad x_1 \geqslant 0, \quad x_2 \geqslant 0.$

The optimal solution to the NBM model is given in the following simplex tableau.

Basic Variable	x_1	x_2	s_1	s_2		Value
x_1	1	0	$\frac{1}{2}$	$-\frac{1}{2}$	$=$	500
x_2	0	1	$-\frac{1}{4}$	$\frac{3}{4}$	$=$	250
Z	0	0	5	25	$=$	35,000

Thus, the optimal monthly plan is to produce

$x_1 = 500$ manual typewriters

and $x_2 = 250$ electric typewriters,

yielding a total contribution to profit $Z = \$35,000$.

PROBLEM. NBM is uncertain as to the exact unit profits they will receive from selling typewriters. In fact, if we let

$$c_1 = \text{unit profit for a manual typewriter}$$

and $\quad c_2 = \text{unit profit for an electric typewriter,}$

then the accounting department at NBM believes that any one of the following pairs of profits given in the following table are possible.

Unit Profits

c_1	c_2
$20	$60
40	60
40	30

That is,

$$c_1 = \$20 \text{ or } \$40 \text{ for a manual typewriter}$$

and $\quad c_2 = \$30 \text{ or } \$60 \text{ for an electric typewriter.}$

Note that NBM has ruled out the possibility of prices $c_1 = \$20$ and $c_2 = \$30$ both occurring in any month.

QUESTION. Given these different unit profits, what should be the optimal monthly production plan?

Answer. Let $Z(c_1, c_2) = c_1 x_1 + c_2 x_2$ denote the total profit from producing at levels x_1 and x_2 with unit profits $\$c_1$ and $\$c_2$, respectively. Then we know that either

$$Z(20, 60) = 20x_1 + 60x_2$$

or $\quad\quad\quad\quad\quad Z(40, 60) = 40x_1 + 60x_2$

or $\quad\quad\quad\quad\quad Z(40, 30) = 40x_1 + 30x_2$

will be the profit function for NBM in any given month.

Consider the following three different linear programming models:

NBM MODEL 1

maximize $Z(20, 60) = 20x_1 + 60x_2$

subject to $\quad\quad\quad\quad 3x_1 + 2x_2 \leqslant 2000$

$\quad\quad\quad\quad\quad\quad\quad\quad\; x_1 + 2x_2 \leqslant 1000$

$\quad\quad\quad\quad x_1 \geqslant 0, \quad\quad x_2 \geqslant 0.$

```
┌─────────────────────────────────────────────────────┐
│                    NBM MODEL 2                        │
│                                                       │
│   maximize Z(40, 60) = 40x₁ + 60x₂                    │
│                                                       │
│   subject to              3x₁ + 2x₂ ≤ 2000            │
│                            x₁ + 2x₂ ≤ 1000            │
│                                                       │
│              x₁ ≥ 0,     x₂ ≥ 0.                      │
└─────────────────────────────────────────────────────┘
```

$$\text{maximize } Z(40, 60) = 40x_1 + 60x_2$$

subject to

$$3x_1 + 2x_2 \leq 2000$$
$$x_1 + 2x_2 \leq 1000$$
$$x_1 \geq 0, \quad x_2 \geq 0.$$

NBM MODEL 3

$$\text{maximize } Z(40, 30) = 40x_1 + 30x_2$$

subject to

$$3x_1 + 2x_2 \leq 2000$$
$$x_1 + 2x_2 \leq 1000$$
$$x_1 \geq 0, \quad x_2 \geq 0.$$

Note that the three models differ only in the form of their profit functions. Solving each of the three models above, by the simplex method, yields the following optimal solution.

Model Number	UNIT PROFIT c_1	c_2	Maximum Profit $Z(c_1, c_2)$	OPTIMAL MONTHLY PRODUCTION LEVELS x_1	x_2
1	$20	$60	$30,000	0	500
2	40	60	35,000	500	250
3	40	30	$26,666\frac{2}{3}$	$666\frac{2}{3}$	0

Which pair of production levels should NBM choose? That is, which model—1, 2, or 3—is the true model for next month? To answer this question, we need to decide on a suitable selection criterion.

Criterion 1 *Optimistic Criterion.* The optimistic criterion assumes that the unit profits that actually occur will be such that the largest maximum profit is obtained. We note from the table that the highest profit is $35,000. Thus, using the optimistic criterion, NBM will choose

$$x_1 = 500$$

and

$$x_2 = 250.$$

Note that NBM in this case is assuming $c_1 = \$40$ and $c_2 = \$60$ are the true prices

Criterion 2 *Pessimistic Criterion.* Note from the table that NBM expects to receive at least $26,666\frac{2}{3}$ to at most $35,000 depending upon the true (but unknown) unit profits c_1 and c_2. Using a pessimistic criterion, NBM will choose

$$x_1 = 666\tfrac{2}{3} \quad \text{and} \quad x_2 = 0$$

since they expect a profit of $26,666\frac{2}{3}$.

PROBLEM. NBM has the following additional information concerning the likelihood of certain unit profits occurring.

UNIT PROFIT		Probability
c_1	c_2	of Occurence
$20	$60	$\frac{1}{5}$
40	60	$\frac{3}{5}$
40	30	$\frac{1}{5}$
		$\overline{1.0}$

That is, NBM's total profit function will be, for given feasible production levels x_1 and x_2,

$$Z(20, 60) = 20x_1 + 60x_2 \text{ with probability } \tfrac{1}{5}$$

$$Z(40, 60) = 40x_1 + 60x_2 \text{ with probability } \tfrac{3}{5}$$

$$Z(40, 30) = 40x_1 + 30x_2 \text{ with probability } \tfrac{1}{5}.$$

Using the additional information of probability of occurrence, what should be NBM's optimal monthly production plan?

Solution. Again we need a selection criterion. We can use what is called the *expected profit criterion.* That is, we use as our objective function $E(Z)$, where $E(Z)$ is calculated as follows.

$$Z(20, 60) \times \tfrac{1}{5} = (20x_1 + 60x_2) \times \tfrac{1}{5} = 4x_1 + 12x_2$$

$$Z(40, 60) \times \tfrac{3}{5} = (40x_1 + 60x_2) \times \tfrac{3}{5} = 24x_1 + 36x_2$$

$$Z(40, 30) \times \tfrac{1}{5} = (40x_1 + 30x_2) \times \tfrac{1}{5} = 8x_1 + 6x_2$$

$$E(Z) = \overline{36x_1 + 54x_2}$$

Next, solve the following linear programming model.

> ## NBM EXPECTED PROFIT MODEL
>
> maximize $E(Z) = 36x_1 + 54x_2$
>
> subject to
> $$3x_1 + 2x_2 \leqslant 2000$$
> $$x_1 + 2x_2 \leqslant 1000$$
>
> $$x_1 \geqslant 0, \qquad x_2 \geqslant 0.$$

Note that the NBM expected profit model above differs only in the form of the profit function when compared to the previous NBM models.

Applying the simplex method to the NBM expected profit model yields the following optimal solution:

$$x_1 = 500 \quad \text{and} \quad x_2 = 250$$

with an expected profit of

$$\begin{aligned} E(Z) &= 36x_1 + 54x_2 \\ &= 36(500) + 54(250) \\ &= \$31{,}500. \end{aligned}$$

PROBLEM. Assume that NBM will have perfect information for each of the next 10 months concerning the values of c_1 and c_2. That is, NBM will know *with certainty* that

$$c_1 = \$20 \quad \text{and} \quad c_2 = \$60 \text{ for 2 out of the next 10 months}$$
$$c_2 = \$40 \quad \text{and} \quad c_2 = \$60 \text{ for 6 out of the next 10 months}$$
and
$$c_1 = \$40 \quad \text{and} \quad c_2 = \$30 \text{ for 2 out of the next 10 months.}$$

Furthermore, they will know the true values of c_1 and c_2 for any month at the beginning of that month prior to making any production decision. What is the average maximum profit for NBM over the next 10 months?

Solution   AMP = average maximum profit

$$= \underset{(model\ 1)}{\$30{,}000 \times \tfrac{1}{5}} + \underset{(model\ 2)}{\$35{,}000 \times \tfrac{3}{5}} + \underset{(model\ 3)}{\left(\$26{,}666\tfrac{2}{3}\right) \times \tfrac{1}{5}}$$

$$= \$32{,}333\tfrac{1}{3}.$$

Note that NBM will use model 1 $\tfrac{1}{5}$ or 20% of the time, model 2 $\tfrac{3}{5}$ or 60% of the time, and model 3 $\tfrac{1}{5}$ or 20% of the time yielding an average, over the next 10 months, maximum profit of $\$32{,}333\tfrac{1}{3}$.

Also note that average maximum profit under perfect information minus expected maximum profit

$$= \text{AMP} - E(Z)$$

$$= \$32{,}333\tfrac{1}{3} - \$31{,}500$$

$$= \$833\tfrac{1}{3}.$$

$\text{AMP} - E(Z) = \$833\tfrac{1}{3}$ is called the *expected value of perfect information.*

Recall that NBM has the following information concerning expected future unit profits for their product line.

UNIT PROFIT		Prior
c_1	c_2	Probabilities
$20	$60	$\frac{1}{5}$
40	60	$\frac{3}{5}$
40	30	$\frac{1}{5}$
		$\overline{1.00}$

That is,

$$P(c_1 = \$20,\ c_2 = \$60) = \tfrac{1}{5}$$

$$P(c_1 = \$40,\ c_2 = \$60) = \tfrac{3}{5}$$

$$P(c_1 = \$40,\ c_2 = \$30) = \tfrac{1}{5}$$

$$\overline{1.00}$$

are *prior* estimates of what NBM expects unit profits to be in the future. NBM conducts quarterly test market surveys on their product lines in order to determine expected sales as well as expected unit profits. The following table summarizes the results of all their past surveys concerning expected *future unit profits*.

Joint Probability Table (unit profits in following month)

Market Survey Outcomes	$c_1 = \$20, c_2 = \$60$	$c_1 = \$40, c_2 = \$60$	$c_1 = \$40, c_2 = \$30$	Marginal Probabilities
Good sales (G)	0.1	0.2	0.1	0.4
Average sales (A)	0.1	0.4	0.1	0.6
Marginal probabilities	0.2	0.6	0.2	1.0

We note from the following joint probability table that the marginal probabilities are:

MARGINAL PROBABILITIES

(1) P(survey indicates good sales)
  $= P(G) = 0.1 + 0.2 + 0.1 = 0.4.$
  P(survey indicates average sales)
  $= P(A) = 0.1 + 0.4 + 0.1 = 0.6.$

(2) P(unit profits are \$20 and \$60)
  $= P(c_1 = \$20, c_2 = \$60) = 0.1 + 0.1 = 0.2.$
  Similarly
    $P(c_1 = \$40, c_2 = \$60) = 0.2 + 0.4 = 0.6.$
    $P(c_1 = \$40, c_2 = \$30) = 0.1 + 0.1 = 0.2.$

Also,

SOME CONDITIONAL PROBABILITIES

(3) P(survey indicated good sales in previous period
  given actual unit profits of $c_1 = \$20$
  and $c_2 = \$60$ in subsequent period)
  $= P(G|c_1 = \$20, c_2 = \$60)$
  $= \dfrac{0.1}{0.2} = \dfrac{1}{2}$
  and $P(A|c_1 = \$20, c_2 = \$60) = \dfrac{0.1}{0.2} = \dfrac{1}{2}.$

The following table gives the conditional probability predictions of G or A given the unit profits.

Conditional Probability Prediction of Market Survey Outcome In Previous Month Given the Actual Unit Profits c_1 and c_2 In Subsequent Month

Market Survey Outcome	$c_1 = \$20, c_2 = \$60$	$c_1 = \$40, c_2 = \$60$	$c_1 = \$40, c_2 = \$30$
Good sales (G)	$\frac{1}{2}$	$\frac{1}{3}$	$\frac{1}{2}$
Average sales (A)	$\frac{1}{2}$	$\frac{2}{3}$	$\frac{1}{2}$
	$\overline{1.0}$	$\overline{1.0}$	$\overline{1.0}$

QUESTION. Assume that NBM has just completed a market survey that yields a prediction that typewriter sales will be average (A) next month. What should be NBM's optimal monthly production plan for next month?

Answer. We expect, based on the market survey results, that next month's sales will be average or A.

Thus, we need to compute, using Bayes' formula, the following probabilities

(1) $P(c_1 = \$20, c_2 = \$60|A)$

(2) $P(c_1 = \$40, c_2 = \$60|A)$

(3) $P(c_1 = \$40, c_2 = \$30|A).$

Now (1) is:

$$P(c_1 = \$20, c_2 = \$60|A) = \frac{P(A|c_1 = \$20, c_2 = \$60)P(c_1 = \$20, c_2 = \$60)}{P(A)}$$

$$= \frac{\frac{1}{2} \times \frac{1}{5}}{\frac{3}{5}} = \frac{1}{6}.$$

(2):

$$P(c_1 = \$40, c_2 = \$60|A) = \frac{P(A|c_1 = \$40, c_2 = \$60)P(c_1 = \$40, c_2 = \$60)}{P(A)}$$

$$= \frac{\frac{2}{3} \times \frac{3}{5}}{\frac{3}{5}} = \frac{2}{3}$$

(3):

$$P(c_1 = \$40, c_2 = \$30|A) = \frac{P(A|c_1 = \$40, c_2 = \$30)P(c_1 = \$40, c_2 = \$30)}{P(A)}$$

$$= \frac{\frac{1}{2} \times \frac{1}{5}}{\frac{3}{5}} = \frac{1}{6}.$$

The expected profit function *given* the survey outcome A is

$$E(Z \text{ given } A) = (20x_1 + 60x_2) \times P(c_1 = 20, c_2 = 60|A)$$
$$\left(\tfrac{1}{6}\right)$$
$$+ (40x_1 + 60x_2) \times P(c_1 = 40, c_2 = 60|A)$$
$$\left(\tfrac{2}{3}\right)$$
$$+ (40x_1 + 30x_2) \times P(c_1 = 40, c_2 = 30|A)$$
$$\left(\tfrac{1}{6}\right)$$
$$= \left(20 \times \tfrac{1}{6} + 40 \times \tfrac{2}{3} + 40 \times \tfrac{1}{6}\right)x_1$$
$$+ \left(60 \times \tfrac{1}{6} + 60 \times \tfrac{2}{3} + 30 \times \tfrac{1}{6}\right)x_2$$
$$= 36\tfrac{2}{3}x_1 + 55x_2.$$

Thus, we need to solve

NBM EXPECTED PROFIT MODEL (GIVEN OUTCOME A)

maximize $E(Z \text{ given } A) = 36\frac{2}{3}x_1 + 55x_2$

subject to
$$3x_1 + 2x_2 \leqslant 2000$$
$$x_1 + 2x_2 \leqslant 1000$$

$$x_1 \geqslant 0, \qquad x_2 \geqslant 0.$$

The optimal solution is

$$x_1 = 500, \qquad x_2 = 250$$

with a maximum expected profit of

$$Z = \$32,083\tfrac{1}{3}.$$

11.1.2. Uncertainty in the Right-Hand Sides

Again consider the NBM model with uncertainty as to the actual values of the production capacities: O_1 and O_2. We initially assumed that

2000 hours of O_1 is available monthly

1000 hours of O_2 is available monthly

and then solved the following problem

NBM MODEL

maximize $Z = 40x_1 + 60x_2$

subject to
$$3x_1 + 2x_2 \leqslant 2000 \quad (O_1)$$
$$x_1 + 2x_2 \leqslant 1000 \quad (O_2)$$

$$x_1 \geqslant 0, \qquad x_2 \geqslant 0.$$

---

yielding the optimal solution

$$x_1 = 500, \qquad x_2 = 250, \qquad \text{profit} = Z = \$35,000.$$

However, the true situation is that O_1 and O_2 vary from month to month as shown below.

Variations in Monthly Capacity

O_1:   1900 hours to 2100 hours
O_2:   800 hours to 1200 hours.

Consider the medians and extremes of O_1 and O_2 as listed in the following table.

O_1	O_2	*Model Number*
1900	800	1
1900	1000	2
1900	1200	3
2000	800	4
2000	1000	5
2000	1200	6
2100	800	7
2100	1000	8
2100	1200	9

To determine an optimal production plan for NBM, we first solve each of the following nine models using the simplex method.

NBM MODEL 1

maximize $Z(1900, 800) = 40x_1 + 60x_2$

subject to
$$3x_1 + 2x_2 \leqslant 1900$$
$$x_1 + 2x_2 \leqslant 800$$

$$x_1 \geqslant 0, \qquad x_2 \geqslant 0.$$

NBM MODEL 2

maximize $Z(1900, 1000) = 40x_1 + 60x_2$

subject to
$$3x_1 + 2x_2 \leqslant 1900$$
$$x_1 + 2x_2 \leqslant 1000$$

$$x_1 \geqslant 0, \qquad x_2 \geqslant 0.$$

$\vdots$

NBM MODEL 9

maximize $Z(2100, 1200) = 40x_1 + 60x_2$

subject to
$$3x_1 + 2x_2 \leqslant 2100$$
$$x_1 + 2x_2 \leqslant 1200$$

$$x_1 \geqslant 0, \qquad x_2 \geqslant 0.$$

The optimal solution for each model is given below.

Model Number	VALUES OF O_1	VALUES OF O_2	Maximum Profit Z	OPTIMAL x_1	OPTIMAL x_2
1	1900	800	$29,500	550	125
2	1900	1000	34,500	450	275
3	1900	1200	30,500	350	425
4	2000	800	30,000	600	100
5	2000	1000	35,000	500	250
6	2000	1200	42,000	400	400
7	2100	800	30,500	650	75
8	2100	1000	35,000	550	225
9	2100	1200	40,500	450	375

QUESTION. Which production plan in the table above should NBM use?

Answer. Notice in the table that the smallest maximum profit is $29,500 when we choose $x_1 = 550$ and $x_2 = 125$. Of course, this is assuming that the minimum number of hours of O_1 and O_2 occur—1900 hours of O_1 and 800 hours of O_2.

The largest maximum profit is $42,000 by choosing $x_1 = 400$ and $x_2 = 400$. This assumes that there will be 2000 hours of O_1 available and 1200 hours of O_2 available next month.

We see from the previous table that NBM can lose sales and hence profit by choosing production levels that are too low. Also, NBM can expect losses from choosing production levels that are too high and being required to purchase additional hours (overtime) of O_1 and O_2.

Thus, using the *pessimistic criterion*, NBM's optimal plan is $x_1 = 550$, $x_2 = 125$, yielding a profit of $29,500.

Using the *optimistic criterion*, NBM's optimal plan is $x_1 = 400$, $x_2 = 400$, yielding a profit of $42,000.

REFERENCES BIERMAN, H., C. P. BONINI, and W. H. HAUSMAN. *Quantitative Analysis for Business Decisions*, 4th ed. Homewood, Ill.: Richard D. Irwin, Inc., 1973.

DAELLENBACH, H. G., and E. J. BELL. *User's Guide to Linear Programming*. Englewood Cliffs, N.J.: Prentice-Hall, Inc., 1970.

DANTZIG, G. B., *Linear Programming and Extensions.* Princeton, NJ.: Princeton University Press, 1963.

DRIEBEEK, N. J. *Applied Linear Programming.* Reading, Mass.: Addison-Wesley Publishing Co., Inc.,1969.

HILLIER, F. S., and G. J. LIEBERMAN. *Introduction to Operations Research*, 2nd ed. San Francisco: Holden-Day, Inc., 1974.

HOROWITZ, I. *An Introduction to Quantitative Business Analysis*, 2nd ed. New York: McGraw-Hill Book Company, 1972.

KIM, C. *Introduction to Linear Programming.* New York: Holt, Rinehart and Winston, Inc., 1972.

KWAK, N. K. *Mathematical Programming with Business Applications.* New York: McGraw-Hill Book Company, 1973.

LAPIN, L. *Quantitative Methods for Business Decisions.* New York: Harcourt Brace Jovanovich, Inc., 1976.

LEVIN, R., and C. KIRKPATRICK. *Quantitative Approaches to Management*, 3rd ed. New York: McGraw-Hill Book Company, 1975.

SHAMBLIN, J. E., and G. T. STEVENS, JR. *Operations Research—A Fundamental Approach.* New York: McGraw-Hill Book Company, 1974.

SIMMONS, D. M. *Linear Programming for Operations Research.* San Francisco: Holden-Day, Inc., 1972.

STRUM, J. E. *Introduction to Linear Programming.* San Francisco: Holden-Day, Inc., 1972.

TAHA, H. A. *Operations Research: An Introduction.* New York: Macmillan Publishing Co., Inc., 1971.

WAGNER, H. M. *Principles of Operations Research with Applications to Managerial Decisions.* Englewood Cliffs, N.J.: Prentice-Hall, Inc., 1975.

KEY CONCEPTS

Sensitivity analysis	Optimistic criterion
Linear programming under uncertainty	Expected profit criterion
	Expected value of perfect
Pessimistic criterion	information

REVIEW PROBLEMS

11.1. Consider the following product mix problem. Let

x_1 = number of units of product 1 to produce

x_2 = number of units of product 2 to produce daily.

The production of both products requires processing time in two departments, D_1 and D_2. The hourly capacities of D_1 and D_2, unit profits for products 1 and 2, and processing time requirements in D_1 and D_2 are given in the following production table.

	PRODUCT		
Department	1	2	Capacity (hours)
D_1	1	2	32
D_2	0	1	8
	$200	$300	

Thus, to build 1 complete unit of product 1 requires 1 hour in D_1 and 0 hours in D_2. To build 1 complete unit of product 2 requires 2 hours in D_1 and 1 hour in D_2.

The solution to the following programming model determines the optimal product mix.

PRIMAL MODEL

maximize $Z = 200x_1 + 300x_2$

subject to

$$1x_1 + 2x_2 \leqslant 32 \quad (D_1)$$
$$0x_1 + 1x_2 \leqslant 8 \quad (D_2)$$

$$x_1 \geqslant 0, \qquad x_2 \geqslant 0.$$

The optimal solution to this primal model is given in the following tableau.

Basic Variable	Z	x_1	x_2	S_1	S_2		Value
x_1	0	1	2	1	0	=	32
S_2	0	0	1	0	1	=	8
Z	1	0	100	200	0	=	6400

Optimal Solution $x_1 = 32$ units $x_2 = 0$ units
         $S_2 = 8$ hours $S_1 = 0$ hours.

The profit = Z = $6400.

How much must the unit profit of product 2 increase in order for x_2 to have a positive value?

11.2. Consider the profit-maximization problem given in question 11.1.

maximize $Z = 200x_1 + 300x_2$

subject to

$$1x_1 + ②x_2 \leqslant 32 \quad (D_1)$$
$$0x_1 + 1x_2 \leqslant 8 \quad (D_2)$$

$$x_1 \geqslant 0, \qquad x_2 \geqslant 0.$$

Recall that the optimal solution is

$$x_1 = 32 \text{ units} \qquad S_1 = 0 \text{ hours}$$
$$x_2 = 0 \text{ units} \qquad S_2 = 8 \text{ hours},$$
$$\text{so } Z = \$64,000.$$

Note that the number 2 circled in the D_1 constraint is the number of hours of D_1 time required to process 1 unit of product 2. How much must this time decrease in order for it to be profitable for x_2 to have a positive value?

11.3. Consider the product mix problem given in Problem 11.2. Now the firm is considering the addition of a new product, called product 3, to its line. Product 3 requires 1 hour of D_1 time and 1 hour of D_2 time. What must be product 3's unit profit in order for the firm to profitably add it to its product line?

11.4. Consider the following linear programming problem:

$$\text{maximize } Z = 1x_1 + 3x_2$$

$$\text{subject to} \qquad 1x_1 + 6x_2 \leqslant 18$$
$$1x_1 \qquad \leqslant 6.$$

The optimal solution is given in the following Tableau.

Basic Variable	Z	x_1	x_2	S_1	S_2		Value
x_2	0	0	1	$\frac{1}{6}$	$-\frac{1}{6}$	=	2
x_1	0	1	0	0	1	=	6
Z	1	0	0	$\frac{1}{2}$	$\frac{1}{2}$	=	12

Thus, optimal solution is

$$x_2 = 2 \qquad \text{nonbasic} \quad \begin{cases} S_1 = 0 \\ S_2 = 0. \end{cases}$$
$$x_1 = 6 \qquad \text{variables}$$

Now the firm achieves a maximin profit of $Z = \$12$ provided that $b = 18$ in the first constraint. However, there is considerable uncertainty concerning the true value of b.

POSSIBLE VALUES OF b

$$b = 6$$
$$b = 12$$
$$b = 18.$$

Determine an optimal solution for both the pessimistic and optimistic criteria. Using the following additional information, determine the maximum expected profit and the expected value of perfect information.

Additional Information

Value	Probability
$b = 6$	$P(b = 6) = \frac{1}{3}$
$b = 12$	$P(b = 12) = \frac{1}{3}$
$b = 18$	$P(b = 18) = \frac{1}{3}$
	$\overline{1.0}$

ANSWERS TO REVIEW PROBLEMS

11.1. Let p_2 denote the increase in the unit profit received from selling product 2. Then we have the following revised profit maximization problem.

REVISED PRIMAL MODEL

maximize $Z = 200x_1 + (300 + p_2)x_2$

subject to
$$1x_1 + 2x_2 \leqslant 32$$
$$0x_1 + 1x_2 \leqslant 8$$
$$x_1 \geqslant 0, \quad x_2 \geqslant 0.$$

The initial tableau and final tableau for the revised model are given below.

Initial Tableau

Basic Variable	Z	x_1	x_2	S_1	S_2		
S_1	0	1	2	1	0	=	32
S_2	0	0	1	0	1	=	8
Z	1	-200	$-300 - p_2$	0	0	=	0

Final Tableau

Basic Variable	Z	x_1	x_2	S_1	S_2		Value
x_1	0	1	0	1	0	=	32
S_2	0	0	1	0	1	=	8
Z	1	0	$100 - p_2$	200	0	=	6400

Note that the coefficient of x_2 (a nonbasic variable) in the profit function Z is $100 - p_2$, where p_2 is to be our price increase for product 2. Thus, for it to be profitable that x_2 have a positive value, $100 - p_2$ must be negative. $100 - p_2$ will be negative if $p_2 > \$100$. For example, let $p_2 = \$125$. Then $100 = p_2 = 100 - 125 = -25$, and it is profitable to bring x_2 into the basis. Note in the final tableau that if x_2 is the entering basic variable, S_2 becomes the leaving basic variable.

11.2. Let D denote the amount of decrease in hours to process 1 unit of product 2 in D_1. This change yields the following revised profit-maximization problem.

$$\text{maximize } Z = 200x_1 + 300x_2$$

$$\text{subject to} \qquad 1x_1 + (2 - D)x_2 \leqslant 32 \qquad (D_1)$$

$$0x_1 + 1x_2 \leqslant 8 \qquad (D_2)$$

$$x_1 \geqslant 0, \qquad x_2 \geqslant 0.$$

The initial and final tableaus for the revised problem are given below.

Initial Tableau

Basic Variable	Z	x_1	x_2	S_1	S_2		Value
S_1	0	1	$2 - D$	1	0	=	32
S_2	0	0	1	0	1	=	8
Z	1	-200	-300	0	0	=	0

Final Tableau

Basic Variable	Z	x_1	x_2	S_1	S_2		Value
x_1	0	1	$2 - D$	1	0	=	32
S_2	0	0	1	0	1	=	8
Z	1	0	$100 - 200D$	200	0	=	6400

Note that the coefficient of x_2 in the profit function Z is $100 - 200D$. Thus, it is profitable for x_2 to have a positive value if $100 - 200D$ is negative.

Now $100 - 200D$ is negative provided that $D > \frac{1}{2}$. Thus, if the unit processing time D_2 required for product 2 decreases by at least $\frac{1}{2}$ hour, then it is profitable for x_2 to have a positive value.

11.3. Let x_3 denote the number of units of product 3 to produce. Let p_3 be the unit profit associated with product 3. This yields the following revised profit-maximization problem.

$$\text{maximize } Z = 200x_1 + 300x_2 + p_3x_3$$

$$\text{subject to} \quad 1x_1 + 2x_2 + 1x_3 \leqslant 32$$

$$0x_1 + 1x_2 + 1x_3 \leqslant 8$$

$$x_1 \geqslant 0, \quad x_2 \geqslant 0, \quad x_3 \geqslant 0.$$

The initial and final optimal tableau for the revised model are given below.

Initial Tableau

Basic Variable	Z	x_1	x_2	x_3	S_1	S_2		Value
S_1	0	1	2	1	1	0	=	32
S_2	0	0	1	1	0	1	=	8
Z	1	-200	-300	$-p_3$	0	0	=	0

Final Tableau

Basic Variable	Z	x_1	x_2	x_3	S_1	S_2		Value
x_1	0	1	2	1	1	2	=	32
S_2	0	0	1	①	0	1	=	8
Z	1	0	100	$200 - p_3$	200		=	6400

Note that the coefficient of x_3 in the profit function is $200 - p_3$. Thus, it is profitable for x_3 to have a positive value only if the price p_3 exceeds \$200. For example, if $p_3 = \$250$, then $200 - p_3 = -50$, then profit $= Z$ will increase \$50 if x_3 has the value $+1$. Note in the final tableau that if x_3 is the entering basic variable, then s_2 becomes the leaving basic variable.

11.4. The optimal solutions to the following three models are given in the table at the foot of page 420.

MODEL 1

$$Z(b = 6) = 1x_1 + 3x_2$$

subject to

$$1x_1 + 6x_2 \leqslant 6 = b$$
$$1x_1 \qquad \leqslant 6$$

$$x_1 \geqslant 0, \qquad x_2 \geqslant 0.$$

MODEL 2

$$Z(b = 12) = 1x_1 + 3x_2$$

$$1x_1 + 6x_2 \leqslant 12 = b$$
$$1x_1 \qquad \leqslant 6$$

$$x_1 \geqslant 0, \qquad x_2 \geqslant 0.$$

MODEL 3

$$Z(b = 18) = 1x_1 + 3x_2$$

$$1x_1 + 6x_2 \leqslant 18 = b$$
$$1x_1 \qquad \leqslant 6$$

$$x_1 \geqslant 0, \qquad x_2 \geqslant 0.$$

Optimal Solution

$(b = 6)$	$(b = 12)$	$(b = 18)$
Model 1	*Model 2*	*Model 3*
$x_1 = 6$	$x_1 = 6$	$x_1 = 6$
$x_2 = 0$	$x_2 = 1$	$x_2 = 2$
$Z(6) = \$6$	$Z(12) = \$9$	$Z(18) = \$12$
$S_1 = 0$	$S_1 = 0$	$S_1 = 0$
$S_2 = 0$	$S_2 = 0$	$S_2 = 0$

Pessimistic Criterion (b = 6 occurs). The optimal decision is:

$$x_1 = 6, \quad x_2 = 0 \quad \text{with } Z(6) = \$6.$$

Optimistic Criterion (b = 18 occurs). The optimal decision is:

$$x_1 = 6, \quad x_2 = 2 \quad \text{with } Z(18) = \$12.$$

Expected Value Criterion. Replace b in the original model with $E(b)$, where

$$E(b) = 6\left(\tfrac{1}{3}\right) + 9\left(\tfrac{1}{3}\right) + 12\left(\tfrac{1}{3}\right)$$
$$= 9.$$

Thus, model 2 applies, yielding

$$x_1 = 6, \quad x_2 = 1, \quad Z(12) = \$9.$$

Average Maximum Profit Under Perfect Information.

$$Z(b = 6)\left(\tfrac{1}{3}\right) + Z(b = 12)\left(\tfrac{1}{3}\right) + Z(b = 18)\left(\tfrac{1}{3}\right)$$

$$= \quad \$6\left(\tfrac{1}{3}\right) \quad + \quad \$9\left(\tfrac{1}{3}\right) \quad + \quad \$12\left(\tfrac{1}{3}\right)$$

$$= \quad \$9.$$

expected value of perfect information $= \$9 - \$9 = \$0.$

EXERCISES

POSTOPTIMALITY ANALYSIS **11.1.** Plot the following constraints showing each corner point:

$$\text{machine time:} \quad 3x_1 + 7x_2 \leqslant 21 \text{ hours}$$

$$\text{labor:} \quad 5x_1 + 15x_2 \leqslant 60 \text{ hours.}$$

(a) Assume that the profitability x_1 is \$50, and the profitability of x_2 is \$70. What is the optimal corner point?

(b) What will be the product mix at the next best corner point?

(c) Now, what range of profits for x_2 would suggest that a move to the next best corner point would be optimal?

POSTOPTIMALITY ANALYSIS **11.2.** The Kansas Company manufactures three products p_1, p_2, and p_3. Each product requires two raw materials—steel and aluminum. Management desires production levels x_1, x_2, and x_3 for p_1, p_2, and p_3, which maximize total profit.

The following linear programming model describes the Kansas Company's production problem.

$$\text{maximize} \quad Z = 30x_1 + 10x_2 + 50x_3$$

$$\text{subject to} \quad 6x_1 + 3x_2 + 5x_3 \leqslant 450 \quad \text{(steel)}$$

$$3x_1 + 4x_2 + 5x_3 \leqslant 300 \quad \text{(aluminum)}$$

$$x_1 \geqslant 0, \quad x_2 \geqslant 0, \quad x_3 \geqslant 0.$$

The optimal production plan is given in the following tableau.

Basic Variable	Z	x_1	x_2	x_3	S_1	S_2		Value
S_1	0	3	-1	0	1	-1	=	150
x_3	0	$\frac{3}{5}$	$\frac{4}{5}$	1	0	$\frac{1}{5}$	=	60
Z	1	0	30	0	0	10	=	3000

Answer the following questions using the tableau above.
(a) The unit profit of p_2 is $10. How much must its price increase in order for it to be profitable for x_2 to have a positive value?
(b) The unit profit of p_1 is $30. How much must this price increase so that p_1 is produced by the Kansas Company?
(c) The company has a daily supply of 450 tons of steel. Suppose that an additional 30 tons may be obtained at a cost of $100 per ton. Should the company purchase the additional steel?
(d) The company has a daily supply of 300 tons of aluminum. Suppose an additional 30 tons may be obtained at a cost of $8.50 per ton. Should the company purchase the additional 30 tons of aluminum?
(e) The company has a fourth product, p_4, under consideration. Its estimated unit profit is $60. To produce 1 unit of p_4 requires 6 tons of steel and 10 tons of aluminum. Should the company produce p_4?

DUAL OPTIMAL **11.3.** Ohio Steel produces two types of steel beams at their Warren, Ohio,
SOLUTIONS AND plant. Both types of beams require machining and finishing before they can be
POSTOPTIMALITY sold. The production and finishing requirements are given in the following
ANALYSIS table:

Type of Beam	Machining (hours required)	Finishing (hours required)
1	1.00	2.00
2	2.00	3.00

The Warren, Ohio, plant has a weekly capacity of:

300 machining hours, and
200 finishing hours.

Type 1's contribution to profit is $12 per unit, type 2's is $8.
(a) How many beams of type 1 and type 2 should be produced in Warren if Ohio Steel's objective is the maximization of weekly profit?
(b) How much should Ohio Steel be willing to pay for an additional hour of machining time?

(c) How should the Warren plant optimally use an additional hour of machining time?

(d) How should the Warren plant optimally use an additional hour of finishing time?

DUAL OPTIMAL
SOLUTIONS AND
POSTOPTIMALITY
ANALYSIS

11.4. Alaska Snowbiles Inc. (ASI) produces two major lines of snowmobiles. The two lines, called the Aleutian and Kodiak, go through the same assembly and testing lines. ASI considers both of these lines to be *scarce resources* because of limited labor time available on each line.

To produce and test one Aleutian requires 2 hours on the assembly line and 1 hour on the testing line. To produce and test one Kodiak requires 3 hours on the assembly line and 1.5 hours on the testing line. ASI has a maximum of 16 hours per day available on the assembly line (two shifts) and a maximum of 18 hours per day on the testing line.

Each Aleutian yields a contribution to profit of $150 and each Kodiak $200. ASI's goal is to use their production facilities in such a manner that total profit achieved per day is maximized.

How many Aleutian and Kodiak snowmobiles should ASI produce daily to achieve their goal?

Interpret the optimal solution to the dual model.

Perform a sensitivity analysis on assembly-line capacity.

DUAL OPTIMAL
SOLUTIONS AND
POSTOPTIMALITY
ANALYSIS

11.5. Vermont Foods Inc. has a financial policy that every monthly production plan must, on the average, satisfy the following asset restrictions:

Restriction 1: raw materials cannot exceed 10,000 bushels per month.

Restriction 2: cash outflows must not exceed $40,000 per month.

Restriction 3: accounts receivable must not exceed $35,000 per month.

Vermont Foods on the average has an accounts receivable balance of $5000 at the beginning of each month.

Produce	Selling Price per Case
Apple jelly	$10
Apple jam	$15
Apple cider	$20

All of Vermont Foods' sales are on a monthly credit basis. Four bushels of apples to produce one case of jam or jelly are required. A case of cider requires 10 bushels of apples. Cash outflows for jam and jelly are $2 for each case produced (labor, sugar, preservatives). Cider has a cash outflow of $1 for each case produced. Profits per case are $1, $3, and $4 for jelly, jam, and cider, respectively.

(a) Determine the optimal monthly product mix for Vermont Foods.

(b) Interpret the optimal solution to the dual model.

POSTOPTIMALITY
ANALYSIS

11.6. Montana Silver Corporation (MSC) produces three different types of silver tea sets for commercial sale: a deluxe set called the Hanover; a regular set, the Concord: and an economy set, the Manchester. The marketing department of MSC has done a market survey to determine the numbers of each setting that can reasonably be expected to be sold each month. The results of the survey concluded that the probability of selling more than 150 Hanovers each month is very small. However, as many sets of the Concord and Manchester settings as can be produced can be sold.

Each of these settings requires certain amounts of gold, silver, and lead. MSC purchases gold and lead from outside suppliers at a cost of $130.00 and $0.60 per ounce, respectively. MSC's production cost for silver is estimated to be about $45 per ounce. A finished Hanover requires 2 ounces of gold, 6 ounces of silver, and 300 ounces of lead. A finished Concord requires 1.5 ounces of gold, 4 ounces of silver, and 250 ounces of lead. A finished Manchester requires 1.0 ounce of gold, 2 ounces of silver, and 200 ounces of lead. The monthly supply of the metals is limited to 100 ounces of gold, 700 ounces of silver, and 5000 ounces of lead.

MSC is only one of many producers of sets similar to the Hanover, Concord, and Manchester, and therefore must sell these sets at a price established by the market. Presently, the Hanover can be sold for $2000 per set, the Concord for $1500 per set, and the Manchester for $1000 per set.

(a) MSC desires to find out how many of each set to produce to maximize monthly profit. What is the "worth" of an additional unit of each of the scarce metals? How should these additional metals be used?

(b) If the cost of gold is increased to $135 per ounce, what changes should be made in MSC's optimal production plan?

POSTOPTIMALITY
ANALYSIS

11.7. The Nevada Gold Company (NGC) produces top-quality, handcrafted men's and women's 14K gold necklaces. Each necklace requires two processes: molding and finishing. A woman's necklace requires 8 units of molding and 12 units of finishing. A man's necklace requires 10 units of molding and 8 units of finishing. A total of 200 units of molding and 240 units of finishing are available daily for the manufacture of necklaces. $30 and $45 are the contributions to profit of men's and women's necklaces, respectively.

(a) NGC desires to know what combination of men's and women's necklaces it should produce in order to maximize daily profits. Set up the appropriate linear programming model. Solve by the simplex method.

(b) Do a postoptimality analysis on unit profits.

LINEAR
PROGRAMMING
UNDER
UNCERTAINTY

11.8. Consider the following profit-maximization problem.

$$\text{maximize } Z = px_1 + 2x_2$$

$$\text{subject to} \quad x_1 + x_2 \leqslant 2$$

$$x_1 + 2x_2 \leqslant 3$$

$$x_1 \geqslant 0, \quad x_2 \geqslant 0,$$

where the true value of p is uncertain. In fact,

$$p = 1 \quad \text{or} \quad 2 \quad \text{or} \quad 3.$$

(a) Obtain an optimal solution using the pessimistic criterion.

(b) Obtain an optimal solution using the optimistic criterion.

(c) Consider the use of the following additional information concerning the true (but unknown) value of p.

Positive Values of p	Probability
1	$\frac{1}{2}$
2	$\frac{1}{3}$
3	$\frac{1}{6}$
	$\overline{1.0}$

Solve for an optimal solution using the maximum expected value criterion. What is the expected value of having perfect information on p?

LINEAR PROGRAMMING UNDER UNCERTAINTY

11.9. Consider the following profit-maximization problem.

$$\text{maximize } Z = 1x_1 + 2x_2$$

$$\text{subject to} \quad x_1 + x_2 \leqslant 2$$

$$x_1 \quad\quad \geqslant b$$

$$x_1 \geqslant 0, \quad x_2 \geqslant 0,$$

where the true value of b is *uncertain*. In fact, $b = 0$, 1, or 2.
(a) Obtain an optimal solution using the pessimistic criterion.
(b) Determine an optimal solution using the optimistic criterion.
(c) Consider the use of the following additional information concerning the true value of b.

Possible Values of b	Probability
0	$\frac{1}{3}$
1	$\frac{1}{3}$
2	$\frac{1}{3}$
	$\overline{1}$

Replace b by $E(b)$ in the model and determine the optimal solution.

LINEAR PROGRAMMING UNDER UNCERTAINTY

11.10. Consider the following cost-minimization problem.

$$\text{minimize } C = 2x_1 + 4x_2$$

$$\text{subject to} \quad x_1 + x_2 \geqslant 4$$

$$ax_1 \leqslant 1$$

$$x_1 \geqslant 0, \quad x_2 \geqslant 0,$$

where the true value of a is *uncertain*. In fact, $a = 0, \frac{1}{2}$, or $\frac{1}{4}$.

(a) Determine an optimal solution using the pessimistic criterion.

(b) Determine an optimal solution using the optimistic criterion.

(c) Consider the following additional information concerning the true (but unknown) value of a.

Possible Values of a	Probability
0	0
$\frac{1}{2}$	$\frac{1}{2}$
$\frac{1}{4}$	$\frac{1}{2}$
	$\overline{1}$

Replace a by $E(a)$ and solve for an optimal solution.

CASE 11.1 Illustrative Case Study Application of
Mathematical Programming to Marketing Management

MEDIA-SELECTION
PROBLEM

The objective of the case is to give you added experience in model building and postoptimality analysis in a marketing management setting.

A critical problem in building a media selection model is that management may not be able to impute specific changes in media effectiveness to specific changes in spending levels for each media. Since most companies are concerned with both the optimal selection of media and the relative change in market coverage for changes in spending levels, a methodology must be used to allow for sensitivity analysis and optimal selection.

Advertising-Media Selection Problem. The marketing department of Marshall-Sears in Chicago is faced with the problem of how to effectively advertise color TV sets. There are three basic media in Chicago through which the firm can advertise: newspaper, radio, and television. The decision variables are the dollars to be spent on advertising with each media:

$$x_1 = \text{dollars spent on newspaper}$$

$$x_2 = \text{dollars spent on radio}$$

$$x_3 = \text{dollars spent on television.}$$

In Table 1 the specific subclassification of media, its cost per standard length, and average audience size are given.

The initial problem is to determine an objective function that will give a measure of the sales response to the various media forms. The manager of the marketing department has decided that the firm's objective function should be "Maximize the number of potential buyers exposed to the advertising." To develop this criterion, the department needs to estimate an effectiveness rating

Table 1. Subclassification of Media[a]

$ Variables	Subclassification	Cost per unit	Audience
x_{11}	Unclassified—newspaper	$28.00	25,000
x_{12}	Classified—newspaper	19.00	20,000
x_{21}	Prime time—radio	21.00	20,000
x_{22}	Other time—radio	11.00	5,000
x_{31}	Daytime—TV	30.00	10,000
x_{32}	Prime time—TV	54.00	60,000
x_{33}	Late time—TV	23.00	10,000

[a]$$x_{ij}$'s are dollars spent on each subclassification.

for each media form. Suppose that a market research study in the Chicago area has shown that there are two major characteristics of individuals who are potential buyers of color TV sets—age and income of the head of the family. The relative importance of each of these characteristics was empirically determined and are listed in Table 2.

Table 2. Consumer Characteristics

Income	AGE	
($000s)	18–33	33 and Over
0–5	0	0.10
5–10	0.10	0.25
10 and over	0.20	0.35

The weights in Table 2 can be interpreted as the probability that a make in the given classification is a potential customer. For example, 25% of the individuals over 33 and in the $5000–10,000 income group are expected to be potential buyers of color TV sets.

In Tables 3–9, the percentage of individuals from the total audience reached by the various media are listed for each category.

Table 3. Unclassified—Newspaper

Income	AGE	
($000s)	18–33	33 and Over
0–5	0.05	0.05
5–10	0.20	0.10
10 and over	0.10	0.10

Table 4. Classified—Newspaper

Income	AGE	
($000s)	18–33	33 and Over
0–5	0.02	0.03
5–10	0.10	0.10
10 and over	0.14	0.06

Table 5. Prime Time—Radio

Income	AGE	
($000s)	18–33	33 and Over
0–5	0.02	0.15
5–10	0.03	0.10
10 and over	0.05	0.10

Table 6. Other Time—Radio

Income	AGE	
($000s)	18–33	33 and Over
0–5	0.01	0.14
5–10	0.03	0.07
10 and over	0.02	0.08

Table 7. Daytime—TV

Income	AGE	
($000s)	18–33	33 and Over
0–5	0.004	0.005
5–10	0.002	0.004
10 and over	0.003	0.003

Table 8. Prime Time—TV

Income	AGE	
($000s)	18–33	33 and Over
0–5	0.05	0.10
5–10	0.10	0.20
10 and over	0.15	0.10

Table 9. Late Time—TV

Income	AGE	
($000s)	18–33	33 and Over
0–5	0.10	0.05
5–10	0.20	0.10
10 and over	0.20	0.05

Assignment

1. Using Table 1 and Tables 2–9, find the expected number of potential customers per dollar spent exposed to each media subclassification. If Marshall-Sears' objective is to maximize the sum of the expected number of potential customers exposed to each classification, what is the form of the objective function?
2. Assume that the firm has allowed a $2000 weekly budget for advertising of color TV sets. In determining the cost per ad, quantity discounts were taken into account and the store agreed to spend at least $100 weekly on newspaper advertising and $400 on radio advertising. Formulate a linear programming model for the firm. Solve for an optimal solution.
3. Perform a postoptimality analysis on
   (a) Weekly budget
   (b) Minimal newspaper requirement
   (c) Minimal radio requirement

CHAPTER 12
Network Programming: Transportation Models

OBJECTIVES: Upon successful completion of this chapter, you should be able to:

1. Formulate distribution problems as transportation models.
2. Find low-cost feasible shipping plans for transportation problems.
3. Solve for optimal shipping plans for transportation problems.

12.1. FORMULATING TRANSPORTATION MODELS

The *transportation model* (or distribution model) is an important example of a network optimization problem. It has been applied to many business problems, such as the control and design of manufacturing plants, determining sales territories, and locating distribution centers and warehouses. Tremendous cost savings have been achieved through the efficient (or least cost) routing of goods from supply points to demand points.

THE GOAL AND CONSTRAINTS OF A TRANSPORTATION MODEL

The goal of a transportation model is to minimize the total cost of shipping a product (or products) from supply points to demand points under the following *constraints*:

1. Each demand point receives its requirement.
2. Shipments from a supply point do not exceed its available capacity.

12.1.1. Example—Formulating a Transportation Model

Consider a product distribution network with two supply points and three demand points, as shown in Figure 12.1.

The number of units of the product *available* for shipment from the two supply points is as follows:

Supply Point Number	Amount Available
1	10
2	15
	25 = total availability (or total supply)

The number of units of the product *required* at each of the three demand points is as follows:

Demand Point Number	Amount Required
1	10
2	5
3	10
	25 = total demand (or total requirements)

Note that the total availability equals the total supply. When this is the case we say that the transportation model is *balanced*.

Figure 12.1

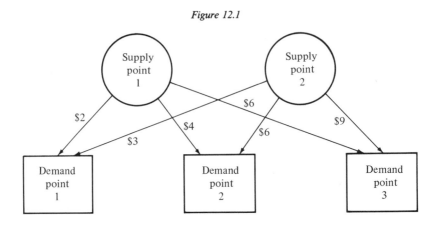

The cost to ship 1 unit of the product from a given supply point to a given demand point can be found in the following shipping-cost table for all pairings of supply and demand points.

Shipping Cost ($/unit shipped)

Supply Point	DEMAND POINT NUMBER		
Number	1	2	3
1	2	4	6
2	3	6	9

Thus, it costs $2 to ship 1 unit of the product from supply point 1 to demand point 1, $4 to ship 1 unit of the product from supply point 1 to demand point 2, $6 to ship from supply point 1 to demand point 3, and so forth.

MODEL FORMULATION. It is common to use double-subscripted variables of the form x_{ij} to denote the number of units of the product shipped from supply point i to demand point j. For example, x_{11} denotes the number of units shipped from supply point 1 to demand point 1, x_{23} denotes the number of units shipped from supply point 2 to demand point 3.
   In general,

$$x_{ij} = amount\ shipped\ from\ point\ i\ to\ point\ j$$

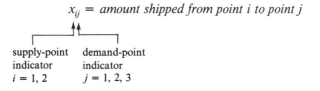

supply-point   demand-point
indicator   indicator
$i = 1, 2$ $j = 1, 2, 3$

The goal is to minimize total shipping costs subject to availability and requirement constraints. That is, choose x_{ij} ($i = 1, 2$ and $j = 1, 2, 3$) to

$$\text{minimize } Z = 2x_{11} + 4x_{12} + 6x_{13} + 3x_{21} + 6x_{22} + 9x_{23} \qquad (O)$$

$$\text{subject to} \quad x_{11} + x_{12} + x_{13} \qquad\qquad\qquad = 10 \qquad (a)$$

$$x_{21} + x_{22} + x_{23} = 15 \qquad (b)$$

$$x_{11} \qquad\qquad + x_{21} \qquad = 10 \qquad (c)$$

$$x_{12} \qquad\qquad + x_{22} \quad = 5 \qquad (d)$$

$$x_{13} \qquad\qquad x_{23} = 10 \qquad (e)$$

$$x_{ij} \geqslant 0 \quad (i = 1, 2, \text{ and } j = 1, 2, 3).$$

Constraints (a) and (b) are availability or supply constraints; (c), (d), and (e) are requirement or demand constraints.

Again, note that supply = 10 + 15 = 25 units equals demand = 10 + 5 + 10 units. What if supply exceeds demand? Consider the following example, which is a revision of Example 12.1.1.

12.1.2. Example—Unbalanced Transportation Problem: Supply Exceeds Demand

Consider a two-supply-point and three-demand-point transportation network with the following data:

Shipping Cost ($/unit shipped)

Supply Point	DEMAND POINT		
	1	2	3
1	2	4	6
2	3	6	9

Supply Point	Amount Available	Demand Point	Amount Required
1	15	1	10
2	15	2	5
	$\overline{30}$ = total supply	3	10
			$\overline{25}$ = total demand

Note that the total supply = 30 exceeds total demand = 25 by 30 − 25 = 5 units.

To construct a balanced model we create a "fictitious" demand point with an amount required equal to 5 units. Call this fictitious demand point "number 4." This yields the following balanced transportation problem.

minimize $Z = 2x_{11} + 4x_{12} + 6x_{13} + 0x_{14} + 3x_{21} + 6x_{22} + 9x_{23} + 0x_{24}$

subject to

$$x_{11} + x_{12} + x_{13} + x_{14} = 15$$
$$x_{21} + x_{22} + x_{23} + x_{24} = 15$$
$$x_{11} + x_{21} = 10$$
$$x_{12} + x_{22} = 5$$
$$x_{13} + x_{23} = 10$$
$$x_{14} + x_{24} = 5$$

$$x_{ij} \geqslant 0 \quad (i = 1, 2 \text{ and } j = 1, 2, 3, 4).$$

The two variables in this constraint (see the rectangular box) are fictitious variables. x_{14} and x_{24} actually represent the amount of product at supply points 1 and 2, respectively, that is not shipped (e.g., the amount of product that is stored at supply points 1 and 2, respectively).

12.1.3. Example—Unbalanced Transportation Problem: Demand Exceeds Supply

Consider again the two-supply-point and three-demand-point transportation network with the following data:

Shipping Cost ($/unit shipped)

Supply Point	DEMAND POINT 1	2	3
1	2	4	6
2	3	6	9

Supply Point	Amount Available	Demand Point	Amount Required
1	10	1	10
2	15	2	10
		3	10
	$\overline{25}$ = total supply		$\overline{30}$ = total demand

Thus, total demand = 30 units exceeds total supply = 25 units by the amount of $30 - 25 = 5$ units.

To create a balanced transportation network (supply = demand), we create a new "ficitious" supply point with an amount available = demand − supply = 5 units. We label the new supply point number 3. This new supply point will yield three new fictitious variables: x_{31}, x_{32}, and x_{33}. The new balanced transportation model is as follows.

minimize $Z = 2x_{11} + 4x_{12} + 6x_{13} + 3x_{21} + 6x_{22} + 9x_{23} + 0x_{31} + 0x_{32} + 0x_{33}$

subject to

$$x_{11} + x_{12} + x_{13} = 10$$
$$x_{21} + x_{22} + x_{23} = 15$$
$$\boxed{x_{31} + x_{32} + x_{33} = 5}$$
$$x_{11} + x_{21} + x_{31} = 10$$
$$x_{12} + x_{22} + x_{32} = 10$$
$$x_{13} + x_{23} + x_{33} = 10$$

$$x_{ij} \geqslant 0 \quad (i = 1, 2, 3 \text{ and } j = 1, 2, 3).$$

The fictitious variables in the rectangular box—x_{31}, x_{32}, and x_{33}—represent the amount of requirements at demand points 1, 2, and 3, respectively, that are not satisfied (shortages).

Any distribution or transportation problem can be balanced by adding either a fictitious supply point if total demand exceeds total supply or by adding a fictitious demand point if total supply exceeds total demand.

These two cases are illustrated in Examples 12.1.2 and 12.1.3.

12.1.4. Example—Heinson Fisheries Incorporated

Heinson Fisheries Incorporated (HFI) has cold storage warehouses located in Boston, New York, and Washington, D.C. At each warehouse location HFI processes and *distributes* lobsters to fish brokers located in various cities throughout the country. Estimated weekly orders for lobsters are as follows:

HFI—Next Week's Lobsters Demand

Location	Number of Boxes
Miami	30
Chicago	50
Philadelphia	65
Dallas	55
	200

The air-freight costs (transportation costs) per box between the warehouses and brokers are as follows:

Transportation Cost ($1 box of lobsters)

From \ To	Miami	Chicago	Philadelphia	Dallas
Boston	14	16	12	20
New York	12	14	10	8
Washington, D.C.	10	16	8	15

Next week HFI expects to have the following supply of lobsters available to meet estimated demand:

HFI—Next Week's Lobster Supply

Warehouse	Supply
Boston	100
New York	40
Washington, D.C.	60
	200

Note that total supply = 200 boxes = total demand. Thus, the problem is *balanced*.

The problem facing HFI's management is how to construct a minimum-cost shipping plan between the warehouses and the fish brokers.

QUESTION. What is a *feasible shipping plan* for HFI?

Answer. A *feasible shipping plan* is a schedule (or plan) that specifies shipments between warehouses and fish brokers in such a manner that (1) a broker does not receive more boxes of lobsters than ordered, and (2) the total shipment out of any warehouse does not exceed its supply.

The following table gives an example of a feasible shipping plan for HFI.

Feasible Shipping Plan for HFI (number of boxes shipped)

From \ To	Miami	Chicago	Philadelphia	Dallas	Supply
Boston	30	50	20	0	100
New York	0	0	40	0	40
Washington, D.C.	0	0	5	55	60
Demand	30	50	65	55	200

Note that the total supply of 200 boxes is shipped which equals the total demand of 200 boxes.

QUESTION. What is the total transportation cost of the preceding feasible shipping plan?

Answer. To compute the total shipping costs, we need to sum the products of the positive shipments given in the preceding table by their corresponding unit shipping costs. This calculation can be simplified by combining the feasible shipping-plan table and the transportation-cost table into one table.

Feasible Shipping Plan for HFI (with unit shipping costs)

From \ To	Miami	Chicago	Philadelphia	Dallas	Supply
Boston	14 / 30	16 / 50	12 / 20	20 / 0	100
New York	12 / 0	14 / 0	10 / 40	8 / 0	40
Washington, D.C.	10 / 0	16 / 0	8 / 5	15 / 55	60
Demand	30	50	65	55	200

Unit shipping costs (unit = 1 box of lobsters) are indicated in the table by the numbers in the upper right-hand corner of each cell. The quantities to be shipped from the warehouses to the various cities are indicated by the numbers in each cell below the unit shipping cost. The total demand and the total supply for each customer and warehouse appear in the bottom row and the right-hand column at the right in the table. Thus, the total cost of this feasible shipping plan is $2725, the calculation of which is as follows:

$$
\begin{aligned}
\text{Boston:} \quad & 30 \times \$14 + 50 \times \$16 + 20 \times \$12 + 0 \times \$20 = \$1460 \\
\text{New York:} \quad & 0 \times \$12 + 0 \times \$14 + 40 \times \$10 + 0 \times \$8 = \$\ 400 \\
\text{Washington, D.C.:} \quad & 0 \times \$10 + 0 \times \$16 + 5 \times \$8 + 55 \times \$15 = \$\ 865 \\
& \hspace{5cm} \overline{\$2725.}
\end{aligned}
$$

QUESTION. Can you find a feasible shipping plan that has a total cost less than $2725? To answer this question *we need an algorithm* to solve for minimum-cost shipping plans.

12.2. FINDING INITIAL FEASIBLE SOLUTIONS TO TRANSPORTATION PROBLEMS

Algorithms for solving transportation problems are similar in structure to the linear programming algorithm given in Chapter 9. See Figure 12.2.

12.2.1. Example—Finding an Initial Basic Feasible Solution

The following problem has three origins and four destinations. The supplies at origins O_1, O_2, and O_3 are 20, 6, and 9 units, respectively. The requirements at the destinations D_1, D_2, D_3, and D_4 are 5, 20, 5, and 5 units, respectively. The problem is balanced because the total supply and total requirements are both equal to 35 units. Supplies and demands, together with unit shipping costs, are shown in Figure 12.3.

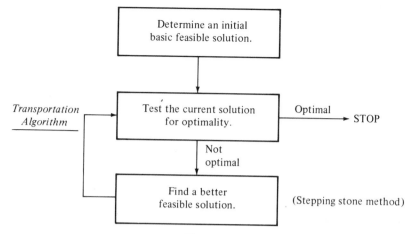

Figure 12.2

	D_1	D_2	D_3	D_4	Supply
O_1	20	30	40	20	20
O_2	60	30	50	40	6
O_3	20	10	40	70	9
Requirement	5	20	5	5	35

Figure 12.3

NORTHWEST CORNER PROCEDURE. The northwest corner procedure is generally considered to be the easiest method to use in determining an initial basic feasible solution. It is also considered to be the least likely to give a good "low-cost" initial solution because it *ignores* the relative magnitude of the costs C_{ij}. This procedure is given by the following three steps.

Step 1. Select the northwest (upper left-hand) corner cell for a shipment.

Step 2. Make as large a shipment as possible in the northwest corner cell.
     This operation will completely exhaust either the supply available at one origin or the remaining requirement at one destination.

Step 3. Adjust the supply and requirement numbers to reflect the remaining supply and requirement and return to step 1.

RULES FOR THE NORTHWEST CORNER PROCEDURE. The northwest corner procedure can be carried out in one transportation-cost table if certain rules are followed.

Rule 1   Shipments are to be indicated within each cell.

Rule 2   Supplies and requirements remaining can be entered to the right of the original numbers.

Rule 3   Rows corresponding to origins can be eliminated or *checked* after their requirements are completely filled.

The six tables in Figure 12.4 illustrate the six iterations of the northwest corner procedure as applied to the preceding table.

The sixth iteration of the northwest corner procedure resulted in the *simultaneous* filling of the remaining demand of 5 units at D_4 and the elimination of the remaining supply of 5 units at O_3.

Iteration 1

	D_1 ✓	D_2	D_3	D_4	Supply
O_1	20 / 5	30	10	20	15
O_2	60	30	50	40	6
O_3	20	10	40	70	9
Demand	0	20	5	5	35

A shipment of 5 units from O_1 to D_1 is indicated: $x_{11} = 5$. Column 1 is checked. Row 1 has a new supply of 15 units.

Iteration 2

	D_1 ✓	D_2	D_3	D_4	Supply
O_1 ✓	20 / 5	30 / 15	10	20	0
O_2	60	30	50	40	6
O_3	20	10	40	70	9
Demand	0	5	5	5	35

A shipment of 15 units from O_1 to D_2 is indicated: $x_{12} = 15$. Column 2 has a new demand of 5 units. Row 1 is checked.

Iteration 3

	D_1 ✓	D_2 ✓	D_3	D_4	Supply
O_1 ✓	20 / 5	30 / 15	10	20	0
O_2	60	30 / 5	50	40	1
O_3	20	10	40	70	9
Demand	0	0	5	5	

A shipment of 5 units from O_2 to D_2 is indicated: $x_{22} = 5$. Row 2 has a new supply of 1 unit. Column 2 is checked.

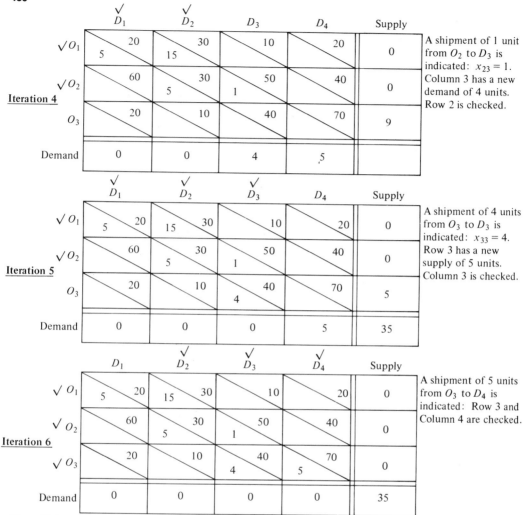

Figure 12.4

The six iterations of the northwest corner procedure yield the following feasible shipping plan:

Feasible Shipping Plan

	FROM O_1		FROM O_2		FROM O_3	
	Shipments	*Cost*	*Shipments*	*Cost*	*Shipments*	*Cost*
	$x_{11} = 5$	$5 \times \$20$	$x_{21} = 0$	$0 \times \$60$	$x_{31} = 0$	$0 \times \$20$
	$x_{12} = 15$	$15 \times \$30$	$x_{22} = 5$	$5 \times \$30$	$x_{32} = 0$	$0 \times \$10$
	$x_{13} = 0$	$0 \times \$10$	$x_{23} = 1$	$1 \times \$50$	$x_{33} = 4$	$4 \times \$40$
	$x_{14} = 0$	$0 \times \$20$	$x_{24} = 0$	$0 \times \$40$	$x_{34} = 5$	$5 \times \$70$
	20	\$550	6	\$200	9	\$510

Total cost = \$550 + \$200 + \$510 = \$1260.

440 Chap. 12: Transportation Models

It is unlikely that this feasible plan is also the minimum-cost feasible shipping plan, since we ignored the relative magnitude of the unit costs in each iteration. Note that it required six iterations of the northwest corner procedure to construct an initial feasible shipping plan.

In general, a transportation problem of size $m \times n$ (m = number of origins and n = number of destinations) requires *at most* $n + m - 1$ iterations of the three steps of the northwest corner rule.

MINIMUM-COST-CELL METHOD FOR FINDING AN INITIAL FEASIBLE SOLUTION. The minimum-cost-cell method differs from the northwest corner procedure only in step 1.

New Step 1. Consider all cells that are not contained in either a checked row or a checked column. Select that cell which has the lowest cost. In the cell selected, make a shipment equal to the minimum of the supply and demand for the row and column containing the selected cell.

To illustrate the minimum-cost-cell method, consider the transportation problem of Example 12.2.1.

12.2.2. Example—Finding an Initial Basic Feasible Solution by the Minimum-Cost-Cell Method

See Figure 12.5

Iteration 1

	D_1	D_2	D_3	D_4	Supply
O_1	20	30	10	20	20
O_2	60	30	50	40	6
✓ O_3	20	10 (9)	40	70	0
Demand	5	11	5	5	35

A shipment of 9 is indicated from O_3 to D_2: $x_{32} = 9$. Column 2 has a new demand of 11. Row 3 is checked.

Minimum cost cells are
(3, 2) and (1, 3).
($10 is the smallest unit cost)

Iteration 2

	D_1	D_2	D_3 ✓	D_4	Supply
O_1	20	30	10 (5)	20	15
O_2	60	30	50	40	6
✓ O_3	20	10 (9)	40	70	0
Demand	5	11	0	5	35

A shipment of 5 is indicated from O_1 to D_3: $x_{13} = 5$. Row 1 has a new supply of 15. Column 3 is checked.

Minimum cost cell is (1, 3).
($10)

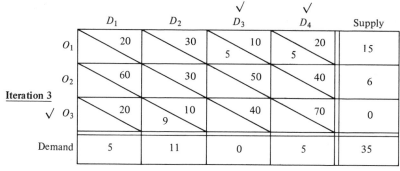

Iteration 3

	D_1	D_2	D_3 ✓	D_4 ✓	Supply
O_1	20	30	10 (5)	20 (5)	15
O_2	60	30	50	40	6
✓ O_3	20	10 (9)	40	70	0
Demand	5	11	0	5	35

Minimum cost cells are (1, 1) and (1, 4)
($20)

A shipment of 5 is indicated from O_1 to D_4: $x_{14}=5$. Row 1 has a new supply of 10. Column 4 is checked.

Iteration 4

	D_1 ✓	D_2	D_3 ✓	D_4 ✓	Supply
O_1	20 (5)	30	10 (5)	20 (5)	5
O_2	60	30	50	40	6
✓ O_3	20	10 (9)	40	70	0
Demand	0	11	0	0	35

Minimum cost cell is (1, 1).
($20)

A shipment of 5 is indicated from O_1 to D_1: $x_{11} = 5$. Row 1 has a new supply of 5. Column 1 is checked.

Iteration 5

	D_1 ✓	D_2	D_3 ✓	D_4 ✓	Supply
✓ O_1	20 (5)	30 (5)	10 (5)	20 (5)	0
O_2	60	30	50	40	6
✓ O_3	20	10 (9)	40	70	0
Demand	0	6	0	0	

Minimum cost cells are (1, 2) and (2, 2)
($30)

A shipment of 5 is indicated from O_1 to D_2: $x_{12} = 5$. Column 2 has a new demand of 6. Row 1 is checked.

Iteration 6

	D_1 ✓	D_2 ✓	D_3 ✓	D_4 ✓	Supply
✓ O_1	20 (5)	30 (5)	10 (5)	20 (5)	0
✓ O_2	60	30 (6)	50	40	0
✓ O_3	20	10 (9)	40	70	0
Demand	0	0	0	0	35

A shipment of 6 is indicated from O_2 to D_2: $x_{22} = 6$. Column 2 and Row 2 are checked.

Minimum, cost cell is (2, 2)
($30)

Figure 12.5

Feasible Shipping Plan

FROM O_1		FROM O_2		FROM O_3	
Shipments	Cost	Shipments	Cost	Shipments	Cost
$x_{11} = 5$	$5 \times \$20$	$x_{21} = 0$	$0 \times \$60$	$x_{31} = 0$	$0 \times \$20$
$x_{12} = 5$	$5 \times \$30$	$x_{22} = 6$	$6 \times \$30$	$x_{32} = 9$	$9 \times \$10$
$x_{13} = 5$	$5 \times \$10$	$x_{23} = 0$	$0 \times \$50$	$x_{33} = 0$	$0 \times \$40$
$x_{14} = 5$	$5 \times \$20$	$x_{24} = 0$	$0 \times \$40$	$x_{34} = 0$	$0 \times \$70$
20	\$400	6	\$180	9	\$90

Total cost = $400 + $180 + $90 = $670.

Notice that the minimum-cost-cell procedure gives a lower-cost initial basic feasible solution than the northwest corner procedure:

northwest corner procedure	= \$1260
minimum-cost-cell procedure	= \$ 670
difference:	\$ 590.

12.2.3. Example—Feasible Shipping Plans for Heinson Fisheries Incorporated

Review Example 12.1.4

Consider the shipping problem of Example 12.1.4. The transportation matrix is given in Figure 12.6. It is accompanied by an initial basic feasible solution determined by the northwest corner procedure.

Feasible Shipping Plan

(Determined by the Northwest Corner Procedure)

FROM BOSTON		FROM NEW YORK		FROM WASHINGTON, D.C.	
Shipments	Cost	Shipments	Cost	Shipments	Cost
$x_{11} = 30$	$30 \times \$14$	$x_{21} = 0$	$0 \times \$12$	$x_{31} = 0$	$0 \times \$10$
$x_{12} = 50$	$50 \times \$16$	$x_{22} = 0$	$0 \times \$14$	$x_{32} = 0$	$0 \times \$16$
$x_{13} = 20$	$20 \times \$12$	$x_{23} = 40$	$40 \times \$10$	$x_{33} = 5$	$5 \times \$ 8$
$x_{14} = 0$	$0 \times \$20$	$x_{24} = 0$	$0 \times \$8$	$x_{34} = 55$	$55 \times \$15$
Total 100	\$1,460	40	\$400	60	**\$865**

Total cost = $1,460 + $400 + $865 = $2,725.

To From	D_1 Miami	D_2 Chicago	D_3 Philadelphia	D_4 Dallas	Supply
O_1 Boston	14 30	16 50	12 20	20	100
O_2 New York	12	14	10 40	8	40
O_3 Washington, D.C.	10	16	8 5	15 55	60
Demand	30	50	65	55	200

Figure 12.6. Feasible shipping plan (determined by the northwest corner procedure).

QUESTION. What is the initial basic feasible solution found by using the minimum-cost-cell procedure?

Answer. The minimum-cost-cell procedure's initial basic feasible solution is given in Figure 12.7.

To From	$D_1:$ Miami	$D_2:$ Chicago	$D_3:$ Philadelphia	$D_4:$ Dallas	Supply
$O_1:$ Boston	14 30	16 50	12 5	20 15	0
$O_2:$ New York	12	14	10	8 40	0
$O_3:$ Washington, D.C.	10	16	8 60	15	0
Demand	0	0	0	0	200

Figure 12.7

QUESTION. What is the total cost of the shipping plan determined by the minimum-cost-cell procedure?

Answer

Feasible Shipping Plan (determined by minimum-cost-cell procedure)

FROM BOSTON		FROM NEW YORK		FROM WASHINGTON, D.C	
Shipments	*Cost*	*Shipments*	*Cost*	*Shipments*	*Cost*
$x_{11} = 30$	$30 \times \$14$	$x_{21} = 0$	0	$x_{31} = 0$	0
$x_{12} = 50$	$50 \times \$16$	$x_{22} = 0$	0	$x_{32} = 0$	0
$x_{13} = 5$	$5 \times \$12$	$x_{23} = 0$	0	$x_{33} = 60$	$60 \times \$8$
$x_{14} = 15$	$15 \times \$20$	$x_{24} = 40$	$40 \times \$8$	$x_{34} = 0$	0
$\overline{100}$	$\overline{\$1580}$	$\overline{40}$	$\overline{\$320}$	$\overline{60}$	$\overline{\$480}$

Total cost = $1580 + $320 + $480 = $2380.

QUESTION. What is the difference in total cost between the two shipping plans determined by the northwest corner procedure and the minimum-cost-cell procedure for Heinson Fisheries Inc. ?

Answer

northwest corner procedure	= $2725
minimum-cost-cell procedure	= $2380
difference:	$ 345.

Is the feasible shipping plan determined by the minimum-cost-cell procedure optimal? To answer this question we need a procedure to test for optimality.

12.3. OPTIMALITY-TEST ALGORITHM FOR TRANSPORTATION PROBLEMS

12.3.1. Stepping-Stone Method

Consider the initial basic feasible solution determined by the minimum-cost-cell procedure for Heinson Fisheries Inc. In this feasible solution 200 boxes of lobsters are shipped from the three warehouses to four cities. The total cost of the initial shipping plan is $2380. This shipping plan is feasible, but is it optimal? We now give a procedure, called the *stepping-stone method*, to test this solution for optimality.

The optimality test begins by examining the empty cells in the transportation tableau containing the initial feasible shipping plan. Each empty cell (an empty cell is one containing a zero shipment) is evaluated to determine if the cost of shifting a unit to that cell from a cell containing a positive shipment will decrease. If we cannot lower total transportation costs by reallocating shipments between cells, then the current basic feasible shipping plan is optimal.

The stepping-stone method has three steps.

Step 1—Determine an Initial Feasible Shipping Plan. This can be done by use of either the northwest-corner or the minimum-cost-cell procedure.

Step 2—Compute a Cell Evaluator for Each Empty Cell. A cell evaluator for each empty cell is determined by computing the *net cost* of shifting 1 unit from a cell containing a positive shipment to the empty cells. Next, the sign of cell evaluators are checked for optimality.

Step 3. If the shipping plan is not optimal, that is, if a cell evaluator fails the sign test, we determine a new lower total cost shipping plan. This is accomplished by shifting the maximum amount to that empty cell so that the supply or demand constraints are not violated. Then return to step 2.

To illustrate the computation of cell evaluators for empty cells and to illustrate the sign test for optimality, we next solve the Heinson Fishery problem using the stepping-stone method.

12.3.2. Example—Determining Optimal Shipping Plans— Heinson Fisheries Inc.

Step 1—Initial Feasible Shipping Plan Determined by the Minimum-Cost-Cell Procedure. See Figure 12.8.

To / From	D_1: Miami	D_2: Chicago	D_3: Philadelphia	D_4: Dallas	Supply
O_1: Boston	14 / 30	16 / 50	12 / 5	20 / 15	100
O_2: New York	12	14	10	8 / 40	40
O_3: Washington, D.C.	10	16	8 / 60	15	60
Demand	30	50	65	55	200

Figure 12.8

Step 2. There are six empty cells in the matrix. They are

(2, 1)—shipping from O_2 to D_1
(2, 2)—shipping from O_2 to D_2
(2, 3)—shipping from O_2 to D_3
(3, 1)—shipping from O_3 to D_1
(3, 2)—shipping from O_3 to D_2
(3, 4)—shipping from O_3 to D_4.

Let's consider shifting 1 unit to cell (2, 1). By so doing we must take 1 unit away from cell (2, 4). That is, the 40 units must be decreased to 39 in order to maintain the supply constraint of 40 units (row 2). Also, we must decrease the shipment of 30 boxes in column 1, cell (1, 1), to maintain the demand constraint of D_1 for 30 boxes. Next we can add $+1$ to cell (1, 4) to maintain the supply constraint of 100 boxes for S_1. These four shifts of 1 unit are shown next in a simplex tableau (Figure 12.9). The arrows indicate the transfer of 1 unit from (1, 1) into (2, 1) and 1 unit from (2, 4) into (1, 4).

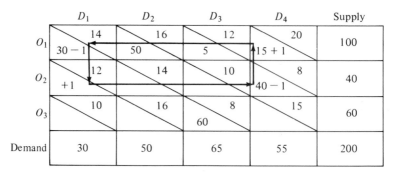

Figure 12.9

The cost of shifting 1 unit into (2, 1) [cell evaluator for cell (1, 2)] is

$$\begin{bmatrix} \$12 \times 1 & + & \$20 \times 1 & - & (\$14 \times 1 & + & \$8 \times 1) \\ \text{cell (2, 1)} & & \text{cell(1, 4)} & & \text{cell (1, 1)} & & \text{cell (2, 4)} \end{bmatrix}$$

$$= \$12 + \$20 - (\$14 + \$8) = \$10.$$

Thus, the shift of 1 unit into empty cell (2, 1) *increases* cost by $10; that is, this shift will increase—not decrease—total transportation costs.

Notice that the cell evaluator is equal to the sum of the unit transportation costs for all cells that gained 1 unit *minus* the sum of the costs for all cells that lost 1 unit.

Also, note that if we trace a *path* from the empty cell which is to receive 1 unit to each cell that receives or loses 1 unit (to maintain balance), we have a *closed loop. This must always be the case in empty-cell evaluations.*

Let us compute the cell evaluator for cell (3, 4). Reproducing the preceding tableau, we obtain the tableau in Figure 12.10.

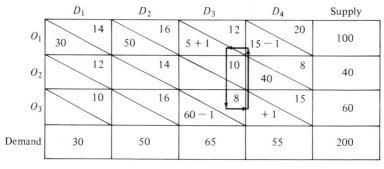

Figure 12.10

Notice that we have a closed loop, beginning with the empty cell (3, 1) and going to cell (1, 4) to cell (1, 3) to cell (3, 3). The evaluator is

$$\begin{bmatrix} \$15 & + & \$12 & - & (\$20 & + & \$8) \\ \text{cell (3, 4)} & & \text{cell (1, 4)} & & \text{cell (1, 4)} & & \text{cell (3, 3)} \end{bmatrix}$$

$$= \$27 - \$28 = \$ - 1.$$

Thus, shifting 1 unit into empty cell (3, 1) *decreases* the cost by \$1.

The cell evaluators, together with their associated closed loops, are as follows:

Empty Cell	Closed Loop	Cost		Cell Evaluator
(2, 1)	(2, 1) → (2, 4) → (1, 4) → (1, 1)	(12 + 20) − (8 + 14)	=	\$10
(2, 2)	(2, 2) → (2, 4) → (1, 4) → (1, 2)	(14 + 20) − (8 + 16)	=	10
(2, 3)	(2, 3) → (2, 4) → (1, 4) → (1, 3)	(10 + 20) − (8 + 12)	=	10
(3, 1)	(3, 1) → (3, 3) → (1, 3) → (1, 1)	(10 + 12) − (8 + 14)	=	0
(3, 2)	(3, 2) → (3, 3) → (1, 3) → (1, 2)	(16 + 12) − (8 + 16)	=	4
(3, 4)	(3, 4) → (1, 4) → (1, 3) → (3, 3)	(15 + 12) − (20 + 8)	=	−1

The only negative cell evaluator is for (3, 4).

Thus, by shifting 1 unit to cell (3, 4) we can decrease transportation costs by \$1. We now go to step 3 of the stepping-stone method.

Step 3. From step 2 we know that transportation costs will decrease by shifting 1 unit into cell (3, 4). We now make the amount of the shift as *large as possible*. However, we cannot violate any supply or demand constraint. Let S denote the amount shifted to empty cell (3, 4) in Figure 12.11.

Note that the largest value that we can assign to S is 15 units. For if we choose S to be larger than 15, say $S = 20$, then cell (1, 4) will have a negative shipment of S. So in cell (3, 4), $S = 15$ units. That is, $x_{14} = 15$. This decreases transportation

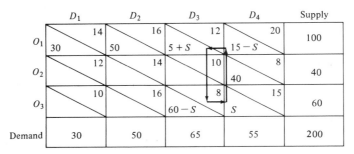

Figure 12.11

costs from \$2380 to

$$\$2380 - S \times \$1 = \$2380 - 15 \times \$1$$
$$= \$2365.$$

The new feasible shipping plan is shown in Figure 12.12.

	D_1	D_2	D_3	D_4	Supply
O_1	14 / 30	16 / 50	12 / 20	20 /	100
O_2	12 /	14 /	10 /	8 / 40	40
O_3	10 /	16 /	8 / 45	15 / 15	60
Demand	30	50	65	55	200

Figure 12.12. Initial feasible shipping plan.

We now return to step 2 and check the signs of all the empty-cell evaluators.

Step 2. The cell evaluators, together with their associated closed loops, are as follows:

Empty Cell	Closed Loop	Costs		Cell Evaluator
(1, 4)	(1, 4) → (1, 3) → (3, 3) → (3, 4)	(20 + 8) − (12 + 15)	=	\$1
(2, 1)	(2, 1) → (1, 1) → (1, 3) → (3, 3) → (3, 4) → (2, 4)	(12 + 12 + 15) − (14 + 8 + 8)	=	9
(2, 2)	(2, 2) → (1, 2) → (1, 3) → (3, 3) → (3, 4) → (2, 4)	(14 + 12 + 15) − (16 + 8 + 8)	=	9
(2, 3)	(2, 3) → (3, 3) → (3, 4) → (2, 4)	(10 + 15) − (8 + 8)	=	9
(3, 1)	(3, 1) → (1, 1) → (1, 3) → (3, 3)	(10 + 12) − (14 + 8)	=	0
(3, 2)	(3, 2) → (1, 2) → (1, 3) → (3, 3)	(16 + 12) − (16 + 8)	=	4

Note that all the cell evaluators in the table above are either zero [cell (3, 1)] or positive. Thus, total transportation costs will either stay the same or increase if a shift of the unit is made to any one of the empty cells.

The preceding tableau provides an optimal shipping plan for Heinson Fisheries:

O_1: $\quad x_{11} = 30, \quad x_{12} = 50, \quad x_{13} = 20, \quad x_{14} = 0$

O_2: $\quad x_{21} = 0, \quad x_{22} = 0, \quad x_{23} = 0, \quad x_{24} = 40$

O_3: $\quad x_{31} = 0, \quad x_{32} = 0, \quad x_{33} = 45, \quad x_{34} = 15$

with total transportation cost $= Z = \$2365.$

12.3.3. Example—Stepping-Stone Method

Let us now apply the stepping-stone method to Example 12.2.2.

Step 1—Initial Feasible Shipping Plan. See Figure 12.13.

	D_1	D_2	D_3	D_4	Supply
O_1	20 5	30 5	10 5	20 5	20
O_2	60	30 6	50	40	6
O_3	20	10 9	40	70	9
Demand	5	20	5	5	35

Figure 12.13

Step 2—Empty-Cell Evaluations. There are six empty cells in the tableau of step 1. Consider cell (2, 4). The closed loop for this cell is

$$(2, 4) \rightarrow (1, 4) \rightarrow (1, 2) \rightarrow (2, 2)$$

as shown in Figure 12.14.

	D_1	D_2	D_3	D_4	Supply
O_1	20 5	30 5	10 5	20 $5-S$	20
O_2	60	30 $6-S$	50	40 S	6
O_3	20	10 9	40	70	9
Demand	5	20	5	5	35

Figure 12.14

The cell evaluator is

$$\$(40 + 30) - \$(20 + 30) = \$20,$$

so each unit we shift to cell (2, 4) increases cost by \$20.

The cell evaluators for each empty cell, together with their associated closed loops, are as follows:

Empty Cells	Closed Loops	Cost		Cell Evaluation
(2, 4)	(2, 4) → (1, 4) → (1, 2) → (2, 2)	(40 + 30) − (20 + 30)	=	$20
(2, 1)	(2, 1) → (2, 2) → (1, 2) → (1, 1)	(60 + 30) − (30 + 20)	=	40
(2, 3)	(2, 3) → (1, 3) → (1, 2) → (2, 2)	(50 + 30) − (10 + 30)	=	40
(3, 1)	(3, 1) → (3, 2) → (1, 2) → (1, 1)	(20 + 30) − (10 + 20)	=	20
(3, 3)	(3, 3) → (1, 3) → (1, 2) → (3, 2)	(40 + 30) − (10 + 10)	=	50
(3, 4)	(3, 4) → (2, 4) → (2, 2) → (3, 2)	(70 + 30) − (40 + 10)	=	50

Since all the cell evaluators are positive, the current shipping plan is optimal.

12.3.4. Alternative Optimal Solutions

In the optimal solution to Example 12.3.2, empty cell (3, 1) has a cost evaluation of $0. This means that if we shift 1 unit to cell (3, 1), transportation costs will decrease by an amount of $1 \times \$0 = 0$. That is, total transportation costs do not change. Let's make such a shift to cell (3, 1) and see what happens using the tableau in Figure 12.15.

Letting S equal 30, we have the tableau in Figure 12.16 on the facing page.

Solution One

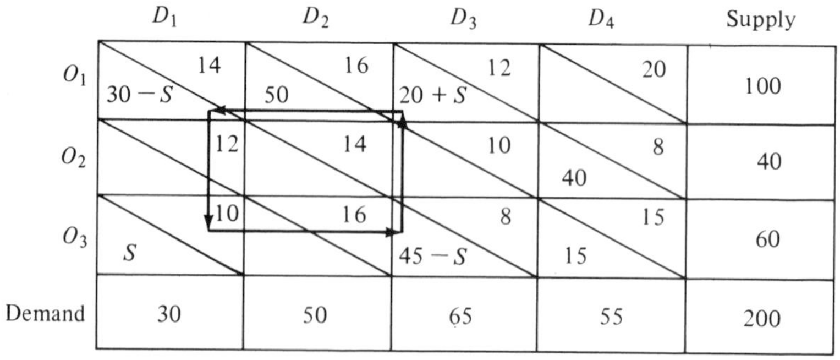

	D_1	D_2	D_3	D_4	Supply
O_1	14 $30 - S$	16 50	12 $20 + S$	20	100
O_2	12	14	10	8 40	40
O_3	10 S	16	8 $45 - S$	15 15	60
Demand	30	50	65	55	200

Figure 12.15. Optimal shipping plan for Heinson Fisheries (given in Example 12.3.1).

	D_1	D_2	D_3	D_4	Supply
O_1	14 / 0	16 / 50	12 / 50	20 /	100
O_2	12 /	14 /	10 /	8 / 40	40
O_3	10 / 30	16 /	8 / 15	15 / 15	60
Demand	30	50	65	65	200

Figure 12.16

Solution 1	Solution 2
$x_{11} = 30$ ⟷	$x_{11} = 0$
$x_{12} = 50$	$x_{12} = 50$
$x_{13} = 20$ ⟷	$x_{13} = 50$
$x_{14} = 0$	$x_{14} = 0$
$x_{21} = 0$	$x_{21} = 0$
$x_{22} = 0$	$x_{22} = 0$
$x_{23} = 0$	$x_{23} = 0$
$x_{24} = 40$	$x_{24} = 40$
$x_{31} = 0$ ⟷	$x_{31} = 30$
$x_{32} = 0$	$x_{32} = 0$
$x_{33} = 45$ ⟷	$x_{33} = 15$
$x_{34} = 15$	$x_{34} = 15$
Total cost = $2365.	Total cost = $2365.

Notice that the two shipping plans are *different* in four cells (or four shipments) but that the minimum total cost is the same. Thus, we can conclude that there are multiple optimal solutions.

> If in an optimal shipping plan there exists an empty cell (or a zero shipment) with a cell evaluator equal to zero, and if we can shift 1 unit of product to this empty cell without violating any demand or supply constraint, then there are multiple optimal solutions.

12.4. DEGENERACY IN TRANSPORTATION PROBLEMS

In applying either the northwest corner procedure or the minimum-cost-cell procedure to a transportation problem with m origins and n destinations, we *often* end up with a solution with less than $m + n - 1$ positive shipments. Such a solution is called *degenerate*.

12.4.1. Example—Degenerate Transportation Problem

Consider the following problem with $m = 2$ origins and $n = 3$ destinations (Figure 12.17).

	D_1	D_2	D_3	Supply
O_1	1 / 10	2 / 5	3	15
O_2	3	2	1 / 10	10
Demand	10	5	10	25

Figure 12.17

Note that we have a feasible shipping with exactly three positive shipments. Thus, the solution is degenerate. We need to have $m + n - 1 = 2 + 3 - 1 = 4$ positive shipments in order to apply the stepping-stone procedures. To remedy this situation we arbitrarily assign a positive "small" number D to any empty cell (say $D = 0.000000001$) and add D to the appropriate supply and demand. This is illustrated in Figure 12.18.

	D_1	D_2	D_3	Supply
O_1	1 / 10	2 / 5	3 / D	$15 + D$
O_2	3	2	1 / 10	10
Demand	15	5	$10 + D$	$25 + D$

Figure 12.18

Note that there are now four cells with positive shipments. We now have a feasible shipping plan for which we can apply the appropriate cell-evaluation procedures.

12.5. DUAL OF THE TRANSPORTATION MODEL

Since the transportation problem is a special case of a linear programming problem, it has a dual with the usual pricing interpretations. However, if supply equals demand in a transportation problem, then special care has to be used in interpreting the optimal values of the dual variables. This is best illustrated by use of the following example.

12.5.1. Example—Dual Programs

See Figure 12.19.

	D_1	D_2	Supply
O_1	5 1	5 1	10
O_2	3	5 1	5
Demand	5	10	15

Figure 12.19

This problem has two origins and two destinations. In the table we have also indicated the optimal solution. The primal model is:

PRIMAL MODEL

minimize $Z = 1x_{11} + 1x_{12} + 3x_{21} + 1x_{22}$

subject to

supply constraints $\begin{cases} x_{11} + x_{12} = 10 \\ x_{21} + x_{22} = 5 \end{cases}$

demand constraints $\begin{cases} x_{11} + x_{21} = 5 \\ x_{12} + x_{22} = 10 \\ x_{ij} \geqslant 0. \end{cases}$

The dual model has four variables, one for each constraint. Let u_1 and u_2 be the dual variable for the first two supply constraints and let v_1 and v_2 be the dual variables for the two demand constraints. We have:

DUAL MODEL

maximize $Z = 10u_1 + 5u_2 + 5v_1 + 10v_2$

$u_1 + v_1 \leqslant 1$	(a)
$u_1 + v_2 \leqslant 1$	(b)
$u_2 + v_1 \leqslant 3$	(c)
$u_2 + v_2 \leqslant 1.$	(d)

In the dual model, u_i can be interpreted as the value of the product f.o.b. at the ith origin, and v_j as its value (delivered) at the j destination. Thus, in the objective function we are maximizing the total of the f.o.b. value plus the delivered value of the product.

Consider constraint (O). We have

$$u_1 + v_1 \leqslant \$1 \quad \text{or} \quad v_1 \leqslant \$1 - u_1.$$

Thus, the delivered value of the product at D_1 cannot be greater than the unit cost of shipping 1 unit from O_1 to D_1 minus the f.o.b. unit value at D_1.

The optimal solution to the primal and dual model is given in the following table.

Optimal Solutions

Primal	Dual
$x_{11} = 5$	$u_1 = 1$
$x_{12} = 5$	$u_2 = 1$
$x_{21} = 0$	$v_1 = 0$
$x_{22} = 5$	$v_2 = 0.$

QUESTION. If we increase 1 unit of supply at D_1, then to maintain a balanced problem, we must increase 1 unit of demand. Say that we increase 1 unit at D_1. How much will total transportation costs increase?

Answer. $u_1 + v_1 = \$1.$

QUESTION. Say that we increase 1 unit at O_2 and 1 unit at D_2. How much will total transportation costs increase?

Answer. $u_2 + v_2 = \$1 + \$0 = \$1.$

REFERENCES BIERMAN, H., C. P. BONINI, and W. H. HAUSMAN. *Quantitative Analysis for Business Decisions*, 4th ed. Homewood, Ill.: Richard D. Irwin, Inc., 1973.

DAELLENBACH, H. G., and E. J. BELL. *User's Guide to Linear Programming*, Englewood Cliffs, N.J.: Prentice-Hall, Inc., 1970.

DANTZIG, G. B. *Linear Programming and Extensions*. Princeton, N.J.: Princeton University Press, 1963.

DRIEBEEK, N. J. *Applied Linear Programming*, Reading, Mass.: Addison-Wesley Publishing Co., Inc., 1969.

HILLIER, F. S., and G. J. LIEBERMAN. *Introduction to Operations Research*, 2nd ed. San Francisco: Holden-Day, Inc., 1974.

HOROWITZ, I. *An Introduction to Quantitative Business Analysis*, 2nd ed. New York: McGraw-Hill Book Company, 1972.

KIM, C. *Introduction to Linear Programming*. New York: Holt, Rinehart and Winston, Inc., 1972.

KWAK, N. K. *Mathematical Programming with Business Applications*. New York: McGraw-Hill Book Company, 1973.

LAPIN, L. *Quantitative Methods for Business Decisions*, New York: Harcourt Brace Jovanovich, Inc., 1976.

LEVIN, R., and C. KIRKPATRICK. *Quantitative Approaches to Management*, 3rd ed., New York: McGraw-Hill Book Company, 1975.

SHAMBLIN, J. E., and G. T. STEVENS, JR. *Operations Research—A Fundamental Approach*. New York: McGraw-Hill Book Company, 1974.

SIMMONS, D. M. *Linear Programming for Operations Research*. San Francisco: Holden-Day, Inc., 1972.

STRUM, J. E. *Introduction to Linear Programming*. San Francisco: Holden-Day, Inc., 1972.

TAHA, H. A. *Operations Research: An Introduction*. New York: Macmillan Publishing Co., Inc., 1971.

WAGNER, H. M. *Principles of Operations Research with Applications to Managerial Decisions*. Englewood Cliffs, N.J: Prentice-Hall, Inc., 1975.

KEY CONCEPTS

Transportation model
Balancing a transportation problem
Initial feasible shipping plan

Transportation algorithm
Dual transportation problem
Optimal pricing

REVIEW PROBLEMS

12.1. A weekly product distribution system has the following characteristics:

Plant	Weekly Capacity	Distribution Center	Weekly Demand
O_1	75	D_1	50
O_2	100	D_2	50
	175	D_3	100
			200

Note that total weekly capacity is 175 units, which is $200 - 175 = 25$ less than total weekly demand. Thus, some distribution centers will be in short supply each week.

The following table gives estimates of revenue lost per unit, by distribution center, for being in short supply.

Distribution Center	Revenue Loss ($/unit)
D_1	2
D_2	3
D_3	2

Transportation Costs ($/unit)

From \ To	D_1	D_2	D_3
O_1	3	2	1
O_2	4	5	6

The goal of the company is to determine a feasible shipping plan that minimizes the sum of total transportation costs *plus* total loss revenue.

(a) Construct a balanced transportation model for the company.

(b) Determine a feasible shipping plan using the minimum-cost-cell procedure.

PRODUCTION SCHEDULING **12.2.** The Carter Peanut Company always schedules production 3 months in advance. The plant has a capacity of 1300 boxes per month on regular shifts. Unit-regular-time production costs are $4 per box. Using overtime, up to 500 additional boxes per month can be produced at a unit cost of $6 per box in excess of the unit production cost for regular-time production. It costs $3 per month to hold a box. Monthly sales will be 1000, 1200, and 1800 boxes during the next 3 months. The unit penalty cost for unsold boxes at the end of the third month is $5.

(a) Carter wishes to determine an optimal production schedule. What is the schedule that minimizes total costs of production and storage but still meets monthly demand?

(b) Formulate this production smoothing problem as a transportation model.

ANSWERS TO REVIEW PROBLEMS **12.1.** Since demand exceeds supply by 25 units, we create a fictitious or dummy plant, O_3, with a capacity of 25 units. This requires the addition of three new decision variables: x_{31}, x_{32}, and x_{33}. The values assigned to these three variables denote the amount not shipped to the respective demand centers.

(a) *Transportation model*

minimize

$$Z = 3x_{11} + 2x_{12} + 1x_{13} + 4x_{21} + 5x_{22} + 6x_{23} + 2x_{31} + 3x_{32} + 2x_{33}$$

$$\underbrace{\hspace{5cm}}_{total\ transportation\ costs} \quad \underbrace{\hspace{3cm}}_{total\ revenue\ cost}$$

subject to

$$
\begin{aligned}
x_{11} + x_{12} + x_{13} &&&&&& = 75 \\
&& x_{21} + x_{22} + x_{23} &&&& = 100 \\
&&&& x_{31} + x_{32} + x_{33} &= 25 \\
x_{11} + && x_{21} + && x_{31} && = 50 \\
x_{12} && + x_{22} && + x_{32} && = 50 \\
x_{13} + && x_{23} + && x_{33} &= 100
\end{aligned}
$$

All x_{ij}'s $\geqslant 0$.

The tableau representation of this model is presented in Figure 12.20.

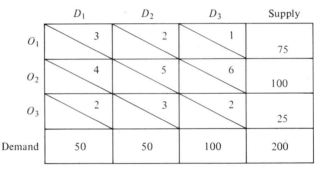

Figure 12.20

(b) The five iterations required to produce a feasible shipping plan are given in the following tableaus.

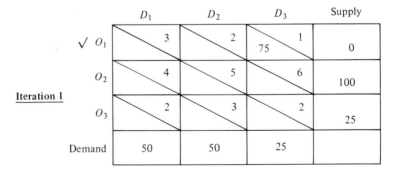

Figure 12.21

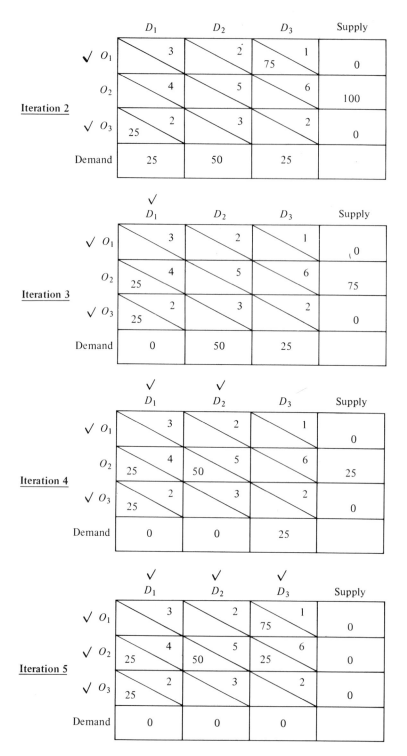

Figure 12.22

The feasible shipping plan given in the tableau of iteration 5 has the following values and costs.

O_1	
$x_{11} = 0$	\$0
$x_{12} = 0$	\$0
$x_{13} = 75$	$75 \times \$1 = \$75$
	$\overline{\$75}$

O_2	
$x_{21} = 25$	$25 \times \$4 = \$100$
$x_{22} = 50$	$50 \times \$5 = \$250$
$x_{23} = 25$	$25 \times \$6 = \underline{\$150}$
	\$500

Total transportation costs = \$75 + \$500 = \$575.

O_3 (fictitious plant)	
$x_{31} = 25$	$25 \times \$2 = \$50$
$x_{32} = 0$	\$ 0
$x_{33} = 0$	$\underline{\$ 0}$
	\$50

Total loss revenue = \$50. Sum of total transportation costs and total loss revenue = \$575 + \$50 = \$625.

12.2. Each month the Carter Peanut Company has two decisions: how many boxes to produce during regular time; and how many boxes to produce in overtime. Thus, a 6-month plan requires $2 \times 6 = 12$ decisions. Now production in each month, regular or overtime, may be used to meet the current month's demand or a future month's demand.

Decision Variables. Thus, for month 1, let x_{11}, x_{12}, and x_{13} be the amounts produced in regular time to meet demand in months 1, 2, and 3, respectively. In general, for months 1, 2, and 3, let x_{ij} be the amount produced in regular time in month i to meet demand in month j:

$$i = 1, 2, 3; \quad j = i, i + 1, \ldots, 3.$$

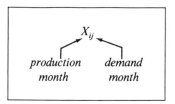

Similarly, for the overtime production decisions we let O_{ij} be the amount produced in overtime in month i to meet demand in month j:

$$i = 1, \ldots, 6; \qquad j = i, i + 1, \ldots, 6$$

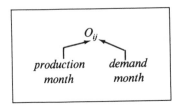

Constraints on the x_{ij}'s and O_{ij}'s. Demand must be satisfied in each month.

$$\text{month 1:} \quad x_{11} + O_{11} \qquad\qquad\qquad \geqslant 1000$$

$$\text{month 2:} \quad x_{12} + x_{22} + O_{12} + O_{22} \qquad \geqslant 1200$$

$$\text{month 3:} \quad x_{13} + x_{23} + x_{33} + O_{13} + O_{23} + O_{33} \geqslant 1800.$$

Capacity Restrictions

$$\text{month 1:} \quad x_{11} + x_{12} + x_{13} \ \leqslant 1300$$

$$O_{11} + O_{12} + O_{13} \leqslant \ 500$$

$$\text{month 2:} \quad x_{22} + x_{23} \qquad \leqslant 1300$$

$$O_{22} + O_{23} \qquad \leqslant \ 500$$

$$\text{month 3:} \quad x_{33} \qquad\qquad \leqslant 1300$$

$$O_{33} \qquad\qquad \leqslant \ 500.$$

Note that the company has a total 3-month capacity of 5400 boxes and a total 3-month demand of $1000 + 1200 + 1800 = 4000$ boxes.

Consider the two types of constraints above. If we treat each of the two types of production each month as two origins, and if we treat each month's demand as the demand at a distribution center, we have the transportation tableau that is shown in Figure 12.23.

The $\times$ed-out cells, in Figure 12.23 denote impossible production decisions. We could leave them in with a "high" cost, say \$∞, which would guarantee that they would never have positive values.

(dummy)

		D_1	D_2	D_3	D_4	
Regular	O_1	c_{11} x_{11}	c_{12} x_{12}	c_{13} x_{13}	c_{14} x_{14}	1300
Overtime	O_2	$\bar{c}_{11}$ O_{11}	$\bar{c}_{12}$ O_{12}	$\bar{c}_{13}$ O_{13}	$\bar{c}_{14}$ O_{14}	500
Regular	O_3		c_{22} x_{22}	c_{23} x_{23}	c_{24} x_{24}	1300
Overtime	O_4		$\bar{c}_{22}$ O_{22}	$\bar{c}_{23}$ O_{23}	$\bar{c}_{24}$ O_{24}	500
Regular	O_5			c_{33} x_{33}	c_{34} x_{34}	1300
Overtime	O_6			$\bar{c}_{33}$ O_{33}	$\bar{c}_{34}$ O_{34}	500
		1000	1200	1800	1400	

Figure 12.23

How do we determine the costs of c_{ij} and $\bar{c}_{ij}$? For example,

c_{11} = unit cost of producing a box in regular time month 1, that is, sold in month 1.

Thus, $c_{11} = \$4.$

c_{12} = unit cost of producing 1 box in period 1 and holding it 1 month for month 2's demand.

Thus, $c_{12} = \$4 + \$3$.
In general,

$$c_{ij} = \$4 + \$3(j - i) \qquad (\text{for } i = 1, 2, 3; \quad j = i, i + 1, \ldots, 3).$$

Now

$$c_{i4} = \$4 + \$3(4 - i) + \$5 \text{ (penalty)}.$$

Similarly,

$$\bar{c}_{ij} = \$(4 + 6) + \$3(j - i) \qquad (i = 1, 2, 3; \qquad j = i, i + 1, \ldots, 3)$$

and

$$\bar{c}_{i4} = \$(4 + 6) + \$3(4 - i) + \$5 \text{ (penalty)}.$$

EXERCISES

TRANSPORTATION PROBLEMS   **12.1.** Solve the distribution problem given in the transportation matrix in Figure 12.22 for a minimum-cost schedule.

SOLVING TRANSPORTATION PROBLEMS   **12.2.** A company has factories at A, B, and C which supply warehouses at D, E, F, and G. Monthly factory capacities are

$$A = 160, \text{ units, } B = 150 \text{ units, and } C = 190 \text{ units.}$$

Monthly warehouse requirements are

$$D = 80 \text{ units, } E = 90 \text{ units, } F = 110 \text{ units, and } G = 160 \text{ units.}$$

Unit shipping costs are as follows:

From \ To	D	E	F	G
A	$40	$50	$40	$40
B	40	50	50	$50
C	50	40	40	$40

Determine a minimum-cost shipping plan.

SOLVING TRANSPORTATION PROBLEMS   **12.3.** A company with factories at A, B, and C supplies warehouses D, E, F, and G. Monthly factory capacities are 20, 30, and 45 units, respectively. Monthly warehouse requirements are 10, 15, 40, and 30 units, respectively. Unit shipping costs are as follows:

From \ To	D	E	F	G
A	$5	$10	$5	$ 0
B	5	9	5	$10
C	10	10	15	$ 5

Determine an optimum distribution plan. What is the minimum total transportation cost?

12.4. The Akron Tire Plant consists of four separate buildings scattered around the outskirts of Akron. The only railroad freight dock is in the center of the city. Normally, the company's own trucks transport tires from the buildings to the central freight dock. However, owing to an expected strike, next month's shipments will be very heavy. Three independent trucking firms have bid on the amount they can carry and the price per 100 tires from the various buildings to the railroad freight dock. The data for this shipping problem are as follows:

	TRANSPORT METHODS				
Buildings	Akron's Own Trucks	Firm 1	Firm 2	Firm 3	Building and Shipping Requirements
A	10	8	2	7	500
B	6	9	5	1	700
C	4	3	7	5	200
D	7	2	4	6	600
	600	1000	600	300	2000

Determine a minimum-cost shipping plan for the Akron Tire Plant.

12.5. The Santa Barbara Oil Company has refineries located in Los Angeles, Houston, and St. Louis. Management needs a minimum-cost distribution plan between the refineries and the regional storage facilities, located in Denver, Seattle, Chicago, and Buffalo.

The following data are representative of a typical month's operation.

Shipping Cost ($/barrel)

From \ To	Buffalo	Seattle	Chicago	Denver
Los Angeles	8	5	8	4
Houston	9	5	5	5
St Louis	9	8	4	4

Refinery	Available Monthly Capacity (millions of barrels)	Variable Costs ($1 barrel)
Los Angeles	150	$5
Houston	80	$4
St. Louis	100	$3

Regional Storage Facility	Monthly Sales (millions of barrels)
Buffalo	50
Seattle	100
Chicago	50
Denver	100

Determine the minimum-cost distribution schedule.

CASE 12.1   Illustrative Case Study

TRANSPORTATION MODELS   The Tyler Radio Company produces automobile radios in four plants: Oakland, Gary, Houston, and Newark. The radios are shipped to three automobile assembly plants, located in Denver, Philadelphia, and Cleveland. Recently, total output has not been able to keep pace with total demand. Consequently, the Tyler Company has decided to build a new plant either in San Francisco or Atlanta.

The production capacities, demands, and transportation costs are given below and on page 465.

Question. Which plant site should be selected by the Tyler Company?

	Supply Data (radios/month)	Unit Production Costs
Oakland	15,000	$50
Gary	10,000	$40
Houston	10,000	$40
Newark	15,000	$50
	50,000	

	Demand Data (radios/month)
Denver	20,000
Philadelphia	20,000
Cleveland	20,000
	60,000

	Estimated Unit Production Costs
Atlanta	$40
San Francisco	60

Transportation Costs (per radio)

From \ To	Cleveland	Denver	Philadelphia
Gary	$10	$14	$11
Houston	11	13	12
Newark	12	12	13
Oakland	13	11	14
San Francisco	14	10	15
Atlanta	9	12	11

CHAPTER 13

Integer Programming and the Branch-and-Bound Method

OBJECTIVES: Upon successful completion of this chapter, you should be able to:

1. Cite several examples of integer programming applications to business problems.
2. Model several business problems as integer programming problems.
3. Solve integer programming problems by the branch-and-bound method.

13.1. INTEGER PROGRAMMING

In many business problems the decision variables make sense only if they have integer values. For example, many business problems require the assignment or allocation of men, machines, and materials to production activities in integer quantitites. The restriction that the decision variables must have integer values has led to the development of special programming algorithms. However, it is common in practice that an integer linear programming problem be first solved by the simplex method (hence ignoring the integer restrictions) and then rounding off the noninteger values to integers in the resulting solution. This is often an inadequate approach, since we may arrive at an integer solution that is drastically different from the optimal integer solution.

13.1.1. Example—Integer Programming Problem

Consider the linear programming problem (LPP) at the top of page 467. The set of feasible solutions to this problem is shown graphically in Figure 13.1.

LINEAR PROGRAMMING PROBLEM

maximize $\quad Z = 6x_1 + 7x_2$

subject to $\qquad x_1 + 2x_2 \leqslant 8$

$\qquad\qquad\quad x_1 - x_2 \leqslant 4$

$\quad x_1 \geqslant 0, \qquad x_2 \geqslant 0.$

The optimal solution occurs at the corner point C determined by the intersection of the equations

$$x_1 + 2x_2 = 8 \quad \text{and} \quad x_1 - x_2 = 4.$$

The coordinates for corner point C are

$$x_1 = \tfrac{16}{3} \quad \text{and} \quad x_2 = \tfrac{4}{3}.$$

That is, note that the optimal values of the decision variables are

$$x_1 = \tfrac{16}{3} \quad \text{and} \quad x_2 = \tfrac{4}{3}.$$

Figure 13.1 Feasible solutions (shaded area) for LPP of Example 13.1.1.

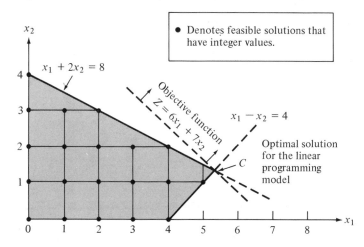

Suppose that we are interested in the optimal integer solution to (LPP). Then our set of feasible solutions is not the shaded area shown in Figure 13.1 but the points depicting integer-valued feasible solutions shown in Figure 13.2.

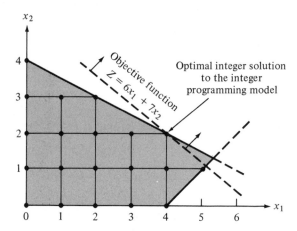

Figure 13.2. Feasible integer solutions (denoted by ●) for IPP of Example 13.1.1.

To determine the optimal integer solution to (LPP) we need to solve the following integer programming model:

INTEGER PROGRAMMING MODEL

maximize $Z = 6x_1 + 7x_2$

subject to $x_1 + 2x_2 \leqslant 8$

$x_1 - x_2 \leqslant 4$

$x_1 \geqslant 0, \qquad x_2 \geqslant 0$

$x_1, \quad x_2$ integers.

The set of feasible integer solutions to (IPP) are listed in Table 13.1, together with their contribution to profit.

We note from Table 13.1 and Figure 13.2 that there are 20 feasible integer-valued solutions to (IPP). By inspecting the second column of Table 13.1 we see that the optimal integer solution is

$$x_1 = 4, \quad x_2 = 2 \qquad \text{with profit } Z = \$38.$$

Table 13.1. Integer Solutions of Example 13.1.1

INTEGER FEASIBLE SOLUTION		
x_1	x_2	Profit $= Z = 6x_1 + 7x_2$
0	0	$0
0	1	7
0	2	14
0	3	21
0	4	28
1	0	6
1	1	13
1	2	20
1	3	27
2	0	12
2	1	19
2	2	26
2	3	33
3	0	18
3	1	25
3	2	32
4	0	24
4	1	31
4	2	38 ← optimal solution to (IPP)
5	1	37 ← round-off solution obtained from (LPP)

Comparing the optimal solution of (LPP) and (IPP) yields the following table:

Model	Optimal Solution	Maximum Profit
LPP	$x_1 = \frac{16}{3}, x_2 = \frac{4}{3}$	$41.33
IPP	$x_1 = 4, x_2 = 2$	$38.00

Note that the integer restriction decreases profit from $41.33 to $38.

QUESTION. Suppose that we solve (LPP) by the simplex method and then round off the resulting solution. Will we obtain the optimal integer solution to (IPP)?

Answer. No. The optimal value of x_1 in (LPP) is $\frac{16}{3} = 5\frac{1}{3}$, which when rounded off gives a value of $x_1 = 5$. But 4 is the optimal value of x_1 in (IPP).

Similarly, the optimal value of x_2 in (LPP) is $\frac{4}{3} = 1\frac{1}{3}$, which when rounded off gives a value of $x_2 = 1$. But 2 is the optimal value for x_2 in (IPP).

Table 13.1 illustrates that rounding off a simplex method solution may not yield the optimal integer solution.

13.1.2. Example—Capital-Budgeting Problem

Bestel Construction Company has the opportunity next year to undertake five different projects, P_1, P_2, P_3, P_4, and P_5, each with an estimated net profit shown in Table 13.2.

Table 13.2. Expected Net Profit for the Projects of Example 13.1.2

Project Number	Expected Net Profit (000s)
1	$100
2	80
3	70
4	60
5	90

Because of the different requirements of each project (manpower, equipment, transportation to project site, etc.), the cost varies from project to project. Also, due to cash-flow requirements, Bestel cannot undertake all five projects.

In Table 13.3 are listed the total cost or cash outlay required for undertaking each project.

Table 13.3. Expected Cost for the Projects of Example 13.1.2

Project Number	Expected Cost (000s)
1	$60
2	40
3	20
4	40
5	50

Bestel estimates (or expects) that it will have cash available in the amount of $150,000 to cover costs next year. Which projects should Bestel undertake next year?

The problem faced by Bestel Construction Inc., can be formulated as an integer programming model with integer-valued decision variables.

Decision Variables

$$x_j = \begin{cases} 1 & \text{if project } j \text{ is selected} \\ 0 & \text{if project } j \text{ is not selected} \end{cases} \quad j = 1, 2, 3, 4, 5.$$

x_1, x_2, x_3, x_4, and x_5 are zero/1 decision variables. Hence, Bestel's problem is an integer programming problem. For example,

$$x_1 = 1, \qquad x_2 = 1, \qquad x_3 = 0, \qquad x_4 = 0, \qquad x_5 = 1$$

would be the decision to select only projects P_1, P_2, and P_5.

GOAL OR OBJECTIVE FUNCTION. Bestel's goal is to select projects that maximize total expected profit.

Let P = total expected profit. Then the objective function is

$$P = 100x_1 + 80x_2 + 70x_3 + 60x_4 + 90x_5.$$

For example, if the decision is to select only projects P_1, P_2, and P_5, that is,

$$x_1 = 1, \qquad x_2 = 1, \qquad x_3 = 0, \qquad x_4 = 0, \qquad x_5 = 1,$$

then expected profit

$$\begin{aligned} P &= 100x_1 + 80x_2 + 70x_3 + 60x_4 + 90x_5 \\ &= 100(1) + 80(1) + 70(0) + 60(0) + 90(1) \\ &= \$270{,}000. \end{aligned}$$

RESTRICTIONS ON THE DECISION VARIABLES. There is a cash restriction of $150,000. The total expected cash outlay is (in thousands of dollars)

$$60x_1 + 40x_2 + 20x_3 + 40x_4 + 50x_5,$$

which must not exceed the expected funds available ($150,000). That is,

$$60x_1 + 40x_2 + 20x_3 + 40x_4 + 50x_5 \leqslant 150.$$

QUESTION. Can Bestel choose all five projects and still not exceed expected funds available?

Answer. No. If $x_1 = 1$, $x_2 = 1$, $x_3 = 1$, $x_4 = 1$, and $x_5 = 1$, then expected cost is

$$60(1) + 40(1) + 20(1) + 40(1) + 50(1) = \$210,$$

which is $60,000 over the available funds.

QUESTION. What is the expected cost of choosing projects P_1, P_2, and P_4?

Answer

$$\begin{aligned} 60x_1 + 40x_2 + 20x_3 + 40x_4 + 50x_5 &= 60(1) + 40(1) + 20(0) + 40(1) + 50(0) \\ &= 140 = \$140{,}000. \end{aligned}$$

SUMMARY OF BESTEL'S INTEGER PROGRAMMING MODEL:
ORIGINAL BESTEL MODEL

Choose x_1, x_2, x_3, x_4, x_5 to

maximize $P = 100x_1 + 80x_2 + 70x_3 + 60x_4 + 90x_5$

subject to $60x_1 + 40x_2 + 20x_3 + 40x_4 + 50x_5 \leqslant 150$

$x_1 = 0$ or 1, $x_2 = 0$ or 1, $x_3 = 0$ or 1,
$x_4 = 0$ or 1, $x_5 = 0$ or 1.

PROBLEM—MUTUALLY EXCLUSIVE PROJECTS. Suppose that management has decided that exactly one project can be selected from the set of projects P_1, P_3, and P_5. However, projects P_2 and P_4 may still be selected subject to the budget restriction. What additional constraint (or constraints) needs to be added to the original Bestel model?

Solution. Since either P_1, P_3, or P_5 must be selected and only one can be selected, exactly one of the three variables x_1, x_3, or x_5 must be equal to 1 and the rest must be equal to zero. That is, x_1, x_3, and x_5 are restricted to be zero/1 and

$$\boxed{x_1 + x_3 + x_5 = 1.}$$ constraint to be added

Note that, for example, if $x_3 = 1$, then $x_1 = 0$ and $x_5 = 0$ in order for the constraint to hold.

PROBLEM—MUTUALLY EXCLUSIVE PROJECTS. Suppose that Bestel has decided that at most one of the two projects, P_2 and P_4, can be selected. What additional constraint needs to be added to the original Bestel model?

Solution. Since at most one of the two projects P_2 and P_4 can be selected, then at most one of the two variables x_2 and x_4 may be equal to 1 and the other must be equal to zero. That is,

$$\boxed{x_2 + x_4 \leqslant 1.}$$ constraint to be added

Note that $x_2 = 0$ and $x_4 = 0$, $x_2 = 1$ and $x_4 = 0$, $x_2 = 0$ and $x_4 = 1$ satisfies this constraint. But $x_2 = 1$ and $x_4 = 1$ violates this constraint, since $1 + 1 = 2 > 1$.

PROBLEM—PRECEDENCE CONSTRAINTS. Suppose that Bestel has decided that if P_3 is selected, then P_4 must be selected. What additional constraint needs to be added to the original model?

$$\boxed{x_3 \leqslant x_4.}$$ constraint to be added

Note that if $x_3 = 1$, then x_4 must be equal to 1. However, x_4 can be equal to 1 and x_3 can be equal to either 0 or 1. That is, the selection of P_4 does not imply that P_3 must be selected.

13.1.3. Example—Fixed-Charge Problem

Jiggs Paint and Supply Company has available three different processes for producing standard white house paint. Each process has a setup cost and a per-gallon processing cost. The capacity of each process is as follows:

Process Number	Setup Cost	Processing Cost (dollars/gallon)	Maximum Daily Capacity (gallons)
1	$100	5	2000
2	200	4	3000
3	300	3	4000

Jiggs expects a daily demand of 3500 gallons. The problem facing Jiggs is what processes to use and at what capacities in order to meet their daily demand at minimum total cost. Jiggs's problem can be formulated as an integer programming model.

MODEL FORMULATION

DECISION VARIABLES.   Let

$$y_1 = \begin{cases} 1 & \text{if process 1 is used} \\ 0 & \text{if process 1 is not used} \end{cases}$$

$$y_2 = \begin{cases} 1 & \text{if process 2 is used} \\ 0 & \text{if process 2 is not used} \end{cases}$$

$$y_3 = \begin{cases} 1 & \text{if process 3 is used} \\ 0 & \text{if process 3 is not used.} \end{cases}$$

Variables y_1, y_2, y_3 are zero/1 variables. For example, $y_1 = 1$, $y_2 = 0$, and $y_3 = 1$ would be the decision to use only processes 1 and 3.

PRODUCTION VARIABLES.   Let

$$x_1 = \text{production level for process 1}$$
$$x_2 = \text{production level for process 2}$$
$$x_3 = \text{production level for process 3.}$$

OBJECTIVE FUNCTION.   The objective is to choose processes and production levels that minimize total cost. Let z denote total cost. Then

$$Z = \underbrace{5x_1 + 4x_2 + 3x_3}_{\substack{\text{total variable} \\ \text{production cost}}} + \underbrace{100y_1 + 200y_2 + 300y_3}_{\text{total setup cost}}.$$

RESTRICTIONS.   We have two types of restrictions on the production
variables. To meet daily demand, we must have

$$x_1 + x_2 + x_3 = 3500 \text{ (gallons).}$$

For the capacity constraints we have

$$\text{process 1:}\quad x_1 \leqslant 2000 \text{ (gallons)}$$
$$\text{process 2:}\quad x_2 \leqslant 3000 \text{ (gallons)}$$
$$\text{process 3:}\quad x_3 \leqslant 4000 \text{ (gallons).}$$

Note that if we use any process at a positive level, we must ensure that the
fixed setup cost is incurred as well as the variable production costs. That is, for
example, if $x_1 > 0$ (we use process 1), then $y_1 = 1$ (we must select process 1).
This leads to the following relationship between the continuous variables x_j
and the integer variables y_j.

$$\text{for process 1:}\quad \text{if } x_1 = 0, \text{ then } y_1 = 0$$
$$\text{if } x_1 > 0, \text{ then } y_1 = 1$$
$$\text{if } y_1 = 0, \text{ then } x_1 = 0.$$
$$\text{for process 2:}\quad \text{if } x_2 = 0, \text{ then } y_2 = 0$$
$$\text{if } x_2 > 0, \text{ then } y_2 = 1$$
$$\text{if } y_2 = 0, \text{ then } x_2 = 0.$$
$$\text{for process 3:}\quad \text{if } x_3 = 0, \text{ then } y_3 = 0$$
$$\text{if } x_3 > 0, \text{ then } y_3 = 1.$$
$$\text{if } y_3 = 0, \text{ then } x_3 = 0.$$

Each set of three constraints given above, together with the corresponding capacity constraint, can be combined into one constraint.

For the first set of three constraints (Process 1) consider the inequality

$$2000y_1 \geqslant x_1.$$

Note that the inequality $x_1 \leqslant 2000y_1$ also includes the capacity constraint for process 1. Recall that y_1 must be either 0 or 1. Thus, if $y_1 = 0$ in $2000y_1 \geqslant x_1$, then $2000y_1 = 0$, which implies that $x_1 = 0$. If $x_1 = 0$, then $y_1 = 0$, since we are minimizing total cost Z. If $x_1 > 0$, then $2000y_1 > 0$ can occur only if $y_1 = 1$.

The model constructed for Jiggs Paint and Supply Company is given below.

INTEGER PROGRAMMING PROBLEM

Choose $y_1, y_2, y_3, x_1, x_2,$ and x_3 to

minimize $Z = 5x_1 + 4x_2 + 3x_3 + 100y_1 + 200y_2 + 300y_3$

subject to $\quad x_1 + x_2 + x_3 = 3500$

$\qquad\qquad x_1 \leqslant 2000y_1$

$\qquad\qquad x_2 \leqslant 3000y_2$

$\qquad\qquad x_3 \leqslant 4000y_3$

$\qquad\qquad y_1 \leqslant 1$

$\qquad\qquad y_2 \leqslant 1$

$\qquad\qquad y_3 \leqslant 1$

$\quad x_1 \geqslant 0, x_2 \geqslant 0, x_3 \geqslant 0 \;\; y_1, \;\; y_2, \;\; y_3$ integers.

Note that the constraints $y_1 \leqslant 1, y_2 \leqslant 1,$ and $y_3 \leqslant 1$ in effect mean that $y_1, y_2,$ and y_3 are zero/1 variables.

13.2. THE BRANCH-AND-BOUND METHOD

As we have seen in Section 13.1, the simplex method for solving linear programming problems may not yield integer values for the decision variables. However, a noninteger linear solution can always be rounded off to yield an integer solution. If the resulting integer solution is feasible and has a profit *close to* the profit obtained from the linear programming solution, then rounding off values of the decision variables can be a good procedure. However, the rounding-off procedure is inadequate in many integer programming problems. In fact, if a problem contains a large number of integer-restricted variables with several constraints, rounding off will likely yield an infeasible solution or a solution that is far from optimal.

Solution procedures specifically designed for integer programming problems include a method called *branch and bound* and another called the *cutting-plane* method. The cutting-plane method is a variant of the simplex method. In fact, it begins with a simplex method solution to the integer programming model with the integer restriction ignored. Then, new constraints are added to the problem which (1) make infeasible the previous noninteger optimal solution and (2) do not exclude any feasible integer solutions. The new constraints added are called *cutting planes* or *cuts*. Next, a new simplex method solution is determined and the process repeated until a feasible integer solution, and hence the optimal integer solution, is obtained.

In an integer programming problem there is most often only a *finite number* of possible feasible solutions. Thus, it is possible (theoretically) to enumerate and evaluate every feasible integer solution in order to find the optimum. If there is a small number of integer variables, complete enumeration is an efficient computational procedure. But, in many realistic integer programming problems, *complete enumeration* of all possible integer solutions is computationally infeasible. It is often the case in using the branch-and-bound method that only *partial enumeration* is necessary, if applied systematically, in finding an optimal integer solution. The branch-and-bound method is a technique for accomplishing this, since it may *eliminate* whole sets of solutions from consideration.

13.2.1. Example—Tree of All Possible Integer Solutions

Consider the following integer programming problem:

$$\text{maximize } Z = 5x_1 + 3x_2 + x_3$$

$$\text{subject to} \quad x_1 + x_2 + x_3 \leqslant 6$$

$$3x_1 + x_2 + 4x_3 \leqslant 9$$

$$x_1 \qquad\qquad \leqslant 1$$

$$x_2 \qquad \leqslant 1$$

$$x_3 \leqslant 4$$

$$x_1, \quad x_2, \quad x_3 \text{ all integers.}$$

The restrictions $x_1 \leqslant 1$ and $x_2 \leqslant 1$ imply that x_1 and x_2 are zero/1 decision variables. The variable x_3 can take on five values. That is, $x_3 = 0, 1, 2, 3,$ or 4. Therefore, considering only the last three constraints of the integer programming problem, there are $2 \times 2 \times 5 = 20$ possible integer solutions.

The complete enumeration of all 20 possible integer solutions is shown graphically in Figure 13.3. Note that the end of the tree has 20 branches—which it must have, one for each possible integer solution. However, the order of the

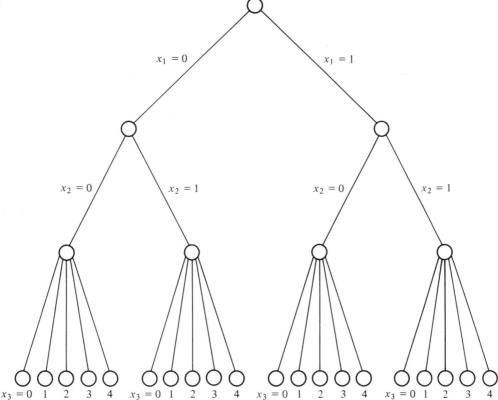

Figure 13.3. Tree of feasible integer solutions for $x_1 \leqslant 1$, $x_2 \leqslant 1$, and $x_3 \leqslant 4$.

variables in the tree is arbitrary. For example, the first pair of branches could require that $x_2 = 0$ and $x_2 = 1$, the second pair could require that $x_3 = 0$ and $x_3 = 1$, and the third pair could require that $x_1 = 0$ and $x_1 = 1$. Also, note that the tree contains several infeasible solutions: that is, integer solutions that do not satisfy the first two constraints of the integer programming model. For a problem such as Example 13.2.1 with 20 possible feasible integer solutions, a computer could evaluate all 20 possibilities quickly. But, for a larger problem, a complete enumeration and evaluation may be inpractical. For example, a problem with 20 zero/1 variables has $2^{20} = 1,048,576$ possible integer solutions.

The *branch-and-bound* method attempts to reduce the amount of enumeration by *eliminating* (or chopping off) connected branches of the tree of all possible integer solutions. The basis for eliminating branches is:

KEY CONCEPT

A branch can be eliminated if it can be shown to contain no integer feasible solution with a higher profit than an integer feasible solution already obtained.

The branch-and-bound procedure requires that an *upper bound* or an *upper limit* be found for the set containing all the possible integer solutions in a given branch. An optimal solution to the integer programming problem obtained by the simplex method with the integer restrictions ignored can provide such an easily obtained upper bound.

The simplex method solution to Example 13.2.1 (ignoring the integer restriction) is

$$x_1 = 1, \qquad x_2 = 1, \quad \text{and} \quad x_3 = 1.20,$$

which is not an integer solution. Profit $Z = 9.20$, which is the maximum profit obtainable over the set of feasible solutions (which, of course, contains the set of

Figure 13.4. Branch-and-bound iterations for Example 13.2.1.

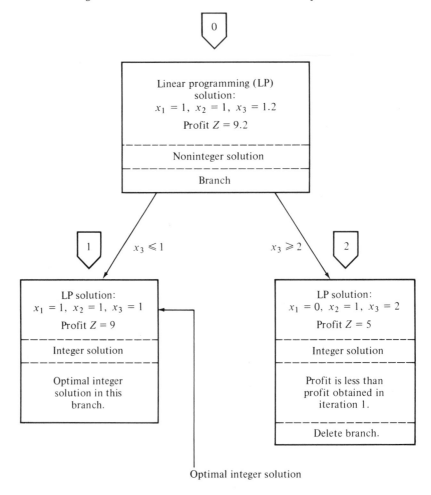

Optimal integer solution

feasible integer solutions). That is, there is no integer solution with a profit higher than 9.20. Thus, profit $Z = 9.20$ is an *upper bound* on all feasible integer solutions to the problem. As we shall illustrate, we can always find an upper bound for any branch by use of the simplex method.

The steps in the branch-and-bound procedure are shown in Figure 13.4 for the problem given in Example 13.2.1.

BRANCH-AND-BOUND SOLUTION OF THE EXAMPLE PROBLEM

ITERATION 0. First solve the problem as a linear programming problem by ignoring the integer restriction. If the solution satisfies the integer restriction, we have obtained an optimal solution to the integer programming problem. The linear programming solution to the example problem is

$$x_1 = 1, \qquad x_2 = 1, \quad \text{and} \quad x_3 = 1.20$$

and profit $Z = 9.20$. Profit $Z = 9.20$ is an *upper bound* on all feasible integer solutions to the problem. However, since this is not an integer solution, we need to continue. But first, we easily see by inspecting the constraints that one feasible integer solution is

$$x_1 = 0, \qquad x_2 = 0, \quad \text{and} \quad x_3 = 0,$$

with a profit of $Z = 0$. It is highly unlikely that this solution is the profit-maximizing integer solution. However, this integer solution does give an *initial lower bound* on maximum profit.

ITERATION 1. Recall that the initial feasible integer solution (obtained in iteration 0) is

$$x_1 = 0, \qquad x_2 = 0, \quad \text{and} \quad x_3 = 0$$

yielding a profit $Z = 0$ (= lower bound on maximum profit).

Step 1—Branching. In this step we select a variable arbitrarily to branch on and then construct the appropriate *branches*. A good selection criterion is to branch on a variable that is noninteger at the current iteration. From iteration 0 only x_3 is noninteger, so we select x_3 for branching. Recall that the previous linear programming solution had $x_3 = 1.2$. Hence, one choice for a pair of branches would be $x_3 \leqslant 1$ and $x_3 \geqslant 2$. This choice for a pair of branches then divides the set of possible integer solutions into *two subsets*, one subset in which $x_3 \leqslant 1$ and the other subset in which $x_3 \geqslant 2$. Since x_3 is restricted to be an integer, it is impossible for x_3 to be between 1 and 2. This step gives the first pair of branches (or partitions) and is shown in Figure 13.4.

Next we arbitrarily select the branch $x_3 \leqslant 1$ for further investigation. For this branch we replace the constraint $x_3 \leqslant 4$ in the original problem by the constraint

$x_3 \le 1$. This replacement yields the following problem:

$$\text{maximize } Z = 5x_1 + 3x_2 + x_3$$

$$\text{subject to} \quad x_1 + x_2 + x_3 \le 6$$

$$3x_1 + x_2 + 4x_3 \le 9$$

$$x_1 \qquad\qquad \le 1$$

$$x_2 \qquad \le 1$$

$$\boxed{x_3 \le 1.} \quad \text{new constraint}$$

The simplex method solution to this problem is

$$x_1 = 1, \qquad x_2 = 1, \quad \text{and} \quad x_3 = 1,$$

yielding a profit $Z = 9$.

Step 2—Bounding. The profit $Z = 9$ for the solution $x_1 = 1$, $x_2 = 1$, $x_3 = 1$ is an *upper bound* on all solutions, including the feasible integer solutions, on the branch $x_3 \le 1$. Also, note that this solution is a feasible integer solution.

Step 3—Comparing and Eliminating. The profit $Z = 9$ for the simplex method solution $x_1 = 1$, $x_2 = 1$, and $x_3 = 1$ is higher than the profit for the best integer solution obtained so far (profit $Z = 0$ with $x_1 = 0$, $x_2 = 0$, and $x_3 = 0$). Thus, $Z = 9$ is a new *lower bound* on maximum profit. Furthermore, we do not need to continue branching further down in the branch $x_3 \le 1$, since we have now determined the optimum feasible integer solution for this branch. That is, for the set of feasible integer solutions for which $x_3 \le 1$, there is no solution that yields a higher profit than the solution just determined,

$$x_1 = 1, \qquad x_2 = 1, \quad \text{and} \quad x_3 = 1,$$

with profit $Z = 9$. Next, we must investigate the other branch in the pair, the branch $x_3 \ge 2$.

ITERATION 2

Step 1—Branching. We now must move back up the tree and investigate the branch $x_3 \ge 2$. That is, we consider the set of possible solutions to the original problem for which the constraint $x_3 \ge 2$ replaces the constraint $x_3 \le 4$. The new problem to be solved by the simplex method is:

$$\text{maximize } Z = 5x_1 + 3x_2 + x_3$$

$$\text{subject to} \quad x_1 + x_2 + x_3 \le 6$$

$$3x_1 + x_2 + 4x_3 \le 9$$

$$x_1 \qquad\qquad \le 1$$

$$x_2 \qquad \le 1$$

$$\boxed{x_3 \ge 2.} \quad \text{new constraint}$$

The optimal solution to this problem is

$$x_1 = 0, \qquad x_2 = 1, \quad \text{and} \quad x_3 = 2$$

with maximum profit $Z = 5$.

Step 2—Bounding. The profit $Z = 5$ for the simplex method solution $x_1 = 0$, $x_2 = 1$, and $x_3 = 2$ is an *upper bound* on all solutions on the branch $x_3 \geq 2$. Note that this solution satisfies the integer restriction. Thus, we have found the optimal integer solution for the branch $x_3 \geq 2$.

Step 3—Comparing and Eliminating. The solution given in step 1 has an upper bound which is associated with a feasible integer solution and is *less than* the previous best lower bound obtained in iteration 1. Thus, we can eliminate this branch from further consideration.

Step 4—Termination. All the branches have been investigated. Thus, the feasible integer solution obtained in iteration 1 is the optimum integer solution for the original problem.

$$\text{optimal solution:} \quad x_1 = 1, x_2 = 1, \text{ and } x_3 = 1$$

with maximum profit $Z = 9$.

13.2.2. Example—Branch-and-Bound Method

Profit Maximization

Consider the following profit-maximization problem:

$$\text{maximize } Z = x_1 + 5x_2 + 7x_3 + 3x_4$$

$$\text{subject to} \quad 7x_1 + 3x_2 + 2x_3 + 4x_4 \leq 15$$

$$8x_1 + 2x_2 + 3x_3 + 5x_4 \leq 17$$

$$x_1 \qquad\qquad\qquad \leq 4$$

$$x_2 \qquad\qquad \leq 4$$

$$x_3 \qquad \leq 1$$

$$x_4 \leq 1$$

$$x_1, \quad x_2, \quad x_3, \quad x_4 \text{ all integers.}$$

Note that the restrictions $x_3 \leq 1$ and $x_4 \leq 1$ imply that x_3 and x_4 are both zero/1 decision variables. The variables x_1 and x_2 can each take on five integer values. That is, $x_1 = 0, 1, 2, 3$, or 4 and $x_2 = 0, 1, 2, 3$, or 4. If we consider only the last four constraints of the integer programming problem, then there are $5 \times 5 \times 2 \times 2 = 100$ possible integer solutions.

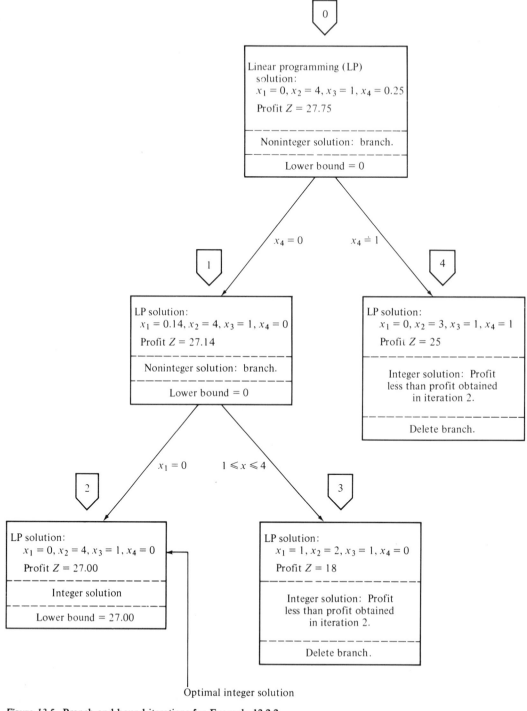

Figure 13.5. Branch-and-bound iterations for Example 13.2.2.

Figure 13.5 shows the results of each iteration of the branch-and-bound method applied to the problem in Example 13.2.2. The number i in the pentagon above each box denotes the ith iteration of the branch-and-bound method.

If the objective is to *minimize* cost rather than *maximize* profit, then the branch-and-bound procedure is unchanged except that the roles of the upper and lower bounds are reversed. Using branch and bound to solve a cost-minimization problem where the decision variables must have integer values is best introduced and understood by an example. A summary of branch and bound for profit maximization is presented in Section 13.2.5 on page 491.

13.2.3. Example—Branch and Bound

Cost Minimization

Consider the following cost-minimization problem:

$$\text{minimize } Z = x_1 + 3x_2 + 5x_3$$

$$\begin{aligned}
\text{subject to} \quad & x_1 + x_2 + x_3 \geqslant 6.5 \\
& 3x_1 + x_2 + 4x_3 \geqslant 9.5 \\
& x_1 \leqslant 1 \\
& x_2 \leqslant 2 \\
& x_3 \leqslant 4
\end{aligned}$$

$$x_1, \quad x_2, \quad x_3 \text{ all integers.}$$

Note that there are $2 \times 3 \times 5 = 30$ possible integer solutions if we consider only the last three constraints of the problem.

Figure 13.6 shows the results of each iteration of the branch-and-bound method applied to the problem above.

ITERATION 0. First solve the problem as a linear programming problem by ignoring the integer restriction. If the solution satisfies the integer restriction, we have an optimal solution to the integer programming problem. The linear programming solution is

$$x_1 = 1, \quad x_2 = 2, \quad \text{and} \quad x_3 = 3.5$$

and cost $Z = 24.5$. Since this is not an integer solution we need to partition the set of solutions. But first note that one feasible integer solution is

$$x_1 = 1, \quad x_2 = 2, \quad \text{and} \quad x_3 = 4$$

with a cost of $Z = 27$. This *feasible integer solution* gives an *initial upper bound* on minimum cost. This integer solution may be the cost-minimizing solution. However, this needs to be determined by application of the branch-and-bound method.

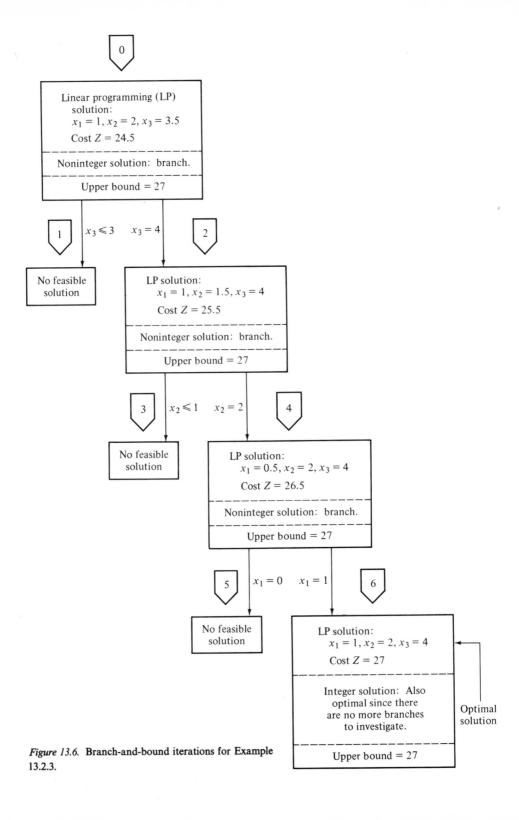

Figure 13.6. Branch-and-bound iterations for Example 13.2.3.

ITERATION 1

Step 1—Branching. In this step we select a variable arbitrarily to branch on and then construct the appropriate branches. From iteration 0 only x_3 is noninteger, so we select x_3 for branching. One choice for a pair of branches is $x_3 \leq 3$ and $x_3 = 4$. Recall that $x_3 = 3.5$ in iteration 0. Next, we arbitrarily select the branch $x_3 \leq 3$ for investigation. In this branch we replace the constraint $x_3 \leq 4$ in the original problem by the constraint $x_3 \leq 3$ and solve the following problem:

$$\text{minimize } Z = x_1 + 3x_2 + 5x_3$$

$$\begin{aligned}
\text{subject to} \quad & x_1 + x_2 + x_3 \geq 6.5 \\
& 3x_1 + x_2 + 4x_3 \geq 9.5 \\
& x_1 \leq 1 \\
& x_2 \leq 2 \\
& \boxed{x_3 \leq 3} \quad \text{new constraint}
\end{aligned}$$

Applying the simplex method to the problem above will show that it has no feasible solution. Note that $x_1 = 1$, $x_2 = 2$, and $x_3 = 3$, the largest possible value of each variable, does not satisfy the first constraint. Thus, we go to the next iteration and investigate the branch $x_3 = 4$.

ITERATION 2

Step 1—Branching. In this step we replace the constraint $x_3 \leq 4$ in the original problem by the constraint $x_3 = 4$ and solve the following problem:

$$\text{minimize } Z = x_1 + 3x_2 + 5x_3$$

$$\begin{aligned}
\text{subject to} \quad & x_1 + x_2 + x_3 \geq 6.5 \\
& 3x_1 + x_2 + 4x_3 \geq 9.5 \\
& x_1 \leq 1 \\
& x_2 \leq 2 \\
& \boxed{x_3 = 4} \quad \text{new constraint}
\end{aligned}$$

The simplex method solution to this problem is

$$x_1 = 1, \quad x_2 = 1.5, \quad \text{and} \quad x_3 = 4$$

with cost $Z = 25.5$.

Step 2—Bounding. The cost $Z = 25.5$ for the solution $x_1 = 1$, $x_2 = 1.5$, and $x_3 = 4$ is a *new lower bound* on all solutions, including the feasible integer solutions. Note that this solution is noninteger.

Step 3—Comparing and Eliminating. Since we have already eliminated the branch $x_3 \leqslant 3$ in iteration 1, we have no other branches to consider for elimination. We do, however, have a *new lower bound* on minimum cost, which is $Z = 25.5$.

ITERATION 3

Step 1—Branching. We now make the obvious choice for a new pair of branches, which is $x_2 \leqslant 1$ and $x_2 = 2$, and select the branch $x_2 \leqslant 1$ for further investigation. Replacing $x_2 \leqslant 2$ by the constraint $x_2 \leqslant 1$ in the problem given in iteration 2 yields the following new problem:

$$\text{minimize } Z = x_1 + 3x_2 + 5x_3$$

$$\text{subject to} \quad x_1 + x_2 + x_3 \geqslant 6.5$$
$$3x_1 + x_2 + 4x_3 \geqslant 9.5$$
$$x_1 \qquad\qquad \leqslant 1$$
$$\boxed{x_2 \qquad \leqslant 1} \quad \text{new constraint}$$
$$x_3 = 4.$$

It can easily be seen by inspection (or by application of the simplex method) that this problem has no feasible solution. Thus, we now move back up the tree and consider the branch $x_2 = 2$.

ITERATION 4

Step 1—Branching. We now consider the set of possible solutions to the problem for which the constraint $x_2 = 2$ replaces the constraint $x_2 \leqslant 2$ in the problem given in iteration 2. This replacement yields the following problem to be solved by the simplex method:

$$\text{minimize } Z = x_1 + 3x_2 + 5x_3$$

$$\text{subject to} \quad x_1 + x_2 + x_3 \geqslant 6.5$$
$$3x_1 + x_2 + 4x_3 \geqslant 9.5$$
$$x_1 \qquad\qquad \leqslant 1$$
$$\boxed{x_2 \qquad = 2} \quad \text{new constraint}$$
$$x_3 = 4.$$

The optimal solution to this problem is

$$x_1 = 0.5, \qquad x_2 = 2, \quad \text{and} \quad x_3 = 4$$

with cost $Z = 26.5$.

Step 2—Bounding. The cost $Z = 26.5$ is a new lower bound on all solutions on the branch $x_2 = 2$. However, note that this solution is noninteger.

Step 3—Comparing and Eliminating. Again, as in iteration 2, there are no branches for comparison that have not already been eliminated.

ITERATIONS 5 AND 6

Step 1—Branching. We now investigate further the branch for which $x_1 = 1$, since by inspection it is easily seen that the branch $x_1 = 0$ has no feasible solutions. Replacing the constraint $x_1 \leqslant 1$ by the constraint $x_1 = 1$ in the problem given in iteration 4 yields the following:

$$\text{minimize } Z = x_1 + 3x_2 + 5x_3$$

$$
\begin{array}{ll}
\text{subject to} & x_1 + x_2 + x_3 \geqslant 6.5 \\
& 3x_1 + x_2 + 4x_3 \geqslant 9.5 \\
& \boxed{x_1 \qquad\qquad = 1} \quad \text{new constraint} \\
& x_2 \qquad\qquad = 2 \\
& x_3 = 4.
\end{array}
$$

By inspecting only the last three constraints, we see that the only solution to this problem is

$$x_1 = 1, \qquad x_2 = 2, \quad \text{and} \quad x_3 = 4$$

with cost $Z = 27$.

Steps 2 and 3—Bounding, Comparing, and Eliminating. The cost $Z = 27$ is a new *lower bound* for all solutions on the branch $x_1 = 1$. It is also an *upper bound* for all solutions on the branch $x_1 = 1$, since it is an integer solution.

Step 4—Termination. All the branches have been investigated. Thus, the feasible integer solution obtained in iteration 5 is the optimum (minimum-cost) solution for the original integer programming problem.

$$\text{optimal solution: } x_1 = 1, x_2 = 2, \text{ and } x_3 = 4,$$

with maximum profit $Z = 27$.

A summary of the steps in the branch-and-bound method for cost minimization appears in Figure 13.7.

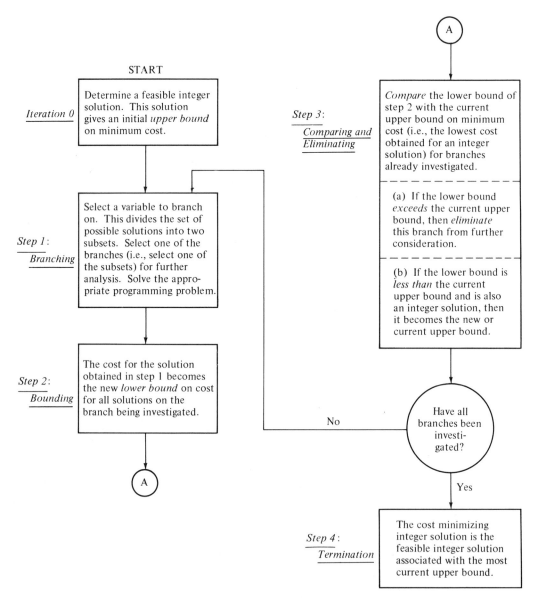

Figure 13.7. Summary of steps in the branch-and-bound method for cost minimization.

13.2.4. Example—Branch and Bound

Cost Minimization

Four different assembly lines are available for producing electronic calculators at Mississippi Electronics (ME). The assembly cost of a calculator in each of the four available lines, the maximum daily capacity of each line, and the corresponding setup costs are given in the production table below. ME has a forecasted demand of 30,000 calculators per day. Management at ME would like a minimum-cost production plan which specifies which lines are to be used, and at what capacity, to meet the minimum daily forecasted demand of 30,000 calculators.

ME Calculator Production Table

Assembly Line	Setup Cost (per day)	Assembly Cost per Calculator	Maximum Capacity
A	$5000	$6	10,000
B	6000	4	20,000
C	1000	7	25,000
D	7000	3	15,000

INTEGER PROGRAMMING MODEL

PRODUCTION DECISION VARIABLES. Let

x_1 = number of calculators produced on line A per day

x_2 = number of calculators produced on line B per day

x_3 = number of calculators produced on line C per day

x_4 = number of calculators produced on line D per day.

ASSEMBLY-LINE SELECTION VARIABLES. Let

$$y_1 = \begin{cases} 0 & \text{if line } A \text{ is not selected for production} \\ 1 & \text{if line } A \text{ is selected for production} \end{cases} \qquad y_2 = \begin{cases} 0 & \text{if line } B \text{ is not selected for production} \\ 1 & \text{if line } B \text{ is selected for production} \end{cases}$$

$$y_3 = \begin{cases} 0 & \text{if line } C \text{ is not selected for production} \\ 1 & \text{if line } C \text{ is selected for production} \end{cases} \qquad y_4 = \begin{cases} 0 & \text{if line } D \text{ is not selected for production} \\ 1 & \text{if line } D \text{ is selected for production.} \end{cases}$$

MODEL

minimize $Z = 5000y_1 + 6000y_2 + 1000y_3 + 7000y_4$

$$\underbrace{}_{\textit{total setup cost}}$$

$$+ 6x_1 + 4x_2 + 7x_3 + 3x_4$$

$$\underbrace{}_{\textit{total variable production costs}}$$

subject to $\quad x_1 + x_2 + x_3 + x_4 = 30{,}000 \quad$ (daily demand)

$\qquad\qquad x_1 \qquad\qquad\quad \leqslant 10{,}000y_1 \quad$ (line A capacity)

$\qquad\qquad\quad x_2 \qquad\qquad \leqslant 20{,}000y_2 \quad$ (line C capacity)

$\qquad\qquad\qquad x_3 \qquad \leqslant 25{,}000y_3 \quad$ (line C capacity)

$\qquad\qquad\qquad x_4 \leqslant 15{,}000y_4 \quad$ (line D capacity)

$\qquad y_1 \qquad\qquad\qquad\quad \leqslant 1$

$\qquad\quad y_2 \qquad\qquad\qquad \leqslant 1$

$\qquad\qquad y_3 \qquad\qquad \leqslant 1$

$\qquad\qquad\qquad y_4 \leqslant 1$

$x_1, \;\; x_2, \;\; x_3, \;\; x_4, \;\; y_1, \;\; y_2, \;\; y_3,$ and y_4 integers (non-negative).

Note that one obvious feasible integer solution is $x_1 = 10{,}000$, $y_1 = 1$, $x_2 = 20{,}000$, and $y_2 = 1$ with a total daily cost of

$$Z = 5000y_1 + 6000y_2 + 1000y_3 + 7000y_4 + 6x_1 + 4x_2 + 7x_3 + 3x_4$$
$$= 5000(1) + 6000(1) + 1000(0) + 7000(0) + 6(10{,}000) + 4(20{,}000)$$
$$+ 7(0) + 3(0)$$
$$= \$151{,}000.$$

This feasible integer solution with a total daily cost of $151,000 gives an initial *upper bound* on minimum total daily cost. The optimal integer solution, obtained after two iterations of the branch-and-bound method is

$$x_1 = 0, \qquad x_2 = 15{,}000, \qquad x_3 = 0, \qquad x_4 = 15{,}000$$
$$y_1 = 0, \qquad y_2 = 1, \qquad\qquad\;\; y_3 = 0, \qquad y_4 = 1$$

with daily cost $Z = \$11{,}000$.

The branch-and-bound method for profit maximization is summarized in Section 13.2.5.

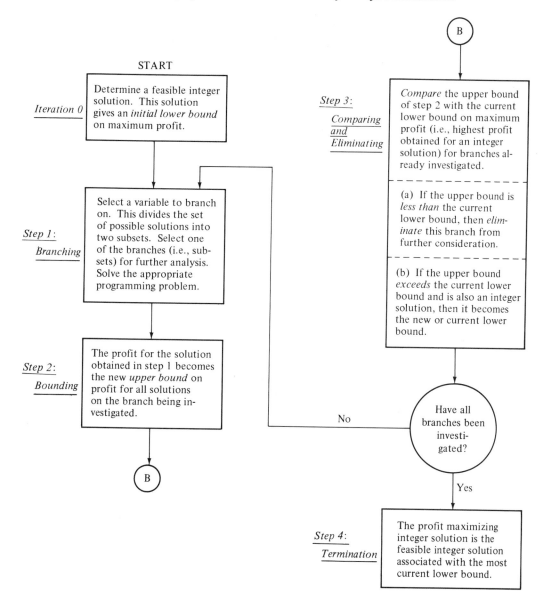

Iteration 0

START

Determine a feasible integer solution. This solution gives an *initial lower bound* on maximum profit.

Step 1:

Branching

Select a variable to branch on. This divides the set of possible solutions into two subsets. Select one of the branches (i.e., subsets) for further analysis. Solve the appropriate programming problem.

Step 2:

Bounding

The profit for the solution obtained in step 1 becomes the new *upper bound* on profit for all solutions on the branch being investigated.

B

B

Step 3:

Comparing and Eliminating

Compare the upper bound of step 2 with the current lower bound on maximum profit (i.e., highest profit obtained for an integer solution) for branches already investigated.

(a) If the upper bound is *less than* the current lower bound, then *eliminate* this branch from further consideration.

(b) If the upper bound *exceeds* the current lower bound and is also an integer solution, then it becomes the new or current lower bound.

Have all branches been investigated?

No

Yes

Step 4:

Termination

The profit maximizing integer solution is the feasible integer solution associated with the most current lower bound.

13.2.6. Example—Assignment Problem

The Cash Trucking Company has four trailers awaiting pickup at different locations in Tennessee. In Arkansas, it has four tractors, each capable of handling any one of the trailers. The assignment of tractors to trailers will affect the total distance traveled to pick up the trailers. Management would like an assignment or pairing of tractors to trailers which minimizes the total distance traveled to pick up the trailers. A tractor can be assigned to pick up one and only one trailer. Also, every trailer must be picked up by a tractor. Table 13.4 gives the distance in miles between each tractor–trailer combination.

Table 13.4. Distance Between Tractor-Trailer Combinations (miles)

		TRAILER				*Minimum*
		1	2	3	4	*Row Number*
	A	36	32	46	38	32
TRACTOR	*B*	50	42	38	46	38
	C	32	34	40	36	32
	D	38	34	50	44	34
						$\overline{136}$ = total

This problem has 24 possible assignments (or feasible solutions), since there are four possible trailers to assign to tractor A and after A is assigned a trailer, there are three trailers left to assign to B, then two left to assign to C; and, finally, one remaining trailer to be assigned to tractor D. Thus, there are $4 \times 3 \times 2 \times 1 = 24$ feasible assignments.

We now apply a branch-and-bound procedure to this assignment problem.

ITERATION 0. First, determine a feasible solution to the problem. This then gives an *upper bound* to the minimum-distance (or minimum-cost) solution. For example, the solution

$$(A-1), \quad (B-2), \quad (C-3), \quad \text{and} \quad (D-4)$$

is feasible and has a total distance equal to

$$\underset{(A-1)}{36} + \underset{(B-2)}{42} + \underset{(C-3)}{40} + \underset{(D-4)}{44} = 162 \text{ miles.}$$

Thus, 162 miles is an *upper bound* to the minimum-distance solution.

Next, to determine a *lower bound* to the minimum-distance solution, we reduce the rows and columns in Table 13.4. To reduce the original distance table we first find the minimum number in each row and subtract it from all numbers in that row. The result of reducing every row is given in Table 13.5.

The optimal assignment of trailers to trucks using Table 13.5 will be exactly the same as for Table 13.4. For example, truck A must be assigned to exactly one of the four trailers. Therefore, the distance traveled by truck A must be *at least* 32 miles. Similarly, the distances traveled by trucks B, C, and D must be *at least* 38, 32, and 34 miles, respectively. Therefore, any assignment including the optimal

Table 13.5. Remaining Distances (obtained by row-reducing Table 13.4)

		TRAILER			
		1	2	3	4
	A	4	0	14	6
TRACTOR	B	12	4	0	8
	C	0	2	8	4
	D	4	0	16	10
Minimum Column Number		0	0	0	4	=4

Total row reduction = 136 miles.

assignment must have a total distance traveled of *at least* 32 + 38 + 32 + 34 = 136 miles.

Next, we reduce the columns of Table 13.5. That is, we subtract the minimum number in each column of Table 13.5 from all numbers in that column. The result of column-reducing Table 13.5 is given in Table 13.6.

Table 13.6. Remaining Distances (obtained by column-reducing Table 13.5)

		TRAILER			
		1	2	3	4
	A	4	0	14	2
TRACTOR	B	12	4	0	4
	C	0	2	8	0
	D	4	0	16	6

Total row reduction + total column reduction
=   136   +   4   = 140 miles.

The total of the row and column reductions is 136 + 4 = 140 miles. Hence, any feasible assignments must have a total distance of *at least* 140 miles. That is, 140 miles is a *lower bound* on the optimal assignment.

Note that if we can make an assignment of all tractors and trailers using zero distances in Table 13.6, we have an optimal assignment. Note in Table 13.6 that the following two solutions, each of whose pairs all have zero distances, are both infeasible.

$$\text{solution 1:} \quad (A\text{–}2), \quad (B\text{–}3), \quad (C\text{–}1), \quad (D\text{–}2)$$
$$\text{solution 2:} \quad (A\text{–}2), \quad (B\text{–}3), \quad (C\text{–}4), \quad (D\text{–}2).$$

ITERATIONS 1 AND 2

Step 1—Branching. Recall that the *lower bound* obtained in iteration 0 equals 140 miles, which is the sum of the numbers required to reduce the original distance (Table 13.4). We now select a pair and construct branches. A good procedure to use is to branch on a pair that has a zero distance.

For example, we could branch on $(A-2)$ and $(\overline{A-2})$, where $(\overline{A-2})$ denotes those solutions that do not pair tractor A with trailer 1. Similarly, we could branch on $(C-1)$ and $(\overline{C-1})$, $(B-3)$ and $(\overline{B-3})$, and so forth. Consider the pair of branches $(A-2)$ and $(\overline{A-2})$. To determine the *lower bound* on the subset of solutions for which $(A-2)$, we cross out row A and column 2 of Table 13.6. This yields Table 13.7.

Table 13.7. Remaining Distances Given (A–2)
(obtained by crossing out row
A and column 2 in Table 13.6)

		TRAILER			Minimum
		1	3	4	Row Number
TRACTOR	B	12	0	4	0
	C	0	8	0	0
	D	4	16	6	4
		0	0	0	

Next, we row- and column-reduce Table 13.7. This yields a net reduction of 4 miles. The reduced Table 13.7 is given in Table 13.8. Thus, the lower bound on the branch $(A-2)$ is $140 + 4 = 144$ miles.

Table 13.8. Remaining Distances Given (A–2)
(obtained by reducing Table 13.7)

		TRAILER		
		1	3	4
TRACTOR	B	12	0	4
	C	0	8	0
	D	0	12	2

To determine the lower bound on the branch $(\overline{A-2})$, we use the following procedure. Since some trailer other than trailer 2 will be assigned to tractor A, we see from Table 13.9 that it must be either trailer 1, 3, or 4 and the remaining distance must be *at least* 2 miles. Similarly, since some tractor other than A will be assigned to trailer 2, we see from the second column of Table 13.9 that it must be either tractor B, C, or D and the distance must be *at least* an additional 0 miles (if, for example, D is assigned to 2). Thus, the set of feasible assignments for which $(\overline{A-2})$ must have a lower bound of $140 + 2 + 0 = 142$ miles. In determining this lower bound, we are in effect row- and column-reducing Table 13.9, with the restriction that the pair $(A-2)$ is not to be considered. Table 13.9 shows $(A-2)$ crossed out to indicate that it is to be prohibited.

Table 13.9. Remaining Distances Given $(\overline{A-2})$
[obtained from Table 13.6 by eliminating $(A-2)$]

TRACTOR		1	2	3	4	Minimum Row Number
	A	4	✕	14	2	2
	B	12	4	0	4	0
	C	0	2	8	0	0
	D	4	0	16	6	0
		0	0	0	0	

Total row reduction = 2 miles

Table 13.10 shows the result of row-reducing Table 13.9.

Table 13.10. Remaining Distances Given $(\overline{A-2})$
(obtained by row-reducing Table 13.9)

TRACTOR		1	2	3	4
	A	2	✕	12	0
	B	12	4	0	4
	C	0	2	8	0
	D	4	0	16	6

Step 2—Bounding. The lower bound on the branch $(A-2)$ is $140 + 4 = 144$ miles and the lower bounding on the branch $(\overline{A-2})$ is $140 + 2 = 142$ miles.

Step 3—Comparing. Since neither branch $(A-2)$ nor $(\overline{A-2})$ has a lower bound which exceeds the upper bound of 162 miles, we return to step 1. The first iteration of the example problem is shown in Figure 13.8. Note the branch (or subset) $(A-2)$ contains six feasible solutions and the branch for which $(\overline{A-2})$ contains 18 feasible solutions.

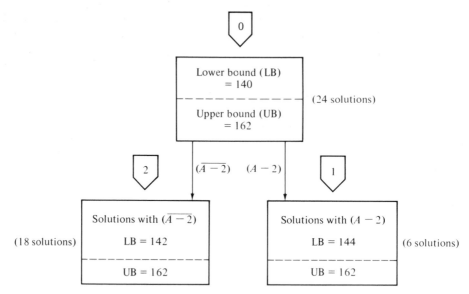

Figure 13.8. Results after two iterations.

ITERATIONS 3 AND 4

Step 1—Branching. We have not yet found a feasible assignment. Hence, we need to proceed farther down the tree. A good choice for further branching is to choose the branch with the smallest lower bound. Since $(\overline{A-2})$ has a smaller lower bound than $(A-2)$, we choose $(\overline{A-2})$ for further branching. In Table 13.10 we see that branch $(B-3)$ has a zero distance. Thus, a good choice for branching is $(B-3)$ and $(\overline{B-3})$.

Step 2—Bounding. To determine a lower bound for the branch $(B-3)$ we cross out row B and column 3 of Table 13.10 and then row- and column-reduce the resulting table. The result of this elimination of column and row reduction is given in Table 13.11. Note that the total reduction is 0 miles. Thus, net addition to the lower bound for the branch $(B-3)$ is 0 miles.

Table 13.11. Remaining Distances Given $(\overline{A-2})$ and (B–3)(obtained from Table 13.10)

		TRAILER		
		1	2	4
TRACTOR	A	2	✕	0
	C	0	2	0
	D	4	0	6

Total reduction = 0 miles

To determine a lower bound for the branch $(\overline{B{-}3})$, we cross out $(B{-}3)$ in Table 13.10 and then row- and column-reduce the resulting table. The results of these two operations on Table 13.10 are shown by Table 13.12. The total addition to the lower bound for the branch $(\overline{B{-}3})$ is 12 miles. Thus, the lower bound on the branch $(B{-}3)$ is $142 + 0 = 142$ miles, and the lower bound on the branch $(\overline{B{-}3})$ is $142 + 12 = 154$ miles.

Table 13.12. Remaining Distances Given $(\overline{A{-}2})$ and $(B{-}3)$ (obtained from Table 13.10)

		TRAILER			
		1	2	3	4
TRACTOR	A	2	✕	4	0
	B	8	0	✕	0
	C	0	2	0	0
	D	4	0	8	6

Total reduction = 12 miles

Figure 13.9. Results after three iterations.

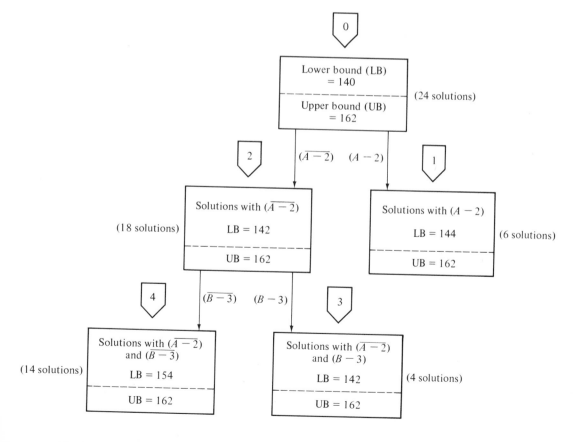

Step 3—Comparing. Since neither branch (B–3) nor $\overline{(B–3)}$ has a lower bound that exceeds the upper bound of 162 miles, we return to step 1 and perform another iteration. The fourth iteration of the example problem is shown in Figure 13.9.

ITERATION 5

Step 1—Branching. We have not found a feasible assignment. Hence, we need to proceed farther down the tree. Since (B–3) has the smallest lower bound we choose (B–3) for further branching.

Figure 13.10. Results of the fifth iteration.

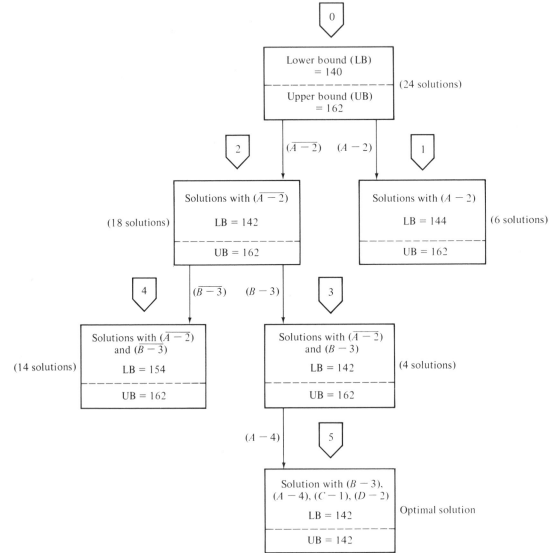

Step 2—Bounding. Note in Table 13.11 for $(\overline{A-2})$ and $(B-3)$ that we can pair $(A-4)$, $(C-1)$, and $(D-2)$ with a net addition to total distance equaling 0 miles. Thus, the lower bound on the branch $(A-4)$ is $142 + 0 = 142$ miles.

Step 3—Comparing and Eliminating. Note that the lower bound on the branch $(A-4)$ is 142 miles and is less than the lower bound on all other branches. Since this branch gives a feasible assignment of

$$(B-3), \quad (A-4), \quad (C-1), \quad \text{and} \quad (D-2),$$

we can eliminate all the remaining branches not yet investigated.

Step 4—Termination. Since all branches have been investigated, we can determine an optimal assignment.

Optimal assignment is

$$(A-4), \quad (B-3), \quad (C-1), \quad \text{and} \quad (D-2)$$

with distance = 142 miles.

The results of performing three branch-and-bound iterations are shown in Figure 13.10.

KEY CONCEPTS

Tree diagrams
  Branches
  Bounds
    Upper bounds
    Lower bounds

Assignment problem
Capital-budgeting problems
Integer-valued solutions

REVIEW PROBLEMS

13.1. A company produces two products, A and B. Each unit of product A requires 1 hour of engineering service and 5 hours of machine time. To produce 1 unit of product B requires 2 hours of engineering and 8 hours of machine time. There are 100 hours of engineering and 400 hours of machine time available. The cost of production is a nonlinear function of the quantity produced, as given in the following table.

PRODUCT A		PRODUCT B	
Production (units)	Unit Cost	Production (units)	Unit Cost
0–50	$10	0–40	$7
50–100	8	40–100	3

The unit selling price of product A is $12 and the unit selling price of product B is $14. The company would like a production plan which gives the number of units of A to produce and the number of units of B that will maximize profit. Formulate an integer programming model for this problem.

13.2. A company must choose a set of projects from the following list. Their goal is to maximize the total net present value of the set of projects selected but not spend more than the estimated budget in any one of the next 3 years.

The data for this capital-budgeting problem are given in the following table. Also given are some additional restrictions on which projects may be selected.

Project Number	Net Present Value (000s)	REQUIRED EXPENDITURES		
		Year 1	Year 2	Year 3
1	$50	$10	$15	$10
2	40	20	10	5
3	30	10	15	10
4	40	20	10	5
5	50	10	15	10
6	60	20	10	5
Estimated budget:		90	80	50

1. The company *must choose* either project 1 or project 6.
2. If project 6 is selected, then project 5 must be selected.

Formulate an integer programming model for this capital budgeting problem.

SUBCONTRACTING PROBLEM (APPLICATION OF DECISION TREES AND BRANCH AND BOUND)

13.3. The ZYX Corporation is considering subcontracting the production of CB aerials during the next 4 years. Management of ZYX believes it may be cheaper in some years to subcontract and in other years to use their existing plant capacity. Management would like a minimum-cost 4-year plan that specifies which years to subcontract production and which years to use existing plant capacity.

Subcontracting production for the first time during the 4-year period will cost ZYX $50,000 per year. If ZYX subcontracts for 2 years *in succession*, the cost for the second year is $40,000. If ZYX subcontracts for 3 years in succession, the cost for the third year is $30,000. Finally, if ZYX skips 1 year between subcontracting, the subcontracting cost during the second year is $45,000.

The following table gives the cost of using existing plant capacity and the cost of subcontracting for each of the next 4 years.

Plant Costs and Subcontracting Costs ($10,000 units)

	YEAR			
	1	2	3	4
Costs of Using Existing Plant Capacity:	2	8	6	$2\frac{1}{2}$
Subcontracting costs given that ZYX subcontracted:				
Previous 0 years	5	5	5	5
Previous 1 year		4	4	4
Previous 2 years			3	3
Previous 3 years				3

13.1. Let

$$x_{A1} = \text{number of units of product } A \text{ produced at a unit cost of \$10}$$

$$x_{A2} = \text{number of units of product } A \text{ produced at a unit cost of \$8.}$$

Then,

$$x_A = x_{A1} + x_{A2}$$
$$= \text{total number of units of product } A \text{ produced.}$$

Similarly, let

$$x_{B1} = \text{number of units of product } B \text{ produced at a unit cost of \$7}$$

$$x_{B2} = \text{number of units of product } B \text{ produced at a unit cost of \$3.}$$

$$x_B = x_{B1} + x_{B2}$$
$$= \text{total number of units of product } B \text{ produced.}$$

Constraints

Engineering: $1x_A + 2x_B$ $\leqslant 100$ hours

or $1(x_{A1} + x_{A2}) + 2(x_{B1} + x_{B2}) \leqslant 100$ hours

Machine time: $5x_A + 8x_B$ $\leqslant 400$ hours

or $5(x_{A1} + x_{A2}) + 8(x_{B1} + x_{B2}) \leqslant 400$ hours.

Objective Function

$$Z = \text{net revenue}$$
$$= (12 - 10)x_{A1} + (12 - 8)x_{A2} + (14 - 7)x_{B1} + (14 - 3)x_{B2}$$
$$= 2x_{A1} + 4x_{A2} + 7x_{B1} + 11x_{B2}.$$

Note that the variable x_{A2} has a larger coefficient than x_{A1}: $4 - 2 = \$2$ larger. Thus, x_{A2} will be positive before x_{A1} in a revenue-maximizing solution. But this cannot be allowed, since x_{A1} must be equal to 50 units before x_{A2} can have a positive value. Similarly, x_{B2} will be positive before x_{B1} in a revenue-maximizing solution. However, x_{B1} must be equal to 40 units before x_{B2} can have a positive value. Thus, we need the following additional constraints.
Consider the three constraints:

$$\boxed{x_{A1} \leqslant 50, \ x_{A1} \geqslant 50y_1, \ x_{A2} \leqslant 50y_1}$$

where y_1 is a zero/1 variable. If we let $y_1 = 0$ in the last two constraints above, then

$$x_{A1} \leqslant 50, \ x_{A1} \geqslant 0, \text{ and } x_{A2} = 0.$$

If we let $y_1 = 1$, then

$$\left.\begin{array}{c} x_{A1} \leqslant 50 \\ x_{A1} \geqslant 50 \end{array}\right\} \text{ or } \quad x_{A1} = 50$$

and $\qquad\qquad x_{A2} \leqslant 50.$

Thus, the addition of the zero/1 variable y_1 in the three constraints above guarantees that $x_{A1} = 50$ if x_{A2} is positive.

Similarly, for product B, let

$$x_{B1} \leqslant 40, \; x_{B1} \geqslant 40y_2, \text{ and } x_{B2} \leqslant 60y_2,$$

where y_2 is a zero/1 variable.

INTEGER PROGRAMMING MODEL

Maximize $Z = 2x_{A1} + 4x_{A2} + \quad 7x_{B1} + 11x_{B2}$

subject to

$$
\begin{aligned}
x_{A1} + x_{A2} + 2x_{B1} + 2x_{B2} &\leqslant 100 \\
5x_{A1} + 5x_{A2} + 8x_{B1} + 8x_{B2} &\leqslant 400 \\
x_{A1} \phantom{+ 5x_{A2} + 8x_{B1} + 8x_{B2}} &\leqslant 50 \\
x_{A1} - 50y_1 \phantom{+ 8x_{B1} + 8x_{B2}} &\geqslant 0 \\
x_{A2} - 50y_1 \phantom{+ 8x_{B1} + 8x_{B2}} &\leqslant 0 \\
x_{B1} \phantom{- 50y_1 + 8x_{B2}} &\leqslant 40 \\
x_{B1} - 40y_2 \phantom{+ 8x_{B2}} &\geqslant 0 \\
x_{B2} - 60y_2 &\leqslant 0 \\
y_1 &\leqslant 1 \\
y_2 &\leqslant 1
\end{aligned}
$$

$$y_1, \; y_2 \text{ integers.}$$

13.2. Let

$$x_i = \begin{cases} 1 & \text{if project } i \text{ is selected} \\ 0 & \text{if project } i \text{ is not selected} \end{cases} \qquad i = 1, 2, 3, 4, 5, 6.$$

There are six zero/1 decision variables in this capital-budgeting problem.

Let Z = total net present value. Then the integer programming model is to choose x_j's to

maximize $Z = 50x_1 + 40x_2 + 30x_3 + 40x_4 + 50x_5 + 60x_6$

subject to $10x_1 + 20x_2 + 10x_3 + 20x_4 + 10x_5 + 20x_6 \leqslant 90$ (budget for Year 1)

$15x_1 + 10x_2 + 15x_3 + 10x_4 + 15x_5 + 10x_6 \leqslant 80$ (budget for Year 2)

$10x_1 + 5x_2 + 10x_3 + 5x_4 + 10x_5 + 5x_6 \leqslant 50$ (budget for Year 3)

(a): $x_1 + \qquad\qquad\qquad\qquad x_6 = 1$

(b): $x_6 \leqslant x_5$ or $x_5 - x_6 \geqslant 0$

$x_1 \leqslant 1, \quad x_2 \leqslant 1, \quad x_3 \leqslant 1, \quad x_4 \leqslant 1, \quad x_5 \leqslant 1, \quad x_6 \leqslant 1$
$x_1, \quad x_2, \quad x_3, \quad x_4, \quad x_5, \quad x_6$ integers.

Note in constraint (a) that if $x_1 = 1$, then $x_6 = 0$, and if $x_1 = 0$, then $x_6 = 1$. However, both solutions $x_1 = 0$, $x_2 = 0$ and $x_1 = 1$, $x_2 = 1$ violate (a).

Note in constraint (b) that if $x_6 = 1$, then $x_5 = 1$. That is, if project 6 is selected, $x_6 = 1$, then project 5 must be selected, $x_5 = 1$. However, we can select project 5, $x_5 = 1$, but not project 6, $x_6 = 0$, and not violate constraint (b).

Constraints of the type given in (a) are called "either/or" constraints. Constraint (b) is what is commonly called a "precedence" constraint.

13.3. At the beginning of each year a decision must be made to subcontract or to use existing plant capacity. This decision *must* be based on a comparison of costs in successive years. We first use a decision-tree technique to solve the problem.

Consider the first year. Let 1 and $\bar{1}$ stand for renting and not renting at a cost of 50,000 and 20,000, respectively, in year 1.

The costs and decisions can be represented as shown in Figure 13.11.

The costs and decisions for 2 years are indicated by branching out from the two end points of the previous tree. See Figure 13.12 on page 504 for the resulting tree.

Figure 13.11. First branch of review problem.

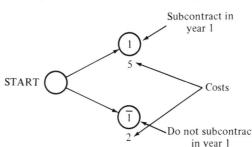

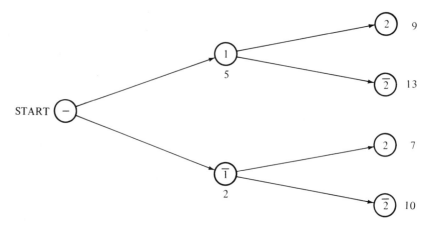

Figure 13.12. Second and third branch of review problem.

Note that if **ZYX** *plans* for only the next 2 years, the optimal decision is to use existing capacity in year 1 but subcontract in year 2 at a total cost of $20,000 + $50,000 = $70,000.

The decision tree shown in Figure 13.13 completely enumerates every possible sequence of decision for **ZYX** over the next 4 years.

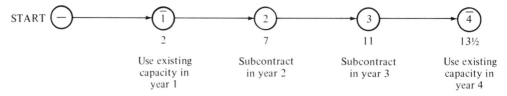

Figure 13.13

The column on the right gives the total cost for each sequence of decisions. Note that the lowest cost is $135,000. To determine the minimum-cost 4-year rental plan in Figure 13.14, we performed a *complete enumeration* of every possible sequence of decisions. We now solve the same problem using a branch-and-bound method.

A Branch-and-Bound Solution. We again start at the beginning of year 1 and branch out from the root of the tree, as shown in Figure 13.15. After constructing the two branches for year 1, we know that total costs for *any* 4-year plan must be at least 2 (or $20,000).

Figure 13.14. Tree showing all possible solutions for the review problem. →

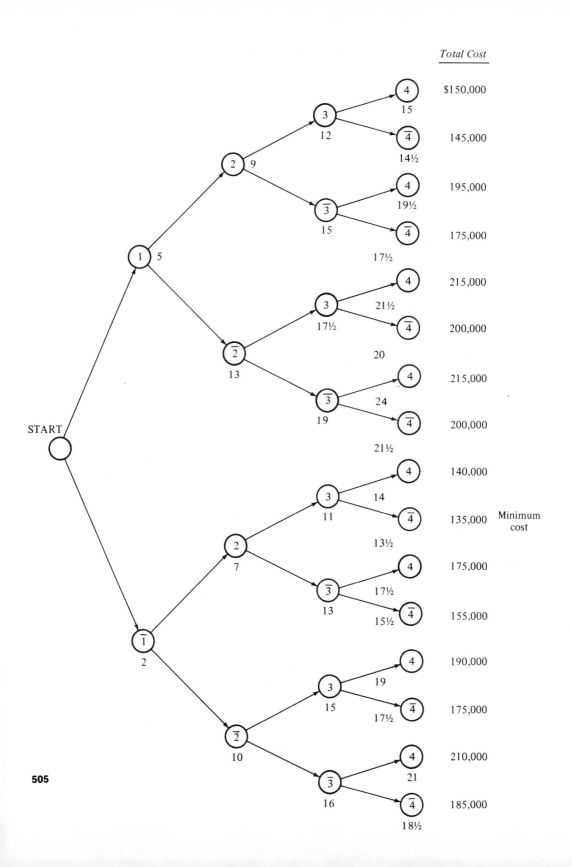

	Total Cost
(4)	$150,000
(4̄)	145,000
(4)	195,000
(4̄)	175,000
(4)	215,000
(4̄)	200,000
(4)	215,000
(4̄)	200,000
(4)	140,000
(4̄)	135,000 Minimum cost
(4)	175,000
(4̄)	155,000
(4)	190,000
(4̄)	175,000
(4)	210,000
(4̄)	185,000

START

1 5
2 9
3 12
15
19½
3̄ 15
17½
2̄ 13
3 17½
21½
20
3̄ 19
24
21½
1̄ 2
2 7
3 11
14
13½
3̄ 13
17½
15½
2̄ 10
3 15
19
17½
3̄ 16
21
18½

505

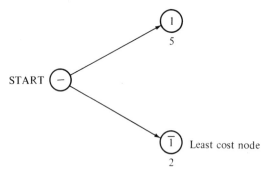

Figure 13.15. First branch of the review problem.

We next *branch* out from the node with the least cost, which is node $\bar{1}$, as illustrated in Figure 13.16.

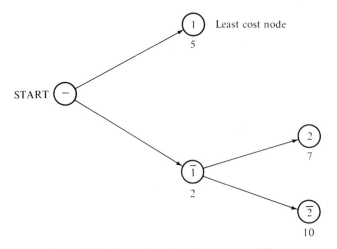

Figure 13.16. Second branch of the review problem.

We now know that the total cost of any 2-year plan must be at least 5 (or $50,000). Again we *branch* out from the least-cost note, which is node 1 (Figure 13.17).

The node with the least total cost is now 2, with a cost of 7. Continuing in this manner, we obtain Figures 13.18–13.20.

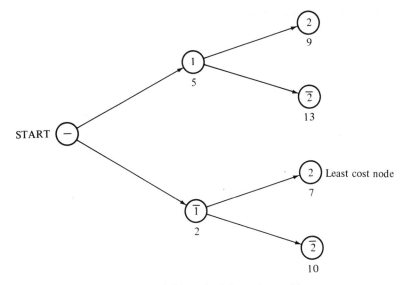

Figure 13.17. Third branch of the review problem.

Figure 13.18. Fourth branch of the review problem.

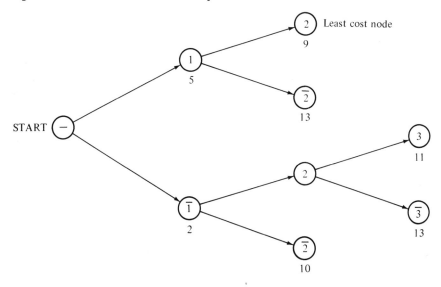

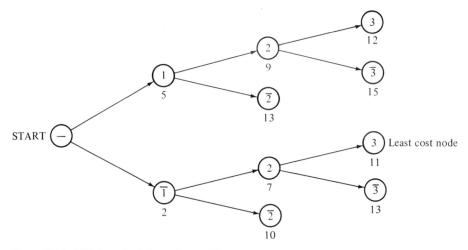

Figure 13.19. Fifth branch of the review problem.

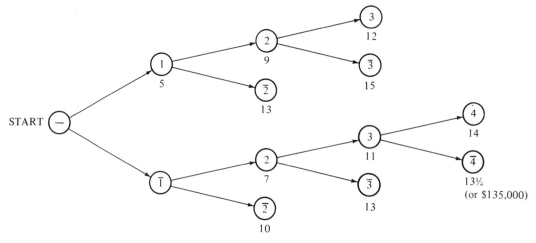

Figure 13.20. Sixth branch of the review problem.

Figure 13.20 indicates the optimal sequence of decisions that is shown in Figure 13.21 and has a cost of $135,000 ($13\frac{1}{2}$), since the minimum cost for any 1-year period is at least $25,000 ($2\frac{1}{2}$). We need not continue branching from the remaining nodes 3, $\bar{3}$, and $\bar{2}$, since the total cost along these paths will be greater than $135,000.

Figure 13.21

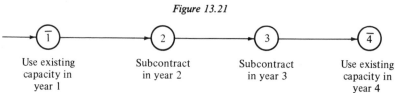

Review. The basic idea of a branch-and-bound method for a minimization problem is as follows. Suppose that the objective function of your model is to be *minimized.* Assume that we can determine an *upper bound* on the optimal value of the objective function. If it is difficult to find an upper bound, this step may be omitted. Next, partition the set of all feasible solutions of the problem into at least two subsets. For each subset determine a *lower bound* on the value of the objective function. Next, we exclude from further consideration any subset with a lower bound exceeding the current upper bound. Of the remaining subsets, the one with the smallest lower bound is further partitioned into subsets. Finally, for this new partition we proceed as above in computing lower bounds and excluding those subsets with lower bounds exceeding the current upper bound. The process of partitioning sets, computing bounds, and eliminating subsets continues until a *feasible solution* is obtained with an objective function value that is equal to or less than the lower bounds for all subsets. This feasible solution is the cost-minimizing solution.

EXERCISES

MODELING AND
INTEGER
PROGRAMMING

13.1. Construct a capital-budgeting integer programming model using the following data.

		COSTS (000S)		
Project Number	Net Present Value	Year 1	Year 2	Year 3
1	$25	$30	$80	$10
2	40	40	70	50
3	70	50	60	70
4	10	60	60	10
5	20	70	40	10
6	35	20	30	90
7	60	20	50	20
8	75	25	80	60
9	15	40	20	15
Estimated budget:		300	320	220

MODELING AND
INTEGER
PROGRAMMING

13.2. Write a constraint to satisfy each of these conditions in a project selection zero/1 integer programming model. The projects are numbered 1, 2, 3, 4, 5, 6, 7, 8, 9, and 10.

Constraint (a): Exactly one project from the set $\{1, 2, 3\}$ must be selected.

Constraint (b): Project 2 can be selected only if number 10 is selected. However, 10 can be selected without 2 being selected.

Constraint (c): No more than one project from the set $\{1, 3, 5, 7, 9\}$ can be selected.

Constraint (d): If number 4 is selected, then number 8 cannot be selected.

Constraint (e): Projects 4 and 10 must both be selected or both be rejected.

13.3. The Tulsa National Bank has six branches located within the city. Once a day, checks are to be picked up at the branches and delivered to the main bank.

Branch Bank Number	Estimated Number of Bags to Be Picked up Daily
1	10
2	30
3	20
4	40
5	80
6	50

The bank can lease four trucks with differed capacities for the pickup and delivery of bags and checks. The costs of a truck per day and their capacities are given in the following table.

Truck Number	Cost / Day	Bag Capacity
1	$50	60
2	100	70
3	90	90
4	125	160

Formulate an integer programming model using the objective of minimizing daily pickup and delivery costs.

13.4. The WCM ("We Charge the Most") Plumbing Company has four men available for assignment to four new contracts. Each plumber will drive directly from his home each morning to his assigned job. The men are paid during the driving time. The union requires that the firm *maximize* the total distances traveled per day by all four men. The following table gives the distances (in kilometers) between the four jobs and the location of the homes of each of the four plumbers.

Plumber Number	JOB NUMBER			
	1	2	3	4
1	2	4	6	8
2	8	6	4	2
3	1	2	3	4
4	4	3	2	1

Construct a zero/1 integer programming model for WCM. The goal of WCM is to assign one and only one plumber to one job so that the total distance traveled per day is maximized.

13.5. Consider the following *make-or-buy* production problem.

A company sells three products, P_1, P_2, and P_3. Estimated weekly demand is 100 units for each product. The company can purchase the products from an independent supplier at the following costs:

Product	Purchasing Cost / Unit
P_1	$3.0
P_2	2.0
P_3	1.0

Also, the company has the production capacity to produce the three products using any one or more of their four assembly lines. The assembly lines differ in their rate of output per hour. Also, each line can be operated at most 40 hours per week. The following table gives the output rates per hour by product and assembly line.

Product		ASSEMBLY LINE		
	L_1	L_2	L_3	L_4
P_1	4	5	6	7
P_2	7	6	5	4
P_3	2	3	4	5

The production costs per unit in the plant are as follows.

Product	Production Cost / Unit
P_1	$2.5
P_2	2.0
P_3	1.20

Construct an integer programming model to use in determining the minimum cost make-or-buy plan for the company.

13.6. Solve the following integer linear programming problem graphically.

$$\text{maximize } Z = 10x_1 + 20x_2$$

$$\text{subject to} \qquad x_1 + x_2 \leqslant 2$$

$$x_1, \quad x_2 \text{ integers.}$$

13.7. Solve the following integer programming problem using a branch-and-bound method.

$$\text{maximize } Z = 10x_1 + 12x_2$$

$$\text{subject to} \qquad x_1 + x_2 \leqslant 2.1$$

$$x_2 \leqslant 1$$

$$x_1, \quad x_2 \text{ integers.}$$

13.8. Solve the following integer programming problem using a branch-and-bound method.

$$\text{minimize } Z = 5x_1 + 6x_2$$

$$\text{subject to} \qquad x_1 + x_2 \geqslant 2.5$$

$$x_2 \geqslant 1$$

$$x_1, \quad x_2 \text{ integers.}$$

13.9. Four jobs can be assigned to four different machines. The setup time for each job on the various machines is given in the following table.

		MACHINE		
Job	1	2	3	4
1	10	11	13	13
2	7	8	9	10
3	5	6	7	8
4	13	14	15	16

Find an optimal assignment of jobs to machines that will minimize the total setup time. Use a branch-and-bound method.

13.10. Use a branch-and-bound method to determine a profit-maximizing assignment using the following data.

		JOB		
Man	1	2	3	4
A	$40	$35	$30	$25
B	40	40	30	40
C	30	30	30	50
D	40	30	40	50

CASE 13.1 Illustrative Case Study
Involving a Financial Management Problem

APPLICATION OF
INTEGER
PROGRAMMING TO
CAPITAL-BUDGETING
PROBLEMS

A capital-budgeting problem occurs when the firm is confronted with a variety of possible investment opportunities and a fixed amount of capital available for these investments. As noted in the finance literature (which you have studied or will be studying in your finance courses), a project yielding a positive net present value is considered a worthwhile investment opportunity, and under various conditions all such investments should be undertaken. However, most firms do not have the funds available or unlimited access to all resources required to invest in every worthwhile investment opportunity. Therefore, the firm is subject to the concept of *capital rationing*.

In order to provide an unbiased measurement of the various investment's "worth," all projects may be subjected to discounted cash-flow calculations and assigned a net present value. It now becomes the firm's objective to select from among the complete set of investment opportunities those which will provide the highest possible returns without exceeding the allowed budget. So far it has been implied that the only constraint is a financial one. This is not necessarily true, for a firm in constructing a capital budget can also be restricted by other constraints, such as manpower or time, in addition to financial constraints. It is obvious that any attempt at selecting an "optimal" set of projects can be tedious and complicated. This is especially true if the possible investment opportunities are interdependent and more than one time period is involved.

Management has a tool available to help solve this problem and to select the best possible combination of projects using the optimal amount of resources available. This tool is provided by applying an integer programming model to the capital-budgeting problem. Such models provide an optimal solution in terms of acceptance or rejection of each individual project. This acceptance or rejection is usually represented by solution values of 1 or zero—1 for acceptance, zero for rejection.

As the name implies, integer programming's objective is to have the optimal solution in terms of whole numbers. Examples of such requirements are numerous and will be omitted, but for the sake of clarity, management needs information of the form: produce 200 cars, as opposed to the form: produce 189.373 cars. With this background in mind consider the following problem.

MSH Inc. is considering investments in plant modernization and plant expansion of its sugar refinery facilities in New Orleans. The data appearing in the tables were prepared by the MSH planning staff, headed by a financial analyst. Management is willing to use the data in selecting the best set of proposals. All projects are to be completed in 2 years, with varying requirements of money and plant engineering.

The planned modernization requires that the modernized or new production line be implemented (Nos. 1 or 2). Project 3 is applicable only to the new line, project 2. Because of an independent present supplier, the company does not want to buy both (No. 6) or build (No. 5). The new trucks (No. 7) are needed; however, project 4 is not mandatory.

Project Number	Description	Net Present Value	Engineering Hours	EXPENDITURES	
				Year 1	Year 2
1	Modernize package line	$100,000	3000	$350,000	$ 0
2	Build new package line	250,000	7000	100,000	300,000
3	Numerical control for new line	35,000	2000	0	200,000
4	Modernize offices and shops	70,000	6000	80,000	100,000
5	Build raw sugar processing facility	130,000	4000	60,000	190,000
6	Buy present subcontractor's facilities for raw-material processing	90,000	500	240,000	0
7	New fleet of delivery trucks	20,000	0	70,000	10,000

The limitations on available capital and manpower provided by the accounting department are:

Expenditures:
Year 1: $550,000
Year 2: $620,000
Engineering hours: 12,000

Assignment

1. Formulate and determine an optimal budget for MSH using integer programming.
2. Assuming that constraints on the availability of funds for each period are planned rather than absolutely fixed, as a financial manager, what benefits might you obtain by permitting partial projects to the solution?
3. To paraphrase an earlier statement—unfortunately (or fortunately) the numbers that come out (solution) of an analysis are related to the numbers put into the analysis. Let us add now another bit of knowledge to the scheme of things. The output (solution) will also be related to the intervening steps (algorithm) employed. In programming it is crucially important that the objective function be logically consistent with the constraints imposed. It is just as important to know when not to use a particular optimization technique as it is to know how to use a technique. Comment on the relevance of mathematical programming in capital budgeting when the constraints are both financial and nonfinancial (see Hughes and Lewellen, 1974).
4. Suppose that one or more constraints are not known with certainty. For example, suppose that for some reason a firm limits its budget to funds generated internally so that future available funds are not known with certainty. How would you incorporate this in your model?

References for Case 13.1

BIERMAN, H., JR., and S. SMIDT. *The Capital Budgeting Decision*. New York: Macmillan Publishing Co., Inc., 1966.

HUGHES, J. S., and W. G. LEWELLEN. "Programming Solutions to Capital Rationing Problems." *Journal of Business, Finance and Accounting,* **1** (1), 1974.

JOHNSON, R. W. *Capital Budgeting*. Belmont, Calif.: Wadsworth Publishing Co., Inc., 1970.

VAN HORNE, J. C. *Financial Management and Policy*. Englewood Cliffs, N.J.: Prentice-Hall, Inc., 1968.

WEINGARTNER, H. M. *Mathematical Programming and the Analysis of Capital Budgeting Problems*. Englewood Cliffs, N.J.: Prentice-Hall, Inc., 1963.

WEINGARTNER, H. M. "Capital Budgeting of Interrelated Projects: Survey and Synthesis." *Management Science,* **12**, 1966, 458–516.

CHAPTER 14
Goal Programming

OBJECTIVES: Upon successful completion of this chapter, you should be able to:

1. Formulate linear and quadratic goal programming models.
2. Use the simplex procedure for single-goal problems, multiple-goal problems, and multiple-goal problems with subgoals.
3. Specify alternative methods of establishing ordinal priorities for the goals.
4. Give examples of situations where goal programming is applicable.

14.1. INTRODUCTION

As we discussed in Chapter 7, most real decision situations, whether personal or professional, are characterized by multiple goals or objectives rather than by a mere single objective. These goals can be complementary, but more often than not, they are generally conflicting as well as incommensurable. For example, an auto producer such as General Motors would like to build a passenger car that would sell for less than $3000, have 250 horsepower, and get 40 miles to the gallon. Consider, for example, the power and fuel-economy goals. The higher the horsepower, the less the fuel economy, indicating that these two goals conflict. Moreover, these two goals are incommensurable, since horsepower and miles per gallon have different scales or dimensions. General Motors is thus faced with a perplexing decision problem regarding the type of car to build, since the objectives it would like to achieve given its capabilities and resources may not be feasible, owing to conflicting and incommensurable objectives.

The problem becomes even more complex in societal decision-making problems. Suppose, for example, that a public utility wishes to build a nuclear power plant in a given location. The goals it would have to consider would be power-generating capacity, reliability, environmental effects such as biological impact at site, health and safety of the population in the vicinity of the nuclear power plant, socioeconomic effects, and system cost. Many of these goals, in addition to being

516

conflicting and incommensurable, are "fuzzy"—biological impact, for example. In fact, such a goal might only be measured and scaled subjectively.

In Chapter 7 we defined four major classes of models and techniques for dealing with problems having multiple objectives. One such class was labeled *mathematical programming models*. In this chapter we develop the concept and techniques of *goal programming* which is a subset of this class.

14.2. LINEAR (NONLINEAR) PROGRAMMING VERSUS GOAL PROGRAMMING

In linear programming, all objectives or goals of management must be included in the objective function and be reducible to a single aggregate measurable criterion or dimension. For example, we maximize total profit (which is the sum of individual product profits), minimize total costs, and so forth. It may not, however, be feasible to reduce all goals of the organization to such a restrictive framework. Thus, when there exists multiple incommensurable goals, in a linear programming framework, one of these goals would have to be chosen and made as the objective function. The goal selected to be in the objective function would be the least important goal. The remaining goals not incorporated into the objective function would then have to be incorporated as constraints in the linear (nonlinear) programming model (Halter and Dean, 1971, pp. 54–57). Thus, the goals in the constraints have absolute priority over the goal in the objective function. The simplex algorithm would then select, from the set of all feasible solutions that satisfy all *resource* and *goal* constraints, a solution that optimizes the objective function. If no feasible solution exists, the goal in the objective function (the least important goal) would be dropped and a new LP formulated. The new formulation would then have the next-least-important goal (taken from the constraints) placed in the objective function. If the solution is again infeasible, one would continue to proceed in the same fashion until a feasible solution is reached. The result is consistent with the choice that would be made by using a lexicographic type of utility function. This model formulation, by requiring that the optimal solution fully satisfy all constraints, implies that all goals specified in the model as *constraints* are equally important. Moreover, they have absolute priority over the goal written as the objective function.

An important new technique for the analysis of decision problems involving the allocation of scarce resources has been developed to supplement linear programming. It is called *goal programming* (GP). GP provides the decision maker with the opportunity to include in the problem formulation objectives or goals that are not reducible to a single dimension. It is also more flexible than LP in that it will allow conflicting and incommensurable goals to be specified and still yield an optimal solution in terms of management's goal priorities. LP under such circumstances would, in many cases, yield an infeasible solution. When contrasted to LP in such situations, GP does not have many of the limitations of LP, while still retaining the characteristic ease of solution using the simplex algorithm.

Goal programming is an extension of linear (nonlinear) programming. Formulating a goal programming model is similar to formulating a linear programming model. The first step is to define the decision variables. Then all managerial goals must be specified and ranked in order of priority. Even though management may not be able to relate the various goals on a cardinal scale, it can usually provide an ordinal ranking to each of its goals or objectives. Thus, a fundamental distinction of goal programming is that it provides for the solution of decision problems having multiple conflicting and incommensurable goals arranged according to management's priority structure.

Goal programming originated in the work of Charnes and Cooper (1961), who sought a way to resolve infeasible linear programming problems stemming from goal–resource constraint interactions. Such interactions occur when goals are conflicting. For example, consider an investor who desires investments that will have a maximal return and minimal risk. These goals are generally incompatible and therefore unachievable. Other examples of multiple conflicting objectives can be found in organizations that want to: (a) maximize profits and increase wages paid to employees; (b) upgrade product quality and reduce product cost; (c) pay larger dividends to shareholders and retain earnings for growth; (d) increase control over channels of distribution and reduce working-capital requirements; and (e) reduce credit losses and increase sales. Basically the method of goal programming consists of formulating an objective function in which optimization "comes as close as possible" to the specified goals. Both Ijiri (1965) and Jaaskelainen (1969) have extended and refined the technique of goal programming. A variety of goal-programming applications can be found in Lee (1972).

Goal programming is capable of handling decision problems with single or multiple goals. In real decision-making situations, typically, goals established by the decision maker are achievable only at the expense of other goals. Furthermore, many of these goals are usually incompatible (i.e., incommensurable). If the decision maker can ordinally rank goals in terms of their importance to the orgainzation, the problem can be formulated and solved as a goal-programming problem. The distinguishing characteristic of goal programming is that goals are satisfied in an *ordinal* sequence. That is, goals that must be ranked in order of priority (importance) by the decision maker are satisfied sequentially by the solution algorithm. Lower-priority goals are considered only after higher-priority goals have been satisfied. Obviously, it is not always possible to achieve every goal to the extent desired by management. In this sense goal programming may be viewed as a *lexicographic* procedure (see Chapter 7). In the sense that the decision maker attempts to achieve a "satisfactory" level of multiple objectives rather than the best possible outcome for a single objective (as with linear programming), goal programming is a *satisficing* procedure.

The fundamental notion of goal programming involves incorporating all managerial goals into the system model formulation. In goal programming, instead of attempting to maximize or minimize the objective function directly, as in linear (nonlinear) programming, the deviations among goals and the achievable limits dictated by the given set of resource constraints are minimized. These deviational variables, which are called "slack" or "surplus" variables in linear programming, take on a new meaning in goal programming. They are partitioned into positive and negative deviations from each subgoal or goal. The objective then becomes the minimization of these deviations within the preemptive priority structure assigned to these deviations.

14.4. GOAL-PROGRAMMING-MODEL FORMULATION

The basic assumptions underlying the linear programming model apply equally to the goal programming model. The significant difference in structure is that goal programming does not attempt to maximize or minimize the objective function as does the linear programming model. Rather, it seeks to minimize the deviations among the desired goals and the actual results according to the priorities assigned. The objective or preference function of a goal programming model is expressed in terms of the deviations from the target goals. That is, the slack or surplus variables of the constraints are placed in the objective function and are to be *minimized*. The general goal programming model can be expressed mathematically as follows:

$$\text{minimize} \quad Z = \sum_{i=1}^{m} w_i(d_i^+ + d_i^-) \tag{14.1}$$

$$\text{subject to} \sum_{j=1}^{n} a_{ij}x_j + d_i^- - d_i^+ = b_i \qquad \text{for all } i \tag{14.2}$$

$$x_j, d_i^-, d_i^+ \geqslant 0 \qquad \text{for all } i, j. \tag{14.3}$$

The variable x_j represents a decision variable, w_i represents the weights (ordinal and/or cardinal) attached to each goal, and d_i^- and d_i^+ represent the degree of underachievement or overachievement of a goal, respectively. Since we cannot have both under- and overachievement of a goal simultaneously, either one or both of these variables will be equal to zero. That is,

$$d_i^- \times d_i^+ = 0. \tag{14.4}$$

Also, the nonnegativity requirement applies to these variables as it does to all other linear programming variables. That is,

$$d_i^-, d_i^+ \geqslant 0. \tag{14.5}$$

Goal programming will move the values of these deviational variables as close to zero as possible within the resource constraints and the goal structure outlined in the model. Once the goal programming model is formulated, the computational procedure is almost identical to the simplex method of linear programming.

Management must analyze each of the goals in the model to determine if under- or overachievement of the goal is satisfactory. For example, if under-achievement is acceptable, the underachievement deviation, d_i^- (called a *slack variable* in LP), can be eliminated from the objective function. Similarly, if overachievement is satisfactory, d_i^+ (called a surplus variable in LP) can be eliminated from the objective function. If exact achievement of the goal is desired, both d_i^- and d_i^+ must be included in the objective function and ranked according to their preemptive priority weights. In goal programming, the most important goal is "optimized" to the maximum extent possible before the second goal is considered. This procedure is followed within the given system constraints of the problem until all goals are fulfilled to the maximum extent possible. One further step must be considered when formulating the goal programming model. Those deviational variables at the same priority level may be given different weights in the objective function so that deviational variables within the same priority have different *cardinal* weights. It must be noted, however, that goals given the same priority level must be commensurable. We shall now use several examples to illustrate the goal programming procedure.

14.4.1. Example—Single Satisficing Goal

A division of the Schwim Manufacturing Company produces two types of bicycles: (1) a 3-speed and (2) a 10-speed. The division realizes a profit of $25 on the 10-speed bike and $15 on the 3-speed bike. Because of the strong demand for these items, during the summer planning period the division believes it can sell, at the prevailing prices, all these two types of bikes it can produce. The division's productive capability is however, limited, since both bikes share common production facilities which are considered to be scarce resources. These scarce resources pertain to the assembly department and the finishing department. The unit processing times and capacities for each department are shown in the following table:

Type of Bike	HOURS REQUIRED TO PROCESS EACH BIKE		Unit Profit Contribution
	In Assembly Department	In Finishing Department	
3-speed	1	1	15
10-speed	3	1	25
Hours available in each department per day	60	40	

If the division has the objective of maximizing profit, the problem can be formulated as a linear programming model and solved for the optimal number of

3-speed and 10-speed bikes to produce per day subject to the assembly and finishing department time constraints. The linear programming formulation is

$$\text{maximize } Z = 15x_1 + 25x_2$$

subject to

$$x_1 + 3x_2 \leqslant 60 \quad \text{(assembly hours)}$$

$$x_1 + x_2 \leqslant 40 \quad \text{(finishing hours)}$$

$$x_1, x_2 \geqslant 0,$$

where x_1 = number of 3-speed bikes produced per day

x_2 = number of 10-speed bikes produced per day.

The optimal solution to this problem can be obtained graphically and is $x_1 = 30$ and $x_2 = 10$, yielding a total profit of $700.

However, the division during this planning period is facing a major reorganizational change and feels that maximizing profit is not a realistic objective. However, it would like to achieve some satisfactory level of profit during this difficult period. Management feels that a daily profit of $600 would be satisfactory and wishes to determine, given the production time constraints, the product mix that would yield this rate of profit contribution. We now have a goal programming problem.

To incorporate the $600 satisficing profit contribution into the goal programming model, we first define the following deviational variables:

d_1^- = underachievement of the target profit
    (i.e., the amount by which actual profit will
    fall short of the target profit)

d_1^+ = overachievement of the target profit
    (i.e., the amount by which actual profit will
    exceed the target profit).

This profit goal is now written into the model as a goal constraint,

$$15x_1 + 25x_2 + d_1^- - d_1^+ = 600 \quad \text{(profit goal constraint)}$$

It is important to note that this constraint is treated and interpreted differently from the type of constraints found in a linear programming model. It is a target rather than an absolute requirement, and deviations below or above the target goal may occur in the final solution.

The goal programming model is thus written as

---

minimize $Z = d_1^- + d_1^+$

subject to
$$x_1 + 3x_2 \qquad\qquad \leqslant 60 \qquad \text{(assembly hours)} \Big\}\; resource$$
$$x_1 + x_2 \qquad\qquad \leqslant 40 \qquad \text{(finishing hours)} \Big\}\; constraints$$

• $\qquad 15x_1 + 25x_2 + d_1^- - d_1^+ = 600 \qquad \text{(target profit)} \qquad goal$
$$\qquad\qquad\qquad\qquad\qquad\qquad\qquad\qquad\qquad\qquad\quad constraint$$

$$x_1,\, x_2,\, d_1^-,\, d_1^+ \;\geqslant\; 0.$$

If the target profit of \$600 is exactly achieved, then both d_1^- and d_1^+ will be equal to zero. Since both d_1^- and d_1^+ appear in the objective function, this implies that management desires to achieve exactly the target profit objective. That is, management wants the model to "drive" both deviational variables as close to zero as possible. If overachievement of the profit goal were acceptable, d_1^+ would be eliminated from the objective function (i.e., the objective function would be min $Z = d_1^-$) and the model would attempt to minimize underachievement of the target profit but would be unconcerned about overachievement. Similarly, if underachievement were acceptable, d_1^- would be eliminated from the objective function (i.e., min $Z = d_1^+$) and the model would attempt to minimize overachievement but would be unconcerned about underachievement.

Since d_1^- and d_1^+ both appear in the objective function and both are assigned equal weights, this indicates that management wishes to achieve the profit goal exactly. If exact achievement of the goal is impossible, management has no preference between overachievement ($d_1^+ > 0$) and underachievement ($d_1^- > 0$) of the target profit goal since the weights assigned to both d_1^- and d_1^+ are equal. Of course, if management felt that it was twice as important to overachieve than to underachieve the target profit goal, we would place twice the weight on d_1^- than on d_1^+. The objective function would thus be

$$\text{minimize } Z = 2d_1^- + d_1^+$$

with the constraints remaining the same as before.

Let us now solve this goal programming problem graphically, using a modified version of the graphical method used in solving LP problems. To do this, the constraints (resource plus goal) are first plotted on a graph, as shown in Figure 14.1. Discounting the profit goal constraint, the feasible solution space is defined by area $OACD$. Now plotting the goal constraint and noting that profit can be less than, equal to, or greater than 600, the feasible solution space can be on either side

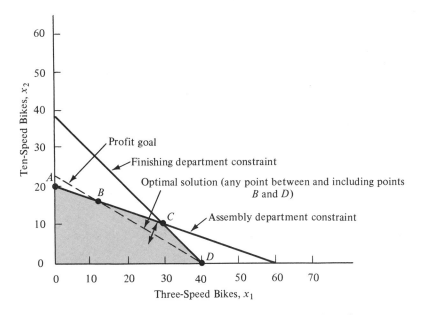

Figure 14.1. Graphical method of goal programming: single goal.

of the straight line defined by this constraint, as noted by the arrow signs. Hence, the feasible solution space is still defined by $OACD$.

Now that we have plotted all constraints on the graph, the next step is to analyze the objective function. The only goal at this point is to avoid the under- and overachievement of the target profit goal, namely the minimization of both d_1^- and d_1^+ to zero. To achieve this goal, the optimal feasible solution must therefore lie at any point between and including points B and D.

Let us now solve the goal programming problem using the simplex method of linear programming. The initial tableau and iterations for the goal programming model are shown in Figure 14.2.* The tableau is set up and solved in an identical fashion as in linear programming. That is, the inequalities are converted to equalities using slack and/or surplus variables wherever required. These variables are given the usual linear programming interpretation. The deviational variable d_1^-, representing the underachievement of the profit goal, initially becomes a basic variable, as do the slack variables, having an initial value of 600. The profit contribution at $x_1 = 0$, $x_2 = 0$ is thus equal to zero, which is $600 below our profit goal.

Since we are minimizing (*as we do in all goal programming problems*), the highest positive value in the objective function row (for convenience, all values in this row are defined as $z_j - c_j$ to denote the marginal per unit reduction in cost by introducing a non-basic variable into the basis) is introduced as a basic variable. This happens to be x_2, whose z_j-c_j value is $25. The interpretation is that actual profit will be increased by $25 for each x_2 produced. Stating this another way, the divergence between actual and targeted profit, which is underachieved by $600 at this point, will be increased by $25 for each x_2 produced. The tableaus are pivoted

---

*The tableau is presented in slightly different form from that in Chapters 8–11.

Initial Tableau

c_B	Basic variable	b	c_j 0 x_1	0 x_2	0 s_1	0 s_2	1 d_1^-	1 d_1^+
0	s_1	60	1	3	1	0	0	0
0	s_2	40	1	1	0	1	0	0
1	d_1	600	15	25	0	0	1	-1
$Z_j - C_j$	Z	600	15	25	0	0	0	-2

Second Tableau

c_B	Basic variable	x_B	c_j x_1	x_2	s_1	s_2	d_1^-	d_1^+
0	x_2	20	$\frac{1}{3}$	1	$\frac{1}{3}$	0	0	0
0	s_2	20	$\frac{2}{3}$	0	$-\frac{1}{3}$	1	0	0
1	d_1	100	$\frac{20}{3}$	0	$-\frac{25}{3}$	0	1	-1
$Z_j - C_j$	Z	100	$\frac{20}{3}$	0	$-\frac{25}{3}$	0	0	-2

using the usual simplex procedure. The final tableau indicates that the profit goal is exactly achieved by producing 15 units of x_1 and 15 units of x_2. There is also 10 hours of slack time in the finishing department.

Since the nonbasic variable s_1 has a $z_j - c_j = 0$, we have an alternative optimal solution. If we introduce s_1 as a basic variable, we drive out s_2 and the alternative optimal solution is $x_1 = 40$ and $x_2 = 0$, with the profit goal being exactly achieved. Hence, any convex combination of solution points between $x_1 = 15$, $x_2 = 15$ and $x_1 = 40$, $x_2 = 0$ will exactly accomplish our goal of achieving \$600 profit per day. This is also shown in Figure 14.1. That is, any point on the line segment between points B and D is an optimal solution to this goal programming problem.

c_B	Basic variable	x_B	x_1	x_2	s_1	s_2	d_1^-	d_1^+
0	x_2	15	0	1	$\frac{3}{4}$	0	$-\frac{1}{20}$	$-\frac{1}{20}$
0	s_2	10	0	0	$\boxed{\frac{1}{2}}$	1	$-\frac{1}{10}$	$\frac{1}{10}$
0	x_1	15	1	0	$-\frac{5}{4}$	0	$\frac{3}{20}$	$-\frac{3}{20}$
$Z_j - C_j$	Z	0	0	0	0	0	-1	-1

Final Alternate Optimal Tableau

c_B	Basic variable	x_B	x_1	x_2	s_1	s_2	d_1^-	d_1^+
0	x_2	0	0	1	0	$-\frac{3}{2}$	$\frac{1}{10}$	$-\frac{1}{10}$
0	s_1	20	0	0	1	2	$-\frac{1}{5}$	$\frac{1}{5}$
0	x_1	40	1	0	0	$\frac{5}{2}$	$-\frac{1}{10}$	$\frac{1}{10}$
$Z_j - C_j$	Z	0	0	0	0	0	-1	-1

Figure 14.2. The goal programming simplex procedure: single goal.

14.4.2. Example—Multiple Goals

Let us now consider the situation using the same problem where management wishes to achieve several goals. We will also assume that management can ordinally rank these goals in order of importance and that the most important goal has absolute priority over the next most important goal, and so on. Under these circumstances conventional linear programming techniques fail, and goal programming becomes applicable.[†]

In goal programming, goals are achieved according to their importance. Hence, negative and/or positive deviations about a given goal must be ranked according to "preemptive" priority factors. In this manner, lower-priority goals are considered only after higher-priority goals are achieved. To do this, goals are

[†]It should be noted that if goals can be assigned cardinal weights (e.g., goal 1 is twice as important as goal 2, and so forth), then conventional linear programming techniques such as used in Example 14.4.1 can be used to solve the goal programming problem.

classified into k ranks and deviational variables associated with the goals are assigned a priority number $P_j (j = 1, 2, \ldots, k)$. The priority factors have the relationship

$$P_1 \ggg P_2 \ggg \cdots \ggg P_j \ggg P_{j+1},$$

where $\ggg$ means "very much greater than." The priority relationship implies that multiplication by n, however large n may be, cannot make a lower-priority goal as important as a higher-priority goal (i.e., $P_j > nP_{j+1}$).‡

Now assume that the management of the Schwim bicycle division, in addition to achieving its \$600 primary profit goal, wishes to fully utilize its assembly and finishing departments during the upcoming reorganization. That is, as a secondary goal, the division desires to minimize idle time. The goal-programming-model formulation is thus as follows:

---

minimize $Z = P_1(d_1^- + d_1^+) + P_2(d_2^- + d_3^-)$

subject to:

$$15x_1 + 25x_2 + d_1^- - d_1^+ = 600 \quad \text{(target profit)}$$

$$x_1 + 3x_2 + d_2^- - d_2^+ = 60 \quad \text{(assembly hours)}$$

$$x_1 + x_2 + d_3^- - d_3^+ = 40 \quad \text{(finishing hours)}$$

$$x_1, x_2, d_i^-, d_i^+ \geq 0, \text{ for all } i.$$

---

where x_1 = number of 3-speed bikes produced per day

x_2 = number of 10-speed bikes produced per day

d_1^-, d_1^+ = underachievement and overachievement of daily target profit, respectively

d_2^-, d_2^+ = daily idle time and overtime in assembly department, respectively

d_3^-, d_3^+ = daily idle time and overtime in finishing department, respectively.

Since both d_1^- and d_1^+ are included in the objective function, the model will attempt to achieve exactly the \$600 per day target profit, minimizing both negative and positive deviations. With d_2^+ and d_3^+ omitted from the objective function, however, the model will be unconcerned about any overtime in either the assembly or finishing department and will attempt only to minimize idle time in these departments. Because the target profit goal is more important than the idle-time

---

‡If values of n can be selected such that this condition holds, then the goal programming problem can be solved as a linear programming problem. The difficulty here is in selecting values for n such that $P_j > nP_{j+1}$.

minimization goal, it is assigned priority P_1. The model will attempt to achieve this goal to the fullest extent possible before it considers the secondary goal of minimizing idle production time.

The graphical solution of this goal programming problem is shown in Figure 14.3. In obtaining the solution graphically, all lines drawn on the graph are interpreted as goals, not constraints in the strict sense of the word. The optimal product mix is $x_1 = 15$ and $x_2 = 15$ (at point B). This results in a total idle time of 10 units, which occurs in the finishing department only. No idle time occurs in the assembly department and no overtime work is performed. Note that in arriving at this solution graphically, we must first satisfy the primary goal of making a $600 profit per day. Hence, any point on the line D–E satisfies this goal. Our next task is to attempt to satisfy our secondary goal of minimizing idle time. The point at which this occurs and which satisfies our primary goal of $600 profit is at point B. As can be seen in Figure 14.3, the idle time at point B is 10 hours, which occurs only in the finishing department. The idle time in the assembly department at this point is zero, and no overtime occurs. To verify that point B is the optimal solution, consider any other point on the line D–E, which represents all feasible values of x_1, x_2 satisfying our primary profit goal of $600. No point on this line has a total idle time less than 10 hours, which occurs at point B. For example, the idle time at point D is 20 hours. At point D, $x_1 = 40$ and $x_2 = 0$, which results in 20 hours of idle time in the assembly department and zero idle time in the finishing department. (This can be also verified analytically by substituting the values for x_1 and x_2 in the algebraic formulation of the goal programming model.)

Figure 14.3. Graphical method of goal programming: multiple goals.

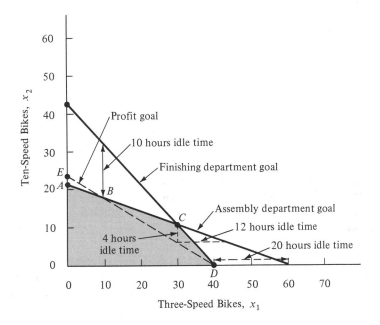

Initial Tableau

c_j			0	0	P_1	P_1	P_2	0	P_2	0
c_B	Basic variables	x_B	x_1	x_2	d_1^-	d_1^+	d_2^-	d_2^+	d_3^-	d_3^+
P_1	d_1^-	600	15	25	1	-1	0	0	0	0
$\leftarrow P_2$	d_2^-	60	1	3	0	0	1	-1	0	0
P_3	d_3^-	40	1	1	0	0	0	0	1	-1
$Z_j - C_j$	P_2	600	2	4	0	0	0	-1	0	-1
	P_1	100	15	25	0	-2	0	0	0	0

Second Tableau

c_j			0	0	P_1	P_1	P_2	0	P_2	0
c_B	Basic variables	x_B	x_1	x_2	d_1^-	d_1^+	d_2^-	d_2^+	d_3^-	d_3^+
$\leftarrow P_1$	d_1^-	100	$\frac{20}{3}$	0	1	-1	$-\frac{25}{3}$	$\frac{25}{3}$	0	0
0	x_2	20	$\frac{1}{3}$	1	0	0	$\frac{1}{3}$	$-\frac{1}{3}$	1	-1
P_2	d_3^-	20	$\frac{2}{3}$	0	0	0	$-\frac{1}{3}$	$\frac{1}{3}$	0	-1
$Z_j - C_j$	P_2	20	$\frac{2}{3}$	0	0	0	$-\frac{4}{3}$	$\frac{1}{3}$	0	-1
	P_1	100	$\frac{20}{3}$	0	0	-2	$-\frac{25}{3}$	$\frac{25}{3}$	0	0

The simplex solution for the model is shown in Figure 14.4. Observe that the two levels of priorities of goals form two z_j-c_j rows (where c_j is actually P_j). The highest priority goal is on the bottom z_j-c_j row. All positive values should be eliminated from this row before positive z_j-c_j values of the next priority goal are considered. A variable having a positive z_j-c_j value of a lower-priority goal cannot be introduced into the solution as long as there is a z_j-c_j value other than zero in the same column of all higher-priority goals.

The first and second tableaus in Figure 14.4 were pivoted on positive values from the P_1 row. Since there were no positive values in the P_1 row of the third tableau, we focused on the P_2 row. Only those columns having a positive value in

Third Tableau

c_B	Basic variable		c_j →	0 x_1	0 x_2	P_1 d_1^-	P_1 d_1^+	P_2 d_2^-	0 d_2^+	P_2 d_3^-	0 d_3^+
← 0	d_2^+		12	$\frac{4}{5}$	0	$\frac{3}{25}$	$-\frac{3}{25}$	-1	1	0	0
0	x_2		24	$\frac{9}{15}$	1	$\frac{1}{25}$	$-\frac{1}{25}$	0	0	0	0
P_2	d_3^-		16	$\frac{6}{15}$	0	$-\frac{1}{25}$	$\frac{1}{25}$	0	0	1	-1
$Z_j - C_j$	P_2		16	$\frac{6}{15}$	0	$-\frac{1}{25}$	$\frac{1}{25}$	-1	0	0	-1
	P_1		0	0 ↑	0	-1	-1	0	0	0	0

Final Optimal Tableau

c_B	Basic variable		c_j →	0 x_1	0 x_2	P_1 d_1^-	P_1 d_1^+	P_2 d_2^-	0 d_2^+	P_2 d_3^-	0 d_3^+
0	x_1		15	1	0	$\frac{3}{20}$	$-\frac{3}{20}$	$-\frac{5}{4}$	$\frac{5}{4}$	0	0
0	x_2		15	0	1	$-\frac{1}{20}$	$\frac{1}{20}$	$\frac{3}{4}$	$-\frac{3}{4}$	0	0
P_2	d_3^-		10	0	0	$-\frac{1}{10}$	$\frac{1}{10}$	$\frac{1}{2}$	$-\frac{1}{2}$	1	-1
$Z_j - C_j$	P_2		10	0	0	$-\frac{1}{10}$	$\frac{1}{10}$	$-\frac{1}{2}$	$-\frac{1}{2}$	0	-1
	P_1		0	0	0	-1	-1	0	0	0	0

Figure 14.4. The goal programming simplex procedure: multiple goals.

the P_2 row along with a zero in the P_1 row were eligible variables to introduce into the basis. Thus, x_1 was introduced into the basis, while d_2^+ was removed from the basis. The fourth tableau provided the optimal solution. However, d_1^+ could not be introduced into the basis, since this would result in a violation of the P_1 goal. d_1^+ would have been an eligible variable to introduce into the basis if its value in the P_1 row was equal to zero.

The optimal tableau indicates that the division should produce 15 units of x_1 and 15 units of x_2. The target profit of $600 will be exactly achieved. The goal of minimizing idle time cannot be fully achieved, as there will be 10 idle hours in the finishing department. However, this is the minimum amount of idle time possible given the exact realization of the $600 profit goal. We could, however, overachieve our profit goal and reduce our idle time to zero, for example, by making 30 units of x_1 and 10 units of x_2 (see Figure 14.3 and the linear programming solution).

Our goal programming model has thus helped us to achieve these incompatible goals as closely as possible within the given resource/goal constraints and management's goal-priority structure. While a linear programming solution to this problem would have resulted in higher profit and lower idle time, in many other problem situations a linear programming solution would have been infeasible. By explicitly modeling our problem in a goal programming format we achieve our satisficing goals to the fullest extent possible, lexicographically achieving our most important goal first, our next most important goal second, and so forth.

14.4.3. Example—Multiple Goals and Subgoals

In our Schwim example, the maximum profit the division could make given 60 hours of assembly time and 40 hours of finishing time was $700, as determined by linear programming. Because of a division reorganization we have considered cases where management would be satisfied (at least temporarily) with a production plan yielding a lower profit of $600.

Suppose that the reorganization has been completed and management now wishes to achieve a daily profit rate of $750. This would mean that some constraints previously adhered to will have to be violated. Assume, however, that the 60 hours and 40 hours represent the production capability of the assembly and finishing departments on regular time only, using the existing workforce. Overtime could be used in either department; hence, deviations above as well as below the 60 and 40 hours are feasible. The overtime pay rate is 3 times higher in the assembly department than in the finishing department. The goal priorities of management, from most to least important, are as follows:

$$P_1$$

Achieve the daily
target profit rate
of $750.

$$P_2$$

Minimize idle
time in both
departments.

$$P_3$$

Minimize overtime
in both departments.

The goal programming formulation of the problem is as follows:

$$\text{minimize } Z = P_1(d_1^- + d_1^+) + P_2(d_2^- + d_3^-) + 3P_3d_2^+ + P_3d_3^+$$

subject to
$$15x_1 + 25x_2 + d_1^- - d_1^+ = 750 \quad \text{(target profit)}$$
$$x_1 + 3x_2 + d_2^- - d_2^+ = 60 \quad \text{(assembly hours)}$$
$$x_1 + x_2 + d_3^- - d_3^+ = 40 \quad \text{(finishing hours)}$$

$$x_1, x_2, d_i^-, d_i^+ \geqslant 0, \text{ for all } i$$

The objective function indicates that management wishes to achieve its first priority goal of profit exactly, by minimizing deviations from this goal in either direction. As a second priority, the model also wishes to minimize the total idle time in both departments. That is, management is indifferent to balancing the idle time in each department; it is concerned only about minimizing the sum of the idle times. (If the cost of idle time was different in both departments, the objective function would need to be changed to reflect this difference. Suppose the idle time cost in the assembly department was twice that in the finishing department. How would the objective function be changed?) Since overtime (priority 3) in the assembly department is three times as costly as overtime in the finishing department, this is reflected in the objective function as shown. Thus, the model will prefer overtime in the finishing department to overtime in the assembly department. We now have assigned different (cardinal) weights or priorities within a given goal, as well as different priorities (ordinal or cardinal) to different goals.

Figures 14.5 and 14.6 show the graphical and simplex solutions.

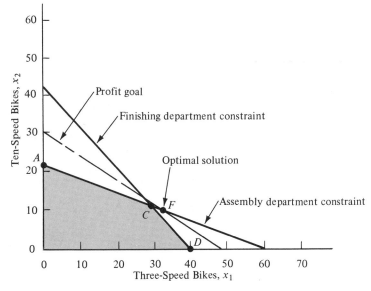

Figure 14.5. Graphical method of goal programming: multiple goals and subgoals.

The goal programming solution is to produce 37.5 units of x_1 and 7.5 units of x_2, achieving the target profit of \$750 exactly. However, this requires 5 hours of overtime in the finishing department. Had we treated both the profit goal and production time as constraints in a linear programming problem, the solution would have been infeasible.

c_B	Basic variable	x_B	x_1 (0)	x_2 (0)	d_1^- (P_1)	d_1^+ (P_1)	d_2^- (P_2)	d_2^+ ($3P_3$)	d_3^- (P_2)	d_3^+ (P_3)
P_1	d_1^-	750	15	25	1	-1	0	0	0	0
P_2	d_2^-	60	1	[3]	0	0	1		0	0
P_2	d_3^-	40	1	1	0	0	0	0	1	-1
$Z_j - C_j$ P_3		0	0	0	0	0	0	-3	0	-1
	P_2	100	2	4	0	0	0	-1	0	-1
	P_1	750	15	25	0	-2	0	0	0	0

c_B	Basic variable	x_B	x_1 (0)	x_2 (0)	d_1^- (P_1)	d_1^+ (P_1)	d_2^- (P_2)	d_2^+ ($3P_3$)	d_3^- (P_2)	d_3^+ (P_3)
P_1	d_1^-	250	$\frac{20}{3}$	0	1	-1	$-\frac{25}{3}$	$\boxed{\frac{25}{3}}$	0	0
0	x_2	20	$\frac{1}{3}$	1	0	0	$\frac{1}{3}$	$-\frac{1}{3}$	0	0
P_2	d_3^-	20	$\frac{2}{3}$	0	0	0	$-\frac{1}{3}$	$\frac{1}{3}$	1	-1
$Z_j - C_j$ P_3		0	0	0	0	0	0	-3	0	-1
	P_2	20	$\frac{2}{3}$	0	0	0	$-\frac{4}{3}$	$\frac{1}{3}$	0	-1
	P_1	250	$\frac{20}{3}$	0	0	-2	$-\frac{25}{3}$	$\frac{25}{3}$	0	0

Figure 14.6. The goal programming simplex tableau: multiple goals with subgoals. See also facing page.

c_j			0	0	P_1	P_1	P_2	$3P_3$	P_2	P_3
c_B	Basic variable	x_B	x_1	x_2	d_1^-	d_1^+	d_2^-	d_2^+	d_3^-	d_3^+
$3P_3$	d_2^+	30	$\frac{4}{5}$	0	$\frac{3}{25}$	$-\frac{3}{25}$	-1	1	0	0
0	x_2	30	$\frac{9}{15}$	1	$\frac{1}{25}$	$-\frac{1}{25}$	0	0	0	0
← P_2	d_3^-	10	$\boxed{\frac{6}{15}}$	0	$-\frac{1}{25}$	$\frac{1}{25}$	0	0	1	-1
$Z_j - C_j$ P_3		90	$\frac{12}{5}$	0	$\frac{9}{25}$	$-\frac{9}{25}$	-3	0	0	-1
P_2		10	$\frac{6}{15}$	0	$-\frac{1}{25}$	$\frac{1}{25}$	-1	0	0	-1
P_1		0	0	0	-1	-1	0	0	0	0

c_j			0	0	P_1	P_1	P_2	$3P_3$	P_2	P_3
c_B	Basic variable	x_B	x_1	x_2	d_1^-	d_1^+	d_2^-	d_2^+	d_3^-	d_3^+
← $3P_3$	d_2^+	10	0	0	$\frac{1}{5}$	$-\frac{1}{5}$	-1	1	-2	$\boxed{2}$
0	x_2	15	0	1	$\frac{1}{10}$	$-\frac{1}{10}$	0	0	$-\frac{3}{2}$	$\frac{3}{2}$
0	x_1	25	1	0	$-\frac{1}{10}$	$\frac{1}{10}$	0	0	0	0
$Z_j - C_j$ P_3		30	0	0	$\frac{3}{5}$	$-\frac{3}{5}$	-3	0	-6	5
P_2		0	0	0	0	0	-1	0	-1	0
P_1		0	0	0	-1	-1	0	0	0	0

c_j			0	0	P_1	P_1	P_2	$3P_3$	P_2	P_3
c_B	Basic variable	x_B	x_1	x_2	d_1^-	d_1^+	d_2^-	d_2^+	d_3^-	d_3^+
P_3	d_3^+	5	0	0	$\frac{2}{5}$	$-\frac{2}{5}$	$-\frac{1}{2}$	$\frac{1}{2}$	-1	1
0	x_2	$\frac{15}{2}$	0	1	$-\frac{1}{2}$	$\frac{1}{2}$	$\frac{3}{4}$	$-\frac{3}{4}$	0	0
0	x_1	$\frac{75}{2}$	1	0	$\frac{9}{10}$	$-\frac{9}{10}$	$-\frac{5}{4}$	$\frac{5}{4}$	0	0
$Z_j - C_j$ P_3		5	0	0	$\frac{2}{5}$	$-\frac{5}{2}$	$-\frac{1}{2}$	$-\frac{2}{5}$	-1	0
P_2		0	0	0	0	0	-1	0	-1	0
P_1		0	0	0	-1	-1	0	0	0	0

14.5. QUADRATIC GOAL PROGRAMMING

Thus far, we have assumed that the goal programming objective function is linear. Hence, the increase in any deviation, d_i, always adds an equal amount of disutility, regardless of the level of all other goal deviations. In economic terms, marginal utilities and rates of substitution are constant. The linear form is realistic in some cases, but economic theory suggests that a diminishing marginal rate of substitution is often more consistent with economic reality. For example, the concave utility function discussed in Chapter 5 is such an example, and typifies many if not most individuals for such commodities as money. In this section we assume that the objective function of the goal programming model is quadratic subject to linear constraints. This presents no computational difficulties, as standard quadratic programming algorithms can be used to solve such problems.

The quadratic goal programming problem can be expressed mathematically as follows:

$$\text{minimize } Z = \sum_{i=1}^{l} \sum_{j=1}^{m} w_i(d_i^- d_j^- + d_i^+ d_j^+ + d_i^- d_j^+) \qquad (14.6)$$

$$\text{subject to } \sum_{j=1}^{n} a_{ij}x_j + d_i^- - d_i^+ = b_i \qquad \text{for all } i \qquad (14.7)$$

$$x_j, d_i^-, d_i^+ \geq 0 \qquad \text{for all } i, j. \qquad (14.8)$$

As before, we wish to find variables x_j, d_i^-, and d_i^+ to minimize the objective function above, which is composed of squared terms (e.g., d_1^{-2}) and interaction or cross-product terms (e.g., $d_1^- d_2^+$). The objective function, of course, must be a convex function to guarantee a global optimal solution to this minimization problem using an existing quadratic programming algorithm.

14.5.1. Example—Quadratic Symmetric Goals

In an effort to facilitate the understanding of the quadratic goal programming formulation, let us go back to Example 14.4.3. Assuming the same goal priority structure, we now assume that the deviations from the goals are quadratic and symmetric (i.e., no interaction or cross-product terms). The quadratic formulation with symmetric preferences can be written:

$$\text{minimize } Z = P_1(d_1^{-2} + d_1^{+2}) + P_2(d_2^{-2} + d_3^{-2}) + 3P_3 d_2^{+2} + P_3 d_3^{+2}$$

subject to the same constraints as in Example 14.4.3.

The interaction terms can be used to obtain a formulation that reflects the asymmetrical nature of the preference function. Asymmetric preferences merely imply that the marginal utility of each deviational variable depends in principle on the other deviational variables. Asymmetric utilities are undoubtedly realistic for some goals. For example, a sales manager would prefer to miss the expected sales target on the high side rather than on the low side.

In order to show an example with asymmetric preferences, assume that the bicycle division manager of Schwim in Example 14.4.3 has set an additional goal. This goal is to achieve the target of minimizing overtime in both the assembly and finishing departments while achieving the target profit. This additional goal is assumed to be less important than all the other goals stated. Assuming quadratic preferences, the corresponding quadratic goal programming formulation can be written as follows:

$$
\begin{aligned}
\text{minimize } Z = {} & P_1\big(d_1^{-2} + d_1^{+2}\big) + P_2\big(d_2^{-2} + d_3^{-2}\big) + 3P_3 d_2^{+2} + P_3 d_3^{+2} \\
& + 3P_4\big(d_1^- d_2^+\big) + P_4\big(d_1^- d_3^+\big)
\end{aligned}
$$

subject to the constraints of Example 14.4.3. Note that since overtime in the assembly department is three times as costly as overtime in the finishing department, this again is reflected in the objective function interaction terms, as shown.

14.6. RANKING MULTIPLE GOALS

In this section we discuss several ways of establishing ordinal priorities for the goals in a goal programming problem. One possible method of obtaining a priority scale for multiple goals is to present a list of goals to the decision maker and simply ask him to rank them in order of importance or preference. As a consistency check, the Churchman–Ackoff approximate-measure-of-value procedure could be used (1954). For a more comprehensive treatment of various ranking and rating procedures, see Eckenrode (1965) and Torgerson (1958).

A second method, which provides some check on the consistency in the value judgment of the decision maker, is the method of paired comparisons. In this method, the decision maker is simply asked to compare the goals two at a time and indicate which goal is the more important one in the pair. This procedure is applied to all combinations of goal pairs. This analysis results in a complete ordinal ranking of the goals in terms of their importance.

To illustrate the paired-comparison procedure, let us assume that a decision maker has identified the following four goals or factors to be considered in purchasing a new car: G_1 (price), G_2 (operating economy), G_3 (maintainability), and G_4 (comfort). If there are n goals, the total combination of paired comparisons would be $[n(n - 1)]/2.$[†] For four goals there are a total of six paired comparisons. Note that this procedure becomes quite cumbersome when there are many goals. For example, 10 goals would require 45 paired comparisons. Fortunately, from a practical viewpoint, most organizational goals can be limited to considerably less than 10 goals, making paired comparisons a workable procedure.

Let us assume that the decision maker's preferences for the six paired comparisons of our four goals are as follows:

$$G_1 > G_2 \qquad G_2 < G_3$$
$$G_1 < G_3 \qquad G_2 > G_4$$
$$G_1 > G_4 \qquad G_3 > G_4,$$

where " $>$ " denotes "more important than." To obtain the ordinal ranking of goals, we rearrange the preferences so that all the "more important than" signs point in the same direction, as follows

$$G_1 > G_2 \qquad G_3 > G_2$$
$$G_3 > G_1 \qquad G_2 > G_4$$
$$G_1 > G_4 \qquad G_3 > G_4$$

The most important goal should be more important than all three other goals. That is, the most important goal should appear on the "more important than" side three times. The next-most-important goal should appear on the "more important than" side twice, and so forth. In general, if there exist n conflicting goals, the goal whose ranking is r should appear $n - r$ times on the "more important than" side of the list of preferences. In this example, the ordinal ranking of the four goals is:

Ranking (Priority)	Goal	$n - r$
1	G_3 (maintainability)	3
2	G_1 (price)	2
3	G_2 (operating economy)	1
4	G_4 (comfort)	0

[†]This formula is obtained using the combination formula

$$_nC_r = \frac{n!}{r!\,(n - r)!}, \qquad \text{where } r = 2.$$

This gives

$$_nC_2 = \frac{n!}{2!\,(n - 2)!} \quad \text{or} \quad \frac{n(n - 1)(n - 2)!}{2!\,(n - 2)!},$$

which by canceling terms is equal to $[n(n - 1)]/2.$

A basic assumption of this procedure is that the decision maker's preferences are *consistent*. If he or she is not consistent, the paired-comparison procedure may not produce a complete ordinal ranking of goals. Should inconsistencies occur, these should be cleared up by having the decision maker reflect on his or her choices.

14.7. SOME APPLICATIONS OF GOAL PROGRAMMING

Goal programming is an approach for dealing with managerial decision problems that involve multiple, incommensurable goals, according to the attached importance of the goals. The decision maker thus must be able to establish at least an ordinal importance ranking of goals. An important advantage of goal programming is its flexibility, in the sense that it allows the decision maker to experiment with a multitude of variations of constraints and goal priorities in grappling with a multiple-objective decision problem.

Goal programming can and has been applied to a large variety of managerial decision problems both in the private and public sectors. For example, it has been applied in such functional management areas as marketing (advertising media planning and scheduling, product mix selection, sales effort allocation), finance (portfolio selection, financial planning, capital budgeting), production (planning and scheduling, transportation), accounting, and manpower planning. In the public sector, goal programming has been applied to problems of academic planning (assigning faculty teaching schedules, university admissions planning), municipal economic planning, urban planning, and medical care planning. Illustrations of these applications are found in Lee (1972); Lee and Nicely (1974); Lee and Moore (1973); Lee, Lerro, and McGinnis (1973); Lee and Bird (1970); and references cited therein. Goal programming is also applicable to such methodological areas as regression analysis. Using case examples, formulation of goal programming problems in several of the areas mentioned above is developed below.

14.7.1. Application 1—Production Scheduling

The Aegis Company has recently developed three new products which can be produced by making use of excess capacity in their three existing branch plants. Each product can be manufactured in any of the three plants. Analysis has shown that it would be profitable to use the excess capacity to produce these new products. In fact, management's principal purpose in developing the new products was to achieve complete utilization of excess productive capacity on a profitable basis. While Aegis's plants generally operate at full capacity on their existing product lines, production at less than full capacity does occur infrequently, presenting problems with the labor force. Although the company does not need the full labor force during these slack periods, the cost of layoffs would be substantial, and Aegis would like to avoid this as much as possible.

Moreover, management would like to balance the utilization of excess capacity among branch plants. This serves to equitably distribute the workload on salaried supervisory personnel and reduces the grievences of the hourly paid labor force, who otherwise would feel discriminated against with respect to workloads and/or layoffs.

For the period under consideration, the plants have the following excess production capacity (in terms of units of new products) and available shipping capacities allocated to the new products:

Plant	Excess Production Capacity (units)	Shipping Capacity (cubic feet)
1	750	12,000
2	300	10,000
3	450	6,500

Products 1, 2, and 3 require 30, 20, and 15 cubic feet per unit, respectively. The unit profit contributions of products 1, 2, and 3 are $15, $18, and $12, respectively. Sales forecasts indicate that Aegis can anticipate selling as many as 900, 1000, and 700 units of products 1, 2, and 3, respectively, during the planning period under consideration.

Given the problem situation, management has expressed the following goal preferences in order of decreasing importance (P_1 = most important):

P_1. Achieve a target profit of $15,000.
P_2. Use as much of the excess plant capacity as possible. Because of lower labor costs, management feels that it is 1.5 times as important to use excess capacity in plant 1 than in plants 2 and 3.
P_3. Achieve a workload balance in the use of excess capacity among all plants. Because of certain extra demands on plant 1 workers, management feels that if a workload imbalance occurs, it is twice as important that it is in favor of having plant 1 do less work than more work relative to plants 2 and 3.
P_4. Achieve the sales forecast for product 2, since it has the largest profit contribution per unit.
P_5. Produce a sufficient amount of products 1 and 3 to meet forecasted sales.
P_6. Not exceed the available shipping capacity.

MODEL FORMULATION. The following steps are required to formulate the goal programming model.

1. *Excess capacity constraints*

$$x_{11} + x_{21} + x_{31} \qquad +d_1^- - d_1^+ \qquad = 750$$
$$x_{12} + x_{22} + x_{32} \qquad +d_2^- - d_2^+ \qquad = 300$$
$$x_{13} + x_{23} + x_{33} \qquad +d_3^- - d_3^+ \quad = 450,$$

where x_{ij} = number of units of product i produced in plant j

d_1^-, d_2^-, d_3^- = excess capacity not used in plants 1, 2, and 3, respectively

d_1^+, d_2^+, d_3^+ = amount by which excess capacity is exceeded in plants 1, 2, and 3, respectively.

2. *Space requirement constraints*

$$30x_{11} + 20x_{21} + 15x_{31} \qquad\qquad +d_4^- - d_4^+ \qquad\qquad = 12{,}000$$
$$30x_{12} + 20x_{22} + 15x_{32} \qquad\qquad +d_5^- - d_5^+ \qquad = 10{,}000$$
$$30x_{13} + 20x_{23} + 15x_{33} \qquad +d_6^- - d_6^+ = 6{,}500,$$

where d_4^-, d_5^-, d_6^- = number of units of available shipping capacity not used in plants 1, 2, and 3, respectively

d_4^+, d_5^+, d_6^+ = number of units of additional shipping capacity required in plants 1, 2, and 3, respectively.

3. *Expected sales constraints*

$$x_{11} + x_{12} + x_{13} \qquad\qquad +d_7^- - d_7^+ \qquad\qquad = 900$$
$$x_{21} + x_{22} + x_{23} \qquad\qquad +d_8^- - d_8^+ \qquad = 1000$$
$$x_{31} + x_{32} + x_{33} \qquad +d_9^- - d_9^+ = 700,$$

where d_7^-, d_8^-, d_9^- = number of units of underachievement of expected sales for products 1, 2, and 3, respectively

d_7^+, d_8^+, d_9^+ = number of units of overachievement of expected sales for products 1, 2, and 3, respectively.

4. *Workload balance*

$$\frac{x_{11} + x_{21} + x_{31}}{750} = \frac{x_{12} + x_{22} + x_{32}}{300}$$
$$\frac{x_{11} + x_{21} + x_{31}}{750} = \frac{x_{13} + x_{23} + x_{33}}{450}.$$

These balance equations can be written as goal constraints by a simple division and transposition of the right-hand side as follows (by transitivity, only two balancing constraints are necessary):

$$0.002x_{11} + 0.002x_{21} + 0.002x_{31} - 0.005x_{12} - 0.005x_{22} - 0.005x_{32} + d_{10}^- - d_{10}^+ = 0$$
$$0.002x_{11} + 0.002x_{21} + 0.002x_{31} - 0.0033x_{13} - 0.0033x_{23} - 0.0033x_{33} + d_{11}^- - d_{11}^+ = 0,$$

where d_{10}^-, d_{11}^- = number of units produced too low relative to that produced in plants 2 and 3, respectively

d_{10}^+, d_{11}^+ = number of units produced in excess relative to that produced in plants 2 and 3, respectively.

5. *Profit constraint*

$$15(x_{11} + x_{12} + x_{13}) + 18(x_{21} + x_{22} + x_{23}) + 12(x_{31} + x_{32} + x_{33}) + d_{12}^- - d_{12}^+$$
$$= 15,000,$$

where d_{12}^- = dollar amount under target profit goal

d_{12}^+ = dollar amount above target profit goal.

If no profit goal is stated, we can constrain the right-hand side of this equation to be equal to zero to determine what profit would be. Since all real variables (x_{ij}) and deviational variables $(d^-$ or $d^+)$ are nonnegative, the value of d_{12}^+ would be the actual profit.

6. *Objective function*

$$\text{minimize } Z = P_1(d_{12}^- + d_{12}^+) + 1.5P_2 d_1^- + P_2(d_2^- + d_3^-)$$
$$+ 2P_3(d_{10}^- + d_{11}^-) + P_3(d_{10}^+ + d_{11}^+) + P_4 d_8^- + P_5(d_7^- + d_9^-)$$
$$+ P_6(d_4^+ + d_5^+ + d_6^+).$$

Since management would like to achieve a target profit of $15,000 with the highest priority, we assign P_1 to the deviational variables in the profit goal constraint. The second goal of management was to use as much excess plant capacity as possible. However, it preferred to use the excess in plant 1 over plants 2 and 3 by a ratio of 1.5 to 1. This presumably represents a differential in operational costs at the different plants. In order to reflect the relative priorities of management, we modify the standard objective function formulation [which would be $P_2(d_1^- + d_2^- + d_3^-)$] to $1.5P_2 d_1^- + P_2(d_2^- + d_3^-)$, which places $1\frac{1}{2}$ times as much weight on achieving the minimization of d_1^-. P_2 is the second general level of managerial priorities regarding the problem. The third goal of management was to achieve workload balance. However, it was twice as important to avoid an imbalance which overworked rather than underworked plant 1—because of additional unfavorable factors which existed there and not in plants 2 and 3. Hence, we assigned $2P_3$ to d_{10}^- and d_{11}^- and P_3 to d_{10}^+ and d_{11}^+. Since the fourth goal was to achieve expected sales on product 2, P_4 is assigned to d_8^-. P_5 is assigned to d_7^- and d_9^-, as the fifth goal is the achievement of these expected sales. Here we are not concerned with the overachievement of the sales forecast, since we can produce for inventory if space is available. If it is not, shipping capacity constraints, which have a higher priority, will take care of this. Since the sixth goal of management is not to exceed currently available shipping space, P_6 is assigned to d_4^+, d_5^+, and d_6^+.

GOAL PROGRAMMING MODEL SUMMARIZED

minimize $\quad Z = P_1(d_{12}^- + d_{12}^+) + 1.5P_2d_1^- + P_2(d_2^- + d_3^-) + 2P_3(d_{10}^- + d_{11}^-) + P_3(d_{10}^+ + d_{11}^+)$

$\qquad\qquad + P_4d_8^- + P_5(d_7^- + d_9^-) + P_6(d_4^+ + d_5^+ + d_6^+)$

subject to:

$$x_{11} + x_{21} + x_{31} \qquad\qquad\qquad\qquad +d_1^- - d_1^+ = 750$$

$$x_{12} + x_{22} + x_{32} \qquad\qquad\qquad +d_2^- - d_2^+ = 300$$

$$x_{13} + x_{23} + x_{33} + d_3^- - d_3^+ = 450$$

$$30x_{11} + 20x_{21} + 15x_{31} \qquad\qquad\qquad\qquad +d_4^- - d_4^+ = 12{,}000$$

$$30x_{12} + 20x_{22} + 15x_{32} \qquad\qquad +d_5^- - d_5^+ = 10{,}000$$

$$30x_{13} + 20x_{23} + 15x_{33} + d_6^- - d_6^+ = 6{,}500$$

$$x_{11} + x_{12} + x_{13} \qquad\qquad\qquad\qquad +d_7^- - d_7^+ = 900$$

$$x_{21} + x_{22} + x_{23} \qquad\qquad +d_8^- - d_8^+ = 1000$$

$$x_{31} + x_{32} + x_{33} + \qquad\qquad d_9^- - d_9^+ = 700$$

$$0.002x_{11} + 0.002x_{21} + 0.002x_{31} - 0.005x_{12} - 0.005x_{22} - 0.005x_{32} \qquad + d_{10}^- - d_{10}^+ = 0$$

$$0.002x_{11} + 0.002x_{21} + 0.002x_{31} - 0.0033x_{13} - 0.0033x_{23} - 0.0033x_{33} \qquad + d_{11}^- - d_{11}^+ = 0$$

$$15x_{11} + 18x_{21} + 12x_{31} + 15x_{12} + 18x_{22} + 12x_{32} + 15x_{13} + 18x_{23} + 12x_{33} + d_{12}^- - d_{12}^+ = 15{,}000$$

$$\text{all } x_{ij}, d_i^-, d_i^+ \geq 0.$$

14.7.2. Application 2—Transportation Problem

The Mercury Distributing Company supplies a single product to three customers at various locations from two different warehouses. During the planning period considered, the company is unable to meet customer demand. However, the company has determined that certain customer demands must be satisfied at the expense of others. To avoid serious inequities, it is important to balance the portion of demand satisfied among certain customers. Also due to union agreements, the company must satisfy certain minimum shipment levels along certain routes. Finally, several of the routes over which the product might be shipped are hazardous, and thus these routes should be avoided.

The transportation problem is summarized below with the shipping costs given in each cell and supply and demand values in the margins. Note that total demand exceeds supply by 1500 units.

From \ To	Customer 1	Customer 2	Customer 3	Supply
Warehouse 1	10	4	12	3000
Warehouse 2	8	10	3	4000
Demand	2000	1500	5000	7000 / 8500

Management has expressed the following goal preferences in order of decreasing importance (P_1 = most important):

P_1. Satisfy entire demand of customer 3 (guaranteed delivery).
P_2. Satisfy at least 75% of the demand of each customer.
P_3. Minimize the total transportation costs for goods shipped.
P_4. Ship at least 1000 units over the route from warehouse 2 to customer 1 (union agreement).
P_5. Minimize shipping over the routes from warehouse 1 to customer 3, and warehouse 2 to customer 2 (hazard).
P_6. Balance the percentage of demand satisfied between customers 1 and 2.

MODEL FORMULATION. The following variables are defined:

x_{ij} = number of units to be shipped from warehouse i to customer j

d_i^- = underachievement of a goal in the ith constraint

d_i^+ = overachievement of a goal in the ith constraint.

1. *Supply constraints.* Supply is restricted to the maximum capacity of the warehouse; hence, positive deviations can be excluded from the supply constraints.

$$x_{11} + x_{12} + x_{13} + d_1^- = 3000$$
$$x_{21} + x_{22} + x_{23} + d_2^- = 4000.$$

2. *Demand constraints.* Let us assume that the firm never wishes to overfill a customer's demand. Therefore, positive deviations can be excluded from the demand constraints. However, negative deviations must be included to identify underachievement of demand goals, since total demand exceeds total supply.

$$x_{11} \qquad + x_{21} \qquad\qquad + d_3^- = 2000$$

$$x_{12} \qquad + x_{22} \qquad + d_4^- = 1500$$

$$x_{13} \qquad\qquad + x_{23} + d_5^- = 5000.$$

3. *Union agreement goal.* The union agreement states that at least 1000 units be shipped from warehouse 2 to customer 1. The variable d_6^- represents a negative deviation from this goal, while d_6^+ is the amount of overachievment of this goal.

$$x_{21} + d_6^- - d_6^+ = 1000.$$

4. *Minimal satisfied demand goal.* In order to preclude gross inequities of demand satisfaction among customers, a goal of satisfying at least 75% of each customer's demand is included. The appropriate constraints, including deviational variables, are as follows:

$$x_{11} \qquad + x_{21} \qquad\qquad + d_7^- - d_7^+ = 1500$$

$$x_{12} \qquad + x_{22} \qquad + d_8^- - d_8^+ = 1125$$

$$x_{13} \qquad\qquad + x_{23} + d_9^- - d_9^+ = 3750.$$

5. *Road hazard goal.* Owing to road hazards, the firm wishes to minimize shipping from warehouse 1 to customer 3 and warehouse 2 to customer 2. Hence, the goal level for these constraints are set to zero, and d_{10}^+ and d_{11}^+ are minimized.

$$x_{13} - d_{10}^+ = 0$$

$$x_{22} - d_{11}^+ = 0.$$

6. *Balance-to-customers goal.* The company desires to transport quantities to customers 1 and 2 such that an equal proportion of demand from each is satisfied. This can be expressed as

$$\frac{x_{11} + x_{21}}{2000} = \frac{x_{12} + x_{22}}{1500}.$$

Thus, by transposing and incorporating deviational variables, the goal constraint becomes

$$x_{11} - 1.33x_{12} + x_{21} - 1.33x_{22} + d_{12}^- - d_{12}^+ = 0.$$

7. *Transportation cost goal.* Since the firm wishes to minimize total transportation costs, a goal of zero is set and an attempt is made to minimize the positive deviation from this target goal value.

$$10x_{11} + 4x_{12} + 12x_{13} + 8x_{21} + 10x_{22} + 3x_{23} - d_{13}^+ = 0.$$

8. *Objective function*

$$\text{minimize } Z = P_1 d_5^- + P_2(d_7^- + d_8^- + d_9^-) + P_3 d_{13}^+ + P_4 d_6^-$$
$$+ P_5(1.2d_{10}^+ + d_{11}^+) + P_6(d_{12}^- + d_{12}^+).$$

Note that for P_5, d_{10}^+ has a coefficient of 1.2, since the cost of shipping from warehouse 1 to customer 3 ($c_{13} = 12$) is 1.2 times greater than the cost of shipping from warehouse 2 to customer 2 ($c_{22} = 10$).

GOAL PROGRAMMING MODEL SUMMARIZED

$$\text{minimize } Z = P_1 d_5^- + P_2(d_7^- + d_8^- + d_9^-) + P_3 d_{13}^+ + P_4 d_6^- \\ + P_5(1.2 d_{10}^+ + d_{11}^+) + P_6(d_{12}^- + d_{12}^+)$$

subject to

$$x_{11} + x_{12} + x_{13} + d_1^- = 3000$$
$$x_{21} + x_{22} + x_{23} + d_2^- = 4000$$
$$x_{11} + x_{21} + d_3^- = 2000$$
$$x_{12} + x_{22} + d_4^- = 1500$$
$$x_{13} + x_{23} + d_5^- = 5000$$
$$x_{21} + d_6^- - d_6^+ = 1000$$
$$x_{11} + x_{21} + d_7^- - d_7^+ = 1500$$
$$x_{12} + x_{22} + d_8^- - d_8^+ = 1125$$
$$x_{13} + x_{23} + d_9^- - d_9^+ = 3750$$
$$x_{13} - d_{10}^+ = 0$$
$$x_{22} - d_{11}^+ = 0$$
$$x_{11} - 1.33 x_{12} + x_{21} - 1.33 x_{22} + d_{12}^- - d_{12}^+ = 0$$
$$10 x_{11} + 4 x_{12} + 12 x_{13} + 8 x_{21} + 10 x_{22} + 3 x_{23} - d_{13}^+ = 0$$

$$x_{ij}, d_i^-, d_i^+ \geqslant 0 \qquad \text{for all } i, j.$$

14.7.3. Application 3—Portfolio Analysis

The Sentinal Finance Company, a small firm, wishes to invest in four stocks. The costs of each stock and the rate of return forecasts on each stock made by the company's five analysts are as follows:

	Stock 1	Stock 2	Stock 3	Stock 4
Cost	$30.00	$45.00	$27.00	$53.00
Forecast 1	3.00	13.00	4.00	25.00
Forecast 2	1.00	4.50	.60	15.00
Forecast 3	2.75	1.75	2.75	20.00
Forecast 4	4.50	5.00	1.90	5.00
Forecast 5	3.25	2.75	3.75	35.00
Expected return ($/share)	2.90	5.40	2.60	20.00

Additionally, the finance company would like to invest no more than $100,000. Sentinal has the following goals for its investment portfolio:

P_1. Invest a maximum of $100,000.
P_2. Achieve an expected return of 10% of total amount invested.
P_3. Achieve a minimum risk [as measured by the absolute deviation from the expected returns (a surrogate for variance)].
P_4. Invest 10% of the total investment in stock 4.

MODEL FORMULATION. The portfolio problem can be formulated into a goal programming problem as follows:

1. *Expected return constraint.* Since the target return expected is 10%, both negative and positive deviations are included in the constraint, which is

$$2.90x_1 + 5.40x_2 + 2.60x_3 + 20.00x_4 + d_1^- - d_1^+ = 0.10(30x_1 + 45x_2 + 27x_3 + 53x_4),$$

which simplifies to

$$- 0.10x_1 + 0.90x_2 - 0.10x_3 + 14.70x_4 + d_1^- - d_1^+ = 0,$$

where x_j = number of shares of stock j invested in

d_1^- = amount by which the expected return is underachieved

d_1^+ = amount by which the expected return is overachieved.

2. *Risk minimization constraints*

$$0.10x_1 + 7.60x_2 + 1.40x_3 + 5.00x_4 + d_2^- - d_2^+ = 0$$
$$- 1.90x_1 - 0.90x_2 - 2.00x_3 - 5.00x_4 + d_3^- - d_3^+ = 0$$
$$- 0.15x_1 - 3.65x_2 + 0.15x_3 + 0.00x_4 + d_4^- - d_4^+ = 0$$
$$1.60x_1 - 0.40x_2 - 0.70x_3 - 15.00x_4 + d_5^- - d_5^+ = 0$$
$$0.35x_1 - 2.65x_2 + 1.15x_3 + 15.00x_4 + d_6^- - d_6^+ = 0,$$

where $d_2^-, \ldots, d_6^-$ = amount of negative deviation from the zero goal

$d_2^+, \ldots, d_6^+$ = amount of positive deviation from the zero goal.

The risk constraints, as measured by the absolute deviations of the forecasted returns of a stock from its mean forecasted return, are determined from the table of forecasts above. For example, the first constraint in this section is determined as follows. First, determine the deviations of the forecasted returns for the first analyst (forecaster) from the mean expected return for stocks 1 through 4. The desired total deviations of these forecasts (times the unknown shares invested for each stock, x_j) should be equal to zero, to minimize risk. Since the actual deviations can be above or below zero, both negative and positive deviations are included in these constraints.

3. *Stock 4 investment constraint*

$$53.00x_4 = 0.10(30.00x_1 + 45.00x_2 + 27.00x_3 + 53.00x_4) - d_7^- + d_7^+$$

or $\quad -3.00x_1 - 4.50x_2 - 2.70x_3 + 47.70x_4 + d_7^- - d_7^+ = 0,$

where d_7^- = amount of underachievement of attaining the goal of investing 10% of invested funds in stock 4

d_7^+ = amount of overachievement of this goal.

This constraint states that the company wishes to invest exactly 10% of its invested funds in stock 4. Both negative and positive deviations are included in the constraint and will be in the objective function.

4. *Total investment constraint*

$$30x_1 + 45x_2 + 27x_3 + 53x_4 + d_8^- = 100,000,$$

where d_8^- is the amount of underachievement of this investment goal.

Only a negative deviational variable is included in this constraint, since investment is restricted to the total available amount of funds for investment.

5. *Objective function*

$$\text{minimize } Z = P_1(d_8^-) + P_2(d_1^- + d_1^+) + P_3 \sum_{i=2}^{6} (d_i^- + d_i^+) + P_4(d_7^- + d_7^+).$$

GOAL PROGRAMMING MODEL SUMMARIZED

$$\text{Minimize } Z = P_1(d_8^-) + P_2(d_1^- + d_1^+) + P_3 \sum_{i=2}^{6} (d_i^- + d_i^+) + P_4(d_7^- + d_7^+)$$

$$
\begin{aligned}
-0.10x_1 + 0.90x_2 - 0.10x_3 + 14.70x_4 + d_1^- - d_1^+ &= 0\\
0.10x_1 + 7.60x_2 + 1.40x_3 + 5.00x_4 + d_2^- + d_2^+ &= 0\\
-1.90x_1 - 0.90x_2 - 2.00x_3 - 5.00x_4 + d_3^- - d_3^+ &= 0\\
-0.15x_1 - 3.65x_2 + 0.15x_3 + 0.00x_4 + d_4^- - d_4^+ &= 0\\
1.60x_1 - 0.40x_2 - 0.70x_3 - 15.00x_4 + d_5^- - d_5^+ &= 0\\
0.35x_1 - 2.65x_2 + 1.15x_3 + 15.00x_4 + d_6^- - d_6^+ &= 0\\
-3.00x_1 - 4.50x_2 - 2.70x_3 + 47.70x_4 + d_7^- - d_7^+ &= 0\\
30.00x_1 + 45.00x_2 + 27.00x_3 + 53.00x_4 + d_8^- &= 0,
\end{aligned}
$$

all x_j, d_i^-, $d_i^+ \geqslant 0.$

After a year of promotion of a new tennis shoe, the sales manager of the Wilsom Sporting Company was reviewing the progress made. Since this product represented the first entry of Wilsom into the tennis shoe market, and financial resources were tight, promotion had been confined to cities in the southwestern part of the United States and consisted principally of radio and newspaper advertising. Ten cities of similar character and size were selected as a sample and the following data on promotional effort and results were obtained: (1) monthly sales in 100s, (2) dollar cost per month of radio advertising, and (3) dollar cost per month of newspaper advertising. The data are tabulated below:

City	Monthly Sales (100s)	Radio Advertising (100s of $/month)	Newspaper Advertising (100s of $/month)
Primary data			
1	5.3	2.0	1.0
2	3.9	1.5	3.0
3	3.0	1.5	1.5
4	7.4	2.3	2.0
5	4.0	1.0	5.0
Secondary data			
6	6.0	2.5	2.3
7	5.7	3.0	1.1
8	9.1	3.8	4.1
9	3.3	1.7	2.3
10	6.5	3.8	1.9

The data for the first five cities were collected from officially documented sources. The data for the second five cities unfortunately could only be obtained subjectively from sales representatives' responses. These data were presumed to be one-third as accurate as the documented data for the first five cities. Hence, it is labeled secondary data. No time was available to obtain an additional sample, so the sales manager was "stuck" with the data he had.

In order to plan further promotional campaigns, the sales manager was reviewing the data to evaluate the relative effect of newspaper and radio advertising on his new tennis shoe sales. Regression seemed like an appropriate procedure for relating sales to radio and newspaper advertising. The sales manager thought that while both types of advertising increased sales, newspaper advertising had less of an effect on sales than radio advertising.

†Goal programming was actually originated to obtain "constrained regression" estimates on an executive compensation formula (Charnes and Cooper, 1961). The regression estimates had to conform to certain a priori requirements (signs of the regression coefficients, weighting relationships among coefficients, etc.). These constrained regression estimates were obtained via linear programming. Of course, since then, goal programming has considerably outgrown "constrained regression" characterizations. However, this class of goal programming problems might be called least-square or least-absolute-value estimators, since these are the deviations that we are attempting to minimize in the objective function.

MODEL FORMULATION. To formulate this constrained regression problem as a mathematical programming problem, we use the following general linear model[†]:

$$y = b_0 + b_1 x_1 + b_2 x_2 + e,$$

where y = monthly sales (100s), x_1 = radio advertising ($100s/month), x_2 = newspaper advertising ($100s/month), and e = error term.

Our task is to choose b_0, b_1, and b_2 to minimize the least-square errors from the regression line above. The basic unrestricted regression model is thus written

$$\text{minimize} \quad Z = \sum_{i=1}^{10} e_i^2$$

$$\text{subject to } y_i = e_i + b_{0i} + b_{1i} x_{1i} + b_{2i} x_{2i} \quad \text{for all } i (= 10) \text{ sample data points,}$$

where the b's and e's are the parameters to be estimated. The problem is quadratic in e subject to linear constraints; hence, we have a quadratic programming problem. The objective function minimizes the summed squared errors by choosing appropriate values of b and e. In order to permit negative and positive b's and e's, a simple, well-known transformation may be performed: making each parameter the difference between two positive numbers (e.g., $b_i = b_i^+ - b_i^-$, $e_j = e_j^+ - e_j^-$).[‡]

Given the data in the table above, let us use quadratic goal programming to estimate the parameters of a linear function relating tennis shoe sales to radio and newspaper advertising. The quadratic goal programming formulation is:

$$\text{minimize } Z = 3\left(\sum_{i=1}^{5} e_i^{-2} + \sum_{i=1}^{5} e_i^{+2} \right) + \sum_{i=6}^{10} e_i^{-2} + \sum_{i=6}^{10} e_i^{+2}$$

$$\text{subject to: } e_1^- - e_1^+ + b_0^- - b_0^+ - 2.0 b_1^+ - 1.0 b_2^+ = 5.3$$

$$e_2^- - e_2^+ + b_0^- - b_0^+ - 1.5 b_1^+ - 3.0 b_2^+ = 3.9$$

$$\vdots$$

$$e_{10}^- - e_{10}^+ + b_0^- - b_0^+ - 3.8 b_1^+ - 1.9 b_2^+ = 1.9$$

$$b_1^+ - b_2^+ \geqslant 0$$

$$e_i^-, e_i^+, b_i^-, b_i^+ \geqslant 0 \text{ for all } i.$$

[†]See McCarl, Moskowitz, and Furtan (1976) for reasons for formulating unconstrained and constrained regression problems as "goal programming" problems.

[‡]Of course, if we had taken our objective to be to minimize the absolute deviations of the errors (rather than the squared errors), we would have a linear programming problem, differing only in the objective function (i.e., having the same constraints as the quadratic programming problem). The linear programming objective function would be:

$$\text{minimize } Z = \sum_{i=1}^{10} e_i^- + \sum_{i=1}^{10} e_i^+.$$

where b_0 = intercept term to be estimated

b_1, b_2 = unknown regression parameters associated with radio and newspaper advertising, respectively

$e_1, \ldots, e_{10}$ = unknown error terms.

The reader should note that the b_1^- and b_2^- terms were not included in the constraint equations, since it was known a priori that these regression coefficients must be positive. The last constraint indicates that the b_1 regression coefficient must be greater than the b_2 regression coefficient, since it was known a priori that radio advertising had more of an effect on sales than newspaper advertising.

14.8. SUMMARY AND CONCLUSIONS

Goal programming is a mathematical programming approach for dealing with decision problems having multiple, conflicting, and incommensurable objectives. With goal programming, management must at least ordinally rank the goals in terms of priority or importance. In a goal programming solution, lower-level goal constraints are often violated to achieve higher-priority goals. If a decision maker discovers an intolerable or unsatisfactory goal constraint violation in the final solution, he may reevaluate his goals as well as his goal-priority structure. Consequently, the value of goal programming is in developing the goal-preference structure of the decision maker and in allowing him insights and information as to the consequences and implications of his preference structure. A goal programming computer code provides a simple vehicle for such interactive analysis by management.* Goal programming is finding increasing application in decision problems in business and government.

While we have dealt principally with linear goal programming problems, both integer and nonlinear goal programming formulations and solutions have been developed [Ignizio (1965), Kornbluth (1973), and references cited therein].

REFERENCES ARTHUR, J. L. and A. RAVINDRAN, "A Partitioning Algorithm for Goal Programming," School of Industrial Engineering, Purdue University, April 1977, Report No. 77.

CHARNES, A., and W. W. COOPER. *Management Models and Industrial Applications of Linear Programming*. New York: John Wiley & Sons, Inc., 1961.

CHARNES, A., and W. W. COOPER. "Goal Programming and Constrained Regression—A Comment." *Omega*, **3** (4), 1975, 403–409.

CHURCHMAN, C. W., and R. L. ACKOFF. "An Approximate Measure of Value," *Journal of the OR Society of America*, **2** (10), 1954.

ECKENRODE, R. T. "Weighting Multiple Criteria," *Management Science*, **12** (3), 1965, 180–192.

HALTER, A. N., and G. W. DEAN. *Decisions Under Uncertainty*. Cincinnati, Ohio: South-Western Publishing Co., 1971.

IGNIZIO, J. P. *Goal Programming and Extensions*. Lexington, Mass: D. C. Heath and Company, 1976.

*An efficient goal programming computer code developed by Arthur and Ravindran (1977) is provided in the Instructors Manual.

IJIRI, Y. *Management Goals and Accounting for Control*. Amsterdam: North-Holland Publishing, 1965.

JAASKELAINEN, V. *Accounting and Mathematical Programming*. Helsinki: Research Institute for Business and Economics, 1969.

KORNBLUTH, J. "A Survey of Goal Programming." *OMEGA*, **1** (2), 1973, 193–205.

LEE, S. M. *Goal Programming for Decision Analysis*. Philadelphia: Auerback, 1972.

LEE, S. M., and M. M. BIRD. "A Goal Programming Model for Sales Effort Allocation." *Business Perspectives*, **6**(4), 1970, 17—21.

LEE, S. M., A. J. LERRO, and B. McGINNIS. "Optimization of Tax Switching for Commercial Banks." *Journal of Money, Credit, and Banking*, **3** (2), 1973.

LEE, S. M., and L. J. MOORE. "Optimizing Transportation Problems with Multiple Objectives." *AIIE Transactions*, **5** (4), 1973, 333–338.

LEE, A. M., and R. NICELY. "Goal Programming for Marketing Decisions: A Case Study." *Journal of Marketing*, **38** (1), 1974, 24–32.

McCARL, B. A., H. MOSKOWITZ, and H. FURTAN. "Quadratic Programming Applications." *OMEGA*, 1976.

TORGERSON, W. S. *Theory and Methods of Scaling*. New York: John Wiley & Sons, Inc., 1958.

KEY CONCEPTS

Deviational variables (under- and overachievement)
Preemptive priority weights
  cardinal versus ordinal priority weights
Goal programming formulations
  single satisficing goal
  multiple goals
  multiple goals and subgoals

Solving goal programming problems graphically
  simplex method
Quadratic goal programming
  symmetric goals
  asymmetric goals
Ranking multiple goals

REVIEW QUESTIONS

14.1. What is goal programming? When is it applicable?

14.2. Contrast the differences between linear programming and linear goal programming.

14.3. Show how you would solve a multicriterion problem by linear programming.

14.4. State the key features of a goal programming problem. Formulate the goal programming model in general, defining terms. Construct a simple example problem and formulate it as a linear goal programming problem. Contrast this formulation to a linear programming formulation. Solve both formulations graphically and discuss your results.

14.5. If a goal is to be met exactly, how is this handled in the objective function of a goal programming model? If underachievement (overachievement) of a goal is to be avoided, how is this handled in the objective function? Illustrate with examples.

14.6. What is meant by "preemptive" priority factors in a goal programming problem?

14.7. Can cardinal weights be used in the objective function of a goal programming model? Under what circumstances? What happens to a goal programming model if cardinal weights are attached to all priorities in the objective function of a goal programming model?

14.8. Contrast the differences in solving a linear versus goal programming problem by the simplex method.

14.9. State some problem areas in management where you think goal programming might be applicable. Be as specific as possible.

14.10. Explain and illustrate a method for obtaining importance rankings of multiple goals.

ANSWERS TO REVIEW QUESTIONS

14.1. Goal programming is a mathematical programming technique which treats the constraints of a linear programming problem as goals in the objective function. Optimization means coming "as close as possible" to achieving these goals in order of priority, as prespecified by the decision maker. Goal programming is applicable to single or multiple goals, although its greatest usefulness occurs when the multiple goals are conflicting and cannot all be satisfied simultaneously.

14.2. In linear programming, one goal is chosen as the objective function and the other goals are specified as constraints. Any solution to a problem must satisfy all constraints prior to optimization of the objective function.

In linear goal programming, each goal enters the problem formulation as an equality constraint which contains slack variables, indicating either underachievement or overachievement of goals. The objective function than contains these deviational variables, and a solution will attempt to minimize them in order of priority. Thus goal programming allows for full or partial achievement of goals, while linear programming requires complete satisfaction of all goals represented as constraints.

14.3. To solve a multiple-criterion problem by linear programming, one of the goals would have to be chosen and formulated into the objective function. This would be the least important goal. The remaining goals would then need to be incorporated as constraints in the model. The simplex algorithm would then select an optimal solution which would satisfy all constraints first, and only then be concerned with optimizing the objective function. If no solution exists which satisfies all the constraints, the goal in the objective function would need to be dropped and a new linear program formulated.

The new formulation would then have the next least important goal placed in the objective function. This process could continue until a feasible solution would be attained.

14.4. The key features of a goal programming problem are

1. Goals are satisfied in order of priority established by the decision maker.
2. Goals need not be satisfied exactly but only as close as possible.

The goal programming model in general can be expressed mathematically as follows:

$$\text{minimize } z = \sum_{i=1}^{m} w_i(d_i^+ + d_i^-)$$

$$\text{subject to } \sum_{j=1}^{n} a_{ij}x_j + d_i^- - d_i^+ = b_i$$

$$x_j, d_i^-, d_i^+ \geq 0, \text{ all } i, j$$

where x_j is decision variable j
w_i is the priority attached to goal i
d_i^- is the degree of underachievement of goal i
d_i^+ is the degree of overachievement of goal i

The chief difference between goal programming and linear programming is that in linear programming all objectives except the weakest must be satisfied exactly, while for goal programming each goal is satisfied to the greatest extent possible.

14.5. If exact achievement of a goal is desired, both the deviational variable indicating the amount of underachievement and the deviational variable indicating the amount of overachievement of the goal would be included in the objective function to be minimized. If underachievement is to be avoided, the deviational variable corresponding to underachievement would be included in the objective function, but that for overachievement could be eliminated.

For example, if one wished to make the sum of two variables x_1 and x_2 be equal to 100, a constraint could be formulated as follows:

$$x_1 + x_2 + d_1^- - d_1^+ = 100$$

Here, $d_1^- > 0$ would indicate that the sum of x_1 and x_2 would be less than 100, and $d_1^+ > 0$ would indicate a sum greater than 100. For exact achievement the objective function (to be minimized) would include both d_1^+ and d_1^-. To avoid underachievement, only the d_1^- variable would appear in the objective function.

14.6. Preemptive priority factors are the coefficients associated with deviations from each goal in a goal programming formulation. They have the property that, if goal i is more important than goal j, the factor P_i will be "much larger" than P_j. This means that even if the deviations from goal j are very large compared to the deviations from goal i, the simplex method will minimize the objective function just according to the deviation from goal i.

14.7. Cardinal weights may be used (1) to indicate the relative value of goals (one could assign a priority factor $3P_i$ to a goal three times as important as goal i), or (2) to indicate the relative importance of overachievement versus underachievement of a goal. If cardinal weights are assigned to goals or priorities, the problem can be solved as a conventional linear program.

14.8. In general, a simplex solution of goal programming problems is similar to the simplex solution of linear programming problems. However, in the case of goal programming, we must work with priority factors instead of cardinal weights in the objective function. The result of this is that the evaluation row $(z_j$-$c_j)$ terms will, in general, consist of terms containing one or more priority factors. Thus, in goal programming, in order to choose variables to enter the basis, we look for the z_j-c_j term which has the largest positive value in the highest priority factor remaining. Only after the highest priority z_j-c_j terms are nonpositive, do we consider the lower priority terms. In goal programming, the z_j-c_j terms are vectors, while in linear programming they are scalars.

14.9. Goal programming is applicable in the following areas.

1. *Marketing*—where conflicting goals might be: maximize market share, minimize advertising cost, maximize profit margin per item sold.
2. *Inventory control*—where it is necessary to minimize the number of stockouts, and to minimize storage cost.
3. *Production*—where it is necessary to minimize time of manufacture, minimize cost, maximize quality control, and maximize resource utilization.

14.10. One method for obtaining importance rankings is by paired comparisons. The decision maker is presented with all goals in the form of all possible pairs and is asked which goal of each pair is more important. Each goal is given a score based on the number of times that the goal has the higher ranking in the paired comparisons. If the decision maker is consistent, the most important goal should have the higher ranking in $n - 1$ paired comparisons (where n is the number of goals), the next best should have the higher ranking in $n - 2$ goals, and so on.

EXERCISES **14.1.** A small specialty products office equipment manufacturer produces two kinds of products, chairs and lamps. The gross margin from the sale of a chair is $80; from the sale of a lamp, $40. The goal of the plant manager is to earn a gross profit of $640 in the next week. Formulate this problem as a goal programming problem.

14.2. Consider the problem presented in Exercise 14.1. Suppose that in addition to the goal constraint considered in that example, the following two goal constraints are imposed. The marketing department reports that the maximum number of chairs that can be sold in a week is six. The maximum number of lamps that can be sold is eight. Reformulate this problem as a goal programming problem.

14.3. Again consider the office equipment manufacturer problem illustrated in Exercises 14.1 and 14.2. Assume the manager now wishes to achieve a weekly profit as close to $640 as possible. He also desires to achieve a sales volume for chairs and lamps close to six and to four, respectively. Reformulate the manager's decision problem as a goal program.

14.4. Consider the following modified problem of the office equipment manufacturer. Production of either a chair or a lamp requires 1 hour of production capacity in the plant. The plant has a maximum production capacity of 10 hours per week. Because of the limited sales capacity, the maximum number of chairs and lamps that can be sold are six and eight per week, respectively. The gross margin from the sale of a chair is $80 and $40 for a lamp.

The plant manager has set the following goals, arranged in order of importance:

1. He wants to avoid any underutilization of production capacity.
2. He wants to sell as many chairs and lamps as possible. Since the gross margin from the sale of a chair is set at twice the amount of profit from a lamp, he has twice as much desire to achieve the sales goal for chairs as for lamps.
3. He wants to minimize overtime operation of the plant as much as possible.

Formulate this as a goal programming problem, so that the plant manager will make a decision that will achieve his goals as closely as possible.

14.5. A production manager faces the problem of job allocation between two of his machines. The processing rate on machine 1 is 5 units per hour and 6 units per hour on the second machine. The regular operating time on both machines is 8 hours per day. The production manager has the following goals for the next day in order of priority:

1. Avoid any underachievement of production level, which is set at 120 units of product.
2. Avoid any overtime of machine 2 beyond 3 hours.
3. Minimize the sum of overtime (*note:* assign differential weights according to the relative cost of overtime hours—assume that the operating cost of the two machines is the same).
4. Avoid any underutilization of regular working hours (assign weights according to the relative productivity of the two machines).

14.6. Universal Appliances produces freezers. The company has two production lines. The production rate for line 1 is 3 units per hour and for line 2 it is 2 units per hour. The regular production capacity is 40 hours per week for both lines. The gross profit from an average freezer is $125. The president of the firm has the following goals for the next week, shown in descending order of priority.

1. Meet the production goal of 200 units for the week.
2. Limit the overtime operation of line 2 to 5 hours.
3. Avoid underutilization of regular working hours for both lines.
4. Limit the sum of overtime operation for both teams.

(a) Formulate this problem as a goal programming problem.
(b) Solve this problem by the graphical method of goal programming.
(c) Solve this problem by the simplex method of goal programming. Compare your solution to that obtained by the graphical method.

14.7. Solve the following problem by the graphical and simplex methods of goal programming:

$$\text{minimize } Z = P_1 d_1^- + 2P_2 d_2^- + P_3 d_1^+$$

$$\text{subject to } x_1 + x_2 + d_1^- - d_1^+ = 400$$

$$x_1 \qquad\qquad + d_2^- = 240$$

$$x_2 \qquad + d_3^- = 300.$$

14.8. Solve the following problem by the graphical and simplex methods of goal programming:

$$\text{minimize } Z = P_1 d_1^- + P_2 d_2^+ + 6P_3 d_3^+ + 5P_3 d_4^+ + 6P_4 d_4^- + 5P_4 d_3^-$$

$$\text{subject to } 50x_1 + 60x_2 + d_1^- - d_1^+ = 1200$$

$$10x_2 + d_2^- - d_2^+ = 110$$

$$10x_1 \qquad + d_3^- - d_3^+ = \quad 80$$

$$100x_2 + d_4^- - d_4^+ = 800 \ .$$

14.9. In planning the construction of nuclear power systems, an electric utility company considers the following goals:

G_1. Provide adequate capacity of generation to meet the power demand (megawatt-hours of generation).
G_2. Maximize the reliability of the system.
G_3. Minimize total system cost.
G_4. Maximize system safety (of site population).
G_5. Minimize effects on the environment (emission of particulates, e.g., sulfur dioxide, nitric oxide, and biological impacts at site).
G_6. Minimize socioeconomic impact.

The utility, wishing to determine the order of importance of these goals, uses the method of paired comparisons to obtain a ranking from the various groups affected. In this method, a decision maker is asked to compare all combinations of these goals taken two at a time and indicate which goal is more important in the pair. Since there are six goals, the total combination of paired comparisons is $6(5)/2 = 15$. One decision maker's judgments for the paired comparisons are as follows:

$$G_1 > G_2 \quad G_2 < G_3 \quad G_3 < G_4 \quad G_4 > G_5 \quad G_5 < G_6$$

$$G_1 > G_3 \quad G_2 < G_4 \quad G_3 > G_5 \quad G_4 > G_6$$

$$G_1 < G_4 \quad G_2 > G_5 \quad G_3 > G_6$$

$$G_1 > G_5 \quad G_2 > G_6$$

$$G_1 > G_6$$

(a) For the data above, derive the complete ordinal ranking of this decision maker's goals in terms of order of importance.

Goal	Priority
G_1	
G_2	
G_3	
G_4	
G_5	

(b) Criticize the use of the paired-comparison method in determining the priorities of goals.
(c) What other schemes might be used to obtain an ordinal priority ranking of goals?

14.10. (a) Consider the simplex criterion portion of the following imaginary goal programming tableau:

$z_j - c_j$	VARIABLES			
	x_1	x_2	x_3	x_4
P_3	0	0	0	0
P_2	4	7	0	-5
P_1	2	2	-1	0

Given this configuration, which variable should enter the basis?

(b) Given the following configuration which variable should enter the basis?

$z_j - c_j$	VARIABLES			
	x_1	x_2	x_3	x_4
P_3	280	0	500	0
P_2	110	0	1000	-4
P_1	2	3	-1	0

(c) In light of your answers to parts (a) and (b), discuss an obvious short-coming of goal programming.

14.11. The production plant of a small tennis manufacturer has a maximum operational capacity of 8 hours per day. With this capacity, the company produces two products: a pro-line wooden tennis racket and an aluminum tennis racket. Production of either a wooden or an aluminum racket requires 6 and 10 minutes, respectively, in the factory. Because of limited sales capacity, the expected sales of wooden and aluminum rackets are 60 and 50, respectively. The unit profit from the sale of a wooden racket is $5, while the profit from an aluminum racket is $10. The manager of the company has listed the following goals in order of importance:

1. Avoid any underutilization of production capacity.
2. Achieve the expected sales for both wooden and aluminum rackets. (*Note:* Since the profit from the sale of a wooden racket is half the amount of an aluminum racket, he is half as concerned about achieving the sales goal for wooden as he is for aluminum rackets.)

(a) Formulate this problem as a goal programming problem and solve for an optimal production schedule.
(b) Let us now treat the deviational variables from the target goals in the objective function as squared terms. That is, our disutility for not achieving a given target goal varies as the square of our deviation (rather than linearly) from that goal. Formulate this problem as a quadratic goal programming problem and solve for an optimal production schedule using an appropriate quadratic programming algorithm.
(c) Assume again that the manager has quadratic preferences as in (b); however, he has set one additional goal. This goal is to achieve the expected sales for both products on the high side *and* to minimize the overtime required for production. (*Note:* This suggests asymmetric preferences, or interaction terms involving the deviational variables.) This additional goal is assumed to have the same degree of importance as achieving the expected sales. Formulate and solve this problem as a quadratic goal programming problem.

14.12. Given the following data, we wish to estimate the parameters of a linear function relating TV sales to price and production.

Regression Data Relating TV Sales to Price and Production

Observation	Sale of TVs	Price of TVs	Production of TVs
Primary data			
1	100	10	100
2	50	15	100
3	130	13	70
Secondary data			
4	200	13	150
5	170	15	200

Assume we have a priori knowledge that the price increase of TVs has a nonnegative effect on the quantity produced. Note also that we consider the primary data to be twice as important as the secondary data, since they are believed to be twice as accurate.
(a) Formulate this problem as a quadratic goal programming problem.
(b) Using minimization of the absolute deviation of errors as a criterion, formulate this problem as a linear goal programming problem.

CASE 14.1 Illustrated Case Study
Involving Farm Planning via Goal Programming

SELECTING A CROPPING PLAN FOR A VEGETABLE FARM *PART A—LINEAR PROGRAMMING PROBLEM.* A medium-size vegetable farm in southern Indiana is faced with the problem of choosing a 1-year cropping plan, such that, initially, the sum of gross margins from all its crops grown are maximized. The farm owner considers the following four cropping activities: (1) carrots, (2) celery, (3) cucumbers, and (4) peppers. The farm owner must consider his decision subject to three resource constraints: (1) the available acreage of land (200 acres), (2) hours of labor available (10,000), and (3) a rotational and market outlet constraint (this requires that the total acreage of celery and peppers be less than or equal to the total acreage of carrots and cucumbers).

A time series of gross margins over the six most recent years was obtained from a sample of actual fresh market vegetable farms in Georgia and Florida, and the mean gross margins used as forecast values for the Indiana farmer's gross margins. These gross margins are shown in Table 1.

Formulate and solve this problem as a linear programming problem.

PART B—GROSS MARGIN AND ACREAGE GOALS. Now assume a change in the problem that would make it suitable as a goal programming problem. Besides the goal of maximization of gross margins, the farmer has a goal of utilizing all his available acreage. When asked which goal was more

Table 1. Activity Gross Margins per Acre

Year	Carrots	Celery	Cucumbers	Peppers
1	292	− 128	420	579
2	179	560	187	639
3	114	648	366	379
4	247	544	249	924
5	426	182	322	5
6	259	850	159	569
Mean	253	443	284	516

important, the farmer replies that the gross margin goal is far more important than the acreage goal. Formulate and solve this problem as a goal programming problem and discuss your solution in Part B with Part A.

PART C—ACREAGE SUBGOALS. Now assume that it is possible for the farmer to acquire more land, but that he dislikes this 5 times more than he dislikes not using all his 200 acres. Formulate and solve this as a goal programming problem. Compare and discuss your solution in Part C with those of Parts A and B.

PART D—GOAL PRIORITIES REVERSED. Again consider Part C. Now assume that the farmer says that the acreage goal is more important than the gross margin goal. Formulate and solve this as a goal programming problem. Compare and interpret your results relative to Parts A, B, and C.

PART E. Now assume that the farmer wishes to achieve a target gross margin of at least $75,000. The farmer has a goal of utilizing all his available acreage. The farmer can acquire more land, but, again, he dislikes this 5 times more than he dislikes not using all of his 200 acres. The gross margin goal he considers far more important than his acreage goal. Formulate and solve this as a goal programming problem.

PART F. Consider the farmer's problem once again. From Table 1 we have the activity gross margin deviations from their sample means in a sample consisting of 6 years of observations on gross margins. The most important goal for the decision maker is still to achieve a sum of gross margins of $75,000, but a subgoal is to minimize the sum of deviations in gross margins from their sample means. Strictly speaking, it is the sum of the absolute deviations that is minimized. Thus, this is a measure of the decision maker's risk aversion. Assume that at most 200 acres are available. Formulate and solve this as a goal programming problem.

PART III *Operations Research Applications*

CHAPTER 15
Inventory Models: Deterministic Demand

OBJECTIVES: Upon successful completion of this chapter, you should be able to:

1. Specify the functions of inventory.
2. Specify the characteristics of inventory systems.
3. Calculate and apply the optimal EOQ decision rules: (a) in the classical situation; (b) with shortages permitted; (c) with quantity discounts given; (d) for production runs of single products; (e) for production runs of multiple products; and (f) with constraints specified.

15.1. INTRODUCTION

Unlike the previous chapters, which are technique-oriented, this and subsequent chapters are devoted to application areas. The topic in this and the next chapter deals with inventory models under deterministic and probabilistic demand, respectively.

One of the first applications of quantitative methods to managerial decision making has been to inventory problems. This is not surprising, since inventories usually represent a considerable percentage of the total capital invested in a business organization, often greater than 25%. Moreover, inventories provide the operating flexibility which ensures that an organization's operations perform smoothly and efficiently. With so many billions of dollars invested in inventory today, proper inventory management and control can effect substantial savings to a company and more globally to the national and international economy.

Development of the first inventory model is credited to Harris (1915). Raymond (1931) extended Harris's work in the early 1930s. Since then, particularly since World War II, the development of inventory theory and inventory models has proliferated to a point of high development. Inventory models cover practically every imaginable inventory situation.

The basic inventory decisions involve *how many units to order* and *when to order*. In this and the next chapter we shall introduce you to how quantitative models can be developed and used in making the decisions above. While there exist many fundamental similarities in all inventory systems, each system is sufficiently unique to preclude the use of a general inventory decision model for all situations. In this chapter we shall introduce several classical inventory decision models and some of the more common and useful variations. In this chapter demand for the commodities in question is assumed to be deterministic, that is, known in advance. Inventory models under uncertain demand are treated in Chapter 16. While the study of inventory models is practically useful, it is also useful from a conceptual viewpoint by providing experience in model development and the use of quantitative techniques and tools that are broadly applicable to other management problem areas.

15.2. THE FUNCTIONS OF INVENTORY

Inventory can be broadly defined as the quantity of goods, commodities, or other economic resources that are stored or idle at any given point in time. The economic resources vary in quantity over time in response to a *demand* process which operates to reduce the inventory level, and a *replenishment* process which operates to increase it. Normally demand is an uncontrollable variable, but the magnitude and timing of the replenishments are controllable.

Inventory, for example, may include raw materials waiting to be used in producing goods (raw-material inventory), semifinished goods or goods in process temporarily stored during the production process (work-in-process inventory), finished goods awaiting shipment from the factory, wholesaler, or retailer (finished-goods inventory). In addition to such physical goods as lightbulbs, toothpaste, and automobiles, cash, human resources, human body parts, and library space available for new books can be viewed as inventoriable items. For example, patients waiting in a doctor's office can be regarded as inventory. The rate at which the doctor sees and treats the patients is the demand process. As this is occurring, new patients arrive to replenish those that have been seen and treated. The how-many and when decisions are determined by how the doctor schedules his appointments.

To illustrate the functions of inventory, let us consider a production–distribution system. Here, inventories exist continuously throughout the entire system, fulfilling some of the following basic functions:

1. *Transit or pipeline inventories.* These are inventories made up of supplies to cover delays in handling and transit.
2. *Lot-size or cycle inventories.* These are inventories that we order in lot sizes because it is more economical to do so than is ordering on an as-needed basis to satisfy demand. For example, it may be more economical to carry a certain amount of inventory by ordering or producing in large lots in order to achieve reduced order or setup costs or to obtain quantity discounts on the items purchased.

3. *Buffer inventories (safety stock)*. These are inventories to prevent stock-outs due to uncertain demand fluctuations.

4. *Decoupling inventories*. Inventories serve the function of decoupling operations, for example, throughout an entire production–distribution system. This permits the various production activities to operate more independently, without complete reliance on the schedule of output of prior activities in the production process. For example, in manufacturing, work-in-process inventories are essential to preclude each individual part from being carried from machine to machine. Similarly, in assembly-line operations, work-in-process inventory at each station effectively reduces the dependence of each station on the speed and performance of the line.

5. *Seasonal inventories*. Inventories used for this purpose are designed to more economically meet seasonal demand than by varying production levels to meet such demand fluctuations. In other words, these inventories are used to smooth out the level of production operations so that workers do not have to be as frequently hired, retrained, and fired.

Inventories can also be used for other purposes. For example, inventory on display serves as a promotional instrument. Raw-material and finished-goods inventories are frequently accumulated to hedge against price rises, inflation, and strikes. Inventories serve to smooth out irregularities in supply. For example, corn is harvested in late summer but is used in feeding animals and is produced into corn products for the consumer throughout the year. Our government stockpiles strategic materials, such as oil, magnesium, rubber, uranium, and so forth, because of the unpredictability of its sources of supply, which often come from unstable and potentially unfriendly governments. When dealing with perishable items, such as fish, fruit, and vegetables which are caught or grown only a few months in each year, inventories are necessary to meet demand for the entire year, until the next fishing or growing season.

The simple fact that inventories serve these functions implies that they have value to management. They should not necessarily be minimized. Organizations who carry minimal inventory levels can incur extremely high production and distribution costs. What is needed is a way to determine optimal inventory levels in a given situational context. This requires balancing a set of costs that increases with higher inventory levels against a set of costs that decreases with higher inventory levels.

In sum, inventories act to decouple organizational activities, thereby achieving lower-cost operations. Inventories act to reduce procurement costs, and inventories act to provide good customer service by providing on-time delivery and avoiding costly stock shortages. Inventories resulting from ordering in large quantities can result in lower freight charges and price discounts. On the other hand, inventories require tying up capital that would otherwise be invested elsewhere. Inventory requires costly storage space; and such costs as insurance, spoilage, obsolescence, pilferage, and taxes must be incurred as a result of maintaining inventory. Thus, management seeks decision rules that will optimally balance these counterveiling costs for a given system.

15.3. BASIC INVENTORY DECISIONS

The basic inventory decisions (decision variables) of every inventory problem are as follows:

1. What *quantity* to order?
2. *When* to order?

As alluded to earlier, in making these decisions, management is faced with a trade-off. On the one hand, management would like to order or produce large lot sizes to minimize procurement or production costs. On the other hand, management desires to minimize inventory holding costs. This can only be achieved if small lots are procured or produced. The optimum strategy is to achieve a balance between these two extremes. By using classical quantitative tools, we can formulate models and develop decision rules for obtaining the optimal economic order quantity, as well as optimally when to order. In many cases these two decisions are independent. In other cases, they are interdependent (i.e., they interact) and therefore must be considered simultaneously. Whether the decisions are independent or not depends on the implicit assumptions of a given model.

15.4. CHARACTERISTICS OF INVENTORY SYSTEMS

Sections 15.5 through 15.11 present the various inventory decision models. This section describes the characteristics of an inventory system.

15.4.1. Inventory Costs (Economic Parameters)

The usual criterion considered in an inventory analysis (i.e., deciding on how much and when to order) is minimization of an appropriate cost function which balances the costs of (1) *ordering*, (2) *holding*, and (3) being *short* of inventory.

ORDERING (OR SETUP) COSTS. Ordering (or setup if produced in-house) costs are those incremental costs associated with inventory replenishment. These costs vary with the number of orders made. Such typical costs each time an order is made include requisitioning costs, costs of issuing and following up on the purchase order, receiving inspection costs and placing goods into inventory, payment to the supplier, accounting costs, and administrative costs such as supplies, stationery, and so on. Salaries of the individuals involved in such activities constitute the major part of the ordering cost.

HOLDING COSTS. These costs are associated with holding a given level of inventory on hand, and vary with the level and length of time inventory is held.

Holding costs include:

1. *Opportunity cost* on investment tied up in inventory (based on cost of capital).
2. *Storage costs* (rent, heat, lights, refrigeration, security, etc.).
3. Product *deterioration* or *obsolescence*.
4. *Taxes*, *depreciation*, and *insurance*.

Holding costs are expressed as the dollar cost of holding 1 unit in inventory per unit time (usually 1 year). Another commonly used form is to specify holding cost per year as a percentage of average inventory value (e.g., 10% of average inventory value).

SHORTAGE (STOCKOUT) COSTS. These are the penalty costs incurred as a result of running out of stock when the commodity is needed. They generally include costs due to loss of customers' goodwill and potential loss in profit due to loss in sales. In the case where the unsatisfied demand can be satisfied at a later date (by means of back orders), these costs usually vary directly with the shortage quantity and delay time. If the unfilled demand is lost completely (no back orders), shortage costs become proportional to only the shortage quantity.

PURCHASE PRICE. This parameter is of special interest when *quantity discounts* or *price breaks* can be secured, or when large production runs may result in a decrease in the production cost. Under these conditions, the order quantity must be adjusted to take advantage of these price breaks.

15.4.2. Demand

The demand pattern of a commodity may either be deterministic or probabilistic. By deterministic we mean that the quantities demanded over subsequent periods are known with certainty. The demand over equal periods of time may be constant or may vary as well as being deterministic. These two cases are referred to as *static* and *dynamic* demand, respectively.

Probabilistic demand occurs when the demand over a certain time period is uncertain, but can be described in terms of a probability distribution. Analogous to the static and dynamic demands in the deterministic case, the probability distribution can either be *stationary* or *nonstationary* over time. In Chapter 16 we deal only with probabilistic inventory models having stationary demand distributions.

Demand for a given time period may be satisfied *instantaneously* at the start of the period or *uniformly* during the period. As you will see, instantaneous and uniform demands affect inventory levels and hence inventory holding costs directly.

15.4.3. Order Cycle

An *order cycle* is identified by the time period between two successive order placements. This may be initiated as follows:

1. *Continuous review.* The record of the inventory level is monitored continuously until a specified trigger (or reorder) point is reached where a new order is placed. This is often referred to as the "two-bin system." This name derives from the fact that continuous monitoring could be effected by using two bins of inventory. Items are drawn from only one bin, and when it is empty, a new order is placed.
2. *Periodic review.* Orders are placed at equal time intervals.

15.4.4. Lead Times

When an order is placed, it may be received immediately or it may take some time before it is received. The time between the placement and receipt of an order is known as the *lead time*. Lead time may be deterministic or probabilistic.

15.4.5. Inventory Replenishment

The actual replenishment of a stock may occur instantaneously or uniformly over time. *Instantaneous replenishment* results when items are purchased from outside sources. *Uniform replenishment* usually occurs when the item is produced locally within the organization.

15.4.6. Time Horizon

The *time horizon* defines the period over which the inventory level will be controlled. This horizon can be finite or infinite, depending on the nature of demand.

15.4.7. Number of Items

An inventory system usually involves many different commodities. Usually, these commodities compete for such limited resources as floor space or capital. When this is the case, an interaction exists among the different commodities and inventory models must be developed for this kind of situation.

An inventory system may have several stocking points rather than a single stocking point. Often these stocking points are organized in such a way that one point is a supply source for several other points. This type of structure may be repeated at various levels in a production–distribution system, where a demand point may again become a new supply point. Such situations are called "multiechelon systems" and will not be dealt with in either this or the next chapter because of their complexity. For a discussion and development of such systems, see Hadley and Whitin (1963).

The attributes discussed above represent the basic elements that need to be considered in modeling inventory situations, demand being perhaps the most important. It should also be pointed out that it is virtually impossible to formulate a general inventory model which accounts for all the variations found in real inventory systems. Hence, we intend to present a set of models that have been found useful and illustrative of some of the various types of inventory systems. The following six models will be discussed in this chapter, generally proceeding from the simplest to the most complex (and presumably most realistic) case:

1. Classic EOQ model (shortages not permitted).
2. EOQ model (shortages permitted).
3. EOQ model with quantity discounts.
4. EOQ model for production runs: single product.
5. EOQ model for production runs: multiple products.
6. EOQ model with resource constraints.

Four of these models deal with a single inventory item. Two models treat the several-commodity system with limited and competing resources. The first model (the classic economic-order-quantity model) will present the basic inventory model. Succeeding models are effectively extensions of this model, which reflect one or more changes in the basic assumptions of this model.

15.5. CLASSIC ECONOMIC-ORDER-QUANTITY (EOQ) MODEL

We begin with the best-known and most fundamental inventory decision model known as the economic-order-quantity (EOQ) model. Although it is too oversimplified to represent most real-world decision situations, it is an excellent starting point from which to develop more realistic and complex inventory decision models. This model is potentially applicable when the entire quantity ordered (or produced) can be considered to arrive in the inventory simultaneously and when the demand rate for the item (which is assumed with certainty) is constant. Typical situations to which the classic EOQ model may apply are:

1. Use of clerical supplies, such as paper clips, pens, pencils, and notebooks in an office.
2. Use of certain industrial supplies, such as nuts, bolts, and washers.
3. Use of toilet supplies in a building.

With little thought you could easily envisage many other possible applications of the model.

The basic assumptions of the classic EOQ model are as follows:

1. Demand (usage) is known with certainty.
2. Demand rate is constant.
3. Inventory is replenished when the inventory is exactly equal to zero (i.e., there are no stock overages or shortages).
4. Lead time is constant and is equal to or greater than zero.
5. Unit price, ordering cost, unit inventory holding costs are constant.

As indicated earlier, in actual situations many of these assumptions may be violated, and an important question that may arise concerns the usefulness of a decision based on a model that does not describe the true situation. In brief, if the violations of the assumptions are not too extreme, this model may indeed be quite robust (insensitive) in the sense that decisions may result in an order quantity and cost that is not far off from optimal.

Figure 15.1 illustrates the variation of the inventory level over time for the classic EOQ model. The downward-sloping line indicates that the inventory level is being reduced at a constant rate over time (known and constant demand rate— assumptions 1 and 2). When the inventory level reaches the reorder point level, Q units of goods are ordered. The order is received at the time when the inventory level is reduced to zero during the lead time (L). This raises the inventory to Q (the maximum inventory level) and the cycle is repeated. Note the "sawtooth" pattern, which is typical of inventory models.

Q in any given cycle will always be equal because we are implictly assuming an infinite planning time horizon and a process that is not changing over time. Hence, the future looks the same at time T_2 as it did at time T_1. Since Q_2 is calculated the same way as Q_1, its value must be the same.

Figure 15.2 shows inventory profiles for two different order quantities. Note that the smaller the Q, the more frequent will be the placement of orders. However, the average inventory level will be reduced. Larger order quantities indicate a larger inventory level with less-frequent order placements. Because these are costs associated with placing orders and holding inventory, the quantity Q is chosen by balancing these two costs in a way that minimizes total costs. This is the basis for formulating the inventory model. We shall now use an example as a starting point for developing the EOQ model and illustrating its application.

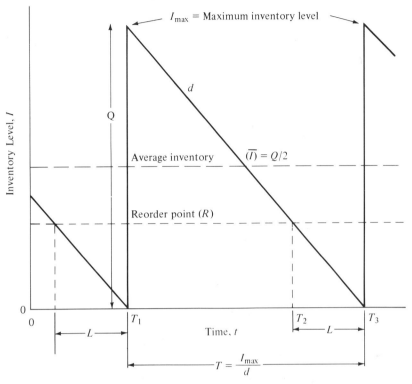

T = length of an inventory cycle (time between orders or runs)
d = demand (usage) rate

I_{max} = Maximum inventory level

d

Average inventory $(\overline{I}) = Q/2$

Reorder point (R)

Q

0

T_1 T_2 T_3

L Time, t L

$$T = \frac{I_{max}}{d}$$

Figure 15.1. Inventory profile of classic EOQ model.

Figure 15.2. Inventory profiles of low- and high-order frequencies.

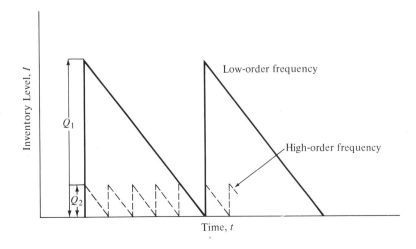

Low-order frequency

High-order frequency

Q_1

Q_2

Time, t

15.5.1. Example—The Lover Tennis Supply Company

Let us consider the situation faced by the Lover Tennis Supply (LTS) Company. LTS is a distributor of tennis products in the Midwest. From a main warehouse facility in Indianapolis, LTS supplies about 500 retail outlets, including sporting goods stores, tennis shops, and tennis clubs with tennis equipment.

LTS's tennis shoe inventory comprises about 10% of LTS's total inventory, currently consisting of approximately 100,000 pairs. The average cost per pair is estimated at $12, resulting in a total tennis shoe inventory of $1,200,000. LTS's cost of capital is estimated to be at an annual rate of 5%. LTS's insurance, taxes, breakage, pilferage, and warehouse overhead costs are estimated at an annual rate of 5% of its inventory value.

Art Ash, the warehouse manager has done a preliminary analysis of LTS's overall inventory costs to assure that the inventory decision rules being used minimize inventory costs. As a further part of his investigation, he wants to do a careful study of LTS's most popular tennis shoe "ILY"—a light, all-leather shoe endorsed by the controversial tennis star Ily Nastie.

Art got together with the LTS purchaser responsible for "ILY" sales, Jamie Conors, in order to find out more about how purchase decisions for this product were being made. He found that Jamie tends to order large quantities in advance and always maintains a large inventory so that LTS would never run into a stock shortage. Jamie appears to give little if any attention to inventory holding costs or costs associated with placing purchasing orders. The records showed that over the past year, Jamie had placed 10 orders of 1000 pairs each (he orders about every 5 weeks), at a cost of $20 per pair. The manufacturer guarantees that each order will be filled in 3 days. Moreover, the records show that each order was received exactly 3 days after it was placed.

Art has also collected demand data on "ILY" for the past year. Demand appears highly predictable and relatively constant throughout the year. A sample of the demand data for the past 10 weeks is as follows:

Week	Demand (pairs)
1	200
2	195
3	203
4	210
5	200
6	204
7	198
8	190
9	200
10	200
Total pairs	2000
Average pairs per week	200
Pairs sold per year (based on a 50-week year)	10,000

Although demand is not exactly constant, given its low variability and high predictability, Art felt it was plausible to assume that demand was known and constant at 200 pairs per week.

Art also analyzed LTS's ordering costs. He found that the major part of order costs involved paying the salaries of LTS's purchasing agents, such as Jamie. For example, it took about 30 minutes to prepare and process an order for the "ILY" tennis shoe, irrespective of the quantity ordered. The standard wage rate and fringe benefit cost for purchasers was $16 per hour. Other costs of ordering, which included allowances for paper, postage, telephone, typing, and transportation, amount to $1 per order.

Art was thus faced with the following problem. Should he (1) keep small inventories and order frequently, or (2) should he keep large inventories and order infrequently? Art knew that the first alternative could give excessive ordering costs, while the second alternative would probably result in excessively high inventory costs. Perhaps some compromise between these two alternatives would result in a lower total inventory cost. A consultant was then called in to develop a quantitative model that would select the optimal order quantity based on minimizing the total inventory costs, comprised of holding and inventory costs.

15.5.2. EOQ Model Formulation

As the consultant would, the first step in constructing the inventory model is to define its variables and parameters. Let

Q = order quantity (units)

T = length of time between orders

c_p = order (preparation, or setup) cost ($ per order)

c_h = inventory holding cost ($ per unit per time; typically the time unit is 1 year as in our example, but may be any time unit provided all time units are consistent)

D = annual demand requirements (units per year)

c = unit purchase cost ($ per unit)

L = lead time

N = number of orders or manufacturing runs per year

TIC = total incremental cost

OBJECTIVE. The next step the consultant would do is to define the decision variables. In this case, there is really only one, Q, the order quantity. The objective is next defined, which is to determine the optimum order quantity Q^* that minimizes TIC, the sum of ordering costs and inventory holding costs. The objective should now be defined in terms of the decision variable Q in order to evaluate and find a Q which minimizes TIC [i.e., TIC = $f(Q)$, where f denotes the function]. TIC is also affected by the parameters of the model: c_p, c_h, and D. Hence, TIC = $f(Q; c_p, c_h, D)$, where the decision variable is to the left of the semicolon and parameters are to the right. The purchase cost, cD, is not an incremental cost, and since it does not affect Q, it is not included in the objective function. LTS's cost function to be minimized is thus

$$\text{TIC} = \text{inventory holding cost} + \text{order costs}$$

$$(\text{total cost/year}) = \left(\begin{array}{l} \text{inventory holding} \\ \text{cost/year} \end{array} \right) + (\text{order cost/year}).$$

Considering each of the above cost components, LTS's annual inventory holding cost is

$$\left(\begin{array}{l} \text{inventory} \\ \text{holding cost} \end{array} \right) = \left(\begin{array}{l} \text{average} \\ \text{inventory} \end{array} \right) \times \left(\begin{array}{l} \text{holding cost} \\ \text{per unit per year} \end{array} \right)$$

$$= \tfrac{1}{2} Q c_h.$$

The average inventory level is equal to $\tfrac{1}{2}Q$, since demand has been assumed constant and the maximum inventory level is equal to Q (refer back to Figure 15.1). For the "ILY" tennis shoe, the annual unit inventory holding cost, c_h, is equal to the cost of capital rate times the unit purchase price; that is, $c_h = (10\%)(\$20$ cost per unit) = \$2$ per unit per year.

$$(\text{order cost/year}) = (\text{cost/order})(\text{number of orders/year})$$

$$= c_p \frac{D}{Q},$$

where the number of orders per year is equal to the annual demand requirements divided by the number of units obtained per order. The unit order cost, c_p (for the "ILY" shoe), which is independent of the order quantity, Q, is equal to the hourly wage and fringe benefit rate times the order processing time plus incremental administrative costs; that is, $c_p = (\$16 \text{ per hour} \times \tfrac{1}{2} \text{ hour}) + \$1 = \$9$.

The TIC model is thus

$$\text{TIC} = \tfrac{1}{2} Q c_h + c_p \frac{D}{Q}$$

$$= \tfrac{1}{2} Q(2) + 9 \left(\frac{10{,}000}{Q} \right) \tag{15.1}$$

$$(\text{cost/year}) = \left[\begin{array}{l} \text{units of} \\ \text{average} \\ \text{inventory} \end{array} \right] \left(\begin{array}{l} \text{holding cost} \\ \text{year/unit} \end{array} \right) + \left(\begin{array}{l} \text{cost/} \\ \text{order} \end{array} \right) + \left(\begin{array}{l} \text{number of} \\ \text{orders/year} \end{array} \right).$$

The cost components of TIC are depicted graphically in Figure 15.3.

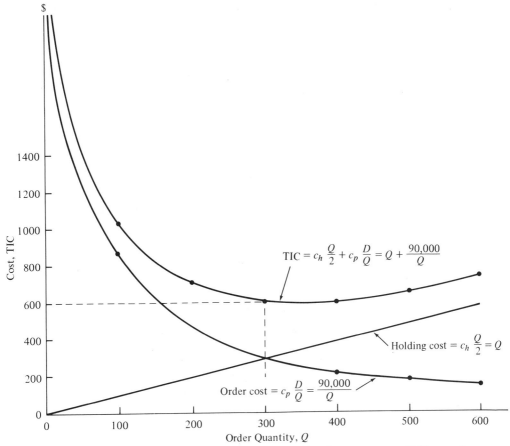

$$TIC = c_h \frac{Q}{2} + c_p \frac{D}{Q} = Q + \frac{90,000}{Q}$$

$$\text{Holding cost} = c_h \frac{Q}{2} = Q$$

$$\text{Order cost} = c_p \frac{D}{Q} = \frac{90,000}{Q}$$

Cost, TIC

Order Quantity, Q

Figure 15.3. Cost curves of classic EOQ model (D = 10,000 units per year, c_h = $2.00 per unit per year, c_p = $9.00 per order).

DETERMINING Q^*: HOW MUCH TO ORDER. As shown in Figure 15.3, as Q is increased, the average inventory level $Q/2$ increases and hence so will inventory holding costs. However, the number of orders annually, and hence order costs, will decrease nonlinearly, asymptotically approaching zero. TIC, which is the sum of annual holding and order costs, thus first decreases as Q increases, reaches some minimum point, and then increases. LTS's objective is to find the minimum cost order quantity Q^*. Table 15.1 shows the inventory costs for selected values of Q. Q^*, obtained by this trial-and-error procedure, is found to be equal to 300 units with a TIC* equal to $600 per year.

We can develop a general optimal EOQ decision rule for problems of this type by making use of the elementary techniques of differential calculus (see Section 15A.1).† It is shown that the value of Q^* which minimizes TIC is expressed by the

†A marginal analysis can also be used to derive this and many of the other inventory models. While a total cost analysis requires the use of classical optimization techniques (and more computational effort), it is simpler conceptually.

Table 15.1 Inventory Costs for Various Order Quantities of "ILY" Tennis Shoes

(1) Order Quantity Q	(2) Inventory Holding Cost $= Q$	(3) Order Cost $= 90,000/Q$	(4) = (2) + (3) Total Incremental Cost
$100	$100	$900	$1,000
150	150	600	750
200	200	450	650
250	250	360	610
$Q^* = 300$	300	300	600
350	350	257	607
400	400	250	650

following well-known EOQ formula:

$$Q^* = \sqrt{\frac{2Dc_p}{c_h}}$$

$$\left(\text{units}/\atop\text{order}\right) = \sqrt{\frac{\left(\text{units}/\atop\text{year}\right)\left(\text{cost}/\atop\text{order}\right)}{\text{cost}/\text{unit per year}}} . \qquad (15.2)$$

In terms of the LTS company,

$$Q^* = \sqrt{\frac{2(10,000)(9)}{2}} ,$$

which is equal to 300 units. This is identical to the result we obtained by trial and error in Table 15.1.

The cost of an optimal solution computed by (15.2) may be easily derived by substituting (15.2) into the cost formula of (15.1) and solving for TIC*. This gives

$$\text{TIC*} = \sqrt{2c_p c_h D}$$

$$\left(\text{cost}/\atop\text{year}\right) = \sqrt{\left(\text{cost}/\atop\text{order}\right)\left(\text{cost}/\atop\text{unit ordered}/\text{year}\right)\left(\text{units}/\atop\text{year}\right)} . \qquad (15.3)$$

With respect to the LTS company, we obtain

$$\text{TIC*} = \sqrt{2(9)(2)(10,000)} ,$$

which yields a TIC* equal to $600. Again, this is identical to our results in Table 15.1.

The question of how frequently to order can now also be answered. The optimal number of orders (or production runs) per year N^* is equal to the total annual demand D divided by the optimal order quantity Q^*; that is,

$$N^* = \frac{D}{Q^*}$$

$$\left(\begin{array}{c}\text{orders}/\\\text{year}\end{array}\right) = \left(\begin{array}{c}\text{units}/\\\text{year}\end{array}\right) \div \left(\begin{array}{c}\text{units}/\\\text{order}\end{array}\right). \tag{15.4}$$

In LTS's case, N^* is equal to $10,000 \div 300 = 33$ orders per year. If, for a given D, the order cost were higher relative to the holding cost, LTS would order less frequently and carry a higher inventory level.

The time between orders (often called the *cycle time*) is the reciprocal of equation (15.4); that is,

$$T^* = \frac{1}{N^*}$$

or
$$T^* = \frac{Q^*}{D}$$

$$(\text{year}/\text{order}) = (\text{units}/\text{order}) \div (\text{units}/\text{year}). \tag{15.5}$$

For the "ILY" tennis shoe, it is equal to 0.03 year or, assuming a 350-day year, 10.5 days. That is, an order should be placed every 10.5 days.

DETERMINING WHEN TO ORDER. Now that we have found Q^* (how much to order) and T^* (how often to order), we wish to answer the second question *of when to order*. The when-to-order decision is often expressed in terms of the reorder point (R), which is the inventory level at which an order should be placed (Figure 15.1). For LTS, there was a known 3-day delivery or lead time. Hence, with a constant demand rate for "ILY" of 200 pairs per week or (based on a 5-day workweek) 40 pairs per day, Art expects 120 pairs of "ILY" tennis shoes ($=40$ pairs/day×3 days) to be sold during the 3 days it takes a new order to reach the LTS warehouse. This 3-day delivery period is the *lead time* for a new order and the 120 pairs of demand anticipated during the lead time period is called the demand during lead time (DDLT). Thus, the reorder point chosen is at 120 units of inventory. This indicates when LTS should place an order for a new shipment of "ILY" tennis shoes from the manufacturer.

SENSITIVITY ANALYSIS. One of the important characteristics of the EOQ model is its "robustness." It tends to give reasonably good results even when parameter values are in error or vary. To see why this is so, let us refer again to the LTS example. Although Art had spent considerable time in determining his inventory holding cost ($= 10\%$) and order cost ($= \$9$) values, he realized that these figures were estimates and could either be in error or change somewhat from period to period. He asked himself, "Suppose the ordering and holding costs were different; how would this affect Q^* and TIC*?" To determine this, he calculated

Table 15.2. Sensitivity of Q* and TIC* to c_h and c_p

Cost of Capital (%)	Inventory Holding Cost ($/unit/year)	Possible Cost per Order ($/order)	Optimal Order Quantity (units)	Total Incremental Cost ($/year)
7.5	1.50	7	305	459
7.5	1.50	11	378	575
12.5	2.50	7	237	590
12.5	2.50	11	297	740

Q^* under several different combinations of c_h and c_p. The results of these calculations are shown in Table 15.2.

15.6. EOQ MODEL WITH SHORTAGES PERMITTED

In the EOQ model just presented it was assumed that an order was received precisely at the time when the inventory level fell to zero. Shortages were not allowed to occur, and thus shortage cost was ignored in the inventory decision model.

While in many inventory situations stockouts should be avoided, there are cases where it is economically justifiable to plan for and allow stockouts. Practically speaking, these types of situations usually exist when the value per unit of inventory is high, resulting in high unit inventory costs. An example of this type of situation is an individual who purchases a new car which is not in stock from a dealer, who back-orders it for the customer.

We now relax the assumption of no stockouts and permit inventory shortages to occur. We add a further assumption that all demands not satisfied as a result of an inventory shortage are *back-ordered* and eventually filled. The assumptions of the classic EOQ model still apply except, of course, for assumption (3), which does not permit stockouts.

Intuitively, the notion is that the cost of running out of stock may be sufficiently small relative to the cost of holding inventory that the cost trade-off indicates to do both. The inventory profile, where stockouts occur, is shown in Figure 15.4. The pattern of inventory is still observed to be "sawtoothed," but drops below the zero inventory level. Here negative inventory represents commodities that are "sold," but "back-ordered" rather than "delivered." Since back orders (shortages) are filled when an order is received, the maximum inventory level does not reach the order quantity Q, as it does in the classic EOQ model. Rather, shortages (S) are filled immediately upon receipt of an order, and the inventory level returns to a level $I_{\max} = Q - S$, the maximum inventory level. Since $I_{\max}$ is less when stockouts are permitted than when they are not, likewise, the inventory carrying cost is reduced. An extreme case would be one in which all demands are

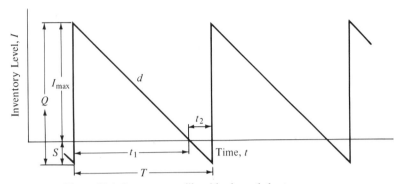

t_1 = time during which inventory is on hand
t_2 = time during which there are shortages
T = cycle time (time between orders)
S = number of shortages per order
d = demand (usage) rate

Figure 15.4. Inventory profile with planned shortages.

back-ordered, resulting in zero inventory and hence zero holding costs. However, the reduction in holding costs must be balanced against the stockout costs associated with these back orders. In this extreme case they presumably would be excessively high.

15.6.1. Model Formulation

In addition to the notation already used, let us define the following terms:

c_s = (stockout) back-order penalty cost, proportional to both the number of back orders and time; shortage cost per unit of shortage per year

S = number of shortages per order (back-order quantity)

I_{max} = maximum inventory level $(Q - S)$.

t_1 = time during which inventory is on hand

t_2 = time during which a shortage exists

T = time between receipt of orders (cycle time $T = t_1 + t_2$).

OBJECTIVE: TOTAL COST EXPRESSION. The annual overall cost function for the inventory model with permissible shortages is

TIC = ordering cost + holding cost + shortage cost

ORDER COST. The cost per order is c_p, as before. Multiplying c_p times the number of orders placed per year gives us the total annual order costs; that is,

$$\text{order costs} = c_p \frac{D}{Q}$$

$$\left(\frac{\$}{\text{year}} \right) = \left(\frac{\$}{\text{order}} \right) \left(\frac{\text{orders}}{\text{year}} \right).$$

HOLDING COST. In a given cycle, inventory holding cost occurs during period t_1, when there is a positive inventory level. Since the maximum inventory level is

$$I_{\max} = Q - S, \tag{15.6}$$

the average inventory level during the time in which inventory is on hand (t_1) is

$$\frac{I_{\max}}{2} = \frac{Q - S}{2}. \tag{15.7}$$

The holding cost during a given cycle T is thus

$$c_h \frac{I_{\max}}{2} t_1 = c_h \frac{Q - S}{2} t_1, \tag{15.8}$$

where t_1 is the time period in which inventory is at a positive level.

To determine annual inventory holding cost, we note that the usage rate d (= demand per unit time) is equal to

$$\frac{Q - S}{t_1}, \tag{15.9}$$

which is equal to (by similar triangles)

$$\frac{Q}{T}. \tag{15.10}$$

Setting (15.9) is equal to (15.10), and solving for t_1, we obtain

$$t_1 = \frac{T(Q - S)}{Q}. \tag{15.11}$$

Substituting (15.11) into (15.8) yields the following holding cost per cycle:

$$\text{holding cost per cycle} = \frac{c_h(Q - S)^2 T}{2Q}. \tag{15.12}$$

Since there are N orders per year, the annual holding cost is N times (15.12), that is,

$$\text{holding cost per year} = \frac{c_h(Q - S)^2 TN}{2Q},$$

where $TN = 1$ (year). Hence,

$$\text{holding cost per year} = \frac{c_h(Q - S)^2}{2Q}. \tag{15.13}$$

SHORTAGE COST. We must now develop an expression for the average number of shortages and the shortage cost. Since S represents the maximum level of shortages, the average level of shortages during the period in which there is a shortage (t_2) will be $S/2$. The shortage cost in a given cycle (T) is thus

$$c_s \frac{S}{2} t_2. \tag{15.14}$$

Again, to determine the annual shortage cost, we note that

$$d = \frac{S}{t_2} \tag{15.15}$$

or

$$d = \frac{Q}{T}.$$

Setting these relationships equal to each other and solving for t_2, we obtain

$$t_2 = T\frac{S}{Q}. \tag{15.16}$$

Substituting (15.16) into (15.14), the shortage cost per cycle is

$$\text{shortage cost per cycle} = c_s \frac{S^2}{2Q} T. \tag{15.17}$$

Again, since the annual shortage cost is N times (15.17), and since $TN = 1$ (year), the annual shortage cost is

$$\text{annual shortage cost} = \frac{c_s S^2}{2Q}. \tag{15.18}$$

Thus, the annual TIC expression is

$$\text{TIC} = c_p\frac{D}{Q} + \frac{c_h(Q - S)^2}{2Q} + \frac{c_s S^2}{2Q}. \tag{15.19}$$

15.6.2. Optimal Decision Rules

Given the model parameters (c_p, c_h, c_s, and D) and the annual TIC expression (15.19), we can determine the optimal decision rules and decisions for our two decision variables: (1) the order quantity Q and (2) the maximum inventory level $I_{\max}$. The safety stock S can be determined simply by computing $Q - I_{\max}$. The optimal decision rules, which are derived in Section 15A.2 using the differential calculus are as follows:

$$Q^* = \sqrt{\frac{2c_p D}{c_h}} \sqrt{\frac{c_h + c_s}{c_s}} \qquad (15.20)$$

$$I_{\max}^* = \sqrt{\frac{2c_p D}{c_h}} \sqrt{\frac{c_s}{c_h + c_s}} \qquad (15.21)$$

$$\text{TIC} = \sqrt{2c_h c_p D} \sqrt{\frac{c_s}{c_h + c_s}}. \qquad (15.22)$$

Note that the difference between (15.20) and (15.22) and the classic EOQ formulas (without shortages) of (15.2) and (15.3) is the inclusion of the second square root terms. Observe that the effect of including shortage costs is to increase Q^*, since annual inventory holding costs are smaller due to the smaller average inventory, and TIC* is smaller than for the classical EOQ model without shortages because both inventory holding costs and order costs are lower. Note also that as the shortage cost c_s becomes large relative to the inventory holding cost c_h, the quantities $(c_h + c_s)/c_s$ and $c_s/(c_h + c_s)$ in (15.20) to (15.22) approach 1. In this case the back-order model and the regular EOQ model give similar results. As c_h becomes large relative to c_s, Q^* increases while $I_{\max}^*$ decreases; hence, $S^* = Q^* - I_{\max}^*$, increases. This explains why many high-valued items (which have a very high per-unit cost and hence high per-unit inventory cost) are handled on a back-order basis.

15.6.3. Example—The LTS Company Revisited

Suppose that we reconsider LTS's "ILY" tennis shoe again. This time the company is considering the possibility of allowing some back orders to occur for this product. Art Ash estimates the shortage cost c_s based on loss of goodwill, potential loss in profit due to lost sales, and delay costs is about four times the holding costs, or $8 per unit per year. Recall that $D = 10,000$ units per year,

$c_h = \$2$ per unit per year, and $c_p = \$9$ per order. Using (15.20) to (15.22),

$$Q^* = \sqrt{\frac{2(10,000)(9)}{2}} \sqrt{\frac{2+8}{8}} = 335 \text{ units}$$

$$I^*_{\max} = \sqrt{\frac{2(10,000)(9)}{2}} \sqrt{\frac{8}{2+8}} = 259 \text{ units}$$

$$S^* = Q^* - I_{\max} = 76 \text{ units}$$

$$\text{TIC}^* = \sqrt{(2)(9)(2)(10,000)} \sqrt{\frac{8}{2+8}} = \$539.$$

Thus, if this model is implemented, the system as compared with the classic EOQ model will have the following characteristics:

Characteristics	EOQ Shortages Permitted	EOQ Shortages Not Permitted
Q^* (units)	335	300
$I^*_{\max}$ (units)	259	300
$T^* = Q/D$ (days)	10.5	11.7
TIC* ($)	539	600

Thus, in this example, permitting shortages would result in a savings of $61 (= 600 - 539)$ or a little over 10% in cost from the no-stockout EOQ model. The comparison above is based on an accurate assessment of the stockout cost, which in actuality is a very difficult parameter to estimate. If LTS has strong concerns that stockouts might lead to a serious deterioration in goodwill and lost sales, then the savings anticipated might not be sufficient to warrant switching to an inventory model that allows for planned shortages. Sensitivity analysis on c_s would be a useful way of deciding this issue.

15.7. EOQ MODEL WITH QUANTITY DISCOUNTS

It is common for suppliers to offer quantity discounts to purchasers to provide an incentive for purchasing large quantities by offering lower unit costs when commodities are purchased in larger lots or quantities. In this section we extend the basic EOQ model to allow for such quantity discounts.

15.7.1. Example—The LTS Company

Again consider the case of the LTS Company. We saw, for example, that the basic EOQ model was an appropriate model for making inventory decisions for the company's products, as exemplified by its application to the "ILY" tennis shoe. Now consider that instead of a fixed unit purchase price of $20 on the "ILY" tennis shoe, LTS's supplier quotes the following price discount schedule, which is dependent on the order quantity, Q:

Order Quantity (Q) (units)	Discount (%)	Unit Cost, c ($)
0–249	0	20
250–999	10	18
1000 and over	25	16

The discounts indeed look quite appealing, especially the 25% discount for the 1000-unit minimum order quantity. Higher order quantities, however, mean higher inventory costs but lower order costs. Hence, purchase costs, holding costs, and order costs must be balanced to achieve a minimum-cost order quantity.

15.7.2. Model Formulation

The quantity discount model is formulated in the same way as the classic EOQ model, except that the cost of goods purchased (in addition to holding and order costs) must be included as an incremental cost in the TIC expression. The TIC expression is thus

$$TIC = \text{order cost} + \text{holding cost} + \textit{purchase cost}.$$

or

$$TIC = c_p \frac{D}{Q} + c_h \frac{Q}{2} + cD \tag{15.23}$$

15.7.3. Determining the Optimal Decision Rule

In the usual manner, Q^* can be determined by differentiating the TIC function of (15.23) with respect to Q and setting the result equal to zero. This yields the basic EOQ formula of equation (15.2). The reason for this is that since the last term in the total-cost equation (15.23) does not include Q, it does not enter into the derivation of Q^*. However, the purchase price, cD, must be considered in choosing an optimal economic order quantity. Alternatively stated, we will also need to consider other order quantities in addition to those determined by the EOQ formula. These additional order quantities to be examined are at the price breaks. The reason for this is that the Q^*'s obtained for the various inventory holding costs (which are a function of the unit purchase price) may fall outside the regions where the quantity discounts apply. Hence, some of the Q^*'s obtained using the EOQ formula are infeasible, since the assumed unit price (and hence holding cost) is unrealistic.

The following procedure can be used to determine an optimal EOQ when quantity discounts apply.

Step 1—Compute a Q^* using the EOQ formula (15.2) for the unit purchase cost associated with each type of discount. In our "ILY" tennis shoe example, the following Q^*'s are obtained:

Number	Discount (%)	c	c_h	Q^*	Feasibility
1	0	$20	$2.0	300	Infeasible
2	10	18	1.8	316	Feasible
3	25	16	1.6	352	Infeasible

Since the only differences in the EOQ computations above are small differences in c_h, the resulting EOQs do not differ very much. This is the usual case for such problems. Note, however, that the Q^*'s for $c = 16$ and 20 are infeasible, as these EOQ computations were based on $c_h = \$1.60$ and $\$2.00$, respectively, because the resulting EOQs fall outside the 250–999 range, where c_h is actually $\$1.8$. For the order quantities for which the assumed price (and hence unit holding cost c_h) is incorrect, the following procedure is used next.

Step 2—For those Q^*'s which are too small to qualify for the assumed discount price, increase the order quantity to the nearest order quantity that will allow the product to be purchased at the assumed price. This implies that a lower-cost order quantity can occur at a price break.

In our example, the only breakpoint we need to evaluate is at 1000, since $Q_3^* = 352$ (computed using a 25% discount) is less than the minimum quantity necessary ($= 1000$) for that price break to be applicable. Because Q_1^* ($= 300$) is greater than the higher order quantity providing that particular discount price ($= 249$), the price break at $Q^* = 250$ need not be evaluated, since it cannot lead to an optimal solution.

Step 3—For each of the order quantities determined in steps 1 and 2, compute the total annual cost using equation (15.23), and select the minimum cost EOQ.

The results of this cost evaluation are as follows:†

Q	Discount (%)	TIC	=	Order Cost	+	Holding Cost	+	Item Purchase Cost
316	10	$18,510		$285		$225		$18,000
1000	25	16,890		90		800		16,000

The 1000-unit order quantity having the 25% discount rate is thus the minimum-cost solution. Note the differences in component costs between the 1000- and

Figure 15.5. Inventory model with quantity discounts.

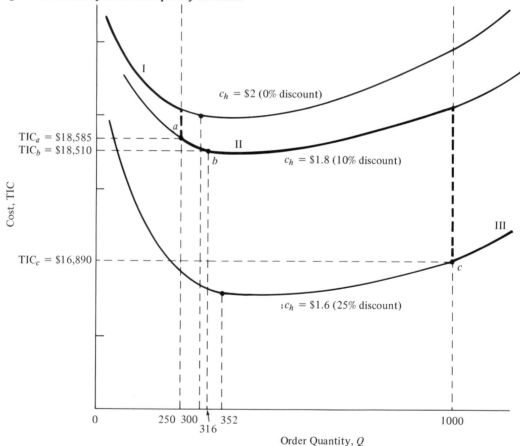

†As already indicated, the order quantity of 250 need not be evaluated, since Q_1^* (determined by the EOQ formula using a 0% discount) is equal to 300. To verify this, the TIC for an order quantity of 250 turns out to be equal to $18,585. The order, holding, and purchase costs are $360, $225, and $18,000, respectively.

316-unit order quantity. For the 25% discount rate solution, order cost is less, since the order quantity is greater, but the order frequency is less. Holding costs, however, are higher, since with fewer orders the average inventory level is higher (although this is somewhat offset by the lower purchase cost, which tends to reduce the average value of inventory held). Purchase cost is less since the price is lower.

The relationship between TIC and Q for the given discount schedule is shown graphically in Figure 15.5. It is made up of portions of three curves. Each of the curves is determined using one of the possible fixed-unit purchase prices. The higher the unit purchase price, the higher the total cost curve. The minimum order quantity required to receive the price discount is indicated by the vertical lines. The darkened portion of the three curves is the relevant curve for analysis, reflecting the feasible portions of the three curves.

Note in Figure 15.5 that if Q is less than 250, then no discount is given and the upper cost curve (I) is relevant. If Q is equal to or greater than 250 but less than 1000, then a 10% discount is given, and the middle cost curve (II) is relevant. If Q is equal to or greater than 1000, then a 25% discount is given, and the lower cost curve (III) is relevant. The objective is to determine the lowest point on the curve (darkened). This is determined by comparing the lowest points on the relevant portions of the upper (I), middle (II), and lower (III) curves. In our example, the lowest point on (I) is at point a, where $Q = 249$; on (II) it is at point b, where $Q = 316$; and on (III) it is at point c, where $Q = 1000$. Since the cost at point c is less than at points a and b, $Q^* = 1000$ and the 25% discount should be taken.

15.8. EOQ MODEL FOR PRODUCTION RUNS: SINGLE PRODUCT

We shall now consider the case where goods are received for inventory at a constant rate over time as units are being consumed. This is in contrast to the basic EOQ model, where the entire order quantity is received instantaneously (assumption 3). This model is typically designed for production situations in which an order is placed, production begins, and a constant number of units are added to inventory each day until the production run has been completed. At the same time, units are being demanded and consumed at a constant rate. It is assumed that the production rate is greater than the demand rate. Otherwise, there will be no inventory buildup and stockouts will occur.

15.8.1. Model Formulation

Let us define the following additional parameters:

p = production rate, or more generally, the rate at which goods are placed into inventory over time; this rate is assumed constant

d = usage or demand rate, also assumed to be constant

All other model symbols are the same as for the original EOQ model.

OBJECTIVE FUNCTION. The annual overall cost function for this inventory model is, as with the EOQ model,

$$TIC = \text{order cost} + \text{holding cost}.$$

The order cost is as before equal to $c_p D/Q$. The interpretation of the order cost in a production situation is more aptly referred to as production setup cost. This cost, which includes man-hours, material, and lost production costs incurred while preparing the production system for operation is a fixed cost which occurs for every production run, regardless of the production quantity. The preparation costs represent the costs to develop production plans for the item, write shop orders and perform other necessary paperwork, set up machines, and control the flow of the order through the manufacturing facility. The holding cost is also equal to, as before, the annual unit holding cost times the average inventory. However, since the production of the total order quantity Q takes place over a period of time (defined by the production rate p), and the parts go into inventory, not in one large batch (as in the basic EOQ model) but in smaller quantities as production and consumption continues, an inventory pattern similar to Figure 15.6 results. The maximum inventory level, and hence the average inventory level, will not only be a function of the lot size as in the classic EOQ model but also a function of the production rate (p) and demand rate (d).

Let us examine Figure 15.6 more closely. First, recall from the classic EOQ model that the average inventory level was $Q/2$, half the maximum inventory level. In this model, the maximum (and hence average) inventory level must be adjusted for the fact that goods are being received and consumed simultaneously. The

Figure 15.6. Inventory profile as a function of time, with noninstantaneous receipt of goods.

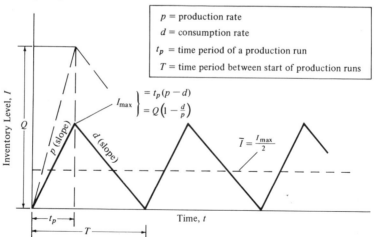

average inventory level is thus determined as follows:

$$t_p = \frac{Q}{p},$$

where t_p represents the length of the production run or, more generally, the time it takes to produce (receive) the entire order quantity Q.

The maximum inventory level I_{max} is

$$I_{max} = t_p(p - d) \tag{15.24}$$

where $p - d$ is the rate of inventory buildup per unit time (p was assumed greater than d) and t_p is the total length of the production run. Hence, the average inventory level is

$$\text{average inventory} = \frac{t_p(p - d)}{2}. \tag{15.25}$$

To obtain the average inventory level in terms of the decision variable Q, substitute (Q/P) for t_p in (15.25), which yields

$$\text{average inventory} = \frac{Q}{2}\left(1 - \frac{d}{p}\right). \tag{15.26}$$

The annual holding cost is thus

$$c_h\frac{Q}{2}\left(1 - \frac{d}{p}\right).$$

The total-cost expression is

$$\text{TIC} = c_p\frac{D}{Q} + c_h\frac{Q}{2}\left(1 - \frac{d}{p}\right). \tag{15.27}$$

OPTIMAL DECISION RULES. Given the objective function in (15.27) and the model parameters (c_h, c_p, D, d, p), we can use a trial-and-error approach to compute TIC for various Q. However, we can also derive an optimal decision rule for Q^* by means of the differential calculus (Section 15A.3). The results are

$$Q^* = \sqrt{\frac{2c_p D}{c_h[1 - (d/p)]}} \tag{15.28}$$

and

$$\text{TIC}^* = \sqrt{2c_p c_h D\left(1 - \frac{d}{p}\right)}. \tag{15.29}$$

The optimal number of production runs of size Q^* is, of course, as before,

$$N^* = \frac{D}{Q^*},$$

and the optimal time between production runs is

$$T^* = \frac{1}{N^*} = \frac{Q^*}{D}.$$

15.8.2. Example—LTS Revisited

Suppose that LTS's "ILY" tennis shoe was manufactured by a division of this company which happened to have its manufacturing facilities next door. Let us also assume that its production rate p was equal to 15,000 units per year. Assuming also that $c_h = \$2$, $c_p = \$9$, as before:

$$Q^* = \sqrt{\frac{(2)(9)(10,000)}{2\left(1 - \frac{10}{15}\right)}} = 510 \text{ units}$$

and

$$TIC^* = \sqrt{(2)(9)(2)(10,000)\left(1 - \frac{10}{15}\right)} = \$347.$$

Also, $N^* = 19.6$ and $t^* = 0.051$ year or 18.4 days ($= 0.051$ year $\times$ 350 days/year). A comparison of these results to the basic EOQ model is as follows:

	Q^* (units)	$TIC =$ ($/year)	Order Costs + ($/year)	Holding Costs ($/year)	N^*, Order Frequency (years)	T^*, Days Between Orders or Runs
Basic EOQ	300	600	300	300	33	10.5
Production run	510	347	177	170	19.6	18.4

Note that with the production-run model, the order quantity Q^* is greater and holding costs are less, since inventory levels are lower. If, for example, the production rate was considerably greater than the demand rate, the basic EOQ model would then be appropriate, since the decision rule for the production-run model would approach that of the basic EOQ model. If the production and demand rate were equal, there would be no inventory buildup. In essence, we would have one continual production run throughout the year, meaning that we were producing to meet demand.

15.9. EOQ'S FOR PRODUCTION RUNS OF MULTIPLE PRODUCTS

Often the same equipment is used to produce a variety of products on a cyclical basis. These resources become a constraint and the independent determination of EOQs for each product by equation (15.28) is no longer applicable due to the interference among production runs for the various items. Instead, we must determine the production runs (and EOQs) jointly so that scheduling incompatibilities are avoided.

To illustrate the difficulties encountered, consider the situation shown in Table 15.3, which gives annual demand, production rates, and cost parameters for five commodities to be produced on the same equipment. The demand rates, production rates, holding costs, and setup costs vary considerably among products. It appears that the equipment has sufficient capacity to produce all five products to meet demand, since the total number of production days, 235, is less than the 250-production-day capacity per year.

Table 15.3. Inventory-Parameter Data for Five Products Produced on Common Equipment

(1)	(2)	(3) = (2) ÷ 250 *days/year*	(4)	(5) = (2) ÷ (4)	(6)	(7)
Product Number	Annual Demand, D	Demand Rate (units/day), d	Production Rate (units/day), p	Required Production (days)	Annual Unit Inventory Holding Cost, c_h	Setup Cost per Run, c_p
1	1,000	4	25	40	$1.00	$20
2	10,000	40	100	100	0.50	15
3	5,000	20	200	25	0.75	25
4	20,000	80	1000	20	0.40	10
5	25,000	100	500	50	0.25	15
				235		

Table 15.4 shows the EOQs computed independently for each product using equation (15.28). The number of production days required to produce the lot size for each product in a given production cycle (i.e., where each product is produced once in a given cycle in the amount Q^*) is 115.44 days (bottom of column 5). Column 7 of Table 15.4 shows the number of production days required to use up the lot sizes produced for each product at the given demand rates. If the number of production days to use up the lot size for a given product (column 7) is greater than the total number of days to complete the production cycle (= 115.44 days), then the lot size produced is not large enough to last through one complete cycle at the

Table 15.4. Independent EOQ Determination for the Five Products Produced on Common Equipment

(1)	(2)	(3)	(4)	(5) = (2) ÷ (4)	(6)	(7) = (2) ÷ (6)	(8)
Product Number	Q^{*a}	$N^* = D/Q$	p	$t_p = Q/p$	d	Q/d	TIC
1	218	4.58	25	8.70	4	54.50	$183
2	1000	10.00	10	100.00	40	25.00	300
3	605	8.30	200	1.82	20	30.25	425
4	1040	19.90	1000	1.04	80	13.00	385
5	1940	12.90	500	3.88	100	19.40	386
				115.44		142.15	$1679

$^a Q^*$ determined by equation (15.28).

given demand rates (i.e., stockouts occur). In our example, stockouts occur in all five products. Thus, while Table 15.3 appears to indicate that capacity is, in an aggregate sense adequate, there will be scheduling conflicts if we produce in accordance with the lot sizes computed in Table 15.4.

We therefore need to develop a procedure for determining the production runs (or lot sizes) for all products simultaneously (jointly) to avoid such scheduling conflicts.

15.9.1. *Model Formulation*

Conceptually, the formulation of the model is identical to the single product EOQ model for production runs which yielded equation (15.28). The only difference is that we must determine a cycle length that minimizes inventory holding plus setup costs jointly for the entire set of products.

OBJECTIVE FUNCTION. The annual overall cost function for the n products is the sum of the setup costs plus inventory holding costs, or

$$\text{TIC} = \sum_{i=1}^{n} \text{order cost for product } i + \sum_{i=1}^{n} \text{holding cost for product } i$$

$$= \sum_{i=1}^{n} \frac{D_i}{Q_i} c_{p_i} + \sum_{i=1}^{n} \frac{c_{h_i} Q_i (1 - d_i/p_i)}{2}. \tag{15.30}$$

Since $N = D_i/Q_i$ (the common number of production runs annually), we can substitute this in equation (15.30) to obtain

$$\text{TIC} = N \sum_{i=1}^{n} c_{p_i} + \frac{1}{2N} \sum_{i=1}^{n} c_{h_i} D_i \left(1 - \frac{d_i}{p_i} \right). \tag{15.31}$$

OPTIMAL DECISION RULE. Equation (15.31) expresses the total incremental cost function in terms of the decision variable N (the length of the production run) rather than the lot size Q. The minimum cost N can be determined by the use of the differential calculus. That is, we differentiate (15.31) with respect to N, set the result equal to zero, and solve for N^* (Section 15A.4). The following rule for N^* results:

$$N^* = \sqrt{\frac{\sum_{i=1}^{n} c_{h_i} D_i (1 - d_i/p_i)}{2 \sum_{i=1}^{n} c_{p_i}}} \tag{15.32}$$

Since $Q_i^* = D_i/N^*$, we can thus determine the optimal lot size for all n products.

By substituting (15.32) for N in the total-cost expression of (15.31), we obtain

$$\text{TIC}^* = \sqrt{2 \sum_{i=1}^{n} c_{p_i} \sum_{i=1}^{n} c_{h_i} D_i (1 - d_i/p_i)} \ . \tag{15.33}$$

The joint determination of the production cycle using equation (15.32) is determined from the computations in Table 15.5, yielding $N^* = 11$ cycles per year

Table 15.5. Determination of Optimal Joint Production Cycle for Five Products Using Equation (15.32)

(1) Product Number	(2) d_i/p_i	(3) $1 - d_i/p_i$	(4) $c_{h_i} D_i$	(5) $(1 - d_i/p_i)c_{h_i} D_i$	(6) c_{p_i}
1	0.16	0.84	1,000	840	$20
2	0.10	0.90	5,000	3,000	15
3	0.10	0.90	3,750	3,375	25
4	0.08	0.92	8,000	7,360	10
5	0.20	0.80	6,250	5,000	15
				19,575	$85

$$N^* = \sqrt{\frac{19,575}{2 \times 85}} \approx 11$$

$$\text{TIC}^* = \sqrt{2 \times 85 \times 19,575} = \$1830.$$

This means that each of the five products would be produced 11 times each year in lot sizes equal to one-eleventh of the annual demand requirements. The calculations in Table 15.5 verify that $N^* = 11$ is feasible.

The production days required to produce Q_i is shown in column 4 of Table 15.6 to be 21.38 days. In column 6 of Table 15.6 we see that each lot produced provides less than a month's supply or 22.75 production days of supply so that the

Table 15.6. Lot Sizes Determined Jointly; Determination of Actual Production Cycle and Adequacy of Inventory to Cover Usage During the Cycle

(1) Product Number	(2) Lot Size Based on Joint Determination of Cycle, $Q_i = D_i/N^*$	(3) p_i	(4) Production Days Required to Produce Q_i, Q_i/p_i	(5) d_i	(6) Number of Production Days Required to Use Up Q_i at Average Demand Rates, Q_i/d_i
1	91	25	3.64	4	22.75
2	910	100	9.10	40	22.75
3	455	200	2.28	20	22.75
4	1820	1000	1.82	80	22.75
5	2270	500	4.54	100	22.75
			21.38		

joint cycle accommodates all products. The total incremental cost of the joint cycling plan is $1830 as compared with $1679 if lot quantities and cycles are established independently. The additional cost of $151 is due largely to a higher average inventory requirement, but the joint cycle plan is feasible. In some instances the joint plan reduces the lot size considerably (products 1, 2, and 3), while in other instances the plan increases the lot size considerably (products 4 and 5).

15.10. EOQ MODEL WITH CONSTRAINTS

Sometimes an EOQ model produces a result that is infeasible. We saw this occur in the quantity discount model and also in the production-run model for multiple products using the same production facilities. There is another situation we have not yet considered where an infeasible result can occur. For example, this can occur when inventory is constrained by such factors as storage space and/or the total amount of capital that may be invested in inventory.

If only one item of inventory is considered, this presents no difficulty. Suppose, for example, that storage space and/or capital constraints limit the order quantity to some maximum value, say 1000 units. Then one would proceed by first determining the EOQ using the appropriate EOQ formula, completely ignoring the constraint. If the computed EOQ turns out to be feasible (e.g., $Q^* = 750$, which is less than 1000), then the optimal order quantity is 750 units. If the computed EOQ is not feasible (e.g., $Q^* = 1350$, which is greater than 1000), then the optimal order quantity is 1000 units, which is the maximum feasible order quantity. Figure 15.7 shows these two situations and illustrates that this procedure yields the optimal feasible EOQ.

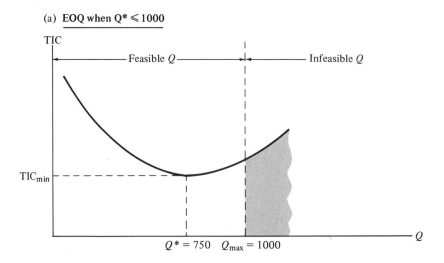

(a) **EOQ when $Q^* \leqslant 1000$**

(b) **EOQ when Q* > 1000**

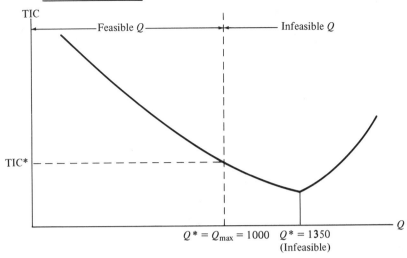

Figure 15.7. **EOQ with constraints.**

However, if multiple items are competing for the same limited space, capital, or other resources, the problem becomes more complex. Let us take an example and use this to develop a procedure for dealing with the multiple-product case having constrained resources.

15.10.1. Example—Constrained Multiple-Product Inventories

You are the manager of a warehouse containing many different purchased items. The volume of your storage space is limited. For each item, there is a demand D_i per year, an order cost c_{p_i}, carrying charges of c_{h_i} dollars per unit per year, and storage volume of k_i per unit. The cubic-foot content of the warehouse is K, and rental of the warehouse is at the rate of w dollars per cubic foot per year.

Assume that two items with the following characteristics are to be purchased:

Characteristics	Item 1	Item 2
Demand, D_i (units/year)	325	1000
Order cost, c_{p_i} ($/order)	20	20
Holding cost, c_{h_i} ($/unit/year)	2	1
Volume, k_i (ft³/unit)	1	2

The maximum storage capacity available for these two units (K) is equal to 300 ft³ and the rental charge (w) is $.20/ft³/year. We wish to find the optimal order quantities for these two items that will minimize total incremental cost subject to the storage constraint.

15.10.2. Model Formulation

Using the example above, let us first write the total incremental cost expression for the two products:

$$
\begin{aligned}
\text{TIC} &= \sum_{i=1}^{2} \text{TIC}_i \\
&= \sum_{i=1}^{2} \left(c_{p_i} \frac{D_i}{Q_i} + c_{h_i} \frac{Q_i}{2} + w_i k_i Q_i \right).
\end{aligned}
\tag{15.34}
$$

Note that the warehouse costs $(w_i k_i Q_i)$ in the problem above are treated separately from inventory holding costs. It is often the case that warehouse costs are treated separately, because in many cases they are not linear in average inventory. For example, warehouse space may have to be allotted and charged on the basis of maximum inventory, as is the case in this problem. The holding costs in this problem thus do not include any storage component.

Equation (15.34) implicitly assumes that the two items are independent of each other. If there are no binding constraints, the EOQs for each item would be determined independently using the following EOQ formula, derived from the total-cost expression of (15.34):[†]

$$
Q_i^* = \sqrt{\frac{2 D_i c_{p_i}}{c_{h_i} + 2 w_i k_i}} .
\tag{15.35}
$$

Determination of the separate EOQs, using (15.35) and ignoring the constraint, yields

$$
Q_1^* = \sqrt{\frac{2(325)(20)}{2 + (2)(.2)(1)}} = 74
$$

$$
Q_2^* = \sqrt{\frac{2(1000)(20)}{1 + (2)(.2)(2)}} = 149.
$$

Let us now consider the constraint. The maximum available storage space is $K = 300$ ft^3, unit 1 occupying $k_i = 1$ ft^3/unit and unit 2 occupying $d_i = 2$ ft^3/unit.

[†]This formula, which is left to the reader to derive using the differential calculus, is similar to the classic EOQ formula of equation (15.2), the difference being accounted for by the extra term resulting from the incremental storage-space cost, $w_i k_i Q_i$.

The constraint is then

$$k_1 Q_1 + k_2 Q_2 \leqslant K$$

$$(\text{ft}^3/\text{unit } 1)(\text{number of units } 1) + (\text{ft}^3/\text{unit } 2)(\text{number of units } 2) \leqslant \text{ft}^3. \quad (15.36)$$

Again, as with a single unit, there are two situations to consider. It is possible that the optimal solution to the problem results in less than full use of the available storage space. That is, the storage space constraint is not violated. If this is true, the solution is the one obtained using (15.35), the unconstrained solution (which treats products independently). So as a first step, we should obtain the two (unconstrained) optimal order quantities, substitute them into the storage-space constraint of (15.36) and determine whether or not the constraint is satisfied. If it is, we are finished. If the constraint is violated, then one or more of the Q_i will have to be revised downward until the total quantity will just fit into the 300-ft^3 space available. Substituting into equation (15.36), we obtain

$$(1)(74) + 2(149) \leqslant 300$$

$$372 \leqslant 300.$$

Since the constraint is violated, we must find a procedure for adjusting the Q_i's downward. Mathematically, we speak of this problem as a constrained optimization problem. That is, we can view this problem as one of minimizing the total-cost function subject to an equality constraint,

$$\text{TIC} = \sum_{i=1}^{2} c_{p_i} \frac{D_i}{Q_i} + c_{h_i} \frac{Q_i}{2} + w_i k_i Q_i$$

subject to
$$\sum_{i=1}^{2} k_i Q_i = K. \quad (15.37)$$

This optimization can be accomplished through the method of Lagrangian multipliers (Section 15A.5). To do this, let us introduce the Lagrangian multiplier λ, and form the Lagrangian function $L(Q_1, Q_2, \lambda)$. This is done by first transposing the constraint to

$$\sum_{i=1}^{n} k_i Q_i - K = 0,$$

multiplying it by λ, and adding it to the TIC expression. This gives

$$L(Q_1, Q_2, \lambda) = \sum_{i=1}^{2} \left(c_{p_i} \frac{D_i}{Q_i} + c_{h_i} \frac{Q_i}{2} + w_i k_i Q_i \right)$$

$$+ \lambda \left(\sum_{i=1}^{2} k_i Q_i - K \right), \quad (15.38)$$

which now makes the problem an unconstrained optimization problem. We then differentiate the Lagrangian function with respect to the unknowns Q_1, Q_2, and λ (decision variables), set each partial derivative equal to zero, and solve the resulting (nonlinear) equations simultaneously. The theory of Lagrangian multipliers for the type of cost function we are considering guarantees that the resulting values solve the original problem (since the function is convex).

Let us illustrate the procedure on the above numerical problem. Taking partial derivatives of the Lagrangian function with respect to Q_1, Q_2, and λ, setting these equal to zero, and solving gives (the derivation is given in Section 15A.5),

$$Q_i = \sqrt{\frac{c_{p_i} D_i}{c_{h_i} + 2k_i(\lambda + w_i)}} . \tag{15.39}$$

Observe that (15.39) is similar to (15.35). The effect of the constraint is to introduce an additional term in the denominator $(2k_i\lambda)$, which has the same effect as an increase in the holding cost c_{h_i}. The amount of increase depends on the space occupied by product i (k_i) and the Lagrangian multiplier λ. The dimension of λ is in $\$/\text{ft}^3$, so λ can be interpreted as a rental rate for space.

The problem is not yet solved, since we have to first find λ before Q_1 and Q_2 can be determined. We can do this if we substitute (15.39) into the constraint (15.36). This gives

$$\sum_{i=1}^{2} k_i \sqrt{\frac{2D_i c_{p_i}}{c_{h_i} + 2k_i(\lambda + w_i)}} = K,$$

or, after substituting the values of the known parameters and simplifying,

$$\sqrt{\frac{2(325)(20)}{2 + 2(1)(\lambda + 0.2)}} + 2\sqrt{\frac{2(1000)(20)}{1 + 2(2)(\lambda + 0.2)}} = 300$$

$$\sqrt{\frac{13,000}{2.4 + 2\lambda}} + 2\sqrt{\frac{40,000}{1.8 + 4\lambda}} = 300. \tag{15.40}$$

Note that as λ gets larger the left-hand side of (15.40) decreases. At $\lambda = 0$, we have the unconstrained situation where the value would be equal to 372. Thus, (15.40) will be satisfied when λ is greater than zero. Table 15.7 shows several trial-and-error attempts to find λ^*, which turns out to be equal to 0.28.[†]

Substituting λ^* into (15.39), we obtain the following optimal EOQs:

$$Q_1^* = 67$$
$$Q_2^* = 118.$$

[†]More sophisticated algorithms could be used to find λ^*. This would be appropriate when the problem involves many items and constraints and a computer program of the algorithm is available.

Table 15.7. Finding λ by Trial and Error

λ	Value of Left-Hand Side of Equation (15.40)
0	372
λ* = 0.28	300
0.30	296
0.50	266

The total annual cost using these constrained order quantities as compared to the nonconstrained order quantities is as follows:

	Q_1^*	Q_2^*	TIC*
Constrained	67	118	$446.1
Unconstrained	74	149	$444.9

15.11. OTHER DETERMINISTIC INVENTORY MODELS

All the inventory decision models we have studied thus far have been based on the assumption that demand for a given product was known (deterministic) and *constant*. With this assumption we have developed optimal order quantities, production runs, reorder points, and related inventory decisions that minimize total cost for a specific type of inventory system.

Although the constant-demand rate assumption may be valid for many inventory items, obviously not all items experience this type of demand. For example, we

Table 15.8. Known Variable Versus Constant Demand from Period to Period

Week	Variable Demand[a]	Constant Demand (ILY)
1	200	200
2	50	195
3	150	203
4	400	210
5	25	200
6	275	204
7	50	198
8	350	190
9	500	200
10	100	200
Total pairs	2000	2000
Average pairs per week	200	200

[a]Compare these demand data to the demand data for the "ILY" tennis shoe, which is in the next column.

may encounter inventory situations where demand is known but does not occur at a constant rate (Table 15.8). Rather, demand from period to period is highly variable. In this situation, where demand is known but changing each period, an application of one of the previous decision models would be inappropriate. We can, however, determine the minimum cost *how-much-to-order* and *when-to-order* decisions by using the technique of dynamic programming (Hadley and Whitin, 1963).

There are many other inventory models that we have not covered. Many of these are variants of the models presented in this chapter.

15.12. SUMMARY

In this chapter we have developed inventory decision models to assist managers in establishing and managing inventory systems at minimal cost. We specifically considered situations where demand for a commodity was known and constant. Our procedure was to develop total-cost models which consisted of ordering costs, holding costs, and in some cases shortage costs, and by means of the differential calculus to develop minimum-cost decision rules for choosing the order quantity, Q. From this the order frequency, time between orders (order cycle), and reorder point could be easily established.

In conclusion, it must be emphasized that these models at best approximate most real-life situations. Many real-world problem situations exist for which no appropriate model has yet been developed. We have really only treated the simplest kinds of situations. However, while it is easy to criticize the models developed in this chapter, that does not negate their value. Inventory models can and often do provide useful decision aids for the decision maker, as well as providing insights into the structure of the problem. It is this latter factor that perhaps provides its most significant benefit. Other models couple inventory systems with production systems and use such classical optimization techniques as linear, integer, and quadratic programming in determining optimal inventory policies.

There are also situations where demand (and/or lead time) is uncertain and can only be expressed in probabilistic terms (as probability distributions). With these different demand conditions, we need different solution procedures to arrive at optimal inventory decisions. These procedures will increase somewhat in complexity. We will consider inventory decision models with probabilistic demands and lead times in Chapter 16.

REFERENCES BUFFA, E. S., and W. H. TAUBERT. *Production–Inventory Systems: Planning and Control.* Homewood, Ill.: Richard D. Irwin, Inc., 1972.

FETTER, R. B., and W. C. DALLECK. *Decision Models for Inventory Management.* Homewood, Ill.: Richard D. Irwin, Inc., 1961.

601

HADLEY, G., and T. M. WHITIN. *Analysis of Inventory System*. Englewood Cliffs, N.J.: Prentice-Hall, Inc., 1963.

HARRIS, F. *Operations and Cost* (Factory Management Series). Chicago: A. W. Shaw Co., 1915, pp. 48–52.

RAYMOND, F. E. *Quantity and Economy in Manufacture*. Princeton, N.J.: D. Van Nostrand Co., Inc., 1931.

STARR, M. K., and D. W. MILLER. *Inventory Control: Theory and Practice*. Englewood Cliffs, N.J.: Prentice-Hall, Inc., 1962.

KEY CONCEPTS

Functions of inventory
  transit or pipeline
  lot-size or cycle
  buffer (safety stock)
  decoupling
  seasonal
Basic inventory decisions
  quantity
  timing
Characteristics of inventory
   decisions
  costs (ordering, holding, shortage,
    purchase price)
  demand (stationary,
    nonstationary; deterministic,
    probabilistic)
  order cycle (continuous, periodic)
  lead time

Inventory replenishment
  (instantaneous, uniform)
  time horizon
  number of items
  number of supply echelons
EOQ models
  classic
  planned shortage
  quantity discounts
  production runs: single product
  production runs: multiple
    products with constraints

REVIEW QUESTIONS

15.1. How might we classify different kinds of inventories (by function)? What functions do each of the different kinds of inventories perform?

15.2. What are the basic inventory decisions?

15.3. Discuss the basic characteristics of inventory systems.

15.4. What are the basic cost categories associated with inventory systems? What do these basic costs include?

15.5. Discuss the classic EOQ model. Give some typical situations to which the model may apply. What are the assumptions of the model? Illustrate how inventory varies over time for the classic EOQ model. Write the objective function and the optimal EOQ formula for the model.

15.6. State the rationale for developing an EOQ model that permits shortages to occur. Write the objective function of this model. Write the optimal EOQ formula and compare it to the EOQ formula for the classic inventory model without shortages permitted.

15.7. Give the circumstances under which the EOQ model with quantity discounts would apply. Describe how to derive an optimal order quantity when quantity discounts are offered.

15.8. Describe the essential differences between the classic EOQ model and the single-product EOQ model for production runs. Write the objective function and EOQ formula for the single-product production-run EOQ model. Relate these expressions to the comparable expressions for the classic EOQ model. Define all terms in these expressions. Illustrate how inventory varies over time for the production-run model.

15.9. Describe the difficulty that can be encountered when trying to apply the production-run EOQ model for single products to multiple products.

15.10. Suppose that inventory is constrained by such limited resources as storage space and/or capital. What optimization procedure could be used to derive an optimal EOQ? Describe the procedure in words.

15.11. When demand is deterministic and nonconstant, what optimization procedure might be used to make the minimum-cost, *how-much-to-order* and *when-to-order* decisions?

15.12. Comment on the following statement made by a retailer named Harry. "My sales next year are going to triple for sure. Where am I going to get the three times as much space I need to satisfy my customers' demand?" Having studied this chapter, what is the fallacy in Harry's thinking and what advice might you give him concerning his inventory problems?

15.13. Suppose that you operate a company in which you have found the "economic-order-quantity" formulas to be useful tools in the planning and management of inventories. Suppose also that you are going to open a plant in a country where (like Italy) inflation is a serious problem. Various measures of inflation have shown a rise in the past of about 20% per year, and you have no reason to believe this will be diminished in the near future. Will this inflation have any effect upon your inventory policy? Discuss the question, noting any assumptions or suppositions upon which your analysis is based.

ANSWERS TO REVIEW QUESTIONS

15.1. Listed below are five types of inventories and the functions they perform:

1. *Transit* or *pipeline*. Supplies to cover delays in handling and transit.
2. *Lot size* or *cycle*. Goods are ordered in lot sizes because it is economical to do so.
3. *Buffer*. Inventories to prevent stockouts due to demand fluctuations.
4. *Decoupling*. Inventories that permit production activities to operate more independently.
5. *Seasonal*. Inventories provided to meet seasonal demand and smooth out the production levels.

15.2. The basic inventory decisions are what quantity to order and when to order.

15.3. Basic characteristics of an inventory system include the various inventory costs, nature of demand pattern, order cycle, lead times, inventory replenishment, time horizon, number of items, and number of supply echelons.

15.4. Types of inventory costs include:

1. Ordering (or set-up) costs, which include incremental costs associated with inventory replenishment, such as administrative costs and costs of issuing a purchase order.
2. Holding costs, which include opportunity cost on investment tied up in inventory, storage costs, product deterioration or obsolescence, taxes, depreciation, and insurance.
3. Shortage or stockout costs, which include penalty costs incurred as a result of running out of stock.
4. Purchase price of item.

15.5. The classic EOQ model is applicable when the entire quantity ordered can be considered to arrive at one time and when the demand rate for the item is constant. Typical situations where the model may apply are:

1. Use of clerical supplies.
2. Use of industrial supplies such as nuts and bolts.
3. Use of toilet supplies in a building.

The assumptions of the model are:

1. Demand is known with certainty.
2. Demand rate is constant.
3. Inventory is replenished when inventory is equal to zero.
4. Lead time is constant and equal to or greater than zero.
5. Unit price, ordering cost, and unit inventory holding cost are constant.

Inventory varies in a sawtooth pattern as shown in Figure 15.8.

Figure 15.8

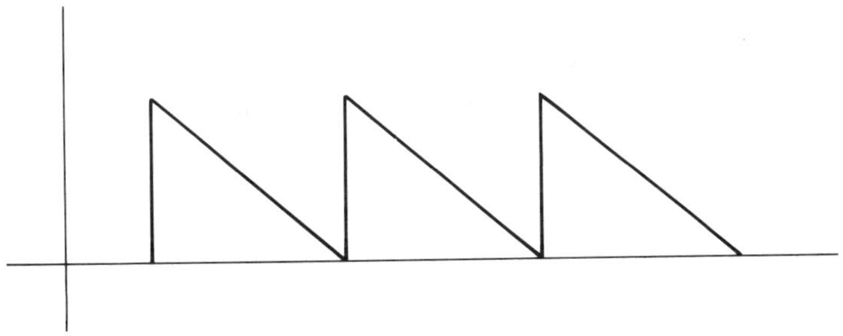

The objective function is written as:

$$\text{TIC} = \tfrac{1}{2}Qc_h + c_p\frac{D}{Q}$$

and

$$Q^* = \sqrt{\frac{2Dc_p}{c_h}}$$

15.6. An EOQ model permitting stockouts is reasonable when the value per unit of inventory is high. This will result in high unit inventory costs.

The objective function is

$$\text{TIC} = c_p \frac{D}{Q} + \frac{c_h(Q - S)^2}{2Q} + \frac{c_s S^2}{2Q}$$

The EOQ is given by

$$Q^* = \sqrt{\frac{2c_p D}{c_h}} \cdot \sqrt{\frac{c_h + c_s}{c_s}}$$

The EOQ is higher with holding costs, although when c_s becomes large compared to c_h, Q^* approaches Q^* without planned stockouts.

15.7. The EOQ model with quantity discounts applies when suppliers offer quantity discounts to purchasers as an incentive for purchasing large quantities.

To determine an optimal order quantity, the cost of goods purchased must be included in the TIC expression. A three-step procedure for determining an EOQ is:

1. Compute a Q^* using the EOQ formula for the unit purchase cost associated with each type of discount.
2. For those Q^*s that are too small to qualify for the assumed discount price, increase the order quantity to the nearest order quantity that will allow the product to be purchased at the assumed price.
3. For each of the order quantities determined in steps 1 and 2, compute the total incremental cost using the TIC equation, and select a Q^* having the minimum cost.

15.8. The basic difference between the classic and production run EOQ models is that for single-product production runs a constant number of units is added to inventory each day. With the classic model, the entire supply arrives at once.

The inventory as a function of time has the profile that is shown in Figure 15.9.

Figure 15.9

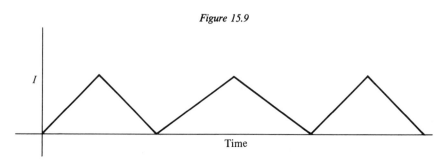

I

Time

The objective function and EOQ formula for the production run model are:

$$Q^* = \sqrt{\frac{2c_p D}{c_h\left(1 - \dfrac{d}{p}\right)}}$$

$$\text{TIC} = c_p \frac{D}{Q} + c_h \frac{Q}{2}\left(1 - \frac{d}{p}\right)$$

where c_p = order cost

D = annual demand requirements

c_h = holding cost

Q = order quantity

d = demand rate

p = production rate

15.9. When the same equipment is used to produce a variety of products, these resources may be a constraint. When this occurs, the independent determination of EOQs for each product is no longer applicable because of the interference among production runs for the various items. Production runs must therefore be determined jointly to preclude scheduling incompatibilities.

15.10. We should first obtain the unconstrained optimal order quantities, substitute them into the storage space constraint, and determine whether or not the constraint is satisfied. If it is, there is no problem. If the resource constraint is violated, then the optimal solution is not feasible and the EOQs must be adjusted downward. A mathematical method for finding constrained Q^*s involves the use of Lagrangian multipliers to make this an unconstrained optimization problem by the substitution of resource constraints into the objective function.

15.11. Dynamic programming can be used to make minimum-cost, how-much-to-order and when-to-order decisions when demand is deterministic and nonconstant.

15.12. If Harry is using the basic EOQ model, then if D increases by 3, Q^* increases by $1.73 (= \sqrt{3})$. Harry thus needs less than twice as much space to accommodate a threefold demand increase.

15.13. If the price of the inventory supplies is increasing as a result of inflation, then there is an additional "holding loss" which must be added to the current holding cost in the TIC expression.

EXERCISES **15.1.** The Brown Company has determined through analysis of accounting data that the administration cost of a raw material is $30. The company expects to use $60,000 of this material in the coming year; its carrying charge is 10% of the average inventory. How many times should raw material be ordered in the coming year?

15.2. Mike O'Neil, the inventory control manager at the FNC Company, has just discovered an error in the computer program used by the firm to determine economic lot sizes. This error caused the economic order quantities to be 25% too high.

Don Fink, the firm's chief accountant, has written a memo to Mike's superior criticizing him for this error. In this memo Don used the data for one product, a widget, to argue that the firm's total inventory carrying cost per year was 25% larger than need be.

Widget: annual requirements = 1000 units

inventory carrying cost = $1/unit/year

ordering cost = $5/order

In a fit of anxiety, Mike loses several nights sleep worrying about what he is going to tell his superior. He asks for help in preparing a statement for his boss which will set forth the consequences of his error in less damaging terms.

15.3. Air Force Captain Henry Burger is responsible for procuring frankfurters for the 8th Bomb Wing. The standard Air Force menu guide specifies that 10,000 boxes will be used throughout the year (27.4 boxes/day) on a uniform basis. (A box contains 200 pounds of frankfurters.) If Captain Burger orders less than 1000 boxes at a time, the price is $100/box, but for orders of 1000 boxes or more, the price is only $99 each. Inventory holding cost is 10% of the item cost. It costs him $5 to place an order.

(a) How many boxes should he order at a time to minimize total incremental costs?

(b) How much does he save using the preferred plan versus the minimum cost possible using the other plan?

15.4. A vendor has made you the following price-discount offer. For orders of 6000 or greater, he will reduce the price per unit for all units ordered by $1. Your monthly inventory holding cost per unit is $0.50 and the cost of placing an order is negligible. Assuming a constant sales rate per month and a no-stockout policy, above what monthly sales level would you recommend taking advantage of the price discount? How large an order would you then place, and why?

15.5. If demand equals 10,000 units per year, c_P = $10 per order, c_h = 25% of the value of the item per year, and the warehousing cost is w = $0.02 per unit per year based on maximum inventory, in what quantities should items be purchased if the price per unit (c) varies according to the number of units ordered as follows:

C (price/unit)	Quantity (units)
$1.00	0–99
0.96	100–999
0.95	≥ 1000

Note: Treat the warehousing cost separately from the inventory holding cost.

(a) Set up a generalized total incremental cost expression, TIC, using c as the price per unit.

(b) Derive an expression for the optimal order quantity, EOQ, using c as the price per unit.

(c) Sketch the curve showing the relationship between TIC (dependent variable) and order quantity, Q, for the various discount prices.

(d) In what quantities (Q^*) should the items be purchased?

15.6. Assume the following conditions:

1. Usage rate = 1800 units/year.
2. Acquisition cost = $5.50.
3. No safety stock required.
4. Annual carrying cost (not including storage) = 10% of average inventory value.
5. Annual storage cost = $0.05 per unit of average inventory.
6. Unit purchase price is $2, but a 5% discount for 50 or more, additional 4% discount for 100 or more, additional 3% discount for 200 or more, additional 2% discount for 400 or more, additional 1% discount for 800 or more.

(a) Determine the economic order quantity.

(b) What would be the effect (in direction) on the EOQ if a $10 storage cost were assigned? Justify. (No computations required.)

(c) Construct a decision flowchart which shows the flow of calculations and decision branching required to develop an optimal solution for three price breaks in the situation described by (a).

15.7. A contractor has to supply 10,000 bearings per day to an automobile manufacturer. He finds that when he starts a production run, he can produce 25,000 bearings per day. The cost of holding a bearing in stock for 1 year is 2 cents, and the setup cost of a production run is $18. How frequently should production runs be made? Assume that there are 250 working days per year.

15.8. A manufacturer requires 15,000 units of a part annually for an assembly operation. The manufacturer can produce this part at the rate of 100 units per day and the setup cost for each production run is $24. To hold 1 unit of this part in inventory costs the manufacturer $5 per year.

(a) Assuming 250 working days per year, what is the optimum number of production runs?

(b) What is the maximum inventory level?

(c) Assume that the manufacturer has the alternative of purchasing these units from an outside vendor. If the cost of placing the order is $200, the cost of each unit is $10, warehouse costs are $0.50 per unit per year, and cost of capital is 10% of the inventory valuation, what is the economic lot size to purchase?

(d) What is the relationship between demand (D) and order quantity (Q)?

15.9. Let

d = demand rate for an item

p = production rate for the item

c = production cost of the item per unit

c_p = setup costs for producing the item

i = carrying-cost rate for the demand period
(covers interest on capital invested in inventory, taxes, insurance, obsolescence, etc., and applies to the average inventory level).

(a) Derive an economic-order-quantity (EOQ) formula that will minimize total costs of setting up, producing, and storing the item over a demand period. Indicate clearly the steps of your derivation, and illustrate graphically the contribution of various costs to the total cost function.

(b) Upon what assumptions are the EOQ formula based?

(c) Will the EOQ defined above always be the best choice of an order quantity to be used in production scheduling?

15.10. An assembly plant of an auto company orders various parts from fabrication plants of the same company. On part no. 9342, next year's requirement is estimated at 20,000 units. The plant uses an annual inventory carrying charge of 20% on the average value of the inventory. Part 9342 is valued at $20 per unit and all orders are delivered in one batch. The variable cost of processing an order is estimated to be $100. The plant operates 250 days a year.

(a) Compute the economic order quantity.

(b) How many orders will be placed a year?

(c) If the average lead time is 10 working days, disbursements continuous and uniform, and safety stock level set at 500 units, what is the reorder point?

15.11. The Reihle Toy Company has found that its cost to purchase Bobby Dolls is $40 per order and the carrying charge on average inventory is 10%. They currently purchase $20,000 of Bobby Dolls per year and make these purchases on an optimum basis. They have been offered a 3% discount on the dolls if they purchase quarterly. Should they accept?

15.12. In Exercise 15.10, suppose that the assembly plant produced part 9342 itself, employing continuous processing and delivery to assembly stations:

(a) If the production rate is 160 units per day and the rate of disbursement averages 80 units per day, what should be the EOQ?

(b) How many orders should be placed per year with the production department?

(c) If the production rate is cut to 100 units per day, what is the EOQ?

15.13. The following are data for three products:

Characteristics	ITEM NUMBER		
	1	2	3
Demand/year	12,000	25,000	6000
Item cost/unit	$3	$2	$6
Inventory holding cost (%/year)	20	20	20
Order cost	$20	$20	$20
EOQ (unrestricted)	890	1580	445

Determine the most economical order quantities if *average inventory investment* for the three items is limited to a total of $3700. Assume that average inventory investment is one-half the maximum investment.

15.14. The production manager at the Kanine Dog Food plant is trying to determine the production lot size for two of the firm's products: Puppies and Doggies. The two products are the only products that are manufactured by one of the firm's processing and packaging lines. The production manager has indicated that only one of the products can be produced at a time by the line and that the firm is willing to carry a finished-goods inventory for the two items. Furthermore, he has supplied the following data:

Product	Annual Sales (units)	Daily Sales (units)[a]	Daily Production Rate (units)[a]	Changeover Cost	Annual Inventory Carrying Cost per Unit
Puppies	400	2	8	$300	$32
Doggies	800	4	8	$500	$40

[a]Assuming 250 working days per year.

Assuming that the production manager wishes to produce each product the same number of times per year to simplify his production scheduling:
(a) Write the formula for the total-cost expression needed to solve for the minimum-cost production frequency.
(b) Compute the minimum-cost production frequency and show how you arrived at this solution.
(c) Compute the minimum-cost production lot size for each product, Puppies and Doggies.

CASE 15.1 Illustrative Case Study
Involving the Establishment of Economic Order Quantities
with Quantity Discounts

CALCON
CORPORATION

In the fall of 1978, John Hancock, operations manager of Calcon Corporation, a maker of industrial electronic calculators, received a letter from Gerry Day, marketing manager of Roadrunner Trucking Company. In the letter John was told that a new shipping rate schedule was just approved by the president of the Roadrunner Transportation Inc., which could result in a significant savings on the chassis, which are manufactured elsewhere and shipped to Calcon. These new rates were to be instituted at the beginning of next month and could result in no less than a 20% savings in Calcon's transportation costs on these chassis. The new rates were as follows: (1) $4 per hundredweight (cwt) for a minimum truckload weight of 5000 pounds; (2) $4 per hundredweight for the first 5000 pounds and $3 for the next 7000 pounds, for a truckload minimum of 10,000 pounds and a truckload maximum 12,000 pounds. Thus, if 10,000 pounds per truck were shipped, the average cost per cwt would be $3.50. This would be a 30% savings over the current rate of $5 per hundredweight.

In response to the letter, Hancock checked his current shipping rates from the company he was currently doing business with, the Rider Trucking Company. The rate Rider was charging was a flat $5 per cwt, with a truckload minimum of 2500 pounds.

Hancock needed to decide whether it was worth it to change from Rider to Roadrunner. To do this required a careful inventory analysis of the situation to determine whether he should order a truckload of 5000 pounds or greater.

Hancock queried his people in the purchasing, distribution and warehouse departments and came up with the following data on Calcon's past purchases of chassis.

Type of Data	Data
Total annual demand	10,000 chassis
Orders per year	20
Units per order	500
Weight per unit	100 pounds
Transportation cost	$5 per hundredweight
Purchase price (excluding transportation)	$200 per unit
Clerical cost per order	$7
Expediting cost per order	$3
Inventory carrying cost (includes interest 10%, obsolescence 8%, taxes 4%, and insurance 3%)	25%
Costs of unloading into warehouse	0.25 per hundredweight

There was sufficient space in the warehouse to store up to 2000 chassis at one time without incurring additional warehousing costs. The transportation and ordering lead time averaged 15 days per order cycle. Over the last year

610

Calcon has ordered about two truckloads per month. Calcon thought that the less-than-truckload rate of $10 per cwt was too high to justify less-than-truckload shipments.

Should Hancock give his business to the Roadrunner Company? How many units should Hancock order, how frequently should he order, and what is his minimum total incremental costs?

CASE 15.2 Illustrative Case Study
Involving the Establishment of a Production Run
and EOQs for Multiple Products

THE STELLER
COMPANY:
INVENTORY
MANAGEMENT OF
VALVES FOR ENERGY
APPLICATIONS

The Steller Company manufactures 10 control valves for energy-related applications (different sizes and types) on the same equipment. Past practice has been to set up and run each item in lots of 1000 for the faster-moving items and in lots of 500 for the slower-moving items. The items were run in sequence and then the cycle was repeated. When the policy was originally set up, the relationship between equipment capacity and sales rate of the items was such that no great difficulties were encountered, since there was plenty of slack capacity. Minimum stock levels of 1 month's supply had also been set up for each item originally. More recently, sales have increased and the company has been unable to maintain the minimum stock levels, and special runs of items have been made frequently. The result has been to upset the cycle sequence, delaying the run of certain items, and increasing the risk of stockout for the delayed items as well. Some company officials felt that it was simply a capacity problem and more equipment was needed so that the size of runs could be doubled. Other officials felt that the present equipment was not being properly utilized and that the inventory policies were at fault. A consultant was called in to review the entire situation and recommend a solution. After a thorough study, the consultant said that he could work out a plan of production runs that would eliminate the scheduling conflicts with no new equipment. The consultant was given the following data for the 10 items involved:

Product Number	Annual Sales (units)	Sales per Production Day (250 days/year)	Daily Production Rate	Annual Inventory Holding Cost	Set up Cost per Run	EOQ Units
1	10,000	40	250	$0.05	$ 20	3,125
2	20,000	80	500	0.10	15	2,670
3	5,000	20	200	0.15	35	1,612
4	13,000	52	600	0.02	40	7,650
5	7,000	28	1,000	0.30	25	1,093
6	8,000	32	800	0.40	37	1,230
7	15,000	60	500	0.02	42	8,325
8	17,000	68	500	0.05	50	6,300
9	3,000	12	200	0.35	16	535
10	1,000	4	125	0.10	12	500
					$292	

The lot sizes shown in the data (EOQ) were computed by the common formula (15.28)

$$Q^* = \sqrt{\frac{2c_p D}{c_h(1 - d/p)}} \quad .$$

Given the data above, what should the consultant recommend with respect to (1) the length of the production run, (2) the lot sizes, (3) total average inventory (in units), and (4) total annual cost which will meet the consultant's requirements of no scheduling conflicts.

CHAPTER 15 APPENDIX

The EOQ Model

15A.1. DERIVATION OF Q^* FOR EOQ MODEL

Given the total incremental cost equation (15.1) for the EOQ model,

$$\text{TIC} = \tfrac{1}{2}Qc_h + c_p\frac{D}{Q},$$

we can derive the optimal order quantity Q^* that minimizes TIC by use of the differential calculus. We first take the derivative of TIC with respect to Q (i.e., $d\text{TIC}/dQ$), set it equal to zero, and then solve for Q^*:

$$\frac{d\text{TIC}}{dQ} = \tfrac{1}{2}c_h - \frac{D}{Q^2}c_p = 0.$$

Solving for Q^* yields

$$Q^* = \sqrt{\frac{2Dc_p}{c_h}} \quad .$$

We can check to make sure that the derived decision rule for Q^* is a minimum cost solution by determining if the second derivative is greater than zero:

$$\frac{d^2\text{TIC}}{dQ^2} = \frac{2D}{Q^3}c_p.$$

Since the value of the second derivative is greater than zero for positive D, c_p, and Q, Q^* is the minimum cost solution.

15A.2. DERIVATION OF Q, I^*, AND S^*
FOR EOQ MODEL WITH SHORTAGES PERMITTED

The method for deriving the optimal decision rules to the EOQ model with permissible shortages involves partially differentiating the total-cost function with respect to each of the decision variables, Q^* and S^*, setting each partial derivative equal to zero, and simultaneously solving the two resulting equations. The total-cost equation (15.19) is

$$\text{TIC} = c_p\frac{D}{Q} + \frac{c_h(Q-S)^2}{2Q} + \frac{c_sS^2}{2Q}.$$

This can be rewritten as follows:

$$\text{TIC} = c_p\frac{D}{Q} + c_h\frac{Q^2 - 2QS + S^2}{2Q} + c_s\frac{S^2}{2Q}$$

$$= c_p\frac{D}{Q} + c_h\frac{Q}{2} + \frac{c_h + c_s}{2Q}S^2 - c_hS.$$

Taking the partial derivative $\partial\text{TIC}/\partial Q$ and setting it equal to zero, we obtain

$$\frac{\partial\text{TIC}}{\partial Q} = -c_p\frac{D}{Q^2} + \frac{c_h}{2} - \frac{(c_h + c_s)^2}{2Q^2} = 0. \qquad (15A.1)$$

Similarly, taking the partial derivative $\partial\text{TIC}/\partial S$ and setting it equal to zero, we obtain

$$\frac{\partial\text{TIC}}{\partial S} = \frac{c_h + c_s}{Q}S - c_h = 0. \qquad (15A.2)$$

Solving (15A.2) for S^*, we obtain

$$S^* = Q\frac{c_h}{c_h + c_s}. \qquad (15A.3)$$

By substituting (15A.3) for S^* in (15A.1),

$$Q^* = \sqrt{\frac{2Dc_p}{c_h}}\,\sqrt{\frac{c_h + c_s}{c_s}}. \qquad (15A.4)$$

The second-order conditions show that (15A.3) and (15A.4) are the minimum-cost decision rules. $I^*_{\max}$ is simply computed from the relationship $I^*_{\max} = Q^* - S^*$.

15A.3. DERIVATION OF THE OPTIMAL LOT SIZE $Q*$ FOR THE PRODUCTION-LOT-SIZE MODEL

Given equation (15.27) as the total-annual-cost formula for the production-lot-size model

$$\text{TIC} = \tfrac{1}{2}(1 - d/p)Qc_h + \frac{D}{Q}c_p,$$

we can find the order quantity Q that minimizes the total cost by setting the derivative $d\text{TIC}/dQ$ equal to zero and solving for $Q*$.

$$\frac{d\text{TIC}}{dQ} = \tfrac{1}{2}\left(1 - \frac{d}{p}\right)c_h - \frac{D}{Q^2}c_p = 0.$$

Solving for $Q*$ we have

$$\tfrac{1}{2}\left(1 - \frac{d}{p}\right)c_h = \frac{D}{Q^2}c_p$$

$$\left(1 - \frac{d}{p}\right)c_h Q^2 = 2Dc_p$$

$$Q^2 = \frac{2Dc_p}{(1 - d/p)c_h}.$$

Hence,

$$Q* = \sqrt{\frac{2Dc_p}{(1 - d/p)c_h}} \ .$$

The second derivative is

$$\frac{d^2\text{TIC}}{dQ^2} = \frac{2Dc_p}{Q^3}.$$

Since the value of the second derivative is greater than zero for D, c_p, and Q greater than zero, $Q*$ is a minimum-cost solution.

15A.4. DERIVATION OF $N*$ FOR PRODUCTION RUNS OF MULTIPLE PRODUCTS

Given the TIC expression of equation (15.31),

$$\text{TIC} = N \sum_{i=1}^{n} c_{p_i} + \frac{1}{2N} \sum_{i=1}^{n} c_{h_i} D_i \left(1 - \frac{d_i}{p_i}\right),$$

we can derive N^* that minimizes TIC by differentiating this cost expression with respect to N, setting the result equal to zero, and then solving for N^*:

$$\frac{d\text{TIC}}{dN} = \sum_{i=1}^{n} c_{p_i} - \frac{1}{2N^2} \sum_{i=1}^{n} c_{h_i} D_i\left(1 - \frac{d_i}{p_i}\right) = 0$$

$$\frac{1}{2N^2} \sum_{i=1}^{n} c_{h_i} D_i\left(1 - \frac{d_i}{p_i}\right) = \sum_{i=1}^{n} c_{p_i}$$

$$N^* = \sqrt{\frac{\sum c_{h_i} D_i(1 - d_i/p_i)}{2 \sum_{i=1}^{n} c_{p_i}}} \ .$$

We can again check second-order conditions to assure that the derived decision rule is a minimum-cost solution by determining if the second derivative is positive (which it is).

15A.5. DERIVATION OF CONSTRAINED EOQS USING LANGRANGIAN FUNCTION

The total-cost expression (15.34) we wish to minimize is

$$\text{TIC} = c_{p_1}\frac{D_1}{Q_1} + c_{h_1}\frac{Q_1}{2} + Q_1 k_1 w_1 + c_{p_2}\frac{D_2}{Q_2} + c_{h_2}\frac{Q_2}{2} + Q_2 k_2 w_2$$

subject to

$$k_1 Q_1 + k_2 Q_2 = K.$$

Writing the Lagrangian function, we obtain

$$L(Q_1, Q_2, \lambda) = \frac{c_{p_1}D_1}{Q_1} + \frac{c_{h_1}Q_1}{2} + k_1 w_1 Q_1$$
$$+ \frac{c_{p_2}D_2}{Q_2} + \frac{c_{h_2}Q_2}{2} + k_2 w_2 Q_2$$
$$+ \lambda(k_1 Q_1 + k_2 Q_2 - K),$$

taking partial derivatives with respect to Q_1, Q_2, and λ, we obtain

$$\frac{\partial L}{\partial Q_1} = -\frac{c_{p_1}D_1}{Q_1^2} + \frac{c_{h_2}}{2} + k_1(\lambda + w_1)$$

$$\frac{\partial L}{\partial Q_2} = -\frac{c_{p_2}D_2}{Q_2^2} + \frac{c_{h_2}}{2} + k_2(\lambda + w_2)$$

$$\frac{\partial L}{\partial \lambda} = k_1 Q_1 + k_2 Q_2 - K.$$

Setting these equal to zero and solving the first two for Q_1 and Q_2, respectively, gives

$$Q_1 = \sqrt{\frac{2c_{p_1}D_1}{c_{h_1} + 2k_1(\lambda + w_1)}}$$

$$Q_2 = \sqrt{\frac{2c_{p_2}D_2}{c_{h_2} + 2k_2(\lambda + w_2)}} \ .$$

The last partial derivative, when set equal to zero, merely reexpresses the original constraint.

CHAPTER 16
Probabilistic Inventory Model and Demand Forecasting

OBJECTIVES: Upon completion of this chapter, you should be able to:

1. Calculate optimal order quantities and reorder points under demand and lead-time uncertainty.
2. Specify the various qualitative and quantitative approaches to demand forecasting.
3. Use the moving-average method of demand forecasting.
4. Use the simple exponential smoothing method of demand forecasting.
5. Specify the relationship between the moving-average and exponential smoothing methods.
6. Use more sophisticated versions of the simple exponential smoothing model.

16.1. PROBABILISTIC INVENTORY MODELS

The inventory models developed in Chapter 15 have assumed that demand was constant and known with certainty. In the first part of this chapter we consider inventory decision models in which the exact demand and lead time for an item is uncertain and therefore can only be described in terms of a probability distribution. The second half of this chapter is devoted to forecasting, with emphasis on the development of forecasting models that can be used to forecast demand and demand during lead time in inventory problems.

Even when demand is probabilistic, the inventory manager still must decide: (1) how much to order, and (2) when to order in order to minimize his total incremental costs. The relevant incremental cost elements of total cost are ordering, holding, and stockout costs.

The basic assumptions of the inventory model we shall develop are as follows:[†]

1. Demand is uncertain.
2. Lead time is uncertain.
3. Lot sizes are being purchased rather than produced internally.
4. Back orders are permitted (i.e., stockouts are penalized but not lost).

[†]The procedure we develop also applies with slight modification to models having different assumptions from those stated. For example, it can be adapted to items produced internally rather than purchased and to situations where back orders are lost.

5. Unit price, ordering cost, unit inventory holding cost, and unit stockout cost are constant.

The presentation that follows outlines an approach for determining an *economic order quantity* (Q^*) and reorder point (R^*) in an inventory system with uncertain demand and replenishment lead time. We will show that, under conditions of uncertainty, these two quantities cannot be determined independently.

When demand is known with certainty (or can assumed to be), determination of the optimal order quantity is straightforward. In this case, the total cost associated with inventory over a given time period (year) is the sum of holding costs and ordering costs, and the *economic order quantity*, Q^*, is that order quantity which yields minimum total cost, as shown in Chapter 15. The determination of the *reorder point* (R^*) when conditions are known with certainty is also relatively straightforward. For these cases, when there is a lead time associated with receipt of goods ordered, the reorder point is easily calculated as the demand per day times the number of days lead time. For example, if item demand is equal to 2 units per day and item lead time is equal to exactly 2 days, then stockouts can be avoided by reordering when the inventory level drops to 4 units.[†] That is, in 2 days the new order will arrive and the 4 units on hand when the order was placed will have just been consumed. Thus, the stock level of the item will drop to zero at the moment a new shipment arrives, and with the arrival of the new shipment, a stockout is just avoided. Note that the reorder point here is determined independently of the value of the order quantity, Q.

In contrast to the above, when item demand and lead time are uncertain, determination of the economic order quantity Q^* and reorder point R^* becomes considerably more complex. Because of the uncertainties involved, a probability distribution of demand during lead time (DDLT) must be determined. These uncertainties cause an interaction between order quantity Q and reorder point R, which preclude their independent determination.

In the following sections determination of the cost components under uncertain demand and lead time is first developed and contrasted to the deterministic classic EOQ model. An illustrative calculation procedure for determination of an economic order quantity and reorder point for the uncertainty case is then presented. This is followed by a more formal development. Let us, however, begin with an example and carry it through, to illustrate the procedures to be developed.

16.1.1. *Example—The Lover Tennis Supply (LTS) Company Revisited*

Let us again consider another situation faced by the LTS company. As you recall, LTS is a distributor of tennis products in the Midwest. From their main warehouse facility in Indianapolis, LTS supplies approximately 500 retail outlets,

---

[†]The objective of stockout avoidance, while common, is not always imposed. If stockouts are allowed, this discussion of reorder-point determination still holds, but with slight modification, as was shown in Chapter 15.

including sporting goods stores, tennis shops, and tennis clubs with tennis equipment.

In addition to their tennis shoe inventory, LTS is very much concerned about a novel tennis racket they distribute exclusively. Ron Lover, the founder of the company, designed it himself a year ago and is having it manufactured by a small firm in Missouri. The Lover racket is made from a special metal alloy that was originally developed for space vehicles. The racket, while extremely light, has tremendous power as well as control. Although sales are presently rather small, this racket promises to become very popular within a few years. Unlike their tennis shoes, demand for the racket is rather unpredictable. The racket costs LTS $50, unstrung. Recall that LTS's cost of capital is annualized at 5%; also LTS's annual insurance, taxes, breakage, pilferage, and warehouse overhead costs are 5% of its total inventory value.

Art Ash, the warehouse manager, has collected demand data on the "Lover" racket since it was introduced last year. Owing to its newness and the unpredictability of tastes, demand has been highly variable throughout the year. Moreover, the records show that the lead times were also variable, taking anywhere from 1 to 3 days to receive an order after it was placed. A sample inventory history of the racket is shown in Table 16.1 for a typical 20-day (4-workweek) period.

Art also analyzed the order cost for the racket and found it to be the same as that of the "ILY" tennis shoe, which was equal to $9. Since demand was uncertain, Art knew that the classic EOQ model would not be applicable for determining the optimal inventory policy. This was because unplanned shortages could and did

Table 16.1. Sample of Lover Tennis Racket Inventory History

(1) Day	(2) Beginning Inventory	(3) Order Received	(4) Demand	(5) Ending Inventory
[a]1	4	0	0	4
2	4	4	2	6
[a]3	6	0	1	5
4	5	3	0	8
[a]5	8	0	0	8
6	8	0	2	6
[a]7	6	2	1	7
8	7	0	1	6
[a]9	6	1	2	5
10	5	0	0	5
[a]11	5	1	2	4
12	4	0	1	3
[a]13	3	2	0	5
14	5	0	1	4
[a]15	4	2	2	4
16	4	0	0	4
[a]17	4	2	0	6
18	6	1	1	6
[a]19	5	2	0	7
20	7	2	2	7

[a]Order placed every 2 days.

occur as a result of uncertain demand. This resulted in considerable loss of customer goodwill, and in some cases lost customers. Art valued this stockout cost to be equal to $10 per unit. He then went back to his consultant and asked him to develop a procedure or model that would select the optimal order quantity Q^* and reorder point R^* based on minimizing the total inventory costs, consisting of ordering, holding, and stockout costs.

16.1.2. Model Formulation

A graphical illustration of inventory level as a function of time is shown in Figure 16.1. Note that safety stock must be carried to reduce the chance of a stockout, because of unpredictable demand. Note that the maximum inventory level during the lead-time period is the reorder point R. This is composed of

Figure 16.1. Inventory profile with safety stock.

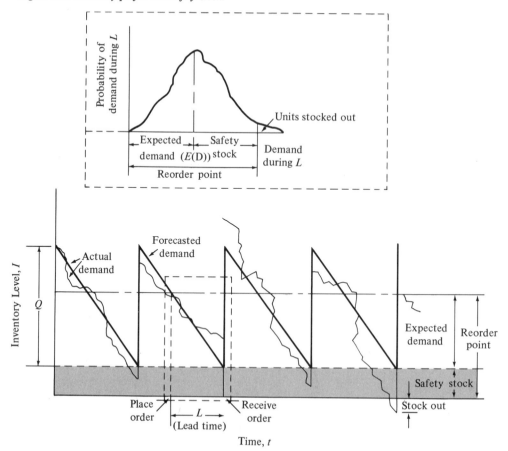

expected demand during lead time, $E(DDLT)$, plus the safety stock. If demand during lead time is less than R, no stockouts will occur; if it is greater than R, stockouts will occur. Only in the fourth cycle would a stockout have occurred, since in this period demand during lead time is greater than R, the inventory level on hand during this period. However, if no safety stock were carried, inventory shortages would have occurred in the first and third cycles in Figure 16.1. In the second cycle, a surplus of inventory would have occurred, even if no safety stock were carried.

From Figure 16.1 we see that the annual total expected inventory cost associated with an item is the sum of three cost components: (1) order cost, (2) holding cost, and (3) stockout cost:

$$\text{TEC} = \text{expected order cost} + \text{expected holding cost} + \text{expected stockout cost}$$

Note that the costs are expected costs rather than deterministic costs, since we are dealing with uncertain demands and lead times. These component costs are determined as follows.

ORDER COST. As in the case of known demand, this cost is equal to the cost of placing each order (c_p) times the number of orders placed each year. The only difference between the deterministic case and the probabilistic case is that instead of using actual demand (D) in determining the number of orders per year, we use expected (average) demand, $E(D)$. Using the same notation as in Chapter 15,

$$\text{order cost per year} = c_p \frac{E(D)}{Q},$$

where $E(D)$ = expected demand, units per year
   Q = order quantity, units.

To determine the annual order cost for our example problem, we must first use the data of Table 16.1 to determine $E(D)$. $E(D)$ can be determined by obtaining a probability distribution of daily demand, determining its expected value, and then multiplying its expected value by the 250 working days in the year. The probability distribution of daily demand is obtained from column 4 of Table 16.1 and is shown in Table 16.2. Daily expected demand is thus

$$0(0.4) + 1(0.3) + 2(0.3) = 0.9$$

Table 16.2. Probability Distribution of Daily Demand

Demand / Day	Frequency	Relative Frequency $\Rightarrow$ Probability
0	8	0.4
1	6	0.3
2	6	0.3
	20	1.0

Multiplying 0.9 by 250 gives an $E(D) = 225$. Given $c_p = \$9$ and $E(D) = 225$, the annual order cost for the "Lover" racket is

$$\text{order cost per year} = \$9\frac{225}{Q}.$$

HOLDING COST. Again, as in the case of known demand, this cost is equal to the cost of holding 1 unit in inventory for the year times the average number of units in inventory. Here, however, the average inventory level is *not* simply $Q/2$ but is a function of the reorder point R and the expected demand during lead time, $E(\text{DDLT})$. The quantity $E(\text{DDLT})$ must be calculated in a special way, which will be explained shortly. We can, however, see from Figure 16.1 that average inventory is

$$\text{average inventory} = \frac{Q}{2} + \text{safety stock}.$$

The safety stock, however, is the difference between the reorder point R and the expected demand during lead time $E(\text{DDLT})$. Hence,

$$\text{average inventory} = \frac{Q}{2} + R - E(\text{DDLT}).$$

The expression for holding cost then becomes

$$\text{annual holding cost} = c_h\left[\frac{Q}{2} + R - E(\text{DDLT})\right],$$

where c_h is the unit holding cost per year (usually expressed as a fraction of item cost c). In our example, $c_h = \$5[c_h = ic = (0.10)(50)]$. $E(\text{DDLT})$ is also a computable parameter but will be determined later. Thus,

$$\text{annual holding cost} = 5\left[\frac{Q}{2} + R - E(\text{DDLT})\right].$$

STOCKOUT COST. The cost of expected stockouts *per lead time period* is the expected number of units demanded but not available during a given lead-time period times the cost per unit stockout. Clearly, stockout cost is related to the reorder point R, since stockouts occur when the demand during lead time is greater than the number of units on hand when the order was placed.

The expected cost of stockouts for the entire year is the expected cost of stockouts per lead time period times the expected number of lead-time periods during the year. But the number of lead-time periods per year is equal to the number of orders placed per year, which is expected yearly demand divided by the order quantity. The expression for stockout cost is then:

$$\text{stockout cost per year} = c_s \cdot E(S) \cdot \frac{E(D)}{Q},$$

where c_s = estimated stockout cost per unit

$E(S)$ = expected stockouts during lead time in units

and other terms are as defined earlier. In our example, c_s = \$10; hence,

$$\text{stockout cost per year} = \$10 \cdot E(S) \cdot \frac{225}{Q}.$$

In this expression for stockout cost, $E(S)$ must be determined for specific reorder-point values, by actually computing the expected demand during lead time greater than a given reorder point (as we shall explain shortly).

The annual total incremental inventory cost is thus

$$\text{TEC} = \text{order cost} + \text{holding cost} + \text{stockout cost}$$

$$= c_p \frac{E(D)}{Q} + c_h\left[\frac{Q}{2} + R - E(\text{DDLT})\right] + c_s E(S) \frac{E(D)}{Q}.$$

From the discussion above and the TEC expression, we can see that the expected cost of stockouts is a function of both Q and R. Furthermore, as pointed out in the discussion of holding cost, both Q and R influence the average inventory level and hence holding cost. Therefore, with uncertain demand, the total cost is dependent upon both Q and R. We cannot, as in the case of known demand and lead time, determine either Q or R independently of the other. Instead, we must search for that *combination* of Q and R that gives minimum total expected cost. We now present a trial-and-error procedure and then a mathematical model for determining Q^* and R^* that minimizes total cost under the condition of uncertain demand and uncertain lead time.

16.1.3. Trial-and-Error Solution Procedure

This procedure consists of five steps—namely, the determination of the demand distribution, of lead-time distribution, of demand during lead-time distribution, of the expected number of stockouts, and of Q^* and R^*.

Step 1—Determine Demand Distribution. Prepare a frequency and relative frequency (probability) distribution of daily demand for the item from actual inventory records by counting the number of days that a certain demand occurs. For example, from Table 16.1, the demand distribution for the "Lover" tennis racket is shown in Table 16.2.

Step 2—Determine Lead-Time Distribution. In a similar way, prepare a frequency and relative-frequency (probability) distribution of lead time for the item from actual inventory records by counting the number of days it takes to receive an order after it is placed. Again, from Table 16.1, the *lead-time* distribution is determined in the following way. Note that we order every 2 days. Of the 10 times we order in the 20-day period, 4 of those times we receive the order in 1 day and 6 of those times in 2 days. The resulting lead-time distribution is thus shown in Table 16.3.

Table 16.3. Probability Distribution of Lead Time

Lead Time	Frequency	Probability (lead time)
1	4	0.4
2	6	0.6
	$\overline{10}$	$\overline{1.0}$

Step 3—Determine Demand During Lead-Time Distribution. We next calculate the demand during lead-time distribution. Given the demand and lead-time distributions, we develop a probability tree that depicts all possible lead times. As an illustration, given the demand and lead-time distributions of Tables 16.2 and 16.3, respectively, we form the probability tree shown in Figure 16.2. Computing the path probabilities and combining the outcomes by DDLT, we obtain the probability distribution of demand during lead time shown in Table 16.4. (See Section 16A.1 for a brief discussion of alternative procedures for obtaining the demand during lead-time distribution.) The expected demand during lead time $E(\text{DDLT})$ is thus

$$E(\text{DDLT}) = \sum_0^4 (\text{DDLT}) \cdot P(\text{DDLT})$$

$$= (0)(0.256) + (1)(0.264) + \cdots + 4(0.054) = 1.440.$$

Table 16.4. Probability Distribution of Demand During Lead Time

DDLT (units/day)	Probability p(DDLT)	Probability of a Stockout for a Given Reorder Point, P(S)
0	0.256	0.744
1	0.264	0.480
2	0.318	0.162
3	0.108	0.054
4	0.054	0.000
	$\overline{1.000}$	

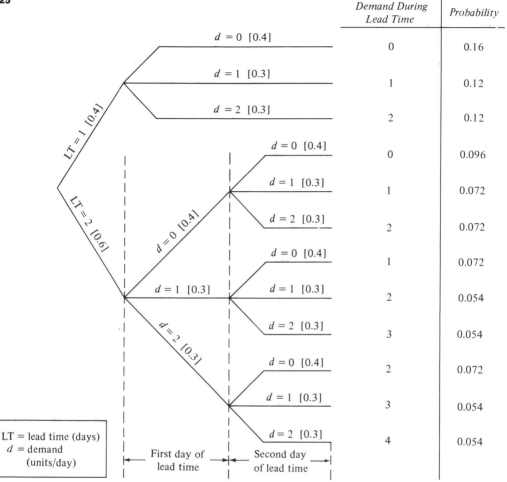

	Demand During Lead Time	Probability
d = 0 [0.4]	0	0.16
d = 1 [0.3]	1	0.12
d = 2 [0.3]	2	0.12
d = 0 [0.4]	0	0.096
d = 1 [0.3]	1	0.072
d = 2 [0.3]	2	0.072
d = 0 [0.4]	1	0.072
d = 1 [0.3]	2	0.054
d = 2 [0.3]	3	0.054
d = 0 [0.4]	2	0.072
d = 1 [0.3]	3	0.054
d = 2 [0.3]	4	0.054

Figure 16.2. Probability tree for determining expected demand during lead time.

Step 4—Determine Expected Number of Stockouts. We next calculate the expected number of stockouts per order $E(S)$ for each possible reorder point R. Because, in our example, we attach zero probability to demand during lead time greater than 4, we need not consider any reorder points larger than 4. Thus, we only need to examine all possible reorder points from 0 to 4. In calculating the expected number of stockouts per lead-time period $E(S)$ for a particular reorder point R, we use the probabilities $p(\text{DDLT})$ in Table 16.4 to determine the expected value of demand *greater than* the reorder point. That is, for each possible value of demand during lead time (DDLT), with associated probability $p(\text{DDLT})$, the number of units unavailable upon occurrence of this demand when the reorder point R is used is $(\text{DDLT} - R)$. Since the probability of this occurring is $p(\text{DDLT})$, the expected number of units stocked out is

$$E(S) = \sum_{\text{DDLT}>R}^{\infty} (\text{DDLT} - R) \cdot p(\text{DDLT}).$$

For each possible R we must examine each possible demand. In our "Lover" tennis racket example, the computations of $E(S)$ for each R are shown in Table 16.5. Figure 16.3 graphically illustrates these calculations used in this step for $R = 2$.

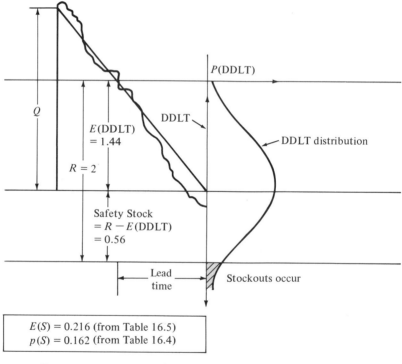

$E(S) = 0.216$ (from Table 16.5)
$p(S) = 0.162$ (from Table 16.4)

Figure 16.3. Inventory profile and resulting DDLT distribution showing E(S) computations for R = 2.

Table 16.5. Computations of E(S) for each R

(1)	(2)	(3)	(4) = (2) × (3)
R	$(DDLT - R)$	$P(DDLT)$	$(DDLT - R) \cdot P(DDLT)$
0	(4 − 0)	0.054	0.216
	(3 − 0)	0.108	0.324
	(2 − 0)	0.318	0.636
	(1 − 0)	0.264	0.264
			$\overline{E(S) = 1.440}$

Table 16.5. Computations of E(S) for each R (continued)

(1) R	(2) (DDLT − R)	(3) P(DDLT)	(4) = (2) × (3) (DDLT − R) · P(DDLT)
1	(4 − 1)	0.054	0.162
	(3 − 1)	0.108	0.216
	(2 − 1)	0.318	0.318
			$E(S) = 0.696$
2	(4 − 2)	0.054	0.108
	(3 − 2)	0.108	0.108
			$E(S) = 0.216$
3	(4 − 3)	0.054	$E(S) = 0.054$
4	(4 − 4)	0.054	$E(S) = 0$

Step 5—Determine Q* and R*. At this point the only unknown quantities in the component costs of the total-cost equation are the decision variables Q and R. That is,

$$\text{TEC} = c_p \frac{E(D)}{Q} + c_h \left[\frac{Q}{2} + R - E(\text{DDLT}) \right] + c_s E(S) \frac{E(D)}{Q}$$

or

$$\text{TEC} = 9\frac{225}{Q} + 5\left(\frac{Q}{2} + R - 1.440 \right) + 10E(S)\frac{225}{Q}.$$

We can try different combinations of Q and R to find the pair that yields a minimum total cost. We know R will vary from 0 to 4. A good starting point for Q can be obtained using the classic EOQ formula,

$$Q = \sqrt{\frac{2c_p D}{c_h}}.$$

In our tennis racket problem,

$$Q = \sqrt{\frac{2(9)(225)}{5}}$$
$$= 28.46.$$

Computations for various values of Q and R are shown in Table 16.6. The optimal order quantity Q^* and reorder point R^* appears to be $Q^* = 30$ and $R^* = 3$. Once we have found the optimal Q, R combination, we can then (if we wish) perform sensitivity analysis to determine the effect of changes in some of the cost parameters. For example, if we are uncertain of the stockout cost c_s, we can examine how the TEC deviates from the optimum value and how Q^* and R^* change as c_s is varied over a range of possible values. In this fashion management can assess the relative importance of the various cost parameter estimates and their impact on inventory policy.

Table 16.6. Determining Q* and R*

Q	R	TEC	Order Cost = $9(225/Q)$	Holding Cost = $5(Q/2 + R - 1.44)$	Stockout Cost = $10 \cdot E(S)225/Q$
28	4	$155.12	$72.32	$82.80	$ 0.00
	3	154.46		77.80	4.34
	2	162.48		72.80	17.36
	1	196.05		67.90	55.93
30[a]	4	155.30	67.50	87.80	0.00
	3[a]	154.35[a]		82.80	4.05
	2	161.50		77.80	16.20
	1	192.50		72.80	52.20
32	4	156.08	63.28	92.80	0.00
	3	154.88		87.80	3.80
	2	161.27		82.80	15.19
	1	190.02		77.80	48.94
34	4	157.36	59.56	97.80	0.00
	3	155.93		92.80	3.57
	2	161.65		87.80	14.29
	1	188.42		82.80	46.06

[a]$Q^* = 30$, $R^* = 3$, TEC = $154.35.

We have just described a trial-and-error procedure for determining the order quantity Q^* and reorder point R^* when demand and lead time are uncertain, for a particular type of inventory management system—the "fixed-order-quantity, fixed-reorder-point" system. We shall now mathematically develop decision rules for Q^* and R^* that will reduce the effort involved in determining Q^* and R^*.

16.1.4. Optimal Decision Rules for Q* and R*

We can develop optimal decision rules for Q and R for problems of this type by use of the differential calculus. In the Appendix to this chapter it is shown that[†]

$$Q^* = \sqrt{\frac{2E(D)\left[c_p + c_s E(S)\right]}{c_h}} \tag{16.1}$$

and

$$p(S)^* = \frac{c_h Q}{c_s E(D)}. \tag{16.2}$$

Note that equations (16.1) and (16.2) cannot be solved independently. Rather, they

[†]In Section 16A.2, decision rules for Q^* and R^* are also developed for the lost-back-order case. The rules are applied in the same manner as equations (16.1) and (16.2).

interact in a slow way, and thus must be solved by a back-and-forth trial-and-error procedure. That is, assume an R^* and solve for Q^*. Now having Q^*, solve again for R^*. With new R^*, solve again for Q^*, and so forth, until the solutions "settle down."

Let us now use these formulas for determining Q^* and R^* for the "Lover" racket problem. Using equation (16.1) and assuming that $E(S) = 0$, we obtain

$$Q^* = \sqrt{\frac{2(225)9}{5}} = 28.46.$$

Substituting $Q^* = 29$ into equation (16.2) gives

$$p(S)^* = \frac{(5)(28.46)}{(10)(225)} = 0.063.$$

From Table 16.4, determine the R which gives a $p(S) = 0.063$. This is between $R = 2[p(S) = 0.162]$ and $R = 3[p(S) = 0.054]$. Hence, the nearest safe R is $R = 3$. Using $R = 3$, calculate a new Q^* using equation (16.1), that is,

$$Q^* = \sqrt{\frac{2(225)[9 + 10(0.054)]}{5}} = 29.30,$$

where $E(S) = 0.054$ for $R = 3$ as obtained from Table 16.5. Again, substituting $Q^* = 29.30$ into equation (16.2) gives

$$p(S)^* = \frac{(5)(29.30)}{(10)(225)} = 0.065.$$

From Table 16.4, we see that R^* is still equal to 3. Hence, the minimum total expected cost solution is $Q^* = 30$ (rounded to nearest integer) and $R^* = 3$.

In summary, the inventory model and solution procedures developed in this chapter are designed to determine the optimal order quantity Q^* and reorder point R^* under demand and lead-time uncertainty. It should again be emphasized that the discussion has been confined only to one particular type of inventory management system—the "fixed-order-quantity, fixed-reorder-point" (R, Q) system. There are several other such systems which can be applied in given situations, and are covered in Buchanan and Koenigsberg (1963) and Hadley and Whitin (1963) and references cited therein.

16.2. FORECASTING

In this second half of this chapter we shall discuss the subject of forecasting. Our intent is to cover the rudiments of two statistical forecasting models, moving average and exponential smoothing. These models are based strictly on historical data. For a more extensive treatment of these models and forecasting in general, see Brown (1959); Brown (1963); Chambers, Satinder and Smith (1971); and Winters (1960).

Statistical forecasting techniques are widely used in the management of production and inventory systems and have also found frequent application in a variety of other problem areas in management, including quality control, financial planning, marketing, investment analysis, and distribution planning. Forecasts provide the inputs into the decision-making process. From a decision theoretic perspective, forecasts can be viewed as predictions of the state of nature (the uncontrollable variable) or consequences that will occur, manifested in terms of either a point estimate (most likely value, expected value, etc.) or a probability distribution. The better the forecast, the better the decision. For this reason, management functions for planning and controlling organizational activities typically include a forecasting function, which may be more or less formally defined.

There are many situations where forecasts are important. Take inventory management, for example. As was the case for the "Lover" tennis racket, in controlling finished-goods inventory, it was necessary to obtain an estimate of annual demand and demand during lead time in order to determine economic order quantities, reorder points, and safety stocks.

From the example above and others that readily come to mind, we see that a forecast is simply a prediction of future events. The purpose of forecasting is to reduce the risk in decision making. Forecasts are rarely, if ever, perfect, but by allocating more resources to forecasting, forecasts should improve, thereby reducing the losses resulting from uncertainty in the decision-making process. Of course, one must balance the value of an improved forecast against the increased cost of making more sophisticated and better forecasts in choosing the appropriate forecasting procedure. This concept is in essence the notion of expected value of perfect information (EVPI) and expected value of sample (or forecast) information covered in Chapter 4.

Forecasting systems should provide a description of the forecast error as well as a forecast. Ideally, the forecasting process should result in an assessment of a probability distribution of the variable being predicted rather than just a point estimate. This permits risk to be incorporated into the decision-making process, as we saw in Chapters 4 and 5. The forecast is not management's ultimate aim, but serves as a conduit toward the goal of better decision making.

16.2.1. Defining the Forecasting Problem

We shall focus our discussion of forecasting techniques to repetitive types of decision problems where there exists a historical data base, such as in inventory management. In inventory management we would thus be concerned with forecasting demand for a product.

More generally, to define the forecasting problem, we must begin with the decision problem. The information from the forecasting process is to be used as input to improve the decision-making process. Hence, the nature of the decisions to be made will dictate many of the desired characteristics of the forecasting system. A study of the decision problem should help answer such questions as:

1. What are we forecasting?
2. What form should the forecast take?
3. What are the time elements?
4. What is the desired accuracy of the forecast?

WHAT IS BEING FORECAST? Here we are defining the variables or parameters that are to be predicted. The level of detail required is an important consideration. A production planning system may require a forecast of demand in units for each finished product produced in order to schedule production and plan and control inventories. On the other hand, we may require a more aggregated forecast of demand; for example, by value class of unit—high, medium, and low. In the first case, the forecast is made on each item; in the second case, it is on a more aggregated value class basis. While these may be the final forms for the forecasts required, they may not necessarily be the variables we would use in the analysis of the decision problem. For example, we may make aggregate demand forecasts and, with secondary calculations, disaggregate these into value class demand forecasts or individual product forecasts. The level of detail of a forecast is influenced by many factors, such as data availability, cost, managerial preferences, and accuracy attainable.

FORM OF FORECAST. The variable we are forecasting can be viewed as a random variable. This implies that our forecast of that variable should be a probability distribution. The common practice, however, is to state a single value (point estimate) for the forecast, which represents some characteristic of its probability distribution (usually a measure of central tendency) such as its mean, median, or mode (most probable value). To capture the uncertainty in a forecast, one must estimate either the standard deviation, a confidence interval, or the entire probability distribution itself. If the distribution can be assumed to be of a standard form, such as the normal distribution, then estimates of its two parameters, its mean and variance, would suffice to characterize the distribution. If it cannot be assumed to be a standard probability distribution, the entire distribution should be assessed. By incorporating uncertainty into the forecast, attention is immediately focused on the fact that forecasts are not perfect and decisions should account for this uncertainty, for example, by establishing buffer and safety stocks.

TIME ELEMENTS INVOLVED. The following time elements must be considered in developing a forecast: (1) the *forecasting period*, (2) the *forecasting horizon*, and (3) the *forecasting interval*. The *forecasting period* is the basic unit of time for which forecasts are made. For example, we might wish a forecast of demand by month, in which case the period is 1 month. The *forecasting horizon* is the number of periods in the future covered by the forecast. For example, we could require a monthly forecast for the next 6 months (i.e., in July we forecast demand for August, September, . . . , January). The period is 1 month, and the horizon is 6 months. The *forecasting interval* is the forecasting frequency (i.e., how often new forecasts are prepared). Often, the forecasting interval is the same as the forecasting period. In this way, forecasts are revised each period using the most recent period's demand and other current information as the basis for revision.

The forecasting period and horizon are usually dictated by the decision process or model requiring the forecasted input information. For a forecast to have value, the forecast horizon must be no less than the lead time for implementing the decision. How far into the future one must forecast depends on the nature of the decision problem. Since forecasts usually become less accurate as we go further into the future (i.e., as the forecast horizon lengthens), we can often improve our decision process by shortening the decision lead time, thereby reducing the forecast horizon and permitting a quicker reaction to forecast error.

The forecasting interval often is determined by the nature and frequency of the data provided by the information-processing system on the variable being forecasted. If, for example, demand is reported monthly, a monthly (rather than a weekly or daily) forecast interval would probably be most appropriate.

FORECAST ACCURACY. The forecast accuracy required by the decision problem will affect the forecasting system adopted. An important quality of good decision making is the ability to make rational (optimal) decisions in the face of uncertainty. While improved forecast accuracy will reduce uncertainty, it may not be economically justified. Here again, the notion of EVPI and EVSI are relevant.

ADDITIONAL FACTORS. There are several other additional factors that should also be considered in defining the forecasting problem. One concerns the behavior of the process being generated (e.g., the demand pattern). If the process is stable, the forecasting model may be quite different from that required when the process is unstable. A stable process would make considerable use of historical data (assuming that it is available) to predict the future, while an unstable process would more heavily rely on subjective estimates, since the process is always changing and hence historical data are irrelevant.

Another important factor is data availability; also its quantity, accuracy, timeliness, and representativeness. The computational limitations imposed on the forecasting system is also an important consideration and must be defined. If only a few variables are forecasted infrequently, more elaborate analysis procedures are possible than if a large number must be analyzed often. In the latter case, considerable effort must be devoted to efficient data-processing procedures. Hence, the cost and ease of development, installation, and operation must be considered. Implementation of the forecasting system is critical. Without management's comprehension of the system and its cooperation, the best forecasting system will fail. Thus, the interests and capabilities of the people involved in the forecast must be carefully considered in defining the forecasting problem. Unless managers and users of the forecast can be convinced that the forecasting procedure is sound, they may make little, if any, use of the forecasts given them.

16.2.2. Forecasting Methods

Forecasting methods can be broadly classified into two categories: (1) qualitative (or intuitive) and (2) quantitative, depending upon the extent to which mathematical and statistical methods are used in making the forecast.

QUALITATIVE (INTUITIVE) PROCEDURES. Qualitative procedures involve subjective estimation and are primarily used when data are scarce or unavailable—for example, when a product is first introduced into a market. They use human judgment and rating schemes to turn qualitative information into quantitative estimates. Techniques range from the use of individual expert opinion and simple opinion polls, to the use of expert panels (discussion groups) and the Delphi technique to secure a consensus from a group of experts. The panel approach is designed to effect a desirable interaction among several experts by bringing them into personal contact with one another. This technique is based on the assumption that several experts can arrive at a better forecast than one person. There is no secrecy and communication is encouraged. The forecasts are sometimes influenced by social factors, and may not reflect a true consensus. One disadvantage to this approach is that it provides the opportunity for more forceful personalities present to dictate the group opinion.

The Delphi technique is an organized, systematic method to obtain a consensus of expert opinion and avoids many shortcomings of the panel and polling approaches. Some of the undesirable features of group or committee discussions are avoided by the use of questionnaires. The technique is carried out in such a manner that many of the advantages of expert interaction are still achieved.

In the Delphi approach direct debate is replaced by a carefully designed program of sequential interrogations, usually conducted by questionnaires, with controlled feedback. Without allowing personal or face-to-face contact, the experts are provided with iterative controlled feedback to raise questions where divergent opinions exist and to identify areas of reasonable agreement. However, again the opinions are only as good as the experts that have been selected. In all these procedures, the experts' responses may be based on objective as well as subjective data. As is often the case, the variable being forecasted can be assessed in terms of a subjective probability distribution, as we have shown in Chapter 5. A discussion of the biases and difficulties managers have in making probabilistic predictions (using subjective probability assessments) is presented in Moskowitz, Schaefer, and Borcherding (1976) and references cited therein.

QUANTITATIVE PROCEDURES. Quantitative or statistical forecasting procedures explicitly define how the forecast is determined. The logic is clearly explicated and the procedure is strictly mathematical. The techniques rely on historical data and the assumption that the process is stable, and use this knowledge to extrapolate the process into the future. Quantitative forecasting models can be basically categorized into two types: (1) time-series models, and (2) causal models.

TIME-SERIES MODELS. These models rely entirely on historical data and focus entirely on data patterns and data-pattern changes. These statistical techniques are used when several years' data are available and when relationships and trends are both clear and relatively stable.

All statistical techniques are based on the assumption that existing patterns will continue into the future. This assumption is more likely to be correct over the short term than it is over the long term, and for this reason these techniques provide us with reasonably accurate forecasts for the immediate future but do quite poorly further into the future (unless the data patterns are extraordinarily stable).

For this same reason, these techniques ordinarily cannot predict when the rate of growth in a trend will change significantly—for example, when a period of slow growth in sales will suddenly change to a period of rapid decay.

Some types of time-series analysis models in order of increasing sophistication and complexity include (1) trend projections, (2) moving average, (3) exponential smoothing, and (4) Box-Jenkins[†]

1. *Trend projections.* This technique fits a trend line to a mathematical equation and then projects it into the future by means of this equation.
2. *Moving average.* Each forecasted point of a moving average of a time series is the arithmetic average or weighted average of a number of prior consecutive data points of the series, where the number of data points is chosen so that the effects of trends, seasonality, and irregularity are eliminated.
3. *Exponential smoothing.* This technique is similar to the moving average, except that more recent data points are given more weight. Descriptively, the new forecast is equal to the old one plus some proportion of the past forecasting error. There are many variations of exponential smoothing: some are more versatile than others, some are computationally more complex, some require more computer time.
4. *Box–Jenkins.* Exponential smoothing is a special case of the Box–Jenkins technique. In the Box–Jenkins model, the time series is fitted with a mathematical model that is optimal in the sense that it assigns smaller errors to history than any other model. The type of model must be identified and the parameters then estimated. This seems to be the most accurate statistical routine presently available but also one of the most costly and time-consuming ones.

CAUSAL MODELS. Causal models attempt to define relationships among system elements. As with time-series analysis, past data are important to causal

---

[†]The technique of pattern recognition is another sophisticated statistical approach to time-series forecasting.

models. Thus, when historical data are available and enough analysis has been performed to spell out explicitly the relationships between the factor to be forecast and other factors (such as related businesses, economic forces, and socioeconomic factors), the forecaster often constructs a causal model.

A causal model is the most sophisticated kind of forecasting tool. It expresses mathematically the relevant causal relationships. It is, in essence, a mathematical description of the underlying process. Hence, the purpose of a causal model is often not merely to predict, but also or rather to explain the process.

Causal models are by far the best for predicting turning points and preparing long-range forecasts. Regression and econometric models are examples of such models.

1. *Regression model.* This functionally relates the variable being forecasted (the dependent variable) to other economic, competitive, or internal variables (independent variables) and estimates a regression equation using the method of ordinary least squares. Relationships are primarily analyzed statistically, although any relationship should be selected for testing on a rational basis.

2. *Econometric model.* An econometric model is a more sophisticated regression approach often involving a system of interdependent regression equations that describes some sector of economic sales or profit activity. The parameters of the regression equations are usually estimated simultaneously. As a rule, these models are relatively expensive to develop. However, owing to the system of equations inherent in such models, they will better express the causalities involved than an ordinary regression equation and hence should predict more accurately.

The same type of forecasting technique is not used at all stages of the life cycle of a product. For example, a technique that relies on historical data is not appropriate in forecasting sales of a new product that has no history. Moreover, in making a particular forecast, forecasting systems often use a combination of quantitative and qualitative methods. Usually, statistical methods are used to routinely analyze historical data and prepare a forecast. This lends objectivity to the forecast, resulting in an effective synthesis of the information content of the historical data. The statistical forecast then becomes an input to a subjective evaluation by informed managers, who may alter the forecast in view of other relevant information and their perception of the future. In fact, one can extend and formalize a useful variant of this procedure in the following way. If we treat the statistical forecast and the manager's subjective forecast as independent variables, then a forecast can be made by taking some linear combination of the two:

$$\text{forecast} = b_1 \cdot \text{statistical forecast} + b_2 \cdot \text{manager's forecast},$$

where b_1 and b_2 are the normalized weights attached to each of these forecasts. These weights can be determined by means of regression analysis. This method has the desirable feature of formally integrating both historical information and the manager's information: There is much to be said for such a procedure, in terms of making a forecasting system work.

Our focus in the remainder of this chapter will be on short-term forecasting. Our orientation will be toward systems requiring periodic forecasting of many items each period, as is the case in inventory control. Under these conditions, the economics usually dictate a relatively simple forecasting model. The two models we shall consider are the ones most often used in practice under these conditions: (1) moving average, and (2) exponential smoothing. Both these models provide estimates of the parameters of the probability distribution of the random variable we are trying to predict; usually the mean (but also the variance).

We shall begin with an example, then develop each of these models and apply them to our example problem.

16.2.3. Example—Forecasting Handy Sales
at Clark Tools Inc.

Clark Tools Inc. (CTI), a manufacturer of standard hardware tools, was experiencing difficulty in controlling its finished-goods inventories. Mr. Ford, the merchandising manager, said, "Our inventories are always either excessive or insufficient!" He was advised by the operations research staff that CTI's inventory problems could be alleviated by improving its sales-forecasting procedure. Specifically, the OR staff recommended that Merchandising consider one of the following forecasting techniques: (1) moving average, or (2) exponential smoothing.

Before deciding which of these techniques to incorporate into CTI's inventory control system, Ford decided first to better understand these techniques and evaluate their performance on a sample product. He therefore reviewed the monthly sales history of the pliers product—the Handy brand. These data are listed in Table 16.7.

Table 16.7. CTI Handy Sales Data (hundred units)

| Month | YEAR | | |
	1974	1975	1976
January		44	50
February		39	59
March		38	57
April		36	55
May		38	64
June		47	55
July	45	51	61
August	47	48	45
September	46	50	49
October	54	50	46
November	45	53	
December	48	46	

To evaluate the moving-average and exponential smoothing models, Ford decided to prepare moving-average and exponentially smoothed sales forecasts for each month in 1976, including November and December. In making these forecasts he also planned to test various-size moving averages and smoothing-constant values and to study their implications. For comparison purposes, he decided on a beginning sales average for January 1976 of 45 units. (Ford determined this beginning value by simply calculating the average monthly sales during 1975.) For the exponential smoothing technique, he also thought he would begin with a smoothing constant (α) equal to 0.2.

After making these forecasts, Ford thought that he would test the performance of his forecasting procedures by comparing the sales forecasts to the actual sales and observing the forecast errors. He decided to use two measures of the forecast error: (1) the average error, and (2) the average absolute forecast error (a surrogate measure of the forecast error standard deviation, which is simpler to calculate than the standard deviation). Ford was aware that the average absolute forecast error (and forecast error standard deviation) measure is directly related to the need to carry buffer inventory (safety stock). On the other hand, the average forecast error measure reflects the tendency of the forecasting model to under/overforecast sales. He was, however, not sure which of these two measures to use in selecting the size of the moving average or the exponential smoothing-constant value.

16.2.4. The Moving Average

We first discuss the moving average and then use it to forecast CTI's Handy sales. In using the moving average, one simply employs the most recent n observations to calculate a simple (or weighted) average, to forecast the next period. Suppose, for example, that we wished to obtain next month's forecasted sales for Clark Tool's Handy brand using a three-period moving average. This means that we will take an average of the most recent past three periods in Table 16.7 to forecast next period's sales. For example, to predict sales in February 1976, we would average actual sales in January, December, and November[†]:

$$\text{forecast for February 1976} = \frac{50 + 46 + 53}{3}$$
$$= \tfrac{1}{3}(50) + \tfrac{1}{3}(46) + \tfrac{1}{3}(53)$$
$$= 49.67.$$

What we have effectively done in making the forecast is to give equal weight to the most recent three periods of data and zero weight to the rest of the older data. Note that the sum of the weights should equal 1. Actual demand in February turned out to be equal to 59. Our forecast error (= actual demand minus forecasted demand)

[†]Our forecast of demand in January was equal to 45, based on an average of the previous year's sales. This initial forecast was used so that the moving average forecasts and exponential smoothing forecasts could be compared.

is thus 9.33. Our forecast for March 1976 (i.e., our new moving average) would now be based on the average actual sales in February, January, and December:

$$\text{forecast for March 1976} = \tfrac{1}{3}(59) + \tfrac{1}{3}(50) + \tfrac{1}{3}(46)$$

$$= 51.67.$$

We could also make forecasts beyond the immediate forthcoming period. For example, if at the end of January, we wished to forecast March's sales as well as February's sales using a three-month moving average, both forecasts would be based on January, December, and November sales. Hence, February's forecast and March's forecast made at the end of January (not February) would be identical and equal to 49.67. Of course, March's forecast made at the end of February would be different since it is based on February, January, and December sales. (What would be April's forecast made in February? March?)[†]

Table 16.8 shows next month's forecasts made for the months of 1976 using a 1-, 3-, and 6-month moving average. Since November sales data are unavailable, forecasted sales in December are made at the end of October (i.e., it is forecasted 2 months in advance). The average forecast errors and average absolute forecast errors are also shown in Table 16.8. Observe that the forecast for the 1-month moving average is simply last month's sales. In other words, we give all the weight (= 1) to the most recent sales datum and zero weight to the older data in making the forecast. A forecast of this nature would imply that the demand process is very unstable (dynamic), and therefore all data except the most recent are irrelevant in terms of predicting future sales. With a three-period moving average we give $\tfrac{2}{3}$ weight to "older" data and $1/3$ to the most recent datum. With a six-period moving average, we give $5/6$ weight to "older" data and $1/6$ weight to the most recent datum. Thus, the larger our sample (size of moving average), the less our forecast is influenced by our most recent datum.

Our choice of the number of periods to employ in a moving average is a measure of the relative importance we attach to old versus current data. Clearly, if we feel the process is stable or is changing slowly, we should use a large moving average (sample) to filter out the noise. Conversely, if we feel that the process is unstable or is changing rapidly, we should adopt a small moving average (sample) to keep pace with the changing process. From a statistical standpoint, what we are actually doing is trading off bias against precision. For example, if a process is known to be stable, the larger sample we take, the more accurate the estimate of expected demand. This is because the sampling distribution of the mean gets tighter as the sample size is increased.

Thus, in forecasting with the moving average, the accuracy of the forecast (which is composed of bias and precision) depends on the number of observations,

---

[†]These forecasts would be different if, for example, a trend existed. A moving average of the trend would then have to be calculated and factored into the forecast, which would then result in different forecasts for December and January.

Table 16.8. CTI Handy Sales Moving-Average Forecasts for 1976

Month	Actual Sales	n = 1[a] Forecast[b]	Forecast Error	Absolute Forecast Error	n = 3 Forecast	Forecast Error	Absolute Forecast Error	n = 6 Forecast	Forecast Error	Absolute Forecast Error
T = 1 Dec. 1975	46									
T = 2 Jan. 1976	50	45.00	5.00	5.00	45.00	5.00	5.00	45.00	5.00	5.00
T = 3 Feb.	59	50.00	9.00	9.00	49.67	9.33	9.33	49.50	9.50	9.50
T = 4 Mar.	57	59.00	−2.00	2.00	51.67	5.33	5.33	51.33	5.67	5.67
T = 5 Apr.	55	57.00	−2.00	2.00	55.33	−0.33	0.33	52.50	2.50	2.50
T = 6 May	64	55.00	9.00	9.00	57.00	7.00	7.00	53.33	10.67	10.67
T = 7 June	55	64.00	−9.00	9.00	58.67	−2.33	2.33	55.17	−0.17	0.17
T = 8 July	61	55.00	6.00	6.00	58.00	3.00	3.00	56.67	4.33	4.33
T = 9 Aug.	45	61.00	−16.00	16.00	60.00	−15.00	15.00	58.50	−13.50	13.50
T = 10 Sept.	49	45.00	4.00	4.00	53.67	−4.67	4.67	56.17	−7.17	7.17
T = 11 Oct.	46	49.00	−3.00	3.00	51.67	−5.67	5.67	54.83	−8.83	8.83
T = 12 Nov.		46.00			46.67			53.33		
T = 13 Dec.										
Average forecast error			0.10			1.66			0.80	
Average absolute forecast error				6.50			5.77			6.73

[a] n = sample size (size of moving average).

[b] forecast error = actual sales − forecasted sales.

639

and the optimum number of observations depends on the rate of change in the process.

To find the optimal-size moving average for the Handy sales data, we would have to try many different-size moving averages and select the one that results in both the smallest average forecast error (bias) and smallest average absolute forecast error (precision or "noise"). It rarely occurs that a given-size moving average will dominate all other-size moving averages on both criteria. The choice thus rests on the problem situation and the tastes of the decision maker. Since precision is less controllable than bias (which can be adjusted for), it would seem that the average absolute forecast error would be a more important criterion than forecast error. For example, in inventory control, if we knew that forecasts were biased, we could easily adjust our inventory levels to account for this. However, if there exists forecast-error variability, we can only account for this by carrying safety stock to avoid stock-outs.

We can extend the moving-average concept by assigning variable weights to older data, where the weights decrease with increasing age of data. For example, in

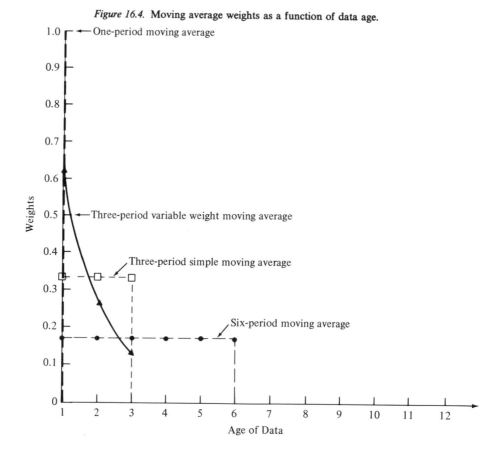

Figure 16.4. Moving average weights as a function of data age.

a three-period moving average, we might assign $\frac{5}{8}$, $\frac{2}{8}$, and $\frac{1}{8}$ to the most recent, next most recent, and oldest data, respectively. In this case, our forecast for Handy sales in February 1976 would be

$$\text{forecast for February 1976} = \tfrac{5}{8}(50) + \tfrac{2}{8}(46) + \tfrac{1}{8}(53)$$

$$= 49.67.$$

We could further extend this notion to using a moving average that assigns positive weights to all past data, such that the weights are monotonically decreasing with increasing age of data. This assures that all data are used in the forecast, but the older the data, the less its influence. A plot of the illustrative moving-average weights as a function of the age of the data is shown in Figure 16.4.

We would prefer to have a forecast that uses all the data, but emphasizes the more recent data, which is assumed to be more representative of recent events. We would also like this forecast to be easy to compute by hand as well as by computer. Exponential smoothing has both these desirable characteristics.

16.2.5. Exponential Smoothing

A moving average has the following shortcomings which limit its attractiveness as a forecasting technique: (1) weights of all the data in the sample are usually given equal weight rather than giving the more recent data greater weight, (2) only part of all past data are used in making the forecast, and (3) it is computationally onerous in the sense that a good deal of data must be retained from period to period to make the forecast. If our moving-average size is 300, this could be a bit computationally inconvenient, even with a large computer.

Exponential smoothing circumvents these shortcomings. In exponential smoothing we assign weights to past data, such that the weights monotonically decrease with its increasing age. This is in keeping with the premise that in a changing process, recent data are more valid than older data. Moreover, with exponential smoothing we need only (1) the current period's forecast, (2) a smoothing constant value, and (3) the actual current period's datum to make a forecast into the future, thus eliminating the need for storing large amounts of past data.

Simple exponential smoothing forecasts are made as follows: the new forecast is equal to the last forecast plus a fraction of the difference between the last datum and the last forecast. The fraction α is called the smoothing constant and varies from 0 to 1. Symbolically,

$$\bar{F}_t = \bar{F}_{t-1} + \alpha\left(D_{t-1} - \bar{F}_{t-1}\right), \tag{16.3}$$

where $\bar{F}_t$ = new forecast (e.g., for February)

$\bar{F}_{t-1}$ = last forecast (e.g., for January)

α = smoothing constant between 0 and 1

D_{t-1} = last datum (e.g., January's actual sales).

Alternatively stated, our new forecast is the last forecast plus a correction factor that is proportional to the error in our last forecast. When we forecast with equation (16.3), we are actually estimating (as we did with the moving average) the mean of the process that is currently generating our data. [We could also use equation (16.3) to estimate the variance or some other parameter of the process under consideration, as we shall indicate later.]

We can rearrange equation (16.3) into the following more computationally convenient form:

$$\bar{F}_t = \alpha D_{t-1} + (1 - \alpha)\bar{F}_{t-1}. \tag{16.4}$$

We can now use equation (16.4) to show that an exponential smoothing forecast (1) uses all the past data, (2) emphasizes the more recent data, and (3) is essentially a weighted average of all past data. To show this, using equation (16.4), let us make a forecast for period $t - 1$,

$$\bar{F}_{t-1} = \alpha D_{t-2} + (1 - \alpha)\bar{F}_{t-2} \tag{16.5}$$

and similarly let us make a forecast for period $t - 2$,

$$\bar{F}_{t-2} + \alpha D_{t-3} + (1 - \alpha)\bar{F}_{t-3}. \tag{16.6}$$

Substituting (16.6) into (16.5), and (16.5) into (16.4) yields

$$\bar{F}_t = \alpha D_{t-1} + (1 - \alpha)\{\alpha D_{t-2} + (1 - \alpha)[\alpha D_{t-3} + (1 - \alpha)\bar{F}_{t-3}]\}.$$

Expanding, we obtain

$$\bar{F}_t = \alpha D_{t-1} + \alpha(1 - \alpha)D_{t-2} + \alpha(1 - \alpha)^2 D_{t-3} + (1 - \alpha)^3 \bar{F}_{t-3}.$$

We now have an equivalent expression for $\bar{F}_t$ in equation (16.4) which involves α, the three previous actual data, and the forecast made three periods ago. If we continue this process of recursion through all the past data involving n periods, we obtain

$$\bar{F}_t = \alpha D_{t-1} + \alpha(1 - \alpha)D_{t-2} + \alpha(1 - \alpha)^2 D_{t-3} + \alpha(1 - \alpha)^3 D_{t-4}$$
$$+ \cdots + \alpha(1 - \alpha)^n D_{t-n+1} + (1 - \alpha)^{n+1}\bar{F}_{t-n+1}. \tag{16.7}$$

Note that equation (16.7) includes all past data, α, plus the original forecast made $n + 1$ periods ago. If we ignore the term $(1 - \alpha)^{n+1}\bar{F}_{t-n+1}$, since $(1 - \alpha)^{n+1}$ approaches zero for large n, equation (16.7) is effectively a weighted average of all the actual past data. The original forecast could be determined in a number of different ways; it could be based on subjective judgment, or a moving average, and so on.

To illustrate the use of this simple exponential smoothing model, let us apply equation (16.4) to the Handy sales data, initially using $\alpha = 0.2$ and $\bar{F}_0 = 45$ as given in the CTI case example, where $\bar{F}_0$ is the original forecast made for January 1976, based on an average of 1975's monthly sales.

$$\bar{F}_{February} = \alpha D_{January} + (1 - \alpha)\bar{F}_{January}$$
$$= (0.2)(50) + (0.8)(45)$$
$$= 46.$$

The forecasts made for the entire year of 1976 are shown in Table 16.9. We could also make forecasts beyond the immediate future period, as we did with the moving average. For example, if our planning horizon was two periods into the future, then our forecasts in a given period would be made for next period as well as the following period. Thus, a forecast made at the end of January would include forecasts for February and March. The forecast for February was equal to 46 as calculated above. This forecast would also be the forecast for March (assuming that no trend existed and was taken into account). Of course, March's forecast would be revised at the end of February, owing to the fact that monthly forecasts are being made one and two periods into the future, and the new information provided by February sales data should alter and more accurately predict March's sales.

Let us now examine the rationale for choosing α and the effect of the value of α on the forecast. From equation (16.7) we see that the weight given each of the data (D) depends on the value of α selected and that the weights are monotonically decreasing with increasing age of the data. Note that the weights are decreasing exponentially, hence the term "exponential smoothing." Table 16.10 shows the

Table 16.9. Handy Sales Simple Exponential Smoothing Forecasts for 1976 ($\alpha = 0.2$)

t Month	Actual Sales D_t	New Forecast (smoothed sales average), $\bar{F}_t$	Last Sales Forecast, $\bar{F}_{t-1}$	Forecast Error, $D_t - \bar{F}_t$	Absolute Forecast Error, $|D_t - \bar{F}_{t-1}|$
1 Dec.	46	45.0	—	—	—
2 Jan.	50	46.0	45.0	5.0	5.0
3 Feb.	59	48.6	46.0	13.0	13.0
4 Mar.	57	50.3	48.6	8.4	8.4
5 Apr.	55	51.2	50.3	4.7	4.7
6 May	64	54.2	51.2	13.8	13.8
7 June	55	53.4	54.2	1.8	1.8
8 July	61	54.9	53.4	7.6	7.6
9 Aug.	45	52.9	54.9	−9.9	9.9
10 Sept.	49	52.1	52.9	−3.9	3.9
11 Oct.	46	50.8	52.1	−5.1	5.1
12 Nov.			50.8		
13 Dec.					
			Average	3.54	7.32

weights given to past data for several different values of α. When α is equal to zero, no weight is given to past data. In this case we see from equation (16.4) that last period's forecast is next period's forecast, implying a completely stable process. At the other extreme, when α is equal to 1, all the weight is given to the most recent datum and zero weight to the older data. Table 16.10 also shows the difference in weightings for $\alpha = 0.2$ and 0.9.

Table 16.10. Exponential Weights as a Function of Age of Data

Period	Weight	\(\alpha\) (SMOOTHING CONSTANT)			
		0	0.2	0.9	1.0
t	α	0	0.200	0.900	1.00
$t-1$	$\alpha(1-\alpha)$		0.160	0.090	0
$t-2$	$\alpha(1-\alpha)^2$		0.128	0.009	
$t-3$	$\alpha(1-\alpha)^3$		0.102	0.001	
$t-4$	$\alpha(1-\alpha)^4$		0.082	0.000	

Now we can return to equation (16.4), which is the one we would use for computational purposes. It is deceptively simple, but remember that the term $\bar{F}_t$ has been generated by a recursive process which in fact represents all the past actual demands. We have shown that the selection of α, the smoothing constant, can be made in such a way that recent data are emphasized as heavily as desired. A relatively large value of α will cause the forecasted average $\bar{F}_t$ to respond quickly to changes in actual demand, reflecting a fraction of random changes in demand as well as actual shifts in the average demand. A small value of α will respond more slowly and smoothly. Figure 16.5 shows the exponentially smoothed forecast of demand for the Handy brand using the smoothing constant of $\alpha = 0.2$ (Table 16.9). Note that the forecast is stable even though there are relatively wide fluctuations in actual demand but that the forecast does change gradually when actual demand changes. At the beginning of this section we alluded to the fact that the forecast would lag behind an upward or downward trend. We can correct for this lag by forecasting the trend using exponential smoothing. This will be discussed later.

We can gain further insight into the nature of exponential smoothing by observing how this forecasting procedure responds to sudden impulses and sudden step changes in the process. Figures 16.6 and 16.7 show the forecasts provided by our forecasting system immediately before, during, and after an impulse and step response has occurred. Note that the forecast asymptotically approaches (but never reaches) the true parameter of the process. The larger the α, the more responsive is the forecast to the signals (i.e., less lag occurs).

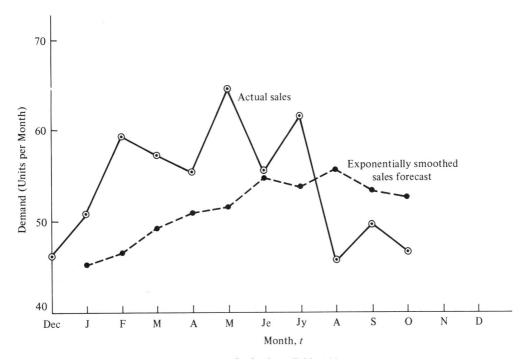

Figure 16.5. Exponential forecast versus actual sales from Table 16.9.

Figure 16.6. Exponential forecasts with impulse response.

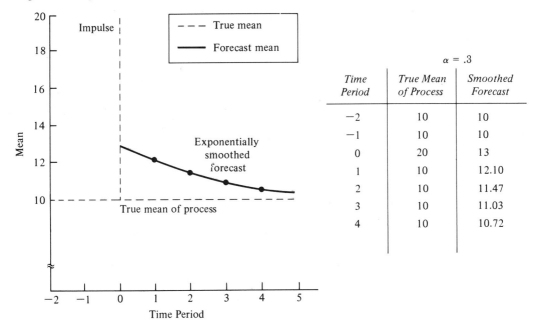

Time Period	True Mean of Process	$\alpha = .3$ Smoothed Forecast
−2	10	10
−1	10	10
0	20	13
1	10	12.10
2	10	11.47
3	10	11.03
4	10	10.72

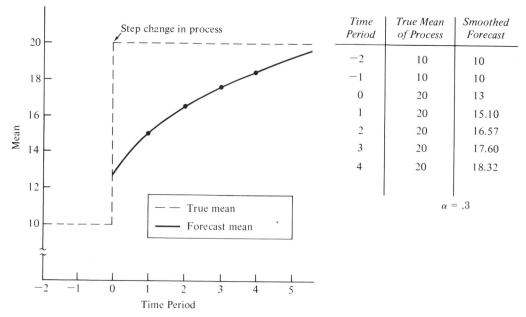

Time Period	True Mean of Process	Smoothed Forecast
−2	10	10
−1	10	10
0	20	13
1	20	15.10
2	20	16.57
3	20	17.60
4	20	18.32

$\alpha = .3$

Figure 16.7. Exponential forecasts with a step response.

Real forecasting systems require a considerable degree of subjectivity. With exponential smoothing, we exercise judgment in selecting α and an initial forecast. If we believe that the process is stable, we make α small. In this way we increase the precision of our forecast without worrying too much about bias. If, however, we believe that the process is changing, we would want a larger α to give us a quicker response.

We can identify process changes by continually surveilling the forecast errors. If the process is stable, our forecasts should be unbiased, which means that the sum of our forecast errors should approach zero. If we find that our forecast errors do not sum to zero but are increasing to some positive value, our forecast is lagging actual demand. If our forecast errors sum to a growing negative value, our predictions are lagging in the opposite direction. In the former case, the parameter of the process we are predicting probably has increased. In the latter case, it has probably decreased. By keeping a running sum of our forecast errors, we should be able to detect such process changes. The forecast errors are also useful for estimating and monitoring the variance (or its surrogate, the mean absolute deviation) of the process. This parameter is useful in inventory management in estimating a demand during lead-time distribution for a standard two-parameter (e.g., mean and variance) theoretical distribution such as the normal distribution. With the forecasted mean and variance, the demand during lead-time distribution is thus defined and can be used to determine the expected number of stock-outs associated with various reorder points. With this, an optimal order quantity and reorder point can be selected that minimizes the total expected costs of ordering, holding, and being short of inventory.

To estimate the variance of the process (or its surrogate measure, the mean absolute deviation), we might simply keep a running sum of the forecast errors squared or the absolute forecast errors, interpreting their mean as an estimate of the variance of the process. We could also use exponential smoothing to estimate the variance, using equation (16.8). That is,

$$\text{var } F_t = \alpha\left(\overline{E}_{t-1}\right)^2 + (1 - \alpha)\,\text{var } F_{t-1} \tag{16.8}$$

where var F_t = forecast of the variance

$\overline{E}_{t-1}$ = last period's forecast error $\left(D_{t-1} - \overline{F}_{t-1}\right)$

var F_{t-1} = last period's forecast of the variance.

Or, as a surrogate for variance

$$\text{ABS}\left(\overline{E}_t\right) = \alpha\text{ABS}(E_{t-1}) + (1 - \alpha)\text{ABS}\left(\overline{E}_{t-1}\right), \tag{16.9}$$

where $\text{ABS}\left(\overline{E}_t\right)$ = absolute forecasted error

$\text{ABS}(E_{t-1})$ = last period's absolute value of actual forecast error

$\text{ABS}\left(\overline{E}_{t-1}\right)$ = last period's absolute value of forecasted error.

EQUIVALENCE RELATIONSHIP BETWEEN MOVING AVERAGE AND EXPONENTIAL SMOOTHING. In exponential smoothing, the weights placed on past data are exponentially proportional to their ages, so that some weight is given to even very old data. With an n-period moving average, all data older than the nth-oldest datum receive zero weight. However, by appropriately selecting the smoothing constant α, we can obtain essentially the same forecast from exponential smoothing that we get from a moving average. To show this, let us determine relationships for the average age of data for both types of forecasting procedures.

For the moving average, the expected age of the nth datum used in the forecast is

$$\text{expected age of moving average} = \frac{1}{n}(0) + \frac{1}{n}(1) + \frac{1}{n}(2) + \cdots + \frac{1}{n}(n - 1)$$

$$= \frac{n - 1}{2}, \tag{16.10}$$

where 0 is the age of the current datum, 1 is the age of the next most recent datum, and so forth.

In the case of exponential smoothing, the expected age of the data used in the forecast (i.e., all the data are used in the forecast) is

$$\text{expected age of exponential smoothing} = \alpha(0) + \alpha(1 - \alpha)(1)$$

$$+ \alpha(1 - \alpha)^2(2) + \cdots$$

$$= \frac{1 - \alpha}{\alpha}. \tag{16.11}$$

Setting (16.10) equal to (16.11) and solving for α, we get

$$\alpha = \frac{2}{n+1}.$$
(16.12)

What we have done is to define an α that is equivalent to an n-period moving average by equating the expected ages of both models. We can thus use equation (16.12) to determine the smoothing constant α that will give us exponential smoothing forecasts that are approximately equivalent to forecasts obtained by means of an n-period moving average. Selected smoothing constants and corresponding values of n in a moving-average model are shown in Table 16.11. Note how α influences the weight attached to older data; the larger the α, the less weight is attached to older observations. Table 16.12 computes exponential smoothing forecasts using smoothing constants that correspond to one-, three-, and six-period moving averages. The reader is urged to compare these results to those obtained by the corresponding moving-average forecasts given in Table 16.8. While the results are different to some extent, note their general similarity.

Table 16.11. Equivalence Relationship Between
α and n

Smoothing Constant, α	Corresponding Number of Data in a Moving Average, n
0.050	39
0.100	19
0.200	9
0.286	6
0.500	3
0.900	1.22
1.000	1

16.2.6. Adaptive Exponential Smoothing

We can modify forecasting models employing exponential smoothing by varying the response rate, which can be made dependent on the value of what is known as a tracking signal. In a simple system, this is tantamount to varying the smoothing constant α according to the extent to which biased forecasts are being obtained. Such a forecasting model will react quicker to changes in the process (e.g., a step change), while still retaining the ability to provide a high degree of precision (i.e., filter out random noise).

In practice, it is customary to use an α value equal to or less than 0.2, in order to filter out a major part of the noise in the process. However, with such a model, a problem then arises if the process suddenly changes. With low values of α, the forecasting model will take an unacceptably long time to "home" in to the new

Table 16.12. Exponentially Smoothed Handy Sales Forecasts for 1976 (smoothing constants correspond to 1-, 3-, and 6-period moving averages)

t Month	Actual Sales, D_t	$\alpha = 1$ ($n = 1$)			$\alpha = 0.5$ ($n = 3$)			$\alpha = 0.286$ ($n = 6$)		
		Forecast, $\bar{F}_{t-1}$	Forecast Error	Absolute Forecast Error	Forecast	Forecast Error	Absolute Forecast Error	Forecast	Forecast Error	Absolute Forecast Error
1 Dec.	46	45[a]			45			45		
2 Jan.	50	50	5	5	47.50	5	5	46.43		
3 Feb.	59	59	9	9	53.25	11.50	11.50	50.03	12.57	12.57
4 Mar.	57	57	−2	2	55.13	3.75	3.75	52.02	6.97	6.97
5 Apr.	55	55	−2	2	55.07	−0.13	0.13	52.87	2.98	2.98
6 May	64	64	9	9	59.54	8.93	8.93	56.05	11.13	11.13
7 June	55	55	−9	9	57.27	−4.54	4.54	55.75	−1.05	1.05
8 July	61	61	6	6	59.14	3.73	3.73	57.25	5.25	5.25
9 Aug.	45	45	−16	16	52.07	−14.14	14.14	52.58	−12.25	12.25
10 Sept.	49	49	4	4	50.54	−3.07	3.07	51.55	−3.58	3.58
11 Oct.	46	46	−3	3	48.27	−4.54	4.54	49.97	−5.55	5.55
12 Nov.										
13 Dec.										
Average			0.10	6.50		0.649	5.933		2.147	6.633

[a]As a common starting point, the initial forecast was the same in all conditions.

level. Hence, biased forecasts will occur and will continue for some time. Such a situation may be detected quickly by means of a tracking signal. It has been the practice in many forecasting systems, particularly when run on a computer, to create deviation messages that invite manual intervention by people in charge of the system, when the tracking signal exceeds certain levels. Unfortunately, when forecasts are being made regularly for many items, it may not be operationally feasible for them to intervene effectively, owing to demands on their time, nor may it be economically justifiable to do so. Consequently, an adaptive exponential smoothing forecasting model was developed that would react automatically to system changes when the tracking signal showed that biased forecasts were occurring. In this section we present one such adaptive forecasting scheme which varies the response rate according to the value of a tracking signal.

PROCEDURE. The procedure we present was developed by Trigg and Leach (1967). The steps are as follows:

Step 1—Compute Smoothed Error. This is a measure of bias. That is,

$$\bar{E}_t = \gamma E_{t-1} + (1 - \gamma)\bar{E}_{t-1}, \tag{16.13}$$

where $\bar{E}_t$ = smoothed (forecasted) error

E_{t-1} = actual forecast error

$\bar{E}_{t-1}$ = last period's smoothed (forecasted) error

γ = another smoothing constant, $0 \leqslant \gamma \leqslant 1$.

Step 2—Compute Absolute Smoothed Error. This is a surrogate measure of forecast standard deviation.

$$\text{ABS}(\bar{E}_t) = \gamma\text{ABS}(E_{t-1}) + (1 - \gamma)\text{ABS}(\bar{E}_{t-1}), \tag{16.14}$$

where ABS denotes absolute value.

Step 3—Compute the Tracking Signal. This is the detection rule, which is similar to the statistical concept of the coefficient of variation—the mean divided by the standard deviation.

$$\text{TS} = \frac{\bar{E}_t}{\text{ABS}(\bar{E}_t)}, \tag{16.15}$$

where TS denotes the tracking signal. If the forecasting system is in control, the tracking signal will fluctuate around zero. If biased errors occur, the tracking signal will move toward ± 1, according to the direction of bias. Since $\bar{E}_t$ is always equal to or less than $\text{ABS}(\bar{E}_t)$, the limits on the tracking signal are

$$-1 \leqslant \text{TS} \leqslant +1$$

or

$$0 \leqslant \text{ABS(TS)} \leqslant 1.$$

Step 4—Compute the Smoothing Constant α. Set $\alpha = $ ABS(TS). The most obvious way for the system to react automatically when forecasts go out of control is to increase the value of α so as to give more weight to recent data and therefore more rapid "homing in" to the changed process. Once the system has "homed in," however, it becomes necessary to reduce the value of α again in order once more to filter out the noise. This is achieved by this step of setting α equal to the tracking signal. Note that α will change automatically from period to period, that is, each time a forecast is made. The value of TS (and hence α) is affected by both $\bar{E}_t$ and ABS($\bar{E}_t$). The larger $\bar{E}_t$ is relative to ABS($\bar{E}_t$), the larger is ABS(TS), and hence α, which in the limit approaches 1. The smaller $\bar{E}_t$ is relative to ABS($\bar{E}_t$), the smaller is ABS(TS), and hence α, which in the limit approaches zero. (What happens to α if we underforecast? If we overforecast?).

Step 5—Make Forecast Using Exponential Smoothing Model, Equation (16.4)

$$\bar{F}_t = \alpha D_{t-1} + (1 - \alpha)\bar{F}_{t-1}.$$

16.2.7. *Example—Clark Tools Inc.*

Let us now apply this five-step adaptive smoothing procedure to our problem of forecasting Handy sales for the month of February 1976. For convenience, let us start with $\gamma = 0.5$ and $\bar{E}_{t-1}$ initially equal to zero.

Step 1

$$\bar{E}_{Feb.} = \gamma E_{Jan.} + (1 -)\bar{E}_{Jan.}$$
$$= (0.5)(5) + (0.5)(0)$$
$$= 2.5.$$

Step 2

$$\text{ABS}(\bar{E}_{Feb.}) = (0.5)(5) + (0.5)(0)$$
$$= 2.5.$$

Step 3

$$\text{TS} = \frac{2.5}{2.5} = 1.$$

Step 4

$$\alpha = \text{ABS(TS)} = 1.$$

Step 5

$$\bar{F}_{Feb.} = \alpha D_{Jan.} + (1 - \alpha)\bar{F}_{Jan.}$$
$$= (1)(50) + (0)(45)$$
$$= 50.$$

The computations and forecasts for all the remaining months of 1976 are shown in Table 16.13. The results of these forecasts should be compared to the forecasts obtained using simple exponential smoothing in Tables 16.9 and 16.12; also compare the average forecast errors and average absolute forecast errors. A comparison of the adaptive smoothing forecasts (Table 16.13) and the simple exponential smoothing forecast using $\alpha = 0.2$ (Table 16.9) is shown in Figure 16.8.

The method presented is simple and expedient. If the process is stable then noise is filtered out as effectively as by the conventional exponential smoothing model with a fixed smoothing constant α. However, when the process is unstable or

Table 16.13. Handy Sales Forecasts for 1976 Made by Adaptive Exponential Smoothing ($\gamma = 0.5$, $E_{t-1} = 0$)

t Month	Actual Sales, D_t	Smoothed Sales Average, $\bar{F}t$	Sales Forecast, $\bar{F}_{t-1}$	Forecast Error, $D_t - \bar{F}_t$	Absolute Forecast Error, $|D_t - \bar{F}_t|$	Smoothing Constant, $\alpha = |TS|$	Smoothed Error, $\bar{E}_t$	Absolute Smoothed Error, $|\bar{E}_t|$
1 Dec.	46	45	—	—	—	—	0	
2 Jan.	50	50	45	5	5	1	2.50	2.50
3 Feb.	59	59.00	50	9	9	1	5.75	5.75
4 Mar.	57	52.90	59	−2	2	0.485	1.88	3.88
5 Apr.	55	54.20	52.90	2.10	2.10	0.670	1.99	2.99
6 May	64	63.33	54.20	9.80	9.80	0.920	5.895	6.395
7 June	55	61.97	63.33	−8.33	8.33	0.165	−1.218	7.363
8 July	61	61.10	61.97	−0.97	0.97	0.260	−1.094	4.167
9 Aug.	45	45.97	61.10	−16.10	16.10	0.940	−7.503	10.138
10 Sept.	49	47.00	45.97	3.03	3.03	0.340	−2.240	6.590
11 Oct.	46	46.57	47.00	−1.00	1.00	0.430	−1.620	3.800
12 Nov.			46.57					
13 Dec.								
			Average	0.53	5.733			

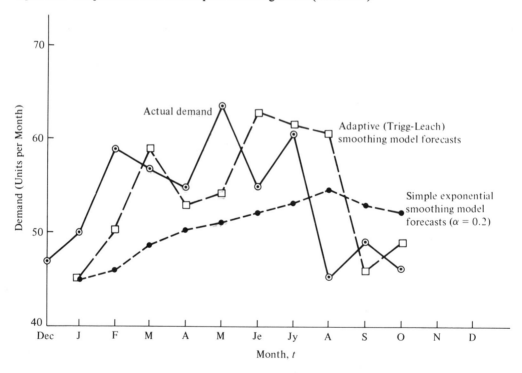

Figure 16.8. Comparison of fixed and adaptive smoothing models (Table 16.13).

subject to step responses, adaptation is much more rapid with an adaptive smoothing model.

Adaptive smoothing is relatively insensitive to the initial smoothing constant (α) used. It should, therefore, be sufficient to make only crude estimates of the coefficient α in this forecasting model. If widely in error, the tracking signal should tend quickly to high absolute values, and the system will adjust this value rapidly. Hence, this method obviates the dilemma of determining the optimal value of α. However, it does leave the problem of determining the best value of α to be used in calculating the tracking signal. The value of α chosen should be based on how rapid a response rate is desired.

16.2.8. Exponential Smoothing with Trend Adjustment

We shall now consider how to forecast by exponential smoothing when a trend is involved.

Step 1—Compute Current Apparent Trend. The apparent trend from period to period is simply defined as the difference in the average forecasts from period to period as computed from equation (16.4), that is, $\bar{F}_t - \bar{F}_{t-1}$. This difference is, of course, subject to noise and can be smoothed (forecast) using exponential smoothing just as we did with average demand using equation (16.4). The current apparent trend is just simply

$$\text{current apparent trend} = \bar{F}_t - \bar{F}_{t-1}. \tag{16.16}$$

Step 2—Compute the New Average Trend Adjustment $\bar{T}_t$. The forecast of trend is

$$\bar{T}_t = \omega(\text{current apparent trend}) + (1 - \omega)(\text{last trend adjustment})$$

$$= \omega(\bar{F}_t - \bar{F}_{t-1}) + (1 - \omega)\bar{T}_{t-1}. \tag{16.17}$$

Step 3—Compute Forecasted (Expected) Demand. The forecasted or expected demand, which now includes an adjustment for trend is, then, the new average forecast $\bar{F}_t$ as determined by equation (16.4) plus a fraction of the new average trend adjustment computed by equation (16.17); that is,

$$E(D_t) = \bar{F}_t + \frac{1 - \omega}{\omega} \bar{T}_t. \tag{16.18}$$

We will now use the Handy sales data to illustrate the methods for forecasting sales by exponential smoothing when a trend is involved, using the procedure above. Table 16.14 shows the results of the computations. Column 3 shows the exponentially smoothed forecast averages computed by equation (16.14). Column 4 gives the current apparent trend computed from equation (16.16). Column 5 shows the forecasted trend $\bar{T}_t$ computed from (16.17). Column 6 shows the forecasted demand adjusted for trend. The forecast without trend adjustment (column 3) and the forecast with trend adjustment (column 6) are graphed in Figure 16.9 in

Table 16.14. Computations of Smoothed Demand, Average Trend Adjustment, and Expected Demand ($\alpha = 0.2$, $T_{initial} = 0$, $\delta = 0.5$)

(1)	(2)	(3)	(4)	(5)	(6)	(7)	(8)
Date	Demand, D_t	Smoothed Demand, $F_t = \alpha D_{t-1} + (1-\alpha)F_{t-1}$	Current Apparent Trend, $F_t - F_{t-1}$	Smoothed Trend Adjustment, $T_t = \omega(F_t - F_{t-1}) + (1-\omega)T_{t-1}$	Expected Demand, $E(D_t) = F_t + \frac{1-\delta}{\delta}T_t$	Forecast Error, $FE = D_t - E(D_t)$	Absolute Forecast Error, $ABSFE = |D_t - E(D_t)|$
Dec. 1975							
Jan. 1976	50	45.0	0.0	0.00	45.00	5.00	5.00
Feb.	59	46.0	1.0	0.50	46.50	12.50	12.50
Mar.	57	48.6	2.6	1.55	50.15	6.85	6.85
Apr.	55	50.3	1.7	1.63	51.93	3.07	3.07
May	64	51.2	0.9	1.27	52.47	11.53	11.53
June	55	54.2	3.0	1.64	55.84	-0.84	0.84
July	61	53.4	-0.8	0.78	54.18	6.82	6.82
Aug.	45	54.9	1.5	1.14	56.04	-11.04	11.04
Sept.	49	52.9	-2.0	-0.43	52.47	-3.47	3.47
Oct.	46	52.1	-0.8	-0.62	51.48	-5.48	5.48
Nov.		50.8	-1.3	-0.96	49.84		
Dec.							
					Average	2.49	6.66

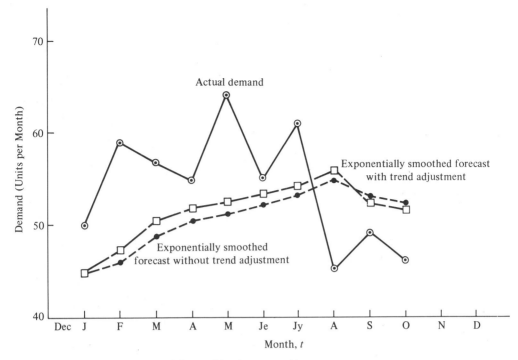

Figure 16.9. Comparison of exponential smoothing forecasts, with versus without a trend adjustment (Table 16.14).

relation to actual demand. Observe the smoothing effects of both these forecasts and also the effect of the trend adjustment in correcting for the lag in the simple exponential smoothing forecast. Note that the forecast average (without trend adjustment) lags the expected demand curve, being below it when the trend is positive and above it when the trend is negative.

The demand for some commodities can also exhibit seasonal effects for such obvious reasons as the weather, which may, for example, dominate the demand for bikini bathing suits. We will not discuss seasonal forecasting methods or the use of exponential smoothing in this context. Such methods for forecasting with a seasonality adjustment can be found in Brown (1959), Brown (1963), Montgomery and Johnson (1976), and Winters (1960). It should also be mentioned that exponential smoothing with trend and seasonal adjustments can easily be incorporated into an adaptive exponential smoothing model.

16.3. SUMMARY

This chapter has been divided into two topics: (1) inventory models under uncertainty and (2) forecasting models. In the first part of this chapter we have attempted to deal with the inventory problem under the more complex and realistic situation of demand and lead-time uncertainty. Thus, we first attempted to specify procedures that allowed us to develop a demand during lead-time distribution. A knowledge of the demand during lead-time distribution made it possible to prescribe safety (buffer) stock levels for specified stockout risk levels. The basic inventory model we developed was the fixed reorder point, fixed order quantity model (often called the *R, Q* model), of which there are several versions, depending upon the assumptions made about back orders and whether lots are produced externally or internally. There are a variety of other inventory models under uncertainty which are discussed in many of the references given at the end of the chapter.

The second half of the chapter was concerned with forecasting. We first defined the forecasting problem and then classified forecasting techniques into qualitative and quantitative models. We then focused on the statistical forecasting techniques of the moving average and exponential smoothing, with principal emphasis on the latter because it is simple, computationally efficient, and widely used. Exponential smoothing techniques covered included simple exponential smoothing (without trend adjustment), adaptive smoothing, and exponential smoothing with trend adjustment. Additional elaboration of these techniques and other methodologies may be found in Brown (1959), Brown (1963) and Montgomery and Johnson (1976).

REFERENCES   BROWN, R. G. *Statistical Forecasting for Inventory Control.* New York: McGraw-Hill Book Company, 1959.

BROWN, R. G. *Smoothing, Forecasting and Prediction.* Englewood Cliffs, N.J.: Prentice-Hall, Inc., 1963.

BUCHANAN, J. and E. KOENIGSBERG. *Scientific Inventory Management.* Englewood Cliffs, N.J.: Prentice-Hall, Inc., 1963.

CHAMBERS, J. C., K. M. SATINDER, and D. D. SMITH. "How to Choose the Right Forecasting Technique." *Harvard Business Review*, July–August 1971, 45–74.

FETTER, R. B., and N. C. DALLECK. *Decision Models for Inventory Management.* Homewood, Ill.: Richard D. Irwin, Inc., 1961.

GEOFFRION, A. M. "A Summary of Exponential Smoothing." *Journal of Industrial Engineering*, **13** (4), 1962.

HADLEY, G., and T. M. WHITIN. *Analysis of Inventory Systems.* Englewood Cliffs, N.J.: Prentice-Hall, Inc., 1963.

MONTGOMERY, D. C., and L. A. JOHNSON. *Forecasting and Time Series Analysis.* New York: McGraw-Hill Book Company, 1976.

MOSKOWITZ, H., R. E. SCHAEFER, and K. BORCHERDING. " 'Irrationality' of Managerial Judgments: Implications for Information Systems." *OMEGA*, **4** (2), 1976.

TRIGG, S. W. "Monitoring a Forecasting System." *Operational Research Quarterly*, **15**, 1964, 271–274.

TRIGG, D. W., and A. G. LEACH. "Exponential Smoothing with an Adaptive Response Rate." *Operations Research Quarterly*, March 1967, 53–59.

WINTERS, P. R. "Forecasting Sales by Exponentially Weighted Moving Averages." *Management Science*, **6** (3), 1960, 324–342.

KEY CONCEPTS

Inventory models under uncertainty
  demand during lead time
  reorder point
Probability of a stockout
  expected number of stockouts
RQ model

Forecasting
  qualitative models
  quantitative models (time-series and causal)
Moving average
Simple exponential smoothing
Adaptive smoothing
Exponential smoothing with trend adjustment

REVIEW QUESTIONS

16.1. Contrast the difference between determining Q^* and R^* when demand and lead time is certain versus uncertain in inventory models.

16.2. Contrast the difference between the objective functions for inventory models under certainty versus uncertainty.

16.3. Using data, state and show two different ways to determine the demand during lead-time distribution. If no historical data were available, how could you subjectively assess a demand during lead-time distribution? Develop an instrument for obtaining a demand during lead-time distribution by means of subjective probability assessment (see Chapter 5 and Case 5.2).

16.4. Describe and illustrate the trial-and-error solution procedure for determining Q^* and R^*.

16.5. State the optimal decision rules (formulas) for determining Q^* and R^*. Show how you would use them. Comment on the point that Q and R are interdependent.

16.6. State the differences in the R, Q model with back orders permitted versus back orders not permitted.

16.7. What do we mean by forecasting and what is the purpose of forecasting for management?

16.8. Define the forecasting problem. Discuss the following forecasting issues: (a) what is being forecast, (b) form of the forecast, (c) time elements involved, (d) forecast accuracy, and (e) additional factors.

16.9. Forecasting methods can be classified into two categories: (1) qualitative and (2) quantitative. Discuss the difference between these two approaches and describe several forecasting techniques that fit into each category.

16.10. Describe the differences between time series forecasting models and causal models.

16.11. What is a moving average? Describe how you would forecast using this procedure.

16.12. What is exponential smoothing? Show how you would make forecasts using the simple exponential smoothing model.

16.13. What are the advantages of exponential smoothing over the moving average, as a forecasting technique?

16.14. Comment on and verify the following statement: "Exponential smoothing assigns weights to all past data such that the weights monotonically decrease with increasing age."

16.15. Show how you would use simple exponential smoothing to predict the variance of a process.

16.16. State the equivalence relationship between the smoothing constant and size of moving average. How was this equivalence relationship derived?

16.17. What is adaptive exponential smoothing? State and illustrate how you would make forecasts using this procedure. What is different about this procedure from simple exponential smoothing?

16.18. State and illustrate the procedure of forecasting by exponential smoothing when a trend is involved.

16.19. Give some examples where seasonality must be taken into account in forecasting.

ANSWERS TO REVIEW QUESTIONS

16.1. When demand is known with certainty, determination of an optimal order quantity is straightforward. Total cost is the sum of holding and ordering costs; Q^* is that order quantity which minimizes total cost, and the reorder point is easily and independently calculated as the demand per day times the number of days lead time.

When demand and lead time are uncertain, a probability distribution of demand during lead time must be determined. The uncertainties cause an interaction between the order quantity and reorder point, which preclude their independent determination.

16.2. The objective function for certainty models differs from those for uncertainty models in two ways:

1. Uncertainty models use expected values—such as expected demand during lead time and expected number of stockouts—rather than deterministic values as in certainty models.
2. Uncertainty models include two decision variables in the objective function—Q and R—while certainty models only have one (Q).

16.3. One way to determine a demand during lead time distribution would be to first generate separate distributions for demand per unit time period and lead time, and then combine these distributions analytically—for example, by use of a tree diagram, assuming independence of the two distributions. A second way would be to count directly all lead times that have occurred along with the demands that actually were obtained during those time periods. This is a simpler, more direct method and does not assume independence between lead times and demand.

The demand during lead time distribution can be assessed subjectively (when no historical data is available), by means of the fractile method covered in Case 5.2. Assessments can be made either separately on the lead time and demand distribution, and then combined mathematically to obtain the DDLT, or they can be obtained by directly assessing the DDLT.

16.4. The trial-and-error solution procedure for determining Q^* and R^* has five steps.

1. Determine the demand distribution (subjectively or from past frequency data).
2. Determine the lead time distribution (subjectively or from past frequency data).
3. Determine the demand during lead time distribution using the above two distributions with a probability tree.
4. Determine the expected number of stockouts for each possible reorder point by calculating the expected value of demand greater than the reorder point.
5. Determine an optimal Q by trial and error iterations to find a pair which minimizes expected total cost.

16.5. The optimal decision rules for determining Q^* and R^* are:

$$Q^* = \sqrt{\frac{2E(D)[c_p + c_S E(S)]}{c_h}} \qquad p(S)^* = \frac{c_h Q}{c_s E(D)}$$

where Q^* is the optimal order quantity and $p(S)$ is the probability of a stockout.

To use these rules, one should use an iterative trial and error procedure. First, assume an R^* which in turn determines $E(S)$, enabling us to solve for Q^* in the first equation. Q^* determines $p(S)$ and also a new R^*. R^* can then be used to solve for Q^*, and so on, until the solutions stabilize.

Since both $E(S)$ and $p(S)$ depend on R, both equations show a relationship between Q and R and any solution must satisfy both equations.

16.6. If backorders are not permitted, then $E(S)$ must be 0 (zero), and the formula for optimal Q reduces to

$$Q^* = \sqrt{\frac{2E(D) \cdot [c_p + (c_s - c) \cdot E(S)]}{c_h}}$$

$$P(S^*) = \frac{c_h Q}{E(D)(c_s - c) + c_h Q}$$

16.7. Forecasting is predicting unknown (usually future) events. Forecasts provide the input information for the decision-making process. From a decision theoretic viewpoint, forecasts can be viewed as predictions of the state of nature or consequences that will occur, manifested in terms of either a point estimate (most likely value, mean, median, and so on) or a probability distribution. The purpose of forecasting is to reduce the risk in decision making.

16.8. The forecasting problem is determining the best way to provide information about unknown events to be used as input information to improve the decision-making process. Forecasting issues include:

1. What is being forecast—the definitions of the uncertain quantities to be predicted.
2. The form of the forecast—should the forecast be in the form of a probability distribution or some summary statistics, such as the mean and variance?
3. The time elements involved, including forecasting period, forecasting horizon, and forecasting interval. The three are, respectively, the unit of time for which forecasts are made, the number of periods in the future covered by the forecast, and the frequency with which new forecasts are to be prepared.
4. Forecast accuracy, which depends on the nature of the decision problem and the economics of generating a forecast (i.e., value of the information).
5. Additional factors, which include whether the process being studied is static or dynamic and how available, accurate, timely, and representative are the data.

16.9. Qualitative forecasts involve subjective estimation and are primarily used when data are scarce, unavailable, or costly—for example, when a new product is first introduced into a market. Such procedures employ human judgment and rating schemes to transform qualitative information into quantitative estimates. Techniques are often implemented through expert opinion polls, discussion groups, and the Delphi procedure.

Quantitative or statistical forecasting procedures are mathematical techniques relying on historical data which are used to forecast. Some such techniques are trend projections, moving averages, exponential smoothing and regression.

16.10. Time series models rely on historical data and focus on data patterns and data pattern changes. These techniques are used when past data are available and usually when relationships and trends are relatively clear and stable.

Causal models attempt to define relationships among system elements, also using past data. These models attempt to describe explicitly the relationships between the uncertain quantity to be forecast and other factors (causal variables). The purpose of a causal model is to: (1) predict and (2) describe the underlying process.

16.11. A moving average is a forecast based on an arithmetic or weighted average of a number of the most recent data points of a series. The number of data points chosen depends on the presumed stability of the process generating the data. To forecast using a moving average, simply follow the above procedure; then, in the next time period, add the most recent and drop the oldest datum, then calculate the average with this new set of points.

16.12. Exponential smoothing is similar to the moving average, except that more recent data points are exponentially given more weight. To make a forecast using this technique, simply take the previous forecast and add a fraction of the difference between the most recent datum and forecast. The magnitude of the fraction or smoothing constant indicates how much weight is being placed on the most recent observations. A value close to 1 indicates considerable reliance on the most recent data; a value close to 0 indicates little reliance.

16.13. The advantages of exponential smoothing over a moving average include: (1) with exponential smoothing, more recent data are weighted more heavily than older data; (2) with exponential smoothing all past data are used in the forecast, and (3) exponential smoothing is computationally simpler since only the most recent observation and the previous forecast are needed to make a forecast.

16.14. The exponential smoothing model forecasts by forming a weighted average of the most recent data point and the previous forecast. However, the previous forecast was formed from the second most recent observation and an earlier forecast, and so on. The net effect is to include all past data points into the current forecast as a weighted average. Moreover, a data point which is one period older than another will have a weight $(1 - \alpha)$ times the other. Since α is between 0 and 1, $(1 - \alpha)$ will also be between 0 and 1, and the older data point's weight will thus be smaller than the more recent weight in an exponential manner.

16.15. To estimate the variance of a process, one could simply keep a running sum of the forecast errors squared or absolute forecast errors, interpreting their mean as an estimate of the variance of the process. Alternatively, one could use exponential smoothing to estimate the variance, where a forecast of the variance would be made as a weighted sum of last period's forecast error squared and last period's forecast of the variance.

16.16. For the smoothing constant and the size of moving average to be approximately equivalent, the smoothing constant, α, should be equal to $2/(n + 1)$. The equivalence relationship is derived by calculating the expected age of a moving average set of data (n) and an exponential smoothing set in terms of α, and by setting the two expressions equal.

16.17. Adaptive exponential smoothing varies the smoothing constant alpha according to the extent to which biased forecasts are made. To implement this procedure, a "tracking signal" is used to detect biased forecasts, which indicates a change in the underlying process. One such procedure described in this chapter involves the following four steps:

1. Computing the smoothed error as a weighted average of all past forecast errors.
2. Computing the absolute smoothed error, which is a weighted average of the absolute value of all past forecast errors.
3. Computing the tracking signal, which is the smoothed error divided by the absolute smoothed error.
4. Setting the smoothing constant to the absolute value of the tracking signal.

Adaptive exponential smoothing models react quickly to changes in the process while they still retain the ability to provide a high degree of precision.

16.18. Exponential smoothing with a trend adjustment involves three steps:

1. Computing the current apparent trend, which is the difference in the average forecasts from period to period.
2. Computing the new average trend adjustment, which is a weighted average of all past and current apparent trends.
3. Computing the forecasted variable, which will be the new forecast (from the basic model) plus a fraction of the new average trend adjustment.

16.19. Seasonality would be important in sales of Christmas toys, winter sports equipment, bathing suits; predictions of energy usage by consumers; and use of vacation accommodations in resort areas.

EXERCISES **16.1.** Given a lead time of 20 working days for a particular article and a usage rate of 1000 pieces per working day, what would be the reorder point? Assume that the order quantity is 80,000 pieces and the minimum inventory is 10,000 pieces.

16.2. Average reorder time for the Carter Peanut Company is 5 days. Average use per day is 20 units. Following are facts about use during the reorder period.

Usage During Past Reorder Period	Number of Times This Quantity Was Used
70	3
80	5
90	22
100	60
110	6
120	4

The optimum number of orders is 5 per year. If the stockout cost per unit is $50 and the carrying charge per unit per year of safety stock is $15, what level of safety stock should be carried?

16.3. An item is sold at the rate of 10 per day, with a paperwork cost of ordering of $20 per order. There is a carrying charge of 4 cents per day per unit in inventory.

(a) Compute the economic order size for this item.
(b) What would the total incremental cost be for this economic order quantity?
(c) If a safety stock is used to take care of variations in demand and supply time, what should its size be if we desire to run out no more than 10% of the days we operate, given the chart below?
(d) Diagram the inventory level through at least two cycles. Label the diagram, including both axes with dimensions.
(e) What will our average inventory level be?
(f) How often would orders of this size be placed?
(g) What would be the total cost to the firm per unit of the product for this optimum quantity?
(h) If the order quantity were reduced to one-half of that suggested by the formula, what would be the cost per unit?
(i) If the order quantity were doubled, what would be the cost per unit?
(j) What conclusion can you draw from these data with regard to the sensitivity of the order quantity?

Daily Demand	Days that Demand Exceeds a Given Level (%)
4	100
5	95
6	90
7	85
8	80
9	60
10	50
11	40
12	30
13	20
14	10
15	5
16	0

16.4. The High Cost Inventory Company desires to reduce inventory costs. Its demand has been determined to be normally distributed with a mean value of 20 per day with a standard deviation of 1. The time lag between ordering and receiving is 4 days.

(a) What reorder level should they use if they desire to incur back orders 50% of the time?
(b) Draw a diagram showing the inventory level over a period of several reordering cycles for the company.
(c) If holding costs increase relative to back-order costs, should the reorder level change and in what direction?

16.5. The Thompson Co. uses a fixed-order-quantity inventory system. The company's inventory analyst is currently facing the problem of determining the inventory rules for a 3-inch spiral gear. The reorder quantity has already been computed; consequently, the number of reorder cycles per year is determined. What remains to be done is to set the reorder point. The cost of shortages is $10; that is, this is the cost of loss incurred for each unit demanded when there is no stock available. The cost of carrying inventory during one reorder cycle is $2 per unit. You are to assist in determining the optimum reorder point. Both demand and lead time are uncertain, but they are independent. Their distribution is given below.

DEMAND DISTRIBUTION		LEAD-TIME DISTRIBUTION	
Probability	Demand/Week	Probability	Weeks
0.4	5	0.3	1
0.6	10	0.7	2

(a) What is the distribution of demand over the lead-time period? (That is, what distribution of demand is anticipated between the time an order is placed and the time it is received?)
(b) Given the distribution of demand over the lead time (as calculated above), what is the expected value of the penalty cost if the reorder point is set at 5 units? 10 units? 15 units?
(c) Which is the preferred reorder point (i.e., the inventory that should be on hand when an order is placed)—5, 10 or 15 units?

16.6. Determine an optimal inventory policy, consisting of an economic lot size (Q) and a reorder point (R), using the following information:

Annual sales:	325 units/year
Ordering cost:	$20/order
Inventory carrying cost:	$2 /unit
Shortage cost:	$20/unit

Sales per Day

Units	Probability
0	0.40
1	0.30
2	0.20
3	0.10

Production Lead Time (days)

Days	Probability
1	0.25
2	0.50
3	0.25

Distribution of Sales During the Replenishment Lead Time

Units	Probability	Units	Probability
0	0.1960	5	0.0477
1	0.2310	6	0.0190
2	0.2260	7	—
3	0.1797	8	—
4	0.0935	9	—

(a) Assume that the inventory level is monitored continuously.

(b) Assume 325 working days/year.

(c) Assume that lost sales are not backordered.

16.7. A firm using the classical EOQ formula has determined that six orders should be placed per year for its raw material and will use a safety stock of 1 unit based on the following distribution of demand during the reorder lead-time period:

Usage During Lead-Time Period	Frequency of Occurrence
5	0.05
6	0.10
7	0.05
8	0.50
9	0.20
10	0.10

The inventory carrying charge per unit per year is $12.

(a) What is the reorder point?

(b) What is the expected number of stockouts?

(c) What is the probability of a stockout?

(d) What is the implicit stockout cost per unit that management has assumed in its choice of safety stock?

16.8. Two methods of short-term forecasting are the moving average and exponential smoothing.

(a) What are the advantages of exponential smoothing over the moving average?

(b) If old forecast = 2000, $\alpha = 0.20$, and actual demand last period = 1800, what is the new forecast for the next period using single exponential smoothing?

(c) What size of α should be chosen when a process is unstable?

16.9. The inventory control manager at the HIJ Company is presently considering the use of an exponential smoothing model to forecast the demand for a single product. He has provided the quarterly record of demand for the product shown in the tables on page 666.

(a) Prepare a one-period-in-advance sales forecast for each quarter in 1979 using a simple exponential smoothing model (without trend and seasonal adjustments) and a smoothing constant of 0.1. [You may assume that the sales average (average sales per quarter at the end of 1979) to be 175 units.] Use the table below to summarize and present the results of your calculations.[†]

Quarter	1979 Demand	Forecast ($\alpha = 0.1$)	Forecast Error (Demand Forecast)	Forecast Mean Absolute Deviation (MAD)[‡]
1	207	_____	_____	_____
2	179	_____	_____	_____
3	197	_____	_____	_____
4	232	_____	_____	_____
		Totals	_____	_____

(b) Do the same using a smoothing constant of 0.9.

Quarter	1979 Demand	Forecast ($\alpha = 0.9$)	Forecast Error (Demand Forecast)	Forecast Mean Absolute Deviation (MAD)
1	207	_____	_____	_____
2	179	_____	_____	_____
3	197	_____	_____	_____
4	232	_____	_____	_____
		Totals	_____	_____

(c) The inventory control manager is concerned about what smoothing-constant value to use. As an alternative to a smoothing-constant value of 0.1, he considered a value of 0.9. Please specify a criterion for deciding between the smoothing-constant values of 0.1 and 0.9. Why did you pick this particular criterion? Now contrast the results in (a) and (b) and choose one of these two smoothing constants.

[†]You may round off your forecasts to the nearest whole number (integer).
[‡]MAD is a surrogate for forecast error standard deviation.

16.10. Tom Hormone, the inventory control manager at the High Products Company, is considering using exponential smoothing to forecast sales for the products stored in the firm's warehouse. He has prepared the following data to try out exponential smoothing on one product—the widget:

Week Number:	2	3	4	5	6
Sales (units)	106	118	104	80	98
Smoothed sales average	—	—	—	—	—
Forecast error	—	—	—	—	—

Tom decided to use a smoothing constant of $\alpha = 0.5$ in his evaluation. He estimated the sales average at the end of week 1 to be 95 units.

(a) Fill in the table above and prepare a forecast for the sales in week 7. Also estimate the mean and standard deviation of the forecast errors:

sales forecast for week 7 = _____

mean forecast error = _____

forecast error standard
deviation = _____ .

(b) Consider the smoothed sales average at the end of week 6. How much weight is placed on the sales in weeks 4, 5, and 6 and on the weighted average at the end of week 3 in calculating the smoothed average at the end of week 6?

weight placed on sales in week 4 = _____

weight placed on sales in week 5 = _____

weight placed on sales in week 6 = _____

weight placed on the smoothed average
at the end of week 3 = _____ .

16.11. Simulate the forecasts one period ahead for the following time series, using a simple exponential smoothing model and the Trigg–Leach adaptive smoothing model (Trigg and Leach, 1967).

Period	1	2	3	4	5	6	7	8	9	10	11	12
Time Series	10	20	20	20	20	10	20	10	20	10	10	10

Use the following beginning estimates and parameter values: initial forecast = 10, $\gamma = 0.1$, and $\bar{E}_0 = 0$. You might plot the time series and forecasts to gain an understanding of their performance. Compute the mean absolute deviation (MAD) for both forecasts for the series.

Illustrative Case Study
Involving an Inventory Problem Using the R, Q Model

THE MUDVILLE MAULERS: INVENTORY MANAGEMENT OF BASEBALLS

The Mudville Maulers, a baseball team in the Bottom-of-the-Barrel League, were faced with the problem of supplying baseballs for their games. Manager Pinkie Tucarera was in the habit of ordering 10 new balls before every Tuesday's game. The team lost at most three balls a game, since the team batting average was 0.120 and slugger Stan Brughanship was out for the season after breaking his ankle while doing a TV commercial.

Each Tuesday Pinkie would send batboy, Alphons Schlantz, downtown to the sporting goods store to buy 10 new balls. This ended up costing the team $2. Alphons would get lost every time and show up either Wednesday or Thursday. (The $2 was so Alphons could eat during his trip.)

A decree from League Commissioner Angelo Cappazello levied a fine of $8 on every ball Mudville had to borrow from the other team in case they ran out, so it actually cost $10 for each of these balls. Also, Angelo required that all league balls be kept in his exclusive baseball warehouse so that no tampering or doctoring of the balls would occur. The charge was $2 per ball.

The data in the table below represent the history of baseball usage through the first 25 games of the season. The Maulers play 5 games per week through a 50-week season, so they expect to use a total of 450 balls.

The projected cost of the present system is at least $2(50) + $2(5) = $110. Pinkie thinks that this can be reduced. Do you?

Game	Number of Balls on Hand Before Game	Alphons Returns	Balls Lost in Game	Number of Balls On Hand After Game
1	3	0	1	2
a2	2	0	1	1
3	1	10	2	9
4	9	0	2	7
5	7	0	3	4
6	4	0	1	3
a7	3	0	2	1
8	1	10	1	10
9	10	0	2	8
10	8	0	2	6
11	6	0	2	4
a12	4	0	1	3
13	3	0	2	1
14	1	10	1	10
15	10	0	3	7
16	7	0	2	5
a17	5	0	1	4
18	4	10	2	12
19	12	0	3	9
20	9	0	2	7
21	7	0	2	5
a22	5	0	1	4
23	4	0	2	2
24	2	10	1	11
25	11	0	3	8

aOrder placed.

Illustrative Case Study
Involving Forecasting by Exponential Smoothing

JAYNES & CO.:
PREDICTING
SHOP DEMAND

Mr. Tabor, the president of Jaynes & Co., was very dejected as he reviewed the financial statements for the past period. Wages, overtime, and idle time in his production process were taking huge bites out of profits.

After talking with his general foreman, Tabor found that the foreman had no idea of what to expect in terms of demand in his shop. Whenever an upswing in demand came along he would have to authorize overtime until he could find new workers to hire. About the time new hirees became productive, the demand would fall off and there would be no work for new as well as old workers.

Tabor decided that there must be some way of forecasting future demand so that these swings in demand would not result in the tremendous expenses of the past. He asked one of his new employees to experiment with the data shown in the table and see if he could find a model that would make reasonable forecasts at a minimal cost. He suggested use of (1) simple exponential smoothing, (2) exponential smoothing with trends, and (3) adaptive exponential smoothing. Tabor also wanted to know if there was any trend in the data that would help him with his long-range planning.

Questions

1. Given these data, what α gives the best forecast?
2. Which of the three models gives the best predictions?
3. What kind of trend is the company experiencing?

Data Item	Demand	Data Item	Demand	Data Item	Demand	Data Item	Demand
1	80	13	76	25	44	37	26
2	95	14	75	26	75	38	48
3	110	15	100	27	91	39	80
4	118	16	136	28	100	40	108
5	157	17	143	29	115	41	127
6	176	18	148	30	108	42	134
7	182	19	122	31	113	43	126
8	154	20	102	32	104	44	105
9	120	21	76	33	70	45	79
10	85	22	56	34	56	46	41
11	63	23	38	35	36	47	6
12	60	24	32	36	15	48	4

16A.1. ALTERNATIVE METHODS FOR DETERMINING DDLT DISTRIBUTION

We can compute the demand during lead-time distribution directly from Table 16.1 by observing demand in each lead-time period. For example, demand during the first lead-time period is 4; demand in the second lead-time period is 3, and so forth. The resulting demand during lead-time distribution is shown in the table below. This distribution, however, differs considerably from that in Table 16.4. There are several reasons for this. First, the sample size for obtaining the latter distribution is smaller than that of the former procedure (10 versus 20 in our example). Hence, the direct approach would tend to be less accurate for small sample sizes (i.e., only a small amount of data was available). Second, the first procedure assumes that demand and lead time are independent. If this assumption were not true, then this demand during lead-time distribution would have been inaccurately computed. The direct approach makes no such assumption. Which procedure one uses to determine the demand during lead-time distribution depends on data availability and the independence assumption. Realistically, it would be wise to use both procedures as a crosscheck. If standard density functions are assumed for demand and lead time, the demand during lead-time distribution could be obtained analytically. If empirical distributions are available and calculations are too tedious, Monte Carlo simulation can be used.

DDLT	Frequency	P(DDLT)
0	0	0.0
1	2	0.2
2	3	0.3
3	3	0.3
4	2	0.2
	$\overline{10}$	$\overline{1.0}$

16A.2. DERIVATION OF Q* AND R* FOR FIXED ORDER QUANTITY AND REORDER POINT MODEL UNDER UNCERTAINTY

16A.2.1. No Lost Back Orders

First express total expected cost as follows:

$$\text{TEC} = cE(D) + c_p \frac{E(D)}{Q} + c_h \left[\frac{Q}{2} + R - E(\text{DDLT}) \right] + c_s \left[E(S) \frac{E(D)}{Q} \right].$$

Taking partial derivatives of the total-expected-cost expression with respect to Q and R, respectively, and setting the results equal to zero, we obtain the following:

$$\frac{\partial \text{TEC}}{\partial Q} = \frac{-c_p E(D)}{Q^2} + \frac{c_h}{2} - \frac{c_s E(S)E(D)}{Q^2} = 0,$$

which gives

$$Q^* = \sqrt{\frac{2E(D)\left[c_p + c_s E(S)\right]}{c_h}}.$$

$$\frac{\partial \text{TEC}}{\partial R} = c_h - \frac{c_s E(D)}{Q} \sum_{\text{DDLT}=R+1}^{\infty} p(\text{DDLT}) = 0,$$

since

$$\frac{d[E(S)]}{dR} = \frac{d\left[\displaystyle\sum_{\text{DDLT}=R+1}^{\infty} (\text{DDLT} - R)p(\text{DDLT})\right]}{dR}$$

$$= -\sum_{\text{DDLT}=R+1}^{\infty} p(\text{DDLT}) = p(S).$$

Hence,

$$p(S^*) = \frac{c_h Q}{c_s E(D)}.$$

Recall, that in the development of the total-expected-cost expression we have assumed purchased lots and that back orders are not lost. Let us now assume that back orders are lost (also purchased lots) and see how this affects the decision rules for Q^* and R^*.

16A.2.2. Lost Back Orders

When back orders are lost, total expected sales are less than total expected demand by the expected number of stockouts during a reorder period times the number of reorder periods, or approximately $[E(D)]E(S)/Q$. Then, the total expected cost expression becomes approximately

$$\text{TEC} = \left[E(D) - \frac{E(D)}{Q} \cdot E(S)\right]c + \frac{E(D)}{Q}\left[c_p + c_s E(S)\right]$$

$$+ c_h\left[\frac{Q}{2} + R - E(\text{DDLT}) + E(S)\right].$$

Note that the average inventory level is higher by the amount $E(S)$ when back orders are lost, since the average usage during the demand-during-lead-time period is decreased by the expected amount of lost sales. In other words, when the new order Q arrives, inventory on hand increases by the full amount Q rather than by Q less the items needed to fill back orders [which is equal to $E(S)$]. Taking partial derivatives of the TEC expression with respect to Q and R and setting these equal to zero gives

$$\frac{\partial \text{TEC}}{\partial Q} = \frac{cE(D)}{Q^2}E(S) - \frac{E(D)}{Q^2}\big[c_p + c_s E(S)\big] + \frac{c_h}{2} = 0,$$

which gives

$$Q^* = \sqrt{\frac{2E(D)\big[c_p + (c_s - c)E(S)\big]}{c_h}}$$

$$\frac{\partial \text{TEC}}{\partial R} = \frac{-c \cdot E(D)}{Q}\left(-\sum_{\text{DDLT}=R+1}^{\infty} p(\text{DDLT})\right) + \frac{E(D)\cdot c_s}{Q}\left(-\sum_{\text{DDLT}=R+1}^{\infty} p(\text{DDLT})\right)$$

$$+ c_h + c_h\left(-\sum_{\text{DDLT}=R+1}^{\infty} p(\text{DDLT})\right) = 0$$

$$p(S^*) = \frac{c_h Q}{E(D)(c_s - c) + c_h Q}.$$

CHAPTER 17
Queueing Models and Simulation

OBJECTIVES: Upon successful completion of this chapter, you should be able to:

1. Explain the assumptions of a single server Poisson queueing system.
2. Apply the formulas for a single source and single/multiple server Poisson queueing system.
3. Understand some of the basic techniques used in a simulation analysis.
4. Apply simulation analysis to some important business problems.
5. Use a table of random numbers to generate observations for stochastic variables.

17.1. INTRODUCTION TO QUEUEING MODELS

The effort of A. K. Erlang in 1909 to analyze telephone traffic congestion with the objective of meeting *uncertain* demand for services at the Copenhagen telephone system resulted in a new theory called *queueing* or *waiting-line* theory. This theory is now a valuable tool in business because many business problems can be characterized as arrival–departure congestion problems.

In queueing systems the term *customers* is used to refer to:

People *waiting* for open telephone lines.
Machines *waiting* to be repaired.
Airplanes *waiting* to land.
People *waiting* in a checkout line at a grocery store; and so forth.

The term *service facilities* is used in queueing systems, referring to:

Telephone lines.
Repair shops.
Airport runways.
Checkout counters; and so forth.

Queueing systems also often involve a *variable rate of arrivals* and a *variable rate of service*. For example,

The demand (or arrival rate) at a telephone exchange is 60 per minute.

Machines breakdown (or arrive at a repair facility) at a rate of 3 per week or 15 per month.

Airplanes arrive (require a runway) between 6:00 P.M. and 7:00 P.M. at a rate of 1 per minute.

Customers arrive at a checkout counter at the rate of 25 per hour.

Examples of service rates could be the following:

A telephone system between two cities can handle 90 calls per minute.

A repair facility can, on the average, repair machines at the rate of 4 per day (or four per 8 hours).

An airport runway can handle (land) two planes per minute (or one every 30 seconds, or 120 per hour).

On the average, a checkout counter can process one customer every 4 minutes.

Congestion in waiting lines can be created by customers waiting in line because there are too many customers arriving for service at inadequate service facilities. That is, more often than not, the arrival rate exceeds the service rate. This causes waiting lines (or queues) to form, resulting in some customers leaving and thus, for some systems, loss of revenue. Service facilities may be empty (waiting for customers) because of too many service facilities and/or existing facilities may have a total service rate in excess of the rate of demand (or rate of arrivals). Thus, the system is overcapacitated.

The more ideal situation is when service facilities are only waiting temporarily for customers and customers are waiting only temporarily for service. This case typifies a "balanced system" tending toward an equilibrium or stable system. In summary, what is sometimes called critical to a queueing (or waiting line) problem is a *trade-off decision*: *comparing* the cost of providing a level of service (for example, 10 telephone lines, 15 repairmen, 4 runways, 9 checkout counters, and so forth) with the cost of waiting (dissatisfied customers, down production lines, loss of revenue, and so forth).

17.1.1. Queueing-System Characteristics

A queueing system is comprised of a set of physical units operating in unison. First, queueing analysis involves understanding the behavior of the system by first predicting the behavior of the system. Next, using these predictions, queueing analysis involves studying the balance between the costs of customers waiting for service and the costs of service facilities.

There is a large variety of queueing systems (models). Some of the more standard systems are illustrated in Figures 17.1, 17.2, and 17.3, where the symbol "0" denotes a customer.

Figure 17.1. Single server model.

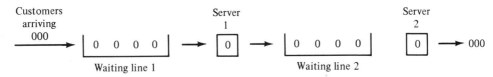

Figure 17.2. Multiserver multiqueue single channel queueing system.

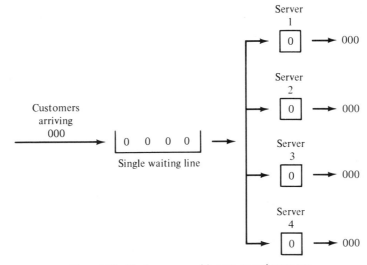

Figure 17.3. Single queue multiserver queueing system.

17.2. SINGLE-SERVER POISSON QUEUEING SYSTEM

In single-server Poisson queueing systems, the following assumptions are made with respect to the rate of customer arrivals and the rate of customer service.

Assumption 1 *Arrival of Customers*: We assume that customers arrive according to a Poisson distribution. That is, let

$$A = \text{number of customers arriving in a specified time interval.}$$

Then

$$P\{A = n\} = \frac{e^{-\lambda}\lambda^n}{n!}, \qquad (n = 0, 1, \ldots,)$$

where λ is the expected (or average) arrival rate in the specified time interval.

The assumption that customers arrive for service according to a Poisson distribution implies the following:

> Arrivals occur "randomly." The probability of an arrival during a specified time interval remains constant and independent of the number of previous arrivals and the length of the waiting time.

QUESTION. Suppose that the expected arrival rate is 3 per minute, $\lambda = 3$. What is the *expected time between arrivals* of individual customers?

Answer. If on the average customers arrive at a rate of 3 per minute, the average (or expected) time between arrivals is $1/\lambda = \frac{1}{3}$ minute, or 20 seconds between customers. Thus, if λ is the expected (or average) arrival rate, $1/\lambda$ is the expected time between two successive arrivals.

Assumption 2 *Queueing Discipline*: We are assuming that when a customer arrives at the system the service rule is *first come, first served*. We also assume that no customer will depart from the system before he receives service.

Assumption 3 *Number of Servers*: We assume that there is one server in the system.

Assumption 4 *Service Distribution*: The service time is assumed to follow the negative exponential distribution. That is, let S be the service time for a typical customer. Then

$$P\{S \leqslant t\} = 1 - e^{-t/\mu} \qquad (\text{for } t \geqslant 0),$$

where μ = expected (or average) service rate.

QUESTION. Suppose that service can be performed at an expected rate of $\mu = 4$ per minute. What is the expected time between completion of two successive services?

Answer. Since the rate of service is on the average $\mu = 4$ per minute, the *expected time* between two successive services is $1/\mu = \frac{1}{4}$ minute, or 15 seconds.

There are a number of important statistics that are useful in evaluating a queueing system. First, can the single server handle the demand? By comparing λ the mean arrival rate (per unit of time) with μ the mean service rate per unit of time as given below,

$$U = \frac{\lambda}{\mu} \qquad \text{(utilization factor)}$$

yields a measure of utilization for the system called the *utilization factor*. If $\lambda \geqslant \mu$, that is, $U > 1$, we would expect the system to be overcongested more often than not. If $\lambda < \mu$, that is, $U < 1$, we would not expect the system to be congested, more often than not.

For example, if $\lambda = 30$ per hour and $\mu = 40$ per hour, utilization $U = \lambda/\mu = \frac{30}{40} = 0.75$. Thus, we would expect the server to be busy 75% of the time.

QUESTION. Given that the arrival rate is $\lambda = 30$ per hour and the average rate of service is 40 per hour, what is the probability that an arriving customer will not have to wait for service?

Answer. Let $P_0 =$ probability that an arriving customer will not have to wait for service. That is, P_0 is the probability that the system is empty. Then it can be shown that

$$P_0 = 1 - U$$
$$= 1 - \frac{\lambda}{\mu}.$$

Thus, if $\lambda = 30$ per hour and $\mu = 40$ per hour, then

$$P_0 = 1 - \frac{30}{40}$$
$$= 0.25.$$

Thus, on the average, the system will be empty 25% of the time. The definition of the probability P_0 suggests the following additional probabilities.

Let P_n be the probability that there are n customers in the system (in queue plus being serviced). Then it can be shown that

$$P_n = P_{n-1} \cdot U \qquad (n = 1, \ldots)$$
$$= P_0 U^n$$
$$= (1 - U)U^n$$
$$= \left(1 - \frac{\lambda}{\mu}\right)\left(\frac{\lambda}{\mu}\right)^n.$$

QUESTION. Given that the arrival rate is 30 per hour and given that the average rate of service is 40 per hour, what is the probability that there are 0, 1, 2, 3, and 4 customers in the system (in queue plus being serviced)?

Answer. $\lambda = 30$ and $\mu = 40$. Thus, $U = \frac{30}{40} = 0.75$ and

$$P_0 = 1 - U = 0.25$$
$$P_1 = (1 - U)U^1 = (0.25)(0.75) = 0.1875$$
$$P_2 = (1 - U)U^2 = (0.25)(0.75)^2 = 0.1406$$
$$P_3 = (1 - U)U^3 = (0.25)(0.75)^3 = 0.1055$$
$$P_4 = (1 - U)U^4 = (0.25)(0.75)^4 = 0.0791.$$

Several other important statistics describing the behavior of the single-server Poisson queueing system are given below.

$E(N)$ = mean (or expected or average) number of customers in the system—both waiting and in service

$$= \frac{U}{1 - U} = \frac{\lambda/\mu}{1 - \lambda/\mu} = \frac{\lambda}{\mu - \lambda} \checkmark$$

$E(L)$ = mean (or expected or average) length of the waiting line (not including the customer in service)

$$= \frac{\lambda^2}{\mu(\mu - \lambda)}$$

$E(W)$ = mean (or expected or average) waiting time of an arrival in the queue

$$= \frac{\lambda}{\mu(\mu - \lambda)}$$

$E(T)$ = average time an arrival spends in the system

$$= \frac{1}{\mu - \lambda}.$$

QUESTION. Given $\lambda = 30$ per hour and $\mu = 40$ per hour, what are $E(N)$, $E(L)$, $E(W)$, and $E(T)$?

Answer

$E(N)$ = average number of customers in the system

$$= \frac{\lambda}{\mu - \lambda} = \frac{30}{40 - 30} = 3 \text{ customers}$$

$E(L)$ = average number of customers in the waiting line

$$= \frac{\lambda^2}{\mu(\mu - \lambda)} = \frac{(30)^2}{40(40 - 30)} = 2.25 \text{ customers}$$

$E(W)$ = average waiting time in the queue

$$= \frac{\lambda}{\mu(\mu - \lambda)} = \frac{30}{40(40 - 30)} = 0.075 \text{ hour} \quad \text{or} \quad 4.5 \text{ minutes}$$

$E(T)$ = average waiting time in the system

$$= \frac{1}{\mu - \lambda} = \frac{1}{40 - 30} = 0.1 \text{ hour} \quad \text{or} \quad 6 \text{ minutes}.$$

17.2.2. Example—Determining the Number of Waiters

The Nebraska Steak House is faced with the problem of determining the number of waiters to use during rush hours.

Management has observed that customers arrive on the average every 4 minutes and the average time to take and process an order is 2 minutes. Also, it has been observed that the pattern of the number of arrivals A follows the Poisson distribution and that the service times (or order processing times) follow the negative exponential distribution with a mean of $\frac{1}{2}$. Thus,

$$\lambda = \text{arrival rate per minute}$$
$$= \tfrac{1}{4} = 0.25 = \tfrac{1}{4} \text{ customer per minute}$$
$$\mu = \text{service rate per minute}$$
$$= \tfrac{1}{2} = 0.50 \qquad \left(\text{service } \tfrac{1}{2} \text{ customer per minute}\right)$$
$$P\{A = n\} = \frac{e^{-0.25}(0.25)^n}{n!} \qquad (n = 0, 1, \dots)$$
$$P\{T \leqslant t\} = 1 - e^{2t} \qquad (t \geqslant 0).$$

QUESTION 1. What is the present utilization for the existing service capacity?

Answer $\qquad U$ = utilization

$$= \frac{\lambda}{\mu} = \frac{0.25}{0.50} = 0.50 \quad \text{or} \quad 50\%.$$

QUESTION 2. What is the probability that an arriving customer will be served immediately?

Answer $\qquad$ P(an arriving customer will be served)

$$= P_0 = \text{probability of the system not being busy}$$
$$= 1 - U$$
$$= 1 - 0.50$$
$$= 0.50 \quad \text{or} \quad 50\%.$$

QUESTION 3. What is the probability that an arriving customer will find a waiting line of length n? $n = 1, 2, \ldots$

<u>*Answer*</u>
$$P_1 = P_0 U^1$$
$$= (0.5)(0.5)$$
$$= 0.25$$
$$P_2 = P_0 U^2$$
$$= (0.5)(0.5)^2$$
$$= 0.125$$
$$P_3 = P_0 U^3$$
$$= (0.5)^4$$
$$= 0.0625; \quad \text{and so forth.}$$

Thus, $P_n = (0.5)^{n+1}$ = probability of n customers in the system (including the customer being served).

Hence, the probability that an arriving customer will find n customers waiting to be served equals the probability of $n + 1$ customers in the system (one being serviced plus n waiting) $= P_{n+1} = (0.5)^{n+2}$.

QUESTION 4. What is the expected number of customers in the system?

<u>*Answer*</u>
$$E(N) = \frac{\lambda}{\mu - \lambda}$$
$$= \frac{0.25}{0.5 - 0.25}$$
$$= 1.0 \text{ customer}$$

QUESTION 5. What is the expected or average queue length.?

<u>*Answer*</u>
$$E(L) = \text{expected queue length}$$
$$= \frac{\lambda^2}{\mu(\mu - \lambda)}$$
$$= \frac{(0.25)^2}{0.5(0.5 - 0.25)} = 0.5 \text{ customer.}$$

QUESTION 6. What is the average time that a customer can expect to wait in the system?

<u>*Answer*</u>
$$E(T) = \frac{1}{\mu - \lambda}$$
$$= \frac{1}{0.5 - 0.25}$$
$$= 4 \text{ minutes.}$$

QUESTION 7. What is the average waiting time that a customer spends in the queue?

Answer

$$E(W) = \frac{\lambda}{\mu(\mu - \lambda)}$$

$$= \frac{0.25}{0.5(0.5 - 0.25)}$$

$$= \frac{0.25}{0.125}$$

$$= 2 \text{ minutes.}$$

We observe, based on our calculations, that if the utilization factor $U = 0.50$ is considered to be high, and, consequently $E(N)$ and $E(T)$ are large, then to reduce waiting time, management should consider the hiring of a second waiter.

17.2.3. Example—Who Is the Best Server?

Management has to decide which of two repairmen, X or Y, to hire. The frequency of machine breakdown in the plant is known to follow the Poisson distribution at a rate of $\lambda = 1$ machine per hour. The company loses revenue from down machines at a cost of \$25 per hour. Repairman X asks for \$20 per hour and repairman Y asks for \$12 per hour. X is able to repair machines at a rate of 1.8 machines per hour and Y is able to repair machines at a rate of 1.2 machines per hour.

QUESTION. Which repairman, X or Y, should be hired? Management's goal is to minimize daily costs (= labor cost + cost of nonproductive machine time).

Answer. To solve this problem, we need to compare total expected daily costs for repairman X with total expected daily costs for repairman Y and choose the lower of the two costs:

total daily expected costs = (total wages per day) + (cost of machines waiting to be repaired and in repair)

Since $\lambda = 1$, we have

$$E(N) = \frac{1}{1.8 - 1.0} = 1.25 \text{ machines for } X$$

and

$$E(N) = \frac{1}{1.2 - 1.0} = 5.00 \text{ machines for } Y.$$

If X is hired, the expected number of nonproductive machines (measured in hours per day) in an 8-hour day is

$$8 \times (1.25) = 10 \text{ hours } \left(\text{or } \tfrac{10}{8} = 1.25 \text{ machines per day}\right).$$

The total daily cost if X is hired is

labor cost + cost of nonproductive machine time = 8($20) + 10($25)
$$= \$410.$$

If Y is hired, the nonproductive machine time per day is $8 \times (5.0) = 40$ (or $\frac{40}{8} = 5$ machines per day), and the total daily cost is

$$8(\$12) + 40(\$25) = \$1096.$$

	SUMMARY OF DAILY COSTS	
Type of Cost	*Repairman X*	*Repairman Y*
Labor costs	8($20) = $160	8($12) = $96
Nonproductive machine time costs	10($25) = $250	40($25) = $1000
	$410	$1096

Thus, X is cheaper than Y.

17.2.4. Example—Choosing the Optimal Repair Facility

Ohio Truckers Incorporated is considering the construction of two repair facilities, each with different characteristics. On the average, 24 trucks require repair each month. The probability distribution of truck breakdowns each month follows the Poisson distribution. That is,

$$P\{A = n\} = \frac{e^{-24}(24)^n}{n!}, \quad (n = 0, 1, \dots).$$

The loss of revenue (opportunity cost) to the firm of having a truck in repair is estimated to be $300 per month.

The two facilities under consideration have the following characteristics (we ignore interest rates and returns on investment):

Characteristics	*Facility A*	*Facility B*
Installment cost	$200,000	$600,000
Labor cost (per month)	$80,000	$80,000
Repair rates (estimated)	$\mu_A = 30$ trucks per month	$\mu_B = 60$ trucks per month
Economic life	8 years	8 years
	$\lambda = 24$ trucks per month	$\lambda = 24$ trucks per month

To determine which facility to build, we need to compare the total annual costs of the two facilities.

$$\text{total annual cost} = \underset{(1)}{\tfrac{1}{4}(\text{total investment expenditure})} + \underset{(2)}{(\text{annual labor cost})}$$

$$+ \underset{(3)}{(\text{annual cost of lost revenue due to down trucks})}$$

TOTAL ANNUAL COSTS FOR FACILITY A. For repair facility A:

1. Annual capital recovery cost $= \tfrac{1}{4}(\$200,000) = \$50,000 = (1)$.
2. Annual labor cost $= 12(\$80,000) = \$960,000 = (2)$.
3. Computing the cost of truck down time $= (3)$:
   (a) Time waiting to be repaired is:

$$\text{average waiting time of an arrival} = E(W) = \frac{\lambda}{\mu(\mu - \lambda)} = \frac{24}{30(30 - 24)}$$

$$= 0.1333 \text{ month.}$$

Thus, total waiting time per year is

$$(\lambda)(12 \text{ months})[E(W)] = 24(12)(0.1333)$$
$$= 38.39 \text{ months.}$$

(b) Time being repaired is:

$$\text{mean time per repair} = \frac{1}{\mu_A} = \tfrac{1}{30} \text{ month.}$$

Thus, total repair time per year is

$$(\lambda)(12 \text{ months})\left(\tfrac{1}{\mu_A}\right) = 24(12)\left(\tfrac{1}{30}\right)$$
$$= 9.6 \text{ months.}$$

Therefore,

$$\text{total lost time per year} = 38.39 + 9.6$$
$$= 47.99 \text{ months.}$$

And finally,

$$\text{total cost of lost revenue} = \$300(47.99)$$
$$= \$14,397.00.$$

Therefore,

$$\text{total annual cost for facility A} = \underset{(1)}{\$50{,}000} + \underset{(2)}{960{,}000} + \underset{(3)}{14{,}397.00}$$

$$= \$1{,}024{,}397.00$$

TOTAL ANNUAL COSTS FOR FACILITY B. For facility B we have

1. Annual capital recovery cost = $\$150{,}000 = (1)$.
2. Annual labor cost = $12(\$80{,}000) = \$960{,}000 = (2)$.
3. Cost due to loss of revenue = (3):
   (a) Time waiting to be repaired $= \dfrac{24}{60(60 - 24)} = 0.0111$ month
   Thus,

   total waiting time per year = $24(12)(0.0111) = 3.1968$ months.

   (b) Time being repaired is:

$$\text{mean time per repair} = \tfrac{1}{60} \text{ month}$$

Thus,

$$\text{total repair time per year} = 24(12)\left(\tfrac{1}{60}\right) = 4.8 \text{ months,}$$
and $\text{total lost time per year} = 3.1968 + 4.8 = 7.997 \text{ months.}$

And finally,

$$\text{total cost of loss of revenue per year} = \$300(7.997) = \$2{,}399.10.$$

Therefore,

$$\text{total annual cost for facility } B = \underset{(1)}{\$150{,}000} + \underset{(2)}{\$960{,}000} + \underset{(3)}{\$2{,}399.10}$$

$$= \$1{,}112.399.10.$$

	SUMMARY OF ANNUAL COSTS	
Type of Cost	*Facility A*	*Facility B*
Capital recovery costs	$50,000.00	$150,000.00
Labor costs	960,000.00	960,000.00
Cost of lost revenue	14,397.00	2,399.10
	$1,024,397.00	$1,112,399.10

As shown in the table, facility A proves to be the least expensive in the long run.

17.3. INTRODUCTION TO SIMULATION

We have reviewed some of the basic characteristics of queueing systems. The formulas we used in computing the characteristics of the Poisson queueing system were easy to use. However, this is not always the case for queueing systems. More complicated arrival patterns, as well as more complicated service systems, usually lead to more complicated queueing formulas. Another method for studying a congestion system is Monte Carlo simulation. Monte Carlo simulation can easily be adapted to studying a wide variety of business situations, provided that alternatives are easily specified and that the data are available.

Simulation is a process of solving a problem by simulating a process with random-number generators. There are two basic requirements for using simulation.

Requirement 1   A *model* representing the essential characteristics of the system

Requirement 2   A *mechanism* to *simulate* the model

Usually, the *model* is one or more probability distributions describing the stochastic variables being studied. The *mechanism* can be a random-number generator, a table of random numbers, or a programmed simulation language.

In summary, simulation is a method to simulate, using "random devices," real-world systems that have key elements that are probabilistic in nature. We now consider some examples to illustrate the basic concepts of simulation.

17.3.1. Example—Simulating the Number of Service Counters

The manager of the Nebraska Steak House wishes to determine the optimal number of counters for a new restaurant in Lincoln, Nebraska. The procedure he is going to use is *simulated* random sampling. He has decided to simulate thirty 1-minute rush-hour periods. He has hypothesized the following distributions concerning the arrival distribution and counter service distribution.

Let $A_1, A_2, \ldots, A_{30}$ be the number of customers arriving at a counter for service in minute $1, 2, \ldots, 30$. Then

$$P\{A_1 = 1\} = \tfrac{1}{2}, \qquad P\{A_1 = 0\} = \tfrac{1}{2}$$
$$P\{A_2 = 1\} = \tfrac{1}{2}, \qquad P\{A_2 = 0\} = \tfrac{1}{2}$$
$$\vdots \qquad\qquad\qquad \vdots$$
$$P\{A_{30} = 1\} = \tfrac{1}{2} \quad \text{and} \quad P\{A_{30} = 0\} = \tfrac{1}{2}.$$

That is, he expects either 0 or 1 arrivals each minute, and the total number of arrivals over a 30-minute period has the binomial distribution.

For each period he will simulate arrivals by tossing a coin. A head (= 1) denotes an arrival and a tail (= 0) will denote no arrival. According to past experience, he knows that the time S a customer spends at the counter is between 1 and 6 minutes. The manager is very uncertain as to what is the exact distribution of service times. Thus, he postulates that the service-time distribution is *discrete uniform* between 1 and 6 minutes. See Figure 17.4.

As mentioned previously, it has been decided to simulate the service time for each customer by tossing a fair die. Table 17.1 gives the simulated results for one service counter. Column 2 (under A_i) of Table 17.1 gives the results of simulating the arrival distribution for each 1-minute period i. For example, arrivals occurred in periods 1, 2, 4, 6, 7, 9, 11, and so forth. Column 3 (under S_i) gives the results of simulating the service times for each arriving customer. For example, the customer who arrives in period 1 has a service time of 1 minute, period 2 of 3 minutes, period 4 of 6 minutes, period 6 of 3 minutes, and so forth.

Furthermore,

(in column 4): B_i = time the customer who arrived in period i *begins* to receive service

(in column 5): E_i = time the customer who arrives in period i completes his service (or leaves the system).

For example, for period 1 we have

$B_1 = 1$ and $E_1 = S_1 = 1$

$B_2 = 2$ since the customer who arrived at the beginning of period 1 completed service at the end of period 1

$E_2 = E_1 + S_2 = 1 + 3 = 4$

= (time last customer finished service) + (service time for customer 3).

B_3 and S_3 have no values, since no customer arrived at the beginning of period 3.

$$B_4 = E_2 + 1 = 4 + 1 = 5$$
$$E_4 = E_2 + S_4 = 4 + 6 = 10.$$

In general, for a customer who arrives at the beginning of period i:

$$B_i = \begin{cases} i & \text{if he is the only customer in the queue} \\ E_{i-1} + 1 & \text{if there is a customer in the queue and the customer arrived at the beginning of period } i - 1. \end{cases}$$

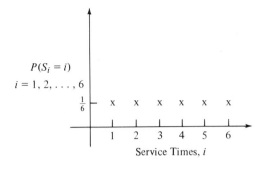

$P(S_i = i)$
$i = 1, 2, \ldots, 6$

Service Times, i

Figure 17.4

Table 17.1. Simulation Table for One Service Counter

Period i (length = 1 minute)	A_i	S_i	B_i	E_i	W_i	T_i
1	1	1	1	1	0	1
2	1	3	2	4	0	3
3	0					
4	1	6	5	10	1	7
5	0					
6	1	3	11	13	5	8
7	1	2	14	15	7	9
8	0					
9	1	2	16	17	7	9
10	0					
11	1	5	18	22	7	12
12	0					
13	1	4	23	26	10	14
14	0					
15	0					
16	1	1	27	27	11	12
17	0					
18	1	5	28	32	10	15
19	0					
20	0					
21	1	4	33	36	12	16
22	1	3	37	39	15	18
23	1	5	40	44	17	22
24	1	1	45	45	21	22
25	0					
26	1	3	46	48	20	23
27	0					
28	0					
29	1	6	49	54	20	26
30	0					
	$\overline{16}$	$\overline{54}$			$\overline{163}$	$\overline{217}$

Also,

$$E_i = E_{i-1} + S_i \text{ if a customer arrived at the beginning of period } i - 1.$$

(in column 6): W_i denotes the waiting time for the ith customer.

Now

$$W_i = B_i - i$$
$$= \text{(time the customer who arrived in period } i \text{ begins to receive service)}$$
$$- \text{(time he arrives at the counter)}.$$

(in column 7): T_i denotes the time the ith customer spends in the system
$$= S_i + W_i.$$

Upon completion of the simulation we are able to estimate two important statistics describing the behavior of the one-server counter as shown below.

Estimated Waiting Time

$$\text{estimated } E(W) = \frac{\text{total waiting time}}{\text{total number of arrivals}}$$

$$= \frac{163}{16} = 10.19 \text{ minutes per customer.}$$

Estimated Time Spent in System

$$\text{estimated } E(T) = \frac{\text{total time spent in the system}}{\text{total number of arrivals}}$$

$$= \frac{217}{16} = 13.56 \text{ minutes per customer.}$$

Table 17.2 gives the results for the simulation of the system with two checkout counters. The first three columns of Table 17.2 are identical to the corresponding columns in Table 17.1. The other computational formulas for E_i, W_i and T_i also hold for the two-counter system except for determining B_i, the time the ith customer begins to receive service.

Now B_i is determined by E_{i-1} and E_{i-2}, the preceding two service times. If $i > E_{i-1}$ or $i > E_{i-2}$, then $B_i = i$. If $i \leqslant E_{i-1}$ and $i \leqslant E_{i-2}$, then $B_i = \min(E_{i-1}, E_{i-2}) + 1$.

Period	A_i	S_i	B_i	E_i	W_i	T_i
1	1	1	1	2	0	1
2	1	3	2	5	0	3
3	0					
4	1	6	4	9	0	6
5	0					
6	1	3	6	8	0	3
7	1	2	9	10	2	4
8	0					
9	1	2	9	10	0	2
10	0					
11	1	5	11	15	0	5
12	0					
13	1	4	13	16	0	4
14	0					
15	0					
16	1	1	16	16	0	1
17	0					
18	1	5	18	22	0	5
19	0					
20	0					
21	1	4	21	24	0	4
22	1	3	23	25	1	4
23	1	5	25	29	2	7
24	1	1	26	26	2	3
25	0					
26	1	3	26	28	0	3
27	0					
28	0					
29	1	6	29	34	0	6
30	0					
	$\overline{16}$				$\overline{7}$	$\overline{61}$

Estimated Waiting Time

$$\text{estimated } E(W) = \frac{\text{total waiting time}}{\text{total number of arrivals}}$$

$$= \frac{7}{16} = 0.44 \text{ minute per customer.}$$

Estimated Time Spent in the System

$$\text{estimated } E(T) = \frac{\text{total time spent in the system}}{\text{total number of arrivals}}$$

$$= \frac{61}{16} = 3.81 \text{ minutes per customer.}$$

We note that a two-server counter has a substantially lower waiting time and waiting-plus-service time per customer.

| | *SIMULATION STATISTICS* | |
	One Counter	*Two Counters*
Estimated waiting time	10.19 minutes per customer	0.44 minute per customer
Time in the system	13.56 minutes per customer	3.81 minutes per customer

17.3.2. Generating Chance Outcomes: Random-Number Tables

From Example 17.3.1 we have seen that simulation requires the *generation of chance outcomes*. We used two devices in generating these chance outcomes.

Device 1   A fair coin to generate arrivals

Device 2   A fair die to generate service times

A third device for generating outcomes is to use a table of random numbers (often generated by use of a computer program).

By use of the following example we will illustrate the use of random-number tables.

17.3.3. Example—Simulating Product Demand

From past experience the daily demand D for a particular item has varied between 300 and 800 per day. The record of the past sales for 100 days is given in the following table.

Demand per Day	Number of Days	Relative Frequency
350	10	$\frac{10}{100} = 0.1$
450	30	$\frac{30}{100} = 0.3$
550	20	$\frac{20}{100} = 0.2$
650	30	$\frac{30}{100} = 0.3$
750	10	$\frac{10}{100} = 0.1$
	$\overline{100}$	$\overline{1.00}$

We can estimate the probability distribution of demand by use of the relative frequencies given in the table above. That is,

$$P(D = 350) = 0.1$$
$$P(D = 450) = 0.3$$
$$P(D = 550) = 0.2$$
$$P(D = 650) = 0.3$$
$$\underline{P(D = 750) = 0.1}$$
$$1.00$$

Also, we can estimate expected daily demand as follows.

$$\text{expected demand} = E(D) = (350)P(D = 350) + (450)P(D = 450)$$
$$+ (550)P(D = 550) + (650)P(D = 650)$$
$$+ (750)P(D = 750) = 550 \text{ units.}$$

We can also plot the cumulative distribution of demand (Figure 17.5) using the following table.

**Cumulative Distribution
of Daily Demand $P(D \leqslant d)$**

d	$P(D \leqslant d)$
350	0.1
450	0.4
550	0.6
650	0.9
750	1.0

Figure 17.5. Cumulative distribution of daily demand.

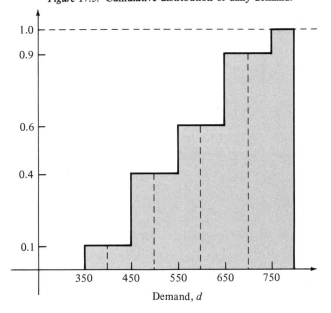

We are now ready to generate a sequence, say 10 days, of demand. To do this we use the preceding empirically derived distributions plus a table of random numbers.

Using the preceding relative frequencies (or estimated probabilities) we first define the following random-number intervals.

Random-Number Interval	Demand per day	Relative Frequency = Estimated Probability
00–09	350	0.10
10–39	450	0.30
40–59	550	0.20
60–89	650	0.30
90–99	750	0.10
		1.00

Any entry 00–09 will correspond to 10% of the numbers, 10–29 to 10%, . . . , and 90–99 to 10% of the 100 uniform numbers between 00 and 99. Table 17.3 gives 350 random numbers.

Table 17.3 Random Numbers

.06784734	.39867459	.90587769	.17800808	.81074892	.87641351	.67964074
.44093363	.79427581	.31478793	.75057190	.28248398	.26862750	.12484033
.23882080	.82137096	.51758536	.24722987	.23896633	.93059766	.94078414
.33414700	.89999697	.73622003	.85895934	.36824675	.89999500	.36952170
.14510138	.05046793	.01534527	.46997282	.12718882	.35159230	.55903312
.64881141	.64309242	.32693554	.57236665	.74242489	.68045131	.42780132
.00632860	.87196973	.90596776	.95629297	.38489603	.27803790	.06566831
.25298284	.88459413	.54105242	.62235237	.93190067	.66121592	.31786451
.47555731	.38854782	.52135444	.34084567	.70849622	.55050739	.86505157
.83996956	.00898240	.21424194	.34591914	.77920069	.16675046	.77524021
.81164022	.90617038	.69969379	.86086355	.08021944	.03690458	.47454397
.20469742	.42155839	.63281955	.72814593	.83870061	.63270933	.19585840
.63849252	.47146085	.31269571	.01820498	.16823064	.49799872	.70761434
.36951487	.12119545	.92391464	.04732475	.51315307	.61489122	.09115676
.82279667	.09620714	.17799886	.09435477	.12260965	.35716898	.36669258
.94515971	.51533057	.23271006	.53187227	.57170831	.10909059	.06854512
.41041222	.35688697	.83327828	.57822894	.75233898	.44724914	.22876762
.70576486	.76071123	.00602937	.13294285	.19561706	.95866564	.35982877
.29345982	.81569562	.33279952	.89642321	.02646312	.47101324	.93328343
.61082361	.38919659	.37392794	.17397264	.10199563	.43909315	.95540755
.93240813	.18864299	.84961797	.28618296	.30329204	.33110877	.94745347
.48837360	.76985899	.02257087	.43411480	.60329907	.74130361	.81236225
.81566128	.93660681	.30621194	.24239105	.87757156	.39840616	.90510067
.05619836	.46127101	.18021157	.26996549	.36189712	.11021179	.92107072
.37578158	.46507126	.07947389	.15830058	.75709224	.87057337	.79544369
.34299217	.55322814	.67867600	.72991016	.47428481	.35111131	.96191807
.95674084	.81342456	.28657032	.46011389	.63491058	.23848306	.90929505
.00809523	.95477691	.97806630	.25612091	.43439207	.25151677	.78913585
.48813304	.95841783	.19762526	.03985783	.59637034	.07759955	.01082144

Table 17.3 (Continued) Random Numbers

.36298610	.96232607	.21257818	.42648977	.23408995	.57414542	.08587970
.30525481	.94948152	.56838949	.88885995	.16409113	.40305276	.45974553
.57412607	.48234392	.57803769	.12587063	.80273190	.49006379	.61249010
.78102651	.27433584	.45743561	.73252199	.99919527	.09647039	.21554865
.76638860	.56972021	.77215842	.35370601	.29532314	.90911336	.91013287
.01704074	.29749992	.39187238	.81054715	.29092584	.79308639	.75327183
.42808557	.49482727	.93925880	.31171442	.22708566	.83460565	.83584110
.87424339	.43518129	.26450833	.81733716	.11462719	.40995689	.53881371
.20892449	.82668323	.07241445	.14659150	.62468671	.76547142	.71953440
.39403135	.97839488	.46271915	.93446610	.54246868	.43857356	.16659543
.15500524	.91093203	.68541131	.36191485	.41263212	.87359303	.28883151
.64054682	.14029919	.51139329	.80799005	.96245051	.39355131	.55800986
.58159602	.96164083	.56956582	.01141878	.05619704	.21647345	.02555350
.84481664	.90942904	.71315107	.64239813	.99679250	.51666307	.44660269
.77382363	.54470798	.56914611	.83080362	.60618360	.06273297	.70889513
.29878354	.50102981	.32996093	.13228094	.89592936	.03308038	.11435113
.84397813	.71500348	.70391880	.88304509	.98966273	.40470462	.16197524
.76735944	.41483866	.90021850	.00181875	.79167548	.93253627	.05912016
.36577314	.12376185	.98591585	.44605403	.60608256	.24065470	.43602234
.48205666	.06769564	.14071613	.17800578	.38283485	.32803685	.72028933
.54202676	.11924422	.45502162	.06228707	.64861469	.99841533	.81246213

PROCEDURE. The following steps are taken to obtain a sample.

Step 1. Enter the table in a random manner. For example, close your eyes and point a pencil to the table. The two closest columns to the point of the pencil becomes your starting point. Next read the table vertically, following the rules given in step 2.

Hand Simulation

Day	Random Number	Demand
1	69	650
2	63	650
3	31	450
4	92	750
5	17	450
6	23	450
7	83	650
8	00	350
9	33	450
10	37	450
		Total = 5300

Estimated average daily
demand = 5300/10 = 530 units.

Step 2. Read N (= sample size) numbers from the table. If the two-digit number is in the interval 00–09, record it as a demand of 350 units. If the two-digit number is in the interval between 10 and 39, record it as a demand of 450; and so forth.

The preceding table lists the results of the hand simulation. Note in Table 17.3 the location of the 10 random numbers used for the hand simulation.

We have seen an example of an important queueing model and been exposed to some basic characteristics of simulation analysis. We now turn to a study of some other queueing systems.

17.4. OTHER QUEUEING SYSTEMS

17.4.1. *Single-Server Poisson Arrivals / Exponential Service Times with a Maximum Queue Length*

Suppose that a congestion system operates as follows. Customers arrive according to a Poisson distribution with mean arrival rate $= \lambda$. There is one server in the system with service times exponentially distributed with mean service rate $= \mu$. However, if an arrival occurs when there are more than M customers in the system, he or she will not enter the system but will *balk* (or leave the system). Then it can be shown that the following formulas are valid for this system. Recall that $U = \lambda/\mu$.

$E(N)$ = expected number in the system

$$= \frac{U}{1 - U} - \frac{(M + 1)U^{M+1}}{1 - U^{M+1}}$$

$E(L)$ = expected number of customers waiting for service

$$= E(N) - 1 + \frac{1 - U}{1 - U^{M+1}}$$

$E(T)$ = expected waiting time of an arriving customer

$$= \frac{1}{\mu(1 - U)} - \frac{MU^M}{\mu(1 - U^M)}$$

$E(W)$ = expected waiting time of an arriving customer for service

$$= E(T) - \frac{1}{\mu}.$$

It is important to note that $E(T)$ and $E(W)$ are waiting times for only those customers who enter the system.

17.4.2. Example—Service Center Congestion Statistics

The Marshall–Sears garage in Lebanon, New Hampshire, can service an average of 6 cars per hour ($\mu = 6$). However, an average of 18 cars arrive each hour ($\lambda = 18$). Given that there is parking space for only 2 cars ($M = 3$), determine the garage's congestion statistics.

First,

$$U = \frac{\lambda}{\mu} = \frac{18}{6} = 3.$$

Hence,

$E(N)$ = expected number of cars in the system

$$= \frac{3}{1-3} - \frac{4(3)^4}{1-(3)^4}$$

$$= -1.5 + \frac{324}{80}$$

$$= 2.55 \text{ cars.}$$

$E(L)$ = expected number of cars waiting for service

$$= (2.55) - 1 + \frac{1-3}{1-(3)^4}$$

$$= 1.575 \text{ cars.}$$

$E(T)$ = expected waiting time of an arriving customer

$$= \frac{1}{6(1-3)} - \frac{3(3)^3}{6[1-(3)^3]}$$

$$= -\frac{1}{12} + \frac{81}{6(26)}$$

$$= -0.083 + 0.519$$

$$= 0.44 \text{ hour} \quad \text{or} \quad 26.17 \text{ minutes.}$$

$E(W)$ = expected watiting time of an arriving customer for service

$$= E(T) - \tfrac{1}{3}$$

$$= 0.44 \text{ hour} - \tfrac{1}{3} \text{ hour}$$

$$= 0.11 \text{ hour} \quad \text{or} \quad 6.6 \text{ minutes.}$$

17.4.3. k Servers, Poisson Arrivals, and Exponential Service Times

Next we consider a system with k servicing stations, each with an average service rate μ, where arrivals occur at an average rate λ. The formulas for expected number in the queue, expected number in the system, expected waiting time for service, and expected time in the system are given below, where $U = \lambda/\mu$.

$E(N)$ = expected number in the system

$$= \frac{\lambda\mu U^k}{(k-1)!\,(k\mu - \lambda)^2}\,P_0 + U$$

$E(L)$ = expected number waiting for service

$$= \frac{\lambda\mu U^k}{(k-1)!\,(k\mu - \lambda)^2}\,P_0$$

$E(T)$ = expected time spent in the system

$$= \frac{\mu U^k}{(k-1)!\,(k\mu - \lambda)^2}\,P_0 + \frac{1}{\mu}$$

$E(W)$ = expected time spent in the queue waiting for service

$$= \frac{\mu U^k}{(k-1)!\,(k\mu - \lambda)^2}\,P_0,$$

where P_0 = probability of 0 customers in the system

$$= \frac{1}{\left[\displaystyle\sum_{n=0}^{k-1} \frac{1}{n!}\,U^n\right] + \dfrac{1}{k!}\,U^k\,\dfrac{k\mu}{k\mu - \lambda}}.$$

This formula for P_0 is valid only if $k\mu > \lambda$.

17.4.4. Example—Service Center Congestion Statistics

The Marshall–Sears garage in Manchester, New Hampshire, has three identical stalls, each of which can service an average of 6 cars per hour ($\mu = 6$). An average of 12 cars arrive each hour ($\lambda = 12$). Also, the center has virtually unlimited parking facilities. Determine the center's congestion statistics.

$$U = \frac{\lambda}{\mu} = \frac{12}{6} = 2$$

$$P_0 = \frac{1}{1\,U^0 + 1\,U^1 + \dfrac{1}{2}\,U^2 + \dfrac{1}{3!}\,U^3\,\dfrac{3(6)}{3(6) - 12}}$$

$$= \frac{1}{1 + 2 + 2 + \frac{1}{6}(8)\left(\frac{18}{6}\right)}$$

$$= \frac{1}{5 + 4}$$

$$= 0.11 \quad \text{or} \quad 11\%.$$

$$E(N) = \frac{12(6)2^3}{2!\,(6)^2}0.11 + 2$$

$$= 2.88 \text{ cars.}$$

$$E(L) = 0.88 \text{ cars.}$$

$$E(T) = \frac{6(2)^3}{2!\,(6)^2}0.11 + \frac{1}{6}$$

$$= 0.24 \text{ hour} \quad \text{or} \quad 14.4 \text{ minutes.}$$

$$E(W) = 0.07 \text{ hour} \quad \text{or} \quad 4.2 \text{ minutes.}$$

17.5. GENERAL SIMULATION PROCEDURE

A general procedure for doing a simulation analysis can be described by the flow chart in Figure 17.6.

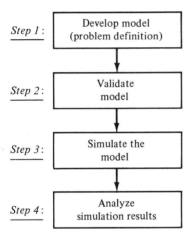

Step 1: Develop model (problem definition)

Step 2: Validate model

Step 3: Simulate the model

Step 4: Analyze simulation results

Figure 17.6

For step 1 we need to develop a model that describes the key characteristics of the system being studied. In developing a model it is important to determine the *decision variables* and the *uncontrollable variables*. It is also important to specify all the relationships between the decision variables and the uncontrollable variables.

The second step is to verify or validate the simulation model. This can be accomplished by comparing the statistics developed for the model with similar statistics obtained from other historical data of the same system.

Some of the critical aspects of steps 3 and 4 are sample-size determination (or how many simulations to perform) and using the correct statistical techniques to analyze the results of a simulation. We will illustrate steps 1, 2, and 3 by use of an example. Those interested in a more detailed treatment of step 4 can consult the references at the end of the chapter.

17.5.1. Example—Simulating an Inventory Control System

Let D_t be the monthly demand for tennis rackets (received at a sporting goods distributor). From historical data the following probability distribution of D_t has been estimated.

Monthly Demand

Number Demanded, D_t	Probability
100	0.25
200	0.50
300	0.25
	$\overline{1.00}$

D_t for any month t is an *uncontrollable variable*. The controllable variable is supply 0_t for any month t. Let S_t be the number of rackets sold in month t. Then

$$S_t = D_t \quad \text{if} \quad D_t \leqslant 0_t,$$

since it is the policy of the firm to sell any excess rackets to their foreign subsidiary in Japan, at cost, **the** total profit derived from a month's operation is

(net unit selling price) $\cdot$ (number of rackets sold) $= \$20S_t$.

To summarize,

MODEL TO BE SIMULATED

$$S_t = D_t \quad \text{if} \quad D_t \leqslant 0_t$$
$$S_t = 0_t \quad \text{if} \quad D_t > 0_t.$$

Total profit $= \$20S_t$.

The firm is considering the following two ordering policies.

Policy 1   Let $0_t = D_{t-1}$

and

Policy 2   Let $0_t = \dfrac{D_{t-1} + D_{t-2}}{2}$

Which policy will yield the highest profit?

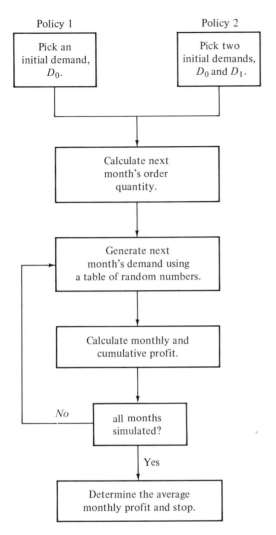

Policy 1

Pick an
initial demand,
D_0.

Policy 2

Pick two
initial demands,
D_0 and D_1.

Calculate next
month's order
quantity.

Generate next
month's demand using
a table of random numbers.

Calculate monthly and
cumulative profit.

No

all months
simulated?

Yes

Determine the average
monthly profit and stop.

Figure 17.7

A general flowchart for simulating the tennis racket problem is shown in Figure 17.7.

We first simulate policy 1. Using the monthly demand distribution, we obtain the following three-digit intervals required by the Monte Carlo method.

Number Demanded, D_t	*Probability*	*Three-Digit Intervals*
100	0.25	000–224
200	0.50	225–749
300	0.25	750–999
	$\overline{1.00}$	

Let

$$D_0 = \text{expected demand} = (0.25)(100) + (0.50)(200) + (0.25)(300)$$
$$= 25 + 100 + 75$$
$$= 200.$$

The simulation calculations are given in the following table.

Policy 1

Demand, D_t: $D_0 = 200$	Random Number	Order Quantity, O_t Rackets	Monthly Profit
$D_1 = 300$	810	$O_1 = D_0 = 200$	40,000
$D_2 = 200$	282	$O_2 = D_1 = 300$	40,000
$D_3 = 200$	238	$O_3 = D_2 = 200$	40,000
$D_4 = 200$	368	$O_4 = D_3 = 200$	40,000
$D_5 = 100$	127	$O_5 = D_4 = 200$	20,000
$D_6 = 200$	742	$O_6 = D_5 = 100$	20,000
$D_7 = 200$	384	$O_7 = D_6 = 200$	40,000
$D_8 = 300$	931	$O_8 = D_7 = 200$	40,000
$D_9 = 200$	708	$O_9 = D_8 = 300$	40,000
$D_{10} = 300$	779	$O_{10} = D_9 = 200$	40,000
			$\overline{\$360,000}$

Average monthly profit = $360,000/10 = $36,000.

Note in Table 17.3 the list of the random numbers used in the analysis above.

Let $D_0 = D_1 = 200$ units for policy 2. A 9-month simulation for policy 2 is given in the following table.

Policy 2

Demand, D_t: $D_0 = D_1 = 200$	Random Number	Order Quantity $O_t = \dfrac{D_{t-1} + D_{t-2}}{2}$	Monthly Profit
$D_2 = 100$	068	$O_2 = 200$	20,000
$D_3 = 200$	228	$O_3 = 150$	30,000
$D_4 = 200$	359	$O_4 = 150$	30,000
$D_5 = 300$	933	$O_5 = 200$	40,000
$D_6 = 300$	955	$O_6 = 250$	50,000
$D_7 = 300$	947	$O_7 = 300$	60,000
$D_8 = 300$	842	$O_8 = 300$	60,000
$D_9 = 300$	905	$O_9 = 300$	60,000
$D_{10} = 300$	921	$O_{10} = 300$	60,000
			$\overline{\$410,000}$

Average monthly profit = $410,000/9 = $45,556.

Based on simulating 10 and 9 months, we see that policy 2 yields a larger contribution to average monthly profit than does policy 1. However, because of the small sample size ($n = 10$ and 9) we should be hesitant about proposing policy 2 for implementation. In fact, a simulation of 30 or more months would be more desirable.

Example 17.5.1 illustrates several of the important steps in a simulation analysis. Several comments are now appropriate for the purpose of performing a good simulation analysis.

17.5.2. Model Development—Problem Definition

Model development for purposes of a simulation analysis differs very little from model development using any of the other tools discussed in this text for solving business problems. Basically, it involves the specification of goals (obtaining a policy that yields the highest average profit in Example 17.5.1) and identifying the relevant decision or controllable variables as well as the uncontrollable variables of the problem to be analyzed. Obviously, the decision variables and the uncontrollable variables determine the extent to which the goal (or goals) are achieved. The goal of the tennis racket distributor in Example 17.5.1 was to choose that ordering policy (policy 1 or policy 2) that yields the highest average profit. The decision variable was the ordering policy; the uncontrollable variable was the monthly demand for tennis rackets.

17.5.3. Specification of Probability Distributions

Two types of probability distributions can be used in a simulation analysis: empirical distributions and mathematical distributions. In Example 17.5.1, the tennis racket inventory problem, an empirical distribution was used based on observing the relative frequency of past demands for tennis rackets. It is conceivable (after more analysis of past demand history) that the demand for tennis rackets "closely" approximated some known distribution, such as, for example, the Poisson or the normal. If this were the case, the input to the simulation analysis may be simplified.

17.5.4. Determining Starting Conditions for a Simulation Analysis

Decision variables and uncontrollable variables, by definition, will assume different values as the simulation progresses. However, a decision must be made at the beginning of a simulation analysis as to the appropriate value of each of these variables. In Example 17.5.1 we assume an average demand of $D_0 = 200$ tennis rackets for month 0 for policy 1 and we assume an average demand of $D_0 = D_1 = 200$ tennis racquets for policy 2. After month 0 (or month 1 using policy 2), the generation of random numbers determined the values of demand in successive months.

The value for the cost parameter in Example 17.5.1 was \$20/racket for the unit selling price. As used in the simulation analysis, the value of this parameter did not change. However, it may change as different ordering and selling policies were to be studied in other simulations.

To determine "good" starting values for variables and other parameters, the analyst can ignore data obtained from the initial periods of the simulation analysis.

17.5.5. *Determination of the Number of Periods to Simulate*

The length of the simulation run (usually given in time periods) depends critically on the goal of the simulation. One of the most common approaches is to run the simulation model until the results exhibit what is called an *equilibrium condition*. In Example 17.5.1, an equilibrium condition is achieved when the relative frequencies of the simulated demands are "close to" their historical relative frequencies.

Another approach is to run the simulation for a period of fixed lengths, such as 3 months, 1 year, or 3 years, and so forth, and analyze the end results for reasonableness in terms of total and average costs as well as relative frequencies.

17.5.6. *Special-Purpose Simulation Languages*

The widespread interest in the use of simulation as a means of analyzing complex business problems has given rise to the development of several special-purpose simulation languages. These languages are such that certain operations that are commonly needed in the simulation studies can be carried out very easily. Although FORTRAN is capable of doing almost anything that these special-purpose languages can do, FORTRAN is often less efficient on large-scale problems. Representative of the popular special-purpose languages are SIMSCRIPT (General Purpose Systems Simulator), and DYNAMO is a language written specifically to accommodate a development by Jay W. Forrester called "industrial dynamics."

REFERENCES   AQUILANO, N. J., and R. B. CHASE. *Production and Operations Management.* Homewood, Ill.: Richard D. Irwin, Inc., 1973.

EMSHOFF, J. R., and R. L. SISSON. *Design and Use of Computer Simulation Models.* New York: Macmillan Publishing Co., Inc., 1970.

FISHMAN, G. S. *Concepts and Methods in Discrete Event Digital Simulation.* New York: John Wiley & Sons, Inc., 1973.

GROSS, D., and C. M. HARRIS. *Fundamentals of Queueing Theory.* New York: John Wiley & Sons, Inc., 1974.

703

LEE, A. *Applied Queueing Theory.* New York: St. Martin's Press, 1966.

MAISEL, H., and G. GNUGNOLI. *Simulation of Discrete Stochastic Systems.* Chicago: Science Research Associates, Inc., 1972.

MEIR, R. C., W. T. NEWELL, and H. L. PAZER. *Simulation in Business and Economics.* Englewood Cliffs, N.J.: Prentice-Hall, Inc., 1969.

PANIRO, J. A. *Queueing Theory.* Englewood Cliffs, N. J.: Prentice-Hall, Inc., 1969.

REITMAN, J. *Computer Simulation Applications.* New York: John Wiley & Sons, Inc., 1971.

SAATY, T. L. *Elements of Queueing Theory with Applications.* New York: McGraw-Hill Book Company, 1961.

SCHMIDT, J. W. and R. E. TAYLOR. *Simulation and Analysis of Industrial Systems.* Homewood, Ill.: Richard D. Irwin, Inc., 1970.

WAGNER, H. *Principles of Operations Research.* Englewood Cliffs, N.J.: Prentice-Hall, Inc., 1969.

KEY CONCEPTS

Customers
Queues or waiting lines
Service facilities
Arrival rate
Service rate
Poisson queues
Utilization factor

Average waiting times
Average number of customers in the system
Random numbers
Simulation model
Simulation analysis

REVIEW PROBLEMS

17.1. What is a queueing problem? What are some of the basic characteristics of a queueing system? What are some of the important assumptions of the basic models discussed in this chapter?

17.2. How would you propose to improve service at each of the following?
(a) A TV repair shop
(b) A local savings and loan institution
(c) An airline ticket counter

17.3. Self-service at a local gas station, at an average rate of 7 minutes per car, is slower than attendant service, which has a rate of 6 minutes per car. The station manager wishes to calculate the average number of customers in the station, the average time each car spends in the station, and the average time each car spends waiting for service. Assume that customers arrive randomly at each line, at the rate of 5 cars per hour. Calculate the appropriate operating statistics for this gas station.

17.4. A repairman is to be hired to repair machines that break down at an average rate of 4 per hour. Breakdowns occur randomly (Poisson) over time. Nonproductive time on any machine is considered to cost the company $0.50/hour. Management has narrowed the choice to two repairmen: one slow but cheap, the other fast but expensive. The slow but cheap repairman has a salary of $30 per hour; in return he will service broken-down machines at an average rate of 5 per hour. The fast but expensive repairman has a salary of $50 per hour and will repair machines at an average rate of 7 per hour. Which repairman should the company hire? Assume exponential repair times for both repairmen.

17.5. What are some important advantages of simulation as a business-problem-solving technique?

17.6. What are the general steps in designing and running a simulation model?

ANSWERS TO REVIEW PROBLEMS

17.1. A queueing problem is essentially the same as a mathematical programming allocation problem. That is, there are competing activities for limited services (or resources). In queueing systems, both the arrival rates and service rates vary over time. Thus, the service facility will be empty part of the time. The goal in "solving" queueing problems is to balance the cost of delays (waiting times and queue lengths) against the cost of providing different amounts of service (more servers or faster servers) with the final objective of minimizing total cost (or total profit). The basic assumptions required to solve the queueing models given in this chapter are that the arrival pattern follows a Poisson distribution and the service time follows an exponential distribution.

17.2. Service can be improved by
(a) For a TV repair shop,
　(1) Scheduling jobs
　(2) Hiring more repairmen
　(3) Establishing priority rules
　(4) Using better (more efficient) test equipment
(b) For savings and loan institution
　(1) Scheduling appointments
　(2) Hiring more or better personnel
(c) For airline ticket counter,
　(1) Hiring more personnel
　(2) Having priority counters
　(3) Installing a curbside baggage-checking facility

17.3.

Self-Service Line	*Attended Line*
$\mu = \frac{1}{7} = 0.143$ customer per minute	$\mu = \frac{1}{6} = 0.167$ customer per minute
$\lambda = \frac{5}{60} = 0.083$ customer per minute	$\lambda = \frac{5}{60} = 0.083$ customer per minute

Self-Service Line

$E(N)$ = expected number of cars in the self-service line

$$= \frac{\lambda}{\mu - \lambda} = \frac{0.083}{0.143 - 0.083} = 1.38 \text{ customers}$$

$E(L)$ = expected number of cars waiting for service

$$= \frac{\lambda^2}{\mu(\mu - \lambda)} = \frac{(0.083)^2}{(0.143)(0.143 - 0.083)} = 0.80 \text{ car}$$

$E(T)$ = average time in the system

$$= \frac{1}{\mu - \lambda} = \frac{1}{(0.143) - (0.083)} = 16.67 \text{ minutes}$$

$E(W)$ = average time waiting for service

$$= \frac{\lambda}{\mu(\mu - \lambda)} = \frac{0.083}{(0.143)(0.143 - 0.083)} = 9.68 \text{ minutes.}$$

Attended Line

$E(N)$ = expected number of cars in the attended line

$$\frac{\lambda}{\mu - \lambda} = \frac{0.083}{0.167 - 0.083} = 0.99 \text{ car}$$

$E(L)$ = expected number of cars waiting for service

$$= \frac{\lambda^2}{\mu(\mu - \lambda)} = \frac{(0.083)^2}{(0.167)(0.167 - 0.083)} = 0.492 \text{ car}$$

$E(T)$ = average time in the system

$$= \frac{1}{\mu - \lambda} = \frac{1}{0.167 - 0.083} = 11.90 \text{ minutes}$$

$E(W)$ = average time spent waiting for service

$$= \frac{\lambda}{\mu(\mu - \lambda)} = \frac{0.083}{(0.167)(0.167 - 0.083)} = 5.91 \text{ minutes.}$$

17.4.

Cheap Repairman	Expensive Repairman
μ = 5 per hour	μ = 7 per hour
labor = $30 per hour	labor = $50 per hour

$E(X) = \lambda = 4$ machines per hour.

Cheap Repairman

hourly cost = labor per hour + (breakdown rate per hour)

      $\times$ (average time spent waiting and in repair per machine)

      $\times$ (nonproductive time per machine)

$$= \$30 + \lambda E(T)(\$0.50/\text{hour})$$

$$= \$30 + 4\left(\frac{1}{5 - 4}\right)(\$0.50)$$

$$= \$30 + \$2$$

$$= \$32.$$

Expensive Repairman

$$\text{hourly cost} = \$50 + 4\left(\frac{1}{7-4}\right)(\$0.50)$$
$$= \$50 + \$0.66$$
$$= \$50.66.$$

17.5. Simulation is an appropriate tool to use in solving a business problem when *experimenting on the real system*:
(a) Would be disruptive.
(b) Would be too expensive.
(c) Does not permit replication of events.
(d) Does not permit control over key variables.
Simulation is a desirable tool for solving a business problem when a mathematical model:
(e) Is too complex to solve.
(f) Is beyond the capability of available personnel.
(g) Is not detailed enough to provide information on all important decision variables.

17.6. The important steps in designing and running a simulation model are:
(a) Define the problem.
(b) Construct the simulation model.
(c) Specify the values of the variables and parameters.
(d) Perform (or run) the simulation.
(e) Evaluate the results of the simulation.

EXERCISES **17.1.** Identify the customers and the servers in each of the following queueing systems:
(a) A toll booth on an interstate highway
(b) An ambulance service
(c) A ship unloading dock
(d) A fire station
(e) A secretarial typing pool

17.2. An Air Force flight-line crew during an alert period estimate that they can service aircraft at the rate of one interceptor every 6 minutes. During a 24-hour alert period it is estimated that seven interceptors will be landing every hour. The crew operates as a team on one interceptor at a time. Assume Poisson landings and an exponential service time. Find:
(a) Utilization of each flight-line crew
(b) Average number of aircraft waiting for service
(c) Average time an aircraft waits for service
(d) Total time an aircraft spends in the system (= waiting time + service time)

17.3. An emergency receiving center at a large city hospital has an expected arrival rate of five cases per hour (Poisson). Past statistics show that service

times are on the average of six per hour (exponential).
(a) How many cases are waiting, on the average, to be treated by a doctor?
(b) What is the average waiting time in the center until a doctor treats an arrival?
(c) What is the average number of cases being worked on?

17.4. During the rush "hour," between 7:00 A.M. and 8:30 A.M., the arrival of customers at a self-service restaurant can be characterized by a Poisson distribution, where the average arrival rate is five customers per 6-minute period. If the average service time is 0.5 minutes, what is the probability of *fewer than* four customers waiting?

17.5. FNCB of Harrisburg plans to open a drive-in banking facility (single server) in a suburban shopping center. Statistics indicate that on the average customers will arrive at a rate of 20 per hour (Poisson). Also, it is estimated that 2 minutes on the average will be required to process a customer (exponential).
(a) What fraction of the time will the facility be empty?
(b) What is the average waiting time for a customer for service?

17.6. Assume in Problem 17.5 that FNCB installs two identical (parallel) drive-in facilities. How would this increase in service capacity change your answers to (a) and (b) of Exercise 17.5?

17.7. What is the difference between known probability distributions and "empirical" distributions? What information is needed to simulate using a known mathematical probability distribution?

17.8. The Oklahoma Gas Transport Company controls pipelines between several natural gas fields and out-of-state distributors. The company has a 100,000-unit storage capacity. Because of federal regulations, the company receives either 40,000 or 60,000 units per day. There is an equal probability that on a given day of either quantity being shipped. The actual demand for natural gas is given by the following table of relative frequencies:

Daily Demand	Probability
25,001–45,000	0.3
45,001–55,000	0.3
55,001–65,000	0.4
	1.0

(a) What is the expected daily demand?
(b) Construct a model that can be used to simulate the company's daily shipping and storage activities.
(c) Simulate the daily receiving, storage, and shipping activities using the model developed in part (b).
(d) Discuss your simulation results. Do your results indicate a need for more storage capacity? How much?

17.9. Simulating an Oil Transport Operation: Random Numbers and Descriptive Statistics

The West Coast Oil Transport Company (WCOT) has pipelines coming in from several harbors. It holds oil in a storage field (tank farm) until needed. Most of WCOT's oil is shipped via a pipeline to a large refinery in California. It is *conjectured* that, on the average, daily intake of WCOT's farm is either 40,000 barrels or 60,000 barrels, with a probability $\frac{1}{3}$ and $\frac{2}{3}$, respectively. The demand, D, for oil at the California refinery is also uncertain from day to day. WCOT has estimated the probability distribution of D to be as follows:

Use / Day	Probability
25,001–35,000	0.1
35,001–45,000	0.2
45,001–55,000	0.3
55,001–65,000	0.4
	1.0

(a) What is the expected value of the number of barrels sent to California per day? (Assume that within any use range, the demand averages to the middle; for instance 25,000–35,000 is 30,000.)
(b) Simulate these activities (receiving and shipping oil) for 20 days. (Use a table of random numbers.)
(c) Does your simulation model indicate that WCOT should build more storage capacity? If so, what additional capacity should be constructed? If not, what can be concluded from the results of your simulation?

CASE 17.1   Illustrative Case Study

DECISION MAKING IN QUEUEING-TYPE SYSTEMS

Queueing situations requiring management to make design (e.g., number of servers, maximum allowable queue length, etc.) and control (e.g., arrival rates, service rates, etc.) decisions arise in a wide variety of contexts. Queueing decision making is concerned with improving the performance of the system through the use of appropriate decision models. Models are constructed using the appropriate operating characteristics, and their solution ultimately determines the *optimum design parameters* of the system. Such design parameters may include, for example, the service rates, the number of parallel servers, or the maximum allowable queue length.

Optimization of the design parameters may be viewed in a variety of ways depending on the objective of management. A most common viewpoint is to base management decisions on a cost model that *minimizes the sum of the costs of service and of waiting per unit time.* Obviously, the higher the first is, the lower the second is, and vice versa.

Costs models are ideal for designing and controlling queueing systems if one can obtain reliable estimates of the required cost parameters. However, it is often difficult to estimate the cost parameters associated with the waiting time. In this case one may be forced to search for another "optimality" criterion. Here, we will consider only cost models.

In summary, a large number of queueing management problems involve making one or more of the following decisions:

1. Number of servers at each service facility.
2. Efficiency (rate) of the servers.
3. Number of service facilities.

Case Assignment. Assume that you are the operations manager of the First National City Bank of New Albany (FNCB). The Brooklyn bank, a branch of FNCB, has a remote terminal connected to the foreign account central computer in New Albany.

A recent international monetary crisis has caused a considerable increase in the volume of foreign account transactions in Brooklyn. This has led to the problem of whether or not to add more remote terminals in the Brooklyn branch of FNCB because:

1. Customers in Brooklyn complained of the high waiting time (time a customer spends in the system) for service.
2. The manager of the Brooklyn bank was of the opinion that tellers were waiting too long in line to use the terminal.

The expected time (average time) between requests (expected interarrival time) by customers for changes in their foreign accounts is estimated to be 50 seconds. The *expected* (average) time required (typing, printing, and computing) to process each customer is estimated to be 60 seconds. Given that a terminal rents for $4 per hour and given that the cost of an idle teller is $7 per hour, which of the following four alternatives would you choose?

alternative 1: add one terminal
alternative 2: add two terminals
alternative 3: add three terminals
alternative 4: add four terminals

Would your decision change if labor costs were increased by 25%? What other statistics should you consider, besides expected costs, in determining the optimal alternative?

A model you may want to use is given by the following:

$$C_s = \text{marginal cost of a server per unit time}$$

$$WC = \text{cost of waiting (a random variable)}$$

$$\text{Model:} = \underset{c}{\text{minimize}}\,[\text{expected total cost per unit time}]$$

$$= \underset{c}{\text{minimize}}\,[cC_s + E(WC)]$$

Assignment

1. Give the formula for $E(WC)$ that you are using.
2. Optimal number of terminals is _____ .
   Minimum expected cost = _____ .
   Minimum waiting time W_s = _____ .
   Minimum queue length L_q = _____ .
   Minimum number in the system L_s = _____ .
   Minimum waiting time in the queue W_q = _____ .
3. Assume an idle time cost of $8.75 for each teller. Optimal number of terminals is _____ .

OBJECTIVES: Upon successful completion of this chapter, you should be able to:

1. Specify the differences between PERT and CPM.
2. Calculate the critical path of a project.
3. Make probabilistic statements about the completion time for a project.
4. Calculate the costs and benefits of crashing a project.
5. Formulate a project network and the crashing decision as a linear programming problem.

18.1. INTRODUCTION

Large-scale one-time projects have been around since the beginning of time; witness the building of the pyramids of Egypt and the aqueducts of Rome. But only recently have the managerial problems associated with these projects been studied by operations researchers.

The problem of project management came to the forefront with the Polaris Missile project, starting in 1958. With so many components and subassemblies being produced by many different contractors, a new tool was needed to schedule and control the project. *PERT (program evaluation and review technique)* was developed by scientists from the Navy's Office of Special Projects, Booz Allen and Hamilton, and the Missile Systems Division of Lockheed Aircraft Corporation. The technique proved so useful that it gained wide acceptance in both government and the private sector.

At approximately the same time, the DuPont Company, together with the UNIVAC Division of Remington Rand, developed the *critical path method (CPM)* to control the maintenance of projects for DuPont's chemical plants. CPM is identical to PERT in concept and methodology. The primary difference between them is simply the method by which time estimates are made for the project activities. With CPM, activity times are deterministic. With PERT, activity times are probabilistic or stochastic.

PERT/CPM was designed to provide several useful items of information for project managers. First, PERT/CPM exposes the "critical path" of a project. These are the activities that limit the length of the project. In other words, to get the project done sooner, the activities along the critical path must be completed sooner. On the other hand, if an activity on the critical path falls behind schedule, the project as a whole is behind schedule by a like amount. Activities that are not on the critical path will have a certain amount of slack; that is, they may be started later and still allow the project as a whole to proceed on schedule. PERT/CPM will identify these activities and the amount of time that is available for delays.

PERT/CPM can also look at the resources needed to complete the activities. In many projects, limitations on manpower and equipment make scheduling very difficult. PERT/CPM will identify the times in the project when these constraints will cause problems and with the flexibility allowed by the slack time of noncritical activities allow the manager to move certain activities in order to alleviate these problems.

Finally, PERT/CPM provides a tool to control and monitor the progress of the project. Each activity has its own role in the project and its relevance to project completion is immediately evident to the project manager. Critical-path activities will, of course, receive most of the attention, because the completion of the project depends so heavily on them. Noncritical activities will be moved and replaced in response to resource availability.

PERT/CPM is a very important "management-by-exception" tool of the modern manager, for it allows him to manage the project by concentrating on those critical activities that affect project completion (i.e., those activities on the critical path).

18.2. DIFFERENCES BETWEEN PERT AND CPM

As indicated above, the main difference between PERT and CPM is the manner in which the time estimates are made. PERT assumes that the time to perform each activity is a random variable described by a probability distribution. CPM, on the other hand, infers that the activity times are deterministically known and can be varied by changing the level of resources used.

The time distribution that PERT assumes for an activity is a beta distribution. The distribution for any activity is defined by three estimates: (1) the most probable time estimate, m; (2) the most optimistic time estimate, a; and (3) the most pessimistic time estimate, b. The form of the distribution is shown in Figure 18.1. The most probable time is the time required to complete the activity under normal conditions. The optimistic and pessimistic times provide a measure of the uncertainty inherent in the activity, including equipment malfunctions, labor availability, material delays, and other factors.

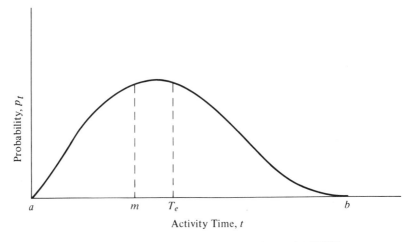

a = optimistic estimate
b = pessimistic estimate
m = most probable estimate
    made
t = activity time
T_e = expected activity time

Figure 18.1. Time distribution of an activity using PERT.

With the distribution defined, the mean (expected) and standard deviation, respectively, of the activity time for activity Z can be calculated by use of the approximation formulas

$$T_e(Z) = \frac{a + 4m + b}{6} \tag{18.1}$$

$$\sigma(Z) = \frac{b - a}{6}. \tag{18.2}$$

The expected completion time of the project is the sum of all the expected times of the activities along the critical path. Likewise, assuming that the activity-time distributions are independent (realistically, a highly questionable assumption), the project variance is the sum of the variances of the activities along the critical path. These properties will be demonstrated later.

Under CPM only one estimate of time is required. All calculations are made with the assumption that the activity times are known. As the project actually proceeds, these estimates are used to control and monitor progress. If slippage should occur in the project, efforts are made to get the project back on schedule by changing allocations of resources.

18.3. MODELING PERT/CPM SYSTEMS

To apply PERT/CPM to a project, thorough understanding of the project requirements and structure is a must. The effort spent in identifying the structure of the project yields valuable insights. In particular, four questions must be answered to begin the modeling procedure:

1. What project activities are required?
2. What are the sequencing requirements or constraints for the activities?
3. Which activities can be conducted simultaneously?
4. What are the estimated time requirements for each activity?

The first step toward building the PERT/CPM network is to list each activity and the activities that must immediately precede it. Table 18.1 lists the activities for a maintenance project on the stadium lighting system at Blue-Gray Stadium.

Table 18.1. Activity List for Light-System-Maintenance Project at Blue-Gray Stadium

Identification Code	Activity	Immediate Predecessor Activity
A	Assemble crew	—
B	Test lights for burned bulbs	—
C	Obtain needed bulbs	B
D	Paint light standards below banks	A
E	Replace burned bulbs	C
F	Deactivate system	B
G	Check all wiring for wear	A, F
H	Obtain needed wire	G
I	Clean lenses on lights	A, F
J	Remove worn wire	G
K	Cut new wire to needed lengths	J, H
L	Check insulators that support wires	J
M	Replace worn insulators	L
N	Replace old wire	M, K
O	Splice new wire with old	N
P	Insulate splices	O
Q	Paint light banks	P
R	Replace broken lenses	E
S	Reactivate system	Q, D, I, R
T	Cleanup	R

Each of the activities will be represented by an arrow. The arrows will connect nodes, represented by small circles.[†] Nodes will represent the state of the project. For example, in general, a typical node would look like Node i in Figure 18.2. Node i represents the end of activities A, B, and C, along with the start of activities D and E.

So, from the activity list in Table 18.1, a network diagram is generated by connecting arrows and nodes representing the structure of the project. In our maintenance project example, activity A must be completed before activity D begins, activity B must be completed before F begins, and so on. Following this procedure it is easy to arrive at the partial network shown in Figure 18.3.

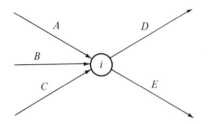

Figure 18.2. Typical node in a network diagram

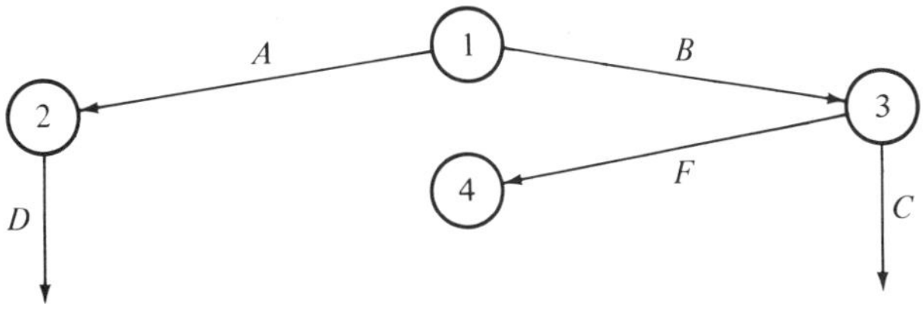

Figure 18.3. Partial network diagram of light system maintenance project of Blue-Gray Stadium.

Activity G cannot start until A and F are completed. There seems to be no way to depict this relationship, because A and F cannot be joined at a node from which G can begin. Separate networks would look as shown in Figure 18.4. To remedy this problem, a dummy activity is used. The dummy activity is represented by a dashed arrow and consumes no time or resources. However, it has the effect

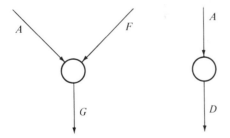

Figure 18.4. Separate networks for activities G and D in light maintenance project at Blue-Gray Stadium.

of requiring that A and F be finished before activity G is begun. (The network would be as in Figure 18.5 after inserting the dummy activity and activity G.)

The partially completed network with activity G is shown in Figure 18.5. Note that the nodes have been numbered to aid identification. There is a convention to this numbering—that the number at the head of an arrow be larger than the

[†]This representation is known as the "activity-on-arrow" representation. Alternatively, the nodes could represent activities and the arrows precedence relationships. The latter is known as the "activity-on-node" representation.

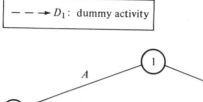

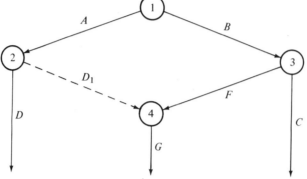

Figure 18.5. Dummy variable in partial network.

number at the origin. This allows the activities to be identified by an ordered pair of numbers (node number of the origin, and node number of the termination). This identification schedule is very useful for automating such networks in the computer, and in developing a mathematical programming formulation for these problems. The activity-node numbers and expected activity times are shown in Table 18.2.

**Table 18.2. Light-Maintenance-Project Data
with Head and Tail Node Numbers Listed**

Activity Code	NODE NUMBER		Expected Activity Duration: T_e
	Begin	End	
A	1	2	1
B	1	3	1
C	3	5	2
D	2	15	14
E	5	7	3
F	3	4	1
Dummy 1	2	4	0
G	4	6	4
H	6	9	2
I	4	15	6
J	6	8	7
Dummy 2	8	9	0
K	9	11	3
L	8	10	2
M	10	11	2

Table 18.2 (*continued*)

Activity Code	NODE NUMBER Begin	NODE NUMBER End	Expected Activity Duration: T_e
N	11	12	4
O	12	13	3
P	13	14	1
Q	14	15	4
R	7	15	4
S	15	16	1
T	16	17	2

18.3.1. *Calculation of ES, LS, EF, and LF*

Once the complete network is developed (Figure 18.6) we wish to find the critical path for the project.[†] This is the path that limits the completion time of the project. To do this, we start at node 1, assigning an arbitrary time for the earliest the project may begin, say time zero. Since node 1 represents the starting point for activities A and B, they are also assigned the *earliest start time* (ES), zero; this is denoted by ES(A), ES(B) = 0.

The earliest an activity may be finished, the *early finish time* (EF), is just the early start time plus the expected activity time (expected activity time is either the deterministic value given by CPM or the mean of the beta distribution estimated by PERT);

$$EF(A) = ES(A) + T_e(A). \qquad (18.3)$$

(T_e is *expected duration of an activity*). So in our example,

$$EF(A) = 0 + 1 = 1$$
$$EF(B) = 0 + 1 = 1.$$

Since activity C depends only on the completion of activity B, it may begin as soon as activity B is completed. Therefore, the earliest start of activity C is equal to the earliest finish (EF) of activity B, or

and
$$ES(C) = EF(B) = 1$$
$$EF(C) = ES(C) + T_e(C)$$
$$= 1 + 2$$
$$= 3.$$

[†]The activity-on-node representation of the completed network is given in the appendix of this chapter.

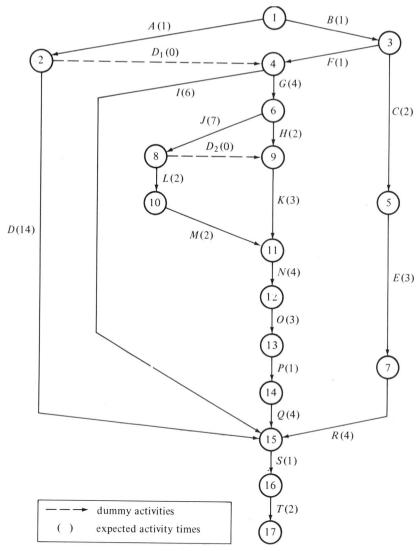

Figure 18.6. Completed network diagram of light system maintenance project at Blue-Gray Stadium.

Similarly, for activity F,

$$ES(F) = EF(B) = 1$$

and

$$EF(F) = ES(F) + T_e(F)$$
$$= 1 + 1$$
$$= 2.$$

Now we want to calculate the earliest start for activity G. However, this time there are two arrows ending at node 4, which signals the beginning of activity G. The first dummy variable (D_1), as you remember, has a duration of zero $[T_e(D_1) = 0]$. Therefore,

$$ES(D_1) = EF(A) = 1$$

and
$$EF(D_1) = ES(D_1) + T_e(D_1)$$
$$= 1 + 0$$
$$= 1.$$

But, as calculated earlier,

$$EF(F) = 2.$$

Activity G cannot begin until both activities D_1 and F are concluded. Therefore,

$$ES(G) = \max[EF(D_1), EF(F)]$$
$$= \max(1, 2)$$
$$= 2$$

and
$$EF(G) = ES(G) + T_e(G)$$
$$= 2 + 4$$
$$= 6.$$

In general, when two or more activities conclude at one node, the earliest start time for the activities emanating from that node is the maximum of the earliest finish times for the activities concluding there. Table 18.3 gives the early start and early finish time for all activities in the project.

Table 18.3. Summary Data for Light-System-Maintenance Project at Blue-Gray Stadium

Activity Code	T_e	ES	EF	LS	LF	TS	FS
A	1	0	1	1	2	1	0
B	1	0	1	0	1	0	0
C	2	1	3	20	22	19	0
D	14	1	15	15	29	14	14
E	3	3	6	22	25	19	0
F	1	1	2	1	2	0	0
Dummy	0	1	1	2	2	1	1
G	4	2	6	2	6	0	0
H	2	6	8	12	14	6	0
I	6	2	8	23	29	21	21
J	7	6	13	6	13	0	0
Dummy	0	13	13	14	14	1	0
K	3	13	16	14	17	1	1

Table 18.3 (*continued*)

Activity Code	T_e	ES	EF	LS	LF	TS	FS
L	2	13	15	13	15	0	0
M	2	15	17	15	17	0	0
N	4	17	21	17	21	0	0
O	3	21	24	21	24	0	0
P	1	24	25	24	25	0	0
Q	4	25	29	25	29	0	0
R	4	6	10	25	29	19	19
S	1	29	30	29	30	0	0
T	2	30	32	30	32	0	0

We now know that the project should be completed 32 days after it is begun. But we have not identified the critical path or any slack that may exist in the project schedule. To do this, we choose an arbitrary time for the completion of the project (let us choose 32) and start backward through the network asking the question: What is the latest this activity can be finished without delaying completion of the entire project?

Obviously, activity T must be completed by day 32; therefore, the latest finish for activity T [LF(T)] is 32. Next, compute the latest time activity T can be started without causing slippage in the project. The latest start for activity T [LS(T)] is just the latest finish time minus the activity time, or

$$LS(T) = LF(T) - T_e(T)$$
$$= 32 - 2$$
$$= 30.$$

Activity S must be finished before activity T may begin. Therefore, the latest S can be finished is 30, or the latest T can start is

$$LF(S) = LS(T)$$
$$= 30.$$

The latest activity S can start is

$$LS(S) = LF(S) - T_e(S)$$
$$= 30 - 1$$
$$= 29.$$

This simple process will continue until we reach a node with two or more arrows originating from it, for example node 6 in Figure 18.6. Activities H and J begin at node 6 while G ends there. The latest start for H is 12, for J it is 6. So activity G must be finished no later than day 6 or activity J will be late causing the whole project to be delayed. For node 11

$$LF(G) = min[LS(H), LS(J)]$$
$$= min(6, 12)$$
$$= 6.$$

In general, for node i in Figure 18.7:

$$ES(X) = ES(Y) = ES(Z) = max[EF(A), EF(B), EF(C)]$$
$$EF(X) = ES(X) + T_e(X) \tag{18.4}$$
$$LF(A) = LF(B) = LF(C) = min[LS(X), LS(Y), LS(Z)]$$
$$LS(A) = LF(A) - T_e(A). \tag{18.5}$$

The late start and late finish times for all activities are also shown in Table 18.3.

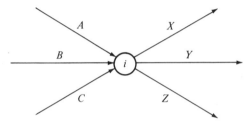

Figure 18.7. ES, EF, LF, LS at node i.

18.3.2. Critical Path and Slack

Having computed ES, EF, LS, and LF for all activities, we are ready to identify the total slack (TS) and free slack (FS) for each activity, and the critical path. The total slack (TS) for any activity is the maximum amount of time the activity can be delayed without affecting the completion time of the project. Recall that LS is defined as the latest time that an activity can be started without delaying the project completion. Subtracting ES (the earliest possible starting time) from LS will give the total slippage allowable for any activity. Denoting total slack at any activity Z by TS:

$$TS(Z) = LS(Z) - ES(Z). \tag{18.6}$$

The critical path of the network, being the *longest path* through the network, must have the smallest total slack of all the activities. This minimum total slack will also be equal for all activities along the critical path. In our maintenance project example, the critical path includes activities $B, F, G, J, L, M, N, O, P, Q, S$, and T (Figure 18.6). This can also be determined from Table 18.3 by observing those activities that have the minimum total slack, which is equal to zero. (Although it did not happen here, it is possible for a dummy activity to be on the critical path.)

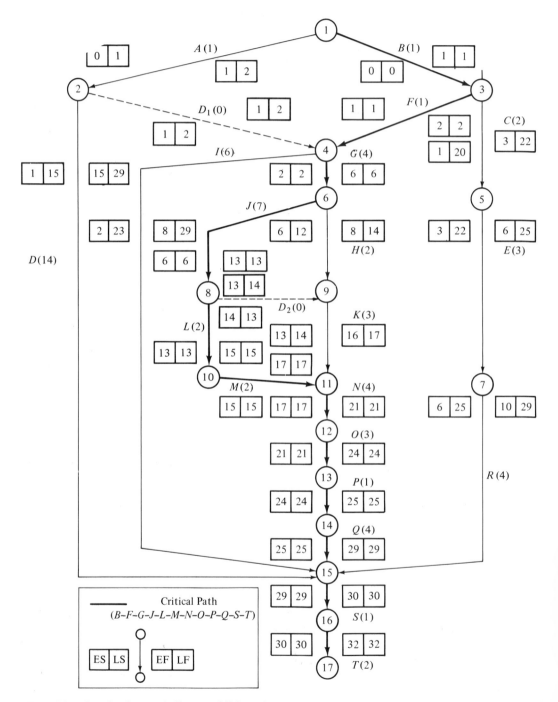

Figure 18.8. Completed network diagram of light maintenance project showing activity times and critical path.

Total slack is a global concept referring to how long a given activity can be delayed before the project as a whole exceeds scheduled completion.

Another useful notion for analyzing a project is called *free slack* (FS). This is the maximum amount of time any activity may be delayed without delaying the start of the next activity. Free slack is a local concept giving the project manager flexibility in scheduling a given activity having free slack, without disturbing the schedule of any other activity in the project. If the manager delays an activity with no free slack he will have to delay other activities subsequent to that activity. Free slack is calculated by

$$\text{EF (current activity)} - \text{ES (successive activity)}. \qquad (18.7)$$

Free slack will only occur on noncritical activities and will never exceed total slack. The free slack for each activity is shown in Table 18.3. Figure 18.8 is the completed network of our maintenance project showing the resulting start times and finish times, free slack and total slack for each activity, as well as the critical path.

18.4. PROBABILITY CONCEPTS WITH PERT

Now that we have found the critical path to the example project, let us assume that we have been working with a PERT system. The time estimates we have been using would have all come from estimates of the three parameters (described earlier), which are shown in Table 18.4.

Table 18.4. PERT Time Estimates for Light Maintenance Project at Blue-Gray Stadium

Activity Code	a	m	b	T_e	σ
A	0	1	2	1	0.33
B	1	1	1	1	0.00
C	0	2	4	2	0.67
D	9	12	27	14	3.00
E	2	3	4	3	0.33
F	1	1	1	1	0.00
G	2	3	10	4	1.33
H	1	1	7	2	1.00
I	2	5	14	6	2.00
J	4	5	14	8	1.67
K	2	3	4	3	0.33
L	1	1	7	2	1.00
M	1	2	3	2	0.33
N	2	4	6	4	0.67
O	1	3	5	3	0.67
P	1	1	1	1	0.00
Q	2	3	10	4	1.33
R	1	4	7	4	1.00
S	1	1	1	1	0.00
T	2	2	2	2	0.00

The *expected time to complete the project* (T_{ep}) is exactly the same as we have already calculated. However, we also have an estimate of the *variance of project completion* σ_p^2, which is the sum of the variances of the activities along the critical path.[†] By adding together these activity distributions, the project distribution approaches a normal distribution based on the central limit theorem. The project manager can then make probabilistic statements about the completion time of the project. To illustrate, in our example the total project time (T_p) is thus assumed to have a normal distribution with mean time T_{ep} equal to 32 and standard deviation σ_p equal to 2.89 (calculations shown in Table 18.5). What if the project manager wanted to know the probability that the project would be finished in 35 days or less? He would compute $p(T \leqslant 35)$. Standardizing T_p to the Z statistic and using the standard normal table (Table IV of Appendix A),

$$P(T_p \leqslant 35) = P\left(Z \leqslant \frac{35 - 32}{2.89}\right)$$

$$= P(Z \leqslant 1.038) = 0.85.$$

Thus, there is an 85% chance that the project will be finished on or before 35 days.

Table 18.5. Calculation of Project Standard Deviation on Light-System-Maintenance Project at Blue-Gray Stadium

Activities on Critical Path	σ	σ^2	
B	0.00	0.00	
F	0.00	0.00	
G	1.33	1.78	
J	1.67	2.78	
L	1.00	1.00	
M	0.33	0.11	
N	0.67	0.44	
O	0.67	0.44	
P	0.00	0.00	
Q	1.33	1.78	
S	0.00	0.00	
T	0.00	0.00	
	$\sigma^2 = \overline{8.33}$		For project completion
	$\sigma = 2.89$		

[†]The assumption that σ_p^2 is the sum of the variance of the activities along the critical path is, strictly speaking, correct only if the activities are independent. If not independent, covariances between activities must be determined to obtain σ_p^2. This is a complex process and beyond the scope of this text. Moreover, from a practical standpoint, this becomes infeasible.

18.5.1. Limited Resources

So far we have not yet discussed how to actually define the schedule for a whole project. We have identified the schedule that the activities along the critical path must have but not the noncritical activities.

Let us now look at a different project, which is shown in Figure 18.9. As you can easily verify, the project is expected to be completed in 9 weeks. To look at the manpower required in each week, it is useful to plot the project on a time chart such as in Figure 18.10; then totaling the men required in each period is easy.

If the manager of this project had unlimited manpower available, he might use a schedule defined by the early start time of each activity. This would result in a manpower profile such as the one given in Figure 18.11. However, very few companies are in such a fortunate position; also, it is very undesirable from a managerial point of view to have wide fluctuations in the manpower requirements in any project. Therefore, the problem is to level the demand for manpower over the duration of this project. For example, what if the company had only 18 men available for this project? Could it get the project done without extending the schedule?

Many heuristic programs have been developed to deal with the problem of resource balancing in PERT/CPM networks. In the project shown in Figures 18.9 and 18.10, primary attention should be given to those activities having the most slack, delaying these as much as possible. For example, delaying activity C until period 3 allows activities A and B to proceed simultaneously. Then we could move activity I to periods 8 and 9, and D to period 5. This opens periods 6 and 7 for activity H.

Figure 18.9. Network for problem with limited resources.

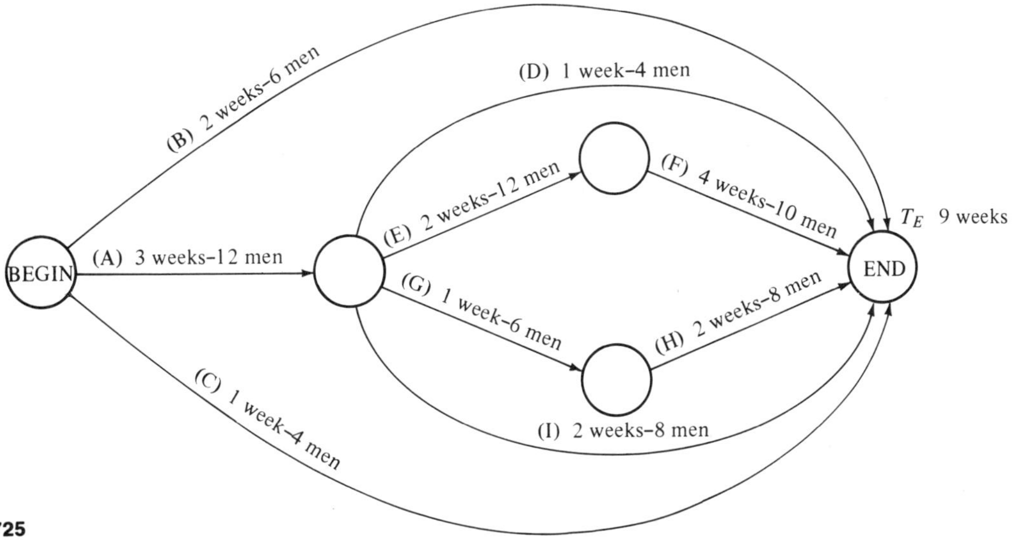

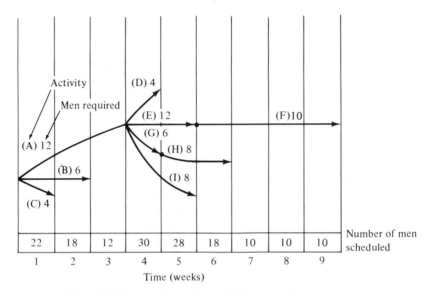

Figure 18.10. Network of Figure 18.9. shown on time graph.

Figure 18.11. Manpower utilization with unlimited resources.

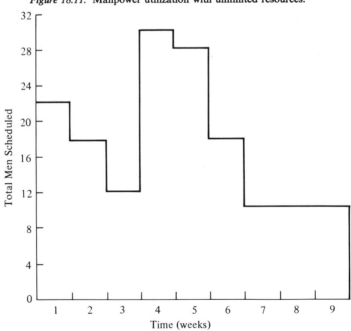

Figure 18.12 shows the resulting schedule for this project. You will notice that even in this very small problem, the resources required in each period cannot be perfectly balanced. In a larger project, the problems may be much greater and decisions may have to be made on delaying some activities beyond their late starts because of manpower restrictions. However, PERT/CPM will alert the manager to these problems in advance and allow time for corrective action.

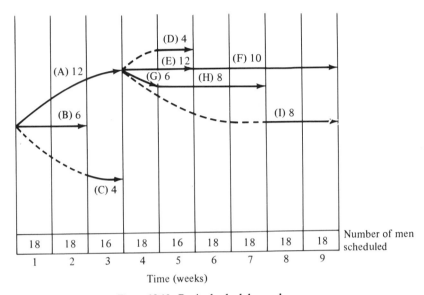

Figure 18.12. Revised schedule graph.

It should be noted that the heuristic applied here, like all others, does not guarantee an optimal solution and will not always work as easily or clearly as it did here. For discussions of other methods, see Davis (1966) and references cited therein.

18.5.2. Crashing

In some situations it may pay to get a project done earlier than the normal schedule would permit. This may mean hiring additional people, working present people overtime, or buying more equipment to help the workers finish early. The process of reducing project completion time by these means is called *crashing*. Table 18.6 depicts a project with normal and crashed activity times and crashing costs. The project network diagram is shown in Figure 18.13.

The first step is to calculate the project completion time, critical path, and costs under both normal and fully crashed conditions.[†] (Assume that the normal

---

[†]That is, all activities are fully crashed to their minimum times.

Table 18.6. Project with Normal and Crashed Activity Times and Costs

Activity	Predecessors	$T_e(S)$ Normal (weeks)	$T'_e(S)$ Fully Crashed (weeks)	Crash Cost per Week
A	None	14	6	100
B	None	12	8	200
C	B	4	2	100
D	A	6	4	200
E	A	18	14	200
F	C, D	8	6	100
G	E, F	12	8	100

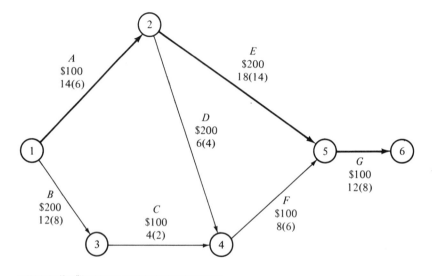

Critical Path

Normal time $(A$–E–$G) = 44$ ($6400)
Crash time $(A$–E–$G) = 28$ ($10,000)

Figure 18.13. Network diagram of project in Table 18.6, with crashing permissible.

project cost is $6400.) These conditions are summarized as follows:

	Critical Path	Project Time	Project Cost
Normal times	A–E–G	44	$ 6,400
Crash times	A–E–G	28	10,000

The critical path for the crashed times need not be the same as for the normal times. (If, for example, a noncritical activity can be crashed in excess of its total slack, it will become a critical activity.)

We have now identified the normal time–normal cost schedule for the project and the least time–highest cost schedule. What if the project manager wanted to know what would be the least-cost schedule to complete the project in 30 weeks, 35 weeks, or any other time between 44 and 28 weeks? To reduce the project time we must obviously reduce the time needed to complete the critical path. Also, we want to do this at the least possible cost. Therefore, we must choose that activity along the critical path that has the least cost of crashing. In our example, activities A and G both cost $100 per week to crash. (In case of a tie, we choose the activity that can reduce the project duration by the greatest amount, which is A.)

Now fully crash A from 14 weeks to 6 weeks. This adds $800 to the project cost (8 weeks $\times$ $100/week), giving a total of $7200. We must now revise the network to reflect the crashing of activity A, as shown in Figure 18.14. The crashing of activity A has reduced the previous critical path, A–E–G, to 36 weeks (Figure 18.14). But also notice that crashing now makes path B–C–F–G critical as well ($= 36$ weeks). (This is an example of noncritical activities becoming critical when activities are crashed.)

Realizing that activity G is the only activity that can reduce the project time alone, we choose it to crash next. We reduce $T_e(G)$ from 12 weeks to 8 weeks at a

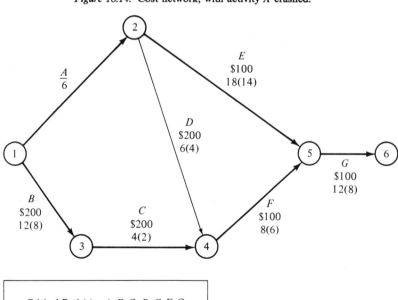

Figure 18.14. Cost network, with activity A crashed.

Critical Path(s): A–E–G; B–C–F–G
Time = 36
Cost = $7200

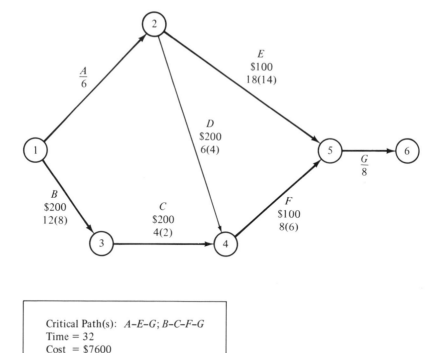

Critical Path(s): A–E–G; B–C–F–G
Time = 32
Cost = $7600

Figure 18.15. Cost network, with activities A and G crashed.

cost of $400. The network is now as shown in Figure 18.15, with total project cost being $7600 with a duration of 32 weeks.

With the two critical paths A–E–G and B–C–F–G—both equal to 32 weeks —we must now choose one activity from each branch to reduce the project time. Since F has the lowest crash cost remaining, it will be chosen. Activity E is the only one left on the other path. Although E could be crashed 4 weeks, it is not worthwhile crashing more than 2 weeks, since this is the limit of activity F. This crashing results in increasing the project cost by $600 (2 × 100 for activity F plus 2 × 200 for activity E). The total project cost is thus $8200, with a duration of 30 weeks. The resulting network is shown in Figure 18.16.

As you can probably see by now, the final step is to crash activity E and either B or C. This step costs $600, making the total cost of the crashed project $8800, which is less than crashing all the activities, as shown earlier. Figure 18.17 shows the final network. Notice that crashing either activity B or D will not result in a reduction in the project time. The results of this analysis can be graphed so as to show the cost of crashing for any project completion time between a normal and a fully crashed schedule (Figure 18.18).

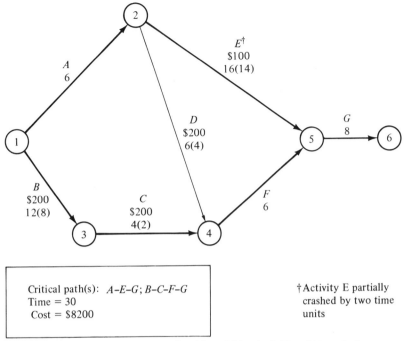

Critical path(s): A–E–G; B–C–F–G
Time = 30
Cost = \$8200

†Activity E partially
crashed by two time
units

Figure 18.16. Cost network, with activities *A, G, F,* and *E* crashed.

Figure 18.17. Cost network, with activities *A, G, F, E,* and *C* crashed.

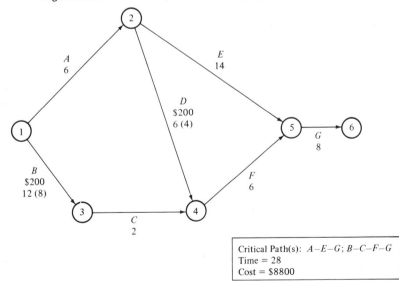

Critical Path(s): A–E–G; B–C–F–G
Time = 28
Cost = \$8800

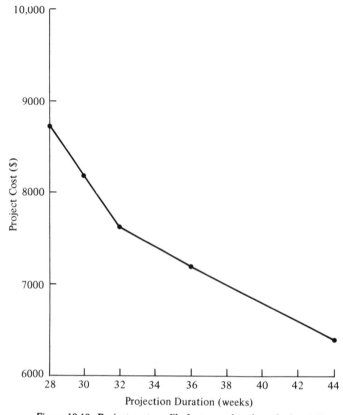

Figure 18.18. Project cost profile for normal and crashed activities.

18.6. LINEAR PROGRAMMING FORMULATION OF PERT/CPM NETWORKS

PERT/CPM networks can very easily be modeled as linear programming problems. The formulation of PERT/CPM networks as linear programming problems provides valuable insights into the project structure and modeling techniques per se. However, from a practical viewpoint it is infeasible to solve a large project network as a programming problem because of the large number of constraints and variables involved, which would exceed existing computer capability.

18.6.1. Critical-Path Determination with Unlimited Resources

If we define $T_e(i)$ as being the expected time at which node i is reached, then the objective function, which is to find the critical path of a PERT/CPM network, is

$$\text{minimize } Z = T_e(n) - T_e(o), \tag{18.8}$$

where node o is the project beginning and node n is the project end. This expression just means we want to minimize the time needed to get from the start to the finish of the network.

The constraints are constructed from the fact that for any activity M, starting at node i and ending at node j, the time needed to get from node i to node j is at least the activity time for M (in fact, the time needed is the activity time plus total slack). Therefore, the constraints are of the form

$$T_e(j) - T_e(i) \geqslant T_e(M)$$

or
$$T_e(j) - T_e(i) = T_e(M) + \text{TS}(M) \tag{18.9}$$

The linear programming formulation for the Blue-Gray Stadium light-system-maintenance project depicted in Tables 18.1 and 18.2 is then:

Node	Minimize $Z = T_e(17) - T_e(1)$ subject to:	Node	Minimize $Z = T_e(17) - T_e(1)$ subject to:
1	$T_e(2) - T_e(1) \geqslant 1$	12	$T_e(11) - T_e(10) \geqslant 2$
2	$T_e(3) - T_e(1) \geqslant 1$	13	$T_e(12) - T_e(11) \geqslant 4$
3	$T_e(4) - T_e(3) \geqslant 1$	14	$T_e(13) - T_e(12) \geqslant 3$
4	$T_e(15) - T_e(4) \geqslant 6$	15	$T_e(14) - T_e(13) \geqslant 1$
5	$T_e(15) - T_e(2) \geqslant 14$	16	$T_e(15) - T_e(14) \geqslant 4$
6	$T_e(6) - T_e(4) \geqslant 4$	17	$T_e(4) - T_e(2) \geqslant 0$
7	$T_e(9) - T_e(6) \geqslant 2$	18	$T_e(5) - T_e(3) \geqslant 2$
8	$T_e(8) - T_e(6) \geqslant 7$	19	$T_e(7) - T_e(5) \geqslant 3$
9	$T_e(9) - T_e(8) \geqslant 0$	20	$T_e(15) - T_e(7) \geqslant 4$
10	$T_e(10) - T_e(8) \geqslant 2$	21	$T_e(16) - T_e(15) \geqslant 1$
11	$T_e(11) - T_e(9) \geqslant 3$	22	$T_e(17) - T_e(16) \geqslant 2$
	$T_e(i) \geqslant 0$ (for all i).		
	[Assume that $T_e(1) = 0$.]		

The critical path can be identified by finding those constraints that have no slack; these will correspond to the activities on the critical path. Also the dual variables that are nonzero will specify the constraints that denote the activities on the critical path.

The computer solution output to the linear programming formulation for the Blue-Gray Stadium light maintenance project is replicated in Table 18.7. Note that this solution tells that we will reach node 17 (column 2, under "Var Name"), the end of the project, in 32 days (column 5, under "Activity Level"), just as we have found previously using normal PERT/CPM procedures (see Figure 18.8). To find the critical path, we need to identify those constraints that have no surplus variables; in other words, those constraints that are strict equalities in the solution. By the complementary slackness theorem in LP, those equations whose corresponding dual variables are not equal to zero must be strict equalities; hence, the corresponding slack surplus (negative) variables are equal to zero. The surplus variables that are not equal to zero are those in the "Opportunity Cost" column (column 6) having a value of 1 (the "shadow price"). These are: 2, 4, 7, 9, 11, 13, 14, 15, 16, 17, 18, and 22. Therefore, the constraints of the same numbers (see the LP formulation) must be equalities, meaning that they have no slack; that is, associated activities specified by these nodes are on the critical path (e.g., since constraint 22 is an equality, activity T is on the critical path, as shown in Figure 18.8).

Table 18.7. Linear Programming Solution to Blue-Gray Stadium Project (summary of results)

Var No.	Var Name	Row No.	Status	Activity Level	Opportunity Cost
1	X1	–	NB	–	0.0000000
2	X2	–	B	2.0000000	–
3	X3	–	B	1.0000000	–
4	X4	–	B	2.0000000	–
5	X5	–	B	22.0000000	–
6	X6	–	B	6.0000000	–
7	X7	–	B	25.0000000	–
8	X8	–	B	13.0000000	–
9	X9	–	B	14.0000000	–
10	X10	–	B	15.0000000	–
11	X11	–	B	17.0000000	–
12	X12	–	B	21.0000000	–
13	X13	–	B	24.0000000	–
14	X14	–	B	25.0000000	–
15	X15	–	B	29.0000000	–
16	X16	–	B	30.0000000	–
17	X17	–	B	32.0000000	–
18	–SLACK	1	B	1.0000000	–
19	–SLACK	2	NB	–	1.0000000
20	–SLACK	3	NB	–	0.0000000
21	–SLACK	4	NB	–	1.0000000
22	–SLACK	5	B	21.0000000	–
23	–SLACK	6	B	13.0000000	–
24	–SLACK	7	NB	–	1.0000000
25	–SLACK	8	B	6.0000000	–
26	–SLACK	9	NB	–	1.0000000
27	–SLACK	10	B	1.0000000	–
28	–SLACK	11	NB	–	1.0000000
29	–SLACK	12	NB	–	0.0000000
30	–SLACK	13	NB	–	1.0000000
31	–SLACK	14	NB	–	1.0000000
32	–SLACK	15	NB	–	1.0000000
33	–SLACK	16	NB	–	1.0000000
34	–SLACK	17	NB	–	1.0000000
35	–SLACK	18	NB	–	1.0000000

Table 18.7 (*continued*)

Var No.	Var Name	Row No.	Status	Activity Level	Opportunity Cost
36	–SLACK	19	B	19.0000000	–
37	–SLACK	20	NB	–	0.0000000
38	–SLACK	21	NB	–	0.0000000
39	–SLACK	22	NB	–	1.0000000
40	–ARTIF D-	1	NB	–	0.0000000
41	–ARTIF D-	2	NB	–	1.0000000
42	–ARTIF D-	3	NB	–	0.0000000
43	–ARTIF D-	4	NB	–	1.0000000
44	–ARTIF D-	5	NB	–	0.0000000
45	–ARTIF D-	6	NB	–	0.0000000
46	–ARTIF D-	7	NB	–	1.0000000
47	–ARTIF D-	8	NB	–	0.0000000
48	–ARTIF D-	9	NB	–	1.0000000
49	–ARTIF D-	10	NB	–	0.0000000
50	–ARTIF D-	11	NB	–	1.0000000
51	–ARTIF D-	12	NB	–	0.0000000
52	–ARTIF D-	13	NB	–	1.0000000
53	–ARTIF D-	14	NB	–	1.0000000
54	–ARTIF D-	15	NB	–	1.0000000
55	–ARTIF D-	16	NB	–	1.0000000
56	–ARTIF D-	17	NB	–	1.0000000
57	–ARTIF D-	18	NB	–	1.0000000
58	–ARTIF D-	19	NB	–	0.0000000
59	–ARTIF D-	20	NB	–	0.0000000
60	–ARTIF D-	21	NB	–	0.0000000
61	–ARTIF D-	22	NB	–	1.0000000

MINIMUM VALUE OF THE OBJECTIVE FUNCTION = 32.0000000

CALCULATION TIME WAS 0.3300 SECOND FOR 23 ITERATIONS.

DATA STORAGE MEMORY = 003076(OCTAL) TOTAL MEMORY = 040000(OCTAL)

18.6.2. Linear Programming Formulation of Crashing

It is also possible to model the crashing situation as a linear programming problem. First let us specify the following notation:

$$T_e(M) = \text{normal activity time for activity } M$$
$$T_e'(M) = \text{activity time for } M \text{ at maximum crashing}$$
$$K(M) = \text{cost per unit time of crashing}$$
$$T_e(i) = \text{expected time of reaching node } i$$
$$C(M) = \text{amount of crash time used for activity } M$$
$$D = \text{deadline for project completion.}$$

The problem is to finish the project in a time that is equal to or less than the duration of the critical path under normal conditions. The project manager wants to know the lowest-cost schedule for doing this. The objective function of the linear programming formulation is thus

$$\text{minimize } Z = \sum_M K(M)C(M),\qquad(18.10)$$

which is the cost of crashing, which we wish to minimize.
The constraints are as follows:

1. We must meet the deadline set for the project,

$$T_e(n) - T_e(o) \leqslant D.\qquad(18.11)$$

2. For any activity M, the time needed to get from beginning node i to ending node j is greater than or equal to the normal activity time for M less any crashing done on M,

$$T_e(j) - T_e(i) \geqslant T_e(M) - C(M).\qquad(18.12)$$

3. The crash time for any activity M cannot exceed the defined maximum crash time,

$$C(M) \leqslant T_e(M) - T_e'(M).\qquad(18.13)$$

With $T_e(M)$, $T_e'(M)$, $K(M)$, and D given, all equations are in terms of the variables $T_e(i)$ and $C(M)$.

Formulating the crashing problem discussed in Section 18.5.2 (Figure 18.13) would result in the following linear programming problem [assuming that $T_e(1) = 0$]:

$$\text{minimize } Z = 6400 + 100 \cdot C(A) + 200 \cdot C(B) + 100 \cdot C(C)$$
$$+200 \cdot C(D) + 200 \cdot C(E) + 100 \cdot C(F) + 100 \cdot C(G)$$

subject to:

Constraint Set 1:   *Meet Deadline Set for Project.* This limit on project length can be parametrically varied to yield the project cost versus time duration profile shown in Figure 18.18

$$T_e(6) \leqslant 28.$$

Constraint Set 2: The project structural constraints are as follows:

$$T_e(2) - T_e(1) \geqslant 14 - C(A)$$
$$T_e(3) - T_e(1) \geqslant 12 - C(B)$$
$$T_e(4) - T_e(2) \geqslant 6 - C(D)$$
$$T_e(6) - T_e(5) \geqslant 12 - C(G)$$
$$T_e(5) - T_e(4) \geqslant 8 - C(F)$$
$$T_e(5) - T_e(2) \geqslant 18 - C(E)$$
$$T_e(4) - T_e(3) \geqslant 4 - C(C).$$

Constraint Set 3: The limits on crashing are as follows:

$$C(A) \leqslant 8 \quad C(E) \leqslant 4$$
$$C(B) \leqslant 4 \quad C(F) \leqslant 2$$
$$C(C) \leqslant 2 \quad C(G) \leqslant 4$$
$$C(D) \leqslant 2 \quad T_e(i) \geqslant 0 \quad \text{(for all } i).$$

Table 18.8 shows the results of solving this LP model. As you can see, activity A is crashed 8 units; C, 2 units; E, 4 units; F, 2 units; and G, 4 units. The cost of the entire project is now $8800. All these results coincide with the solution obtained through manual crashing techniques discussed in Section 18.5.2 and shown in Figures 18.17 and 18.18. If the right-hand side of the constraint in constraint set 1 were parametrically varied from 28 to 44 days and solved, the results would be identical to those shown in Figure 18.18.

Table 18.8. Linear Programming Solution to Crashing Project (summary of results)

Var No.	Var Name		Row No.	Status	Activity Level	Opportunity Cost	Bound Value
1	X1	Te(1)	–	NB	–	0.0000000	INF
2	X2	Te(2)	–	B	6.0000000	–	INF
3	X3	Te(3)	–	B	12.0000000	–	INF
4	X4	Te(4)	–	B	14.0000000	–	INF
5	X5	Te(5)	–	B	20.0000000	–	INF
6	X6	Te(6)	–	AB	28.0000000	300.0000000	28.0000
7	X7	C(A)	–	AB	8.0000000	100.0000000	8.0000
8	X8	C(B)	–	NB	–	100.0000000	4.0000
9	X9	C(C)	–	AB	2.0000000	0.0000000	2.0000
10	X10	C(D)	–	NB	–	200.0000000	2.0000
11	X11	C(E)	–	B	4.0000000	–	4.0000
12	X12	C(F)	–	B	2.0000000	–	2.0000
13	X13	C(G)	–	AB	4.0000000	200.0000000	4.0000
14	–SLACK		1	NB	–	200.0000000	INF
15	–SLACK		2	NB	–	100.0000000	INF
16	–SLACK		3	B	2.0000000	–	INF
17	–SLACK		4	NB	–	300.0000000	INF
18	–SLACK		5	NB	–	100.0000000	INF

Table 18.8 (*continued*)

Var No.	Var Name	Row No.	Status	Activity Level	Opportunity Cost	Bound Value
19	–SLACK	6	NB	–	200.0000000	INF
20	–SLACK	7	NB	–	100.0000000	INF
21	–ARTIF D-	1	NB	–	200.0000000	INF
22	–ARTIF D-	2	NB	–	100.0000000	INF
23	–ARTIF D-	3	NB	–	0.0000000	INF
24	–ARTIF D-	4	NB	–	300.0000000	INF
25	–ARTIF D-	5	NB	–	100.0000000	INF
26	–ARTIF D-	6	NB	–	200.0000000	INF
27	–ARTIF D-	7	NB	–	100.0000000	INF

MINIMUM VALUE OF THE OBJECTIVE FUNCTION = 8800

CALCULATION TIME WAS 0.1370 SECOND FOR 15 ITERATIONS.

DATA STORAGE MEMORY = 000752(OCTAL); TOTAL MEMORY = 040000(OCTAL)

18.7. SUMMARY

PERT and CPM have been applied to many project situations. Beginning with their initial application to the Polaris project and maintenance of chemical plants, today they (and their variants) are applied to highway and building construction, and to the development and production of high-technology items such as aircraft, aerospace vehicles, ships, and computers.

PERT was developed for projects where there existed uncertainty in the time activities (usually because the project had never been attempted before and therefore there was no data base for activity times). This led to the probabilistic approach taken. While PERT time estimates and their time distributions have been controversial, PERT has been a useful tool in project management. The major drawback is that it can become dysfunctional for very large projects because of the three time estimates required on each activity and the limited capability of current computers to store this vast amount of data. Moreover, the cost of updating and maintaining project information over time in such dynamic environments can be excessively prohibitive.

On the other hand, CPM was developed to deal with recurring or similar projects (e.g., maintaining chemical plants). Obviously, experience is gained in such situations over a period of time, even though no two projects may be the same. Such experience led to the development of the crashing analysis techniques used in CPM networks.

While CPM and PERT are essentially the same, their nuances make each more applicable than the other in different situations. In both methods the essential information desired is the critical path and slack. These allow the project manager to make informed decisions, based on the principle of management by exception, about the actual work plans and schedules and to monitor the progress of the project.

REFERENCES DAVIS, E. W. "Resource Allocations in Project Network Models—A Survey." *Journal of Industrial Engineering*, **17** (4), 1966.

LEVY, F. K., G. L. THOMPSON, and J. D. WIEST. "The ABC's of the Critical Path." *Harvard Business Review*, September–October, 1963, 98–108.

MODER, J. J. and C. R. PHILLIPS. *Project Management with CPM and PERT.* New York: Reinhold Publishing Corporation, 1964.

PHILLIPS, D., A. RAVINDRAN, and J. SOLBERG. *Operations Research.* New York: John Wiley & Sons, Inc., 1976.

KEY CONCEPTS

CPM
PERT
  most likely, optimistic, pessimistic time estimates
Critical path
Total slack
Free slack
Early start

Late start
Early finish
Late finish
Activity on node diagram
Activity on arrow diagram
Dummy activities
Crashing activities

REVIEW QUESTIONS

18.1. Define:
(a) Total slack
(b) Free slack
(c) Critical path

18.2. What are the meanings and purposes of the following variables?
(a) ES
(b) LS
(c) EF
(d) LF

18.3. Describe the information needed to
(a) Find the critical path
(b) Crash costs
(c) Determine a resource-leveled schedule.

18.4. What are the three time estimates needed for PERT analysis and what do they represent? Show how you would use these estimates to compute the expected activity time and the variance in activity time.

18.5. What is the assumed distribution of the completion time of a project and why is it important?

18.6. What is crashing and when is it used?

18.7. What is leveling and when is it used?

18.8. Would PERT/CPM models be categorized as planning, scheduling, and control tools or as optimization models? Discuss.

18.9. Would PERT/CPM be used for a one-time project or for repetitive projects?

18.10. Under what circumstances would you use PERT as opposed to CPM in project management? Give some examples of projects where each would be more applicable than the other.

18.11. Discuss the notion of using three time estimates and assuming a beta distribution for activity times with PERT. What are the advantages and shortcomings of this from a theoretical and practical standpoint? From a conceptual viewpoint, consider what constitutes a beta distribution (Chapter 2) and what was learned in Chapter 5 about assessing subjective probability distributions of random variables. From a practical viewpoint, consider the number of estimates that need to be made in a given project.

18.12. Can you think of any advantages or disadvantages of formulating and solving a PERT/CPM problem via linear programming?

18.13. Project control is a key requirement in R&D management.
(a) How is PERT used in R&D control?
(b) How does the budget provide control?
(c) What is the basis for controlling the selection of new R&D projects?

ANSWERS TO REVIEW QUESTIONS

18.1. The following are the definitions for "total slack," "free slack," and "critical path."
(a) Total slack for any activity is the maximum amount of time the activity can be delayed without affecting the completion time of the project.
(b) Free slack is the maximum amount of time any activity may be delayed without delaying the start of the next activity.
(c) The critical path is the longest path through the network.

18.2. For ES, LS, EF, and LF, the meanings and purposes are as follows:
(a) ES is the earliest start time of an activity and is equal to the time the project begins plus the longest time path to that activity.
(b) LS is the latest starting time of an activity that will allow the activity to be finished without delaying the completion of the project.
(c) EF is the earliest finish time of an activity and is equal to ES plus the expected time of the activity.
(d) LF is the latest finishing time of an activity that will not delay the project, and is equal to LS plus the time to complete the activity.

18.3. To find the critical path, to crash costs, and determine a resource-leveled schedule, the following information is needed:
(a) To find the critical path, one must know which project activities are required, what the sequencing requirements or constraints on the activities are, which activities can be conducted simultaneously, and what are the estimated time requirements for each activity.
(b) To crash costs, it would be necessary to know the critical path as well as the cost of hiring additional workers, working present employees overtime, or buying more equipment to help the workers complete activities early.
(c) To determine a resource-leveled schedule, primary attention should be given to those activities having the most slack, delaying these as much as possible.

18.4. The three time estimates in PERT are a most probable (m), optimistic (a), and pessimistic estimate (b). Once these estimates are obtained, the expected activity time and standard deviation of an activity time can be computed using the following formulas:

$$T_e(Z) = \frac{a + 4m + b}{6}$$

where $T_e(Z)$ is the expected activity time and

$$\sigma(Z) = \frac{b - a}{6}.$$

18.5. The assumed distribution of completion time of a project (not activity) is normal distribution, justified on the basis of the Central Limit Theorem. It is important because it permits the determination of the probability of completion of the project in a given time.

18.6. Crashing is the hiring of additional people, working present people overtime, or buying more equipment to help workers finish the project earlier than normal. It is used in situations where it might pay to complete a project earlier than the normal schedule would permit.

18.7. Leveling is smoothing the demand for employee man-power or for other limited resources over the duration of a project. It is appropriately used to avoid wide fluctuations in employee man-power requirements resulting in excessive hiring and firing costs.

18.8. Both PERT/CPM provides a tool for planning, scheduling, and controlling a project. The relationships among activities are depicted in a project network, each showing its potential impact on project completion.

PERT/CPM can also be viewed in terms of an optimization model, where the objective function is to minimize project completion time subject to scheduling and activity time constraints.

18.9. Both PERT and CPM should generally be used for one-time projects.

18.10. PERT would generally be used where uncertainty exists in the time activities, such as in research and development projects involving new technology.

CPM would generally be used for projects where the technology is known and thus there is low uncertainty in the activity time estimates; for example, CPM would be used for overhauling a chemical plant.

18.11. There are many different ways of generating subjective probability distribution assessments from individuals. Methods such as the fractile method may require up to nine points on the CDF to define the distribution. Having to assess three points, as in PERT, is advantageous relative to these methods, especially when the number of estimates required is very large. However, even three estimates of the many activities in a project usually make the application of PERT onerous and often unworkable.

The rationale for assuming the Beta distribution is that it is computationally easy to work with and it is "flexible," taking on a wide variety of possible shapes. With proper combinations of parameters, it may be u-shaped, uniform, or bell-shaped. Most subjective probability distributions (as long as they are not multimodel) would fit into one of these categories.

18.12. The formulation of PERT/CPM networks as LP problems provides valuable insights into the project structure and modeling techniques per se. However, from a practical viewpoint, it is infeasible, at present, to solve a large project network as a programming problem. This is because the large number of constraints and variables involved would exceed the capacity of the computer.

18.13. The use of PERT, budgeting, and the selection of new R&D projects are all related to project control.

(a) PERT allows the R&D manager to assess the probabilities that a project will be finished at various times in order to determine whether a project milestone will be met. It allows the manager to focus on the critical activities, which could also include those having a high variance with respect to completion time.

(b) The budget provides control by limiting the amount, distribution and scheduling of manpower or other scarce resources.

(c) New projects are selected on the basis of whether they can be completed in a reasonable length of time and whether they exceed the limitations on the use of scarce resources.

EXERCISES   **18.1.** Using the critical path method (CPM), determine the following for the problem specified below:
(a) Critical path
(b) Earliest completion time
(c) Free slack for jobs, *C*, *D*, and *F*

Job	Immediate Predecessors	Job Time
A	—	2
B	A	3
C	B	3
D	B	1
E	F, C, D	2
F	A	5

18.2. Given the following information:

Activity	Immediate Predecessors	Activity Time
A	—	4
B	A	1
C	A	2
D	B, C	5
E	B, D	3
F	C	8
G	E, D, F	2

(a) Find the ES, LS, EF, LF, TS, and FS for each activity.

(b) Find the critical path.

(c) List two major differences between PERT and CPM.

18.3. A research and development department is developing a new power supply for a console television set. It has broken the job down into the following form:

Job	Description	Immediate Predecessors	Time (days)
a	Determine output voltages	—	5
b	Determine whether to use solid-state rectifiers	a	7
c	Choose rectifiers	b	2
d	Choose filter	b	3
e	Choose transformer	c	1
f	Choose chassis	d	2
g	Choose rectifier mounting	c	1
h	Lay out chassis	e, f	3
i	Build and test	g, h	10

(a) Draw a critical-path scheduling-arrow diagram, identifying jobs by letters and associating times with each. Indicate the critical path.

(b) What is the minimum time for completion of the project?

(c) What is the early start for job c?

(d) What is the free slack for job h?

18.4. An architect has been awarded a contract to prepare plans for an urban renewal project. The job consists of the following activities and their estimated times:

Activity	Description	Immediate Predecessors	Time (days)
A	Prepare preliminary sketches	—	2
B	Outline specifications	—	1
C	Prepare drawings	A	3
D	Write specifications	A, B	2
E	Run off prints	C, D	1
F	Have specifications printed	B, D	3
G	Assemble bid packages	E, F	1

(a) Draw a critical-path arrow diagram for this project, indicate the critical path, and calculate the total slack and free slack for each activity.

(b) How long will the preparation take for the architect working alone?

(c) How long with two architects (neither working on the same activity at once)?

(d) What would the minimum completion time be if PERT were used instead of CPM?

18.5. In putting a job together to run at a data-processing center, certain steps need to be taken. These jobs can be described as follows:

Job	Time (minutes)	Immediate Predecessors	Description
A	180	—	Design flowchart and write FORTRAN statements
B	30	A	Punch control cards
C	20	A	Punch comment cards
D	60	A	Punch program cards
E	10	B, C, D	Obtain brown folder
F	20	B, C, D	Put deck together
G	10	E, F	Submit deck

(a) Draw a critical-path scheduling diagram and indicate the critical path. What is the minimum time to completion?
(b) What is the free slack of job C?
(c) Assuming the table accurately represents the jobs to be done and their times, if you were performing this project, would the minimum time to completion obtained above be the minimum time for you to complete the project? If yes, what conditions would change your answer? If no, why not, and what would the correct time be?

18.6. Electronic Production Inc. is nearly through with a project to produce a small warning-signal generator. Owing to a reduction in required performance characteristics, the remainder of the work is simpler to do than was originally planned. A new estimate of time to completion must be made. The following is known:

Activity	Time (days)	Immediate Predecessors	Description
a	1	—	Check total weight and approve
b	2	—	Check power consumption
c	2	—	Check temperature requirements
d	2	a, b	Choose connecting plug
e	4	b, c	Fix resistors final values
f	1	c	Choose encapsulating foam
g	4	d	Ensure hermetic seal
h	8	g, e, f	Perform final test

(a) Draw a critical-path scheduling diagram and indicate the critical path.
(b) What is the minimum time to completion?
(c) If the starting day is day zero, what is the early start for activity d?
(d) What is the free slack for activity d? What is the total slack for this activity?

(e) During the second day of work (day 1), it is discovered that activity f (choose encapsulating foam) will take 4 days instead of 1. Will this delay the project? If the activity takes 6 days, will the project be delayed?

(f) Electronic Production Inc. has a limited number of men available to work on the project. Only two activities can be under way at the same time. Will this delay the project over what the time would have been with unlimited resources? (Activity f takes 6 days to complete.) Try creating a schedule with this limited resource restriction.

(g) To meet government requirements, Electronic Production must have a PERT chart. Draw such a chart with the assumption of unlimited resources. How does using a PERT chart instead of a critical-path scheduling diagram (CPM) change the minimum time to completion?

18.7. The following table lists a set of nine activities together with their sequence requirements, estimated activity times, and the daily number of men required for each activity. These nine activities make up a complete project.

Activity Code	Code of Immediate Predecessor	Time Required (days)	Men Required per day
A	—	10	3
B	—	8	4
C	—	5	7
D	A	6	5
E	B	4	2
F	C	10	4
G	F	4	3
H	F	8	3
I	D, E, G	7	3

(a) Use this information to develop a network diagram.

(b) Determine the earliest start (ES), earliest finish (EF), latest start (LS), and latest finish (LF) times for each activity.

(c) List the activities on the critical path.

(d) What is the earliest finish time of the project without resource constraints (assuming that we have an unlimited number of men)?

(e) Assume that we have only 11 men available but that each man is completely interchangeable. That is, any man can do any task. Also assume that the activities must use exactly the number of men and days specified. For example, you *cannot* use twice the manpower and complete the activity in one-half the time. Now determine (if possible) a schedule of activity starting times that will allow these 11 men to complete the project by the earliest finish date. If this is not possible, show a schedule that will finish the project as soon as possible with 11 men. (Start with day 1, *not* day 0.)

18.8. In the project network in Figure 18.19, activities are represented by arrows, and the number above each activity is both its identification and its normal duration, in days.

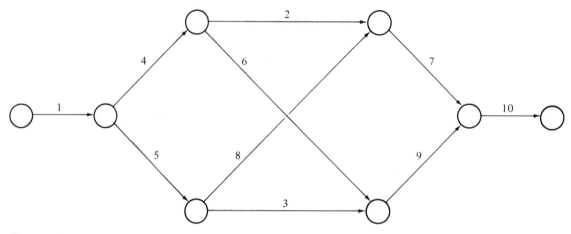

Figure 18.19

(a) Determine the minimum length of the project and identify activities on the critical path.

(b) Answer part (a) by formulating and solving this problem as a linear programming problem.

(c) Assume that the project due date is equal to its minimum length. Calculate the late start time, total slack, and free slack for activities 2, 3, 6, and 8.

(d) Assume that each activity (except 1 and 2) can be shortened up to 2 days at a cost per day equal to the activity number. (For example, activity 6 could be shortened to 5 days at a cost of $6, or to 4 days at a cost of $12.) Determine the least-cost 26-day schedule. Show the new durations of activities that have been shortened, and the total cost of shortening the schedule.

CASE 18.1   Illustrative Case Study
Involving Project Planning Using PERT

RUBINOWITZ,   Parnelli Rubinowitz, a famous race driver turned car owner, was faced with
PENNISKI   the problem of getting his new car ready for the coming racing campaign.
RACING TEAM   Roland Tyre, Parnelli's chief mechanic and car designer, had just discovered a new concept and believed he could design a car that could not be beaten. The only trouble was that the first race was just 2 months from the present date.

Roger Penniski, the team manager, decided to use PERT to analyze the chances of getting the car ready for the coming season. He sat down with Roland and came up with an activity list (Table 1) and a project diagram (Figure 1). Even though the team had much experience with car building, Roger knew that there are always problems and delays in assembling a new car. Therefore, he and Roland made careful estimates of the most likely, most optimistic, and most pessimistic completion times for each activity (Table 2).

747

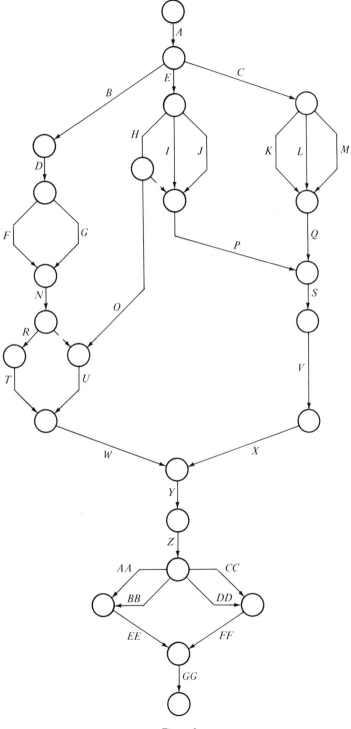

Figure 1

Questions

1. What are the chances that the car will be ready for the first race 2 months (60 days) from today?
2. What are the chances that it would be ready for the second and third races 1 week and 2 weeks later?
3. What are the activities that need to be watched most carefully to keep the project on schedule?

Table 1. Activity List for Racing Car Project

Activity	Description	Predecessors
A	Design specification	—
B	Build scale mock-up for wind tunnel tests	A
C	Blue prints for engine	A
D	Preliminary wind tunnel test	B
E	Trans-axle design	A
F	Analysis and changes to wings	D
G	Aerodynamic changes to body	D
H	Trans-axle housing fabrication	E
I	Gear shift linkage fabrication	E
J	Gear fabrication	E
K	Engine block fabrication	C
L	Valves and cam shaft fabrication	C
M	Crank shaft, piston, and connecting rod fabrication	C
N	Final wind tunnel test	F, G
O	Suspension fabrication	H
P	Decision on gear ratios to be used	H, I, J
Q	Engine assembly	K, L, M
R	Fabrication of body and chassis	N
S	Preliminary dynamometer test on engine	P, Q
T	Wing and body parts fabrication	R
U	Wheel and tire decision	N, O
V	Alterations to engine	S
W	Final assembly of chassis	T, U
X	Final dynamometer test on engine	U
Y	Engine installed in chassis	W, X
Z	Ship car to test track	Y
AA	Test and sort suspension problems	Z
BB	Test different wing settings	Z
CC	Test different gear ratios	Z
DD	Test different engine settings	Z
EE	Aerodynamic and suspension changes	AA, BB
FF	Engine and drive train changes	CC, DD
GG	Ship car to next race track	EE, FF

Table 2. Activity Time Estimates for Racing Car Project

Activity	ESTIMATED COMPLETION TIMES (DAYS)			Activity	ESTIMATED COMPLETION TIME (DAYS)		
	a	m	b		a	m	b
A	2	5	7	Q	1	2	4
B	5	7	9	R	15	21	28
C	1	2	4	S	1	1	1
D	1	1	2	T	2	4	5
E	5	8	12	U	1	2	2
F	3	4	7	V	2	4	8
G	5	6	8	W	1	1	1
H	8	10	14	X	1	1	1
I	2	4	7	Y	3	4	9
J	1	2	3	Z	2	2	2
K	8	10	13	AA	1	4	4
L	10	12	14	BB	1	2	3
M	10	12	14	CC	1	3	4
N	1	1	2	DD	2	2	2
O	4	5	9	EE	1	4	6
P	1	1	1	FF	2	2	2
				GG	5	5	5

CASE 18.2 Illustrative Case Study
Involving Project Planning with CPM
and Its Linear Programming Formulation

CHARLES SLACK'S
HOUSEBUILDING
PROJECT

Charles Slack, a mathematician at a well-known midwestern university, was in the process of building a new house. Being well versed in the area of operations research, he decided to analyze the process as a network.

The activities are shown in Table 1. Slack was particularly interested in linear programming but could not formulate the model he had devised for his house construction project.

Assignment

1. Find the minimum project completion time and critical path using PERT/CPM.
2. Formulate and solve the problem as a linear programming problem.
   (a) How will you find the critical path?
   (b) Where will you find values for total slack?
   (c) Compare solutions.

Table 1. Project Activity Data for Housebuilding Project

	Description	Predecessors	Start	End	Time
A	Excavate and pour footers	—	0	1	3
B	Pour foundation	A	1	2	2
C	Erect wooden frame and roof	B	2	3	6
D	Lay brickwork	C	3	5	10
E	Install basement drains & plumbing	B	2	4	5
F	Pour basement floor	E	4	6	2
G	Install rough plumbing	E	4	8	4
H	Install rough wiring	C	3	8	3
	DUMMY	C	3	6	0
I	Install heating and ventilation	C, F	6	8	5
J	Fasten plasterboard and plaster	H, I, G	8	10	10
K	Lay finish flooring	J	10	12	5
L	Install kitchen fixtures	K	12	13	2
M	Install finish plumbing	K	12	13	3
N	Finish carpentry	K	12	15	5
O	Finish roofing and flashing	D	5	7	2
P	Fasten gutters and downspouts	O	7	9	3
Q	Lay storm drains	B	2	9	1
R	Paint	L, M	13	14	5
	DUMMY	S	14	15	0
S	Sand and varnish flooring	N, S	15	16	3
T	Finish electrical work	S	14	16	2
U	Finish grading	P, Q	9	11	8
V	Pour walk, driveway, and complete landscape	U	11	16	7
X	FINISH		16	17	

Activity-on-Node Representation of Light-System-Maintenance Project (See Tables 18.1 and 18.2 and Figure 18.6)

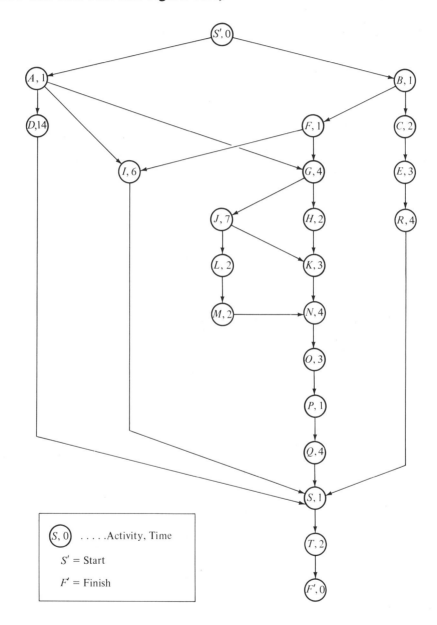

(S, 0) . . . . . Activity, Time

S' = Start

F' = Finish

APPENDICES *Tables,*
Matrix Notation,
and Matrix Operations

APPENDIX A
Tables

CONTENTS: The following tables are contained within this appendix.

Table I. Binomial Probabilities

n	x	.05	.10	.15	.20	θ .25	.30	.35	.40	.45	.50
1	0	.9500	.9000	.8500	.8000	.7500	.7000	.6500	.6000	.5500	.5000
	1	.0500	.1000	.1500	.2000	.2500	.3000	.3500	.4000	.4500	.5000
2	0	.9025	.8100	.7225	.6400	.5625	.4900	.4225	.3600	.3025	.2500
	1	.0950	.1800	.2550	.3200	.3750	.4200	.4550	.4800	.4950	.5000
	2	.0025	.0100	.0225	.0400	.0625	.0900	.1225	.1600	.2025	.2500
3	0	.8574	.7290	.6141	.5120	.4219	.3430	.2746	.2160	.1664	.1250
	1	.1354	.2430	.3251	.3840	.4219	.4410	.4436	.4320	.4084	.3750
	2	.0071	.0270	.0574	.0960	.1406	.1890	.2389	.2880	.3341	.3750
	3	.0001	.0010	.0034	.0080	.0156	.0270	.0429	.0640	.0911	.1250
4	0	.8145	.6561	.5220	.4096	.3164	.2401	.1785	.1296	.0915	.0625
	1	.1715	.2916	.3685	.4096	.4219	.4116	.3845	.3456	.2995	.2500
	2	.0135	.0486	.0975	.1536	.2109	.2646	.3105	.3456	.3675	.3750
	3	.0005	.0036	.0115	.0256	.0469	.0756	.1115	.1536	.2005	.2500
	4	.0000	.0001	.0005	.0016	.0039	.0081	.0150	.0256	.0410	.0625
5	0	.7738	.5905	.4437	.3277	.2373	.1681	.1160	.0778	.0503	.0312
	1	.2036	.3280	.3915	.4096	.3955	.3602	.3124	.2592	.2059	.1562
	2	.0214	.0729	.1382	.2048	.2637	.3087	.3364	.3456	.3369	.3125
	3	.0011	.0081	.0244	.0512	.0879	.1323	.1811	.2304	.2757	.3125
	4	.0000	.0004	.0022	.0064	.0146	.0284	.0488	.0768	.1128	.1562
	5	.0000	.0000	.0001	.0003	.0010	.0024	.0053	.0102	.0185	.0312
6	0	.7351	.5314	.3771	.2621	.1780	.1176	.0754	.0467	.0277	.0156
	1	.2321	.3543	.3993	.3932	.3560	.3025	.2437	.1866	.1359	.0938
	2	.0305	.0984	.1762	.2458	.2966	.3241	.3280	.3110	.2780	.2344
	3	.0021	.0146	.0415	.0819	.1318	.1852	.2355	.2765	.3032	.3125
	4	.0001	.0012	.0055	.0154	.0330	.0595	.0951	.1382	.1861	.2344
	5	.0000	.0001	.0004	.0015	.0044	.0102	.0205	.0369	.0609	.0938
	6	.0000	.0000	.0000	.0001	.0002	.0007	.0018	.0041	.0083	.0156
7	0	.6983	.4783	.3206	.2097	.1335	.0824	.0490	.0280	.0152	.0078
	1	.2573	.3720	.3960	.3670	.3115	.2471	.1848	.1306	.0872	.0547
	2	.0406	.1240	.2097	.2753	.3115	.3177	.2985	.2613	.2140	.1641
	3	.0036	.0230	.0617	.1147	.1730	.2269	.2679	.2903	.2918	.2734
	4	.0002	.0026	.0109	.0287	.0577	.0972	.1442	.1935	.2388	.2734
	5	.0000	.0002	.0012	.0043	.0115	.0250	.0466	.0774	.1172	.1641
	6	.0000	.0000	.0001	.0004	.0013	.0036	.0084	.0172	.0320	.0547
	7	.0000	.0000	.0000	.0000	.0001	.0002	.0006	.0016	.0037	.0078
8	0	.6634	.4305	.2725	.1678	.1001	.0576	.0319	.0168	.0084	.0039
	1	.2793	.3826	.3847	.3355	.2670	.1977	.1373	.0896	.0548	.0312
	2	.0515	.1488	.2376	.2936	.3115	.2965	.2587	.2090	.1569	.1094
	3	.0054	.0331	.0839	.1468	.2076	.2541	.2786	.2787	.2568	.2188
	4	.0004	.0046	.0185	.0459	.0865	.1361	.1875	.2322	.2627	.2734

Table I *(continued)*

n	x	.05	.10	.15	.20	.25	.30	.35	.40	.45	.50
8	5	.0000	.0004	.0026	.0092	.0231	.0467	.0808	.1239	.1719	.2188
	6	.0000	.0000	.0002	.0011	.0038	.0100	.0217	.0413	.0703	.1094
	7	.0000	.0000	.0000	.0001	.0004	.0012	.0033	.0079	.0164	.0312
	8	.0000	.0000	.0000	.0000	.0000	.0001	.0002	.0007	.0017	.0039
9	0	.6302	.3874	.2316	.1342	.0751	.0404	.0207	.0101	.0046	.0020
	1	.2985	.3874	.3679	.3020	.2253	.1556	.1004	.0605	.0339	.0176
	2	.0629	.1722	.2597	.3020	.3003	.2668	.2162	.1612	.1110	.0703
	3	.0077	.0446	.1069	.1762	.2336	.2668	.2716	.2508	.2119	.1641
	4	.0006	.0074	.0283	.0661	.1168	.1715	.2194	.2508	.2600	.2461
	5	.0000	.0008	.0050	.0165	.0389	.0735	.1181	.1672	.2128	.2461
	6	.0000	.0001	.0006	.0028	.0087	.0210	.0424	.0743	.1160	.1641
	7	.0000	.0000	.0000	.0003	.0012	.0039	.0098	.0212	.0407	.0703
	8	.0000	.0000	.0000	.0000	.0001	.0004	.0013	.0035	.0083	.0176
	9	.0000	.0000	.0000	.0000	.0000	.0000	.0001	.0003	.0008	.0020
10	0	.5987	.3487	.1969	.1074	.0563	.0282	.0135	.0060	.0025	.0010
	1	.3151	.3874	.3474	.2684	.1877	.1211	.0725	.0403	.0207	.0098
	2	.0746	.1937	.2759	.3020	.2816	.2335	.1757	.1209	.0763	.0439
	3	.0105	.0574	.1298	.2013	.2503	.2668	.2522	.2150	.1665	.1172
	4	.0010	.0112	.0401	.0881	.1460	.2001	.2377	.2508	.2384	.2051
	5	.0001	.0015	.0085	.0264	.0584	.1029	.1536	.2007	.2340	.2461
	6	.0000	.0001	.0012	.0055	.0162	.0368	.0689	.1115	.1596	.2051
	7	.0000	.0000	.0001	.0008	.0031	.0090	.0212	.0425	.0746	.1172
	8	.0000	.0000	.0000	.0001	.0004	.0014	.0043	.0106	.0229	.0439
	9	.0000	.0000	.0000	.0000	.0000	.0001	.0005	.0016	.0042	.0098
	10	.0000	.0000	.0000	.0000	.0000	.0000	.0000	.0001	.0003	.0010
11	0	.5688	.3138	.1673	.0859	.0422	.0198	.0088	.0036	.0014	.0005
	1	.3293	.3835	.3248	.2362	.1549	.0932	.0518	.0266	.0125	.0054
	2	.0867	.2131	.2866	.2953	.2581	.1998	.1395	.0887	.0513	.0269
	3	.0137	.0710	.1517	.2215	.2581	.2568	.2254	.1774	.1259	.0806
	4	.0014	.0158	.0536	.1107	.1721	.2201	.2428	.2365	.2060	.1611
	5	.0001	.0025	.0132	.0388	.0803	.1321	.1830	.2207	.2360	.2256
	6	.0000	.0003	.0023	.0097	.0268	.0566	.0985	.1471	.1931	.2256
	7	.0000	.0000	.0003	.0017	.0064	.0173	.0379	.0701	.1128	.1611
	8	.0000	.0000	.0000	.0002	.0011	.0037	.0102	.0234	.0462	.0806
	9	.0000	.0000	.0000	.0000	.0001	.0005	.0018	.0052	.0126	.0269
	10	.0000	.0000	.0000	.0000	.0000	.0000	.0002	.0007	.0021	.0054
	11	.0000	.0000	.0000	.0000	.0000	.0000	.0000	.0000	.0002	.0005
12	0	.5404	.2824	.1422	.0687	.0317	.0138	.0057	.0022	.0008	.0002
	1	.3413	.3766	.3012	.2062	.1267	.0712	.0368	.0174	.0075	.0029
	2	.0988	.2301	.2924	.2835	.2323	.1678	.1088	.0639	.0339	.0161
	3	.0173	.0852	.1720	.2362	.2581	.2397	.1954	.1419	.0923	.0537
	4	.0021	.0213	.0683	.1329	.1936	.2311	.2367	.2128	.1700	.1208
	5	.0002	.0038	.0193	.0532	.1032	.1585	.2039	.2270	.2225	.1934
	6	.0000	.0005	.0040	.0155	.0401	.0792	.1281	.1766	.2124	.2256
	7	.0000	.0000	.0006	.0033	.0115	.0291	.0591	.1009	.1489	.1934
	8	.0000	.0000	.0001	.0005	.0024	.0078	.0199	.0420	.0762	.1208
	9	.0000	.0000	.0000	.0001	.0004	.0015	.0048	.0125	.0277	.0537

Table I (continued)

n	x	.05	.10	.15	.20	.25	.30	.35	.40	.45	.50
12	10	.0000	.0000	.0000	.0000	.0000	.0002	.0008	.0025	.0068	.0161
	11	.0000	.0000	.0000	.0000	.0000	.0000	.0001	.0003	.0010	.0029
	12	.0000	.0000	.0000	.0000	.0000	.0000	.0000	.0000	.0001	.0002
13	0	.5133	.2542	.1209	.0550	.0238	.0097	.0037	.0013	.0004	.0001
	1	.3512	.3672	.2774	.1787	.1029	.0540	.0259	.0113	.0045	.0016
	2	.1109	.2448	.2937	.2680	.2059	.1388	.0836	.0453	.0220	.0095
	3	.0214	.0997	.1900	.2457	.2517	.2181	.1651	.1107	.0660	.0349
	4	.0028	.0277	.0838	.1535	.2097	.2337	.2222	.1845	.1350	.0873
	5	.0003	.0055	.0266	.0691	.1258	.1803	.2154	.2214	.1989	.1571
	6	.0000	.0008	.0063	.0230	.0559	.1030	.1546	.1968	.2169	.2095
	7	.0000	.0001	.0011	.0058	.0186	.0442	.0833	.1312	.1775	.2095
	8	.0000	.0000	.0001	.0011	.0047	.0142	.0336	.0656	.1089	.1571
	9	.0000	.0000	.0000	.0001	.0009	.0034	.0101	.0243	.0495	.0873
	10	.0000	.0000	.0000	.0000	.0001	.0006	.0022	.0065	.0162	.0349
	11	.0000	.0000	.0000	.0000	.0000	.0001	.0003	.0012	.0036	.0095
	12	.0000	.0000	.0000	.0000	.0000	.0000	.0000	.0001	.0005	.0016
	13	.0000	.0000	.0000	.0000	.0000	.0000	.0000	.0000	.0000	.0001
14	0	.4877	.2288	.1028	.0440	.0178	.0068	.0024	.0008	.0002	.0001
	1	.3593	.3559	.2539	.1539	.0832	.0407	.0181	.0073	.0027	.0009
	2	.1229	.2570	.2912	.2501	.1802	.1134	.0634	.0317	.0141	.0056
	3	.0259	.1142	.2056	.2501	.2402	.1943	.1366	.0845	.0462	.0222
	4	.0037	.0349	.0998	.1720	.2202	.2290	.2022	.1549	.1040	.0611
	5	.0004	.0078	.0352	.0860	.1468	.1963	.2178	.2066	.1701	.1222
	6	.0000	.0013	.0093	.0322	.0734	.1262	.1759	.2066	.2088	.1833
	7	.0000	.0002	.0019	.0092	.0280	.0618	.1082	.1574	.1952	.2095
	8	.0000	.0000	.0003	.0020	.0082	.0232	.0510	.0918	.1398	.1833
	9	.0000	.0000	.0000	.0003	.0018	.0066	.0183	.0408	.0762	.1222
	10	.0000	.0000	.0000	.0000	.0003	.0014	.0049	.0136	.0312	.0611
	11	.0000	.0000	.0000	.0000	.0000	.0002	.0010	.0033	.0093	.0222
	12	.0000	.0000	.0000	.0000	.0000	.0000	.0001	.0005	.0019	.0056
	13	.0000	.0000	.0000	.0000	.0000	.0000	.0000	.0001	.0002	.0009
	14	.0000	.0000	.0000	.0000	.0000	.0000	.0000	.0000	.0000	.0001
15	0	.4633	.2059	.0874	.0352	.0134	.0047	.0016	.0005	.0001	.0000
	1	.3658	.3432	.2312	.1319	.0668	.0305	.0126	.0047	.0016	.0005
	2	.1348	.2669	.2856	.2309	.1559	.0916	.0476	.0219	.0090	.0032
	3	.0307	.1285	.2184	.2501	.2252	.1700	.1110	.0634	.0318	.0139
	4	.0049	.0428	.1156	.1876	.2252	.2186	.1792	.1268	.0780	.0417
	5	.0006	.0105	.0449	.1032	.1651	.2061	.2123	.1859	.1404	.0916
	6	.0000	.0019	.0132	.0430	.0917	.1472	.1906	.2066	.1914	.1527
	7	.0000	.0003	.0030	.0138	.0393	.0811	.1319	.1771	.2013	.1964
	8	.0000	.0000	.0005	.0035	.0131	.0348	.0710	.1181	.1647	.1964
	9	.0000	.0000	.0001	.0007	.0034	.0116	.0298	.0612	.1048	.1527
	10	.0000	.0000	.0000	.0001	.0007	.0030	.0096	.0245	.0515	.0916
	11	.0000	.0000	.0000	.0000	.0001	.0006	.0024	.0074	.0191	.0417
	12	.0000	.0000	.0000	.0000	.0000	.0001	.0004	.0016	.0052	.0139
	13	.0000	.0000	.0000	.0000	.0000	.0000	.0001	.0003	.0010	.0032
	14	.0000	.0000	.0000	.0000	.0000	.0000	.0000	.0000	.0001	.0005
	15	.0000	.0000	.0000	.0000	.0000	.0000	.0000	.0000	.0000	.0000

Table I (continued)

n	x	.05	.10	.15	.20	θ .25	.30	.35	.40	.45	.50
16	0	.4401	.1853	.0743	.0281	.0100	.0033	.0010	.0003	.0001	.0000
	1	.3706	.3294	.2097	.1126	.0535	.0228	.0087	.0030	.0009	.0002
	2	.1463	.2745	.2775	.2111	.1336	.0732	.0353	.0150	.0056	.0018
	3	.0359	.1423	.2285	.2463	.2079	.1465	.0888	.0468	.0215	.0085
	4	.0061	.0514	.1311	.2001	.2252	.2040	.1553	.1014	.0572	.0278
	5	.0008	.0137	.0555	.1201	.1802	.2099	.2008	.1623	.1123	.0667
	6	.0001	.0028	.0180	.0550	.1101	.1649	.1982	.1983	.1684	.1222
	7	.0000	.0004	.0045	.0197	.0524	.1010	.1524	.1889	.1969	.1746
	8	.0000	.0001	.0009	.0055	.0197	.0487	.0923	.1417	.1812	.1964
	9	.0000	.0000	.0001	.0012	.0058	.0185	.0442	.0840	.1318	.1746
	10	.0000	.0000	.0000	.0002	.0014	.0056	.0167	.0392	.0755	.1222
	11	.0000	.0000	.0000	.0000	.0002	.0013	.0049	.0142	.0337	.0667
	12	.0000	.0000	.0000	.0000	.0000	.0002	.0011	.0040	.0115	.0278
	13	.0000	.0000	.0000	.0000	.0000	.0000	.0002	.0008	.0029	.0085
	14	.0000	.0000	.0000	.0000	.0000	.0000	.0000	.0001	.0005	.0018
	15	.0000	.0000	.0000	.0000	.0000	.0000	.0000	.0000	.0001	.0002
	16	.0000	.0000	.0000	.0000	.0000	.0000	.0000	.0000	.0000	.0000
17	0	.4181	.1668	.0631	.0225	.0075	.0023	.0007	.0002	.0000	.0000
	1	.3741	.3150	.1893	.0957	.0426	.0169	.0060	.0019	.0005	.0001
	2	.1575	.2800	.2673	.1914	.1136	.0581	.0260	.0102	.0035	.0010
	3	.0415	.1556	.2359	.2393	.1893	.1245	.0701	.0341	.0144	.0052
	4	.0076	.0605	.1457	.2093	.2209	.1868	.1320	.0796	.0411	.0182
	5	.0010	.0175	.0668	.1361	.1914	.2081	.1849	.1379	.0875	.0472
	6	.0001	.0039	.0236	.0680	.1276	.1784	.1991	.1839	.1432	.0944
	7	.0000	.0007	.0065	.0267	.0668	.1201	.1685	.1927	.1841	.1484
	8	.0000	.0001	.0014	.0084	.0279	.0644	.1134	.1606	.1883	.1855
	9	.0000	.0000	.0003	.0021	.0093	.0276	.0611	.1070	.1540	.1855
	10	.0000	.0000	.0000	.0004	.0025	.0095	.0263	.0571	.1008	.1484
	11	.0000	.0000	.0000	.0001	.0005	.0026	.0090	.0242	.0525	.0944
	12	.0000	.0000	.0000	.0000	.0001	.0006	.0024	.0081	.0215	.0472
	13	.0000	.0000	.0000	.0000	.0000	.0001	.0005	.0021	.0068	.0182
	14	.0000	.0000	.0000	.0000	.0000	.0000	.0001	.0004	.0016	.0052
	15	.0000	.0000	.0000	.0000	.0000	.0000	.0000	.0001	.0003	.0010
	16	.0000	.0000	.0000	.0000	.0000	.0000	.0000	.0000	.0000	.0001
	17	.0000	.0000	.0000	.0000	.0000	.0000	.0000	.0000	.0000	.0000
18	0	.3972	.1501	.0536	.0180	.0056	.0016	.0004	.0001	.0000	.0000
	1	.3763	.3002	.1704	.0811	.0338	.0126	.0042	.0012	.0003	.0001
	2	.1683	.2835	.2556	.1723	.0958	.0458	.0190	.0069	.0022	.0006
	3	.0473	.1680	.2406	.2297	.1704	.1046	.0547	.0246	.0095	.0031
	4	.0093	.0700	.1592	.2153	.2130	.1681	.1104	.0614	.0291	.0117
	5	.0014	.0218	.0787	.1507	.1988	.2017	.1664	.1146	.0666	.0327
	6	.0002	.0052	.0301	.0816	.1436	.1873	.1941	.1655	.1181	.0708
	7	.0000	.0010	.0091	.0350	.0820	.1376	.1792	.1892	.1657	.1214
	8	.0000	.0002	.0022	.0120	.0376	.0811	.1327	.1734	.1864	.1669
	9	.0000	.0000	.0004	.0033	.0139	.0386	.0794	.1284	.1694	.1855

Table I (continued)

n	x					θ					
		.05	.10	.15	.20	.25	.30	.35	.40	.45	.50
18	10	.0000	.0000	.0001	.0008	.0042	.0149	.0385	.0771	.1248	.1669
	11	.0000	.0000	.0000	.0001	.0010	.0046	.0151	.0374	.0742	.1214
	12	.0000	.0000	.0000	.0000	.0002	.0012	.0047	.0145	.0354	.0708
	13	.0000	.0000	.0000	.0000	.0000	.0002	.0012	.0045	.0134	.0327
	14	.0000	.0000	.0000	.0000	.0000	.0000	.0002	.0011	.0039	.0117
	15	.0000	.0000	.0000	.0000	.0000	.0000	.0000	.0002	.0009	.0031
	16	.0000	.0000	.0000	.0000	.0000	.0000	.0000	.0000	.0001	.0006
	17	.0000	.0000	.0000	.0000	.0000	.0000	.0000	.0000	.0000	.0001
	18	.0000	.0000	.0000	.0000	.0000	.0000	.0000	.0000	.0000	.0000
19	0	.3774	.1351	.0456	.0144	.0042	.0011	.0003	.0001	.0000	.0000
	1	.3774	.2852	.1529	.0685	.0268	.0093	.0029	.0008	.0002	.0000
	2	.1787	.2852	.2428	.1540	.0803	.0358	.0138	.0046	.0013	.0003
	3	.0533	.1796	.2428	.2182	.1517	.0869	.0422	.0175	.0062	.0018
	4	.0112	.0798	.1714	.2182	.2023	.1491	.0909	.0467	.0203	.0074
	5	.0018	.0266	.0907	.1636	.2023	.1916	.1468	.0933	.0497	.0222
	6	.0002	.0069	.0374	.0955	.1574	.1916	.1844	.1451	.0949	.0518
	7	.0000	.0014	.0122	.0443	.0974	.1525	.1797	.1443	.0961
	8	.0000	.0002	.0032	.0166	.0487	.0981	.1489	.1797	.1771	.1442
	9	.0000	.0000	.0007	.0051	.0198	.0514	.0980	.1464	.1771	.1762
	10	.0000	.0000	.0001	.0013	.0066	.0220	.0528	.0976	.1449	.1762
	11	.0000	.0000	.0000	.0003	.0018	.0077	.0233	.0532	.0970	.1442
	12	.0000	.0000	.0000	.0000	.0004	.0022	.0083	.0237	.0529	.0961
	13	.0000	.0000	.0000	.0000	.0001	.0005	.0024	.0085	.0233	.0518
	14	.0000	.0000	.0000	.0000	.0000	.0001	.0006	.0024	.0082	.0222
	15	.0000	.0000	.0000	.0000	.0000	.0000	.0001	.0005	.0022	.0074
	16	.0000	.0000	.0000	.0000	.0000	.0000	.0000	.0001	.0005	.0018
	17	.0000	.0000	.0000	.0000	.0000	.0000	.0000	.0000	.0001	.0003
	18	.0000	.0000	.0000	.0000	.0000	.0000	.0000	.0000	.0000	.0000
	19	.0000	.0000	.0000	.0000	.0000	.0000	.0000	.0000	.0000	.0000
20	0	.3585	.1216	.0388	.0115	.0032	.0008	.0002	.0000	.0000	.0000
	1	.3774	.2702	.1368	.0576	.0211	.0068	.0020	.0005	.0001	.0000
	2	.1887	.2852	.2293	.1369	.0669	.0278	.0100	.0031	.0008	.0002
	3	.0596	.1901	.2428	.2054	.1339	.0716	.0323	.0123	.0040	.0011
	4	.0133	.0898	.1821	.2182	.1897	.1304	.0738	.0350	.0139	.0046
	5	.0022	.0319	.1028	.1746	.2023	.1789	.1272	.0746	.0365	.0148
	6	.0003	.0089	.0454	.1091	.1686	.1916	.1712	.1244	.0746	.0370
	7	.0000	.0020	.0160	.0545	.1124	.1643	.1844	.1659	.1221	.0739
	8	.0000	.0004	.0046	.0222	.0609	.1144	.1614	.1797	.1623	.1201
	9	.0000	.0001	.0011	.0074	.0271	.0654	.1158	.1597	.1771	.1602
	10	.0000	.0000	.0002	.0020	.0099	.0308	.0686	.1171	.1593	.1762
	11	.0000	.0000	.0000	.0005	.0030	.0120	.0336	.0710	.1185	.1602
	12	.0000	.0000	.0000	.0001	.0008	.0039	.0136	.0355	.0727	.1201
	13	.0000	.0000	.0000	.0000	.0002	.0010	.0045	.0146	.0366	.0739
	14	.0000	.0000	.0000	.0000	.0000	.0002	.0012	.0049	.0150	.0370
	15	.0000	.0000	.0000	.0000	.0000	.0000	.0003	.0013	.0049	.0148
	16	.0000	.0000	.0000	.0000	.0000	.0000	.0000	.0003	.0013	.0046
	17	.0000	.0000	.0000	.0000	.0000	.0000	.0000	.0000	.0002	.0011
	18	.0000	.0000	.0000	.0000	.0000	.0000	.0000	.0000	.0000	.0002
	19	.0000	.0000	.0000	.0000	.0000	.0000	.0000	.0000	.0000	.0000
	20	.0000	.0000	.0000	.0000	.0000	.0000	.0000	.0000	.0000	.0000

Table II. Poisson Probabilities

$$\lambda\tau$$

x	0.1	0.2	0.3	0.4	0.5	0.6	0.7	0.8	0.9	1.0
0	.9048	.8187	.7408	.6703	.6065	.5488	.4966	.4493	.4066	.3679
1	.0905	.1637	.2222	.2681	.3033	.3293	.3476	.3595	.3659	.3679
2	.0045	.0164	.0333	.0536	.0758	.0988	.1217	.1438	.1647	.1839
3	.0002	.0011	.0033	.0072	.0126	.0198	.0284	.0383	.0494	.0613
4	.0000	.0001	.0002	.0007	.0016	.0030	.0050	.0077	.0111	.0153
5	.0000	.0000	.0000	.0001	.0002	.0004	.0007	.0012	.0020	.0031
6	.0000	.0000	.0000	.0000	.0000	.0000	.0001	.0002	.0003	.0005
7	.0000	.0000	.0000	.0000	.0000	.0000	.0000	.0000	.0000	.0001

$$\lambda\tau$$

x	1.1	1.2	1.3	1.4	1.5	1.6	1.7	1.8	1.9	2.0
0	.3329	.3012	.2725	.2466	.2231	.2019	.1827	.1653	.1496	.1353
1	.3662	.3614	.3543	.3452	.3347	.3230	.3106	.2975	.2842	.2707
2	.2014	.2169	.2303	.2417	.2510	.2584	.2640	.2678	.2700	.2707
3	.0738	.0867	.0998	.1128	.1255	.1378	.1496	.1607	.1710	.1804
4	.0203	.0260	.0324	.0395	.0471	.0551	.0636	.0723	.0812	.0902
5	.0045	.0062	.0084	.0111	.0141	.0176	.0216	.0260	.0309	.0361
6	.0008	.0012	.0018	.0026	.0035	.0047	.0061	.0078	.0098	.0120
7	.0001	.0002	.0003	.0005	.0008	.0011	.0015	.0020	.0027	.0034
8	.0000	.0000	.0001	.0001	.0001	.0002	.0003	.0005	.0006	.0009
9	.0000	.0000	.0000	.0000	.0000	.0000	.0001	.0001	.0001	.0002

$$\lambda\tau$$

x	2.1	2.2	2.3	2.4	2.5	2.6	2.7	2.8	2.9	3.0
0	.1225	.1108	.1003	.0907	.0821	.0743	.0672	.0608	.0550	.0498
1	.2572	.2438	.2306	.2177	.2052	.1931	.1815	.1703	.1596	.1494
2	.2700	.2681	.2652	.2613	.2565	.2510	.2450	.2384	.2314	.2240
3	.1890	.1966	.2033	.2090	.2138	.2176	.2205	.2225	.2237	.2240
4	.0992	.1082	.1169	.1254	.1336	.1414	.1488	.1557	.1622	.1680
5	.0417	.0476	.0538	.0602	.0668	.0735	.0804	.0872	.0940	.1008
6	.0146	.0174	.0206	.0241	.0278	.0319	.0362	.0407	.0455	.0504
7	.0044	.0055	.0068	.0083	.0099	.0118	.0139	.0163	.0188	.0216
8	.0011	.0015	.0019	.0025	.0031	.0038	.0047	.0057	.0068	.0081
9	.0003	.0004	.0005	.0007	.0009	.0011	.0014	.0018	.0022	.0027
10	.0001	.0001	.0001	.0002	.0002	.0003	.0004	.0005	.0006	.0008
11	.0000	.0000	.0000	.0000	.0000	.0001	.0001	.0001	.0002	.0002
12	.0000	.0000	.0000	.0000	.0000	.0000	.0000	.0000	.0000	.0001

Table II. (continued)

$$\lambda\tau$$

x	3.1	3.2	3.3	3.4	3.5	3.6	3.7	3.8	3.9	4.0
0	.0450	.0408	.0369	.0334	.0302	.0273	.0247	.0224	.0202	.0183
1	.1397	.1304	.1217	.1135	.1057	.0984	.0915	.0850	.0789	.0733
2	.2165	.2087	.2008	.1929	.1850	.1771	.1692	.1615	.1539	.1465
3	.2237	.2226	.2209	.2186	.2158	.2125	.2087	.2046	.2001	.1954
4	.1734	.1781	.1823	.1858	.1888	.1912	.1931	.1944	.1951	.1954
5	.1075	.1140	.1203	.1264	.1322	.1377	.1429	.1477	.1522	.1563
6	.0555	.0608	.0662	.0716	.0771	.0826	.0881	.0936	.0989	.1042
7	.0246	.0278	.0312	.0348	.0385	.0425	.0466	.0508	.0551	.0595
8	.0095	.0111	.0129	.0148	.0169	.0191	.0215	.0241	.0269	.0298
9	.0033	.0040	.0047	.0056	.0066	.0076	.0089	.0102	.0116	.0132
10	.0010	.0013	.0016	.0019	.0023	.0028	.0033	.0039	.0045	.0053
11	.0003	.0004	.0005	.0006	.0007	.0009	.0011	.0013	.0016	.0019
12	.0001	.0001	.0001	.0002	.0002	.0003	.0003	.0004	.0005	.0006
13	.0000	.0000	.0000	.0000	.0001	.0001	.0001	.0001	.0002	.0002
14	.0000	.0000	.0000	.0000	.0000	.0000	.0000	.0000	.0000	.0001

$$\lambda\tau$$

x	4.1	4.2	4.3	4.4	4.5	4.6	4.7	4.8	4.9	5.0
0	.0166	.0150	.0136	.0123	.0111	.0101	.0091	.0082	.0074	.0067
1	.0679	.0630	.0583	.0540	.0500	.0462	.0427	.0395	.0365	.0337
2	.1393	.1323	.1254	.1188	.1125	.1063	.1005	.0948	.0894	.0842
3	.1904	.1852	.1798	.1743	.1687	.1631	.1574	.1517	.1460	.1404
4	.1951	.1944	.1933	.1917	.1898	.1875	.1849	.1820	.1789	.1755
5	.1600	.1633	.1662	.1687	.1708	.1725	.1738	.1747	.1753	.1755
6	.1093	.1143	.1191	.1237	.1281	.1323	.1362	.1398	.1432	.1462
7	.0640	.0686	.0732	.0778	.0824	.0869	.0914	.0959	.1002	.1044
8	.0328	.0360	.0393	.0428	.0463	.0500	.0537	.0575	.0614	.0653
9	.0150	.0168	.0188	.0209	.0232	.0255	.0280	.0307	.0334	.0363
10	.0061	.0071	.0081	.0092	.0104	.0118	.0132	.0147	.0164	.0181
11	.0023	.0027	.0032	.0037	.0043	.0049	.0056	.0064	.0073	.0082
12	.0008	.0009	.0011	.0014	.0016	.0019	.0022	.0026	.0030	.0034
13	.0002	.0003	.0004	.0005	.0006	.0007	.0008	.0009	.0011	.0013
14	.0001	.0001	.0001	.0001	.0002	.0002	.0003	.0003	.0004	.0005
15	.0000	.0000	.0000	.0000	.0001	.0001	.0001	.0001	.0001	.0002

$$\lambda\tau$$

x	5.1	5.2	5.3	5.4	5.5	5.6	5.7	5.8	5.9	6.0
0	.0061	.0055	.0050	.0045	.0041	.0037	.0033	.0030	.0027	.0025
1	.0311	.0287	.0265	.0244	.0225	.0207	.0191	.0176	.0162	.0149
2	.0793	.0746	.0701	.0659	.0618	.0580	.0544	.0509	.0477	.0446
3	.1348	.1293	.1239	.1185	.1133	.1082	.1033	.0985	.0938	.0892
4	.1719	.1681	.1641	.1600	.1558	.1515	.1472	.1428	.1383	.1339

Table II. (continued)

$\lambda\tau$

x	5.1	5.2	5.3	5.4	5.5	5.6	5.7	5.8	5.9	6.0
5	.1753	.1748	.1740	.1728	.1714	.1697	.1678	.1656	.1632	.1603
6	.1490	.1515	.1537	.1555	.1571	.1584	.1594	.1601	.1605	.1606
7	.1086	.1125	.1163	.1200	.1234	.1267	.1298	.1326	.1353	.1377
8	.0692	.0731	.0771	.0810	.0849	.0887	.0925	.0962	.0998	.1033
9	.0392	.0423	.0454	.0486	.0519	.0552	.0586	.0620	.0654	.0688
10	.0200	.0220	.0241	.0262	.0285	.0309	.0334	.0359	.0386	.0413
11	.0093	.0104	.0116	.0129	.0143	.0157	.0173	.0190	.0207	.0225
12	.0039	.0045	.0051	.0058	.0065	.0073	.0082	.0092	.0102	.0113
13	.0015	.0018	.0021	.0024	.0028	.0032	.0036	.0041	.0046	.0052
14	.0006	.0007	.0008	.0009	.0011	.0013	.0015	.0017	.0019	.0022
15	.0002	.0002	.0003	.0003	.0004	.0005	.0006	.0007	.0008	.0009
16	.0001	.0001	.0001	.0001	.0001	.0002	.0002	.0002	.0003	.0003
17	.0000	.0000	.0000	.0000	.0000	.0001	.0001	.0001	.0001	.0001

$\lambda\tau$

x	6.1	6.2	6.3	6.4	6.5	6.6	6.7	6.8	6.9	7.0
0	.0022	.0020	.0018	.0017	.0015	.0014	.0012	.0011	.0010	.0009
1	.0137	.0126	.0116	.0106	.0098	.0090	.0082	.0076	.0070	.0064
2	.0417	.0390	.0364	.0340	.0318	.0296	.0276	.0258	.0240	.0223
3	.0848	.0806	.0765	.0726	.0688	.0652	.0617	.0584	.0552	.0521
4	.1294	.1249	.1205	.1162	.1118	.1076	.1034	.0992	.0952	.0912
5	.1579	.1549	.1519	.1487	.1454	.1420	.1385	.1349	.1314	.1277
6	.1605	.1601	.1595	.1586	.1575	.1562	.1546	.1529	.1511	.1490
7	.1399	.1418	.1435	.1450	.1462	.1472	.1480	.1486	.1489	.1490
8	.1066	.1099	.1130	.1160	.1188	.1215	.1240	.1263	.1284	.1304
9	.0723	.0757	.0791	.0825	.0858	.0891	.0923	.0954	.0985	.1014
10	.0441	.0469	.0498	.0528	.0558	.0588	.0618	.0649	.0679	.0710
11	.0245	.0265	.0285	.0307	.0330	.0353	.0377	.0401	.0426	.0452
12	.0124	.0137	.0150	.0164	.0179	.0194	.0210	.0227	.0245	.0264
13	.0058	.0065	.0073	.0081	.0089	.0098	.0108	.0119	.0130	.0142
14	.0025	.0029	.0033	.0037	.0041	.0046	.0052	.0058	.0064	.0071
15	.0010	.0012	.0014	.0016	.0018	.0020	.0023	.0026	.0029	.0033
16	.0004	.0005	.0005	.0006	.0007	.0008	.0010	.0011	.0013	.0014
17	.0001	.0002	.0002	.0002	.0003	.0003	.0004	.0004	.0005	.0006
18	.0000	.0001	.0001	.0001	.0001	.0001	.0001	.0002	.0002	.0002
19	.0000	.0000	.0000	.0000	.0000	.0000	.0000	.0001	.0001	.0001

$\lambda\tau$

x	7.1	7.2	7.3	7.4	7.5	7.6	7.7	7.8	7.9	8.0
0	.0008	.0007	.0007	.0006	.0006	.0005	.0005	.0004	.0004	.0003
1	.0059	.0054	.0049	.0045	.0041	.0038	.0035	.0032	.0029	.0027
2	.0208	.0194	.0180	.0167	.0156	.0145	.0134	.0125	.0116	.0107
3	.0492	.0464	.0438	.0413	.0389	.0366	.0345	.0324	.0305	.0286
4	.0874	.0836	.0799	.0764	.0729	.0696	.0663	.0632	.0602	.0573
5	.1241	.1204	.1167	.1130	.1094	.1057	.1021	.0986	.0951	.0916
6	.1468	.1445	.1420	.1394	.1367	.1339	.1311	.1282	.1252	.1221
7	.1489	.1486	.1481	.1474	.1465	.1454	.1442	.1428	.1413	.1396
8	.1321	.1337	.1351	.1363	.1373	.1382	.1388	.1392	.1395	.1396
9	.1042	.1070	.1096	.1121	.1144	.1167	.1187	.1207	.1224	.1241

Table II. *(continued)*

$\lambda\tau$

x	7.1	7.2	7.3	7.4	7.5	7.6	7.7	7.8	7.9	8.0
10	.0740	.0770	.0800	.0829	.0858	.0887	.0914	.0941	.0967	.0993
11	.0478	.0504	.0531	.0558	.0585	.0613	.0640	.0667	.0695	.0722
12	.0283	.0303	.0323	.0344	.0366	.0388	.0411	.0434	.0457	.0481
13	.0154	.0168	.0181	.0196	.0211	.0227	.0243	.0260	.0278	.0296
14	.0078	.0086	.0095	.0104	.0113	.0123	.0134	.0145	.0157	.0169
15	.0037	.0041	.0046	.0051	.0057	.0062	.0069	.0075	.0083	.0090
16	.0016	.0019	.0021	.0024	.0026	.0030	.0033	.0037	.0041	.0045
17	.0007	.0008	.0009	.0010	.0012	.0013	.0015	.0017	.0019	.0021
18	.0003	.0003	.0004	.0004	.0005	.0006	.0006	.0007	.0008	.0009
19	.0001	.0001	.0001	.0002	.0002	.0002	.0003	.0003	.0003	.0004
20	.0000	.0000	.0001	.0001	.0001	.0001	.0001	.0001	.0001	.0002
21	.0000	.0000	.0000	.0000	.0000	.0000	.0000	.0000	.0001	.0001

$\lambda\tau$

x	8.1	8.2	8.3	8.4	8.5	8.6	8.7	8.8	8.9	9.0
0	.0003	.0003	.0002	.0002	.0002	.0002	.0002	.0002	.0001	.0001
1	.0025	.0023	.0021	.0019	.0017	.0016	.0014	.0013	.0012	.0011
2	.0100	.0092	.0086	.0079	.0074	.0068	.0063	.0058	.0054	.0050
3	.0269	.0252	.0237	.0222	.0208	.0195	.0183	.0171	.0160	.0150
4	.0544	.0517	.0491	.0466	.0443	.0420	.0398	.0377	.0357	.0337
5	.0882	.0849	.0816	.0784	.0752	.0722	.0692	.0663	.0635	.0607
6	.1191	.1160	.1128	.1097	.1066	.1034	.1003	.0972	.0941	.0911
7	.1378	.1358	.1338	.1317	.1294	.1271	.1247	.1222	.1197	.1171
8	.1395	.1392	.1388	.1382	.1375	.1366	.1356	.1344	.1332	.1318
9	.1256	.1269	.1280	.1290	.1299	.1306	.1311	.1315	.1317	.1318
10	.1017	.1040	.1063	.1084	.1104	.1123	.1140	.1157	.1172	.1186
11	.0749	.0776	.0802	.0828	.0853	.0878	.0902	.0925	.0948	.0970
12	.0505	.0530	.0555	.0579	.0604	.0629	.0654	.0679	.0703	.0728
13	.0315	.0334	.0354	.0374	.0395	.0416	.0438	.0459	.0481	.0504
14	.0182	.0196	.0210	.0225	.0240	.0256	.0272	.0289	.0306	.0324
15	.0098	.0107	.0116	.0126	.0136	.0147	.0158	.0169	.0182	.0194
16	.0050	.0055	.0060	.0066	.0072	.0079	.0086	.0093	.0101	.0109
17	.0024	.0026	.0029	.0033	.0036	.0040	.0044	.0048	.0053	.0058
18	.0011	.0012	.0014	.0015	.0017	.0019	.0021	.0024	.0026	.0029
19	.0005	.0005	.0006	.0007	.0008	.0009	.0010	.0011	.0012	.0014
20	.0002	.0002	.0002	.0003	.0003	.0004	.0004	.0005	.0005	.0006
21	.0001	.0001	.0001	.0001	.0001	.0002	.0002	.0002	.0002	.0003
22	.0000	.0000	.0000	.0000	.0001	.0001	.0001	.0001	.0001	.0001

$\lambda\tau$

x	9.1	9.2	9.3	9.4	9.5	9.6	9.7	9.8	9.9	10
0	.0001	.0001	.0001	.0001	.0001	.0001	.0001	.0001	.0001	.0000
1	.0010	.0009	.0009	.0008	.0007	.0007	.0006	.0005	.0005	.0005
2	.0046	.0043	.0040	.0037	.0034	.0031	.0029	.0027	.0025	.0023
3	.0140	.0131	.0123	.0115	.0107	.0100	.0093	.0087	.0081	.0076
4	.0319	.0302	.0285	.0269	.0254	.0240	.0226	.0213	.0201	.0189

Table II. *(continued)*

$$\lambda\tau$$

x	9.1	9.2	9.3	9.4	9.5	9.6	9.7	9.8	9.9	10
5	.0581	.0555	.0530	.0506	.0483	.0460	.0439	.0418	.0398	.0378
6	.0881	.0851	.0822	.0793	.0764	.0736	.0709	.0682	.0656	.0631
7	.1145	.1118	.1091	.1064	.1037	.1010	.0982	.0955	.0928	.0901
8	.1302	.1286	.1269	.1251	.1232	.1212	.1191	.1170	.1148	.1126
9	.1317	.1315	.1311	.1306	.1300	.1293	.1284	.1274	.1263	.1251
10	.1198	.1210	.1219	.1228	.1235	.1241	.1245	.1249	.1250	.1251
11	.0991	.1012	.1031	.1049	.1067	.1083	.1098	.1112	.1125	.1137
12	.0752	.0776	.0799	.0822	.0844	.0866	.0888	.0908	.0928	.0948
13	.0526	.0549	.0572	.0594	.0617	.0640	.0662	.0685	.0707	.0729
14	.0342	.0361	.0380	.0399	.0419	.0439	.0459	.0479	.0500	.0521
15	.0208	.0221	.0235	.0250	.0265	.0281	.0297	.0313	.0330	.0347
16	.0118	.0127	.0137	.0147	.0157	.0168	.0180	.0192	.0204	.0217
17	.0063	.0069	.0075	.0081	.0088	.0095	.0103	.0111	.0119	.0128
18	.0032	.0035	.0039	.0042	.0046	.0051	.0055	.0060	.0065	.0071
19	.0015	.0017	.0019	.0021	.0023	.0026	.0028	.0031	.0034	.0037
20	.0007	.0008	.0009	.0010	.0011	.0012	.0014	.0015	.0017	.0019
21	.0003	.0003	.0004	.0004	.0005	.0006	.0006	.0007	.0008	.0009
22	.0001	.0001	.0002	.0002	.0002	.0002	.0003	.0003	.0004	.0004
23	.0000	.0001	.0001	.0001	.0001	.0001	.0001	.0001	.0002	.0002
24	.0000	.0000	.0000	.0000	.0000	.0000	.0000	.0001	.0001	.0001

$$\lambda\tau$$

x	11	12	13	14	15	16	17	18	19	20
0	.0000	.0000	.0000	.0000	.0000	.0000	.0000	.0000	.0000	.0000
1	.0002	.0001	.0000	.0000	.0000	.0000	.0000	.0000	.0000	.0000
2	.0010	.0004	.0002	.0001	.0000	.0000	.0000	.0000	.0000	.0000
3	.0037	.0018	.0008	.0004	.0002	.0001	.0000	.0000	.0000	.0000
4	.0102	.0053	.0027	.0013	.0006	.0003	.0001	.0001	.0000	.0000
5	.0224	.0127	.0070	.0037	.0019	.0010	.0005	.0002	.0001	.0001
6	.0411	.0255	.0152	.0087	.0048	.0026	.0014	.0007	.0004	.0002
7	.0646	.0437	.0281	.0174	.0104	.0060	.0034	.0018	.0010	.0005
8	.0888	.0655	.0457	.0304	.0194	.0120	.0072	.0042	.0024	.0013
9	.1085	.0874	.0661	.0473	.0324	.0213	.0135	.0083	.0050	.0029
10	.1194	.1048	.0859	.0663	.0486	.0341	.0230	.0150	.0095	.0058
11	.1194	.1144	.1015	.0844	.0663	.0496	.0355	.0245	.0164	.0106
12	.1094	.1144	.1099	.0984	.0829	.0661	.0504	.0368	.0259	.0176
13	.0926	.1056	.1099	.1060	.0956	.0814	.0658	.0509	.0378	.0271
14	.0728	.0905	.1021	.1060	.1024	.0930	.0800	.0655	.0514	.0387
15	.0534	.0724	.0885	.0989	.1024	.0992	.0906	.0786	.0650	.0516
16	.0367	.0543	.0719	.0866	.0960	.0992	.0963	.0884	.0772	.0646
17	.0237	.0383	.0550	.0713	.0847	.0934	.0963	.0936	.0863	.0760
18	.0145	.0256	.0397	.0554	.0706	.0830	.0909	.0936	.0911	.0844
19	.0084	.0161	.0272	.0409	.0557	.0699	.0814	.0887	.0911	.0888
20	.0046	.0097	.0177	.0286	.0418	.0559	.0692	.0798	.0866	.0888
21	.0024	.0055	.0109	.0191	.0299	.0426	.0560	.0684	.0783	.0846
22	.0012	.0030	.0065	.0121	.0204	.0310	.0433	.0560	.0676	.0769
23	.0006	.0016	.0037	.0074	.0133	.0216	.0320	.0438	.0559	.0669
24	.0003	.0008	.0020	.0043	.0083	.0144	.0226	.0328	.0442	.0557

Table II. (continued)

$$\lambda\tau$$

x	11	12	13	14	15	16	17	18	19	20
25	.0001	.0004	.0010	.0024	.0050	.0092	.0154	.0237	.0336	.0446
26	.0000	.0002	.0005	.0013	.0029	.0057	.0101	.0164	.0246	.0343
27	.0000	.0001	.0002	.0007	.0016	.0034	.0063	.0109	.0173	.0254
28	.0000	.0000	.0001	.0003	.0009	.0019	.0038	.0070	.0117	.0181
29	.0000	.0000	.0001	.0002	.0004	.0011	.0023	.0044	.0077	.0125
30	.0000	.0000	.0000	.0001	.0002	.0006	.0013	.0026	.0049	.0083
31	.0000	.0000	.0000	.0000	.0001	.0003	.0007	.0015	.0030	.0054
32	.0000	.0000	.0000	.0000	.0001	.0001	.0004	.0009	.0018	.0034
33	.0000	.0000	.0000	.0000	.0000	.0001	.0002	.0005	.0010	.0020
34	.0000	.0000	.0000	.0000	.0000	.0000	.0001	.0002	.0006	.0012
35	.0000	.0000	.0000	.0000	.0000	.0000	.0000	.0001	.0003	.0007
36	.0000	.0000	.0000	.0000	.0000	.0000	.0000	.0001	.0002	.0004
37	.0000	.0000	.0000	.0000	.0000	.0000	.0000	.0000	.0001	.0002
38	.0000	.0000	.0000	.0000	.0000	.0000	.0000	.0000	.0000	.0001
39	.0000	.0000	.0000	.0000	.0000	.0000	.0000	.0000	.0000	.0001

Table III. Values of e^x and e^{-x}

x	e^x	e^{-x}	x	e^x	e^{-x}
0.0	1.000	1.000	5.0	148.4	0.0067
0.1	1.105	0.905	5.1	164.0	0.0061
0.2	1.221	0.819	5.2	181.3	0.0055
0.3	1.350	0.741	5.3	200.3	0.0050
0.4	1.492	0.670	5.4	221.4	0.0045
0.5	1.649	0.607	5.5	244.7	0.0041
0.6	1.822	0.549	5.6	270.4	0.0037
0.7	2.014	0.497	5.7	298.9	0.0033
0.8	2.226	0.449	5.8	330.3	0.0030
0.9	2.460	0.407	5.9	365.0	0.0027
1.0	2.718	0.368	6.0	403.4	0.0025
1.1	3.004	0.333	6.1	445.9	0.0022
1.2	3.320	0.301	6.2	492.8	0.0020
1.3	3.669	0.273	6.3	544.6	0.0018
1.4	4.055	0.247	6.4	601.8	0.0017
1.5	4.482	0.223	6.5	665.1	0.0015
1.6	4.953	0.202	6.6	735.1	0.0014
1.7	5.474	0.183	6.7	812.4	0.0012
1.8	6.050	0.165	6.8	897.8	0.0011
1.9	6.686	0.150	6.9	992.3	0.0010
2.0	7.389	0.135	7.0	1,096.6	0.0009
2.1	8.166	0.122	7.1	1,212.0	0.0008
2.2	9.025	0.111	7.2	1,339.4	0.0007
2.3	9.974	0.100	7.3	1,480.3	0.0007
2.4	11.023	0.091	7.4	1,636.0	0.0006
2.5	12.18	0.082	7.5	1,808.0	0.00055
2.6	13.46	0.074	7.6	1,998.2	0.00050
2.7	14.88	0.067	7.7	2,208.3	0.00045
2.8	16.44	0.061	7.8	2,440.6	0.00041
2.9	18.17	0.055	7.9	2,697.3	0.00037
3.0	20.09	0.050	8.0	2,981.0	0.00034
3.1	22.20	0.045	8.1	3,294.5	0.00080
3.2	24.53	0.041	8.2	3,641.0	0.00207
3.3	27.11	0.037	8.3	4,023.9	0.00025
3.4	29.95	0.033	8.4	4,447.1	0.00022
3.5	33.12	0.030	8.5	4,914.8	0.00020
3.6	36.60	0.027	8.6	5,431.7	0.00018
3.7	40.45	0.025	8.7	6,002.9	0.00017
3.8	44.70	0.022	8.8	6,634.2	0.00015
3.9	49.40	0.020	8.9	7,332.0	0.00014
4.0	54.60	0.018	9.0	8,103.1	0.00012
4.1	60.34	0.017	9.1	8,955.3	0.00011
4.2	66.69	0.015	9.2	9,897.1	0.00010
4.3	73.70	0.014	9.3	10,088	0.00009
4.4	81.45	0.012	9.4	12,088	0.00008
4.5	90.02	0.011	9.5	13,360	0.00007
4.6	99.48	0.010	9.6	14,765	0.00007
4.7	109.95	0.009	9.7	16,318	0.00006
4.8	121.51	0.008	9.8	18,034	0.00006
4.9	134.29	0.007	9.9	19,930	0.00005

Table IV. Values of the Standard Normal Distribution Function

z	0	1	2	3	4	5	6	7	8	9
−3.	.0013	.0010	.0007	.0005	.0003	.0002	.0002	.0001	.0001	.0000
−2.9	.0019	.0018	.0017	.0017	.0016	.0016	.0015	.0015	.0014	.0014
−2.8	.0026	.0025	.0024	.0023	.0023	.0022	.0021	.0021	.0020	.0019
−2.7	.0035	.0034	.0033	.0032	.0031	.0030	.0029	.0028	.0027	.0026
−2.6	.0047	.0045	.0044	.0043	.0041	.0040	.0039	.0038	.0037	.0036
−2.5	.0062	.0060	.0059	.0057	.0055	.0054	.0052	.0051	.0049	.0048
−2.4	.0082	.0080	.0078	.0075	.0073	.0071	.0069	.0068	.0066	.0064
−2.3	.0107	.0104	.0102	.0099	.0096	.0094	.0091	.0089	.0087	.0084
−2.2	.0139	.0136	.0132	.0129	.0126	.0122	.0119	.0116	.0113	.0110
−2.1	.0179	.0174	.0170	.0166	.0162	.0158	.0154	.0150	.0146	.0143
−2.0	.0228	.0222	.0217	.0212	.0207	.0202	.0197	.0192	.0188	.0183
−1.9	.0287	.0281	.0274	.0268	.0262	.0256	.0250	.0244	.0238	.0233
−1.8	.0359	.0352	.0344	.0336	.0329	.0322	.0314	.0307	.0300	.0294
−1.7	.0446	.0436	.0427	.0418	.0409	.0401	.0392	.0384	.0375	.0367
−1.6	.0548	.0537	.0526	.0516	.0505	.0495	.0485	.0475	.0465	.0455
−1.5	.0668	.0655	.0643	.0630	.0618	.0606	.0594	.0582	.0570	.0559
−1.4	.0808	.0793	.0778	.0764	.0749	.0735	.0722	.0708	.0694	.0681
−1.3	.0968	.0951	.0934	.0918	.0901	.0885	.0869	.0853	.0838	.0823
−1.2	.1151	.1131	.1112	.1093	.1075	.1056	.1038	.1020	.1003	.0985
−1.1	.1357	.1335	.1314	.1292	.1271	.1251	.1230	.1210	.1190	.1170
−1.0	.1587	.1562	.1539	.1515	.1492	.1469	.1446	.1423	.1401	.1379
− .9	.1841	.1814	.1788	.1762	.1736	.1711	.1685	.1660	.1635	.1611
− .8	.2119	.2090	.2061	.2033	.2005	.1977	.1949	.1922	.1894	.1867
− .7	.2420	.2389	.2358	.2327	.2297	.2266	.2236	.2206	.2177	.2148
− .6	.2743	.2709	.2676	.2643	.2611	.2578	.2546	.2514	.2483	.2451
− .5	.3085	.3050	.3015	.2981	.2946	.2912	.2877	.2843	.2810	.2776
− .4	.3446	.3409	.3372	.3336	.3300	.3264	.3228	.3192	.3156	.3121
− .3	.3821	.3783	.3745	.3707	.3669	.3632	.3594	.3557	.3520	.3483
− .2	.4207	.4168	.4129	.4090	.4052	.4013	.3974	.3936	.3897	.3859
− .1	.4602	.4562	.4522	.4483	.4443	.4404	.4364	.4325	.4286	.4247
− .0	.5000	.4960	.4920	.4880	.4840	.4801	.4761	.4721	.4681	.4641

Table IV *(continued)*

z	0	1	2	3	4	5	6	7	8	9
.0	.5000	.5040	.5080	.5120	.5160	.5199	.5239	.5279	.5319	.5359
.1	.5398	.5438	.5478	.5517	.5557	.5596	.5636	.5675	.5714	.5753
.2	.5793	.5832	.5871	.5910	.5948	.5987	.6026	.6064	.6103	.6141
.3	.6179	.6217	.6255	.6293	.6331	.6368	.6406	.6443	.6480	.6517
.4	.6554	.6591	.6628	.6664	.6700	.6736	.6772	.6808	.6844	.6879
.5	.6915	.6950	.6985	.7019	.7054	.7088	.7123	.7157	.7190	.7224
.6	.7257	.7291	.7324	.7357	.7389	.7422	.7454	.7486	.7517	.7549
.7	.7580	.7611	.7642	.7673	.7703	.7734	.7764	.7794	.7823	.7852
.8	.7881	.7910	.7939	.7967	.7995	.8023	.8051	.8078	.8106	.8133
.9	.8159	.8186	.8212	.8238	.8264	.8289	.8315	.8340	.8365	.8389
1.0	.8413	.8438	.8461	.8485	.8508	.8531	.8554	.8577	.8599	.8621
1.1	.8643	.8665	.8686	.8708	.8729	.8749	.8770	.8790	.8810	.8830
1.2	.8849	.8869	.8888	.8907	.8925	.8944	.8962	.8980	.8997	.9015
1.3	.9032	.9049	.9066	.9082	.9099	.9115	.9131	.9147	.9162	.9177
1.4	.9192	.9207	.9222	.9236	.9251	.9265	.9278	.9292	.9306	.9319
1.5	.9332	.9345	.9357	.9370	.9382	.9394	.9406	.9418	.9430	.9441
1.6	.9452	.9463	.9474	.9484	.9495	.9505	.9515	.9525	.9535	.9545
1.7	.9554	.9564	.9573	.9582	.9591	.9599	.9608	.9616	.9625	.9633
1.8	.9641	.9648	.9656	.9664	.9671	.9678	.9686	.9693	.9700	.9706
1.9	.9713	.9719	.9726	.9732	.9738	.9744	.9750	.9756	.9762	.9767
2.0	.9772	.9778	.9783	.9788	.9793	.9798	.9803	.9808	.9812	.9817
2.1	.9821	.9826	.9830	.9834	.9838	.9842	.9846	.9850	.9854	.9857
2.2	.9861	.9864	.9868	.9871	.9874	.9878	.9881	.9884	.9887	.9890
2.3	.9893	.9896	.9898	.9901	.9904	.9906	.9909	.9911	.9913	.9916
2.4	.9918	.9920	.9922	.9925	.9927	.9929	.9931	.9932	.9934	.9936
2.5	.9938	.9940	.9941	.9943	.9945	.9946	.9948	.9949	.9951	.9952
2.6	.9953	.9955	.9956	.9957	.9959	.9960	.9961	.9962	.9963	.9964
2.7	.9965	.9966	.9967	.9968	.9969	.9970	.9971	.9972	.9973	.9974
2.8	.9974	.9975	.9976	.9977	.9977	.9978	.9979	.9979	.9980	.9981
2.9	.9981	.9982	.9982	.9983	.9984	.9984	.9985	.9985	.9986	.9986
3.	.9987	.9990	.9993	.9995	.9997	.9998	.9998	.9999	.9999	1.0000

Note 1: If a random variable X is not "standard," its values must be "standardized": $Z = (X - \mu)/\sigma$. That is,

$$P(X \leq x) = N \left(\frac{x - \mu}{\sigma} \right).$$

Note 2: For $z \geq 4$, $N(z) = 1$ to four decimal places; for $z \leq -4$, $N(z) = 0$ to four decimal places.

APPENDIX B

Matrix Notation and Matrix Operations

B.1. MATRIX NOTATION

We define a matrix to be a rectangular array of numbers. For example, the following array of numbers is a matrix labeled A:

$$A = \begin{bmatrix} 1 & 3 & -2 \\ 0 & -1 & 2 \end{bmatrix}.$$

Note that the matrix A has two rows and three columns. Thus, A consists of $2 \times 3 = 6$ numbers. The *size* or *dimension* of a matrix is defined to be the number of rows and columns in the matrix. That is,

size of matrix A = (number of rows) $\times$ (number of columns).

Consider the following matrices:

$$A = \begin{bmatrix} 1 & 2 & 3 \\ -1 & -2 & -3 \end{bmatrix}$$

$$B = \begin{bmatrix} 1 & -1 \\ 2 & 3 \\ -2 & -3 \end{bmatrix}$$

$$C = \begin{bmatrix} 1 & 2 & 3 \end{bmatrix}$$

$$D = \begin{bmatrix} 2 \\ -2 \end{bmatrix}.$$

A is a 2×3, B is 3×2, C is 1×3, and $D = 2 \times 1$ matrix.

It is common to use capital letters to denote matrices. To identify a particular number in a matrix is equivalent to specifying its row and column position. Consider the following matrix:

$$A = \begin{bmatrix} 1 & 3 & -2 \\ 0 & -1 & 2 \end{bmatrix}.$$

For example, the number 1 appears in row 1 and column 1 of A. This is expressed as

$$a_{11} = 1,$$

where the notation

$$a_{ij} = \text{number in row } i \text{ and column } j \text{ of matrix } A.$$

Thus, in matrix A we have

$$a_{11} = 1 \qquad a_{12} = 3 \qquad a_{13} = -2$$

$$a_{21} = 0 \qquad a_{22} = -1 \qquad a_{23} = 2.$$

B.1.1. Vectors

Matrices with only one column or with only one row are called vectors. Thus,

$$C = \begin{bmatrix} 1 & 2 & 3 \end{bmatrix}$$

is a "row" vector (a 1×3 matrix), and

$$D = \begin{bmatrix} 2 \\ -2 \end{bmatrix}$$

is a "column" vector (a 2×1 matrix)

Instead of using the double-subscript notation c_{ij} for a vector, we use one subscript to denote the position of a number in a vector. For example, in

$$C = \begin{bmatrix} 1 & 2 & 3 \end{bmatrix}$$

we have

$$c_1 = 1, \qquad c_2 = 2, \quad \text{and} \quad c_3 = 3,$$

and in

$$D = \begin{bmatrix} 2 \\ -2 \end{bmatrix}$$

we have

$$d_1 = 2 \quad \text{and} \quad d_2 = -2.$$

B.2. MATRIX OPERATIONS

B.2.1. Transpose

The transpose of a given matrix is a matrix whose ith column is the ith row of the original matrix. For example, the transpose of

$$A = \begin{bmatrix} 1 & 3 & -2 \\ 0 & -1 & 2 \end{bmatrix}$$

is the matrix

$$A^T = \begin{bmatrix} 1 & 0 \\ 3 & -1 \\ -2 & 2 \end{bmatrix}.$$

Note that we use the notation A^T to denote the transpose of a given matrix A. Similarly, if

$$B = \begin{bmatrix} 1 & -1 \\ 2 & 3 \\ -2 & -3 \end{bmatrix},$$

then

$$B^T = \begin{bmatrix} 1 & 2 & -2 \\ -1 & 3 & -3 \end{bmatrix}.$$

If

$$C = [1, 2, 3],$$

then

$$C^T = \begin{bmatrix} 1 \\ 2 \\ 3 \end{bmatrix}.$$

If

$$D = \begin{bmatrix} 2 \\ -2 \end{bmatrix},$$

then

$$D^T = \begin{bmatrix} 2 & -2 \end{bmatrix}.$$

We note from the previous examples that if A is an $m \times n$ matrix, A^T is an $n \times m$ matrix.

B.2.2. Matrix Multiplication

We now illustrate three types of matrix multiplication: (1) *Multiplication of two vectors*. (2) *Multiplication of a vector times a matrix*. And (3) *Multiplication of a matrix times a matrix*.

MULTIPLICATION OF TWO VECTORS. The product of a row vector of dimension $1 \times n$ times a column vector of dimension $n \times 1$ yields a *number* obtained by multiplying the first number in the row vector times the first number in the column vector, the second number in the row vector times the second number in the column vector, and so forth, and then summing all the products. Consider the following example:

$$A = \begin{bmatrix} 1 & 2 \end{bmatrix} \quad \text{and} \quad B = \begin{bmatrix} 3 \\ 4 \end{bmatrix}.$$

Then

$$AB = (1)(3) + (2)(4) = 11.$$

If

$$C = \begin{bmatrix} 1 & -1 & 0 \end{bmatrix} \quad \text{and} \quad D = \begin{bmatrix} 4 \\ 6 \\ 0 \end{bmatrix},$$

then

$$CD = (1)(4) + (-1)(6) + (0)(0) = -2.$$

If

$$C = \begin{bmatrix} 1 & 2 & 3 \end{bmatrix} \quad \text{and} \quad X = \begin{bmatrix} X_1 \\ X_2 \\ X_3 \end{bmatrix},$$

then

$$CX = (1)X_1 + 2(X_2) + 3(X_3).$$

MATRIX-VECTOR MULTIPLICATION. The product of an $m \times n$ matrix times an $n \times 1$ column vector yields an $m \times 1$ column vector whose ith element is obtained by multiplying the ith row of the $m \times n$ matrix times the $m \times 1$ column vector.

Consider the following example:

$$A = \begin{bmatrix} 2 & 3 \\ 4 & 5 \end{bmatrix} \quad \text{and} \quad B = \begin{bmatrix} 5 \\ 6 \end{bmatrix}.$$

Then

$$AB = \begin{bmatrix} 2 & 3 \\ 4 & 5 \end{bmatrix} \begin{bmatrix} 5 \\ 6 \end{bmatrix}$$

$$= \begin{bmatrix} [2 \ 3] & \begin{bmatrix} 5 \\ 6 \end{bmatrix} \\ [4 \ 5] & \begin{bmatrix} 5 \\ 6 \end{bmatrix} \end{bmatrix}$$

$$= \begin{bmatrix} (2)(5) + (3)(6) \\ (4)(5) + (5)(6) \end{bmatrix}$$

$$= \begin{bmatrix} 28 \\ 50 \end{bmatrix}.$$

$$A = \begin{bmatrix} 2 & 3 & 1 \\ -1 & 0 & 2 \end{bmatrix} \quad \text{and} \quad B = \begin{bmatrix} 1 \\ 2 \\ 3 \end{bmatrix}.$$

Then

$$AB = \begin{bmatrix} (2)(1) + (3)(2) + (1)(3) \\ (-1)(1) + (0)(2) + (2)(3) \end{bmatrix}$$

$$= \begin{bmatrix} 11 \\ 5 \end{bmatrix}.$$

$$A = \begin{bmatrix} 2 & 3 & 1 \\ -1 & 0 & 2 \end{bmatrix} \quad \text{and} \quad X = \begin{bmatrix} x_1 \\ x_2 \\ x_3 \end{bmatrix}.$$

Then

$$AX = \begin{bmatrix} (2)x_1 + (3)x_2 + (1)x_3 \\ (-1)x_1 + (0)x_2 + (2)x_3 \end{bmatrix}.$$

MATRIX TIMES A MATRIX. The product of an $m \times n$ matrix and a $n \times p$ matrix yields an $m \times p$ matrix whose ijth element is the vector product of the ith row of the $m \times n$ matrix and the jth column of the $n \times p$ matrix. Consider the following examples:

$$A = \begin{bmatrix} 1 & 2 \\ 3 & 4 \end{bmatrix} \quad \text{and} \quad B = \begin{bmatrix} 4 & 3 \\ 2 & 1 \end{bmatrix}.$$

Then

$$AB = \begin{bmatrix} 1 & 2 \\ 3 & 4 \end{bmatrix} \quad \begin{bmatrix} 4 & 3 \\ 2 & 1 \end{bmatrix}$$

$$= \begin{bmatrix} [1 \ 2]\begin{bmatrix} 4 \\ 2 \end{bmatrix} & [1 \ 2]\begin{bmatrix} 3 \\ 1 \end{bmatrix} \\ [3 \ 4]\begin{bmatrix} 4 \\ 2 \end{bmatrix} & [3 \ 4]\begin{bmatrix} 3 \\ 1 \end{bmatrix} \end{bmatrix}$$

$$= \begin{bmatrix} 4+4 & 3+2 \\ 12+8 & 9+4 \end{bmatrix} = \begin{bmatrix} 8 & 5 \\ 20 & 13 \end{bmatrix}.$$

Consider

$$A = \begin{bmatrix} 1 & 2 \\ 0 & 1 \\ 1 & 0 \end{bmatrix} \quad \text{and} \quad B = \begin{bmatrix} 1 & 0 \\ 0 & 1 \end{bmatrix}.$$

Then

$$AB = \begin{bmatrix} 1 & 2 \\ 0 & 1 \\ 1 & 0 \end{bmatrix} \begin{bmatrix} 1 & 0 \\ 0 & 1 \end{bmatrix}$$

$$= \begin{bmatrix} [1 \ 2]\begin{bmatrix} 1 \\ 0 \end{bmatrix} & [1 \ 2]\begin{bmatrix} 0 \\ 1 \end{bmatrix} \\ [0 \ 1]\begin{bmatrix} 1 \\ 0 \end{bmatrix} & [0 \ 1]\begin{bmatrix} 0 \\ 1 \end{bmatrix} \\ [1 \ 0]\begin{bmatrix} 1 \\ 0 \end{bmatrix} & [1 \ 0]\begin{bmatrix} 0 \\ 1 \end{bmatrix} \end{bmatrix}$$

$$= \begin{bmatrix} 1 & 2 \\ 0 & 1 \\ 1 & 0 \end{bmatrix}.$$

Finally, two vectors are said to be equal if their corresponding elements are equal. For example,

$$\begin{bmatrix} 2 \\ 3 \\ 4 \end{bmatrix} = \begin{bmatrix} 2 \\ 3 \\ 4 \end{bmatrix}$$

$$\begin{bmatrix} 2 \\ 3 \\ 4 \end{bmatrix} \neq \begin{bmatrix} 2 \\ 5 \\ 4 \end{bmatrix} \quad \text{since } 3 \neq 5$$

and

$$\begin{bmatrix} 2 \\ 3 \\ a \end{bmatrix} = \begin{bmatrix} 2 \\ 3 \\ 4 \end{bmatrix} \qquad \text{only if } a = 4.$$

B.3. LINEAR PROGRAMMING MODELS IN VECTOR-MATRIX NOTATION

Consider the following examples.

> **LINEAR PROGRAMMING MODEL**
>
> maximize $Z = 10x_1 \quad + 20x_2$
>
> subject to $\quad (1)x_1 \quad +(0)x_2 = 5$
>
> $\qquad\qquad\quad (2)x_1 +(-3)x_2 = 10$
>
> $\qquad\qquad\quad x_1 \geqslant 0, \qquad x_2 \geqslant 0.$

Let

$$C = \begin{bmatrix} 10 & 20 \end{bmatrix}, \qquad X = \begin{bmatrix} x_1 \\ x_2 \end{bmatrix}, \qquad A = \begin{bmatrix} 1 & 0 \\ 2 & -3 \end{bmatrix}, \quad \text{and} \quad b = \begin{bmatrix} 5 \\ 10 \end{bmatrix}.$$

Then the LP model can be restated as: choose

$$X = \begin{bmatrix} x_1 \\ x_2 \end{bmatrix}$$

to maximize $Z = CX$ subject to

$$AX = b \quad \text{and} \quad X \geqslant \begin{bmatrix} 0 \\ 0 \end{bmatrix}.$$

Consider the following linear programming problem:

$$\text{LP model:} \quad \text{minimize } Z = CX$$
$$\text{subject to } AX = b \quad \text{and} \quad X \geqslant 0,$$

where

$$C = \begin{bmatrix} -1 & 0 & 1 \end{bmatrix}, \qquad A = \begin{bmatrix} 1 & 0 & 2 \\ -1 & 0 & 3 \end{bmatrix}, \qquad b = \begin{bmatrix} 10 \\ 20 \end{bmatrix}, \qquad \text{and} \quad X = \begin{bmatrix} x_1 \\ x_2 \\ x_3 \end{bmatrix}.$$

PROBLEM. Write the LP model in standard form.

Solution. The objective function is

$$Z = CX = \begin{bmatrix} -1 & 0 & 1 \end{bmatrix} \begin{bmatrix} x_1 \\ x_2 \\ x_3 \end{bmatrix} = (-1)x_1 + (0)x_2 + (1)x_3.$$

The constraints are:

$$AX = b$$

or

$$\begin{bmatrix} 1 & 0 & 2 \\ -1 & 0 & 3 \end{bmatrix} \begin{bmatrix} x_1 \\ x_2 \\ x_3 \end{bmatrix} = \begin{bmatrix} 10 \\ 20 \end{bmatrix}$$

or

$$\begin{bmatrix} 1x_1 + 0x_2 + 2x_3 \\ -1x_1 + 0x_2 + 3x_3 \end{bmatrix} = \begin{bmatrix} 10 \\ 20 \end{bmatrix}$$

or

$$1x_1 + 0x_2 + 2x_3 = 10$$
$$-1x_1 + 0x_2 + 3x_3 = 20.$$

and $x_1 \geqslant 0, x_2 \geqslant 0, x_3 \geqslant 0.$

Index